THE SANSKRIT DRAMA

THE SANSKRIT DRAMA

in its Origin, Development Theory & Practice

A. BERRIEDALE KEITH

MOTILAL BANARSIDASS PUBLISHERS
PRIVATE LIMITED • DELHI

Reprint: Delhi, 1998, 2015
First Indian Edition: 1992

ISBN: 978-81-208-0977-2 (Cloth)
ISBN: 978-81-208-1530-8 (Paper)

MOTILAL BANARSIDASS
41 U.A. Bungalow Road, Jawahar Nagar, Delhi 110 007
8 Mahalaxmi Chamber, 22 Bhulabhai Desai Road, Mumbai 400 026
203 Royapettah High Road, Mylapore, Chennai 600 004
236, 9th Main III Block, Jayanagar, Bengaluru 560 011
8 Camac Street, Kolkata 700 017
Ashok Rajpath, Patna 800 004
Chowk, Varanasi 221 001

Printed in India

by RP Jain at NAB Printing Unit,
A-44, Naraina Industrial Area, Phase I, New Delhi–110028
and published by JP Jain for Motilal Banarsidass Publishers (P) Ltd,
41 U.A. Bungalow Road, Jawahar Nagar, Delhi-110007

PREFACE

THIRTY-TWO years have elapsed since the appearance of Professor Sylvain Lévi's admirable treatise, *Le théâtre indien*, the first adequate sketch of the origin and development of the Indian drama and of Indian dramatic theory. Since then the discovery of important fragments of the dramas of the great Buddhist poet Açvaghoṣa, and of the plays of the famous Bhāsa, has thrown unexpected light on the early history of the drama in India; the question of the origin of the drama has been the subject of elaborate investigation by Professors von Schroeder, Pischel, Hertel, Sir W. Ridgeway, Lüders, Konow, and myself; and the real significance and value of the Indian theory of the dramatic art have been brought out by the labours of Professor Jacobi. The time is therefore ripe for a fresh investigation of the origin and development of the drama in the light of the new materials available.

To bring the subject matter within moderate compass, I have confined it to the drama in Sanskrit or Prākrit, omitting any reference to vernacular dramas. I have also omitted from the account of the theory of drama all minor detail which appeared to have no more than the interest of ingenuity in subdivision and classification; I have had the less hesitation in doing so, because I have no doubt that the value and depth of the Indian theory of poetics have failed to receive recognition, simply because in the original sources what is important and what is valueless are presented in almost inextricable confusion. In tracing the development of the drama, I have laid stress only on the great writers and on dramatists who wrote before the end of the first millennium; of later works I have selected a few typical specimens for description; it seemed needless to dwell on plays which in the main show an excessive dependence on older models and on the text-books of dramatic theory, and whose chief merit, when they have any, lies in skill and taste in versification. Valuable bibliographies of the dramas are contained in Mr. Montgomery Schuyler's *Bibliography of the Sanskrit Drama* (1906), and in Professor Konow's treatise, and it has seemed needless to do more than refer to the most important and accessible editions of the plays mentioned and to treatises which have appeared since the publication of these works.

Though the limits of space available have precluded any full investigation of the style of the dramatists, I have not followed Professor Lévi in leaving this aspect out of consideration. The translations given of the passages cited are intended merely to convey the main sense; I have therefore left without discussion difficulties of interpretation and allusion, and have resorted to prose. Verse translations from Sanskrit sometimes attain very real merit, but normally only in a way which has little affinity with Sanskrit poetry. H. H. Wilson's versions of Sanskrit dramas in his *Theatre of the Hindus* for this reason, and also because the prose of the dramas is turned into verse, thus fail, despite their many intrinsic merits, to convey any precise idea of the effect of a Sanskrit drama.

I am indebted to my wife for much assistance and criticism.

A. BERRIEDALE KEITH.

EDINBURGH UNIVERSITY,
April, 1923.

CONTENTS

PART I. THE ORIGIN OF THE SANSKRIT DRAMA

PAGE

I. Dramatic Elements in Vedic Literature.
1. The Indian Tradition of the Origin of the Drama . . . 12
2. The Dialogues of the Veda 13
3. Dramatic Elements in Vedic Ritual 23

II. Post-Vedic Literature and the Origin of the Drama.
1. The Epics 28
2. The Grammarians 31
3. Religion and the Drama 36
4. Theories of the Secular Origin of the Drama . 49
5. Greek Influence on the Sanskrit Drama . . 57
6. The Çakas and the Sanskrit Drama . . . 69
7. The Evidence of the Prākrits 72
8. The Literary Antecedents of the Drama . . 75

PART II. THE DEVELOPMENT OF THE SANSKRIT DRAMA

III. Açvaghoṣa and the Buddhist Drama.
1. The Çāriputraprakaraṇa 80
2. The Allegorical and the Hetaera Dramas . . 83
3. The Language of the Dramas 85
4. The Metres 89

IV. Bhāsa.
1. The Authenticity of Bhāsa's Dramas . . . 91
2. The Date of Bhāsa's Dramas 93
3. The Dramas and their Sources 95
4. Bhāsa's Art and Technique 105
5. Bhāsa's Style 114
6. The Language of the Plays 120
7. The Metres of the Dramas 123

PAGE

V. The Precursors of Kālidāsa and Çūdraka.
1. The Precursors of Kālidāsa 127
2. The Authorship and Age of the Mṛcchakaṭikā . 128
3. The Mṛcchakaṭikā 131
4. The Prākrits 140
5. The Metres 142

VI. Kālidāsa.
1. The Date of Kālidāsa 143
2. The Three Dramas of Kālidāsa 147
3. Kālidāsa's Dramatic Art 155
4. The Style 160
5. The Language and the Metres 166

VII. Candra, Harṣa, and Mahendravikramavarman.
1. Candra or Candraka 168
2. The Authorship of the Dramas ascribed to Harṣa 170
3. The Three Dramas 171
4. Harṣa's Art and Style 175
5. The Language and the Metres of Harṣa's Dramas 181
6. Mahendravikramavarman 182

VIII. Bhavabhūti.
1. The Date of Bhavabhūti 186
2. The Three Plays 187
3. Bhavabhūti's Dramatic Art and Style . . 192
4. The Language and the Metres 203

IX. Viçākhadatta and Bhaṭṭa Nārāyaṇa.
1. The Date of Viçākhadatta 204
2. The Mudrārākṣasa 205
3. The Language and the Metres of the Mudrārākṣasa 211
4. The Date of Bhaṭṭa Nārāyaṇa 212
5. The Veṇīsaṁhāra 212
6. The Language and the Metres of the Veṇīsaṁhāra 219

X. Murāri, Rājaçekhara, their Predecessors and Successors.
1. The Predecessors of Murāri 220
2. Murāri 225
3. The Anargharāghava 226
4. The Date of Rājaçekhara 231
5. The Dramas of Rājaçekhara 232
6. Bhīmaṭa and Kṣemīçvara 239

PAGE

XI. The Decline of the Sanskrit Drama.
1. The Decadence of the Drama 242
2. The Nāṭaka 244
3. The Allegorical Nāṭaka 251
4. The Nāṭikā and the Saṭṭaka 256
5. The Prakaraṇa 257
6. The Prahasana and the Bhāṇa 260
7. Minor Dramatic Types 264
8. The Shadow Play 269
9. Dramas of Irregular Type 270

XII. The Characteristics and Achievement of the Sanskrit Drama 276

PART III. DRAMATIC THEORY

XIII. The Theory of the Dramatic Art.
1. The Treatises on Dramatic Art 290
2. The Nature and the Types of the Drama . . 295
3. The Subject Matter and the Plot 296
4. The Characters 305
5. The Sentiments 314
6. The Dramatic Styles and Languages . . . 326
7. The Dance, Song, and Music 338
8. The Preliminaries and the Prologue . . . 339
9. The Types of Drama 345
10. The Influence of Theory on Practice . . . 352
11. Aristotle and the Indian Theory of Poetics . 355

PART IV. DRAMATIC PRACTICE

XIV. The Indian Theatre.
1. The Theatre 358
2. The Actors 360
3. The Mise-en-scène and Representation of the Drama 364
4. The Audience 369

English Index 373

Sanskrit Index 394

ABBREVIATIONS

AID.	Über die Anfänge des indischen Dramas, Munich, 1914.
AJP.	American Journal of Philology.
AP.	Agni Purāṇa, ed. BI.
BI.	Bibliotheca Indica, Calcutta.
BS.	Bhāsa-Studien, Leipzig, 1918.
BSS.	Bombay Sanskrit Series.
CHI.	Cambridge History of India.
DR.	Daçarūpa, cited from Hall's ed. BI.
EI.	Epigraphia Indica.
GGA.	Göttingische gelehrte Anzeigen.
GIL.	Geschichte der indischen Litteratur, by M. Winternitz, Leipzig, 1904-22.
GN.	Nachrichten der königl. Gesellschaft der Wissenschaften zu Göttingen.
GOS.	Gaekwad's Oriental Series.
GSAI.	Giornale della Società Asiatica Italiana.
HOS.	Harvard Oriental Series.
IA.	Indian Antiquary.
ID.	Das indische Drama, Berlin, 1920.
IS.	Indische Studien.
JA.	Journal Asiatique.
JAOS.	Journal of the American Oriental Society.
JBRAS.	Journal of the Bombay Branch of the Royal Asiatic Society.
JPASB.	Journal and Proceedings of the Asiatic Society of Bengal.
JRAS.	Journal of the Royal Asiatic Society.
KF.	Aufsätze zur Kultur- und Sprachgeschichte Ernst Kuhn gewidmet. Breslau, 1916.
KM.	Kāvyamālā series, Bombay.
N.	Nāṭyaçāstra.
R.	Rasārṇavasudhākara, ed. TSS. 1916.
SBAW.	Sitzungsberichte der königl. Akademie der Wissenschaften zu Berlin.
SP.	Studies in the History of Sanskrit Poetics, I, London, 1923.
SD.	Sāhityadarpaṇa, cited by the sections of the BI. ed.
TI.	Le théâtre indien, Paris, 1890.
TSS.	Trivandrum Sanskrit Series.
VOJ.	Vienna Oriental Journal.
ZDMG.	Zeitschrift der Deutschen Morgenländischen Gesellschaft.

PART I

THE ORIGIN OF THE SANSKRIT DRAMA

I

DRAMATIC ELEMENTS IN VEDIC LITERATURE

1. *The Indian Tradition of the Origin of the Drama*

INDIAN tradition, preserved in the *Nāṭyaçāstra*,[1] the oldest of the texts of the theory of the drama, claims for the drama divine origin, and a close connexion with the sacred Vedas themselves. The golden age had no need for such amusements: ignorant of all pain, the sorrow, which is as essential to the art as joy itself, was inconceivable. The creation of the new form of literature was reserved to the silver age, when the gods approached the all-father and bade him produce something to give pleasure to the ears and eyes alike, a fifth Veda which, unlike the other four, would not be the jealous preserve of the three twice-born castes, but might be shared by the Çūdras also. Brahmā gave ear to the pleading, and designed to fashion a Veda in which tradition (*itihāsa*) should be combined with instruction in all the ends of men. To accomplish his task he took from the *Ṛgveda* the element of recitation, from the *Sāmaveda* song, from the *Yajurveda* the mimetic art, and from the *Atharvaveda* sentiment. Then he bade Viçvakarman, the divine architect, build a playhouse in which the sage Bharata was instructed to carry into practice the art thus created. The gods accepted with joy the new creation; Çiva contributed to it the Tāṇḍava dance, expressing violent emotion, Pārvatī, his spouse, the tender and voluptuous Lāsya, while Viṣṇu was responsible for the invention of the four dramatic styles, essential to the effect of any play. To Bharata fell the duty of transferring to earth this celestial Veda in the inferior and truncated form of the *Nāṭyaçāstra*.

The legend is interesting for its determination to secure the

[1] i. 2 ff.

participation of every member of the Hindu Trinity in the creation of the new art, and for its effort to claim that the fifth Veda of tradition was the Veda of the dramatic art. The older tradition, recorded and exploited by the epic,[1] recognizes as the fifth Veda the mass of traditions, and the *Nāṭyaçāstra* tacitly concedes this by representing the *Nāṭyaveda* as including these traditions. The legend, therefore, is not of great antiquity, nor need we place it long before the compilation of the *Nāṭyaçāstra* itself. The date of that text is uncertain, but we cannot with any assurance place it before the third century A.D. With the Indian tendency to find divine origins, it may well be that the tradition existed much earlier, but in the absence of any corroboration that must remain a mere hypothesis, for which no conclusive ground can be adduced. What is important is that none of the theorists on the drama appeal to any Vedic texts as representing dramas, whence it is natural to draw the conclusion that there was no Indian tradition extant in their time which pointed to the preservation among the sacred texts of dramas. Indeed, if it were worth while, the conclusion might legitimately be drawn that the absence of any drama in the Vedic literature was recognized, since it was necessary for the gods to ask Brahmā to create a completely new type of literature, suitable for an age posterior to that in which the Vedas already existed.

2. *The Dialogues of the Veda*

The silence of Indian tradition is all the more remarkable because there do exist in the *Ṛgveda* itself a number of hymns which are obviously dialogues, and which are expressly recognized as such by early Indian tradition.[2] The number of such hymns is uncertain, for it is possible to add to those which clearly bear that character others whose interpretation might be improved by assuming a division of persons. There are, however, at least fifteen whose character as dialogues is quite undeniable, and most of these hymns are of marked interest. Thus in x. 10 Yama and Yamī, the primeval twins, whence in the legend are derived the races of men, engage in debate;

[1] Hopkins, *Great Epic of India*, pp. 7, 10, 53.
[2] Keith, JRAS. 1911, pp. 981 ff.

the poet, with a more refined sentiment than the legend, is uneasy regarding this primitive incest, and represents Yamī as intent on an effort, fruitless so far as the hymn goes, to induce Yama to accept and make fruitful her proffered love. A tantalizing, but certainly interesting, hymn in the same book (x. 95) gives a dialogue between Purūravas, and the nymph Urvaçī; he rebukes her inconstancy, but does not succeed in making her refrain from withdrawing from his gaze. In viii. 100 Nema Bhārgava utters an appeal to Indra, to which the god is pleased to give a reply. Sometimes there are three interlocutors; thus Agastya, the sage, has a conversation (i. 179) of an enigmatic type with his wife, Lopāmudrā, and their son; not less obscure is the dialogue between Indra and Vasukra, in which the wife of the latter plays a small part, in x. 28; and in iv. 18 we have a most confused dialogue between Indra, Aditi, and Vāmadeva. Even less intelligible is the famous debate between Indra, his wife, Indrāṇī, and Vṛṣākapi (x. 86), each interpreter of which is able to show the absurdity of the versions of his predecessors but seems incapable of recognizing the defects of his own. Or one of the interlocutors may be a troop, not an individual. Thus Saramā, the messenger of Indra, seeking the kine which have been taken away, goes to the demons, the Paṇis, and holds with them lively debate (x. 108). The gods also have a hard business (x. 51–3) to persuade Agni, the living fire, to persevere in the tedious occupation of bearing to them the oblations of mortals, and the dialogue in which they engage is vivid in the extreme, extending even to the breaking of a stanza into portions for two interlocutors. Two dialogues are of interest for their historical allusions, the converse of Viçvāmitra and the rivers (iii. 33) which he seeks to cross, and that of Vasiṣṭha with his sons (vii. 33), if indeed that is the correct interpretation of the speakers of the hymn. Indra again disputes with the Maruts (i. 165 and 170), who had disgraced themselves in his eyes by deserting him in the thick of his contest with the demon Vṛtra, but who succeed at last in placating his anger; in the former hymn Agastya seems also to intervene, by summing up the result at the close, and invoking the favour of the gods for himself. Similarly the account of Viçvāmitra's dialogue ends with the assertion that the Bharatas successfully crossed the rivers in search of booty, having won a passage by the intercession of their priest. The interesting, but obscure, hymn (iv. 42), in which Indra and Varuṇa seem to engage in a dispute as to their relative preeminence, is clearly commented on by the poet himself, and his intervention may be suspected even where it is not essential.

Now it is clear that the tradition of the ritual literature did not know what to make of the dialogues of the *Ṛgveda*. The genre of composition was one which died out in the later Vedic age; it is significant that the *Atharvaveda* knows but one hymn of that type (v. 11) in which the priest, Atharvan, begs the god for the payment due, a cow; the god is little inclined to accord his prayer, but finally is induced to relent and to add to the guerdon due the promise of eternal friendship. It is not in the least surprising, therefore, if we find that Yāska and Çaunaka in the fifth century B.C. were at variance as to whether the hymn x. 95 was a dialogue, as the former held, or a mere legend, as the latter believed.[1] In the commentary of Sāyaṇa we find that the tradition was unable to ascribe any ritual use for nearly all the hymns; the case of x. 86 is an exception, but it is significant that that hymn has little of a true dialogue, the three speakers rather uttering enigmas than conversing, and it was therefore easier to fit it into the inconspicuous part it occupies in the later ritual. We must, therefore, admit that we have in these dialogues the remnant of a style of poetry which died out in the later Vedic period.

Its original purpose is obscure, but a very interesting suggestion was made in 1869 by Max Müller in connexion with his version of *Ṛgveda* i. 165.[2] He conjectured that the 'dialogue was repeated at sacrifices in honour of the Maruts or that possibly it was acted by two parties, one representing Indra, the other the Maruts and their followers'. In 1890 the suggestion was repeated with approval by Professor Lévi,[3] who added to it the argument that the *Sāmaveda* shows that the art of music had been fully developed by the Vedic age. Moreover the *Ṛgveda*[4] already knows maidens who, decked in splendid raiment, dance and attract lovers, and the *Atharvaveda*[5] tells

[1] Sieg, *Die Sagenstoffe des Ṛgveda*, p. 27.
[2] SBE. xxxii. 182 f.
[3] TI. i. 307 f.
[4] i. 92. 4.
[5] xii. 1. 41.

how men dance and sing to music. There is, therefore, *a priori* no fatal objection to assuming that the period of the *Ṛgveda* knew dramatic spectacles, religious in character, in which the priests assumed the rôles of gods and sages in order to imitate on earth the events of the heavens.

The logical consequence of this doctrine is seen in Professor von Schroeder's elaborate theory [1] that the dialogue hymns, and also certain monologues, for instance x. 119, in which Indra appears as glorifying himself in the intoxication of his favourite Soma drink, are relics of Vedic mysteries, an inheritance in germ from Indo-European times. Ethnology shows us the close relation of music, dance, and drama among many peoples, and the curious phenomenon that Vedic religion knows of gods as dancers cannot be explained satisfactorily save on the assumption that the priests were used to see performed ritual dances, in themselves imitations of the cosmic dance in which the world was, on one view, created. Such dances partake of the nature of sympathetic magic, and they have an obvious parallel in the great sacrificial rites, which in the Brāhmaṇa period are undertaken in order to represent on earth the cosmic creation. It is true that we do not find in the *Ṛgveda* the phallic dances which in Greece and Mexico alike are held to be closely connected with the origin of drama, but that was because the priests of the *Ṛgveda* were in many respects austere, and disapproved of phallic deities of any kind. The dramas of the ritual, therefore, are in a sense somewhat out of the main line of the development of the drama; the popular side has survived through the ages in a rough way in the Yātrās well known in the literature of Bengal, while the refined and sacerdotalized Vedic drama passed away without a direct descendant.

Independent support for the view of the dialogues as mystery plays *in nuce* is given by Dr. Hertel,[2] whose argument is largely based on the doctrine that the Vedic hymns were always sung, and that in singing it would have been impossible for a single singer to make the necessary distinction between the different speakers, which would have been possible if the hymns had not

[1] *Mysterium und Mimus im Rigveda* (1908); VOJ. xxii. 223 ff.; xxiii. 1 ff., 270 f.

[2] VOJ. xviii. 59 ff., 137 ff.; xxiii. 273 ff.; xxiv. 117 ff. Cf. Charpentier, VOJ. xxiii. 33 ff.; *Die Suparṇasage* (1922) is somewhat confused and uncritical.

been sung. The hymns, therefore, represent the beginnings of a dramatic art, which may be compared with the form of the *Gītagovinda*.[1] But, what is more important, he seeks to find an actual drama on an extended scale in the *Suparṇādhyāya*,[2] a curious and comparatively late Vedic text. In his view, accordingly, the Vedic drama does not stand isolated; it is seen in the *Ṛgveda* only in its beginnings; the *Suparṇādhyāya* displays it en route to further development, and in the Yātrās we can see a continuation of the old type, which aids us in following the growth from the Vedic drama of the classical drama of India. In this regard there is a distinct divergence of view between the two supporters of the dramatic theory, for Professor von Schroeder regards the Yātrās as genuinely connected with the later drama, being developed in close connexion with the cult of Viṣṇu-Kṛṣṇa and Rudra-Çiva, but as representing a different development from the same root as the Vedic dialogues. Of this other side of the drama he finds hints in the traditional connexion of the Gandharvas and Apsarases with the drama, for these in his view are essentially phallic deities.

There is, of course, no doubt of the possibility of the dialogues really representing portions of the old ritual in which the priests assumed the character of gods or demons, for there are abundant parallels for such a supposition. But there is no sufficient ground to compel us to seek for such an explanation of these hymns; that the *Ṛgveda* contains nothing save what is connected with ritual is a postulate which is not made by the Indians themselves, and has no justification save in the desire for symmetry. On the contrary, it is perfectly legitimate and much more natural to regard the *Ṛgveda* as a collection of hymns, in the vast majority of cases of ritual origin, but including some more secular poetry, to which genus alone can we reasonably attribute the battle hymns of Viçvāmitra and Vasiṣṭha. The fact that such hymns disappear in the later Vedic literature is then natural, for that literature represents unquestionably hymns collected definitely for ritual uses, and therefore nothing was admitted which could not be employed therein. To assume, therefore, that a ritual explanation must

[1] See ch. xi., § 9; Winternitz, GIL. iii. 130 f.

[2] See also Jarl Charpentier, *Die Suparṇasage* (Uppsala, 1922).

be found, and to find it in ritual drama is illegitimate, and the only justification for accepting the view in any case must lie in the fact that it affords a better explanation of the hymn than any which can be given otherwise.

It is impossible to feel any certainty that the necessary proof has been brought in any case. The hymn ix. 112, which describes in four stanzas in a rather humorous style the various ends of men, ending with the refrain in each case, 'O Soma, flow for Indra', is transformed into the marching song of a popular festival at which mummers represent vegetation deities and symbols of fertility are carried. The tradition knows nothing of these happenings, and the hymn certainly suggests none to the average intelligence. On the contrary, it seems a very natural piece of witty sarcasm, to which point is lent by the use of the refrain, and to deny the possibility of sarcasm to the thinkers who produce the advanced and sceptical views expressed in the *Ṛgveda* is certainly unwise.[1] To explain the Vṛṣākapi hymn (x. 86) as a piece of fertility magic in dramatic form is ingenious, but unluckily it in no way contributes towards the explanation of the hymn, and, therefore, is as valueless as the other possible explanations which have been offered. The same condemnation must be passed on the effort to find a mimic race at a festival described in the strange Mudgala hymn (x. 102) which if it is intelligible at all, seems to have a mythological reference, and not to refer either to actual or mimic races.

An ingenious effort is that made to adduce ethnological parallels to prove that the hymn x. 119, which is a straightforward monologue, placed in the mouth of Indra, celebrating the effect of drinking the Soma, must be regarded as part of a ritual in which at the close of the drinking of the Soma in the rite, a priest comes forward, assuming the rôle of Indra, and celebrates in monologue the strength of the juice of the holy plant Among the Cora Indians, after a wine festival, a god is introduced showing the effects of the drink, while a singer celebrates its potent merits. There is, however, a fatal hiatus in the proof; the poem by itself is perfectly clear, and to seek

[1] This is quite consistent with the ritual use in a Soma 'wish' offering suggested by Oldenberg, GGA. 1909, pp. 79 ff. Cf. his remarks on vii. 103 in *Ṛgveda-Noten*, ii. 67.

for an explanation so far-fetched is idle expenditure of energy. The same condemnation must be expressed of the effort to find in the frog hymn (vii. 103) a song sung by men masked as frogs, dancing as a spell to secure rain. If we grant that the hymn is really intended as a rain spell, which is moderately probable though not proved, it needs no further explanation whatever, and, if we do not accept this suggestion but adopt the older view that it satyrizes in an amusing way the antics of certain performers of the ritual, the character of the hymn as a fertility spell vanishes at once. The errors of method are seen excellently in the fantastic conclusion that the gambler's hymn (x. 34), in which a gambler deplores the fatal love for the dice which has led to his reducing even his beloved wife to ruin, is a dramatic monologue in which dancers represent the leaping and falling dice. The dialogue of Yama and Yamī reduces itself to a fertility drama, from which the prudishness of the Vedic age has omitted the vital part of the union of the pair. The curious hymn, iv. 18, which tells of Indra's unnatural birth becomes a drama by the assumption that of thirteen verses seven are ascribed to the poet himself. We are in fact in every case presented with a bare possibility, which sometimes involves absurdities, and in all cases does nothing whatever to help us in interpreting the hymns. There is nothing, it is true, inconceivable in the view that the hymn of Saramā and the Paṇis was actually recited by two different parties, and thus was a ritual drama *in nuce*; what is certain is that the later Vedic period knew nothing whatever of such a practice; the only hymn in dialogue form for which it finds a use (x. 86) is assigned an employment in which there is nothing dramatic whatever. The absurdity of the whole process reaches perhaps its fullest exhibition in the dissertation on the hymn regarding Agastya and Lopāmudrā (i. 179), for it becomes a fertility rite performed after the corn has been cut; Lopāmudrā becomes 'that which has the seal of disappearance upon it', a feat which is impossible in the Vedic language; the hymn itself suits far better the obvious alternative[1] of 'one who enjoys love at the cost of breaking her marital vows'. To explain the hymns of Indra and the Maruts (i. 170, 171, and 165) we are to hold that we

[1] Oldenberg, GGA. 1909, p. 77, n. 4.

have three scenes of a dramatic performance, which takes place at a Soma sacrifice to celebrate the victory of Indra over the serpent Vṛtra, ending with a dance of the Maruts, represented by youths fully armed. This weapon dance is a relic of old vegetation ritual, the driving out of the old year, winter, or death, which is the foundation of the dances of the Roman Salii, the Greek Kouretes, the Phrygian Korybantes, and the German sword dancers. How can it be justifiable to spin theories thus in order to explain hymns which are taken by themselves without serious difficulty save in detail?

It is equally impossible to find any cogency in Dr. Hertel's arguments from the necessity of assuming two sets of performers, since the hymns were sung and a single voice in singing could not distinguish the interlocutors. Doubtless, if we accepted this necessity, we would be inclined to admit *a priori* that the song would tend to be accompanied by action and by the dance, so that drama would be on the way to development. But we do not know that the hymns of the *Ṛgveda* were always sung; on the contrary we do know with absolute certainty that, while the verses of the *Sāmaveda* were sung (*gai*), the verses of the *Ṛgveda* were recited (*çaṅs*). True, we do not have precise information of the exact character of the recitation, but there is not the slightest ground to suppose that a reciter could not have conveyed by differences in his mode of recitation the distinction between two different interlocutors, and the fact that this point is ignored in the argument is fatal to it. Moreover, we must admit that we are wholly ignorant as to the degree in which it was desired by the authors or reciters of these hymns to convey these differences of person. We do not know, and the ritual text-books did not know, exactly in what way these hymns were used. We find in the *Ṛgveda* a number of philosophic hymns; why should we not admit that a philosophic dialogue such as that of Yama and Yamī is possible without demanding that it should be a fragment of ritual? We have historical hymns in Maṇḍala vii; why should we turn the dialogue of Viçvāmitra and the rivers into a drama? Why should we insist that all hymns were composed for ritual use, when we know that ancient tales were among the things used to pass the period immediately following the disposal of the dead, and that during the pauses in the great horse sacrifice, performed to assert the wide sovereignty of the king, both Brahmins and warriors sang songs to fill up the time? We may legitimately assume that in the *Ṛgveda* we have hymns of other than directly ritual or magic purpose; the gambler's hymn cannot by any reasonable stretch of the imagination be taken as ritual.[1]

It is also impossible to accept the view that the Vedic drama died out under the chilling effect of the disapproval of the priests of fertility ritual. We find, on the contrary, that fertility ritual is fully recognized later in the Mahāvrata ceremonial, and also in the horse sacrifice, which are both known to the other Vedic Saṁhitās, though this feature of the rite is not referred to, directly at least, in the *Ṛgveda.* Moreover, even if the disapproval of fertility rites had been real, why should it have brought to a close the drama? The dialogues of Agni and the gods, of Saramā and the Paṇis, of Varuṇa and Indra, of Indra and the singer—and perhaps Vāyu also (viii. 100), have no connexion with fertility, and this aspect of drama need not have perished. Dr. Hertel is certainly right in demanding traces of development, not of decadence, but his great effort to find a full drama in the *Suparṇādhyāya* must definitely be pronounced a failure. It involves an elaborate invention of stage directions, the preparation of a list of *dramatis personae* largely on the basis of imagination, and a translation of the piece based on this theory, which can be shown in detail to be open to the certainty of error. Add to this the fact that there is no hint in Indian tradition that the *Suparṇādhyāya,* on the face of it a late imitation of Vedic work proper, had ever any dramatic intention or use.

A very different theory of the purpose of these hymns is that which we owe to Professors Windisch,[2] Oldenberg,[3] and Pischel.[4] They represent an old type, Indo-European in antiquity, of composition of epic character, in which the verses, representing the points of highest emotion, were preserved, and the connecting links were in prose which was not stereotyped, and therefore

[1] Keith, JRAS. 1911, p. 1006.
[2] Cf. *Sansk. Phil.* pp. 404 ff.
[3] ZDMG. xxxvii. 54 ff.; xxxix. 52 ff.; GGA. 1909, pp. 66 ff.; GN. 1911, pp. 441 ff.; *Zur Geschichte der altindischen Prosa* (1917), pp. 53 ff.; *Das Mahabharata,* pp. 21 ff.
[4] VS. ii. 42 ff. GGA. 1891, pp. 351 ff.

has not come down to us. The theory is capable of combination with the suggestion that these hymns in dialogue were dramatic; thus Prof. Pischel explained the combination of prose and verse in the Sanskrit drama as a relic of this early form of literature, which thus might serve both epic and dramatic ends.[1] Despite the considerable vogue which the theory has at one time or other attained, and the energetic defence of it by Professor Oldenberg, who has based upon it an elaborate theory of the development of Indian prose, it is doubtful whether we can accept the view.[2] It is a very real difficulty here also that the tradition shows no trace of knowledge of this characteristic of the hymns, and we do not find any work actually in this form in the whole of the Vedic literature. The alleged instances of this type, such as those of the tale of Çunaḥçepa in the *Aitareya Brāhmaṇa*, or the working up in the *Çatapatha Brāhmaṇa* of the legend of Purūravas and Urvaçī cannot possibly be made to fit the theory. In the latter case we have a tale, which manifestly does not agree with the verses of the *Ṛgveda*, and which is openly and obviously an attempt to work that hymn into the explanation of the ritual; in the former we have the use of gnomic verses to illustrate a theme, a form of literature which is preserved through the history of Sanskrit prose, and portions of a verse narrative. The true type, verses used at the point of emotion, especially, therefore, to give the vital speeches and replies, is thus not represented by any text of the Vedic literature. Whether it ever existed at all in the sense postulated by the theory, whether there are traces of it in the Pali Jātakas, or whether its existence even there is a misunderstanding, are questions which are not in vital connexion with the origin of Sanskrit drama, and may, therefore, here be left undiscussed. One consideration, however, is germane; if it were necessary to explain the Vedic dialogues by this theory, it would certainly be possible to do so far more effectively and simply than by the theory of their being the remains of ritual dramas. The most serious objection to both theories is that they are not really necessary. Professor Geldner[3] who formerly patronized

[1] Compare Oldenberg, *Die Literatur des alten Indien*, p. 241.

[2] See Keith, JRAS. 1911, pp. 981 ff.; 1912, pp. 429 ff.; *Rigveda Brāhmaṇas*, pp. 68 ff.

[3] *Die indische Balladendichtung* (1913). Cf. G. M. Miller, *The Popular Ballad* (1905)

the theory of Oldenberg has sought to explain the hymns in question as ballads.[1]

Nor of course is it necessary to make any use of this theory in order to explain the mixture of prose and verse in the Sanskrit drama. The use of prose needs no defence or explanation; that of verse is what was essentially to be expected, in view of the importance of song as a form of amusement as well as in worship both in Vedic times and later, and of the fact that our extant dramas draw so largely on epic tradition, preserved in versified texts. Nothing indeed is more noteworthy in Sanskrit literature than the determination to turn everything, law, astronomy, architecture, rhetoric, even philosophy into a metrical form. The theorists on the drama give no suggestion that the prose was regarded as any less fixed in character than the verses, or that it was not the duty of the author of the drama to be as careful in preparing the one as the other, and the manuscript tradition of the drama does not hint at any distinction of the two elements as regards source.

3. *Dramatic Elements in Vedic Ritual*

When we leave out of account the enigmatic dialogues of the *Ṛgveda* we can see that the Vedic ritual contained within itself the germs of drama, as is the case with practically every primitive form of worship. The ritual did not consist merely of the singing of songs or recitations in honour of the gods; it involved a complex round of ceremonies in some of which there was undoubtedly present the element of dramatic representation; that is the performers of the rites assumed for the time being personalities other than their own. There is an interesting instance of this in the ritual of the Soma purchase for the Soma sacrifice. The seller is in some versions at the close of the ceremony deprived of his price, and beaten or pelted with clods. Now there can be no doubt that we have here, not a reflex of a disapproval of trafficking in Soma, but a mimic account of the obtaining of Soma from its guardians the Gandharvas, and there is some truth in the comparison drawn

[1] The existence of this type in the Epic is certainly most improbable, and in the Jātakas it is not frequent; cf. Charpentier, *Die Suparṇasage*, and Winternitz's admissions, GIL. ii. 368 with Oldenberg, GN. 1918, pp. 429 ff.; 1919, pp. 61 ff.

between the Çūdra who plays the role of the mishandled seller and the much misused Devil of the mediaeval mystery plays.[1] But we must not exaggerate the amount of representation; it falls very far short of an approach to drama, a point which is overlooked by Professor von Schroeder throughout his discussions. A drama proper can only be said to come into being when the actors perform parts deliberately for the sake of the performance, to give pleasure to themselves and others, if not profit also; if a ritual includes elements of representation, the aim is not the representation, but the actors are seeking a direct religious or magic result. It would be absurd, for instance, to treat the identification in the marriage ritual of the husband and wife with the sky and the earth as in any sense dramatic or to see any drama in the performance of the royal consecration, which is based carefully on the divine consecration of Indra, doubtless in the view that thus the king was for the time being identified with the great god, and so acquired some measure of his prowess.

In the Mahāvrata[2] we find elements which are of importance as indicating the materials from which the drama might develop. The Mahāvrata is plainly a rite intended to strengthen at the winter solstice the sun, so that it may resume its vigour and make fruitful the earth. Now an essential part of the rite is a struggle between a Vaiçya, whose colour is to be white, and a Çūdra, black in colour, over a round white skin, which ultimately falls to the victorious Vaiçya. It is impossible, without ignoring the obvious nature of this rite, not to see in it a mimic contest to gain the sun, the power of light, the Aryan, striving against that of darkness, the Çūdra. In the face of the ethnological parallels it is impossible also to sever this episode from the numerous forms of the contest of summer and winter, the first represented by the white Aryan, the second by the dark Çūdra. We have in fact a primitive dramatic ritual, and one which it may be added was popular throughout the Vedic age. The same ceremony is also marked by a curious episode; a Brahmin student and a hetaera are introduced as engaged in coarse abuse of each other, and in the older form of the ritual

[1] Hillebrandt, *Ved. Myth.*, i. 69 ff.
[2] Keith, *Śāṅkhāyana Āraṇyaka*, pp. 72 ff.

we actually find that sexual union as a fertility rite is permitted, though later taste dismissed the practice as undesirable. The ritual purpose of this abuse is undeniable; it is aimed at producing fertility, and has a precise parallel in the untranslatable language employed in the horse sacrifice during the period when the unlucky chief queen is compelled to lie beside the slaughtered horse, in order to secure, we may assume, the certainty of obtaining a son for the monarch whose conquests are thus celebrated.[1]

There are, however, nothing but elements here, and we have reasonable certainty that no drama was known. In the *Yajurveda* we have long lists of persons of every kind covering every possible sort of occupation, and the term Naṭa, which is normally the designation of the actor in the later literature is unknown. We find but one term[2] which later ever has that sense, Çailūṣa, and there is nothing whatever to show that an actor here is meant; a musician or a dancer may be denoted, for both dancing and singing are mentioned in close proximity.

Professor Hillebrandt,[3] on the other hand, is satisfied that we have actual ritual drama before us, and Professor Konow[4] insists that these are indeed ritual dramas, but that they are borrowed by the ritual from the popular mime of the time, which accordingly must have known dialogue, abusive conversation and blows, but of which the chief parts were dance, song, and music which are reckoned in the ***Kauṣītaki Brāhmaṇa***[5] as the arts, but of which the *Pāraskara Gṛhya Sūtra*[6] disapproves for the use of men of the three higher castes. The evidence for this assumption is entirely lacking, and it is extremely significant that the Vedic texts ignore the Naṭa,[7] whose activity belongs according to all the evidence to a later period. It is, of course, always possible to deprecate any argument from silence, though the value of this contention is diminished by the very remarkable enumerations of the different forms of occupation given in the Puruṣamedha sections of the

[1] Keith, HOS. XVIII. cxxxv. [2] VS. xxx. 4; TB. iii. 4. 2.
[3] AID. pp. 22 f. [4] ID. pp. 42 ff. [5] xxix. 5. [6] ii. 7. 3.
[7] The Prākritic form of the term as opposed to Vedic *nṛtu* and *nṛtta* is legitimate evidence for the development of pantomimic dancing in circles more popular than priestly. But it does nothing to show that such dancing was originally secular, or that it rather than religious dancing gave a factor to drama.

Yajurveda, where in the imaginary sacrifice of men the imagination of the Brahmins appears to have laboured to enumerate every form of human activity. But in the absence of any proof that secular pantomime is older than religious throughout the world, and in the absence of anything to indicate that it was so in the case of India, it seems quite impossible to accept Professor Konow's suggested origin of drama.

Of other elements which enter into drama we find the songs of the *Sāmaveda*, and the use of ceremonial dances. Thus at the Mahāvrata maidens dance round the fire as a spell to bring down rain for the crops, and to secure the prosperity of the herds. Before the marriage ceremony is completed[1] there is a dance of matrons whose husbands are still alive, obviously to secure that the marriage shall endure and be fruitful. When a death takes place, and the ashes of the deceased are collected, to be laid away, the mourners move round the vase which contains the last relics of the dead, and dancers are present who dance to the sound of the lute and the flute; dance, music, and song fill the whole day of mourning.[2] Dancing is closely associated throughout the history of the Indian theatre with the drama, and in the ritual of Çiva and Viṣṇu-Kṛṣṇa it has an important part. Hence the doctrine which has the approval of Professor Oldenberg[3] and which finds the origin of drama in the sacred dance, a dance, of course, accompanied by gesture of pantomic character; combined with song, and later enriched by dialogue, this would give rise to the drama. If we further accept the view that the dialogue in prose was added from the ritual element seen in the abuse at the horse sacrifice and the Mahāvrata, then within the Vedic ritual we may discern all the elements for the growth of drama present.

In this sense we may speak of the drama as having its origin in the Vedic period, but it may be doubted whether anything is gained by such a proposition. Unless the hymns of the *Ṛgveda* present us with real drama, which is most implausible, we have not the slightest evidence that the essential synthesis of elements and development of plot, which constitute a true

[1] *Çāṅkhāyana Gṛhya Sūtra*, i. 11. 5.

[2] Caland, *Die altindischen Todten- und Bestattungsgebräuche*, pp. 138 ff.

[3] *Die Literatur des alten Indien*, p. 237; Macdonell, *Sanskrit Literature*, p. 347.

drama, were made in the Vedic age. On the contrary, there is every reason to believe that it was through the use of epic recitations that the latent possibilities of drama were evoked, and the literary form created. One very important point in this regard has certainly often been neglected. The Sanskrit drama does not consist, as the theory suggests, of song and prose as its vital elements; the vast majority of the stanzas, which are one of its chief features, were recited, not sung, and it was doubtless from the epic that the practice of recitation was in the main derived. Professor Oldenberg[1] admits in fact the great importance of the epic on the development of drama, but it may be more accurate to say that without epic recitation there would and could have been no drama at all. Assuredly we have no clear proof of such a thing as drama existing until later than we have assurance of the recitation of epic passages by Granthikas, as will be seen below.

[1] *Die Literatur des alten Indien*, p. 241. In Mexico we have the material of a ritual drama (K. Th. Preuss, *Archiv für Anthropologie*, 1904, pp. 158 ff.), but not the epic element.

II

POST-VEDIC LITERATURE AND THE ORIGIN OF THE DRAMA

1. *The Epics*

THE great epic of India, the *Mahābhārata*, in the whole extent of its older portions, does not recognize in any explicit manner the existence of the drama.[1] The term Naṭa indeed occurs, and, if it meant actor, the existence of the drama would be proved, but it may equally well merely denote pantomimist. This conclusion, moreover, is strongly supported by the strange fact that, if the epic knew the drama, it should never mention any of its characteristics or such a standing character as the Vidūṣaka. There is, what is still more significant, even in the later parts of the epic, such as the Çānti and Anuçāsana Parvans, no clear allusion to the art, for the passage in the Çānti[2] in which Professor Hillebrandt has found an allusion to dramatic artists can perfectly well apply to pantomimes, and in the latter text[3] the passage in which the commentator Nīlakaṇṭha finds comedians and dancers (*naṭa-nartakāḥ*) yields perfectly good senses as pantomimists and dancers, both occupations there repudiated by Brahmins. To find the drama we are compelled to have recourse to the *Harivaṅça*,[4] which is a deliberate continuation of the *Mahābhārata*, and there we have explicit evidence, for we learn of players who made a drama out of the *Rāmāyaṇa* legend. But this is of no importance for the purpose of determining the date of the drama; the *Harivaṅça* is of uncertain date, but in all probability, as we have it, it cannot be placed earlier than the second or third century A.D., long after the

[1] Hopkins, *The Great Epic of India*, pp. 55 ff. Nāṭaka in ii. 11. 36 is very late; JRAS. 1903, pp. 571 f.
[2] xii. 140. 21. [3] xiii. 33. 12. [4] ii. 88 ff. See § 3 below.

time when there is no doubt of the existence of a Sanskrit drama.

The *Rāmāyaṇa* lends no aid to the attempt to establish an early existence of drama; we hear of festivals and concourses (*samāja*) where Naṭas and Nartakas delight themselves,[1] and even of the speaking of Nāṭakas;[2] in another passage the term Vyāmiçraka[3] denotes, if we believe the commentator, plays in mingled languages. But, accepting all these references as genuine, which we are not obliged to do, the passages have manifestly no claim to early date, for other reasons than the allusions, and leave us again without any early evidence.

But, while the epics cannot be said to know the drama, there is abundant evidence of the strong influence on the development of the drama exercised by the recitation of the epics. The long continued popularity of these recitations is attested throughout the literature; at the beginning of the seventh century A. D.[4] a Brahmin, Somaçarman, akin to the royal house of Cambodia, presented to a temple in that far-off outpost of Indian civilization a complete copy of the *Bhārata*, in order that regular recitations might take place, and almost contemporaneously Bāṇa in the *Kādambarī* depicts the queen as hastening to the temple of Çiva to hear the recitation of the epic. Four centuries later Kṣemendra reproaches his contemporaries with their equal eagerness to hear such recitations, and their reluctance to carry out in practice the excellent advice contained in them. We have vivid accounts from recent time of such recitations not only in temples but in villages, when the generosity of some rich man has secured the presence, if need be, for three months or longer of the reciters, Kathakas, to go over the hugh poem, which claims to be an encyclopaedia of all useful knowledge as well as the best of poems. The reciters divide themselves into two classes, the Pāṭhakas, who repeat the poem, and the Dhārakas, who expound it in the vernacular for the edification of the people, whose deep interest in the recitations is attested; if the *Rāmāyaṇa* is the epic chosen for recitation, the departure

[1] ii. 67. 15.

[2] ii. 69. 3.

[3] ii. 1. 27; Hillebrandt ZDMG. lxxii. 229, n. 1; *contra*, SBAW. 1916, p. 730.

[4] Barth, *Inscr. Sansc. du Cambodge*, p. 30. At the close of the *Mahābhārata* the existence of such recitations is clearly recognized; Oldenberg, *Das Mahabharata*, p. 20.

of the hero into exile excites their tears and sobs, even to the interruption of the recital; when he returns and ascends the throne the village is illuminated and garlanded.[1] Fortunately we have in a bas-relief[2] from Sānchi, which may safely be placed before the Christian era, a representation of a group of these Kathakas. We see in it that they accompanied with music in some degree their recitations, danced, and indicated by gestures the sentiments of the characters they presented. We have thus something which in its nature is far from undramatic; given the use of dialogue, the drama would be present in embryo. This step is foreshadowed but not actually taken in the account given in the later additions to the *Rāmāyaṇa*[3] of the first recitation of that poem. Vālmīki, the author of the narrative of Rāma's deeds, teaches the poem to Kuça and Lava, the children whom Sītā in exile bears to Rāma; they enter Ayodhyā at the moment when the king performs the horse sacrifice, and excite the curiosity of the king himself, who hears the recitation of his own deeds by the two rhapsodes, and recognizes them for his own sons.

The term Bhārata,[4] which is an appellation of the comedian in the later texts, attests doubtless the connexion of the rhapsodes with the growth of the drama. It has survived in the modern form of Bhāṭ denoting a class of reciters, who are the inheritors of a tradition of recitation of the epics, and who are expert in genealogy, enjoy general consideration, and by their mere presence with a caravan assure its passage in safety. The Bhāratas must be the rhapsodes of the Bhārata tribe,[5] whose fame is great in the early history of India, whose special fire is known to the *Ṛgveda*, and who have a special offering (*hotrā*) of their own. The *Mahābhārata* is the great epic of the family, preserved by their care. With the passage of time the rhapsodes doubtless took upon them the newer art of drama. Bhavabhūti in the *Uttararāmacarita* shows himself conscious of the debts owed by the drama to the epic, and the clearest proof is now available in the dramas of Bhāsa, with their wide indebtedness to the great epic itself.

[1] Max Müller, *India*, p. 81. Cf. Winternitz, GIL. iii. 162, n. 1.
[2] E. Schlagintweit, *India in Wort und Bild*, i. 176.
[3] vii. 93.
[4] Lévi, TI. i. 311 f.
[5] Macdonell and Keith, *Vedic Index*, ii. 94 ff.

The term Kuçīlava, which occasionally denotes actor, is apparently derived from the Kuça and Lava of the *Rāmāyaṇa*; the mode of formation of the compound is indeed strange, for it is not obvious why it should have been formed on the mode of compounds in which the first member represents a woman's name, but it is equally, if not more difficult, to imagine how it could be derived from the prefix *ku* and *çīla* manners, denoting 'of bad morals'. Weber's attempt to compare this name with Çailūṣa of the Vedic texts and Çilālin, who is connected with a Sūtra for Naṭas, is obviously impossible, and it may be that the name, derived originally from Kuça and Lava, was later by a witticism altered to Kuçīlava as a hit against the morals of the actors, which were recognized on every hand to be bad.[1]

2. *The Grammarians*

In Pāṇini[2] we find mention of Naṭasūtras, text-books for Naṭas, ascribed to Çilālin and Kṛçāçva; the fact is recorded because of the formation of the names assumed by their followers, Çailālins and Kṛçāçvins. The names are curious; it has been suggested by Professor Lévi to see in them ironical appellations; the Kṛçāçvins are those whose horses are meagre, with an ironic reference to the great Indo-Iranian hero Kṛçāçva, while the Çailālins have nothing but stones for their beds in pitiful contrast with the fame of the Vedic school of that name, whose *Çailāli Brāhmaṇa* is known to us. But we unfortunately are here as ever in no position to establish the meaning of Naṭa, which may mean no more than a pantomime. The conclusion is important, for Pāṇini's date is most probably the fourth century B.C., and the fact that he has no term certainly denoting drama is of significance.

In Patañjali,[3] the author of the *Mahābhāṣya*, whose date is certainly to be placed with reasonable assurance about 140 B.C., we find much more effective evidence bearing on the existence of drama. We learn from his criticism on a rule laid down by his predecessor Kātyāyana, as to the use of the imperfect tense of things which a person has himself seen, that it was normal

[1] Konow, ID. p. 9; Lévi, TI. ii. 51. On these rhapsodes, cf. Jacobi, *Das Rāmāyaṇa*, pp. 62 ff.; GGA. 1899, pp. 877 f.; Hopkins, *The Great Epic of India*, pp. 364 ff.

[2] iv. 3. 110 f.

[3] iii. 2. 111.

to use in his time phrases describing a past event as if it had occurred before the eyes of the speaker; we can understand this only of a character in a dramatic performance of some kind, and it is significant that the phrase cited in illustration of the usage is 'Vāsudeva has slain Kaṅsa'. The reference is to the famous legend of Kṛṣṇa, son of Vasudeva, and his wicked uncle Kaṅsa, who first sought to destroy him in his childhood, and afterward paid the penalty of his evil deeds by death at the hands of Kṛṣṇa. This notice receives further elucidation by a famous passage, first adduced by Weber, in which Patañjali explains the justification of the use of phrases such as 'He causes the death of Kaṅsa', and 'He causes the binding of Bali'.[1] Both these deeds, the actual killing, the actual binding, are deeds of the remote past; how then can the present be in place? The answer, we learn, is that the events are described in the present because the sense is, not that they are being actually done, but that they are being described. Of the modes of description no less than three are then set out. In the first place we have the case of the Çaubhikas or Çobhanikas, who before the eyes of the spectators actually carry out—naturally in appearance only in the first case—the killing of Kaṅsa and the binding of Bali; they represent in fact by action, without words, so far as this passage formally tells us, the slaying of the wicked Kaṅsa, the binding of the evil Bali. Secondly, we have the painters; they describe by their paintings, for on the canvases themselves we see the blows rained on Kaṅsa and the dragging of him about; a painter, that is to say, kills Kaṅsa and has Bali bound by painting a scene describing these incidents. Thirdly, we have those who use words, and not action of the Çaubhika type, the Granthikas; they also, while relating the fortunes of their subjects from their birth to their death, make them real to the minds of their audience, for they divide

[1] *ye tāvad ete çobhanikā nāmaite pratyakṣaṁ Kaṅsaṁ ghātayanti pratyakṣam Baliṁ bandhayantīti. citreṣu katham? citreṣv apy udgūrṇā nipātitāç ca prahārā dṛçyante Kaṅsakarṣaṇyaç ca. granthikeṣu kathaṁ yatra çabdagaḍumātraṁ lakṣyate te 'pi hi teṣām utpattiprabhṛty ā vināçād ṛddhīr vyācakṣāṇāḥ sato buddhiviṣayān prakāçayanti. ātaç ca sato vyāmiçrā hi dṛçyante: kecit Kaṅsabhaktā bhavanti, kecid Vāsudevabhaktāḥ. varṇānyatvaṁ khalv api puṣyanti: kecit kālamukhā bhavanti, kecid raktamukhāḥ.* See iii. 1. 26. The text, uncertain in detail, must be corrected by replacing *buddhīr* for the absurd *ṛddhīr* of some manuscripts only, defended by Lüders. See Weber, IS. xiii. 487 ff. Çaubhika is a variant.

themselves into two parties, one set adhering to Kṛṣṇa, and one to Kaṅsa, and they adopt different colours, the adherents of Kaṅsa black, and those of Kṛṣṇa red, though, by what is probably an erroneous correction, the colours are ascribed in the inverse order by many of the manuscripts.

This is clear and intelligible, and it is unfortunate that it has recently been misunderstood by Professor Lüders,[1] with disastrous results for the comprehension of the notice. The Çaubhikas are made to be persons who explain to the audience shadow pictures, a view which has not even the merit of Indian tradition, and, as will be seen below, contradicts entirely the facts known as to the shadow play in India, where it is recorded only in late mediaeval times. The traditional rendering in India of the statement is recorded by Kaiyaṭa, more than a thousand years later; it is frankly obscure; Professor Lévi[2] renders it as meaning that the Çaubhikas are those who teach actors, representing Kaṅsa, and so on, the mode of recitation, a version which is doubtless very difficult. The sense accorded to it by Professor Lüders is that the Çaubhikas explain to the audience dumb actors, a form of drama which is recorded as performed by the Jhāṁkīs of Bombay and Mathurā in modern India, but of which in ancient times we have no certainty, since this is the only passage which even remotely can be supposed to allude to it. The obvious view, that of Weber,[3] that we have a reference to a pantomimic killing and binding, seems irresistible; the use of the causative is explained by this fact; if Bali and Kaṅsa were persons of to-day the simple verb would express their binding and slaying; because it is mere actors, the causative is used, and its use denotes that the act is not now real but an exposition of a past act. 'He causes the binding of Bali'

1 SBAW. 1916, pp. 698 ff. Cf. Hillebrandt, ZDMG. lxxii. 227 f.; Keith, *Bulletin of School of Oriental Studies*, I. iv. 27 ff. Winternitz (ZDMG. lxxiv. 118 ff.) ineffectively supports Lüders, though he recognizes the extraordinary difficulties of this view. The error is due to the idea that one can only describe (*ācaṣṭe*) in words, ignoring art and action.

2 TI. i. 315. The words are: *Kaṅsādyanukāriṇāṁ naṭānāṁ vyākhyānopādhyāyāḥ.*

3 Weber might be interpreted as believing in an actual killing, but, if so, he was clearly in error, and in point of fact he merely gives this as possible (IS. xiii. 490). That Çaubhikas did manual acts and were not talkers primarily, if at all, is suggested by the use elsewhere of the term; thus in the *Kāvyamīmāṅsā*, p. 55, they are classed with rope-dancers and wrestlers.

means 'he describes the binding of Bali'. The only legitimate doubt on the passage is that regarding the exact mode of performance of the Çaubhikas; the word *pratyakṣam* in the text insists that it is done before the eyes of the audience, and we may justly assume that the Çaubhikas performed manual acts. Did they also use dialogue? There is nothing in the passage either to show that they did or that they did not; the contrast which follows later with Granthikas, whose medium was words, is sufficiently pointed if they used action as well as words. The most that can be said is that Çaubhika or Çobhanika does not obtain currency later as denoting an actor, which may tell against the view that Patañjali is here actually alluding to drama proper. Further we cannot go; to argue that, if he had known drama proper, he must have clearly mentioned it, is to ignore entirely the manner of Patañjali, whose silence as to what he must have known is as common as his incidental mention of current topics.

The error of Professor Lüders in insisting on a literal interpretation of the passage as referring to different sorts of narrators by words comes out with special clearness as regards the second class of persons alluded to by Patañjali. That they are painters whose canvases are living speeches was clearly recognized by the commentators in India. Haradatta tells us in the simplest and plainest language that when men look at a picture on which is shown the death of Kaṅsa at the hands of Vāsudeva they interpret the picture as the slaying of the wicked Kaṅsa by the blessed Vāsudeva, and thus by the pictured Vāsudeva cause to be slain the pictured Kaṅsa, for this is the conception which they form as they gaze, and he adds, very naturally, that this explains the practice of saying of artists that they cause the slaying of Kaṅsa, the binding of Bali.[1] It would be difficult to see how the idea could have been more forcibly expressed, but Professor Lüders interprets it in the sense that artists occasionally explain their own pictures to others, an idea which is not merely wholly impossible, but renders Haradatta's

[1] *ye 'pi citraṁ vyācakṣate 'yam Mathurāprāsādo 'yaṁ Kaṅso 'yam bhagavān Vāsudevaḥ praviṣṭa etāḥ Kaṅsakarṣiṇyo rajjava etā udgūrṇā nipātitāç ca prahārā ayaṁ hataḥ Kaṅso 'yam ākṛṣṭa iti te 'pi citragataṁ Kaṅsaṁ tādṛçenaiva Vāsudevena ghātayanti. citre 'pi hi tadbuddhir eva paçyatām. etena citralekhakā vyākhyātāḥ.* On Lüders' view the second sentence is useless.

language nonsense. On this basis he finds that the Çaubhikas added to their business of explaining shadow pictures that of showing and explaining other pictures, in this respect again without any support from tradition.

Finally Professor Lüders denies any division of parties among the Granthikas, whose name he derives, like the scholiasts, from the use of manuscript books in recitation, rejecting the idea of cyclic rhapsodes suggested by Dr. Dahlmann.[1] The derivation is too speculative in sense to be relied upon, but there is no doubt that the Granthikas were reciters. Their exact means of expressing the sense is not quite clear owing to the unlucky divergence of reading in the text, and the fact that the precise meaning of the second word in the most probable reading (*çabda-gaḍu-mātram*)[2] is wholly unknown. It is, accordingly, wholly illegitimate to assert that they used words alone, and on the score of that to deny that they could be said to divide themselves into two parties, one of followers of Kańsa, one of adherents of Kṛṣṇa, bearing appropriate colours. This view reduces us to the impossible theory that the division of parties refers to the audience. Apart from all questions of regard for the Sanskrit language, which Patañjali should be assumed capable of writing, the ludicrous result is achieved that among a pious audience of Kṛṣṇa adorers we are to suppose that there were many who favoured Kańsa, the cruel uncle whose vices are redeemed by not a single virtue, and for whose fate Sanskrit literature, pious and devout, shows not a sign of regret. The change of colour, which is asserted to be the only possible sense of the term *varṇānyatvam*, wholly without ground, is referred to the spectators, who turn red with anger if supporters of Kańsa, black with fear if they support Vāsudeva. Professor Hillebrandt, who has unfortunately accepted the new theory to the extent that he believes that there were persons who carried round pictures and explained them for a living, justly declines to believe in the possibility of a Hindu audience containing persons who wished the success of Kańsa, and he accepts the plain fact that the Granthikas took parts. The colours he

[1] *Genesis des Mahābhārata*, pp. 163 ff. Granthika occurs in MBh. xiv. 70. 7; cf. *granthin*, Manu, xii. 103.

[2] SBAW. 1916, p. 26. Hillebrandt (ZDMG. lxxii. 228) criticizes effectively Lüders's interpretation. Cf. *granthagaḍutva* in R. i. 243.

explains, however, as indicating the sentiments which the two parties feel, a view for which there is the authority of the *Nāṭyaçāstra* which ascribes to each sentiment an appropriate colour, and, accepting the reading of Kielhorn, he is compelled to assume that the supporters of Kaṅsa on the stage showed as the dominant sentiment fury, while those of Kṛṣṇa are reduced to manifest fear as the sentiment of their side. But it is frankly incredible that the followers of Kṛṣṇa, the invincible, who calmly and coolly proceeds from victory to victory culminating in the overthrow of his wicked uncle, accomplished with ease and celerity, should show fear as the dominant sentiment, and it is clear that on this view we should accept the reading which inverts the descriptions,[1] thus allotting to the supporters of Kaṅsa the fear, to those of Kṛṣṇa the fury of slaughter and revenge. But in this trait it is more probable, as will be seen below, that we have a trace of the religious origin of the drama.[2]

3. *Religion and the Drama*

We seem in fact to have in the *Mahābhāṣya* evidence of a stage in which all the elements of drama were present; we have acting in dumb show, if not with words also; we have recitations divided between two parties. Moreover, we hear of Naṭas who not only recite but also sing; we find that in the days of the *Mahābhāṣya* the Naṭa's hunger is as proverbial as the dancing of the peacock, that it was no rare thing for him to receive blows, and that a special term, Bhrūkuṅsa, existed to name him who played women's parts, appropriately made up.[3] The *Mahābhāṣya* does not seem to recognize women as other than dancers or singers,[4] so that it may well be that in the infancy of the

[1] It is a confirmation of the incorrectness of Lüders's view that he is driven to render *vṛddhīr*, which he reads for *buddhīr*, as 'Schicksale'. Now *vṛddhi* cannot possibly be used in this sense; it means 'prosperity', and, applied to Kaṅsa or Bali, it is ludicrous. What is meant is that, by forming parties, the Granthikas make real to the audience the feelings of the characters, a doctrine entirely in keeping with the duty of an actor according to N. Hillebrandt's view of the Çaubhikas as explaining the subject of the play to the audience, like the Sthāpaka later (N. v. 154 ff.; DR. iii. 3; SD. 283), contradicts the word *pratyakṣam*.

[2] Winternitz (ZDMG. lxxiv. 122) desires inversion, even on Lüders's theory, although Lüders attaches importance to the text.

[3] i. 4. 29 (*naṭasya çṛṇoti, granthikasya çṛṇoti*); ii. 4. 77 (*agāsīn naṭaḥ*); ii. 3. 67 (*naṭasya bhuktam*); iii. 2. 127 (*naṭam āghnānāḥ*); iv. 1. 3.

[4] vi. 3. 43.

dramatic art the rôles of women were reserved for men, though in the classical drama this was by no means necessarily the case. We cannot absolutely prove that in Patañjali's time the drama in its full form of action allied to speech was present, but we know that all its elements existed, and we may legitimately and properly accept its existence in a primitive form.

That form, from the express mention of the subjects of the dramatic exhibitions, we may deduce to have been of the nature of a religious drama. It is difficult not to see in the Kaṅsavadha, the death of Kaṅsa at the hands of Kṛṣṇa, the refined version of an older vegetation ritual in which the representative of the outworn spirit of vegetation is destroyed. Colour is given to this theory by the remarkable fact that in one reading the partisans of the young Kṛṣṇa are red in hue, those of Kaṅsa are black. Now as Kṛṣṇa's name indicates black, it would be almost inevitable that the original attribution of red to his followers should be corrected by well-meaning scribes to black, and this explains effectively the transposition found in the bulk of the manuscripts. In the red hue of Kṛṣṇa's supporters as against the black of those of Kaṅsa we probably have a distinct reminiscence of another side of the slaying of the vegetation spirit.[1] The contest is often presented as one between summer and winter, and we have seen in the Mahāvrata what is probably a primitive form of this contest; the white Vaiçya fights with the black Çūdra for the sun, and attains possession of its symbolical form. The red of Kṛṣṇa's following then proclaims him as the genius of summer who overcomes the darkness of the winter.

With this view accords most interestingly the theory of the origin of the Greek drama from a mimic conflict of summer and winter, as developed by Dr. Farnell.[2] In the legend of the conflict between the Boiotian Xanthos and the Neleid Melanthos we hear that at the moment of conflict Melanthos descried a form beside his foe, whom he taunted with bringing a friend to aid him. Xanthos turned round, and Melanthos slew him.

[1] Keith, ZDMG. lxiv. 534 f.; JRAS. 1911, pp. 979 ff.; 1912, pp. 411 ff.

[2] *The Cults of the Greek States*, v. 233 ff. The variant theory of Miss Harrison, Prof. Gilbert Murray, and Dr. Cornford in *Themis*, and of Dieterich, *Archiv f. Religionswissenschaft*, xi. 163 ff., is much less plausible.

The form was that of Dionysos Melanaigis, and for his intervention the Athenians rewarded him by admission to the Apatouria, the festival of deceit. Thus the black Melanthos with the aid of Dionysos of the black goatskin slays the fair; the dark winter destroys the light of summer. Even in modern times in Northern Thrace[1] is celebrated a popular festival in which a man clad in a goatskin is hailed as king, scatters seed over the crowd—obviously to secure fertility—and ultimately is cast into the river, the usual fate for the outworn spirit of vegetation. In a similar mummery performed near the ancient Thracian capital there is a band of mummers, clad in goatskins, of whom one is killed and lamented by his wife. It is natural to deduce hence that tragedy had its origin in a primitive passion-play performed by men in goatskins, in which an incarnation of a divine spirit was slain and lamented, whence the dirge-like nature of the Greek drama.

The primitive Indian play differs in one essential from this suggested origin of tragedy; the victory lies, as we have seen, with Kṛṣṇa, with the Vaiçya, not with the dark Kaṅsa, the black Çūdra. We have, therefore, not sorrow, though there is death, and the fact that the Sanskrit drama insists on a happy ending is unquestionably most effectively explained if it be brought into connexion with the fact of the origin of the drama in a passion play whose end was happiness through death, not grief. This view has received a remarkable measure of confirmation from the discovery of the plays of Bhāsa; that dramatist does not conform to the rule of the later theory that there must be no slaying on the stage, but he most assuredly conforms to the principle of the *Kaṅsavadha* that the slaying is to be of an enemy of the god; the *Ūrubhaṅga*, which has erroneously[2] been treated as a tragedy is, on the contrary, the depicting of the deplorable fate of an enemy of Kṛṣṇa, and we have from Bhāsa himself the *Bālacarita* which describes the death of several monsters at Kṛṣṇa's hands, and finally of Kaṅsa himself.

In the recitation of the Granthikas divided into two parties

[1] Dawkins, *Journ. Hell. Stud.*, 1906, pp. 191 ff.

[2] Lüders (SBAW. 1916, p. 718, n. 3) is responsible for the view that Duryodhana is the hero. Lindenau (BS. p. 30) accepts this, but gives the true facts (pp. 32, 33), without apparently realizing that the views are contradictory. The *Ūrubhaṅga's* conclusion is happy, not tragic, for the worshipper of Kṛṣṇa.

we have an interesting parallel to the place played according to Aristotle[1] by the dithyramb in the development of the Greek drama. Action was required neither of the singers of the dithyramb nor of the Granthikas, but it was only necessary in one case and the other to introduce action, and the form of the drama would be complete.

Both in the Greek and the Sanskrit drama the essential fact in the contest, from which their origin may thus be traced, is the existence of a conflict. In the Greek drama in its development this conflict came to dominate the play, and in the Indian drama this characteristic is far less prominent. But it is distinctly present in all the higher forms of the art, and we can hardly doubt that it was from this conflict that these higher forms were evolved from the simplicity of the early material out of which the drama rose.

For the religious origin of drama a further fact can be adduced, the character of the Vidūṣaka, the constant and trusted companion of the king, who is the normal hero of an Indian play. The name denotes him as given to abuse,[2] and not rarely in the dramas he and one of the attendants on the queen engage in contests of acrid repartee, in which he certainly does not fare the better. It would be absurd to ignore in this regard the dialogue between the Brahmin and the hetaera in the Mahāvrata, where the exchange of coarse abuse is intended as a fertility charm.

Another religious element may, it has been suggested, be conjectured as present in the Vidūṣaka, the reminiscence of the figure of the Çūdra who is beaten in the ceremony of the purchase of the Soma; possibly it is to this that the hideous appearance attributed to the Vidūṣaka is due. Professor Hillebrandt[3] compares the history of the Harlequin who was originally a representative of the Devil and not a figure of mirth. It may be that these factors concurred in shaping the character of the Vidūṣaka, but the fact that he is treated as a Brahmin is conclusive that the abusive side of his character is the more

[1] *Poetics*, 1449 *a* 10 ff.

[2] Cf. the connexion of Greek Comedy with ritual cathartic cursing; Keith, JRAS. 1912, p. 425, n. For less plausible theories see F. M. Cornford, *The Origin of Attic Comedy* (1914); Ridgeway, *Dramas and Dramatic Dances*, pp. 401 ff.

[3] AID. p. 27. Cf. below, p. 51, n. 1.

important. It is to this doubtless that his use of Prākrit is due; it cannot be conceived that a dialogue of abuse was carried on by the Brahmin in the sacred language, which the hetaera of the primitive social conditions of the Mahāvrata could not possibly be expected to appreciate. Professor Hillebrandt suggests indeed that there is change in the character of the Vidūṣaka in the literature as compared with the account given in the *Nāṭyaçāstra*, but there is clearly no adequate ground for this view.

There is further abundant evidence of the close connexion of the drama with religion; it is attested in the legend of Kṛṣṇa whose feat of slaying Kaṅsa is carried out in the amphitheatre in the presence of the public, where he defeats the wrestlers of his uncle's court, and finally slays the tyrant. The festival of his nativity is essentially a popular spectacle; as developed later, in detail which has often evoked comparison with the Nativity,[1] the young mother, Devakī, is shown on a couch in a stable, with her infant clinging to her; Yaçodā is also there with the little girl, who in the legend meets the fate intended for Kṛṣṇa by Kaṅsa; gods and spirits surround them; Vasudeva stands sword in hand to guard them; the Apsarases sing, the Gandharvas dance, the shepherdesses celebrate the birth, and all night is spent by the audience in gazing at the gay scene. Kṛṣṇa, again, is the lover of the shepherdesses and the inventor of the ardent dance of love, the Rāsamaṇḍala. Of great importance in this regard is the persistence in popularity of the Yātrās, which have survived the decadence of the regular Sanskrit drama. They tell of the loves of Kṛṣṇa and Rādhā, his favourite among the Gopīs, for cowherdesses replace in the pastoral the shepherdesses of European idyllic poetry. Kṛṣṇa is by no means a faithful lover, but the end is always the fruition of Rādhā's love for him. And in Jayadeva's *Gītagovinda* we have in literary form[2] the expression of the substance of the Yātrā, lyric songs, to which must be added the charms of music and the dance. A further consideration of the highest importance attests the influence of the Kṛṣṇa cult: the normal

[1] Weber, *Ueber die Kṛṣṇajanmāṣṭamī* (1868).

[2] The influence of the Kṛṣṇa legend is suggested on the *Vikramorvaçī*; Gawroński, *Les sources de quelques drames indiens*, pp. 33 ff. Cf. below, p. 130.

prose language of the drama is Çaurasenī Prākrit, and we can only suppose that it is so because it was the ordinary speech of the people among whom the drama first developed into definite shape. Once this was established, we may feel assured, the usage would be continued wherever the drama spread; we have modern evidence of the persistence of the Brajbhāshā, the language of the revival of the Kṛṣṇa cult after the Mahomedan invasions in the ancient home of Çaurasenī, as the language of Kṛṣṇa devotion beyond the limits of its natural home.[1] Mathurā, the great centre of Kṛṣṇa worship, still celebrates the Holi festival with rites which resemble the May-day merriment of older England, and still more the phallic orgies of pagan Rome as described by Juvenal. It is an interesting coincidence with the comparison made by Growse[2] of the Holi and the May-day rites that Haraprasād Śāstrin should have found an explanation of the origin of the Indian drama in the fact that at the preliminaries of the play there is special attention devoted to the salutation of Indra's banner, which is a flagstaff decorated with colours and bunting.[3] The Indian legend of the origin of drama tells that, when Bharata was bidden teach on earth the divine art invented by Brahmā, the occasion decided upon was the banner festival (*dhvajamaha*) of Indra. The Asuras rose in wrath, but Indra seized the staff of his banner and beat them off, whence the staff of the banner (*jarjara*) is used as a protection at the beginning of the drama. The drama was, therefore, once connected with the ceremonies of bringing in the Maypole from the woods at the close of the winter, but in India this rite fell at the close of the rainy season, and the ceremony was converted into a festival of thanksgiving for Indra's victory over the clouds, the Asuras. The theory in itself is inadequate, but the preliminaries of the drama are sufficient to show the extraordinary importance attached to propitiation of the gods, a relic of the old religious service, which would be quite out of place if the origin of the drama had been secular.

The importance of Kṛṣṇa must not cause us to ignore the prominent place occupied by Çiva in the history of the drama.

[1] Lévi, TI. i. 331 f. Cf. Bloch, *Langue Marathe*, pp. ix. 12 f.
[2] *Mathurā*, pp. 91 f., 101 f.
[3] JPASB. v. 351 ff.

To him and his spouse are ascribed the invention of the Tāṇḍava[1] and the Lāsya, the violent and the tender and seductive dances, which are so important an element in the representation of a play. Nor is it surprising that a god who in the Vedic period itself is hailed as the patron of men of every profession and occupation should be regarded as the special patron of the artists. But it is probable that this importance in the drama is later than that of Kṛṣṇa, and it is not without significance that Bhāsa, who is older than any of the other classical dramatists, unlike them, celebrates in full Kṛṣṇa, and is a Vaiṣṇava, while Çūdraka, Kālidāsa, Harṣa, and Bhavabhūti alike are adorers of Çiva in their prefaces. The *Mālavikāgnimitra* of Kālidāsa introduces a dancing-master who speaks of the creation of the dance by the god and its close connexion with the drama. The sect of the Pāçupatas, adorers of Çiva as lord of creatures, include in their ritual the song and the dance, the latter consisting in expressing the sentiments of the devotees by means of corporeal movement in accord with the rules of the *Nāṭya-çāstra*. In the decadent ceremonial of the Tantras the ritual includes the representation of Çiva by men, and of his spouse as Çakti, female energy, by women.

The part of Rāma in the growth of drama was certainly not less important than that of Kṛṣṇa himself, for the recitation of the *Rāmāyaṇa* was popular throughout the country, and has persisted in vogue. The popularity of the story is proved to the full by the effect of the Rām-Līlā or Daçārha festival, at which the story is presented in dumb show, children taking the places of Rāma, Sītā, and Lakṣmaṇa before a vast concourse of pilgrims and others. No effort is made to speak the parts, but a series of tableaux recalls to the minds of the devotees, to whom the whole tale is familiar, the course of the history of the hero, his banishment, his search for Sītā, and his final triumph. In Rāma's case the influence of the epic on the drama appears in its full development.[2]

The religious importance of the drama is seen distinctly in

[1] Megasthenes ascribed the Kordax to the Indian Dionysos (Çiva); Arrian, *Ind.* 7. Bloch (ZDMG. lxii. 655) exaggerates his importance.

[2] Cf. Ridgeway, *Dramas and Dramatic Dances*, p. 190, and pp. 192 ff. on modern Indian drama in general.

the attitude of the Buddhists towards it.[1] The extreme dubiety of the date of the Buddhist Suttas renders it impossible to come to any satisfactory decision regarding the existence of drama at any early date, while the terms employed, such as Visūka-dassana, Nacca, and Pekkhā, and the reference to Samajjas leave us wholly without any ground for belief in an actual drama. We see, however, that the objection of the sacred Canon to monks engaging in the amusement of watching these shows, whatever their nature, was gradually overcome, and it is an important fact that the earliest dramas known to us by fragments are the Buddhist dramas of Açvaghoṣa. With the acceptance of the drama, the *Lalitavistara*[2] does not hesitate to speak of the Buddha as including knowledge of the drama as among his accomplishments; the Buddha is even called one who has entered to gaze on the drama of the Great Law. The legend is willing to admit that even in Buddha's time there were dramas, for Bimbisāra had one performed in honour of a pair of Nāga kings,[3] and the *Avadānaçataka*,[4] a collection of pious tales, places the drama in remote antiquity. It was performed by the bidding of Krakucchanda, a far distant Buddha in the city Çobhāvatī by a troupe of actors; the director undertook the rôle of the Buddha himself, while the other members of the troupe took the rôle of monks; the same troupe in a later age, under Gautama the Buddha himself, performed at Rājagṛha, the actress Kuvalayā gaining enormous fame, and seducing the monks, until the Buddha terminated her career by turning her into a hideous old woman. She then repented and attained the rank of a saint. The same idea of a play bearing on the life of the Buddha himself is preserved in another tale in Tibet where an actor from the south sets up in rivalry with the monks in giving representations of the life of the Buddha. These Buddhist dramas have left their imprint on the form of the *Saddharmapuṇḍarīka*, the Lotus of the Good Law, itself, which has none of the epic character of the *Lalitavistara*, but is pre-

[1] Lévi, TI. i. 319 ff. That any of the early Buddhist texts (e.g. *Padhānasutta*, *Pabbajjāsutta*; *Mārasaṁyutta*, *Bhikkhunīsaṁyutta*; *Chaddanta-*, *Ummadantī-*, *Mahājanaka-*, or *Candakinnara-jātaka*; *Theragāthā*, 866 ff.; *Therīgāthā*, 912 ff.) is really dramatic is out of the question; cf. Winternitz, VOJ. xxvii. 38 f.

[2] xii. p. 178. Drama is alluded to in *Divyāvadāna*, pp. 357, 360, 361.

[3] Schiefner, IS. iii. 483, *Indian Tales*, pp. 236 ff.

[4] ii. 24 (75).

sented as a series of dialogues in which the Buddha himself, now supernatural, is the chief, but not the only interlocutor. The same love of the Buddhists for artistic effects is seen in the use of music, song, dance, and some scenic effects in the ceremonial attaching to the foundation of Thūpas in Ceylon by a prince of the royal house; the *Mahāvaṅsa* assumes that dramas were displayed on such occasions, though this may be an anachronism. The frescoes of Ajaṇṭā show the keen appreciation felt for music, song, and the dance, though they date from a time when there is certain evidence of the full existence of the drama. We find also in Tibet[1] the relics of ancient popular religious plays in the contests between the spirits of good and those of evil for mankind, which are part of the spring and autumn festivals. The actors wear strange garments and masks; monks represent the good spirits, laymen the evil spirits of men. The whole company first sings prayers and benedictions; then an evil spirit seeks to seduce into evil a man; he would yield but for the intervention of his friends; the evil spirits then arrive in force, a struggle ensues, in which the men would be defeated but for the intervention of the good spirits, and the whole ends with the chasing away with blows of the representatives of the spirits of evil.

With Jainism it is as with Buddhism; we find censure of such ideal enjoyments as the arts akin to the drama, but also recognition of song, music, dance, and scenic presentations in the Canon.[2] But it is hopeless, in view of the utter uncertainty of the date of that collection, to draw any conclusion from it as to the age of the drama. As in the case of Buddhism, Jainism in its development was glad to have recourse to the drama as a means of propagating its beliefs.[3]

The evidence is conclusive on the close connexion of religion and the drama, and it strongly suggests that it was from religion

[1] E. Schlagintweit, *Buddhism in Tibet*, p. 233; JASB. 1865, p. 71. Ridgeway's *Dramas, &c.*, ignores Tibet. For similar Chinese performances, see *Annales Guimet*, xii. 416 f.

[2] *Āyāraṅga Sutta*, ii. 11. 14; *Rājapraçnīya*, IS. xvi. 385. The love of the Indians for song and dance is recorded by Greek tradition; Arrian, *Anabasis*, vi. 2.

[3] Unfortunately the date of this change of view is uncertain. No early Jain drama is certainly recorded. A number of mediaeval works have recently been printed; see E. Hultzsch, ZDMG. lxxv. 59 ff.

that the decisive impulse to dramatic creation was given. The importance of the epic is doubtless enormous, but the mere recitation of the epics, however closely it might approach to the drama, does not overstep the bounds. The element which fails to be added is that of the dramatic contest, the Agon of the Greek drama. That this was supplied by the development of such primitive vegetation rituals as that of the Mahāvrata, until they assumed the concrete and human form of the Kṛṣṇa and Kaṅsa legend would be a conjecture worth consideration, but without possibility of proof if we had not the notice of the *Mahābhāṣya* which expressly shows that the story of Kṛṣṇa and Kaṅsa could both be represented by Granthikas, who coloured their faces and expressed vividly the emotions of those whom they represented, but also, in dumb show seemingly, by Çaubhikas. If there did not exist an Indian drama proper, in which these sides were combined when Patañjali wrote, it is fair to say that it would be surprising if it did not develop shortly afterwards, and we have perfectly certain proof that the Naṭas of Patañjali were much more than dancers or acrobats; they sang and recited. The balance of probability, therefore, is that the Sanskrit drama came into being shortly after, if not before, the middle of the second century B.C., and that it was evoked by the combination of epic recitations with the dramatic moment of the Kṛṣṇa legend, in which a young god strives against and overcomes enemies.

The drama which was nascent in Patañjali's time must be taken to have been, like the classical drama, one in which Sanskrit was mingled with Prākrit in the speeches of the characters. The epic recitations of the slaying of Kaṅsa which he records must have been in Sanskrit, but, if the drama was to be popular—and the *Nāṭyaçāstra* in its tale of the origin of the art recognizes both its epic and popular characteristics, the humble people who figured in it must have been allowed to speak in their own vernacular; this accords brilliantly with the presence of Çaurasenī as the normal prose of the drama of the classical stage. A different view is taken by Professor Lévi,[1]

[1] JA. sér. 9, xix. 95 ff. If this had been the case, one would have found references freely to the literature in Hāla, where only v. 344 alludes to the Pūrvaraṅga of the Nāṭaka (*raiṇāḍaapuvvaraṁgassa*).

who conceives that the drama sprang first into being in Prākrit, while Sanskrit was only later applied at the time when Sanskrit, long reserved as a sacred language, re-entered into use as the language of literature; India, he contends, was never anxious for contact with reality, and it is absurd to suppose that the mixture of languages was adopted as a representation of the actual speech-usage of the time and circles in which drama came into being. This contention is supported by the observation that a number of the technical terms of the *Nāṭyaçāstra* are of strange appearance, and the frequency of cerebral letters in them suggests Prākrit origin. The contention can hardly be treated as satisfactory, nor is it clear how it can possibly be reconciled with the evidence of Patañjali. The early drama, it seems clear, was not secular in origin, and Professor Lévi emphasizes its dependence on the cult of Kṛṣṇa; to refuse to use Sanskrit in it, therefore, would be extremely strange, unless we are to assume that the existence of true drama goes back to a period considerably earlier than Patañjali, and that it came into being among a milieu which was not Brahminical. There are very serious difficulties in such a theory; we may legitimately hold that such a literary form as the true drama was not created until the Brahmin genius fused the ethic and religious agonistic motives into a new creation of the highest importance for the literary history of India. The presence of a number of Prākrit terms in the *Nāṭyaçāstra* is probable, but it does not mean that a theory of drama was first excogitated in Prākrit; the main theory in all its essentials is expressed in Sanskrit, and all that is borrowed from Prākrit is some technical terms of subsidiary importance, borrowed, doubtless, from the minor arts, which go to aid but do not constitute the drama, song, music, dancing, and the mimetic art.

The religious origin of the Sanskrit drama in Kṛṣṇa worship is also admitted as part, however, of a wider thesis by Dr. Ridgeway,[1] who contends that Greek drama, and drama all over the world, are the outcome of the reverence paid to the spirits

[1] *The Origin of Tragedy* (1910); *Dramas and Dramatic Dances of non-European Races* (1915); JRAS. 1916, pp. 821 ff.; Keith, JRAS. 1916, pp. 335 ff.; 1917, pp. 140 ff. G. Norwood (*Greek Tragedy*, pp. 2 f.) rejects Ridgeway's view for Greece, and see Keith, JRAS. 1912, pp. 411 ff.

of the dead, which again is the source of all religion, a revival in fact of the doctrine of animism in one of its connotations. The contention as applied to the Indian drama involves the view that the actors in the primitive drama were representatives of the spirits of the dead, and that the performance was meant to gratify the dead. It is supported by the doctrine that not only Rāma and Kṛṣṇa were believed once to be men, but that Çiva himself had this origin;[1] all gods indeed are derived from the memory of noble men. The evidence adduced for this thesis is simply non-existent. A valuable collection of material due to Sir J. H. Marshall proves the prevalence throughout India of popular dramatic performances celebrating the deeds of Rāma and Kṛṣṇa, and the modern Indian drama deals also with the lives of distinguished historical characters such as Açoka or Candragupta. But there is nothing to show that the idea of gratifying the dead by the performances of dramatic scenes based on their history was ever present to any mind in India, either early or late. Rāma and Kṛṣṇa to their worshippers were long before the rise of so late an art as drama, just like Çiva, great gods, of whom it would be absurd to think as dead men requiring funeral rites to give them pleasure. Nor is it necessary further to criticize his reconstruction of Vedic religion on the basis of his animistic theory, for these issues of origins have no possible relevance to the specific question of the origin of the Indian drama. Whether elsewhere the worship of the dead resulted in drama is a matter open to grave doubt; certainly in the case of the Greek drama, which offers the most interesting parallel to that of India, the evidence of derivation from funeral games is wholly defective.

Definite support for this view of the origin of drama may be found in the accounts of dramatic performances which are given in the *Harivaṅça*, the supplement of the *Mahābhārata*. That work cannot, as has been mentioned, be dated with any certainty or probability earlier than the dramas of Açvaghoṣa, and, therefore, it cannot be appealed to as the earliest mention now extant of the dramatic art. But it is of value as showing how closely

[1] *Drama, &c.*, p. 129 asserts this as the view of 'the best authorities'; very wisely he does not refer to these amazing authorities. Cf. E. Arbman, *Rudra* (Uppsala, 1922); Keith, *Indian Mythology*, pp. 81 ff.

connected the drama was in early times with the Kṛṣṇa cult, thus supplementing the conclusions to be derived from the *Mahābhāṣya*, and falling into line with the evidence of Bhāsa.

At the festival performed by the Yādavas after the death of Andhaka, we find that the women of the place danced and sang to music, while Kṛṣṇa induced celestial nymphs to aid the merriment by similar exhibitions, including a representation by the Apsarases, apparently by dancing, of the death of Kaṅsa and Pralamba, the fall of Cāṇūra in the amphitheatre, and various other exploits of Kṛṣṇa. After they had performed, the sage Nārada amused the audience by a series of what may fairly be called comic turns; he imitated the gestures, the movements, and even the laughter of such distinguished personages as Satyabhāmā, Keçava, Arjuna, Baladeva, and the young princess, the daughter of Revata, causing infinite amusement to the audience, and reminding us of the part played by the Vidūṣaka in the drama. The Yādavas then supped, and this enjoyment was followed by further songs and dances by the Apsarases, whose performance thus resembled a modern ballet with songs interspersed.[1]

In a later passage [2] in connexion with the story of the demon Vajranābha, whom Indra asked Kṛṣṇa to dispose of, we learn of an actor Bhadra who delighted all by his excellent power of representation; Vajranābha is induced to demand his presence in his abode, and Kṛṣṇa's son Pradyumna and his friends disguise themselves to penetrate there; Pradyumna is to be the hero, Sāmba the Vidūṣaka, and Gada the assistant of the stage director, while maidens, skilled in song, dance, and music, are the actresses; they delight the demons by presenting the story of Viṣṇu's descent on earth to slay the chief of the Rākṣasas, a dramatised version of the *Rāmāyaṇa*, presenting the figures of Rāma, his brother, and in special the episode of Ṛṣyaçṛṅga and Çāntā, that curious old legend based on a fertility- and rain-ritual.[3] After the play the actors showed their skill in depicting

[1] ii. 88.

[2] ii. 91. 26 ff.; 93. 1 ff. Cf. Hertel, VOJ. xxiv. 117 ff.; Ravivarman, *Pradyumnābhyudaya*, Act III, p. 23.

[3] Cf. von Schroeder, *Mysterium und Mimus*, pp. 292 ff. That this was originally a ritual drama is most improbable.

situations suggested by their hosts, and Vajranābha himself induces them to perform an episode from the legend of Kubera, the rendezvous of Rambhā; after music from the orchestra the actresses sing, Pradyumna enters and recites the benediction, and then a verse on the descent of the Ganges, which is connected with the subject-matter of the piece; he then assumes the role of Nalakūbara, Sāmba is his Vidūṣaka, Çūra plays Rāvaṇa, Manovatī Rambhā. Nalakūbara curses Rāvaṇa, and consoles Rambhā, and the audience was delighted by the skilled acting of the Yādavas, who by a magic illusion had presented mount Kailāsa on the stage.

4. *Theories of the Secular Origin of the Drama*

Professors Hillebrandt[1] and Konow[2] agree in the main in maintaining the view that it is an error to look to religious ceremonies as explaining the origin of the drama. True, these ceremonies have a share in the development of the drama, but they themselves are merely the introduction into the ritual of elements which have a popular origin. We are to believe that a popular mime existed, which, with the epic, lies at the bottom of the Sanskrit drama.

It must be admitted at once that we have extremely little authentic information regarding the performers of these mimes, believed to have existed before the origin of drama. The statements made by Professor Konow, who finds in them experts in song, dance, music, but also in matters such as jugglery, pantomime, and the allied arts, all rest on evidence which is either contemporary with the *Mahābhāṣya* or later than it; the fact that Naṭas sang is recorded for us in the *Mahābhāṣya*, which of course may refer to genuine actors, and not to professors of the mime, and their connexion with sweet words is attested in the Jātaka prose only, which dates several centuries after the existence of the true drama. We need not, of course, doubt that music, song, and dance, popular in the Vedic age, preserved that character throughout the later period, and we have evidence from Açoka's time onwards of the existence of Samājas which he condemned, doubtless because of the fights of animals which took

[1] AID. pp. 22 ff. [2] ID. pp. 42 ff.

place at them.[1] That Naṭas and Nartakas were present at such festivals we learn from the *Rāmāyaṇa*; but we cannot say whether pantomimes and dancers or actors and dancers are referred to. Our knowledge, in fact, of the primitive mime is hypothetical, and it rests in effect on certain considerations which Professor Hillebrandt adduces to show a popular as opposed to a religious origin for drama. His view is supported by the general argument that the drama as comedy is a natural expression of man's primitive life of pleasure and appreciation of humour and wit. It is, however, unnecessary to enter into any examination of this general principle, which he defends against the theory accepted by Dr. Gray that it is highly problematical whether any view of pleasure to the actors or audience is associated with primitive drama. These ultimate origins are a matter of indifference to the concrete question of the origin of so late a production as the classical drama of India. That the mimetic character is natural to man may be granted; the essential point in question is whether the Sanskrit drama in its characteristics shows signs of religious or secular origin.

Of the points adduced by Professor Hillebrandt most have clearly no relevance in the argument. The use of Sanskrit and dialects in the classical drama is claimed as a proof of popular origin; as has been explained above, the Prākrit element is due to the fact that the drama contains an essential popular, but also religious, element, the Kṛṣṇa worship. The mixture of prose and song, and the union of both with music and the dance, are as natural on the theory of religious origin as on that of secular derivation. The simplicity of the Indian stage, which knows no arrangements for providing changes of scenery, is certainly no proof of secular origin; the Vedic religion is singularly sparing in any external apparatus, and there is the strongest similarity between its practice to mark out altars for its great sacrifices at pleasure, and to have no regular sacrificial buildings, and the tradition throughout the Sanskrit dramas which neither requires nor needs fixed theatres.

The popular origin of the Vidūṣaka is obvious, but the point is whether this origin is religious or secular, and we have seen

[1] Hardy, *Album Kern*, pp. 61 f.; Thomas, JRAS. 1914, pp. 392 f.

[2] ERE. iv. 868.

that the Vedic literature offers us in the Brahmin of the Mahāvrata the prototype, possibly with reminiscences of the Çūdra in the Soma sale, of this figure, a fact admitted by the supporters of the theory of secular origin. It is manifestly unnecessary and illegitimate, when the descent of this figure from the Vedic literature is clear, to insist that it was borrowed directly from popular usage, for which there is no proof, but only conjecture.

There remains the argument derived from the fact that the classical drama usually begins with a dialogue between the Sūtradhāra and the Naṭī, who is usually represented as his wife; in this we have, it is said, a reflex of the old popular mime. But an examination of the practice and theory, as found in Bhāsa and the *Nāṭyaçāstra*, shows that we have no simple or naïve arrangement, but a very elaborate literary device by which the actors bridge over the transition from the preliminaries of the drama to the drama itself. The preliminaries are essentially popular religion, and the detail was left largely in the hands of the Sūtradhāra and his assistants, aided by a chorus of dancers and by musicians; they are doubtless older than the drama, and it was an ingenious and happy device which was invented to carry on the preliminaries, so that the transition to the drama was effective and satisfactory. It is, however, a perversion of all probability to find in this item the trace of a primitive popular secular performance.

The evidence, therefore, for a secular origin disappears; it is curious, indeed, that Professor Hillebrandt[1] himself adduces proof that the western parallel of the Vidūṣaka is connected with religious ceremonies rather than a secular creation. But what is most remarkable of all is that Professor Konow adduces as evidence of the secular origin of the drama the Yātrās, which are essentially bound up with the religion of Kṛṣṇa, and the rough dramatic sketches performed at Almora at the Holi festival, also

[1] AID. p. 25. Lindenau (BS. p. 45) sees in Vṛṣākapi of *Ṛgveda*, x. 86, the prototype of the Vidūṣaka, as a maker of mischief and as the god's companion, bu this is far-fetched. Hertel (*Literarisches Zentralbl.* 1917, pp. 1198 ff.) lays stress on the fact that at the royal courts the king had normally a jester to amuse him. This may easily have served to affect the figure of this character, if of religious origin. For older views, cf. J. Huizinga, *De Vidūṣaka en het indisch tooneel* (Groningen, 1897); F. Cimmini, *Atti della reale Accademia di Archeologia, Lettere et Be.. Arti* (Naples, 1893), xv. 97 ff.; M. Schuyler, JAOS. xx. 338 ff.; P. E. Pavolini, *Studi italiani di filologia indo-iranica*, ii. 88 f.

essentially religious.[1] It is indeed to ignore how essentially religion enters into the life of the Hindu to imagine that it is possible to trace the beginnings of drama to a detached love of amusement. It is apparently difficult for the modern mind to appreciate that religion may cover matters which to us appear scarcely connected with it or even repugnant; but this is a delusion largely due to the narrower and more exalted conception of religion of the northern and western lands of Europe.

Less plausible still is the attempt of Pischel[2] to find evidence that the puppet-play is the source of the Sanskrit drama, and that moreover it has its home in India, whence it has spread over the world. The curious and odd art may indeed have an Indian origin, but it would be wholly unwise to suppose that the drama is due to it, nor is the theory apparently accepted on any side at the present time. The existence of such a play is attested by the *Mahābhārata*,[3] though the antiquity of the device is not thus made clear; in the *Kathāsaritsāgara*, following perhaps the *Bṛhatkathā* of Guṇāḍhya, possibly of the third century A.D., we hear of a damsel, daughter of the wonderful craftsman Asura Maya, who amused her companion with puppets which could speak, dance, fly, fetch water, or pluck and bring a garland. In the *Bālarāmāyaṇa* of Rājaçekhara Rāvaṇa is represented as deceived by a puppet made to resemble Sītā, in whose mouth a parrot was placed to give his entreaties suitable replies. Shaṅkar Pāṇḍuraṅg Paṇḍit[4] records of his time that in the Marāṭha and Kanarese country there are travelling marionette theatres, the only form of drama known in the villages; the puppets made of wood or paper are managed by the director, whose style is Sūtradhāra; they can stand or lie, dance or fight. From this puppet-play, it was suggested, the names of the Sūtradhāra, as the puller of the strings, and of the Sthāpaka, arranger, his assistant, passed over to the legitimate drama. The Vidūṣaka, in Pischel's view, owed also his origin to the puppet-play.

Professor Hillebrandt[5] has argued against this theory on the ground that the puppet-play assumes the pre-existence of the

[1] TD. pp. 43 f. Cf. Nisikânta Chattopâdhyâya, *The Yâtrâs* (1882).

[2] *Die Heimat des Puppenspiels* (1902). Obvious objections are given by Ridgeway, *Dramas, &c.*, pp. 164 ff.

[3] iii. 30. 23; v. 39. 1.

[4] *Vikramorvaçīya*, pp. 4 f.

[5] AID. p. 8; ZDMG. lxxii. 231.

drama, on which it must essentially be based, and he then uses the early date of the puppet-play as a proof of the still earlier existence of the drama. The latter argument, however, is unsatisfactory on various grounds. Apart from the fact that we cannot date the epic references or prove them earlier than the *Mahābhāṣya*, we have the doubt whether such a contention can possibly be justified. The use of puppets is primarily, of course, derived from the make-belief of children in playing with dolls; the terms for puppets which denote 'little daughter' (*putrikā*, *puttalī*, *puttalikā*, *duhitṛkā*), show this clearly enough, and the popularity of puppets is indicated by the erotic game known as the imitation of puppets, where the word for puppet (*pāñcālī*) suggests that the home of the puppet-play in India was the Pañcāla country. The growth of the drama doubtless brought with it the use of puppets to imitate it in brief, and from the drama came the Vidūṣaka, and not *vice versa*.

Though Pischel's theory [1] of the puppet-play as the origin of drama has failed to find supporters, the shadow play, on whose importance in India he was the first to lay stress, has emerged in lieu in the hands of Professor Lüders [2] as an essential element in the development of the Sanskrit drama, a position accepted by Professor Konow. The place found for the drama is in connexion with the displays of the Çaubhikas of the *Mahābhāṣya*. Owing to the misinterpretation of that passage it is held that the Çaubhikas were persons who explained matters to the audience to supplement either dumb actors [3] or shadow figures. It is admitted by Professor Lüders that there is no proof which of these two eventualities is correct, but he endeavours both to prove the existence of the shadow-play in early India and to show that the Çaubhikas had the function of showing them. Based on this misinterpretation of the *Mahābhāṣya* and on the hypotheses—wholly in the air—which it necessitates, is his view that the influence of the epic on the drama was conveyed through

[1] SBAW. 1906, pp. 481 ff.

[2] SBAW. 1916, pp. 698 ff. *Contra*, Hillebrandt, ZDMG. lxxii. 230 f. Winternitz (ZDMG. lxxiv. 120) reduces the Çaubhikas to people who tell tales of what is depicted on pictures, a clearly impossible version, but valid against Lüders.

[3] Based on Kaiyaṭa's version of Çaubhika: *Kaṁsādyanukāriṇāṁ naṭānāṁ vyākhyānopādhyāyāḥ*. This is clearly incompatible with Lüders's view, as he admits (pp. 720 f.). Kaiyaṭa is far too late or useful evidence.

the use of shadow-figures to illustrate the epic recitation; this, united with the art of the old Naṭas, gave birth to drama, though he is not certain whether such a real drama existed or not at the time of Patañjali, and Konow sets its appearance much later.

The early evidence adduced for the existence of the shadow-drama is wholly unreliable. Professor Konow suggests that the term Rūpa used in the fourth Rock Edict of Açoka, where he speaks of exhibiting spectacles of the dwellings of the gods, of elephants and bonfires, refers to a shadow device, in apparent ignorance of the true sense abundantly illustrated by the attested facts as to the mode of such representations in Buddhist literature;[1] he accepts the wholly absurd view that Rūpaka as a name of the drama is derived from such shadow projections, while in fact it obviously denotes the visible presentation, the normal and early sense of Rūpa. Equally unfortunate is the effort to discover that the Sītābengā cave[2] shows signs of grooves in front, which might have served in connexion with the curtain necessary for a shadow play, and much more so is the effort to explain Nepathya, the name of the tiring-room behind the curtain in the Sanskrit drama, from a misunderstood Prākrit *nevaccha*, which in its turn might represent a Sanskrit *naipāṭhya*—never found—denoting the place for the reader; apparently the shadows are in this view explained by some person behind the curtain. The philological combination is quite impossible.

Pischel's evidence for the early existence of the shadow-drama is all of it without value. The term *rupparūpakam* occurs in v. 394 of the comparatively old *Therīgāthā* of the Buddhist Canon, but it may indicate a puppet-play, and this is rendered very probable by the mention of a puppet only just before in the text; if not, it doubtless means, as taken by the commentator, a piece of jugglery, an art always loved in India; unfortunately the age of the text is uncertain, so that even for the puppet-play it gives no precise date. It is certain that *rūpadakkha*, a term used in the *Milindapañha*[3]—a work of dubious date—has no such reference, nor *lūpadakha* in a cave at Jogīmārā. To find *rūpopajīvana* in the *Mahābhārata* used in the sense of shadow-

[1] See Vincent Smith, *Asoka*, (ed. 3), pp. 166 f.

[2] Bloch, *Arch. Survey of India Report*, 1903-4, pp. 123 ff.

[3] p. 344.

play is impossible; the explanation is given by Nīlakaṇṭha,[1] and proves the existence in his time, the seventeenth century A.D., of the custom, but the term is used in close proximity with appearing on the stage (*rañgāvataraṇa*), and there is conclusive evidence that the word refers to the deplorable immorality of the players, who actually have as a synonym in the lexicons the style of 'living by (the dishonour of) their wives (*jāyājīva*)'. The same fact explains the term *rūpopajīvin* used by Varāhamihira in the sixth century A.D. in proximity to painters, writers, and singers: the actor is essentially mercenary.[2] It is impossible to accept the suggestion that the Aindrajālikas, who appear working magic results in the *Ratnāvalī*, the *Prabodhacandrodaya*, and the Pūrvapīṭhikā of the *Daçakumāracarita*, were really shadow-dramatists; Indian magicians are well known even at present, and the illusions which to some extent they produce have nothing whatever to do with shadow-plays. The scenes which the magician describes to the king in the *Ratnāvalī* were doubtless left to the imagination of the audience, just as was the apparent fire which burned the inner apartments and enveloped the princess. To believe in realism in these cases runs contrary to the stage directions of the play itself. From the name Çaubhika, with its Prākrit equivalent Sobhiya, nothing whatever can be made out; the word has no relation to shadows and is never explained by any authority in that sense.

We are left, therefore, with the evidence to be derived from the term Chāyānāṭaka, which is interpreted by Pischel as a 'shadow-drama', and is applied to several dramas, among which the oldest which can be dated with sufficient certainty is the *Dūtāñgada* of Subhaṭa in the thirteenth century A.D. The exact meaning of the term is uncertain, as it might denote a 'drama in the state of a shadow', and this would accord perfectly with the *Dūtāñgada* itself. That such a drama was a shadow-drama is best supported by the *Dharmābhyudaya* of Meghaprabhācārya,[3] which is styled a Chāyānāṭyaprabandha, and in which a definite stage direction is found directing that, when the king expresses his intention to become an ascetic, a puppet is to be placed inside the curtain in the attire of an ascetic. But the

[1] xii. 295. 5. [2] *Bṛhatsaṁhitā*, v. 74; see Hillebrandt, ZDMG. lxxii. 227.
[3] ZDMG. lxxv. 69 f.

date of this play is uncertain, and it is extremely difficult to argue with any certainty from it to the *Dūtāṅgada*; why, it is inevitable to ask, should the latter play contain no stage direction of this kind? We know that the shadow-drama arose in some part of India, for Nīlakaṇṭha recognizes it, but we have no evidence that it existed at the time of the *Dūtāṅgada*.

Whatever judgement be passed on this view,[1] and the matter must be left undecided in the absence of any effective evidence, it is wholly impossible to accept the argument of Professor Lüders which would take the *Dūtāṅgada* as the type of Chāyānāṭaka, and thence deduce that the *Mahānāṭaka* and the *Haridūta* are shadow-dramas. The one Chāyānāṭya which we know to have been a shadow-drama in fact is an ordinary play without kinship to the *Dūtāṅgada*, and the same remark applies to the other dramas known to us which are styled Chāyānāṭakas. There are, however, points of similarity between the *Dūtāṅgada* and the *Mahānāṭaka*; the prevalence of verse, often epic in character, over prose, the absence of Prākrit, the large number of characters, and the omission of the Vidūṣaka, which explain themselves easily in the latter case by the assumption that we have literary drama before us, a play never intended to be acted. The conviction is strengthened by the shameless plagiarisms of the plays from earlier Rāma dramas. In any case, however, we are dealing with the late developments of the Sanskrit drama, and it is clear that nothing can be gained from any assumption of a part played by the shadow-play in the evolution of the Sanskrit drama. Even on Professor Lüders's own interpretation of the *Mahābhāṣya*, all that is requisite is dumb players, and this form of drama is attested for India in modern times.

That the Sūtradhāra and Sthāpaka derive their names from manipulating the puppets for either the puppet- or the shadow-drama is a suggestion which, though recently repeated by Dr. Hultzsch, cannot be regarded as plausible.[2] The term Sthāpaka is colourless, and may merely denote 'performer'; if it comes from the puppet-play, it is difficult to see why such a person was needed beside the Sūtradhāra, who moved the strings. Moreover, the theory recognizes the Sūtradhāra clearly

[1] See ch. xi, § 8 below.

[2] See ch. xiv, § 2 below.

as the man who lays out the temporary playhouse needed for the exhibition, and this sense passes easily over into that of director; this derivation is preferable on the whole to the other, accepted by Professor Hillebrandt,[1] which would make him the man who knows the rules of his art.

The shadow-play, we have seen, cannot have influenced the progress of the early drama, and we may, therefore, leave aside the question whether it does not essentially presuppose the drama, as Professor Hillebrandt contends; the parallel from Java adduced to refute this opinion is clearly wholly inadequate, unless and until it can be proved that the shadow play sprang up in Java without any previous knowledge of real drama.

5. *Greek Influence on the Sanskrit Drama*

It is undoubtedly a matter far from easy for any people to create from materials such as existed in India a true drama, and it was a perfectly legitimate suggestion of Weber's[2] that the necessary impetus to creation may have been given by the contact of Greece with India, through the representation of Greek plays at the courts of the kings in Baktria, the Punjab, and Gujarāt, who brought with them Greek culture as well as Greek forces. This view suffered modification in view of further consideration of the evidence of an Indian drama in the *Mahābhāṣya*, and the final opinion of Weber was content with the view that a certain influence might have been exerted by the Greek on the Sanskrit drama. The vehement repudiation of this opinion by Pischel[3] was followed by the elaborate effort of Windisch[4] to trace the extent of the influence which he believed he could establish. Windisch's attitude is of special importance because he recognizes fully the elements which made for the development of an independent Indian drama, the epic recitations and the mimetic art of the Naṭa, whose name indicated, as a Prākritism of the root *nṛt*, dance, that he was at first a dancer, in the Indian sense of the term, that is one who represents by

[1] AID. p. 8, n. 2. On Javan drama, cf. Ridgeway, *Dramas, &c.*, pp. 216 ff.

[2] IS. ii. 148; *Ind. Lit.*[2] p. 210; SBAW. 1890, p. 920; cf. IS. xiii. 492.

[3] *Die Recensionen der Çakuntalā* (1875), p. 19; SBAW. 1906, p. 502.

[4] *Der griechische Einfluss im indischen Drama* (1882); *Sansk. Phil.* pp. 398 ff. Cf. E. Brandes, *Lervognen* (1870), pp. iii ff.; Vincent Smith, JASB. lviii. 1. 184 ff.

his postures and gestures emotions of varied kinds, or, in the terminology of the Greek and Roman stage, a pantomime. But he insists on the distinction between the dramatization of the epic material suggested by the *Mahābhāṣya*, and the features of the classical form of the drama. The subject-matter differs, heroic and mythic figures are presented in the relations of everyday life, the chief theme is a comedy of love, the plot is artistically developed and the action divided into scenes, character types are developed, the epic element recedes before the development of dialogue, verse is mingled with prose, Sanskrit with Prākrit. The change is remarkable; was it aided by the influence of the Greek drama? Admittedly on any theory we must allow for powerful causes to produce so splendid a development, and it would be idle to ignore the possibility of such influence.

Since Windisch wrote, the extent of Greek influence on India before and after the Christian era has been the subject of much investigation, which has yielded its richest fruits in the sphere of art. That India borrowed the incitement to the art of Gandhāra from Greece as its ultimate source is undeniable, and it is equally clear that the Buddhist adoption of the practice of depicting the human form of the Buddha, in lieu of merely indicating his presence by some symbol such as his seat, was due to Greek artistic influences. The extent to which the rise of the Mahāyāna school of Buddhism was furthered by the influx of religious and philosophical ideas from the west is still uncertain; but it is noteworthy that Professor Lévi,[1] who most strongly opposed the theory of Windisch, has himself attributed to western influences the development of the new spirit in Buddhism which he traces in Açvaghoṣa, whom he places in the entourage of Kaniṣka, dating the former in the first century B.C. If this were the case, there would be decided difficulties in maintaining any chronological objections such as Professor Lévi[2] originally urged to the theory of Windisch; when he attacked that theory he could place the earliest Sanskrit dramas preserved, those of Kālidāsa in his view, five or six centuries A.D. But now we have dramas of about A.D. 100 which are certainly not the earliest of their

[1] *Mahāyānasūtrālaṁkāra*, ii. 16 f. Cf. Keith, *Buddhist Philosophy*, p. 217.

[2] TI. i. 345.

type, and it is impossible to deny that the Sanskrit drama came into being during the period when Greek influence was present in India. The highest point of that influence politically was doubtless attained under Menander; in the middle of the first century B.C., roughly a century after Menander's conquests, the Greek princes were on the verge of being absorbed by new influences culminating in the establishment of the Kuṣana[1] domination, but there is nothing chronologically difficult in assuming the influence of Greek drama on the drama in India.

The question, however, arises how far there was actual presentation at the courts of Greek princes in India of dramatic entertainments. On this topic the evidence is no doubt scanty.[2] We know indeed that Alexander was fond of theatrical spectacles with which he amused himself in the intervals allowed by his victories, and we hear that at Ekbatana there were no fewer than three thousand Greek artists who had come from Greece. We are told also that the children of the Persians, the Gedrosians and the people of Susa, sang the dramas of Euripides and Sophokles; if we are to believe Philostratos's Life of Apollonios of Tyana,[3] a Brahmin boasted that he had read the *Herakleidai* of Euripides, and Plutarch has described in inimitable fashion the strange scene at the court of Orodes of Parthia when the messenger arrived, bearing the head of Crassus, and the actor Iason substituted the ghastly relic for the head of Pentheus in the *Bakchai*, which he was then performing. We need not doubt from these and other passages the existence of performances of Greek dramas throughout the provinces which formed the Empire of Alexander; the scepticism of Professor Lévi[4] in this regard is clearly inadmissible. It is perfectly true that of dramatic performances in India we have no express mention, but in view of the miserably scanty information we possess regarding these principalities of the Greeks in India there is nothing surprising in the fact. Nor is it likely that princes who could employ artists of sufficient ability to produce

[1] Or Kuṣāṇa; CHI. i. 580 ff.

[2] Plutarch, *Alex.* 72; *Fort. Alex.* 128 D; *Crassus*, 33. Marshall (JRAS. 1909, pp. 1060 f.) suggests a reproduction of a motif of the *Antigone* in a vase at Peshawar, but dubiously.

[3] ii. 32.

[4] TI. ii. 60.

beautiful coins would be indifferent to what is after all the greatest literary creation of Greece.

Nor can we lay much stress on the difficulty of India borrowing anything from the Greek drama, owing to the great difference between the two civilizations, Indian exclusiveness, Indian ignorance of foreign languages, or similar general considerations, because we have really no evidence of value of the feelings and actions of the Indians during the period when the Greek invasion was only the forerunner of invasions by Parthians, Çakas, and Kuṣanas, followed by other less famous but not unimportant immigrants, whose advent vitally affected the population and civilization of the north-west of India. It is plain that in the Gupta dynasty of the fourth century A.D. we find a great Hindu revival, but a revival which evidently drew strength primarily from the east, and we do not know anything definite to enable us to reason *a priori* on what was, or was not, possible as regards assimilation of the drama. The only decisive evidence possible is that of the actual plays, and unfortunately the results to be attained by examination of them are not at all satisfactory.

It is held by Windisch that the New Attic Comedy, which flourished from 340–260 B.C., must be deemed the source of influence on Indian drama; the fact that no mention of this comedy is specifically made in the few notices we have of drama in the east is doubtless not of importance. On the other hand, we know that Alexandria under the Lagidai became a great centre of Greek learning, and that between Alexandria and Ujjayinī through the port of Barygaza[1] there was a brisk exchange of trade which may have aided in intellectual contact,[2] perhaps especially in the period when Menander's conquests gave Greek products of every sort a special vogue. The new comedy by its making its subject of the everyday life of man was far more suited than any other form of drama to attract imitation.

The actual points of contact between the New Comedy and the Sanskrit drama are, however, scanty. The division of both the Roman drama[3] and the Sanskrit into acts, distinguished by

[1] *Periplus*, 48.

[2] Cf. Hultzsch, JRAS. 1904, pp. 399 ff. on the Kanarese words found in a fragment of a Greek comedy preserved in a papyrus of the second century A. D.

[3] This does not appear in the dramas of Menander so far as recovered, and is of uncertain date. Cf. Donatus on Terence, *Andria*, Prol.

the departure of all the actors from the stage and the number of five as normal, though often exceeded in India, are facts which need not be more than casual coincidences: the divisions in the Sanskrit drama rest on an analysis of the action which is not recorded in Greece or Rome. There is similarity in the scenic conventions, in the asides, in the entry and exit of characters, more notably in the practice that the advent of a new character is usually expressly notified to the audience by a remark from one of the actors already on the stage. But these are all matters which must almost inevitably coincide in theatrical performances produced under approximately similar conditions. Even in the modern theatre with its programmes the necessity of indicating at once the identity of the new comers to the stage is keenly felt.

More value attaches to the argument from the use of Yavanikā,[1] or its Prākrit form Javanikā, for the name of the curtain which covered the tiring room and formed the background of the stage. The word primarily is an adjective meaning Ionian, the Greeks with whom India first came into contact. But it was not confined to what was Greek in the strict sense of the word; it applies to anything connected with the Hellenized Persian Empire, Egypt, Syria, Bactria, and it therefore cannot be rigidly limited to what is Greek. As applied to the curtain it is an adjective, and describes doubtless the material of the curtain (*paṭī, apaṭī*) as foreign, possibly as Lévi suggests, Persian tapestry brought to India by Greek ships and merchants. The word Yavanikā has no special application to the curtain of the theatre, as would be the case, if it were borrowed as a detail of stage arrangement from Greece. Nor in fact was there any curtain in the case of Greek drama, so far as is known, from which it could be borrowed; Windisch's contention merely was that the curtain was called Greek because it took the place of the painted scenery at the back of the Greek stage.

As little can any conclusion of Greek borrowing be drawn from the Yavanīs, Greek maidens, who are represented as among the body-guard of the king;[2] for this the Greek drama offers no

[1] Konow, ID. p. 5, n. 5; Lévi, TI. i. 348; for the generic sense, cf. Amara, ii. 6. 3. 22; Halāyudha, ii. 154.

[2] Already in Bhāsa: cf. Lindenau, BS. p. 41, n. 2; Lévi, *Quid de Graecis, &c.*

parallel; it represents the fondness of the princes of India[1] for the fascinating hetaerae of Greece, and the readiness of Greek traders to make the high profits to be derived from shipping these youthful cargoes.

The points of resemblance in regard to the plot are of interest. There is some similarity between the stock theme of the Nāṭikā, the love of a king for a maiden, hindered by various obstacles, and finally successful through events which reveal her as a princess, destined for him in marriage but concealed in this aspect by some accident, and the New Comedy picture of the youth whose affection for a fair lady, apparently of status which forbids marriage by Attic law, but in reality of equal birth, is finally rewarded by the discovery of the mark which leads to her identification. The use of a mark of recognition is undoubtedly common in both dramas. We have in the *Çakuntalā* the ring[2] which gives part of the title of the play *Abhijñāna-Çakuntalā*, and in the *Vikramorvaçī* the stone of reunion (*saṅgamamaṇi*) which enables Purūravas to recognise his beloved despite her change into a creeper. In the *Ratnāvalī* we have the necklace which permitsthe identification of the heroine; in the *Nāgānanda*, the jewel which, falling from the sky, denotes the fate of the prince; in the *Mālatīmādhava* the garland plucked by Mādhava, worn by Mālatī, which Saudāminī produces at the dénouement as a sign of recognition; and in the *Mṛcchakaṭikā* the clay cart in which are placed the jewels used as evidence against the hero. In the same general category fall the ring of the queen in the *Mālavikāgnimitra*, which the Vidūṣaka obtains from her in order to cure a snake-bite, and employs to bring about the release of Mālavikā; the arrow of Āyus, in the *Vikramorvaçī*, which reveals to Purūravas his son; and the seal of Rākṣasa in the *Mudrārākṣasa* of which Cāṇakya makes use to confound his schemes. In

(1890), pp. 41 f.; on Greek influence, cf. Kennedy, JRAS. 1912, pp. 993 ff., 1012 ff.; 1913, pp. 121 ff.; W. E. Clark, *Classical Philology*, xiv. 311 ff.; xv. 10 f., 18 f.; Weber, SBAW. 1890, pp. 900 ff.

[1] *Kauṭilīya Arthaçāstra*, i. 21; Megasthenes, frag. 26; Strabo, xv. 1. 55.

[2] For this motif cf. Gawroński, *Les Sources de quelques drames indiens*, pp. 39 ff. On recognition in the Greek tragic drama see Aristotle, *Poetics*, 1452 *a* 29 ff.; Verrall, *Choephorae*, pp. xxxiii–lxx. Its alleged essential character as an element of primitive tragedy, the recognition of the god, is disposed of by Ridgeway, *Dramas, &c.*, pp. 40 f.

some cases the similarity of use of these emblems is close; Mālavikā, taken away by brigands, and Ratnāvalī, rescued from the sea, are real parallels to the heroine of the *Rudens*, stolen from her father by a brigand, sold to a *leno* and wrecked on the Sicilian coast, whose recognition is brought about by the discovery of her childish ornaments.

These are striking facts, and the only way to meet them is to show that the motifs in Sanskrit drama have an earlier history in the literature, and can, therefore, be regarded as natural developments. The difficulty presented here is that the literature available consists either of tales, which in any form available to us are later than the period of the supposed Greek influence, or the epic which is of uncertain date, so that no strict proof is available that any of its minor issues antedates the Christian era. But we do find in the epic indications that it was not necessary for Greece to give to India the ideas presented in the drama. The story of the love of Kīcaka for Draupadī, when disguised as handmaiden she served Sudeṣṇā, wife of the king Virāṭa, has a tragic outcome, for his love is repulsed, but it has undoubted affinities with the plot of the Nāṭikā. In the case of the old tale of Nala and Damayantī, the heroine is more happy, for, when separated from her husband who has abandoned her in the distraction of losing his kingdom at dice, she lives in peace, guarded securely from interference; at last she is recognized by a birthmark. In the *Rāmāyaṇa* the use of signs of this sort is extended to artificial modes: Sītā, stolen away from Rāma, drops her jewels to the ground; the monkeys bear them to their king, who hands them to Rāma, and the hero thus knows beyond a peradventure the identity of the ravisher. To console her in her detention pending his efforts at rescue he sends Hanumant to her, bearing his messages, and gives him his ring to serve to identify him; Sītā sees it and takes heart. We may admit that such incidents are almost inevitable in a primitive society, in which the means of identification were necessarily material, or personal. Nor in the Sanskrit drama is there any preponderant use of this factor; the letter and the portrait[1] are other means, the use of which is recognized in the theory.

The evidence of borrowing based on the *Mṛcchakaṭikā* by

[1] Cf. Bhāsa's *Svapnavāsavadattā*, vi. pp. 51 ff.

Windisch requires reconsideration in the light of the facts now known regarding the authority of that drama for the early Sanskrit drama. To Windisch it seemed to present every appearance of an early age, and to show close relations to a Greek model. The title he compared with the *Cistellaria*, 'little chest', or the *Aulularia*, 'little pot'; the mixture of a political intrigue and a love drama with the mention—only incidental however—of political events contemporaneous with the action in Plautus's *Epidicus* and *Captivi*; the court scene he held to be of Greek inspiration; the meeting of Cārudatta and Vasantasenā he compared with that of the hero and heroine of the *Cistellaria*; the theft of Çarvilaka, in order to buy the freedom of the slave girl he loves, to the dishonest means adopted by the hero in the new comedy to procure means to purchase his inamorata; the setting free of the slave by Vasantasenā with the attaining of the position of a freedwoman in the Greek drama; finally the elevation of Vasantasenā to the rank of a woman of good character to permit of her legal marriage to Cārudatta is compared with the discovery in the Greek drama of the existence of a free status as the birthright of the maiden whom the hero loves. The *Mṛcchakaṭikā*, however, is not an early representative of the Indian drama in the sense held by Windisch; it is based on the *Cārudatta* of Bhāsa, in which there is no mingling of the political and love intrigue, at any rate as we have that play; the title *Mṛcchakaṭikā*, which departs from the usual model, was probably deliberately chosen to distinguish the new drama from the old. The plays cited have no real combination of political and love intrigues, and the other parallels are far too vague to be taken seriously. The raising of Vasantasenā to a new status is an extraordinary event, which is dependent on an action of the new king Āryaka, who, as an overthrower of the former monarch, exercises the supreme right of sovereignty in favour of the lady, in defiance of the rules of caste. The political intrigue thus becomes a vital element in the play.

Nor can any special value be ascribed to the rule, which is laid down in the theory, and observed in practice, and which confines the events in an act to the limits of a single day, as compared with the rule of Aristotle[1] that the events of a drama should not

[1] *Poetics*, 1449 *b* 12 ff.

exceed, or only by a little, the duration of a day. If the rule was borrowed, it was greatly changed in sense by permitting long periods, up to a year, to elapse between the acts in the Sanskrit drama, and the mere moral needs of the approximation to reality requisite for illusion would produce the state of the Sanskrit drama without external influence.

The characters of the drama present problems which are not solved by the theory of borrowing. The figure of the queen, loving her husband, noble and dignified, is compared by Windisch with that of the *matrona* of the Roman comedy, while her attempts to prevent the union of her husband and the new love are compared to the efforts of the *senex* to dissuade his son from a rash marriage or intrigue. But it is clear that the comparisons are idle; the rivalry of the old love and the new is an incident of the life of the harem inevitable in polygamy, while it affords an admirable opportunity for the poet to depict the contrast of types and the different aspects of love, his chief theme. Windisch, however, lays most stress on his comparison of the three figures of the Viṭa, Vidūṣaka, and Çakāra, with the parasite, the *servus currens*, and the *miles gloriosus* of the Greek drama, and his arguments have a certain weight. It is true that these three, with the Sūtradhāra and his assistant, are given by the *Nāṭya-çāstra* in a list of actors, and that the five correspond fairly closely with the male personnel of a Greek drama; it is also true that, while Kālidāsa and the *Mṛcchakaṭikā* with the *Cārudatta* know the Çakāra, he vanishes from the later drama, and the Viṭa shows comparatively little life, suggesting that the Greek borrowings were gradually felt unsuited to India and died a natural death. But the argument is inadequate to prove borrowing. The Viṭa is, indeed, more closely akin to the parasite than to any other character of the Greek or Roman comedy, but the parasite is lacking in the refinement and culture of his Indian counterpart, who is clearly drawn from life, the witty and accomplished companion who is paid to amuse his patron, but whose dependence does not make him the object of insolence and bad jokes. The Vidūṣaka has, in all likelihood, as has been seen, his origin in the religious drama; his Brahmin caste, and his use of Prākrit can best thus be explained. The alternative views all present far more difficulties; the transformance of the slave into a Brahmin is far too violent a change to be credible, while Lévi's[1] view which makes him a borrowing from the Prākrit drama, which depicted with truth the type of Brahmin who serves as go-between in love affairs, masking his degraded trade under the cloak of religion, renders it unintelligible why the Brahmins should have consented to maintain him in the Sanskrit drama. Equally unconvincing is Professor Konow's[2] effort to explain him as a figure of the popular drama, which loved to make fun of the higher classes, especially the Brahmins. There was no conceivable reason why the Brahmins should have kept such a figure in a drama which never appealed to the lower classes, and it is significant that there is no trace of a comic figure of the Kṣatriya class, although the populace doubtless was as willing to make fun of the rulers as of the priests. The similarity between the Çakāra and the *miles gloriosus* is by no means small, but the argument from borrowing is refuted by the reflexion that such a figure can be explained perfectly easily from the actual life of India in the period of Bhāsa and the *Mṛcchakaṭikā*, when mercenary soldiers must have been painfully familiar to Indians.

The number of actors is certainly not in accord with the Greek practice; not only has Bhāsa large numbers, but the *Çakuntalā* has thirty, the *Mṛcchakaṭikā* twenty-nine, the *Vikramorvaçī* eighteen, the *Mudrārākṣasa* twenty-four, and it is only in the later and less inventive Bhavabhūti that we find but thirteen in the *Mālatīmādhava* and eleven in the *Uttararāmacarita*.

The prologue in both dramas serves the purpose of announcing the author's name, the title of the play, and the desire of the dramatist for a sympathetic reception, but the Indian prologue is closely attached to the preliminaries, and has a definite and independent character of its own in the conversation between the Sūtradhāra and his wife, the chief actress, so that borrowing is out of the question. Nor does any importance attach to the fact that Çiva, who is in a special sense the patron of drama, is the nearest Indian representative of Dionysos, or that the time of the festival at which plays were often shown was spring, as in the case of the Great Dionysia at Athens when new plays were usually presented. There is similarity between the Protagonist and the Sūtradhāra, for both undertake the leading parts in the drama,

[1] TI. i. 358.

[2] ID. p. 15.

but this and other minor points such as can be adduced are of no value as proofs of historical connexion.

Windisch admitted that in regard to the theatrical buildings there was no possibility of comparison, as the Indian theatre was not permanent, but Bloch[1] has endeavoured to show that the Sītābengā cave theatre has marked affinities to the Greek. The attempt, however, is clearly a failure; the construction of the whole is merely that of a small amphitheatre cut out in the rock for a small audience without any special similarity to the Greek theatre of any period.

More recently the tendency of those who seek to find Greek influence in the making of the Sanskrit drama has turned to the mime as the form of art which exercised influence on India, and the older arguments of Windisch have been given a new shape and in part strengthened in this regard.[2] The mime was performed without masks and buskins, as was the Indian drama. Moreover the mime, at any rate in Roman hands, had a curtain (*siparium*), which may be compared with the curtain of India. There was also no scene painting in the mime; different dialects were used, and the number of actors was considerable. Further, some of the standing types of the mime may be paralleled in the Indian drama; the zēlotypos has some similarity to the Çakāra, the mōkos to the Vidūṣaka.

Some of the arguments adduced against this theory of Reich's are admittedly untenable. It is impossible to argue as does Professor Konow that the use of the *Mṛcchakaṭikā* as a work of early date is a mistake, since the oldest dramas preserved are of quite another type and have no similarity with Greek works. True, the *Mṛcchakaṭikā* is not as old as it was thought, but the *Cārudatta* can be substituted in lieu, and there are no dramas older than it, save those of the same author and some fragments of Buddhist drama. Nor have we any very satisfactory evidence of a mime in India at an early date, for a mime means a great deal more than the mere work of a Naṭa. But there are adequate grounds for disregarding the theory. The similarity of types is not at all convincing; the borrowing of the idea of using

[1] *Arch. Survey of India Report*, 1903-4, pp. 123 ff., rashly followed by Lüders, ZDMG. lviii. 868. See Hillebrandt, AID. pp. 23 f.; GIL. iii. 175, n. 1.

[2] *Der Mimus*, i. 694 ff.; DLZ. 1915, pp. 589 ff.; E. Müller-Hess, *Die Entstehung des indischen Dramas* (1916), pp. 17 ff.; Lindenau, *Festschrift Windisch*. p. 41.

different dialects from the mime is really absurd, and the large number of actors is equally natural in either case. The argument from the curtain is wholly without probative power; as we have seen, the term Yavanikā refers to material only; it would be very remarkable that the term Greek should be confined to the curtain alone, if the stage were really a Greek borrowing, and, last not least, we have no proof that the Greek mime had the curtain. The new form of the theory must, therefore, claim no more credence than the old. We cannot assuredly deny[1] the possibility of Greek influence, in the sense that Weber admitted the probability; the drama, or the mime, may, as played at Greek courts, have aided in the development of a true drama, but the evidence leaves only a negative answer to the search for positive signs of influence.

There are, undoubtedly, certain considerations which *a priori* tell against borrowing; to judge from the Roman borrowings from Greece and those of France from the classics, the trace of imitation if it were real would be clear and emphatic. But we can hardly place very great faith in arguments from analogy; India has a strange genius for converting what it borrows and assimilating it, as it did in the case of the image of the Buddha which it fabricated from Greek models. More important is the possibility of tracing the sources of the dramas in the epic and the tales, though here the difficulty of dates prevents the demonstration being complete. The epic and undramatic character of the Sanskrit drama is true enough, but not universally applicable, and the argument is liable to be turned by adopting the view that only Greek influence is contended for, not the exclusion of Indian native influences. The typical nature of the characters, adduced by Professor Konow as a point of difference, seems to indicate a forgetfulness that the Greek drama, and especially the New Comedy, is rich in types, and that the mime depicts types. Nor in that comedy do we find any particularly effective heightening of interest or development of the situation from the characters of the persons, or solutions produced without recourse to cutting the knot by artificial means. In all these matters indeed the Indian drama rather is akin to the Greek than otherwise.

[1] Cf. Oldenberg, *Die Literatur des alten Indien*, pp. 241 ff.

6. *The Çakas and the Sanskrit Drama*

Professor Levi,[1] whose opposition to Windisch regarding the possibility of Greek influence on the Indian drama has been noted, is himself responsible for the suggestion that the rise of the Sanskrit drama, as opposed to the more popular religious drama in Prākrit, is to be attributed to the Çakas, whose advent to India was one of the causes of the rapid decadence of the Greek principalities in the north west. The theory is based on a general view of the elevation of Sanskrit to the rank of the language of literature, as opposed to its restriction to use as the learned and sacred language of the Brahmins. The inscriptions, on the whole, show that Sanskrit as an epigraphic language was introduced by Rudradāman whose Girnār inscription of A.D. 150 is wholly in Sanskrit, though Sanskrit appears in part in Uṣavadāta's inscription of A.D. 124. The Western Kṣatrapas, of Çaka origin, were, he holds, the first to bring Sanskrit down to earth, while not vulgarizing it, as contrasted with the Hindu and orthodox Çātakarṇis of the Deccan who retained Prākrit in their inscriptions down to the third century A.D. The character of the Çakāra may be regarded in this light; in its hostility to the Çakas it reveals a period when either a prince was opposed to the Çaka rule, or the Çaka dominion had just fallen and was fresh in the minds of the people. The *Mṛcchakaṭikā* may retain a confused version of the events of the second century A.D. A specific connexion between the Çakas and the creation of drama may be seen in the terminology of the *Nāṭyaçāstra*, and that of their inscriptions. Rudradāman refers to his grandfather Caṣṭana as Svāmin and Sugṛhītanāman, and Svāmin is freely used in the epigraphic records of the kings of the line from Nahapāna (A.D. 78) onwards. Further Rudrasena in A.D. 205, in referring to his royal ancestors, Caṣṭana, Jayadāman, Rudradāman, and Rudrasena, gives them the epithet of Bhadramukha, 'of gracious countenance'. These terms, Lévi argues, correspond with the use laid down in the *Nāṭyaçāstra*, which must have borrowed from contemporary official usage. Further, Rudradāman uses the term Rāṣṭriya as applying to Puṣyagupta, who under

[1] JA. sér. 9, xix. 95 ff.; IA. xxxiii. 163 ff. Cf. Bloch, *Mélanges Lévi*, pp. 15 f.; Franke, *Pāli und Sanskrit*, pp. 87 ff.; Keith, *Sansk. Lit.* ch. 1.

Candragupta, the Maurya, some four and a half centuries earlier established the reservoir which he had repaired, and this term occurs in the *Çakuntalā* and the *Mṛcchakaṭikā* in the sense of brother-in-law of the king, the sense given to it in the *Amarakosa*, the earliest Sanskrit lexicon of established authority. To these considerations may be added that Ujjayinī, the capital of the Western Kṣatrapas of Mālava, is a centre, round which as a fan radiate the three great literary Prākrits of the drama, Çaurasenī, Māgadhī, and Māhārāṣṭrī, thus accounting for their use, which else would be difficult to explain.

Lévi's suggestion, which was accompanied by an admission that the *Mṛcchakaṭikā* or its source was older than he had formerly argued, and that the possibility of Greek influence was thus increased, has been accepted by Professor Konow[1] with the important modification that in face of the fact that the oldest dramas known to us, the fragments of Açvaghoṣa and those of Bhāsa, ignore Māhārāṣṭrī and that Çaurasenī is the normal prose tongue, he accepts Mathurā as the home of the drama, and ascribes it to about the middle of the first century A.D. This view he supports by the fact that the rulers of Mathurā were also Çaka Kṣatrapas, or Satraps, whose control extends back at least to the beginning of the first century A.D.

It may be feared that neither theory will stand critical investigation, however tempting it may be to obtain an exact date for the Sanskrit drama. The discovery of Açvaghoṣa's fragments shows that the drama has already attained a very definite and complete form, and we really cannot with any probability assume that the creation of drama preceded this by no more than a century. Even a century, however, brings us further back than the middle of the first century A.D., for Konow's date of Kaniṣka, about A.D. 150,[2] is probably considerably too late, and should be placed fifty years earlier at least. We are thus separated from Rudradāman by a period of 150 years, probably more, and the theory that the Western Kṣatrapas introduced Sanskrit into the drama falls hopelessly to the ground on chronological considerations alone.

The argument from the use of technical terms is clearly untenable. That Rāṣṭriya in Rudradāman's inscription has the sense

[1] ID. p. 49. [2] ID. p. 50. Contrast CHI. i. 583.

of 'brother-in-law' is not supported by the slightest evidence, and is most improbable; the term doubtless denotes governor, and the restricted use is a later development. The use of Svāmin as the mode of addressing the king is not recorded in the *Nāṭya-çāstra*, and to argue that it, being given in the *Daçarūpa* and the *Sāhityadarpaṇa*, must be borrowed from Bharata, as Konow does, is quite impossible. On the contrary, Bharata[1] gives the style to the Yuvarāja, or Crown Prince, presumably as distinct from the king. In the extant dramas after Bhāsa it is not used of the king or Crown Prince. Sugṛhītanāman, denoting perhaps 'whose name is uttered with respect', has no parallel in Bharata; only in the later theory do we find Sugṛhītābhidha, which, however, is prescribed merely for the address of a pupil, child, or younger brother to a teacher, father, or elder brother, and therefore stands in no conceivable relation to the term used by Rudradāman. Bhadramukha is the address to a royal prince in Bharata; it is used of kings by Rudrasena, and the literature ignores the specific or royal use. The lack of accord is complete and convincing; if the drama had originated under the Western Kṣatrapas of Ujjayinī, it would not have been so flagrantly out of harmony with the official language.

The whole error of these arguments rests in the belief that the drama developed as a Prākrit drama before it was turned into Sanskrit. The same theory has been applied to every department of secular Sanskrit literature without either plausibility or success; the *Mahābhāṣya* knows Sanskrit Kāvya before any Prākrit Kāvya is recorded.[2] But, apart from this, it is essential to remember that the drama was religious in origin and essentially connected with epic recitations, and that for both reasons Sanskrit claimed in it a rightful place from the inception. It is certain that the recitations known by Patañjali were in Sanskrit, and it is difficult in the extreme to understand how in the view of Lévi and Konow a Prākrit drama proper ever came into being. Before the coalescence of the epic recitation and the primitive mime believed in by Konow, there cannot have been any drama on his own theory; when they coalesced, Sanskrit must have from the first been present.

[1] xvii. 75; cf. *Sāhityadarpaṇa*, 431; R. iii. 314.
[2] Cf. IS. xiii. 483 ff.; Kielhorn, IA. xiv. 326 f.

The discovery of Açvaghoṣa's fragments undoubtedly helps greatly to bring the creation of the drama very close up to the time of Patañjali, if not to that date. The first century B.C. can with fair certainty be assumed to be the very latest period at which the appearance of a genuine Sanskrit drama can be placed. If indeed Professor Lüders's former date for Kaniṣka were correct and he were the founder of the Vikrama era of 57 B.C.,[1] then the Sanskrit drama must be dated a century at least earlier, and we would have the paradoxical position that on Professor Lüders's date of Açvaghoṣa he must place the drama at not later than Patañjali, while when dealing with the *Mahābhāṣya* evidence he doubts the existence of the drama. Professor Lüders has overlooked this dilemma, which, however, we may evade on his behalf by recognising that he erred in assigning to Kaniṣka a date which the evidence available in 1911 already showed to be quite untenable.

7. *The Evidence of the Prākrits*

The discovery of Açvaghoṣa's fragments not only disposes effectively of Professor Lévi's dating of the rise of Sanskrit drama, since he probably preceded Rudradāman by at least half a century, but it casts a vivid light on the question of the Prākrits and Sanskrit. It must be remembered that Açvaghoṣa was the exponent of a faith which had originally insisted on the use of the vernacular as opposed to Sanskrit, and that it is absurd to imagine that it would have occurred to him to use Sanskrit in dramas of Buddhist inspiration and aim, had not the use of that language been established in the drama of the day. This leads us back once more to the conclusion that the drama from the outset was written in part at least in Sanskrit, and that, therefore, it stands in genetic relation with the dramatic recitations described by Patañjali which were in Sanskrit.

That the drama was also in part in Prākrit from the outset seems extremely probable. The mere recitation of the epic

[1] *Bruchstücke buddhistischer Dramen*, pp. 11, 64. Contrast his views in SBAW. 1912, pp. 808 ff., when he accepts the much later date, advocated by Oldenberg, GN. 1911, pp. 427 ff.

indeed did not demand any intervention of Prākrit, but that such recitations by themselves would produce a true drama is most improbable, and we may legitimately hold that it was only the union of these recitations with action from the religious contest that produced the drama. In that contest we may assume that the lower classes were represented and spoke their own language ; in the Vedic Mahāvrata we cannot suppose that the Çūdra who contested the right of the Vaiçya to the symbol of the sun spoke in Sanskrit, nor that the Brahmin and the hetaera exchanged their ritual abuse in the classical tongue, or its Vedic antecedent. The religious festival in which Kṛṣṇa appeared as slaying Kaṅsa must similarly have demanded the use of the vernacular by the humbler members of those who took part in it. The fact that Prākrit appears mainly in the dialogue, Sanskrit pre-eminently in verses, strengthens the view that the new drama derived its verse in the main from the epic recitation, its prose dialogue from the religious contest. The two elements never entirely merged ; the Vidūṣaka who comes from one side of the religious ceremonial, that which in Greece lies at the basis of comedy as opposed to tragedy, is not a figure normal in the dramas of mainly epic inspiration ; but this is not enough to prove that the drama ever in its early days was merely in Sanskrit. It may indeed have been the case ; Bhāsa's *Dūtavākya* has no Prākrit, and so far the probability is rather for than against it, as an alternative form.

The question how many Prākrits were used in the primitive Sanskrit drama presents difficulties. The obvious conclusion is that the vernacular employed would be that of the region where the drama came into being, and that this was the Çūrasena country is not to be denied. Çaurasenī in fact appears throughout as the normal prose of the drama ; it is the language of the Vidūṣaka and the hetaera and normally of all the characters of a play who are born in Āryāvarta, and no other dialect even in theory vies with it in importance. The theory and the practice after Bhāsa ascribe to Māhārāṣṭrī the honour of the language of verses sung by maidens who would in prose speak Çaurasenī. There can be no doubt that this is not primitive, but is a reflex of the growth and development of the fame of the artificial lyric poetry of which we have an anthology under the name of Hāla, perhaps to be ascribed to the third or fifth century A. D.[1]

To what extent any other Prākrit was used in the earliest drama we cannot effectively determine. Bhāsa has only, besides Çaurasenī, Māgadhī of two kinds, and a few hints of what may be styled Ardha-Māgadhī, while Açvaghoṣa has three dialects which suggest much older forms of Çaurasenī, Māgadhī, and Ardha-Māgadhī. The use of these dialects for characters by Açvaghoṣa explains itself naturally from his familiarity with the Buddhist scriptures whose original was very probably in something approximating to the Ardha-Māgadhī[2] he knew, and the fact that the speaker of Old Māgadhī is the Duṣṭa, or bad man, reminds us of the bad character enjoyed[3] by the Magadha. Lévi's[4] suggestion that the Māgadhī of the drama comes from its epic element, and that the Māgadhas were the reciters of Prākrit epic compositions, is clearly untenable, and indeed seems to have been later abandoned by its author in favour of the suggestion that the Prākrits of the drama were evolved, because the drama was produced at Ujjayinī, which was a meeting place of different dialectical forms. This theory might be revised to adapt it to making Mathurā the headquarters of the drama and Māgadhī and Ardha-Māgadhī the other dialects, but the restricted use of anything but Çaurasenī by Bhāsa suggests that the introduction of other Prākrits was a gradual process. In point of fact it never attained great vitality, and in the developed drama Çaurasenī and Māhārāṣṭrī alone play any real part. The ground for the more extended use of dialects when found may be attributed to literary purposes rather than to any attempt to imitate the speech of the day, as Sir George Grierson[5] has suggested. The ground for this conclusion, apart from the improbability of so great an effort at realism, is that the dialects used for instance even in the *Mṛcchakaṭikā* are clearly literary and not attempts to reproduce true vernaculars.

[1] Jacobi, *Ausgew. Erzählungen in Mâhârâshṭrî*, pp. xiv ff., suggests the fifth century A. D. for Sātavāhana. V. Smith's date (first cent. A. D.) is certainly wrong. The poetry may probably be as early as the third century; Weber's ed., p. xxiii; Lévi, TI. i. 326; GIL. iii. 102 f.

[2] Lüders, *Bruchstücke buddhistischer Dramen*, pp. 40f.; SBAW. 1913, pp. 1003 ff.

[3] See Keith in CHI. i. 123 f.

[4] TI. i. 331.

[5] IA. xxx. 556.

The stage reached by the Prākrits of Açvaghoṣa shows clearly how late are the Prākrits of the orthodox classical drama,[1] and reminds us how much more closely akin to Sanskrit must have been the Prākrit of the drama of the time of, or shortly after, Patañjali. The classical drama with its broken-down forms of Prākrit gives a false impression of the original dramatic form in which either perhaps Sanskrit alone, if the matter were epic, or both Sanskrit and a closely akin Çaurasenī appeared.

8. *The Literary Antecedents of the Drama*

The drama owes in part its origin to the epics of India; from them throughout its history it derives largely its inspiration, far more truly so indeed than Greek tragedy as compared with the Greek epic.[2] From the epics also developed the Kāvya, the refined and polished epic, which appears at its best in the *Kumārasambhava* and *Raghuvañça* of Kālidāsa. The parallelism between the developed form of both is close and striking. The *Sāhityadarpaṇa*[3] lays down that it is a composition in several cantos, the hero a god or Kṣatriya of high race, of the type noble and superior; if there are several heroes, they are persons of royal rank of one family. The sentiment which predominates is the erotic, the heroic, or occasionally that of calm; the others serve in a subsidiary rôle. The subject-matter is either taken from tradition or not, but the heroes must be virtuous. The work begins with a prayer, a benediction, or an indication of the subject-matter. The development of the story employs the same five junctures as the theory prescribes for the drama. One or other of the four aims of man, wealth, love, performance of duty, or release, is to be attained by the action. The number of cantos is not to be less than eight; each should end in a different metre, and should announce the subject of the following act. Descriptions of every kind are essential; objects of these are the different times of day, the sun, the moon, night, the

[1] A transitional stage of Prākrit may, perhaps, be seen in the *Nāṭyaçāstra*, but the text is very corrupt; cf. Jacobi, *Bhavisattakaha*, pp. 84 ff.

[2] Cf. Aischylos in Athen., p. 347.

[3] 559. See Daṇḍin, *Kāvyādarça*, i. 14 ff., and cf. the analyses of Mañkha's *Çrīkaṇṭhacarita* (twelfth cent.) and Haricandra's *Dharmaçarmābhyudaya* in Lévi, TI. i. 337 ff.; Keith, *Sansk. Lit.*, pp. 38 ff.

dawn, twilight, darkness, morning, midday, the hunt, mountains, the seasons, forests, the ocean, the sky, a town, the pleasures of love, the misery of separation from one's beloved, a sacrifice, a battle, the march of an army, a marriage, the birth of a son, all of which should be developed in appropriate detail.

The essential feature of these little epics is the enormous development of the art of description, and the feature occurs in the other forms of narrative literature, the Kathā, tale, and the Ākhyāyikā, romance, types which blend with each other. Whether the subject be an imaginary theme, as is the *Vāsavadattā* of Subandhu, or a historical one, as in the *Harṣacarita* of Bāṇa, we find nothing treated as really important save the descriptions as contrasted with the narrative. The Sanskrit lyric also, in Kālidāsa's masterpiece, the *Meghadūta*, is essentially descriptive, as is the Prākrit lyric preserved in the collection of Hāla, which is based on the model of an older lyric in Sanskrit, whose existence is revealed to us by the *Mahābhāṣya*.

The love of description, however, is not new; it is a characteristic of the epic itself, and the *Rāmāyaṇa* in special shows us how the way for the court poetry was being prepared.[1] Hence the fact that the verses of the drama are overwhelmingly descriptive, when not gnomic in character, is no matter for surprise. The peculiarity is a direct inheritance from the epic.

This fact has one important bearing on the history of the drama. The suggestion of Pischel[2] that the verses alone were once preserved, and the prose left to be improvised would have been plausible only if the verses had been essentially the important elements in the dialogue, as in the supposed Vedic Ākhyāna hymns. But this is assuredly not the case; the verses do little to help on the action; as in the epic, they express descriptions of situations and emotions; when movement of the play is requisite recourse is had to prose. Or the verses serve to set out maxims, as is natural in view of the great fondness of India for gnomic poetry, seen already in the verses introduced

[1] See Jacobi, *Das Rāmāyaṇa*, pp. 119 ff.; Walter, *Indica*, III.

[2] Such a drama as the *Haragaurīvivāha* of Jagajjyotirmalla of Nepal (A.D. 1617–33), which is really a sort of opera with the verses, written in dialect, as the only fixed element (Lévi, *Le Népal*, i. 242) is of no cogency for the early drama. The Maithilī beginnings of drama, based on the classical, give song in dialect, dialogue in Sanskrit and Prākrit (Lévi, TI. i. 393).

into the legend of Çunaḥçepa in the *Aitareya Brāhmaṇa.* In this again there is a close parallel with the epic, nor is it surprising that the epic poet, like Açvaghoṣa and Kālidāsa, was often devoted to the drama.

A further source of literary inspiration must undoubtedly be seen in the work of the lyric poets, of whose work clear evidence, as well as some scattered fragments, is preserved to us in the *Mahābhāṣya* of Patañjali.[1] Moreover, to these lyric writers it is probable that the drama owed some of its metrical variety; in the development of the metres with a fixed number of syllables, each of determined length, from the older and freer Vedic and epic forms, it may be taken as certain that the erotic poets, who had a narrow theme to handle, and had every motive to aim at variety of form and effect, must have contributed largely, a conclusion which is also strongly suggested, if not proved, by the very names of the metres with their erotic suggestion.[2]

[1] Kielhorn, IA. xiv. 326 f.; Lüders, *Bruchstücke buddhistischer Dramen*, p. 63.
[2] Cf. Weber, IS. viii. 181 ff.; Jacobi, ZDMG. xxxviii. 615 f.

PART II

THE DEVELOPMENT OF THE SANSKRIT DRAMA

III

AÇVAGHOṢA AND THE BUDDHIST DRAMA

1. *The Çāriputraprakaraṇa*

THE discovery of fragments of manuscripts on palm-leaf, of great antiquity, at Turfan, has through the energy of Professor Lüders revealed to us the existence of at least three Buddhist dramas. Of one of these the authorship is happily certain, for the colophon of the last act has been preserved, and it records that the drama was the *Çāriputraprakaraṇa* of Açvaghoṣa, son of Suvarṇākṣī; it gives also the fuller title *Çāradvatīputraprakaraṇa*, and the number of acts as nine.

Açvaghoṣa is an author whose fame, thanks to his error in being a Buddhist long lost in India, has recently attained renewal by the discovery and publication of his *Buddhacarita*, a court epic in excellent style and spirit on the life of the Buddha. His *Sūtrālaṁkāra* is also known through the medium of a Tibetan translation, and illustrates his ability in turning the tale into an instrument for propaganda in support of the Buddhist faith. If the tradition which ascribes to him the *Mahāyānaçraddhotpāda* is correct, he was also the founder or expounder of a subtle system of metaphysics akin to the Vijñānavāda of the Mahāyāna school, and the *Vajrasūcī* seems to preserve in some measure the record of his onslaught on the caste system, which exalted the Brahmins at the expense of the Kṣatriyas, and condemned Buddhism on the score that it was unfitting that a Kṣatriya like the Buddha should give instructions to Brahmins. Certainly genuine is the *Saundarananda*, in the epic manner, which like all his works is devoted to the effective exposition of Buddhism in the language of polite literature, and also of the Brahmin schools. We recognize in him one who appreciated that it would never do to allow Buddhism to remain buried in a form inferior to the best that

Brahminism could produce, and it is curious that fate should have preserved the work of the rival of the Brahmins, while it has permitted his models to disappear. That he had abundant precedent to guide him is clear from the classical form already assumed by his dramas; the argument of Professor Konow[1] to the contrary, on the ground that many of the standing formulae and characters are derived from the popular drama, and show that the artistic drama had not developed yet full independence, is unintelligible, since these features persist throughout the history of the Sanskrit drama. Nor does any weight attach to the argument that the *Nāṭyaçāstra*, assumed to be of about the same period as Açvaghoṣa, shows knowledge of only a limited variety of dramas. On the contrary it is amazing how much literature must have preceded to permit of the setting up of the main types of drama, some of which were evidently represented by many specimens, though others doubtless rested on a small basis of practice.

The brief fragments preserved of the drama of Açvaghoṣa give us the certainty of his authorship if any doubt could exist after the colophon, for one verse is taken bodily from the *Buddhacarita*, just as he twice refers in the *Sūtrālaṁkāra* to that important work. The story of the play is clear; it deals with the events which led up to the conversion of the young Maudgalyāyana and Çāriputra by the Buddha, and some of the incidents are certain. Çāriputra had an interview with Açvajit; then he discussed the question of the claims of the Buddha to be a teacher with his friend, the Vidūṣaka, who raised the objection that a Brahmin like his master should not accept the teaching of a Kṣatriya; Çāriputra repels the objection by reminding his friend that medicine aids the sick though given by one of inferior caste, as does water one aheat. Maudgalyāyana greets Çāriputra, inquiring of him the cause of his glad appearance, and learns his reasons. The two go to the Buddha, who receives them, and who foretells to them that they will be the highest in knowledge and magic power of his disciples.

[1] ID. p. 50. For the fragments see Lüders, *Bruchstücke buddhistischer Dramen* (1911); SBAW. 1911, pp. 388 ff. For his philosophy, cf. Keith, *Buddhist Philosophy*, Part III, ch. iii. The *Saundarananda* is earlier than the *Buddhacarita* and it than the *Sūtrālaṁkāra*.

In this point there is a deliberate and certainly artistic deviation from the ordinary version of the incident, followed in the *Buddhacarita*, in which the prophecy of the Buddha is addressed, not to the disciples themselves, but to others of the Buddha's followers. The end of the play is marked by a philosophic dialogue between Çāriputra and the Buddha, which includes a polemic against the belief in the existence of a permanent self; it terminates in a praise of his two new disciples by the Buddha, and a formal benediction.

The most remarkable thing regarding this drama is its close correspondence to the classical type as laid down in the *Nāṭyaçāstra*. The piece is a Prakaraṇa, and it has nine acts, which accords perfectly with the rule of the Çāstra; the *Mṛcchakaṭikā* and *Mālatīmādhava* have ten apiece; the Acts bear no titles, but this is in accord with the normal usage, though the *Mṛcchakaṭikā* gives names. The hero is Çāriputra, who corresponds to the Brahmin hero of the Çāstra, and who is emphatically of the noble and calm type enjoined by that authority. Whether the heroine was a lady or a hetaera we do not know, nor does it appear how far the poet altered the subject-matter by invention, which is normally the case with later Prakaraṇas. The Buddha and his disciples, including, beside the two heroes, Kauṇḍinya and a Çramaṇa speak Sanskrit, and use both prose and verse; the Vidūṣaka speaks Prākrit. The presence of this figure is a remarkable proof of the fixed character attained by the drama, for in itself there is nothing more absurd than that a youthful ascetic seeking after truth should be encumbered by one who is a meet attendant on a wealthy merchant, Brahmin, or minister. It can, therefore, only be supposed that Açvaghoṣa was writing a type of drama in which the rôle was far too firmly embedded to permit its omission, and presumably in the story of the drama now lost to us the Vidūṣaka served to introduce comic relief. With natural good taste, he disappears from the last Act, where Çāriputra has no need as a member of the Buddha's fraternity for encumbrances like a jester.

In one point only has it been claimed to find a clear discrepancy between Açvaghoṣa's practice and that of the later drama. At the close the theory[1] requires that the question, 'Is

[1] N. xix. 102.

there anything further that you desire (*ataḥ param api priyam asti*)?' be addressed to the hero by himself or another, to which he replies by uttering a benediction styled the Bharatavākya. In the drama of Açvaghoṣa the phrase is omitted, and the benediction proceeds, without prelude, with the words, 'From now on shall these two ever increase their knowledge, restraining their senses, to gain release', spoken by the Buddha, not by the hero. Lüders concludes hence that the regular form of close was not yet established by Açvaghoṣa's time. The conclusion is clearly fallacious, and rests on a failure to recognize in this the readiness of Açvaghoṣa to give effect to a traditional usage, while not slavishly following it. It would obviously have been absurd to place the last words in the drama in the form of a benediction in the mouth of any one save the Buddha, and therefore he speaks the benediction. To preface it with the usual formula was needless in his case, but the opening words of the verse are *ataḥ param*, which is obviously not an incredible coincidence, but a deliberate reference to the ordinary phrase. Açvaghoṣa shows thus his knowledge of the rule and his power to vary it in case of need. Similarly Bhaṭṭa Nārāyaṇa in the *Veṇīsaṁhāra* puts the Bharatavākya in the mouth of Yudhiṣṭhira, but he makes Kṛṣṇa end the play by according the favour prayed for by Yudhiṣṭhira. He too felt that it would be absurd to leave the omnipotent one in the position of listening without response to the utterance of a benediction by one who cannot be more than an inferior, though nominally the hero.[1]

2. *The Allegorical and the Hetaera Dramas*

The same manuscript which contains portions of the *Çariputraprakaraṇa* has also fragments of two other dramas. There is no evidence of their authorship, other than the fact that they appear in the same manuscript as the work of Açvaghoṣa, and that they display the same general appearance as the work of that writer. That they are Açvaghoṣa's is much more probable than that they are the work of some unknown contemporary.[2]

[1] Similarly in the *Pārthaparākrama* of Prahlādanadeva (twelfth cent.) Vāsava pronounces the benediction.

[2] Açvaghoṣa's dramatic powers are also exhibited in the Māra legend of the

The first of these is specially interesting as it represents a type of which we have otherwise no earlier specimen than the *Prabodhacandrodaya* of Kṛṣṇamiçra. We find the allegorical figures of Buddhi, wisdom, Kīrti, fame, and Dhṛti, firmness, appearing and conversing. This is followed by the advent of the Buddha himself, adorned with the halo which he borrowed from Greek art. We do not know whether he appeared later in actual conversation with the allegorical figures, but for this mixture of the real and the ideal we have to go beyond Kṛṣṇamiçra, who represents all his characters as abstract, Viṣṇu for instance by Faith in Viṣṇu, to Kavikarṇapūra's glorification of Caitanya in the sixteenth century, in which allegorical figures are mingled with Caitanya and his followers, though they do not actually converse together.[1] It must remain uncertain whether there was a train of tradition leading from Açvaghoṣa to Kṛṣṇamiçra, or whether the latter created the type of drama afresh; the former theory is the more likely. The characters all speak Sanskrit, but the fragments are too short to give us any real information on the general trend of the play.

The other drama gives us more interesting matter. It is one in which figures a hetaera named Magadhavatī, a Vidūṣaka named Komudhagandha, a hero styled only Nāyaka, but probably named Somadatta, a Duṣṭa, rogue, without further name, a certain Dhānaṁjaya, who may possibly be a prince if the term 'king's son' (*bhaṭṭidālaka*), which is recognized in the *Nāṭyaçāstra* as the style of the younger princes of the blood, applies to him, a maid-servant, and Çāriputra and Maudgalyāyana. The drama was doubtless intended for purposes of religious edification, but what we have is too fragmentary to do more than show that the author was possessed of humour and that the Vidūṣaka was already a hungry soul. The drama alludes to an old garden as the place where part of the action passed, as in the *Mṛcchakaṭikā*, and also as in that drama the house of the hetaera served as the scene of another part of the action. The characters are often introduced as entering in vehicles (*pravahaṇa*), a further point of

Sūtrālaṁkāra, which is preserved in the *Divyāvadāna* (pp. 356 ff.; Windisch, *Māra und Buddha*, pp. 161 ff.); cf. Huber, BEFEO. iv. 414 f.

[1] In the Jain *Moharājaparājaya* (below, ch. xi, § 3) the real and the ideal characters converse.

similarity to that drama, while an allusion to a Samāja or festival on a hill-top accords with the frequent reference to such amusements in Buddhist literature. An obscure character is a person, obviously of lower rank, who is styled Gobaṁ°.

The drama shows close agreement with the classical model; the name of the Vidūṣaka is evidence of this, for not only is it connected with a real Brahmin family, but it obeys the rule that the name of that character should indicate a flower, the spring, &c., for it means literally 'the offspring of the lotus-smelling'. The name of the hetaera does not observe the rule exemplified in the *Cārudatta* that the hetaera's name should end in *senā*, *siddhā*, or *dattā*, but, apart from the fact that the authority for the rule is very late, the name was very probably given to the poet by the literary tradition. The fact that the Duṣṭa and the Nāyaka appear by these titles only has a parallel in the *Cārudatta* and the Buddhist drama of Harṣa, the *Nāgānanda*, but it is difficult to say whether or not this is a sign of antiquity.

The material available in the case of any of the three dramas is too scanty to give us any assurance as to what the practice was regarding the introduction, especially the use of the Nāndī, or verse of benediction. What is certain is that the Pāripārçvika, or assistant of the Sūtradhāra in the later literature, is found apparently as taking part in the opening of the drama, perhaps the *Çāriputraprakaraṇa*.

3. *The Language of the Dramas*

In accordance with the later rules we find the Buddha, his disciples, the hero of the hetaera play and Dhānaṁjaya speaking Sanskrit; the same is true of the allegorical characters, and this is also in accord with later practice, for in both Kṛṣṇamiçra and Kavikarṇapūra's works some of the allegorical characters speak Sanskrit, though others, of more feminine appeal and character, speak Prākrit. One Çramaṇa speaks Sanskrit, another—conceivably an Ājīvika—a Prākrit.

The Sanskrit contains some errors, which are obvious Prākritisms, and which it would be unjust to attribute to the author, or authors. Genuine departures from the norm are scanty; the use of *ārttha* for *artha* has a precise parallel in the nearly contemporaneous dialect of Mathurā; *tuṣṇīm* is frequent in

Buddhist Sanskrit as well as etymologically correct; *krimi* is found also in the *Buddhacarita* where the reading *kṛmi* would spoil the metre; *pratīgṛhīta* has many Sanskrit parallels. In *pradveṣaṁ* where the metre requires *pradoṣaṁ* Buddhist influence is doubtless present, but *yeva* and *tāva* are probably merely errors of the scribe, to whom may be assigned such a monstrosity as *paçyemas* and *Somadattassa.* But *bhagavāṁ* has the support of the practice of the *Mahāvastu* where stems in *mat* and *vat* end thus, and it explains the Sandhi *çṛṇvam puṣpā.* These are minimal variants; in the main the Sanskrit is excellent and the fragments shows traces of the able versification and style of Açvaghoṣa.

The other characters speak Prākrit, and, by a curious variation from the normal practice, the stage directions, which are freely given as in the classical drama, are normally expressed in the language which the character concerned uses, though there are cases of mixture and apparent confusion which may be due to the scribe. Three different forms of Prākrit may be distinguished, the first spoken by the Duṣṭa, the second by the mysterious Gobaṁ°, and the third by the hetaera and Vidūṣaka.

The Duṣṭa's speech in three important points is similar to the Māgadhī of the Prākrit grammarians; it substitutes *l* for *r*; reduces all three sibilants to *ç*; and has *e* in the nominative singular of masculine nouns in *a.* But it ignores the rules of the grammarians in certain matters; hard letters are not softened (e.g. *bhoti*), nor soft consonants elided (e.g. *komudagandha*), when intervocalic. There is no tendency to cerebralize *n*, and in *kālanā* the dental replaces the cerebral. Fuller forms of consonants remain in *haṅgho* (*haṁho*) and *bambhaṇa* (*baṁhaṇa*). The later forms of development of consonantal combinations are unknown; thus for *rj* we have *jj*, not *yy*, as in *ajja*; *cch* remains in lieu of becoming *çc*; *kṣ* becomes *kkh*, not *sk* or *ẖk*; *ṣṭ* and *ṣṭh* give *ṭṭh*, not *sṭ*. In *kiççа* we have an older form than *kīça*, in *ahakaṁ* than *ahake, hake, hage.* In practically all these details we must see an earlier stage of what becomes Māgadhī in the grammarians. With it may be compared the metrical inscription of the Jogīmārā cave on the Rāmgarh hill which belongs to the period of Açoka.

The Prākrit of the Gobaṁ° agrees with this Old Māgadhī in having *l* for *r* and *e* in the nominative singular, but it reduces all sibilants to *s*. It thus shows a certain similarity to the Ardha-Māgadhī of the grammarians, but that dialect often keeps *r* though it frequently alters it to *l*; for instance it has *r* for the *kaleti* of this Prākrit and the Old Māgadhī. Other points of similarity are the retention of the dental for cerebral in *vanna*; the lengthening of the vowel before the suffix *ka* (*vannīkāhi*); the accusative plural neuter in *pupphā*; and the infinitive *bhuṁjitaye* (*bhuñjittae*). There are points of difference, but they are probably all cases of earlier forms. Thus, as in Old Māgadhī, we have no softening or loss of intervocalic consonants; *n* is not cerebralised, but even introduced in *palinata*; *ḷ* appears in lieu of *l*; the instrumental in *āhi* has no nasal; the nominative of *vat* stems appears as in *vā*, as against *vaṁ* or *vante*; in the infinitive we find no doubling of the consonant in *taye*. The fact, however, of the regular change of *r* to *l* and the use of the form *yeva* after a long vowel as in Māgadhī and Pāli show that the Old Ardha-Māgadhī was more akin to Māgadhī than the later Ardha-Māgadhī, which came steadily under the influence of the western dialects as shown by the tendency to change *e* of the nominative to *o*.

There are strong points of similarity between this Old Ardha-Māgadhī and the language of Açoka's pillar inscriptions. They agree as regards the use of *l*, *s*, and *e*, the dentals in *palinata* and *vannīkāhi*, *yeva* after long vowels, and the long vowel before the suffix *ka*. They disagree in the nominative and accusative plural neuter of *a* stems, which have *āni* in the inscriptions as against *ā*, but that is of no great importance, as these are doublets. The infinitive, however, is in *tave*, which cannot be equated with *taye*; Ardha-Māgadhī *ttae* may be from either.

The Açokan dialect is doubtless the court speech of his kingdom, and a descendant of the Ardha-Māgadhī of Mahāvīra, the founder of the Jain religion, and probably also of the Buddha, whose speech was clearly not akin to the Māgadhī of the grammarians, though it is called Māgadhī in the sacred texts.[1]

The theory of the *Nāṭyaçāstra* assigns Ardha-Māgadhī as the language of savants, sons of kings or Rājputs, and Çreṣṭhins, rich merchants, but, with the exception of Bhāsa's *Karṇabhāra*, it does not appear in the extant dramas. Māgadhī, on the con-

[1] Cf. Lüders, SBAW. 1913, pp. 999 ff.

trary, is required in the case of men who live in the women's apartments, diggers of underground passages, keepers of drink shops, watchers, the hero himself in time of danger, and the Çakāra. Into which category the Duṣṭa falls is not certain; the *Daçarūpa* ascribes this Prākrit to low people in general.

Çaurasenī is ascribed to the hetaera by the Çāstra which gives Prācyā or eastern dialect to the Vidūṣaka, but it is clear that the Prācyā is a mere variety of Çaurasenī, from which it differs only in the use of certain expressions. This is borne out by the dramas, in which there is no real distinction between the speech of these two characters. With the Çaurasenī of the grammarians it shows remarkable parallels. It has *r* in lieu of changing it to *l*; it reduces the sibilants to *s*; and for the nominative masculine it has *o*. Further, it changes *kṣ* into *kkh*, not *cch*; for *chard* it has *chaḍḍ*, for *mard*, *madd*; for *saçrīkam* irregularly *sassirīkaṁ* with the double *s* despite the epenthetic vowel; and in the third singular future *issiti*. The gerund *kariya* is parallel to *karia* in Hemacandra's grammar; *bhaṭṭā* is the vocative of *bhartṛ*; *iyaṁ* is feminine as later *iaṁ* in Çaurasenī alone; *bhavāṁ* as nominative is comparable with *bhavaṁ*; *bhaṇ* is conjugated in the ninth class; *viya* is parallel to *via* for *iva*; and *dāni* with loss of *i* as a particle is similar to *dāṇiṁ*.

In other cases the forms of this Prākrit are clearly older than those of the grammarians' Çaurasenī. As in the other Prākrits of the drama, there is no softening or omission of intervocalic consonants, and no cerebralization of *n*. Further, initial *y* is kept, not reduced to *j*; the interjection *ai* in lieu of *aï* is supported by the language of the Girnār and Udayagiri inscriptions; in *nirussāsam* we have an older form than *ūsasida* of Çaurasenī; *ñ* and *ny* give *ññ*, not the later *ṇṇ*; *dy* gives *yy* (written *y*) for *jj*; *tuvaṁ* and *tava* are both manifestly older than the forms *tumaṁ* and *tuha*, while *karotha* is a remarkable example of the preservation of the old strong base. Old also is the preservation of the long vowel in *bhavāṁ*. In *adaṇḍāraho* and the dubious *arhessi* we have two variants on the rule of Çaurasenī, which has *i* as the epenthetic vowel in *arh*, but this merely illustrates the uncertainty of these epentheses; *duguṇa* in lieu of *diuṇa* is not older, but a variant mode of treating *dviguṇa*, and there is no special difficulty in holding that *dāṇi* and *idāṇi* are forms which were originally doublets of *dāṇiṁ* and *idāṇiṁ* in Çaurasenī, and later were superseded. From other Prākrit passages, presumably in the same Old Çaurasenī, we obtain old forms like *vayaṁ*, we, and *tumhākaṁ* in lieu of *tumhāṇaṁ*; *edisa* for *erisa* or *īdisa*; *dissati* for *dīsadi*; *gahītaṁ* for *gahidaṁ*; *khu* is kept after short vowels in lieu of being doubled; a long vowel is kept before *tti* and such forms as *mhi*. The future in *gamissāma* is probably old, while *nikkhanta* and *bambhaṇa* admit of this explanation against the later *nikkanta* and *bamhaṇa*.

In the words of the hetaera the word *surada* occurs, with softening of *t* to *d*; conceivably the passage might be verse, but in all probability we are merely faced with a sporadic instance of a change which later set in, due perhaps to a copyist's error; to find in it an evidence of Māhārāṣṭrī would be unwise, especially as the very next word (*vimadda*) is not in the Māhārāṣṭrī form (*vimaḍḍa*). In the dialect of the Duṣṭa we have a form *makkaṭaho* which may be genitive, as in Apabhrañça, but is not allowed in Māgadhī; but the sense is too uncertain to permit of any security.

The existence and literary use of these Prākrits is most interesting in the history both of the language and the literature, for they present archaic features which place them on the same plane of change as Pāli and the dialects of the older inscriptions. They may be set beside the inscriptions in the Sītābengā and Jogīmārā caves on the Rāmgarh hill, which both show lyric strophes. The influence of the Kāvya style in Sanskrit can be traced obviously in the later Nāsik inscription in Prākrit of the second century A.D., and even in the inscription of Khāravela of Kaliñga perhaps in the second century B.C.[1] We cannot, therefore, see any plausibility in the idea of the gradual adaptation of Sanskrit, a sacred language, to belles lettres; on the contrary the dramas show that the Prākrits in literature were already under the influence of the Sanskrit Kāvya.

4. *The Metres*

Scanty as the fragments are, they display another feature significant of the development of the drama on the classical

[1] That any date is given in the inscription is wholly uncertain; see discussions in I.A. xlvii. 223 f.; xlviii. 124, 206 f.; xlix. 30, 43 ff.; JRAS. 1910, pp. 324 ff.

lines. The metres employed are very numerous, as is natural in a poetry in which the verse serves essentially the purpose of displaying the skill of the writer. In addition to the Çloka we find the Upajāti (⏓ – ⏑ – – ⏑ ⏑ – ⏑ – –), the Çālinī (– – – –, – ⏑ – – ⏑ – –), Vaṅçasthā (⏑ – ⏑ – – ⏑ ⏑ – ⏑ – ⏑ –), Praharṣiṇī (– – –, ⏑ ⏑ ⏑ ⏑ – ⏑ – ⏑ – –). Vasantatilaka (– – ⏑ – ⏑ ⏑ ⏑ – ⏑ ⏑ – ⏑ – –), Mālinī (⏑ ⏑ ⏑ ⏑ ⏑ ⏑ – –, – ⏑ – – ⏑ – –), Çikhariṇī (⏑ – – – – –, ⏑ ⏑ ⏑ ⏑ ⏑ – – ⏑ ⏑ ⏑ –), Hariṇī (⏑ ⏑ ⏑ ⏑ ⏑ –, – – – –, ⏑ – ⏑ ⏑ – ⏑ –), Çārdūlavikrīḍita (– – – ⏑ ⏑ – ⏑ – ⏑ ⏑ ⏑ –, – – ⏑ – – ⏑ –), Sragdharā (– – – – ⏑ – –, ⏑ ⏑ ⏑ ⏑ ⏑ ⏑ –, – ⏑ – – ⏑ – –), and Suvadanā (– – – – ⏑ – –, ⏑ ⏑ ⏑ ⏑ ⏑ ⏑ –, – – ⏑ ⏑ ⏑ –), the last of these metres being almost a stranger to the drama, though it appears in Bhāsa, in the *Mudrārākṣasa*, and once in Varāhamihira. The tendency to seek sound effects is clear in a Çikhariṇī verse.

That so many metres of elaborate form should be found is of great interest, not merely as testimony of the early development of the Kāvya literature, but also because we see that the drama as early as Açvaghoṣa, and doubtless long before him, had definitely accepted the verses not as essential elements of the dialogue as are the verses in Greek drama, but as more or less ornamental excursions. In the absence of any complete play we cannot say what proportion of Çlokas was observed by Açvaghoṣa; we may suspect that it was not higher than in Bhāsa, if so high. Now the Çloka by its comparative simplicity and brevity, and by the ease of its structure, might well have served the same purpose in the Indian drama as did the trimeter in that of Greece, and it is curious to speculate what might have been the fate of the drama if it had been felt possible to write it throughout in verse. But evidently by Açvaghoṣa's age the distinction between prose and stanzas, essentially lyric in type, was fixed, and the elaborate structure of the stanza, normally with four lines of equal length and identic structure, the longer lines having also caesuras, rendered it quite unsuitable as a medium of conversation. Thus early in the drama we find a defect in form which was gradually to become more and more marked and to render the dialogue, that is the essential feature of the drama, less and less the subject of the labours of the dramatists.

IV

BHĀSA

1. *The Authenticity of Bhāsa's Dramas*

UNTIL 1910 the existence of any drama of Bhāsa's was unknown in Europe, and only in 1912 appeared under the editorship of T. Gaṇapati Çāstrin, the first of a series of thirteen dramas which their discoverer attributed to that poet. The fact, however, that the dramas themselves are silent as to the authorship rendered careful research necessary to determine their provenance, and the proofs adduced have not won entire satisfaction.

What we knew before the publication of Bhāsa was simply his high reputation. Kālidāsa in his first work, the *Mālavikāgnimitra*, refers to Bhāsa, with Saumilla, Kaviputra, and others as his great predecessors in the art, whose fame renders difficult the acceptance of the work of an untried author. Bāṇa,[1] at the beginning of the seventh century, states that Bhāsa attained fame by his dramas, begun by the Sūtradhāra, with many rôles and including episodes, as one might by the erection of temples, begun by the architect, with many stages, and beflagged. It would be unwise to prove by this that Bhāsa innovated in these regards; what is essential to Bāṇa is to celebrate Bhāsa's fame, and to show his wit by the comparison in the same words with some not very obvious object of comparison. A century later Vākpati[2] declares his pleasure in Bhāsa, friend of fire (*jalaṇamitte*), in the author of the *Raghuvaṅça*, in Subandhu and Hāricandra. Rājaçekhara (*c.* A.D. 900) places him among the classical poets, and a verse records a curious incident: 'Critics cast on the fire, to test it, the discus composed of the dramas of Bhāsa; the *Svapnavāsavadattā* did not succumb to the

[1] *Harṣacarita*, intr. v. 16. [2] *Gaüḍavaha*, 800.

flames'.[1] The verse, however, contains a *double entendre* strangely ignored by Professor Konow;[2] it denotes of course the superiority of the *Svapnavāsavadattā* to the other dramas of Bhāsa—a fact which the published plays bear out to the full—but it also alludes to a reason; the play itself contains a fire, which was feigned by the minister to permit the possibility of the king's new marriage, and it is only appropriate that, as that fire could not burn the queen, so the fire which tried the play was unable to prevail against it. The passage throws the necessary light on the term 'friend of fire' of Vākpati, which should not be rendered meaningless by attributing it to the fact that Bhāsa often mentions fire in his dramas.

These facts are, it must at once be admitted, extremely favourable to the authenticity of the dramas; taken all in all they are clearly the work of a very considerable writer; in technique they are less finished than those of Kālidāsa; the Prākrit is clearly earlier than that of the works of Kālidāsa or the *Mṛcchakaṭikā*; the *Svapnavāsavadattā* is clearly the best, and it explains Vākpati and Rājaçekhara's references. Bāṇa's statement regarding the opening of the plays by the Sūtradhāra is proved by the dramas. There is also substantial evidence to be derived from the writers on rhetoric. Bhāmaha, who may belong to the beginning of the eighth century A.D., criticizes severely the plot of the *Pratijñāyaugandharāyaṇa*; Vāmana, in the eighth, cites from that play, the *Svapnavāsavadattā*, and the *Cārudatta*; Abhinavagupta (*c.* A.D. 1000) twice names the *Svapnavāsavadattā*, and mentions the *Cārudatta*. These references are not in themselves conclusive, for they do not mention Bhāsa as the author of the plays, even when these are named,[3] and not merely cited from or discussed, but they show that the critics knew and were prepared to cite these dramas, which means that they accepted the view that they were by an important author. The ascription of the *Svapnavāsavadattā* to Bhāsa gives us the right to accept his authorship of the rest if internal evidence supports it. That this is so is undeniable,

[1] Cf. Chandradhar Guleri, IA. xlii. 52 ff.

[2] ID., p. 51, who also misses the point of *Bhāsanāṭakacakra* by taking it to refer to one play only.

[3] Cf. Lindenau, BS., p. 48, n. 1.

even by those who suspect the attribution to Bhāsa; the coincidences in technique, in the Prākrits, in metre, and in style are overwhelming. Finally, there is the evidence of the *Cārudatta*; it is undeniably and obviously the prototype of the *Mṛcchakaṭikā*, and it proves, therefore, that the dramas are older than that work which was well known by Vāmana, and is certainly a good deal earlier.

The arguments[1] against the authenticity are all inconclusive. They are based on the fact that a drama, *Mattavilāsa*, of Mahendravikramavarman, of the seventh century A. D. presents the same characteristics as regards the form of opening the drama as the plays of Bhāsa, and the suggestion that Rājasiṅha is to be identified with a prince of the south of that name (*c.* A. D. 675). The evidence is clearly inadequate; Bhāsa's fame was evidently more prevalent in the south than in the north, for a scene from one of his plays has survived in a mutilated form in the popular theatre there, and it is easy to understand how a seventh-century writer imitated him in technique. Moreover, the imitation is very partial; the omission of the name of the author and the play is not followed, and this is certainly a sign of a later date for the *Mattavilāsa*. The guess regarding the identification of the king is without probative force, for the term seems deliberately vague, and is in keeping with the silence of the author regarding his own name and that of his drama. The introduction of immediate reality is incongruous, and, therefore, avoided.

2. *The Date of Bhāsa's Dramas*

It is difficult to arrive at any precise determination of Bhāsa's date. That Kālidāsa knew his fame as firmly established is clear, and, if we may fairly safely date Kālidāsa about A. D. 400, this gives us a period of not later than A. D. 350 for Bhāsa. The fact of his priority to the *Mṛcchakaṭikā* leads us to no definite result, for the view that this play is to be placed before Kālidāsa in the third century A. D. is not at all plausible. An upper limit is given by the fact that Bhāsa is doubtless later than Açvaghoṣa, whose *Buddhacarita* is probably the source of a

[1] Barnett, JRAS. 1919, pp. 233 ff.; 1921, pp. 587 ff. Contrast G. Morgenstierne, *Über das Verhältnis zwischen Cārudatta und Mṛcchakaṭikā*, p. 16, n. 1; Keith, IA. lii. 59 f.; Thomas, JRAS. 1922, pp. 79 ff.; Winternitz, GIL. iii. 186, 645.

verse in the *Pratijñāyaugandharāyaṇa*, and whose Prākrit is assuredly and unquestionably older in character. It is useless to seek to estimate by the evidence of the Prākrit whether Bhāsa is more closely allied in date to Kālidāsa than to Açvaghoṣa, because changes in speech and the representation of them in literature are matters which do not in the slightest degree permit of exact valuation in terms of years. The most that can be said is that it may be held without improbability that Bhāsa is nearer to Kālidāsa's period than to Açvaghoṣa's.

An effort at more exact determination is made by Professor Konow[1] on the ground that Bhāsa's dramas in part deal with the story of Udayana, of which Ujjayinī was specially fond, as we know from Kālidāsa. Hence we may assume that the home of the poet was Ujjayinī, an assumption which obviously is not legitimate in any degree. Further we may assume that he lived under one of the Western Kṣatrapas, which again goes too far. Now the usual ending of a drama is not regularly observed in Bhāsa's dramas; the introductory question is found only in the *Avimāraka*, *Pratijñāyaugandharāyaṇa*, *Bālacarita*, and *Dūtavākya*. The description of the final benediction as Bharatavākya is omitted in the *Madhyamavyāyoga*, where Viṣṇu is praised; in the *Dūtaghaṭotkaca*, where his commands are given; in the *Pañcarātra*, where the wish is expressed that the king (*rājasiṅha*) should rule the whole earth; and in the *Ūrubhaṅga*, where the wish is that the prince should conquer his foes and rule the earth. In the other plays a change of form of the Bharatavākya is asserted; in the *Karṇabhāra* there is the desire for the disappearance of misfortune; in the *Pratimānāṭaka* the wish is that the king may fare as Rāma who was reunited with Sītā and his kinsmen; in the *Avimāraka*, the *Abhiṣekanāṭaka*, and the *Pratijñāyaugandharāyaṇa*, that the king should, after destroying his foes, rule the whole earth, while in the *Svapnavāsavadattā*, *Dūtavākya*, and *Bālacarita*, the wish is for universal rule. This suggests that for a time the king reigned in peace; then enemies arose and disturbed his power; finally he again won the upper hand, and his friends could without absurdity pray for his attaining imperial rank. This would agree with the history of the Kṣatrapa Rudrasiṅha, who held from 181–8, and

[1] KF. pp. 109 ff.

again from A.D. 191–6 the high rank of Mahākṣatrapa, and whose name may be hinted at in the use of the term *rājasiṅha*. That the *Pratijñāyaugandharāyaṇa* is older than the *Svapnavāsavadattā* is held to support this suggestion, but it is clearly without any merit save ingenuity.

Nor is there more to be said for Konow's other suggestions of date; the fact that the term Nāṭaka is used, and that the Vidūṣaka appears, cannot show that he is early, for they are used on continuously to the latest days of the drama, and the view that Bhāsa was an innovator who shortened the preliminaries, which is given as a reason for making him early, because the *Nāṭyaçāstra* gives the preliminaries in detail, is abandoned *sub silentio* in the author's later work,[1] where it is candidly admitted that we do not know whether he shortened the preliminaries at all. Nor can we say anything regarding his relation to the *Nāṭyaçastra* which will aid us to a date; there is even a tradition that he himself wrote on the theory of the drama. Nor can any weight be attached to the view that Bhāsa stands nearer Açvaghoṣa in technique than Kālidāsa; these matters do not permit of precise evaluation in time, and, if we place Bhāsa about A.D. 300, we go as far as the evidence allows.

3. *The Dramas and their Sources*

The derivation of the drama in part from epic recitations is peculiarly clear in Bhāsa, who shows the influence of the two great epics in its clearest form. In the *Madhyamavyāyoga*[2] we have a reminiscence of the tale of the love of the demon Hiḍimbā for Bhīma, the third of the five Pāṇḍavas, and their marriage which has Ghaṭotkaca as its fruit, though the parents part. The play opens with preliminary rites, after which the director pronounces a benediction on the audience, and begins to address them, but is suddenly interrupted by a sound, which is revealed as the cry of a Brahmin, who with his three sons and his wife is being pursued by the demon Ghaṭotkaca. The demon has received orders from his mother to bring her a victim; he offers, there-

[1] ID. p. 25; cf. Pischel, GGA. 1891, p. 361; below, p. 126.

[2] All the dramas are ed. in TSS. 1912–15 by T. Gaṇapati Çāstrin; this play is trs. E. P. Janvier, Mysore, 1921; P. E. Pavolini, GSAI. xxix. 1 f. who points out that the Bakavadha of the *Mahābhārata* is used.

fore, to spare the rest of the family, if one is willing to go with him, and the midmost, Madhyama, of the sons decides to go, though there is a generous rivalry among the three in self-sacrifice. He asks, however, time to go to perform a rite of purification, and, as he tarries, the demon in anger calls aloud for him. Bhīma responds, as the midmost of the Pāṇḍavas ; he will go in the boy's place, but not by force. The demon, not knowing his father, seeks to compel him, but, failing, accepts his offer to go willingly. Hiḍimbā greets her husband with joy, and reproaches her son and bids him express regret. She explains that her demand was made expressly to win for her a visit from Bhīma, who suggests that they should all accompany the aged Brahmin and his family to their destination, and with a verse in praise of Viṣṇu the piece ends.

Ghaṭotkaca is again the leading figure of the *Dūtaghaṭotkaca*, which may also be classed as a Vyāyoga, a term indicating primarily a military spectacle. The Kurus are jubilant over the defeat of Abhimanyu, Arjuna's son, at the hands of Jayadratha, though Dhṛtarāṣṭra warns them of the dangers that overshadow them. Ghaṭotkaca appears to them and predicts their punishment at the hands of Arjuna. Of the same general type apparently is the *Karṇabhāra* which deals with Karṇa's armour ; he makes himself ready for his fight with Arjuna, and tells Çalya, the Madra king, of the trick by which he won it from the great Paraçurāma, though the latter retaliated for the deception by the curse that the arms should fail him in the hour of his need. The curse is fulfilled, for Indra comes in the guise of a Brahmin and obtains from Karṇa his weapons and earrings. Karṇa and Çalya go out to battle, and the sound of Arjuna's chariot is heard. In the *Ūrubhaṅga* the fight between Bhīma and Duryodhana, greatest of the Kurus, ends in the breaking of the thigh of the latter, who falls in agony ; his son comes to him in his childish way, but his father is fain to save him the sorrow of his plight. His parents and wives surround him ; he seeks to comfort them ; Açvatthāman swears vengeance despite his counsels of peace ; visions of his brothers and Apsarases float before him, and he passes away.

These four plays have each but one Act ; the *Pañcarātra*, on the other hand, has three, and may perhaps be classed as a

Samavakāra, in so far at least as it is a drama in which there are more heroes of sorts than one, and they more or less attain their ends, which seem to be the chief features of that dubious kind of play in the theory. It reflects the period when efforts are being made to save the Kurus and the Pāṇḍavas from the fatal conflict, which ends in the ruin of the former and grave loss to the latter. Droṇa has undertaken a sacrifice for Duryodhana, and seeks as the fee the grant to the Pāṇḍavas of half the realm to which they had a just claim. Duryodhana promises on condition that they are heard of within five days. Virāṭa, however, is missing from those present at the offering; he has to mourn the loss of a hundred[1] Kīcakas. Bhīṣma suspects that Bhīma must be at the bottom of this illhap, and on his instigation at the end of Act II it is decided to raid Virāṭa's cows, as he hopes thus to bring the facts to light. The foray, however, fails, for the Pāṇḍavas are with Virāṭa in disguise; Abhimanyu is taken prisoner and married to Virāṭa's daughter. The charioteer in Act III brings back the news, showing clearly that Arjuna and Bhīma have taken part in the contest, but none the less Duryodhana decides to keep faith.

The *Dūtavākya*, a Vyāyoga in one act, is again from the *Mahābhārata*, but deals with the Kṛṣṇa legend. Bhīṣma is made chief of the Kuru forces; the arrival of Nārāyaṇa is announced, but Duryodhana forbids that any honour be shown to him, and seats himself before a picture, in which is depicted the indignity shown to Draupadī, when her husband gambled her away at dice. Kṛṣṇa enters, making a deep impression on all by his majesty; even Duryodhana falls from his seat. The messenger demands the half of the realm for the Pāṇḍavas; Duryodhana refuses and seeks to bind the envoy. Enraged, he calls for his magic weapons, but finally he consents to lay aside his wrath, and receives the homage of Dhṛtarāṣṭra. It is interesting to note that the play, in describing the picture, omits any allusion to the miracle by which in the epic Kṛṣṇa himself is represented as providing the unhappy Draupadī with fresh raiment as soon as each garment is dragged from her in insult. But it would be extremely unwise to assume with Professor Winternitz[2] that this

[1] One in the *Mahābhārata*, but Bhīma slays there 105 Sūtas also, the original Kīcaka being of that class.

[2] KF. pp. 301 f.

fact proves that Bhāsa did not know of this episode, and that it was interpolated after his time in the epic. Obviously it would have ruined the effect of the picture if such a fact had been hinted at in it, apart from the difficulty of exhibiting this by the painter's art, and Bhāsa is clearly justified on artistic grounds in allowing this episode to be passed over.

Of far greater importance is the *Bālacarita*,[1] which presents us with a lively and vivid picture of the feats of Kṛṣṇa, culminating in the slaying of Kaṅsa, a brilliant exemplification of the value of Patañjali's evidence as to the growth of drama. The director enters, pronounces a verse of benediction asking the favour of the god, who is Nārāyaṇa, Viṣṇu, Rāma, and Kṛṣṇa in the four ages of the world; he announces the advent of the sage Nārada and retires. Nārada explains that he has come from the heaven to gaze on the young Kṛṣṇa, born in the family of the Vṛṣṇis as son of Devakī and Vasudeva, who is in truth Nārāyaṇa incarnate to destroy Kaṅsa. He sees the infant, pays homage, and departs. Devakī and Vasudeva appear on the stage; they have joy in the birth of a son, but terror, for Kaṅsa has slain already six sons of theirs and will slay the seventh—a deviation in number from our other sources which make Kṛṣṇa the eighth child. Vasudeva takes the infant and decides to remove it from Kaṅsa's reach. He leaves the city, but the child's weight is as colossal as that of Mount Mandara; the darkness is impenetrable, but a marvellous light comes from the child, and the Yamunā makes dry a path for him to cross. The spirit of the tree under which he rests brings to him the cowherd Nanda, bearing a dead maiden, an infant just borne by his wife Yaçodā, who, fallen in a faint, does not know whether the child is a boy or a girl. Nanda gives aid reluctantly, but in memory of past favours. He seeks first to purify himself from contact with the dead, but a spring of water shoots forth and renders labour needless. He takes the boy, but his weight proves too great. Now appear in the guise of herdsmen the weapons of Kṛṣṇa and his steed, who present themselves each with a verse, 'I am the bird, Garuḍa,' &c., 'I am the discus', 'I the bow', 'I the club', 'I the conch', and 'I the sword'. At the request of the discus the infant consents to become light, and Nanda bears him away. Vasudeva finds the dead child awakened

[1] Winternitz, ZDMG. lxxiv. 125 ff.; Lindenau, BS. pp. 22 ff.

to life in his arms, and the weight of it is oppressive, but the Yamunā once more gives dry passage, and he returns to Mathurā and Devakī. Act II opens with an entr'acte in Kaṅsa's palace. The curse pronounced on him by the seer Madhuka enters, guised as a Caṇḍāla in hateful form with a necklace of skulls; he and his retinue of Caṇḍālīs force their way into the heart of the palace; the royal fortune, Rājaçrī, would bar their way, but the curse announces that it is Viṣṇu's will that he enter, and she yields; the curse seizes then hold of Kaṅsa. The Act then presents Kaṅsa uneasy and distressed by the portents of the night; he summons his astrologer and his domestic priests, who warn him that the portents presage the birth of a god. Kaṅsa has Vasudeva summoned, is told of the birth of a daughter, refuses to spare the child, and hurls it against a rock. But part only of the lifeless body falls to earth; the rest rises to heaven, and the dread figure of the goddess Kārtyāyanī appears to the king. Her retinue come also, announcing each his advent with a verse, and declare their purpose to destroy Kaṅsa. In the meantime, in herdsmen's guise they will go to the home of the child to share in the sports of the herdsmen.

The entr'acte before Act III tells us in the mouths of the herdsmen of their joys since Kṛṣṇa came to live with them, and an old man relates in a long Prākrit speech his wonderful deeds, including the destruction of the demons, Pūtanā, Çakaṭa, Yamala and Arjuna, Pralamba, Dhenuka, and Keçin. We are told then that Kṛṣṇa or Dāmodara, the name won from an adventure, has gone to the Vṛndā wood for the Hallīçaka dance; the dance is performed by Dāmodara, his friends, and the maidens, to the music of the drum and to song. The advent of the demon Ariṣṭa is announced; Dāmodara bids the maidens and herdsmen mount a hill, and watch the struggle. It proves unequal; the bull demon recognizes the superiority of his foe, and that he is Viṣṇu himself, and meets death with resignation. The victory accomplished, the news is brought of a new danger, the snake Kāliya has appeared on the Yamunā bank, menacing cows and Brahmins. Act IV shows us the maidens seeking to restrain Kṛṣṇa from the new struggle, but he persists and overcomes the demon, plunging into the waters to grapple with him. He brings him out, learns that he had entered the waters in fear of Garuḍa who slays snakes at pleasure, makes him promise to spare cows and Brahmins, and puts on him a mark that Garuḍa must respect. A herald then enters to challenge Dāmodara and his brother Balarāma to the festival of the boys at Mathurā.

Act V shows us Kaṅsa plotting the overthrow of the youths. A herald reports the arrival of Dāmodara, and his great feats of strength, the mocking of the elephant let loose on him, the making straight of a female dwarf, the breaking of the bow of the guardsman. The king orders at once the boxing to begin; Kṛṣṇa, however, easily overcomes Muṣṭika and Cāṇūra, the king's chosen champions, and completes his victory by a sudden onslaught which leaves the king dead. His soldiers would avenge him, but Vasudeva announces Kṛṣṇa's identity with Viṣṇu, and appoints Ugrasena king in Kaṅsa's place, freeing him from the confinement in which his son had placed him. Nārada with Apsarases and Gandharvas appears to glorify Kṛṣṇa, who graciously permits Nārada to return to heaven, and a benediction, spoken apparently by the actor, closes the play.

The precise source of the drama is unknown; it differs in detail widely from the stories of Kṛṣṇa in the *Harivaṅça*, *Viṣṇu*, and *Bhāgavata Purāṇas*, but none of these works, as we have it, is probably older than Bhāsa. The erotic element, which is so closely associated with Kṛṣṇa in later tradition, is lacking here as in the *Harivaṅça* and the *Viṣṇu Purāṇa*, and similarly the figure of Rādhā is missing.

The merits of the *Bālacarita* are not reproduced in Bhāsa's treatment of the other chief Avatāra of Viṣṇu. The *Pratimānāṭaka* shows us the death of Daçaratha, when he realizes the departure of Rāma, deprived of his inheritance by Kaikeyī's wiles, with Sītā and Lakṣmaṇa into the forest; his statue is added to those of his predecessors in the statue (*pratimā*) hall. Bharata returns from a visit, learns of the news, pursues Rāma, but is induced to return to rule, bearing with him Rāma's shoes as token that he regards himself but as viceroy. Rāma decides to offer the sacrifice for the dead for his sire; Rāvaṇa appears under the guise of an expert, and bids him offer a golden antelope, by this device securing Rāma's absence when Sītā is stolen by him, slaying Jaṭāyu who seeks to protect her. Rāma goes to Kiṣkindhā, and makes alliance with Sugrīva against Vālin. Bharata learns that Kaikeyī's ruse had been induced by the curse of an ascetic, whose son Daçaratha had unwittingly slain, and that she had but meant to ask for a banishment of fourteen days, but had by a slip said years. He sends his army to aid Rāma, who ultimately defeats Rāvaṇa, and recovers Sītā. He brings her with him to Janasthāna, where he is begged to resume his kingdom; all then go by the magic car Puṣpak to Ayodhyā. The seven acts of the play are matched by the six of the *Abhiṣekanāṭaka*,[1] the drama of the consecration of Rāma which follows, like its predecessor, the *Rāmāyaṇa*. It tells of Vālin's death at the hands of Rāma; Hanumant's success in reaching Lañkā and in comforting Sītā and affronting Rāvaṇa. Vibhīṣaṇa advises the coercion of the ocean to attain a passage for the army; Rāvaṇa vainly seeks to win Sītā, showing her in appearance the heads of Rāma and Lakṣmaṇa, but she repudiates his advances; he is compelled to fight, and the play ends with Rāma's coronation. The epic apparently has weighed too heavily on the author, whose resource in incident is remarkable by its absence.

A far more favourable opportunity is afforded to Bhāsa when he derived his story from the Kathā literature,[2] as is doubtless the case in the *Avimāraka*, a drama in six acts. The daughter of king Kuntibhoja, the young Kurañgī, is saved from an elephant by an unknown youth, who, in reality son of the Sauvīra king, is with his father living as a member of a degraded caste for a year, as the outcome of a curse. His low status forbids his aspiring to the princess, but love triumphs, and the maidens of Kurañg, arrange a secret meeting to which the youth comes in the guise of a thief. But the news leaks out and he must fly; in despair of reunion he seeks death in the fire, but Agni repulses him; he would have thrown himself from a rock, but a Vidyādhara dissuades him, giving him a ring which enables him unseen to re-enter the palace and save Kurañgī, likewise desolated, from suicide. The way for a happy issue from the impasse is found by the fact that Nārada reveals the true history of Avimāraka; he is not in fact the son of the Sauvīra king; he is the son of the god Agni by Sudarçanā, the wife of the king of Kāçi, who

[1] Trs. E. Beccarini-Crescenzi, GSAI. xxvii. 1 ff.

[2] Cf. KSS. cxii. and *Kāmasūtravyākhyā* in ed. of *Pratimānāṭaka*, Upodghāta, p. 29, n.; trs. GSAI. xxviii.

gave him over on his birth to Sucetanā, her sister, wife of the Sauvīra king. The marriage thus takes place with the approval of all those connected with the pair.

Equally from the Kathā literature, and in this case from a source known to us, the *Bṛhatkathā* of Guṇāḍhya, which, written in Paiçācī Prākrit has vanished, but is preserved in a version from Nepal and two from Kashmir, is the subject of the *Pratijñāyaugandharāyaṇa*,[1] styled in the prologue a Prakaraṇa, which has four Acts and resembles in part that form of drama as recognized by the theory, though its hero is the minister of Udayana, the Vatsa king. The latter goes on an elephant hunt, armed with his lyre to charm his prey, but is taken prisoner by a clever trick of his enemy, Pradyota Mahāsena, of Ujjayinī, a counterfeit elephant being employed for his overthrow. Yaugandharāyaṇa determines to revenge the king. In Ujjayinī Mahāsena discusses with his wife the question of the marriage of their daughter Vāsavadattā, when the news of the capture of Udayana arrives. They decide that she shall take lessons in music from the captive, and, not unnaturally, the two fall in love. Yaugandharāyaṇa comes to Ujjayinī in disguise with his friends, and through his machinations the king is enabled to escape with Vāsavadattā, though the minister is himself, after a gallant fight, captured. Mahāsena, however, appreciated the minister's cleverness, and has the marriage of the pair depicted.[2]

The play is criticized severely, though not by name, by Bhāmaha,[3] on the score that Udayana could never have been deceived by an artificial elephant, and if deceived his life would not have been spared by the enemy forces. The contentions are obviously of little value in this form ; the essence, of course, is that such an incident which may pass in a tale seems too childish for a drama, but, if this troubles us, we may console ourselves with the reflexion that the trees were thick, and Udayana ardent in the chase. Vāmana[4] cites the end of verse 3 in Act IV which occurs also in the *Arthaçāstra*,[5] a work which need not be older than Bhāsa, and may be a good deal later.

[1] The story is referred to in the *Mālatīmādhava*, ii. 92 ; for the Kathā, see Lacôte, *Le Bṛhatkathā*, pp. 70 ff. ; for the 'Trojan horse' motif, GIL. ii. 155 ; iii. 175, n. 3.

[2] The work is styled a Nāṭikā in the colophon in one manuscript.

[3] iv. 40 ff. [4] v. 2. 28. [5] p. 366.

The *Svapnavāsavadattā*,[1] or the *Svapnanāṭaka*, in six Acts forms in substance the continuation of the *Pratijñāyaugandharāyaṇa*. The minister is anxious to secure for Udayana an extension of his power by wedding him to Padmāvatī, daughter of the king of Magadha. But Udayana will not leave his beloved Vāsavadattā, so that strategy is needed. The minister induces Vāsavadattā to aid in his scheme, and, taking advantage of a temporary separation, he spreads the rumour that the queen and he have perished in a conflagration. The king is thus induced to consider marriage with Padmāvatī, in whose care the minister has entrusted the queen, giving out that she is his sister. Padmāvatī is willing to accept the love of the king, but, learning that he has never ceased to cherish the memory of his beloved, she is seized by a severe headache, and the king comes to comfort her. He does not find her, and lies down, sleep overcoming him; Vāsavadattā who had come to aid Padmāvatī sits down beside the sleeping form which she mistakes for that of her new mistress, but, as he begins to speak in his sleep she rises and leaves him, but not before he has caught a glimpse of her, in a dream as he thinks. He is summoned to the palace, and finds the good news that his foes have been defeated, and a messenger has come from Mahāsena and his wife to console him, bearing the picture of the nuptials of himself and Vāsavadattā. Padmāvatī recognizes in the lady the features of the sister left in her care by Yaugandharāyaṇa, who arrives to explain to the satisfaction of all the plan he has devised to secure Udayana's ends.

The fame of the work in Rājaçekhara's time is attested, and already before him the imaginary conflagration of the queen had excited the imitation of Harṣa in the *Ratnāvalī*; Vāmana[2] cites from it, and Abhinavagupta[3] knew it. Nor is there any doubt that it is the poet's masterpiece and the most mature of his dramas. Great promise, however, in a different vein is shown in the *Cārudatta*, of which we have only a fragment in four

[1] Trs. A. Baston, Paris, 1914 (corr. in GSAI. xxvii. 159 f.); A. G. Shirreff and Panna Lall, Allahabad, 1918. Cf. Lacôte, JA. sér. 11, xiii. 493 ff.

[2] iv. 3. 25, citing iv. 7.

[3] *Dhvanyālokalocana*, p. 152 cites probably a lost verse; comm. on N. in TSS. ed. p. xxii. The play is cited also by Vandyaghaṭīya Sarvānanda (A.D. 1159).

Acts without beginning or final verses. Cārudatta, a merchant whose generosity has impoverished him, has seen a hetaera Vasantasenā at a festival, and they have fallen in love. Pursued by the king's brother-in-law, Saṁsthāna, Vasantasenā takes refuge in Cārudatta's house, and, when she goes, she leaves in his care her gold ornaments. She generously ransoms from his creditors a former servant of Cārudatta, who then renounces the world and becomes a monk. In the night the ornaments, which she had deposited, are stolen by a thief Sajjalaka who breaks into Cārudatta's house, in order to gain the means to purchase the freedom of a slave of the hetaera with whom he is in love. Cārudatta is overcome with shame at learning of the theft of goods deposited in his care, and his noble wife sacrifices a pearl necklace, which she gives to the Vidūṣaka to hand over to Vasantasenā in lieu of her lost jewels. He takes it to the hetaera, who has learned of the theft, but accepts it to have the excuse of visiting the merchant once more. She therefore hands over the slave girl to Sajjalaka, and starts out to Cārudatta's house. At this point the play ends abruptly, but it seems as if Cārudatta were accused of theft, and that Vasantasenā herself is in grave danger of her life.

A verse of this play is cited by Vāmana [1] and another,[2] found also in the *Bālacarita* [3] and the *Mṛcchakaṭikā*,[4] is quoted by Daṇḍin in the *Kāvyādarça*.[5] We need not doubt that Bhāsa is his source, especially as there is possibly elsewhere in the *Kāvyādarça* an allusion to the dream scene of the *Svapnavāsavadattā* and its sequel. The *Daridracārudatta* mentioned by Abhinavagupta is most probably the same work. From it are derived the first four Acts of the *Mṛcchakaṭikā*.[6] The source of the drama is not certain; we have the motif of the love of a merchant and a hetaera elsewhere, but not with the special developments given by Bhāsa.

Verses attributed to Bhāsa are also found which are not contained in the extant dramas, so that, even allowing for misquotation and confusion, it is probable that he may have written

[1] i. 2 in Vāmana, v. i. 3. [2] i. 19. [3] i. 15.
[4] i. 34. [5] ii. 233.
[6] G. Morgenstierne, *Über das Verhältnis zwischen Cārudatta und Mṛcchakaṭikā* (1921). Cf. Mehendale, *Bhandarkar Comm. Vol.* pp. 369 ff.

further plays, or he may have illustrated the book of the dramatic art which he is credited with writing,[1] by inserting examples of his own composition. Why his plays should have fared so badly as to disappear from popular use apparently for centuries does not appear. The most plausible view is that he was a poet of the south, and that his dramas suffered from the general Mahomedan objection to everything Hindu, and especially to the dramas of an earnest devotee of Viṣṇu such as Bhāsa was. But this is mere conjecture.

4. *Bhāsa's Art and Technique*

The number of Bhāsa's dramas, and the variety of their themes, indicate the activity and originality of his talent. Even the limitations imposed by the choice of epic subjects are often successfully surmounted. In the Rāma dramas only is there lacking any sign of his ability; the *Abhiṣekanāṭaka* is a somewhat dreary summary of the corresponding books (IV–VI) of the *Rāmāyaṇa*, nor is the *Pratimānāṭaka* substantially superior. The variations are in the main few and unimportant; the two struggles between Sugrīva and Vālin are condensed into one, which leaves the treacherous slaying of Vālin without shadow of excuse, and casts a blemish on Rāma's character which later dramatists avoid. The pathetic scene of the epic in which Tārā, his wife, laments Vālin's death is omitted, Vālin forbidding any woman to gaze on him in his fall. The two efforts of Rāvaṇa to deceive Sītā, first by showing her Rāma's head, and later Rāma and Lakṣmaṇa bound and seemingly dead, are reduced to one, the showing of the heads of both, and Sītā's constancy is made inhuman by denying her the comfort of a consoler. To secure a happy ending, Agni is made to vindicate Sītā by the test of fire, and to hand her over to Rāma as Lakṣmī and his fit mate. The characters remain stereotyped and dull; Rāvaṇa is nothing more than a *miles gloriosus*, if not comic, and Lakṣmaṇa cuts a very poor figure.[2]

The pieces based on the *Mahābhārata* shows more invention

[1] *Arthadyotanikā*, 2.

[2] In the *Pratimānāṭaka* the poet invents the episode of Bharata's learning of Sītā's abduction, of Rāma's taking over the reins of government from Bharata, and his coronation in the hermitage. In the *Pañcarātra* the gift by Duryodhana of half the realm is new.

and interest. The *Madhyamavyāyoga* exploits neatly the theme of Hiḍimbā's longing to see her husband of many years before, and the obedience of a son to a mother exemplified both by Ghaṭotkaca and by Madhyama ; a mother's bidding outweighs even that of a father. The struggle of father against son, both unknowing, is original, though not tragic. In the *Karṇabhāra* the nobility of the haughty Karṇa is emphasized ; in the epic he surrenders his armour to Indra, but demands a price, the lance that never fails ; in the play it suffices the prince that he has conferred a boon on the god himself. There is the same martial spirit, evoking the sentiment of heroism in the audience, in the *Dūtaghaṭotkaca* where the joy of the Kurus is contrasted effectively with the doubts of Dhṛtarāṣṭra, and the grave warning which Ghaṭotkaca brings of the revenge to be wreaked by Arjuna for his son's death. The *Dūtavākya* is admirable in his contrast between the character of Duryodhana and the majesty of Kṛṣṇa ; the picture motif is effectively elaborated, and the deep admiration of the poet for Kṛṣṇa as the embodiment of the highest of gods Viṣṇu, of whom he was an adorer, is plainly manifest. In the *Ūrubhaṅga* Duryodhana's hauteur to the highest of gods meets with its just punishment ; Duryodhana is the chief subject, but not the hero, of the piece which manifests the just[1] punishment of the impious. The death of Duryodhana is admirably depicted ; his child who loved to sit on his knees comes to him, but must be repulsed ; the touch that brought joy aforetime would now be an agony.[2] But Duryodhana, with all his demerits as a man, remains heroic in his death.

The *Bālacarita* reveals the originality of Bhāsa's genius ; the entr'acte to the second Act is extremely effective in its terrors, and the poet has no hesitation in asking the audience to conceive for themselves the strange figures of the attendants of Viṣṇu or the host of the goddess Kārtyāyanī, or the bull Ariṣṭa, or the snake demon Kāliya, all of whom appear on the stage, but doubtless in costumes which left most to the mind's eye. The miracles of the light emanating from the child Kṛṣṇa, the crossing of the Yamunā, and the water springing from the ground, are innovations on the tradition, as is the apparent death and revival of the child of Yaçodā. Kṛṣṇa is heroism incarnate, Kaṅsa

[1] Recognized by Duryodhana, v. 35. [2] v. 43.

without merit, and his slaying just, but the heroic sentiment is blended with the erotic, and with that of wonder. As a drama, however, the play suffers unquestionably from the wholly undeniable disparity between the two opponents; Kṛṣṇa is never in danger, and his feats are too easily achieved to produce their full effect.

The *Avimāraka* is a drama of love, primitive in its expression and intensity; Bhāsa's love for rapid action is here, as always, strongly marked, as is also his willingness to repeat incidents and situations; the hero twice seeks suicide, and the heroine does so once. The dénouement is artificial, though something of the kind was necessary to secure the possibility of the marriage of the pair. There is a far more interesting hint of youthful love in the amours of Udayana and Vāsavadattā in the *Pratijñāyaugandharāyaṇa*, where the rapidity of action is in entire harmony with the skill attributed to the minister, whose address, courage, and loyalty, make him an attractive figure. The *Svapnavāsavadattā* itself reveals Udayana as a faithful and devoted husband, very different from the careless if courteous gentleman of Harṣa's dramas. His love for the queen he imagines lost ennobles and elevates his character, while motives of statecraft and the affection shown him by Padmāvatī easily explain his wooing of that maiden. Vāsavadattā herself is not the jealous if high-minded wife of Harṣa's plays; she is the devoted and self-sacrificing lover who is willing to postpone her own feelings and wishes to the good of her husband. The king and queen are the finest products of Bhāsa's characterization of lovers. In the *Cārudatta*, however, we have clever studies in the hetaera, the merchant and the minor figures, though the value of the play must seem less to us than when completed and elaborated in the *Mṛcchakaṭikā*.

Bhāsa undoubtedly excels in suggesting heroism; this characteristic is admirably depicted in Yaugandharāyaṇa, and above all in Duryodhana, who is the *Dūtaghaṭotkaca* effectively replies to the menaces of the envoy by promising an answer in deeds war, not in harsh words. But his power is not confined to heroism, love, pathos, or the marvellous. The Vidūṣaka in his hands attains the characteristics which mark him in the later drama, and, though much was doubtless traditional, it may safely be assumed that he tended by his example to stereotype the figure. In the *Avimāraka*[1] he distinguishes himself by devotion to his master; he is set on finding him, dead or alive, when he is missing, and he is prepared if need be to follow him beyond the grave. Avimāraka himself portrays the character of his friend; he places first, doubtless deliberately, the amusement he produces in social intercourse (*goṣṭhīṣu hāsyaḥ*), but he describes him also as brave in battle, a wise friend, a comforter in sorrow, a violent foe to his enemies. If in the *Pratijñāyaugandharāyaṇa*[2] he seems to abandon the idea of succouring his master, it is only because he is convinced thst Vatsa is dead, and that nothing can be done to save him. The other side of his character is his devotion to the pleasures of the table and his feeble attempts at wit and humour. Vāsavadattā he remembers fondly because she used to see that he never lacked sweetmeats.[3] When in the *Avimāraka*[4] the heroine weeps in love-sorrow, he would like to weep also in sympathy; but no tears come, and he recalls that, even when his own father died, he could hardly weep. When addressed as a man, he insists that he is a woman. He is, however, a Brahmin in his prejudices; he will not drink brandy, a pleasure which he permits to the Gātrasevaka, the disguise assumed by one of Yaugandharāyaṇa's following in the attempt to rescue Udayana. This worthy favours us with a eulogy of drink, which is an interesting fragment of the drinking songs which must have existed in ancient India:[5]

dhaṇṇā surāhi mattā dhaṇṇā surāhi aṇulittā;
dhaṇṇā surāhi ṇhādā dhaṇṇā surāhi saṁṇavidā.

'Blessed those that are drunk with drink, blessed those that are soaked with drink; blessed those that are washed with drink, blessed those that are choked with drink.' Amusing also is the figure of Yaugandharāyaṇa as an Unmattaka, devoted to eating and dancing, and of Rumaṇvant in his guise of a Çramaṇaka. There is genuine humour in the scene in the *Pratijñāyaugandharāyaṇa*[6] between the Gātrasevaka and the servant, when the former makes ready the elephant Bhadravatī, which is to be

[1] p. 69 and v. 21.
[2] iii. p. 53.
[3] *Svapnavāsavadattā*, iv. p. 43.
[4] v. p. 83.
[5] *Pratijñāyaugandharāyaṇa*, p. 57.
[6] pp. 59 ff.

the means of carrying off the king and Vāsavadattā beyond the reach of all pursuit, without raising any suspicion on the part of the entourage of Mahāsena. Quiet humour is shown in the episode of the bringing of Bhīma by Ghaṭotkaca to his mother Hiḍimbā; Ghaṭotkaca has difficulty in describing his victim, and is much amazed to find his mother, whose curiosity is aroused by his lack of precision, finding him to be his deity and hers in his capacity as husband and father.[1] In the same vein is the compliment paid by Rāma to Sītā, when the latter accurately predicts the action he would take when his father offered him the throne: 'Thou hast guessed well; few pairs are there of like character in the world (*suṣṭhu tarkitam alpaṁ tulyaçīlāni dvandvāni sṛjyante*)'.[2] Quite distinctly amusing is the scene at the close of the *Avimāraka*,[3] where the facts of the relationships are being disclosed to the king Kuntibhoja. That sovereign may be justly excused his difficulty in apprehending the situation; he is reduced to such confusion that he is dubious about his own capital Vairantya, but finally, when assured that the hero is the son-in-law of Kuntibhoja, asks who that worthy may be, to be reminded politely that he himself is Kuntibhoja, father of Kuraṅgī, son of Duryodhana, and lord of Vairantya. This power explains the description of Bhāsa as the laughter (*hāsa*) of poetry given to him by Jayadeva in the *Prasannarāghava*, a title which is also merited by such verses as one cited in the anthologies,[4] though not found in the extant dramas:

kapāle mārjāraḥ paya iti karāṅl leḍhi çaçinas
tarucchidraprotān bisam iti karī saṁkalayati
ratānte talpasthān harati vanitāpy aṅçukam iti
prabhāmattaç candro jagad idam aho viplavayati.

'When its rays fall on its cheeks the cat licks them, thinking them milk; when they are caught in the cleft of a tree the elephant deems them a lotus; when they rest on the couch of lovers the maiden seizes them, saying, "'Tis my robe"; the moon in truth, proud of its brilliance, doth lead astray all this world.'

Of deeper sentiments we need expect nothing from Bhāsa;

[1] *Madhyamavyāyoga*, p. 22.
[2] *Abhiṣekanāṭaka*, i. p. 13.
[3] vi. p. 102.
[4] *Subhāṣitāvali*, 1994.

in this respect he sets the model for his successors. From Kālidāsa he differs in being a devotee of Viṣṇu rather than Çiva, but he is equally an admirer of the established Brahminical order. In the *Pañcarātra*,[1] the *Pratijñāyaugandharāyaṇa*,[2] and in the character of Nārada in the *Avimāraka*,[3] we find clearly expressed his appreciation of the high rank of the Brahmin, and the obligations due to him from kings and other classes.

Care in the delineation of even minor characters is normally displayed; the number of these is considerable; sixteen each in the *Svapnavāsavadattā* and the *Pratijñāyaugandharāyaṇa*, about twenty in the *Avimāraka*, *Abhiṣekanāṭaka*, and *Pañcarātra*, twelve in the *Cārudatta*, and about thirty in the *Bālacarita*. But there are traces of the anxiety of Bhāsa to avoid adding needlessly to the number of those appearing; in the *Avimāraka* neither the king of Kāçi nor Sucetanā appears on the scene despite their part in the play. The silence of Sītā, though at the close of the *Abhiṣekanāṭaka* she appears on the stage, is doubtless explicable by the same dramatic touch which makes Euripides refuse to assign any words to Alkestis on her return from the dead.

In technique Bhāsa does not accord entirely with the later rules of the theorists. The *Nāṭyaçāstra*, it is true, when it forbids the exhibition of battle scenes contradicts itself, and Bhāsa freely permits them, as must have been the case in the primitive drama in which Kṛṣṇa slew Kaṅsa. The maidens, however, he bids watch the mortal combat of Ariṣṭa and Kṛṣṇa from afar. Daçaratha's death he admits; the bodies of Cāṇūra, Muṣṭika, and Kaṅsa lie on the stage, and Vālin perishes there as well as Duryodhana, but all these are evildoers, and their death evokes no sorrow. The same simplicity doubtless accounts for the introduction of the mythological figures of the *Bālacarita*, whom we need not imagine to have been elaborately costumed; they announce their nature or are described,[4] and the spectator supplies the imagination requisite to comprehend them.

We find already in Bhāsa the formal distinction of introductory scenes into Viṣkambhakas of two kinds, according as Sanskrit alone or Sanskrit and Prākrit are used and Praveçakas:

[1] i. 25. [2] pp. 43 ff. [3] pp. 99 ff.

[4] Cf. Duryodhana's description of Kṛṣṇa's manifestation in the *Dūtavākya*.

in the former the number of interlocutors is three in two[1] cases against one or two as usual later; there are other signs of his fondness for triads.[2] The introduction normally is styled Sthāpanā,[3] not as later Prastāvanā, and it is extremely simple; after a Nāndī, not preserved, has been pronounced--perhaps behind the scene—the director enters, utters a benediction, and is about to make an announcement when a sound is heard which leads up to the actual drama. No mention of the poet's name or the work is found, but these we may suggest were left to the preliminaries which even in the *Nāṭyaçāstra* were elaborate, and which doubtless were performed before Bhāsa's plays, as they were essentially religious rites in honour of the gods. On the other hand, the close, the Bharatavākya, of the later theory is varied in Bhāsa. The conventions as to the use of speech, aloud, aside to another, or to the audience alone are well known, and effective use is made of the voice from the air or behind the scene, as in the *Abhiṣekanāṭaka*, when Rāvaṇa taunts his prisoner and asks, who can set her free when her rescuers are dead; the voice replies, 'Rāma, Rāma'.[4]

There are unquestionably primitive traits in Bhāsa's art; he uses with dangerous freedom the device by which some one departs and returns straightway, to narrate what must have taken long to happen; thus in the *Abhiṣekanāṭaka*, Çañkukarṇa is bidden send a thousand men against Hanumant; he departs at once, to return and tell that they have fallen. Free use is made also, as in the epic, of magic weapons in the conflict, as in the battle of Duryodhana and Kṛṣṇa in the *Dūtavākya*. So also in the *Madhyamavyāyoga* we find Ghaṭotkaca employing his magic power to produce water from a rock; then he binds Bhīma in a magic noose, from which he is delivered by a magic formula. In the *Dūtavākya* the discus of Kṛṣṇa

[1] *Abhiṣekanāṭaka*, vi, where three Vidyādharas describe Rāma and Rāvaṇa's fight; *Pañcarātra*, i, where three Brahmins describe Duryodhana's sacrifice.

[2] In the *Madhyamavyāyoga* there are three sons of the Brahmin; *Ūrubhañga*, where three servants describe the battle. Cf. the Trigata of the preliminaries to the drama.

[3] Prastāvanā is given in the *Karṇabhāra*.

[4] v. p. 56; cf. *Avimāraka*, iii. p. 41. Compare the use of an abrupt interruption in the *Pratijñāyaugandharāyaṇa*, p. 30, where the query of the king as to a husband is answered by the mention of Vatsarāja's capture.

secures water from the heavenly Ganges by magic means; it has the power to move the mountains of the gods, to set the ocean in motion, and to bring down the stars to earth, ideas which are less unintelligible when we remember the wide-spread Indian beliefs in the powers of magicians, which we find later in Harṣa's *Ratnāvalī*, and which are earlier recorded of those who have attained high degrees of intuition in both the Upaniṣads and Buddhism. In the *Avimāraka* we have the magic ring of the Vidyādhara playing a decisive part in the action, since by its use the hero can enter unseen the harem and visit his wife Kuraṅgī in secret. It is clear that both in the epic and in the popular tale Bhāsa found adequate precedent for the stress laid on these means of evoking in his audience the sentiment of wonder.

The use of the dance as an ornament to the drama which is seen in Kālidāsa is frequently resorted to in Bhāsa. In Act III of the *Bālacarita* there is a performance of the Hallīçaka dance, in which both the herdsmen and the cowherdesses take full part; the dance is accompanied by music and song, and the maidens are gaily attired. A similar dance is mentioned in Act II of the *Pañcarātra*,[1] a reflex no doubt of the ritual dance of the winter solstice in the Mahāvrata rite. It is conceivable also that the conception in the *Bālacarita* of the appearance of Viṣṇu's weapons as figures on the stage in the dress of herdsmen is a reminiscence of a cult dance in honour of Viṣṇu, but this idea must not be pressed unduly, for the poet there invents also the figures of the Curse and the King's Fortune as *personae dramatis*. There is, it is clear, a certain similarity between the personification of these abstractions and the allegorical figures of the Buddhist drama, which come again into being in the *Prabodhacandrodaya* of Kṛṣṇamiçra. Song as an important element in the drama again appears in the *Abhiṣekanāṭaka*, where the Gandharvas and Apsarases sing the praises of Viṣṇu.[2]

There are clear traces in the dramas of the overwhelming influence of epic tradition and of epic recitation in the tendency

[1] p. 22. Apparently a dance on the occasion of an eclipse may be meant; Lindenau, BS. p. 43. Cf. L. von Schroeder, *Arische Religion*, ii. 114 ff.

[2] The idea that *prathamakalpa* is a technical term of dramaturgy (DR. i. 60, comm.) appears to be due to the frequent use of the term, apparently as a remark of eulogy, in the manuscripts of Bhāsa's works.

to introduce the description of battle scenes at great length in lieu of dramatic action, while a certain lack of skill is apparent in the attempt to transform the tale into a drama. Thus in the *Avimāraka* the facts essential for a full understanding of the story come out only in the last Act, and the adventures of the hero are there recounted with distinct lack of propriety, as they have formed the subject of the earlier acts of the drama. Neither the *Pratijñāyaugandharāyaṇa* nor the *Svapnavāsavadattā* is constructed in so clumsy a manner, but in both cases the working out of the plot is certainly open to criticism. Thus even in the last Act of the latter drama, which in many respects is effective, the stage directions assume that the queen appears on the stage with Vāsavadattā as her attendant, but that the king either does not see, or does not recognize the latter, both obviously very improbable suppositions; possibly it is assumed that the presence of Vāsavadattā, though obvious to the audience, is concealed from the king in some manner by the use of the curtain, but this is left to be imagined,[1] and it would have been much simpler to invent some ground for securing the entry of Vāsavadattā by herself later on. On the other hand, in Act I of the play, the facts regarding the supposed death of Vāsavadattā and the minister in a fire are effectively brought out by the device of using a Brahmacārin, who arrives at the hermitage at the same time as Yaugandharāyaṇa and Vāsavadattā in their disguise, and tells the tale of the disaster as explaining why he has left that place in sorrow at the event, dilating at the same time on the effect of the news on the unhappy king. The mode in which Vāsavadattā in Act V mistakes the king for Padmāvatī is quite naturally evolved, for the place where he is resting is poorly illuminated and she was naturally unwilling to arouse her mistress from the slumber into which she hoped she had fallen. In Act II of the *Abhiṣekanāṭaka* the conversation of Hanumant with Sītā is made possible only by the somewhat implausible device of assuming that the Rākṣasīs who guard her fall asleep at their post.

A rather marked fondness is shown by Bhāsa for the repetition of the same incident. Thus in the *Avimāraka* we have the

[1] The use of a transverse curtain would explain the scene, but there is no real evidence of this. Cf. chap. xiv. § 1.

twice repeated attempt of the hero at suicide followed by the attempt of the heroine in the same sense, from which he saves her. At the close of the *Pratijñāyaugandharāyaṇa* we have again the idea of the attempted suicide of the heroine's mother, which is obviated by the king's good sense in showing her that the marriage of the runaway pair was quite proper in their rank and in arranging for marrying them in a painting. The dying Vālin in the *Abhiṣekanāṭaka* has a vision of the Ganges and the other great rivers. Urvaçī and the Apsarases, and the chariot drawn by a thousand swans, which bears away the dead, coming for his spirit; Duryodhana in the *Ūrubhaṅga* has a similar vision, and Avimāraka, when on the point of committing suicide he sees the Vidyādhara beside him, imagines that this is a vision such as comes often to dying men. Again in the prologues there is almost a monotonous adoption of the device by which the director is interrupted in making a proposed announcement by a voice from behind the scene, which enables him by a clever transition to lead the audience into the dramatic action proper.

5. *Bhāsa's Style*

The rapidity and directness of the action of Bhāsa's plays is reflected in his style. More than any other dramatist, he uses the verse to further the progress of the play, in lieu of devoting it to descriptions rather poetic than directly aiding the drama, and it is characteristic that he freely employs monostichs, which are rare later. On the other hand, he is ready to resort to monologue; that on the third Act of the *Avimāraka* suggested perhaps the monologue of Çarvilaka in the *Mṛcchakaṭikā*, whose author must have known Bhāsa's works intimately.

The dominating influence on Bhāsa's style was clearly that of the epic and in special of Vālmīki, whose great work inevitably impressed itself on the minds of all his successors. The effects are visible not merely in the dramas with epic subject-matter, but extend throughout Bhāsa's plays. The results of this influence are all to the good; the necessities of the drama saved Bhāsa from the one great defect of the epic style, the lack of measure, which permits the *Rāmāyaṇa* to illustrate by twenty-nine similes the sorrows of Sītā in her captivity, while in the

Abhiṣekanāṭaka the dramatist is content with one. On the other hand he owes to it the relative simplicity of his diction, and his freedom from the excesses of the poetic equivalent of the nominal style, which comes to dominate later Sanskrit literature. The use of long compounds is obviously and plainly undramatic; carried to excess it must have rendered a Sanskrit drama unintelligible even to a highly cultivated audience as far as the verses were concerned, and it is an essential dramatic merit in Bhāsa that his expression is far easier to follow than in much of later dramatic poetry. He possesses in fact that clearness, which is theoretically a merit of the Kāvya style, but which is signally neglected by the average Kāvya writer in his anxiety to display the complete familiarity which he possesses with every side of the art of poetry. As far as we can judge from the scanty fragments of Açvaghoṣa's dramas, that poet was more complex than Bhāsa, and certainly so in his epics, which aided powerfully in the formation of Kālidāsa's epic and dramatic style.

Bhāsa, of course, is not in the slightest degree akin to a poet of the people; he is an accomplished master of the art of poetry, but one whose good sense and taste preserve him from adopting in drama the artifices which are permitted in the court epic and lyric which were intended to be studied at leisure. The simple and sententious is beloved of Bhāsa: thus Karṇa repels the objections of Çalya to his parting with armour and earring to the disguised Indra:[1]

çikṣā kṣayaṁ gacchati kālaparyayāt: subaddhamūlā nipatanti pādapāḥ
jalaṁ jalasthānagataṁ ca çuṣyati: hutaṁ ca dattaṁ ca tathaiva tiṣṭhati.

'Learning decayeth with the passing of time; though firm their roots, trees fall; the water of a lake drieth up; but sacrifices and gifts endure.' When Sītā is forced to undergo the ordeal by fire Lakṣmaṇa exclaims:[2]

vijñāya devyāç çaucaṁ ca çrutvācāryasya çāsanam
dharmasnehāntare nyastā buddhir dolāyate mama.

'I know the queen's chastity; I have heard the bidding of our preceptor; like a swing, my mind doth move 'twixt duty and

[1] *Karṇabhāra*, 22.

[2] *Abhiṣekanāṭaka*, vi. 21.

love.' When Rāma falls at his father's feet on the order being given for his coronation, he tells us:[1]

samaṁ bāṣpeṇa patatā tasyopari mamāpy adhaḥ
pitur me kleditau pādau mamāpi kleditaṁ çiraḥ.

'My father's feet were wet with tears I let fall on them, and my head was wet with tears he let fall over me.' When Devakī must yield, for the sake of saving it, her child, it is said of her:[2]

hṛdayeneha tarañgair dvidhābhūteva gacchati
yathā nabhasi toye ca candralekhā dvidhā kṛtā.

'She is divided; her heart remaineth here, her body goeth yonder, as in cloud and water the digit of the moon is divided.' Rāvaṇa's contempt for Rāma as a foe is forcibly expressed:[3]

kathaṁ lambasataḥ siṅho mṛgeṇa vinipātyate
gajo vā sumahān mattaḥ sṛgālena nihanyate?

'Can the deer bring low the lion with flowing mane? Can the jackal slay the mighty elephant in his wrath?' In the *Cārudatta*[4] the darkness is happily described:

sulabhaçaraṇam āçrayo bhayānāṁ: vanagahanaṁ timiraṁ ca tulyam eva
ubhayam api hi rakṣyate 'ndhakāre: janayati yaç ca bhayāni yaç ca bhītaḥ.

'Affording easy refuge, yet abodes of fear, the forest depths and darkness are akin; for the shadows guard alike him who feareth and him who causeth fear.' More ambitious is a verse given in the *Subhāṣitāvali*:[5]

kaṭhinahṛdaye muñca krodhaṁ sukhapratighātakam
likhati divasaṁ yātaṁ yātaṁ Yamaḥ kila mānini
vayasi taruṇe naitad yuktaṁ cale ca samāgame
bhavati kalaho yāvat tāvad varaṁ subhage ratam.

'Hard-hearted maiden, lay aside the anger that doth impede our joy; death entereth on his register every day as it goeth, disdainful one; not meet is this in thy tender youth, for love is fleeting; rather spend in love the time we lose in this quarrel.'

The simple figures of speech are freely used by Bhāsa, and he shows as usual a marked fondness for the accumulation of similar sounds, as in *sajalajaladhara*, *sanīranīrada*, or ***kuladayaṁ hanti***

[1] *Pratimānāṭaka*, i. 6. [2] *Bālacarita*, i. 13.
[3] *Abhiṣekanāṭaka*, iii. 20. [4] i. 20. [5] v. 1619.

madena nārī: kūladvayaṁ kṣubdhajalā nadīva. More interesting are instances of his power, which is specially manifest in the *Svapnavāsavadattā* and the *Pratimānāṭaka*, of expressing strong emotion adequately and forcibly. Thus we have the indignant upbraiding of Kaikeyī by the angry Bharata:[1]

vayaṁ ayaçasā cīreṇāryo nṛpo gṛhamṛtyunā
pratataruditaiḥ kṛtsnāyodhyā mṛgaiḥ saha Lakṣmaṇaḥ
dayitatanayāḥ çokenāmbāḥ snuṣādhvapariçramair
dhig iti vacasā cogreṇātmā tvayā nanu yojitāḥ?

'Hast thou not brought upon me disgrace and dishonour, on my noble father death at the hands of his dearest, on all Ayodhyā ceaseless lamentation, exile on Lakṣmaṇa, sorrow on the noble ladies, who love their children, for the cruel journey imposed on thy daughter-in-law, and on thyself the hateful reproach of a shameful deed?' Equally effective is Lakṣmaṇa's protest against Rāma's acquiescence in his exclusion from the throne:[2]

yadi na sahase rājño mohaṁ dhanuḥ spṛça mā dayā
svajananibhṛtaḥ sarvo 'py evam mṛduḥ paribhūyate
atha na rucitam muñca mām ahaṁ kṛtaniçcayo
yuvatirahitaṁ kartuṁ lokaṁ yataç chalitā vayam.

'If thou wilt not endure the king's infatuation, take thy bow, show no pity. Hidden among his own folk every weakling is thus overborne. But, if thou wilt not, leave me free at least; my mind is intent to make this world free of that youthful one, since cheated we have been.' Bharata's devotion is expressed happily enough:[3]

tatra yasyāmi yatrāsau vartate Lakṣmaṇapriyaḥ
nāyodhyā taṁ vināyodhyā sāyodhyā yatra Rāghavaḥ.

'Thither will I go where dwelleth Lakṣmaṇa's beloved; without him Ayodhyā is not Ayodhyā; where Rāghava is, there is Ayodhyā.' A martial spirit breathes in Virāṭa's words:[4]

tāḍitasya hi yodhasya çlāghanīyena karmaṇā
akālāntaritā pūjā nāçayaty eva vedanām.

'Instant fame destroys the pangs of the warrior stricken in performing a deed of valour.' There is manly indignation and pathos in Dhṛtarāṣṭra's mourning over Abhimanyu's death:[5]

[1] *Pratimānāṭaka*, iii. 17. [2] *Ibid.*, i. 18. [3] *Ibid.*, iii. 24.
[4] *Pañcarātra*, ii. 28. [5] *Dūtaghaṭotkaca*, 17.

bahūnāṁ samupetānām ekasmin nirghṛṇātmanām
bāle putre praharatāṁ kathaṁ na patitā bhujāḥ.

'How could these cruel men bear to raise their arms to smite one young boy, alone against such a concourse?' The necessity of toil to achieve any end is well brought out in a verse in the *Pratijñāyaugandharāyaṇa*,[1] which has a curious parallel in Açvaghoṣa:[2]

kāṣṭhād agnir jāyate mathyamānād: bhūmis toyaṁ khanyamānā dadāti
sotsahānāṁ nāsty asādhyaṁ narāṇām: mārgārabdhāḥ sarvayatnāḥ phalanti.

'Fire ariseth from the rubbing of timber; the earth when dug giveth water; nothing is there that men may not obtain by effort; every exertion duly undertaken doth bear fruit.' A profound truth, the rareness of gratitude, is emphasized in the *Svapnavāsavadattā*:[3]

guṇānāṁ vā viçālānāṁ satkārāṇāṁ ca nityaçaḥ
kartāraḥ sulabhā loke vijñātāras tu durlabhāḥ.

'There are many to show conspicuous virtue and to do constant deeds of kindness, but few are there who are grateful for such actions.' The heavy burden of the duties of a king is effectively described in the *Avimāraka*:[4]

dharmaḥ prāg eva cintyaḥ sacivamatigatiḥ prekṣitavyā svabuddhyā
pracchādyau rāgaroṣau mṛduparuṣaguṇau kālayogena kāryau
jñeyaṁ lokānuvṛttam paracaranayanair maṇḍalam prekṣitavyam
rakṣyo yatnād ihātmā raṇaçirasi punas so 'pi nāvekṣitavyaḥ.

'First there must be consideration of the injunctions of the law, then the train of the minister's thought must be followed; desire and anger must be concealed; mercy and harshness must be applied as expediency demands; the temper of the people must be ascertained through the aid of spies as well as the demeanour of neighbouring kings; one's life must be guarded with every care, but in the forefront of battle heed for it must be laid aside.' The position of a minister is no enviable one:[5]

[1] i. 18.
[2] *Pratimānāṭaka*, p. xi.
[3] iv. 9.
[4] i. 12.
[5] *Avimāraka*, i. 5.

prasiddhau kāryāṇām pravadati janaḥ pārthivabalam
vipattau vispaṣṭaṁ sacivam atidoṣaṁ janayati
amātyā ity uktāḥ çrutisukham udāraṁ nṛpatibhiḥ
susūkṣmaiṁ daṇḍyante matibalavidagdhāḥ kupuruṣāḥ.

'If policy succeeds, the people acclaim the prince's might; if disaster ensue, it condemns the incompetency of the minister; poor fools, puffed up by their strength of intellect, they receive from kings the noble and sweet sounding style of "counsellor" only to be punished sharply for any failure.'

Bhāsa is fond of expressing typical feelings in simple language which later poets would deem lacking in ornament; thus he expresses a mother's feelings regarding her daughter's marriage in the *Pratijñāyaugandharāyaṇa*:[1]

adattety āgatā lajjā datteti vyathitam manaḥ
dharmasnehāntare nyastā duḥkhitāḥ khalu mātaraḥ.

'Shame were it if she be not betrothed; yet if betrothed sorrow is one's lot; between duty and love mothers are sore vexed in heart.' The responsibility of a teacher is set out by Droṇa in the *Pañcarātra*:[2]

atītya bandhūn avalaṅghya mitrāṇy: ācāryam āgacchati çiṣyadoṣaḥ.
bālaṁ hy apatyaṁ gurave pradātum: naivāparādho 'sti pitur na mātuḥ.

'A pupil's fault passes over relatives and friends and settles on the teacher, for it is no wrong in father or mother to hand over a young child to a preceptor.'

Bhāsa's power of depicting irony is specially prominent in the *Svapnavāsavadattā*,[3] where Vāsavadattā is driven to weave the garland for the new queen's marriage, on the score of her skill in this art. Rāvaṇa shows the heads which he represents as those of Rāma and Lakṣmaṇa to Sītā, only to hear the announcement that his son is slain in the battle, by the very two whose death he has feigned.[4] Effective is the contrast between Vālin's splendour and his fall in his son Aṅgada's lament:[5]

atibalasukhaçāyī pūrvam āsīr harīndraḥ: kṣititalaparivartī kṣīṇasarvāṅgaceṣṭaḥ.

'Soft indeed thy couch aforetime as lord of the apes, who now

[1] ii. 7. [2] i. 18. [3] iii. p. 25.
[4] *Abhiṣekanāṭaka*, v. p. 56. [5] *Ibid.*, i. p. 10.

dost lie on the ground, thy every movement stilled in death', and Duryodhana's fall is not less effectively described.[1]

A characteristic of Bhāsa is his fondness for pithy proverbial phrases, 'Everything suits a handsome figure', 'Misfortunes never come singly', 'Good news sounds more pleasant from a friend's mouth (*piaṇivediamāṇāṇi piāṇi piadarāṇi honti*), 'Man's fate is as mobile as an elephant's trunk', 'There are many obstacles in the road to fortune', 'A small cause begets grave misfortune', are found in the *Avimāraka* alone. An idea once expressed fascinates Bhāsa and is repeated again and again in the same terms, a fact which incidentally helps to assure the genuineness of the plays. For some phrases he has a special fondness; *mā* with the instrumental is normal in lieu of the ordinary *alam*, which he also uses; *aho tu khalu* to introduce a stanza; *kiṁ nu khalu* in a question; *āma* and *bādham* to indicate assent; *sukham āryasya* as a phrase of greeting. Especially is he devoted to the term *vara*, sometimes before, usually after, the noun whose quality it intensifies; the use occurs even twice or thrice in a single stanza.

The harmony and melody of Bhāsa's style, added to its purity and perspicuity, have no better proof than the imitations of his verses which are unquestionably to be traced in Kālidāsa, who attests thus his practical appreciation of the merits of the dramatist, with whose established fame his nascent genius had to contend.

6. *The Language of the Plays*

Bhāsa's Sanskrit[2] is in the main correct according to the rules of the grammarians, but his dependence on the epic is revealed by the occasional use of epic irregularities, almost always for the sake of the metre, which in the epic also is the cause of many deviations from classical grammar. We have thus the irregular contractions *putreti* and *Avantyādhipateḥ*, and a number of middle forms in lieu of active, *gamiṣye*, *garjase*, *drakṣyate*, *pṛcchase*, *bhraçyate*, *ruhyate*, *çroṣyate*. In other cases the active replaces the middle, *āpṛccha*, *upalapsyati*, *pariṣvaja*. There is confusion between the simple and the causative verb in *sravati* and *vījanti*,

[1] *Ūrubhaṅga*, 29.
[2] See *Pratimānāṭaka*, App. i; V. S. Sukhtankar, JAOS. xli. 118 ff.

and in *vimoktukāma*. The forms *rudantī* and *gṛhya* have many epic parallels. Irregular compounds are *sarvarājñaḥ* in verse, and *Kāçirājñe* in prose; *vyūḍhoras* and *tulyadharma* occur in verse. The use in one clause of both *ced* and *yadi* is found in verse and also in prose, as in the epic. Mere blunders perhaps may be styled *pratyāyati*, a haplological form of the causative with the meaning of the simple verb, *samāçvāsitum* with causative sense, and *yudh* as a masculine noun. There are other seeming irregularities, but they are either sanctioned by usage or possible of explanation by reference to variant interpretations of Pāṇini's rules.

The Prākrits[1] found in Bhāsa are normally Çaurasenī, which is present in all the plays save the *Dūtavākya*, which has no Prākrit; Māgadhī found in two different forms; and what may be styled Ardha-Māgadhī. The distinctive feature of his language is its transitional aspect as compared with Açvaghoṣa on the one hand and Kālidāsa on the other. Açvaghoṣa never softens—save in one instance—hard consonants, but both *ṭ* and *t* are changed to *ḍ* and *d* in Bhāsa. Açvaghoṣa never omits consonants, but, though this is less often carried out than in Kālidāsa, we find cases of the loss of *k*, *g*, *c*, *j*, *t*, *d*, *p*, *b*, *v*, and *y* when intervocalic. *y* itself suffers frequent change to *j*, contrary to Açvaghoṣa's usage. The change of *n* initial and medial to *ṇ* is regular, while it is unknown to Açvaghoṣa. The aspirates *kh*, *gh*, *th*, *dh*, *ph*, and *bh* are all often reduced as later to *h*, but never in Açvaghoṣa.

In the case of conjunct consonants we find that *jñ* gives in Bhāsa either *ññ* or *ṇṇ*, possibly the latter by error; Açvaghoṣa has *ññ* only, Kālidāsa *ṇṇ*. For *ny* and *ṇy* Bhāsa has always *ṇṇ* as against Açvaghoṣa's *ññ*. The eliding of a consonant, with the compensatory lengthening of the vowel as in *dīsadi*, is unknown to Açvaghoṣa, where the omission of the consonant twice occurs but without lengthening; it is frequent in Bhāsa and regular in Kālidāsa. The analogous use of a short vowel and a double consonant to represent a long vowel with a single consonant is unknown to Açvaghoṣa, but Bhāsa has it in *evva*, *evvaṁ*, *jovvana*,

[1] W. Printz, *Bhāsa's Prākrit* (1921). The evidence of retention of older forms later in South Indian manuscripts (Barnett, JRAS. 1921, p. 589) is interesting but does not alter the importance of these forms.

devva, *ekka*. On the other hand, like Açvaghoṣa, for *ry* he has *yy* only in lieu of Kālidāsa's *jj*. For the later *metta matta* is always found, and the epenthetic vowel is *u*, not *i*, in *purusa*, and *puruva* is normal.

In inflection we have, in the nominative and accusative plural of neuter stems in *a*, *āni* in Açvaghosa, *āṇi* in Bhāsa, while both *āṇi* and *āiṁ* are allowed later. The accusative plural masculine has also, analogously to *āni* in the Ardha-Māgadhī of the Açoka inscriptions,[1] *āṇi*, and the locative singular feminine is in *āaṁ*, not as later *āe*. For the later *attāṇaaṁ* we have *attāṇaṁ*. For 'we' Açvaghoṣa has *vayaṁ*, Kālidāsa *amhe*; Bhāsa both and *vaaṁ*. In the genitive plural Bhāsa has both *amhāaṁ* and the only form later *amhāṇaṁ*, while Açvaghoṣa would doubtless have used *amhākaṁ*. *kissa* is kept for later *kīsa*, and *kocci* (*kaccid*) disappears later. The root *darç* is represented by *dass* and *daṅs*, *grah* by *gaṇhadi* against the later *geṇhadi*, which, however, is found in Açvaghoṣa. The older form *karia* and *gacchia* or *gamia*, are found in lieu of *kadua* and *gadua*, but the last occurs once. *mā* is used with the gerund in the sense of *alam*.

Many of these peculiarities mark also the Māgadhī, which appears in two slightly varied forms, the first in the *Pratijñāyaugandharāyaṇa* and the *Cārudatta*, the second in the *Bālacarita* and the *Pañcarātra*; in the two latter we have *ṣ* and *o* for the *ç* and *e* of the former. As in Açvaghoṣa there is no trace of obedience to the rules of the grammarians which require *sṭ* for Sanskrit *ṣṭh* or *ṣṭ*, *çc* for *cch*, *sk* or *ẖk* for *kṣ*. For 'I' we find *ahake*, which is an intermediate stage between Açvaghoṣa's *ahakam* and the later *hage*. *ny* becomes *ṇṇ*, not *ññ*, and the use of *y* to denote a dropped consonant is not carried out.

The only passages that can claim to be anything like Ardha-Māgadhī are the remarks of Indra in disguise in the *Karṇabhāra*, where the characteristic signs, the use of *r*, *s*, and *e*, are found; in the speeches of Muṣṭika and Cāṇūra in the *Bālacarita* we have the use of *l* and a locative in *ammi*. A single passage in the *Pañcarātra* suggests Māgadhī Apabhrança, but is probably corrupt.

[1] *āni* in Pāli, *āṇi* in the Ardha-Māgadhī of the Jain Canon; Lüders, SBAW. 1913, pp. 999 ff.

7. *The Metres of the Dramas*

It is characteristic of Bhāsa's close dependence on the epic that his dramas should show a far more frequent use of the Çloka, 436 out of 1,092 verses. No later writer save Bhavabhūti in his Rāma dramas approaches this frequency, which, it must be noted, is not confined to the epic plays, for the *Svapnavāsavadattā* has 26 Çlokas out of 57 verses. In some plays, it is true, such as the *Madhyamavyāyoga* or the *Pañcarātra*, long series of Çlokas suggest incomplete command of the dramatic art on Bhāsa's part, but his general preference is clearly an outcome of his desire for rapid movement and simplicity; it is the later love for elaborate descriptions that encourages the use of sonorous and complex metres. The Çlokas are remarkably regular in construction; the diiambus in the second Pāda is insisted on rigidly; the Vipulās[1] are rare, the fourth is unknown, the second sporadic, the first twice as frequent as the third, and the prior foot is rarely[2] ⏓ – ⏑ –. The sparing use of the irregular forms is doubtless due to the comparatively small number of Çlokas used consecutively, which minimises the desire for change of form.

Of the more elaborate metres, in which each syllable has a fixed length, the favourite is the Vasantatilaka, which occurs 179 times, while the Upajāti occurs 121 times. Next comes the Çārdūlavikrīḍita (92), Mālinī (72), Puṣpitāgrā with the scheme ⏑⏑⏑⏑⏑⏑–⏑–⏑–– ¦ ⏑⏑⏑⏑–⏑⏑–⏑ –⏑–– (66), Vaṅçasthā (35), Çālinī (2), Çikhariṇī (19), and Praharṣiṇī (17). Other metres are purely sporadic; they include the Sragdharā, Hariṇī, Vaiçvadevī,[3] Drutavilambita,[4] Pṛthvī,[5] and Bhujaṅgaprayāta,[6] while the Suvadanā occurs four times. There is one example of the Upagīti with 12 morae in the first and third Pādas, and 15 in the second and fourth, and one of the Vaitalīya with 14 and 16 in the two sets respectively. There is also one example of the shortest form of Daṇḍaka metre, with six short syllables followed by

[1] Verses in which the last four syllables are not ⏑ – – ⏓; viz. (1) ⏑ ⏑ ⏑ ⏓; (2) – ⏑ ⏑ ⏓; (3) –, – – ⏓; (4) – ⏑ – ⏓.

[2] Cf. Jacobi, IS. xvii. 443 f.; V. S. Sukhtankar, JAOS. xli. 107 ff.

[3] – – – – –, – ⏑ – – ⏑ – –. Later only in the *Mṛcchakaṭikā* of classical dramas.

[4] ⏑ ⏑ ⏑ – ⏑ ⏑ – ⏑ ⏑ – ⏑ –.

[5] ⏑ – ⏑ ⏑ ⏑ – ⏑ –, ⏑ ⏑ ⏑ – ⏑ – – ⏑ –.

[6] ⏑ – – ⏑ – – ⏑ – – ⏑ – –. Later first in the *Caitanyacandrodaya*.

seven amphimacers, while there is also one shorter metre with six amphimacers. The rarity of the Āryā is remarkable; beside the one Upagīti, which is in Prākrit, there are only eleven, of of which five are in Prākrit. Contrast the frequency of the Āryā in Kālidāsa where there are 31 out of 163 in the *Vikramorvaçī*, and 35 out of 96 in the *Mālavikāgnimitra*.

Generally the rules of classical prosody are faithfully observed; there is one hiatus between Pādas and once Sandhi; in *niyatī* and *maulī*, as in *anūkarṣa*, the lengthening is probably metrical. The Çlokas shows a great fondness for epic tags, such as *acireṇaiva kālena*, *prasādaṁ kartum arhasi*, and *kampayann iva medinīm*. Especially frequent is the breaking up of a verse between different speakers or by interruptions of one kind or another.

8. *Bhāsa and Kālidāsa*

There is *prima facie* the probability that Kālidāsa should be strongly affected by a predecessor so illustrious and of such varied achievement, and the probability is turned into certainty by the numerous coincidences between the two writers.[1] Inevitably, of course, with such a genius as Kālidāsa's, the matter which is borrowed is transformed and normally improved in the change, and this fact renders strict proof of indebtedness impossible. But the evidence is sufficient to induce conviction to any one accustomed to weighing literary evidence of borrowing.

In Act I of the *Çakuntalā* the king is struck with the elegance of the simple bark dress worn by the heroine in keeping with her station as a maiden of the hermitage; *kim iva hi madhurāṇām maṇḍanaṁ nākṛtīnām*, 'For what does not grace a lovely figure?' he asks, and illustrates his theme.[2] The germ of this pretty idea is found in the *Pratimānāṭaka*, Act I, where Sītā playfully decks herself in a dress of bark, evoking the judgement of her friend: *savvasohaṇīaṁ surūvaṁ ṇāma*.[3] The converse relationship is here incredible; Bhāsa's imitation of Kālidāsa would be feeble and tasteless, while Kālidāsa's improvement on his original is apt and skilful. The fact of borrowing is established by the episode in the same act of the *Çakuntalā* of

[1] T. Gaṇapati Çāstrin, *Pratimānāṭaka*, pp. 1 ff.
[2] i. 17.
[3] p. 7.

the treatment of watering the garden as an act of penance on the maiden's part; an idea which occurs in a closely parallel passage in Act V of the *Pratimānāṭaka*. Bhāsa treats it as bearable, illustrating it by the adduction of an example in the technical form of an Arthāntaranyāsa,[1] while Kālidāsa[2] is more severe in his condemnation, using the technical figure Nidarçanā, clearly a deliberate variation of the idea. In the same Act of the *Pratimānāṭaka*[3] we find Rāma bidding Sītā take farewell of the fawns and the trees, which are her foster-children, and of her dear friends, the Vindhya mountain and the creepers; in the departure of Çakuntalā from the hermitage[4] the trees and the fawns as well as the creepers share in the grief of her departure; of the deer is expressly used the term 'foster-child' found in the *Pratimānāṭaka*. Again in Act VII of that play Sītā is reminded of the distrust felt by the deer in Bharata,[5] just as Çakuntalā describes their distrust of Duḥṣanta.[6] There is a parallel in the *Svapnavāsavadattā*, Act I, where Vāsavadattā is received kindly by the lady of the hermitage, and thanks her for her courteous words, to the scene at the opening of the *Çakuntalā*, in which the king assures Anasūyā that her speech of welcome is sufficient hospitality (*bhavatīnāṁ sūnṛtayaiva girā kṛtaṁ ātithyaṁ*). The parallel is completed by the instruction given by the chamberlain in Bhāsa's play to the servant to avoid disturbance to the hermitage with the commands of the king to the commander-in-chief. Similar also is the scene in Act II of the *Svapnavāsavadattā*, in which during the play of Padmāvatī and Vāsavadattā in disguise reference is made to the former's approaching marriage, to the talk of Çakuntalā's friends with her in Act I. We have also in the sixth Act of either play a parallel treatment of the lute lost by Udayana in the one case,[7] and the ring lost by Çakuntalā in the other;[8] the verses in which these innocent objects of censure are attacked are similar in spirit and taste.

Other traces of Bhāsa's influence are also to be found. The motif of the curse of Durvāsas which in the *Çakuntalā* explains the sufferings of the heroine suggests the curse of Caṇḍabhārgava in the *Avimāraka* which reduces the hero to a humble rank, and

[1] v. 3. [2] i. 16. [3] v. 11. [4] iv. 8, 11, 13.
[5] p. 107. [6] v. [7] vi. 1, 2. [8] vi. 11, 13.

in the *Çakuntalā* the lovers are reunited at the hermitage of the sage Mārīca, as in the *Avimāraka* they meet at the home of Nārada. There is a vague similarity also as regards many expressions in the two poets, but it would be unwise to lay any special stress on such testimony. But the more specific evidence given above of dependence is undeniable, and it is surprising to find it questioned by Professor Hillebrandt,[1] especially when we have Kālidāsa's own recognition of Bhāsa's fame, and Bāṇa's reiteration of it.

The most valid argument which might be adduced against dependence is the fact that Kālidāsa's dramas as they stand do not seem to agree with the rule observed in those of Bhāsa regarding the beginning of the drama. In Bhāsa's works the Sūtradhāra appears on the stage at the close of a Nāndī, the text of which is not given, and recites a verse which obviously is not technically a Nāndī, though it is of the same type, containing a benediction. In the works of Kālidāsa the first verse is the Nāndī, and at the close of it the Sūtradhāra begins the play with a dialogue. But we cannot rely on the manuscripts as giving us the true practice of Kālidāsa's date, for we know that in the case of the *Vikramorvaçī* old manuscripts denied to the first verse the character of a Nāndī, and therefore presented the play in the form affected by Bhāsa, and the same style is sometimes followed in South Indian manuscripts of other plays. It is, therefore, impossible to hold that Kālidāsa rejected the practice of Bhāsa, or to base any argument on the facts.

[1] *Kālidāsa*, p. 103.

V

THE PRECURSORS OF KĀLIDĀSA AND ÇŪDRAKA

1. *The Precursors of Kālidāsa*

KĀLIDĀSA refers in the prologue to the *Mālavikāgnimitra* not only to Bhāsa but to Saumilla and Kaviputra—perhaps rather the Kaviputras—as his predecessors in drama. Saumilla, whose name suggests an origin in Mahārāṣṭra, is mentioned by Rājaçekhara along with Bhāsa and a third poet Rāmila. Further, the same authority tells us that Rāmila and Somila composed a *Çūdrakakathā*, which is compared to Çiva under the form of Ardhanārīçvara, in which he is united with his spouse, perhaps a hint at the union of heroic and love sentiments in the tale. A fine stanza is attributed to them in the *Çārṅgadharapaddhati*:[1]

savyādheḥ kṛçatā kṣatasya rudhiraṁ daṣṭasya lālāsrutiḥ
kiṁcin naitad ihāsti tat katham asau pānthas tapasvī mṛtaḥ?
ā jñātaṁ madhulampaṭair madhukarair ārabdhakolāhale
nūnaṁ sāhasikena cūtamukule dṛṣṭiḥ samāropitā.

'Had he been ill he would have been emaciated; wounded, he would have bled; bitten, have shown the venom; no sign of these is here; how then has the unhappy traveller met his death? Ah! I see. When the bees began to hum as they sought greedily for honey, the rash one let his glance fall on the mango bud'. Spring is the time for lovers' meetings; the traveller, far from his beloved, lets himself think of her and dies of despair.

The Kaviputras, a pair according to the verse cited from them in the *Subhāṣitāvali*[2], were apparently also collaborators, a decidedly curious parallel with Somila and Rāmila, as such collaboration seems later rare. The stanza is pretty:

bhrūcāturyaṁ kuñcitāntāḥ kaṭākṣāḥ: snigdhā hāvā lajjitāntāç ca hāsāḥ
līlāmandaṁ prasthitaṁ ca sthitaṁ ca: strīṇām etad bhūṣaṇam āyudhaṁ ca.

[1] cxxxiii. 40. [2] v. 2227.

'The play of the brows, the sidelong glances which contract the corners of the eyes, words of love, bashful laughter, the slow departure in sport, and the staying of the steps: these are the ornaments and the weapons of women.'

Strange that so scanty remnants should remain of poets who must have deserved high praise to receive Kālidāsa's recognition, but the fame of that poet doubtless inflicted on them the fate that all but overtook Bhāsa himself.

2. *The Authorship and Age of the Mṛcchakaṭikā*

The discovery of the *Cārudatta* of Bhāsa has cast an unexpected light on the age of the *Mṛcchakaṭikā*, but has still left it dubious whether or not the author is to be placed before Kālidāsa. That this rank was due to him was the general opinion before Professor Lévi attacked the theory, and it is curious that later he should have inclined to doubt the value of his earlier judgement. The existence of the *Cārudatta* would explain, of course, the silence of Kālidāsa on the *Mṛcchakaṭikā*, if it existed in his time. Explicit use of the drama by Kālidāsa or the reverse would be conclusive, but unhappily none of the parallels which can be adduced have any effective force, and from rhetorical quotations we only have the fact that Çūdraka was recognized as an author by Vāmana,[1] for Daṇḍin's citation of a verse found in the *Mṛcchakaṭikā* is now clearly known to be a citation from Bhāsa, in whose works the verse in question twice occurs. With this falls the hypothesis of Pischel,[2] who, after ascribing the play to Bhāsa, later fathered it upon Daṇḍin, to make good the number of three famous works with which he is in later tradition credited.

The play itself presents Çūdraka, a king, as its author and gives curious details of his capacities; he was an expert in the *Ṛgveda*, the *Sāmaveda*, mathematics, the arts regarding courtesans, and the science of elephants, all facts which could be concluded from the knowledge shown in the play itself; he was cured of some complaint, and after establishing his son in his place, and performing the horse sacrifice, he entered the fire and

[1] Lévi, TI. i. 198: Vāmana, iii. 2. 4.

[2] *Rudraṭa*, pp. 16 f. But see Hari Chand, *Kālidāsa*, pp. 78 f.

died at the age of a hundred years and ten days. We have a good deal more information of a sort regarding his personality; he was to Kalhaṇa in the *Rājataraṅgiṇī*[1] a figure to be set beside Vikramāditya; the *Skanda Purāṇa*[2] makes him out the first of the Andhrabhṛtyas; the *Vetālapañcaviṅçati* knows of his age as a hundred, and gives as his capital either Vardhamāna or Çobhāvatī, which is the scene of his activities according to the *Kathāsaritsāgara*, which tells of the sacrifice of a Brahmin who saves him from imminent death and secures his life of a hundred years by killing himself. In the *Kādambarī* he is located at Vidiçā, and in the *Harṣacarita* we hear of the device by which he got rid of his enemy Candraketu, prince of Cakora, while Daṇḍin in the *Daçakumāracarita* refers to his adventures in several lives. The fact that Rāmila and Somila wrote a Kathā on him is significant of his legendary character in their time, considerably before Kālidāsa. A very late tradition in the *Vīracarita* and the younger Rājaçekhara[3] brings him into connexion with Sātavāhana or Çālivāhana, whose minister he was and from whom he obtained half his kingdom, including Pratiṣṭhāna.[4]

These references seem to suggest that Çūdraka was a merely legendary person, a fact rather supported than otherwise by his quaint name, which is absurd in a king of normal type. Nevertheless, Professor Konow treats him as historical, and finds in him the Ābhīra prince Çivadatta, who, or whose son, Īçvarasena, is held by Dr. Fleet to have overthrown the last of the Andhra dynasty and to have founded the Cedi era of A.D. 248–9.[5] This remarkable result is held to be supported by the fact that in the play the king of Ujjayinī is Pālaka, and is represented as being overthrown by Āryaka, son of a herdsman (*gopāla*), and the Ābhīras are essentially herdsmen. But this is much more than dubious; we have in fact legendary history in the names of Pālaka, Gopāla—to be taken probably in the *Mṛcchakaṭikā* as a proper name—and Āryaka. The proof is indeed overwhelming, for Bhāsa, who is the source of so much of the *Mṛcchakaṭikā*,

[1] iii. 343. [2] Wilson, *Works*, ix. 194.

[3] IS. xiv. 147; JBRAS. viii. 240.

[4] He is later the hero of a Parikathā, the *Çūdrakavadha* (Rāyamukuṭa, ZDMG. xxviii. 117), and of a drama, *Vikrāntaçūdraka* (*Sarasvatīkaṇṭhābharaṇa*, p. 378).

[5] KF. pp. 107 ff. Cf. Bhandarkar, *Anc. Hist. of India*, pp. 64 f.; CHI. i. 311.

mentions in his *Pratijñāyaugandharāyaṇa* as sons of Pradyota of Ujjayinī both Gopāla and Pālaka, and the *Bṛhatkathā* must have contained the story of Gopāla surrendering the kingdom on Pradyota's death to Pālaka, and of the latter having to make room for Āryaka, his brother's son. To make history out of these events, which belong to the period shortly after the Buddha's death, say 483 B.C., and history of the third century A.D., is really impossible. Çūdraka is really clearly mythical, as is seen by the admission that he entered the fire, for no one can believe that he foresaw his death-day so precisely, or that the ceremony referred to is that performed on becoming an ascetic, or even that the prologue was added after his death; if it had been, it would have doubtless been of a different type. Still less can we imagine that he was helped in his work by Rāmila and Somila.

Windisch,[1] on the other hand, attempted to prove a close similarity between the plot of the political side of the play and the legend of Kṛṣṇa, instancing the prediction of Āryaka's attaining the throne, the jealousy of the king and his efforts to destroy him, and the final overthrow of the tyrant. The similarity, however, is really remote; the story is a commonplace in legend, and nothing can be made of the comparison.

We are left, therefore, to accept the view that the author who wrote up the *Cārudatta*, and combined with it a new play, thought it well to conceal his identity and to pass off the work under the appellation of a famous king. Lévi's suggestion that he chose Çūdraka for this purpose because he lived after Vikramāditya, patron of Kālidāsa, and wished to give his work the appearance of antiquity by associating it with a prince who preceded Vikramāditya, is clearly far-fetched, and insufficient to suggest a date. Nor can anything be deduced from the plentiful exhibition of Prākrits, which is not, to judge from Bhāsa, a sign of very early date; while the use of Māhārāṣṭrī Prākrit would be, if proved, conclusive that he is fairly late. Konow's effort to support Çūdraka's connexion with Pratiṣṭhāna by this use is clearly untenable.

There is more plausibility in the argument from the simple form of the construction of the drama; the manner of Bhāsa is

[1] *Berichte der Sächs. Gesellsch. d. Wissenschaften*, 1885, pp. 439 f.

closely followed; thus in Act IX the absurd celerity with which the officer of the court obeys the order to bring the mother of Vasantasenā on the scene, and secures the presence of Cārudatta, is precisely on a par with Bhāsa's management of the plot in his dramas. The scenes of violence, in which Vasantasenā is apparently killed and Cārudatta is led to death, are reminiscent of Bhāsa's willingness to present such scenes, but they do not depart from the practice of the later drama as in Bhavabhūti's *Mālatīmādhava*. The Çakāra and Viṭa are indeed figures of the early stage, but they are taken straight from Bhāsa and prove nothing. The position of the Buddhist monk is more interesting, but here again it is borrowed, though developed, and we find Buddhism respected in Kālidāsa and Harṣa. The arguments based on the apparent similarity with the Greek New Comedy are without value for an early date, for they apply, if they have any value at all, to the *Cārudatta* of Bhāsa. We are left, therefore, with no more than impressions, and these are quite insufficient to assign any date to the clever hand which recast the *Cārudatta* and made one of the great plays of the Indian drama.[1]

3. *The Mṛcchakaṭikā*

The first four acts of the play are a reproduction with slight changes of the *Cārudatta* of Bhāsa;[2] the very prologue shows the fact in the inexplicable transformation in the speech of the director, who opens in Sanskrit and then changes to Prākrit, while in the *Cārudatta* he speaks Prākrit only as fits the part of the Vidūṣaka which he is to play. The names are slightly changed; the king's brother-in-law is called Saṁsthānaka, and the thief Çarvilaka. Act I carries the action up to the deposit of the gems by Vasantasenā; Act II relates the generosity of the hetaera to the shampooer who turns monk, and the attack made on him as he leaves her house by a mad elephant, from which Karṇapūraka, a servant of Vasantasenā's, saves him, receiving as reward a cloak which Vasantasenā recognizes as Cārudatta's. In Act III we learn of Çarvilaka's success in stealing the jewels, and the generous resolve of the wife of Cārudatta to give her necklace to

[1] Jacobi (*Bhavisattakaha*, p. 83) believes in Çūdraka as a king, but thinks Kālidāsa older.

[2] See G. Morgenstierne, *Über das Verhältnis zwischen Cārudatta und Mṛcchakaṭikā* (1921).

replace them. In Act IV Çarvilaka gives the jewels to Vasantasenā, who, though aware of his theft, sets his love free. As he leaves with her, he hears of the imprisonment of his friend Āryaka by order of the king, who knows the prophecy of his attaining the kingship, and leaving his newly-made bride, he hastens to aid his friend who is reported to have escaped from his captivity. The Vidūṣaka then comes with the necklace, which the hetaera accepts in order to use it as a pretext to see Cārudatta once more. The visit occupies Act V, which passes in a storm forcing Vasantasenā to spend the night in Cārudatta's house. Act VI reveals her next morning offering to return to Cārudatta's wife the necklace, but her gift is refused. The child of Cārudatta appears, complaining that he has only a little earth cart (*mṛcchakaṭikā*), whence the name of the play; Vasantasenā gives him her jewels that he may buy one of gold. She is to rejoin Cārudatta in a neighbouring park, the property of Saṁsthānaka, but by error she enters the car of Saṁsthānaka, while Āryaka, who has been seeking a hiding-place, leaps into that of Cārudatta and is driven away; two policemen stop the cart, and one recognizes Āryaka, but protects him from the other with whom he contrives a quarrel. In Act VII Cārudatta, who is conversing with the Vidūṣaka, sees his cart drive up, discovers Āryaka, and permits him to go off in it, while he himself leaves to find Vasantasenā. In the next act Saṁsthānaka, with the Viṭa and a slave, meets in the park the shampooer turned monk, who has gone there to wash his robe in the tank; he insults him and beats him. The cart with Vasantasenā then is driven up, and the angry Saṁsthānaka first tries to win her by fair words; then, repulsed, orders the Viṭa and the slave to slay her; they indignantly refuse; he pretends to grow calm, dismisses them, and then rains blows on Vasantasenā, who falls apparently dead; the Viṭa, who sees his action, deserts at once his cause and passes over to Āryaka's side. Saṁsthānaka, after burying the body under some leaves, departs, promising himself to put the slave in chains; the monk re-enters to dry his robe, finds and restores to life Vasantasenā, and takes her to the monastery to be cared for. In Act IX Saṁsthānaka denounces Cārudatta as the murderer of Vasantasenā to the court;[1] her

[1] Jolly (*Tagore Law Lectures*, 1883, pp. 68 f.) compares the procedure of the Smṛtis.

mother is summoned as a witness, but defends Cārudatta, who himself is cited; the police officer testifies to the escape of Āryaka, which implicates Cārudatta; the Vidūṣaka who enters the court, while *en route* to return to Vasantasenā the jewels she had given the child, is so indignant with the accuser that he lets fall the jewels; this fact, taken together with the evidence that Vasantasenā spent the night with Cārudatta and left next morning to meet him, and the signs of struggle in the park, deceives the judge, who condemns Cārudatta to exile; Pālaka converts the sentence into one of death. Act X reveals the hero led to death by two Caṇḍālas, who regret the duty they have to perform; the servant of Saṁsthānaka escapes and reveals the truth, but Saṁsthānaka makes light of his words as a disgraced and spiteful slave, and the headsmen decide to proceed with their work. Vasantasenā and the monk enter just in time to prevent Cārudatta's death, and, while the lovers rejoice at their reunion, the news is brought that Āryaka has succeeded Pālaka whom he has slain, and that he has granted a principality to Cārudatta. The crowd shout for Saṁsthānaka's death, but Cārudatta pardons him, while the monk is rewarded by being appointed superior over the Buddhist monasteries of the realm, and, best of all, Vasantasenā is made free of her profession, and thus can become Cārudatta's lawful wife.

To the author we may ascribe the originality of combining the political and the love intrigue, which give together a special value to the play. We know of no precise parallel to this combination of motifs, though in the *Bṛhatkathā* there was probably a story recorded later [1] of the hetaera Kumudikā who fell in love with a poor Brahmin, imprisoned by the king; she allied herself to the fortunes of a dethroned prince Vikramasiṅha, aided him by her arts to secure the throne, and was permitted by the grateful prince to marry her beloved, now released from prison. The idea was doubtless current in some form or another, just as for the incidents of Bhāsa's story we can trace parallels in the Kathā literature of hetaerae who love honest and poor men and desire to abandon for their sakes their hereditary and obligatory calling, which the law will compel them to follow.[2] The conception of the science of theft is neatly paralleled in the *Daçakumāracarita*,

[1] KSS. lviii. 2–54.

[2] *Daçakumāracarita*, ii.

where a text-book of the subject is ascribed to Karṇīsuta, and the same work contains interesting accounts of gambling which illustrate Act II. The *Kathāsaritsāgara*[1] tells of a ruined gambler, who takes refuge in an empty shrine, and describes in Sarga xxxviii the palace of the hetaera Madanamālā in terms which may be compared with the description by the Vidūṣaka in Act IV of the splendours of Vasantasenā's palace.[2] The court scene conforms duly to the requirements of the legal Smṛtis of the sixth and seventh centuries A.D., but the conservatism of the law renders this no sign of date.

Though composite in origin and in no sense a transcript from life, the merits of the *Mṛcchakaṭikā* are great and most amply justify what else would have been an inexcusable plagiarism. The hints given in the *Cārudatta* here appear in full and harmonious development aided and heightened by the introduction of the intrigue, which combines the private affairs of the hero with the fate of the city and kingdom. Cārudatta's character is attractive in the extreme; considerate to his friend the Vidūṣaka, honouring and respecting his wife, deeply devoted to his little son, Rohasena, he loves Vasantasenā with an affection free from all mere passion; he has realized her nobility of character, her generosity, and the depth and truth of her love. Yet his devotion is only a part of his life; aware of the vanity of all human things, he does not value life over-highly; his condemnation affects him most because it strikes at his honour that he should have murdered a woman, and he leaves thus to his child a heritage of shame. Not less attractive is Vasantasenā, bound, despite herself, to a profession which has brought her great wealth but which offends her heart; the judge and all the others believe her merely carried away by sensual passion; Cārudatta and his wife alone recognize her nobility of soul, and realize how much it means for her to be made eligible for marriage to her beloved. There is an admirable contrast with the hero in the Çakāra Saṁsthānaka, who is described vividly and realistically. His position as brother-in-law of the king and his wealth make him believe that he is entitled to whatever he wants; Vasantasenā's repulse of him outrages his sense of his own importance

[1] xii. 92; xviii. 121.

[2] Cf. *Çlokasaṁgraha*, x. 60–163.

more than anything else; brutal, ignorant[1] despite his association with courtiers of breeding and refinement, and cowardly, he has only skill in perfidy and deceit, and is mean enough to beg piteously for the life he has forfeited, but which Cārudatta magnanimously spares. The Viṭa is an excellent foil to him in his culture, good taste, and high breeding; despite his dependence on his patron, he checks his violence to Vasantasenā, strives to prevent his effort to murder her, and when he fails in this takes his life into his own hands and passes over to Āryaka's side. The Vidūṣaka may be fond of food and comfortable living, but he remains faithful in adversity to his master, is prepared to die for him, and consents to live only to care for his son.

The minor characters among the twenty-seven in all who appear have each an individuality rare in Indian drama. Çarvilaka, once a Brahmin, now a professional thief, performs his new functions with all the precision appropriate to the performance of religious rites according to the text-books. The shampooer, turned Buddhist monk, has far too much worldly knowledge to seek any temporal preferment from the favour of Āryaka. Māthura, the master gambler, is a hardened sinner without bowels of compassion, but the two headsmen are sympathetic souls who perform reluctantly their painful duty. The wife of Cārudatta is a noble and gentle lady worthy of her husband, and one who in the best Indian fashion does not grudge him a new love if worthy, while the lively maid Madanikā deserves fully her freedom and marriage with Çarvilaka. Even characters which play so small an actual part as Āryaka are effectively indicated. The good taste of the author is strikingly revealed by the alteration made in the last scene by a certain Nīlakaṇṭha,[2] who holds that the omission to bring upon the stage Cārudatta's wife, his son, and the Vidūṣaka was due to the risk of making the time occupied by the representation of the play too great. He supplies the lacuna by representing all three as determined to commit suicide when Cārudatta rescues them; the author himself would never have consented to introduce the first wife at the moment when a second is about to be taken.

The author is not merely admirable in characterization; he is

[1] His errors in the field of mythology are appalling, e.g. Kuntī for Sītā, i. 21.

[2] Stenzler's ed. pp. 325 ff.; Wilson, i. 177.

master of pathos, as in the parting of Cārudatta from his son who asks the headsman to kill him and let his father go, and above all he abounds in humour and wit; even in the last act Goha, the headman, relieves the tension by the tale of his father who advised him on his death-bed not to slay too quickly the criminal on the off-chance that there might be a revolution or something to save the wretch's life, and, when after deliverance comes the noble Cārudatta forbids the slaying with steel of the grovelling Saṁsthānaka, Çarvilaka cheerfully remarks that is all right: he will be eaten alive by the dogs instead.

These merits and the wealth of incident of the drama more than compensate for the overluxuriance of the double intrigue, and the lack of unity, which is unquestionable. A demerit in the eyes of the writers on poetics is the absence of elaborate descriptions, but the simple and clear diction of the play adds greatly to its liveliness and dramatic effect, and the poet has perfect command of the power of pithy and forcible expression. The Viṭa effectually rebukes the arrogance and pride of family of Saṁsthānaka:

kiṁ kulenopadiṣṭena çīlam evātra kāraṇam
bhavanti sutarāṁ sphītāḥ sukṣetre kaṇṭakidrumāḥ.

'Why talk of birth? Character alone counts. In rich soil the thorn trees grow fastest.' Cārudatta on the point of death asserts his fearlessness:

na bhīto maraṇād asmi kevalaṁ dūṣitaṁ yaçaḥ
viçuddhasya hi me mṛtyuḥ putrajanmasamo bhavet.

'I fear not death, but my honour is sullied; were that stain removed, death would be as dear as the birth of a son.' Admirable is his expression of belief in Vasantasenā who may be dead:

prabhavati yadi dharmo dūṣitasyāpi me 'dya: prabalapuruṣavākyair bhāgyadoṣāt kathaṁcit
surapatibhavanasthā yatra tatra sthitā vā: vyapanayatu kalaṅkaṁ svasvabhāvena saiva.

'If righteousness prevails, though to-day I am undone by the slanderous words of one in power through my unhappy fate, may she, dwelling with the gods above or wherever she be, by her true nature wipe out the blot upon me.' Sadly he apostrophizes his child deemed to be at play:

hā Rohasena na hi paçyasi me vipattim: mithyaiva nandasi paravyasanena nityam.

'Ah! Rohasena, since thou dost not know my plight, ever dost thou rejoice in thy play falsely, for sorrow is in store.'

The character of Cārudatta is effectively portrayed by the Vidūṣaka:[1]

dīnānāṁ kalpavṛkṣaḥ svaguṇaphalanataḥ sajjanānāṁ kuṭumbī
ādarçaḥ çikṣitānāṁ sucaritanikaṣaḥ çīlavelāsamudraḥ
satkartā nāvamantā puruṣaguṇanidhir dakṣiṇodārasattvo hy
ekaḥ çlāghyaḥ sa jīvaty adhikaguṇatayā cocchvasanti cānye.

'A tree of bounty to the poor, bent down by its fruits, his virtues; a support for all good men; a mirror of the learned, a touchstone of virtue, an ocean that never violates its boundaries of virtue; righteous, free from pride, a store-house of human merit, the essence of courtesy and nobility; he gives meaning to life by the goodness which we extol; other men merely breathe.'

The evils of poverty are forcibly depicted by Cārudatta himself:[2]

çūnyair gṛhaiḥ khalu samāḥ puruṣāḥ daridrāḥ
kūpaiç ca toyarahitais tarubhiç ca çīrṇaiḥ
yad dṛṣṭapūrvajanasaṁgamavismṛtānām
evaṁ bhavanti viphalāḥ paritoṣakālāḥ.

'Like empty houses, in truth, are poor men, or wells without water or blasted trees; for fruitless are their hours of relaxation, since their former friends forget them.' The same idea is again expressed by the hero:[3]

satyaṁ na me vibhavanāçakṛtāsti cintā: bhāgyakrameṇa hi dhanāni bhavanti yānti
etat tu māṁ dahati naṣṭadhanāçrayasya: yat sauhṛdād api janāḥ çithilībhavanti.

'My dejection, assuredly, is not born of the mere loss of my wealth, for with the turn of fortune's wheel riches come and go. Nay, what pains me is that men fail in friendship to him whose sometime wealth has taken flight.' The repetition of the idea becomes, indeed, wearisome, but the ingenuity and fancy of the author are undoubted.

[1] i. 48. [2] v. 42. [3] i. 13; cf. *Cārudatta*, i. 5.

Love is also effectively described. The Viṭa is an admirer of Vasantasenā and thus addresses the fleeting lady:[1]

kiṁ tvaṁ padair mama padāni viçeṣayantī
vyālīva yāsi patagendrabhayābhibhūtā?
vegād aham praviçṛtaḥ pavanaṁ nirundhyām
tvannigrahe tu varagātri na me prayatnaḥ.

'Why, surpassing my speed with thine own, dost thou flee like a snake, filled with fear of the lord of birds? Were I to use my speed I could outstrip the wind itself, but I would make no effort to seize thee, O fair-limbed one.' Cārudatta praises the rain:[2]

dhanyāni teṣāṁ khalu jīvitāni: ye kāminīnāṁ gṛham āgatānām
ārdrāṇi meghodakaçītalāni: gātrāṇi gātreṣu pariṣvajanti.

'Happy the life of those whose limbs embrace the limbs of their loved ones, come to their home, dripping wet and cold with the water of the clouds.'

Moreover, while to later Indian critics the descriptive stanzas of the poet are lacking in that elaboration and cleverness which are admitted by developed taste, to us much of the poetic value of the drama depends on the power of the poet to describe with point and feeling in simple terms which require no effort to appreciate. The whole scene of the storm gains by the stanzas in which its beauties are described, once we consent, as we must do in appreciating any Sanskrit play, to ignore the inappropriateness of these lyric effusions in the actual circumstances. In real life a lady seeking eagerly an interview with her beloved, in resplendent attire, would have no time to display her command of Sanskrit poetry in description, when counsels of prudence urged her to her destination with the least possible delay:[3]

mūḍhe nirantarapayodharayā mayaiva: kāntaḥ sahābhiramate kiṁ tavātra?
māṁ garjitair iti muhur vinivārayantī: mārgaṁ ruṇaddhi kupiteva niçā sapatnī.

'"If, foolish one, my beloved has joy clasped in my bosom's embrace, what is that to thee?" Thus night with her thunders, seeking to stay me, blocks my path, like an angry rival.'

meghā varṣantu garjantu muñcantv açanim eva vā
gaṇayanti na çītoṣṇaṁ ramaṇābhimukhāḥ striyaḥ.

[1] i. 22; cf. *Cārudatta*, i. 11, on which it improves. [2] v. 49. [3] v. 15.

'Let the clouds rain, thunder, or cast down the levin bolt; women who speed to their loved ones reckon nothing of heat or cold.'[1]

gatā nāçaṁ tārā upakṛtam asādhāv iva jane
viyuktāḥ kāntena striya iva na rājanti kakubhaḥ
prakāmāntastaptaṁ tridaçapatiçastrasya çikhinā
dravībhūtam manye patati jalarūpeṇa gaganam.

'The stars disappear, like a favour bestowed on a worthless man; the quarters lose their radiance, like women severed from their beloved; molten by the fierce fire of Indra's bolt, the sky, I ween, is poured down upon us in rain.'[2]

unnamati namati varṣati garjati meghaḥ karoti timiraugham
prathamaçrīr iva puruṣaḥ karoti rūpāṇy anekāni.

'The cloud rises aloft, bows down, pours rain, sends thunder and the dark; every show it makes of its wealth like the man newly rich.'[3]

Last we may cite the rebuke of Vasantasenā to the lightning:

yadi garjati vāridharo garjatu tannāma niṣṭhurāḥ puruṣāḥ
ayi vidyut pramadānāṁ tvam api ca duḥkhaṁ na jānāsi?

'If the cloud must thunder, then let him thunder; cruel were men ever; but, O lightning, can it be that thou too dost not know the pangs of a maiden's love?'[4]

The merits of the play are sufficient to enable its author to dispense with praise not deserved. For Çūdraka, regarded as the author, has been credited[5] with the distinction of being a cosmopolitan; however great the difference between Kālidāsa, 'the grace of poetry'[6] and Bhavabhūti, 'the master of eloquence,'[7] these two authors, it is said, are far more allied in spirit than is either of them with the author of the *Mṛcchakaṭikā*; the *Çakuntalā* and the *Uttararāmacarita* could have been produced nowhere save in India, Çakuntalā is a Hindu maid, Mādhava a Hindu hero, while Saṁsthānaka, Maitreya, and Madanikā are citizens of the world. This claim, however, can hardly be admitted; the *Mṛcchakaṭikā* as a whole is a drama redolent of Indian thought and life, and none of the three characters adduced have any special claim to be more cosmopolitan than some of the

1 v. 16. 2 v. 25. 3 v. 26. 4 v. 32.
5 Ryder, *The Little Clay Cart*, p. xvi.
6 Jayadeva, *Prasannarāghava*, i. 22. 7 *Mahāvīracarita*, i. 4.

creations of Kālidāsa. The variety of the characters of the play is unquestionably laudable, but the praise in part is due to Bhāsa, and not to his successor. To the same source also must be attributed the comparative simplicity of the style, which certainly contrasts with the degree of elaboration found even in Kālidāsa, and carried much further in Bhavabhūti. The variety of incident is foreshadowed in Bhāsa, but the development of the drama must be attributed to the author, and frankly it cannot be said to be wholly artistic; that the drama is unnecessarily complex must be conceded, nor can the action be said to proceed with complete ease and conviction. The humour of the play is undoubted, but here again to Bhāsa must honour be given. Bhāsa again is the prototype for the neglect of the rule of the dramaturgy which demands the presence of the hero on the stage in each act; the naming of the play, in defiance of convention, from a minor incident may justly be ascribed to the author himself.

The real Indian character of the drama reveals itself in the demand for the conventional happy ending, which shows us every person in a condition of happiness, with the solitary exception of the evil king. Cārudatta is restored to affluence and power from the depths of infamy and misery; Vasantasenā's virtue and fidelity are rewarded by the signal honour of restoration to the rank of one whom the hero may marry; the monk, who refuses worldly gain, has the pleasure of becoming charged with spiritual oversight, with its attendant amenities—not inconsiderable to judge from our knowledge of the wealth of Buddhist monasteries. Even Saṁsthānaka is spared, to save us, we may assume, the pain of seeing anything so unpleasant as a real, even if well deserved, death on the stage, for the king perishes at a distance from the scene. If, as Cārudatta asserts at the end of the play, fate plays with men like buckets at the well, one rising as another falls, Çūdraka is not inclined to seek realism sufficiently to permit of his introducing even a tinge of sorrow into the close of his drama.

4. *The Prākrits*

No extant play exhibits anything like the variety of Prākrits found in the *Mṛcchakaṭikā*, which seems almost as if intended to illustrate the precepts of the *Nāṭyaçāstra* in this regard.[1] The commentator obligingly provides us with the names of the dialects represented and those who speak them. Çaurasenī is spoken by the director after his Sanskrit exordium, the comedienne, Vasantasenā, Madanikā, her servant, Karṇapūraka, her slave, her mother, the wife of Cārudatta, the Çreṣṭhin or guildsman, and the officer of the court, and Radanikā, Cārudatta's servant. Avantikā is attributed to the two policemen Vīraka and Candanaka. The Vidūṣaka speaks Prācyā. The shampooer who turns monk, Sthāvaraka, servant of the Çakāra Saṁsthānaka, Kumbhīlaka, servant of Vasantasenā, Vardhamānaka, servant of Cārudatta, and the little Rohasena speak Māgadhī. The Çakāra speaks Çākārī, the Caṇḍālas who act as headsmen Cāṇḍālī, and the chief gambler Ḍhakkī. Sanskrit, on the other hand, is spoken by the hero, the Viṭa, the royal claimant Āryaka, and the Brahmin thief Çarvilaka. This distribution of Prākrits agrees with that of the *Nāṭyaçāstra* as we have it in one important aspect; it ignores the Māhārāṣṭrī, though for some not obvious reason Konow claims that this was introduced into the drama by Çūdraka. On the other hand, it does not assign to slaves, Rājputs, or guildsmen the Ardha-Māgadhī of the *Nāṭyaçāstra*. In the case of Rohasena the Māgadhī ascribed to him has been largely converted into Çaurasenī in the manuscripts. The Çāstra ascribes Āvantī to Dhūrtas, which is interpreted as meaning gamblers; the distinction between it and Çaurasenī is minimal; it is said to have *s* and *r* and be rich in proverbs by Pṛthvīdhara, and this accords adequately with the actual speeches of the officers. But the second, Candanaka, expressly gives himself out as a southerner, and we can hardly avoid the conclusion that the dialect is Dākṣiṇātyā which the Çāstra ascribes to warriors, police officers, and gamblers. The Prācyā of the Vidūṣaka is nothing more or less than Çaurasenī, though it is given separately in the Çāstra also; it may have been an eastern dialect of the main language. The Ḍhakkī ascribed to the gamblers should probably[2] be named Ṭakkī, or Ṭākkī, an easy error because of the confusion of the letters in manuscripts. Pischel regarded it as an eastern dialect which had *l*, and preserved two

[1] Cf. Pischel, *Prākrit-Grammatik*, pp. 25 ff.

[2] JRAS. 1913, p. 882; 1918, p. 513. Cf. *Kāvyamīmāṅsā*, p. 51.

sibilants *ç* and *s* in which *ṣ* was merged; Sir G. Grierson finds in it a western dialect, which seems more probable. The Çākārī of Saṁsthānaka is nothing more or less than Māgadhī, which is given as the language of that person by the *Nāṭyaçāstra*, and the Cāṇḍālī is merely another variety of that Prākrit. Thus the rich variety reduces itself in effect to Çaurasenī[1] and Māgadhī with Takkī, of which we have too little to say precisely what it was.

5. *The Metres*

The author of the *Mṛcchakaṭikā* shows considerable skill in metrical handling; his favourite metre is naturally enough the Çloka, which suits his rapid style and is adapted to further the progress of the dialogue. It occurs 83 times, while the next favourite, the pretty Vasantatilaka, appears 39 times, and the Çārdūlavikrīḍita 32 times. The only other important metres are the Indravajrā (26), with the Vaṅçasthā (9), and the Upajāti combination of both (5). But there occur also the Puṣpitāgrā, Praharṣiṇī, Mālinī, Vidyunmālā,[2] Vaiçvadevī, Çikhariṇī, Sragdharā, and Hariṇī, and one irregular stanza. Of the Āryā there are 21 cases, including one Gīti, with 30 morae in each half stanza, and there are two instances of the Aupacchandasika. The Prākrit metres show considerable variety; of the Āryā type there are 53 as against 44 of other types.[3]

[1] Used in verse even, e.g. by the Vidūṣaka.

[2] – – – –, – – – –. In no other classical drama is it found.

[3] The apparent occurrence of Māhārāṣṭrī stanzas is in all probability not in accordance with the original text, which knew only the Prākrits given in § 4; see Hillebrandt, GN. 1905, pp. 436 ff.

VI

KĀLIDĀSA

1. *The Date of Kālidāsa*

It is unfortunate, though as in the case of Shakespeare not surprising, that we know practically nothing of the life and age of Kālidāsa save what we can infer from his works and from the general history of Sanskrit literature. There are indeed stories[1] of his ignorance in youth, until he was given poetic power by the grace of Kālī, whence his strange style of Kālidāsa, slave of Kālī, which is not one *prima facie* to be expected in the case of a poet who shows throughout his work the finest flower of Brahmanical culture. But these tales are late and worthless, and equally without value is the fiction that he was a contemporary of King Bhoja of Dhārā in the first half of the eleventh century A.D. As little value, however, attaches to a tale which has been deemed of greater value, the alleged death of Kālidāsa in Ceylon when on a visit there by the hand of a courtesan, and the discovery of his murder by his friend Kumāradāsa, identified with the king of that name of the early part of the sixth century A.D. The tradition, as I showed in 1901, is very late, unsupported by the earliest evidence, and totally without value.[2]

The most prevalent tradition makes Kālidāsa a contemporary of Vikramāditya, and treats him as one of the nine jewels of that monarch's entourage. Doubtless the king meant by the tradition, which is late and of uncertain provenance, is the Vikramāditya whose name is associated with the era of 57 B.C. and who is credited with a victory over the Çakas. Whatever truth there may be in the legend, and in this regard we have nothing but conjecture,[3] there is not the slightest reason to accept so early a date for Kālidāsa, and it has now no serious supporter outside India. But, based on Fergusson's suggestion[4] that the era of

[1] Hillebrandt, *Kālidāsa* (1921), pp. 7 ff.
[2] JRAS. 1901, pp. 578 ff.
[3] e.g. Konow, SBAW. 1916, pp. 812 ff.
[4] JRAS. xii. (1880), 268 f.

57 B.C. was based on a real victory over Hūṇas in A.D. 544, the reckoning being antedated 600 years, Max Müller[1] adopted the view that Kālidāsa flourished about that period, a suggestion which was supported by the fact that Varāhamihira, also a jewel, certainly belongs to that century, and others of the jewels might without great difficulty be assigned to the same period. The theory in so far as it rested on Fergusson's hypothesis has been definitely demolished by conclusive proof of the existence of the era, as that of the Mālavas, before A.D. 544, but the date has been supported on other grounds. Thus Dr. Hoernle[2] found it most probable that the victor who was meant by Vikramāditya in tradition was the king Yaçodharman, conqueror of the Hūṇas, and the same view was at one time supported by Professor Pathak,[3] who laid stress on the fact that Kālidāsa in his account of the Digvijaya, or tour of conquest of the earth, of the ancient prince Raghu in the *Raghuvañça*[4] refers to the Hūṇas, and apparently locates them in Kashmir, because he mentions the saffron which grows only in Kashmir.

An earlier date, to bring Kālidāsa under the Guptas, has been favoured by other authorities, who have found that the reference to a conquest of the Hūṇas must be held to be allusion to a contemporary event. This date is attained on second thoughts by Professor Pathak,[5] who places the Hūṇas on the Oxus on this view, and holds that Kālidāsa wrote his poem shortly after A.D. 450, the date of the first establishment of their empire in the Oxus valley, but before their first defeat by Skandagupta, which took place before A.D. 455, when they were still in the Oxus valley and were considered the most invincible warriors of the age. On the other hand, Monmohan Chakravarti,[6] who converted Professor Pathak to belief in the contemporaneity of Kālidāsa with the Guptas, places the date at between A.D. 480 and 490, on the theory that the Hūṇas were in Kālidāsa's time in Kashmir. The whole argument, however, appears fallacious; Raghu is represented as conquering the Persians, and there is no

[1] *India* (1883), pp. 281 ff.
[2] JRAS. 1909, pp. 89 ff.
[3] JBRAS. xix. 39 ff.
[4] iv. 68.
[5] *Meghadūta* (ed. 2), pp. vii ff. In v. 67 he reads *Vañkṣū* = Oxus, for *Sindhu*; see Haranchandra Chakladar, *Vātsyāyana*, p. 23.
[6] JRAS. 1903, pp. 183 f.; 1904, pp. 158 f.

contemporary ground for this allegation; manifestly we have no serious historical reminiscences, but, as is natural in a Brahmanical poet, a reference of the type of the epic which knows perfectly well the Hūṇas. The exact identity of the Hūṇas of the epic is immaterial; as the name had penetrated to the western world by the second century A.D. if not earlier, there is no conceivable reason for assuming that it could not have reached India long before the fifth or sixth centuries A.D.[1]

Other evidence is scanty. Mallinātha, as is notorious, finds in verse 14 of the *Meghadūta* a reference to a poet Nicula, a friend of Kālidāsa, and an enemy Dignāga; the latter would be the famous Buddhist logician, and, assuming that his date is the fifth century A.D., we have an argument for placing Kālidāsa in the fifth or sixth century A.D. But the difficulties of this argument are insurmountable. In the first place, it is extremely difficult to accept the alleged reference to Nicula, who is otherwise a mere name, and to Dignāga; why a Buddhist logician should have attacked a poet does not appear, especially as every other record of the conflict is lost. Nor is the *double entendre* at all in Kālidāsa's manner;[2] such efforts are little in harmony with Kālidāsa's age, while later they are precisely what is admitted, and are naturally seen by the commentators where not really intended. It is significant that the allusion is not noted by Vallabhadeva, and that it first occurs in Dakṣiṇāvarta Nātha (*c.* A.D. 1200) and Mallinātha (fourteenth century), many centuries after the latest date assignable to Kālidāsa. Even, however, if the reference were real, the date of Dignāga can no longer be placed confidently in the fifth century A.D., or with other authorities in the sixth century. On the contrary, there is a good deal of evidence which suggests that A.D. 400 is as late as he can properly be placed.[3]

As little can any conclusion be derived from the allusion in Vāmana to a son of Candragupta in connexion with Vasubandhu, which has led to varied efforts at identification. based largely on the fifth century as the date of Vasubandhu. But it is far more

[1] Huth, *Die Zeit des Kālidāsa*, pp. 29 ff.

[2] Thomas's suggestion (Hillebrandt, p. 12) of a reference to the Sārasvata school in the same passage only adds to the improbability of the reference.

[3] Keith, *Indian Logic*, p. 28.

probable that Vasubandhu dates from the early part of the fourth century, and nothing can be derived hence to aid in determining the period of Kālidāsa.[1]

More solid evidence must be sought in the astronomical or astrological data which are found in Kālidāsa. Professor Jacobi has seen in the equalization of the midday with the sixth Kāla in the *Vikramorvaçī* a proof of Kālidāsa's having lived in the period immediately subsequent to the introduction from the west of the system of reckoning for ordinary purposes the day by 12 Horās, Kāla being evidently used as Horā. The passage has been interpreted by Huth as referring to a sixteenfold division, and the argument to be derived from it is not established, but Huth, on the other hand, manifestly errs by making Kālidāsa posterior to Āryabhaṭa (A.D. 499) on the score that in the *Raghuvañça* he refers to eclipses as caused by the shadow of the earth, the reference being plainly to the old doctrine of the spots on the moon. It is, however, probable that Kālidāsa in the *Vikramorvaçī* refers to the figure of the lion in the zodiac, borrowed from the west, and it is certain that he was familiar with the system of judicial astrology, which India owes to the west, for he alludes both in the *Raghuvañça* and the *Kumārasambhava* to the influence of the planets, and above all uses technical terms like *ucca* and even *jāmitra*, borrowed from Greece. A date not probably prior to A.D. 350 is indicated by such passages.[2]

Similar evidence can be derived from Kālidāsa's Prākrit, which is plainly more advanced than that of Bhāsa, while his Māhārāṣṭrī can be placed with reasonable assurance after that of the earlier Māhārāṣṭrī lyric, which may have flourished in the third and fourth centuries A.D. He is also earlier than the Aihole inscription of A.D. 634, where he is celebrated, than Bāṇa (A.D. 620), and above all than Vatsabhaṭṭi's Mandasor Praçasti of A.D. 473. It is, therefore, most probable that he flourished under Candragupta II of Ujjayinī, who ruled up to about A.D. 413 with the style of Vikramāditya, which is perhaps alluded to in the

[1] Pathak, IA. xl. 170 f.; Hoernle, 264; Haraprasād, JPASB. i. (1905), 253; JBORS. ii. 35 f.; 391 f.

[2] Jacobi, ZDMG. xxx. 303 ff.; *Monatsber. d. kgl. Preuss. Akad. d. W.*, 1873, pp. 554 ff.; Huth, *op. cit.*, pp. 32 ff., 49 ff.

name *Vikramorvaçī*, while the *Kumārasambhava's* title may well hint a compliment on the birth of young Kumāragupta, his son and successor.[1] The *Mālavikāgnimitra* with its marked insistence on the horse sacrifice of the drama seems to suggest a period in Kālidāsa's early activity when the memory of the first horse sacrifice for long performed by an Indian king, that of Samudragupta, was fresh in men's minds. Moreover the poems of Kālidāsa are essentially those of the Gupta period, when the Brahmanical and Indian tendencies of the dynasty were in full strength and the menace of foreign attack was for the time evanescent.

2. *The Three Dramas of Kālidāsa*

The *Mālavikāgnimitra*[2] is unquestionably the first dramatic work[3] of Kālidāsa; he seeks in the prologue to excuse his presumption of presenting a new play when tried favourites such as Bhāsa, Saumilla, and the Kaviputras exist, and in the *Vikramorvaçī* also he shows some diffidence, which has disappeared in the *Çakuntalā*. The great merits of the poet are far less clearly exhibited here than in his other plays, but the identity of authorship is unquestionable, and was long ago proved by Weber against the doubts of Wilson.

The play, performed at a spring festival, probably at Ujjayinī, is a Nāṭaka in five Acts, and depicts a love drama of the type seen already in Bhāsa's plays on the theme of Udayana. The heroine Mālavikā is a Vidarbha princess, who is destined as the bride of Agnimitra; her brother, Mādhavasena, however, is captured by his cousin Yajñasena; she escapes and seeks Agnimitra, but *en route* to his capital in Vidiçā her escort is attacked

[1] Keith, JRAS. 1909, pp. 433 ff.; Bloch, ZDMG. lxii. 671 ff.; Liebich, IF. xxxi. 198 ff.; Konow, ID., pp. 59 f.; Winternitz, GIL. iii. 43 f.

[2] Ed. F. Bollensen, Leipzig, 1879; trs. A. Weber, Berlin, 1856; V. Henry, Paris, 1889; C. H. Tawney, London, 1891. The existence of a variant recension is shown by the divergence of a citation from it in comm. on DR. iii. 18 from the manuscript tradition.

[3] That the *Meghadūta* is younger is suggested, not proved, by the lesser lyric power shown (Huth, p. 68). The *Ṛtusaṁhāra*, however, is doubtless earlier; its authenticity is demonstrated by me in JRAS. 1912, pp. 1066 ff.; 1913, pp. 410 ff. The relation of the *Kumārasambhava* and *Raghuvaṅça* to the two later dramas is uncertain.

by foresters, perhaps by order of the rival Vidarbha prince; she escapes again, however, and reaches Vidiçā, where she finds refuge in the home of the queen Dhāriṇī, who has her trained in the art of dancing. The king happens to see a picture in which she is depicted, and falls in love with her. To arrange an interview is not easy, but Gautama, his Vidūṣaka, provokes a quarrel between two masters of the dance, who have recourse to the king to decide the issue of superiority. He in turn refers the matter to the nun Kauçikī, who is in reality a partisan of Mālavikā, who had been in her charge and that of her brother, who was killed when the escort was dispersed. She bids the masters produce each his best pupil; Gaṇadāsa brings out Mālavikā, whose singing and dancing delight all, while her beauty ravishes the king more than ever. She is victorious. In Act III the scene changes to the park, whither comes Mālavikā at the bidding of Dhāriṇī to make the Açoka blossom, according to the ancient belief, by the touch of her foot. The king hidden with the Vidūṣaka behind a thicket watches her, but so also does Irāvatī, the younger of Agnimitra's queens, who is suspicious and jealous of any rival in the king's love. The king overhears Mālavikā's conversation with her friend, and realizes that his love is shared; he comes forth and embraces her, but Irāvatī springs out of her hiding-place and insults the king. Dhāriṇī has Mālavikā confined to prevent any further development of the intrigue. The Vidūṣaka, however, proves equal to the occasion with the aid of Kauçikī; he declares himself bitten by a snake; the only remedy proves to require the use of a stone in the queen's ring, which is accorded for that purpose, but employed for the more useful end of securing the release of Mālavikā, and the meeting of the lovers, which Irāvatī, who has excellent grounds for her vigilance, again disturbs. The king's embarrassment is fortunately mitigated by the necessity of his going to the rescue of the little princess Vasulakṣmī, whom a monkey has frightened. Act V cuts the knot by the advent of two unexpected pieces of news; envoys come bearing the report of victory over the prince of Vidarbha and conveying captives; two young girls introduced before the queen as singers recognize both Kauçikī and their princess Mālavikā among the queen's attendants, and Kauçikī explains her silence on the princess's identity by obedience to a prophecy. Further, Puṣyamitra, Agnimitra's father, sends tidings of victory from the north; the son of Dhāriṇī, Vasumitra, has defeated the Yavanas on the bank of the Indus, while guarding the sacrificial horse, which by ancient law is let loose to roam for a year unfettered before a king can perform rightfully the horse sacrifice, which marks him as emperor. Dhāriṇī already owes Mālavikā a guerdon for her service in causing the Açoka plant to blossom; delighted by the news of her son's success, she gladly gives Agnimitra authority to marry Mālavikā, Irāvatī begs her pardon, and all ends in happiness.

Puṣyamitra, Agnimitra, and Vasumitra are clearly taken from the dynasty of the Çuñgas, formed by the first through the deposition of the last Maurya in 178 B.C.[1] Contact with Yavanas in his time is recorded and the horse sacrifice is doubtless traditional, but equally it may reflect the sacrifice of Samudragupta, the most striking event of the early Gupta history, since it asserted the imperial sway of the family. The rest of the play is based on the normal model.

The *Vikramorvaçī*,[2] by many reckoned as the last work[3] in drama of Kālidāsa, seems rather to fall in the interval between the youthful *Mālavikāgnimitra* and the mature perfection of the *Çakuntalā*. The theme is that of the love of Purūravas, a king, and Urvaçī, an Apsaras, or heavenly nymph. The prologue, which has been unjustly suspected of being proof of the incompleteness and therefore later date of the drama, is followed by screams of the nymphs from whom Urvaçī on her return from Kailāsa has been torn away by a demon; the king hastens to her aid, recovers her, and restores her first to her friends, and then to the Gandharva king, but not before both have fallen desperately in love. In the entr'acte a servant of the queen extracts cleverly from the Vidūṣaka the secret of the change which has come over the king, his love for Urvaçī. The king himself then appears; in conversation with the Vidūṣaka he

[1] For the history, see CHI. i. 519 f.

[2] Ed. F. Bollensen, Leipzig, 1846; S. P. Paṇḍit, Bombay, 1901; M. R. Kale, Bombay, 1898; trs. E. B. Cowell, Hertford, 1851; L. Fritze, Leipzig, 1880 E. Lobedanz, Leipzig, 1861. The Bengālī recension is ed. Pischel, *Monatsber d. kgl. Preuss. Akad. d. W.* 1875, pp. 609 ff.

[3] Cf. Huth, *op. cit.*, pp. 63 ff.

declares his love, to meet with scant sympathy; Urvaçī and a friend appear in the air, and Urvaçī drops a letter written on birch bark breathing her love; the king reads it and gives it to the Vidūṣaka; Urvaçī's friend appears, and finally Urvaçī herself, but after a brief exchange of love passages Urvaçī is recalled to play a part in heaven in a drama produced by Bharata. The message, unluckily, falls into the queen's hands, and she refuses to be appeased by Purūravas's attempts to soothe her. In the entr'acte before Act II we learn from a conversation between two pupils of Bharata that Urvaçī was so deeply in love that she played badly her part in the piece on Lakṣmī's wedding; asked whom she loved, she answered Purūravas instead of Puruṣottama, Viṣṇu's name, and Bharata cursed her; but Indra intervened and gave her leave to dwell on earth with her love until he had seen the face of her child. The Act that follows shows the king, anxious to please the queen, engaged with her in celebrating the festival of the moon's union with Rohiṇī; Urvaçī and her friend, in disguise and unseen by the king in a fairy mist, watch his courtesy which fills the nymph with anguish, though her friend assures her that it is mere courtesy. To her joy she finds that the queen has decided to be reconciled, and to permit the king the enjoyment of his beloved; pressed to stay with the king, she refuses, and Urvaçī joins Purūravas, her friend leaving her, bidding Purūravas to care for her so that she may not miss her friends in the sky.

The prelude to Act IV tells us of misfortune; the nymphs who mourn by the sea her absence learn that, angry at her husband for some trivial cause, she had entered the grove of Kumāra, forbidden to women, and been turned into a creeper. In distraction[1] the king seeks for her; he deems the cloud a demon which has stolen her away, demands of the peacock, the cuckoo, the flamingo, the bee, the elephant, the boar, the antelope what has become of her; he deems her transformed into the stream, whose waves are the movements of her eyebrows while the rows of birds in its waters are her girdle; he dances, sings, cries, faints in his madness, or deems the echo to be answering

[1] The prototype here is clearly Rāma's search for Sītā; *Rāmāyaṇa*, iii. 60. The *Sudhanāvadāna*, cited by Gawroński (*Les sources de quelques drames indiens*, pp. 19, 29) draws probably from the same source.

him, until a voice from heaven tells him of a magic stone, armed with which he grasps a creeper which in his embrace turns into Urvaçī.

From this lyric height the drama declines in Act V. The king and his beloved are back in his capital; the moon festival is being celebrated, but the magic stone is stolen by a vulture, which, however, falls pierced by the arrow of a youthful archer; the arrow bears the inscription, 'the arrow of Āyus, son of Urvaçī and Purūravas'. The king had known nothing of the child, but, while he is amazed, a woman comes from a hermitage with a gallant boy, who, educated in the duties of his warrior caste, has by his slaying the bird violated the rule of the hermitage and is now returned to his mother. Urvaçī, summoned, admits her parentage, but, while Purūravas is glad, she weeps to think of their severance, now inevitable, since he has seen his son. But, while Purūravas is ready to abandon the realm to the boy and retire to the forest in grief, Nārada comes with a message of good tidings; a battle is raging between the gods and the demons; Purūravas's arms will be necessary, and in reward he may have Urvaçī's society for his life.

The play has come down in two recensions, one preserved in Bengālī and Devanāgarī manuscripts and commented on by Rañganātha in A.D. 1656, and the other in South Indian manuscripts, commented on by Kāṭayavema, minister of the Reḍḍi prince, Kumāragiri of Koṇḍavīḍu about A.D. 1400. The most important among many differences is the fact that in Act IV the northern manuscripts give a series of Apabhrañça verses, with directions as to the mode of singing and accompanying them, which are ignored in the southern manuscripts. The northern text calls the play a Troṭaka, apparently from the dance which accompanied the verses, the southern a Nāṭaka which it in essentials is. The arguments against the authenticity of the verses are partly the silence of the theorists, the fact that the existence in Kālidāsa's time of Apabhrañça of the type found is more than dubious,[1] that there is sometimes a degree of discrepancy between the verses and the prose of the drama, and that in the many imitations of the scene (*Mālatīmādhava*, Act IX, *Bālarāmāyaṇa*, Act V, *Prasannarāghava*, Act VI, and *Mahānā-*

[1] Jacobi, *Bhavisattakaha*, p. 58; Bloch, *Vararuci und Hemacandra*, pp. 15 f.

ṭaka, Act IV) there are no similar verses. These reasons are on the whole conclusive, and the problematic fact that the Prākrit of the northern recension is better is not of importance.

The *Çakuntalā*[1] certainly represents the perfection of Kālīdāsa's art, and may justly be assumed to belong to his latest period of work. The prologue with his usual skill leads us up to the picture of the king in swift pursuit of an antelope entering the outskirts of the hermitage; warned of the sacred character of the spot, the king alights from his chariot and decides to pay his respects to the holy man whose hermitage it is; he is absent, but Çakuntalā, his foster-daughter, is there with her friends; pursued by a bee she calls for help; they reply that Duḥṣanta the king should aid as the hermitage is under his protection, and the king gallantly comes forward to help. From the maidens he elicits the tale of Çakuntalā's birth; she is daughter of Viçvāmitra and Menakā, and is being reared not for the religious life but for marriage to some worthy one. The king loves and the maiden begins to reciprocate his affection, when the news that a wild elephant is menacing the hermitage takes him away. Act II reveals his Vidūṣaka groaning over the toils of the king's hunting. But the king gives order for the hunt to end, not to please the Vidūṣaka but for Çakuntalā's sake, and, while he recounts his feelings to his unsympathetic friend, receives with keen satisfaction the request of the young hermits to protect the hermitage against the attacks of demons. The Vidūṣaka he gets rid of by sending him back to the capital to take part in a festival there, assuring him, in order to prevent domestic trouble, that his remarks about Çakuntalā were not serious. In the entr'acte before Act III a young Brahmin praises the deeds of Duḥṣanta, and we learn that Çakuntalā is unwell, and her maidens are troubled regarding her state, as she is the very life breath of Kaṇva. The Act itself depicts Çakuntalā with her maidens; she is deeply in love and writes a letter at their suggestion: the king who has overheard all comes on the scene and a dialogue follows, in which both the king and the maiden express their feelings; the scene is

[1] Bengālī recension, R. Pischel, Kiel, 1877; M. Williams, Hertford, 1876, and M. R. Kale, Bombay, 1908, represent the Devanāgarī version, and so mainly S. Ray, Calcutta, 1908; C. Cappeller, Leipzig, 1909. There are South Indian edd., Madras, 1857, 1882. See also Burkhard, *Die Kaçmirer Çakuntalā-Handschrift*, Vienna, 1884.

ended by the arrival of the nun Gautamī to fetch away her charge. The entr'acte that follows tells us from the conversation of Priyaṁvadā and Anasūyā, Çakuntalā's dear friends, that the king after his marriage with Çakuntalā has departed and seems to have forgotten her; while Kaṇva is about to return and knows nothing of the affair. A loud cry interrupts them; Çakuntalā in her love-sickness has failed to pay due respect to the harsh ascetic Durvāsas, who has come to visit the hermitage: he curses her, and all the entreaties of her friends succeed in no more than mitigating the harshness of his curse; she will be forgotten by her husband, not indeed for ever, but until she presents to him the ring he gave her in token of their union. The curse is essential; the whole action of the play depends on it. The Act itself tells us that the difficulty regarding Kaṇva has been solved; a voice from the sky has informed him at the moment of his return of the marriage and Çakuntalā's approaching maternity. He has decided to send her under escort to the king. Then follows a scene of intense pathos; the aged hermit unwillingly parts with his beloved foster-daughter, with words of advice for her future life, and Çakuntalā is desolated to leave him, her friends, and all that she has loved at the hermitage.

Act V shows us the king in his court, overwhelmed with the duties of office, for Kālidāsa takes care to show us Duḥṣanta as the great and good monarch. News is brought that hermits with women desire an interview, while a song is heard in which the queen Haṅsavatī laments the king's faithlessness to her; the king dispatches the Vidūṣaka to solace her, and receives in state the hermits. They bring him his wife, but, under the malign influence of the curse, he does not recognize her and cannot receive her. The hermits reprove him, and insist on leaving her, refusing her the right to go with them, since her duty is by her husband's side. The king's priest is willing to give her the safety of his house till the babe be born, but a figure of light in female shape appears and bears Çakuntalā away, leaving the king still unrecognizing, but filled with wonder. In the entr'acte which follows a vital element is contributed; policemen mishandle a fisherman accused of theft of a royal ring found in a fish which he has caught; it is Duḥṣanta's ring which Çakuntalā had dropped while bathing. The Act that follows tells us of the recognition by the king of the wrong unwittingly done and his grief at the loss of his wife; he seeks to console himself with her portrait, when he is interrupted by a lady of the harem, and then by the minister, who obtains from him the decision of a law case involving the right of succession; the episode reminds the king of his childlessness. From his despair the king is awakened by the screams of the Vidūṣaka who has been roughly handled by Mātali, Indra's charioteer, as an effective means of bringing the king back to the realization that there are duties superior to private feeling. The gods need his aid for battle. In Act VII Duḥṣanta is revealed victorious, and travelling with Mātali in a divine car high through the air to Hemakūṭa, where dwells in the place of supreme bliss the seer Mārīca and his wife. Here the king sees a gallant boy playfully pulling about a young lion to the terror of two maidens who accompany him in the dress of the hermitage; they ask the king to intervene with the child in the cub's interest, and the king feels a pang as he thinks of his sonlessness. To his amazement he learns that this is no hermit's son, but his own; Çakuntalā is revealed to him in the dress of an ascetic, and Mārīca crowns their happiness by making it clear to Çakuntalā that her husband was guiltless of the sorrow inflicted upon her.

A drama so popular has naturally enough failed to come down to us in a single recension.[1] Four are normally distinguished, Bengālī, Devanāgarī, Kāçmīrī, and South Indian, while a fifth may also be traced. There are, however, in reality, two main recensions, the Bengālī, with 221 stanzas, as fixed by the commentators Çañkara and Candraçekhara, and the Devanāgarī, with 194 stanzas, of Rāghavabhaṭṭa; the Kāçmīrī, which supplies an entr'acte to Act VII, is in the main an eclectic combination of these two representatives of North Indian texts, and the South Indian is closely akin to the Devanāgarī; Abhirāma and Kāṭayavema among others have commented on it. The evidence of superior merit is conflicting; Pischel[2] laid stress on the more correct Prākrit of the Bengālī and the fact that some readings in

[1] Konow, ID., pp. 67 f.; Hari Chand, *Kālidāsa*, pp. 243 ff.; B. K. Thakore, *The Text of the Śakuntalā* (1922); Windisch, *Sansk. Phil.* pp. 344 f.

[2] *De Kâlidâsae Çâkuntali recensionibus* (1870); *Die Recensionen der Çakuntalā* (1875).

the Devanāgarī are best explained as glosses on the Bengālī text, while Lévi[1] proved that Harṣa and Rājaçekhara knew the Bengālī recension in some shape. On the other hand, Weber[2] contended for the priority of the Devanāgarī; certainly some readings there are better, and some of the Bengālī stanzas are mere repetitions of others found in both texts. Unless we adopt the not very plausible view of Bollensen that the Devanāgarī version is the acting edition of the play revised for representation, we must hold that neither recension is of conclusive value: the argument from the Prākrit is not conclusive, for it may merely rest on the superior knowledge of the copyists from whom the Bengālī original ultimately issued.[3]

3. *Kālidāsa's Dramatic Art*

The order of plays here adopted is in precise harmony with the development in a harmonious manner of Kālidāsa's dramatic art. The *Mālavikāgnimitra* is essentially a work of youthful promise and some achievement;[4] the theme is one less banal probably in Kālidāsa's time than it became later when every Nāṭikā was based on an analogous plot, and there is some skill in the manner in which the events are interlaced; the Vidūṣaka's strategems to secure his master the sight of his beloved are amusing, and, though Agnimitra appears mainly as a love-sick hero, the reports of battles and victories reminds us adequately of his kingly functions and high importance. The most effective characterization, however, is reserved for the two queens, Dhāriṇī and Irāvatī: the grace and dignity, and finally the magnanimity of the former, despite just cause for anger, are set off effectively against the passionate impetuosity of the latter, which leads her to constant eavesdropping, and to an outbreak against the king, forgetful of his rank and rights. The heroine is herself but faintly presented, but her friend Kauçikī, who has been driven by a series of misfortunes to enter the religious life, is a noble

[1] TI. ii. 37. The erotic passages in Act III in the Bengālī recension must be judged by Indian taste; cf. Thakore, p. 13 for a condemnation.

[2] IS. xiv. 35 ff., 161 ff. Cf. Bühler, *Kashmir Report*, pp. lxxxv ff.

[3] Cf. above, p. 121, n. 1 as to the variation in correctness in different classes of MSS.

[4] For a warm eulogy, see V. Henry, *Les littératures de l'Inde*, pp. 305 ff.

figure; she comforts and distracts the mind of Dhāriṇī; she is an authority on the dance and on the cure for snake bite, and alone among the women she speaks Sanskrit. The Vidūṣaka is an essential element in the drama, and he plays rather the part of a friend and confidant of the king than his jester; without his skilled aid Agnimitra would have languished in vain for his inamorata. But on the other hand he contributes comparatively little to the comic side of the drama.

In the *Vikramorvaçī* Kālidāsa shows a marked advance in imagination. We have no preçise information of the source he followed; the story is old, it occurs in an obscure form in the *Ṛgveda*, and is degraded to sacrificial application in the *Çatapatha Brāhmaṇa*; it is also found in a number of Purāṇas, and in the *Matsya*[1] there is a fairly close parallel to Kālidāsa's version, for the motif of the nymph's transformation into a creeper, instead of a swan, is already present, Purūravas's mad search for her is known as well as his rescue of her from a demon. The passionate and undisciplined love of Urvaçī is happily displayed, but it is somewhat too far removed from normal life to charm; her magic power to watch her lover unseen and to overhear his conversation is as unnatural as the singular lack of maternal affection which induces her to abandon forthwith her child rather than lose her husband; her love is selfish; she forgets her duty of respect to the gods in her dramatic act, and her transformation is the direct outcome of a fit of insane jealousy. The hero sinks to a diminutive stature beside her, and, effective in the extreme as is his passionate despair in Act IV, his lack of self-restraint and manliness is obvious and distasteful. The minor characters are handled with comparative lack of success; the incident of the boy Āyus is forced, and the ending of the drama ineffective and flat. The Vidūṣaka, however, introduces an element of comedy in the stupidity by which he allows himself to be cheated out of the name of Urvaçī, and the clumsiness which permits the nymph's letter to fall into the hands of the queen. The latter, Auçīnarī, is a dignified and more attractive figure than the nymph;

[1] xxiv; *Viṣṇu*, iv. 6; *Bhāgavata*, ix. 14; Pischel and Geldner, *Ved. Stud.* i. 243 ff.; L. v. Schroeder, *Mysterium und Mimus*, pp. 242 ff. A. Gawroński (*Les sources de quelques drames indiens*, pp. 19 ff.) suggests a popular legend, comparing the *Sudhanāvadāna*, No. 30 of the *Divyāvadāna*.

like Agnimitra in his scene with Irāvatī, Purūravas cuts a sorry figure beside her, seeing how just cause she had to be vexed at his lack of faith and candour towards her.

In the *Çakuntalā* Kālidāsa handles again with far more perfect art many of the incidents found in his earlier drama. He does not hesitate to repeat himself; we have in the first and third Acts the pretty idea of the king in concealment hearing the confidential talk of the heroine and her friends; the same motif is found in Act III of the *Mālavikāgnimitra*. Like Urvaçī, Çakuntalā, when she leaves the king, makes a pretext—her foot pricked by a thorn and her tunic caught by a branch—to delay her going; in the same way both express their love by letters; the snatching by a bird of the magic stone in the *Vikramorvaçī* is paralleled by Mātali's seizure of the Vidūṣaka in Act VI; Āyus has a peacock to play with, as the little Bharata a lion, but in each case the comparison is all to the good of the *Çakuntalā*. The same maturity is seen in the changes made in the narrative of the *Mahābhārata*[1] which the poet had before him. The story there is plain and simple; the king arrives at the hermitage; the maiden recounts to him her ancestry without false shame; he proposes marriage; she argues, and, on being satisfied of the legality of a secret union, agrees on the understanding that her son shall be made heir apparent. The king goes away; the child grows up, until at the due season the mother, accompanied by hermits, takes him to court; the hermits leave her, but she is undaunted when the king out of policy refuses to recognize her; she threatens him with death and taunts him with her higher birth; finally, a divine voice bids the king consecrate the child, and he explains that his action was due solely in order to have it made plain that the child was the rightful prince. This simple tale is transformed; the shy heroine would not dream of telling her birth; her maidens even are too modest to do more than hint, and leave the experienced king to guess the rest. Çakuntalā's dawning love is depicted with perfect skill; her marriage and its sequel alluded to with delicate touches. The king's absurd conduct is now explained; a curse produces it, and for that curse Çakuntalā was not without responsibility, for she allowed her

[1] i. 74. Winternitz's denial (GIL., i. 319 f.) of priority is impossible; cf. Gawroński, *Les sources de quelques drames indiens*, pp. 40, 91.

love to make her forgetful of the essential duty of hospitality and reverence to the stranger and saint. Before the king she utters no threat but behaves with perfect dignity, stunned as she is by his repudiation of their love. The king is a worthy hero, whose devotion to his public duties and heroism are insisted on, and who deserves by reason of his unselfishness to be reunited with his wife. His love for his son is charmingly depicted, and, accepting as an Indian must do the validity of the curse,[1] his conduct is irreproachable; it is not that he despises the lovely maiden that he repulses her, but as a pattern of virtue and morality he cannot accept as his wife one of whom he knows nothing. Çakuntalā's own love for him is purified by her suffering, and, when she is finally united to him, she is no longer a mere loving girl, but one who has suffered tribulation of spirit and gained in depth and beauty of nature.

The other characters are models of skilful presentation. Kālidāsa here shakes himself free from the error of presenting any other woman in competition with Çakuntalā; Duḥṣanta is much married, but though Haṅsavatī deplores his faithlessness he does not meet her, and, when Vasumatī enters in Act VI, the effect is saved by the entry of the minister to ask the king to decide a point of law. The Vidūṣaka, who would have ruined the love idyll, is cleverly dismissed on other business in Act II, while he serves the more useful end of introducing comic relief; Mātali playfully terrifies him to rouse the king from his own sorrows. Kaṇva is a delightful figure, the ascetic, without child, who lavishes on his adopted daughter all the wealth of his deep affection, and who sends her to her husband with words of tender advice; he is brilliantly contrasted with the fierce pride and anger of Durvāsas who curses Çakuntalā for what is no more than a girlish fault, and the solemn majesty of Mārīca, who, though married, has abandoned all earthly thoughts and enjoys the happiness of release, while yet contemplating the affairs of the world and intervening to set them in order with purely disinterested zeal. The companions of the heroine are painted with delicate taste; both are devoted body and soul to their mistress, but Anasūyā is serious and sensible; Priyaṁvadā

[1] The absurd silence as to Mālavikā's origin in the *Mālavikāgnimitra* is rendered acceptable by belief in prophecy.

talkative and gay. There is a contrast between the two hermits who take Çakuntalā to the court; Çārngarava shows the pride and hauteur of his calling, and severely rebukes the king; Çāradvata is calm and restrained and admonishes him in lieu. Equally successful is the delineation of the police officers, whose unjust and overbearing conduct to the fisherman represents the spirit of Indian police from the first appearance in history. The supernatural, which is in excess in the *Vikramorvaçī*, is reduced to modest dimensions, and intervenes hardly at all in the play, until we come to the last Act, where the theory permits and even demands that the marvellous should be introduced, and the celestial hermitage is a fit place for the reunion of two lovers severed by so hard a fate. The episode of the ring whose loss prevents the immediate recognition of the heroine is effectively conceived and woven into the plot.

Kālidāsa excels in depicting the emotions of love, from the first suggestion in an innocent mind to the perfection of passion; he is hardly less expert in pathos; the fourth Act of the *Çakuntalā* is a model of tender sorrow, and the loving kindness with which even the trees take farewell of their beloved one contrasts with the immediate harsh reception which awaits her at the royal court. Kālidāsa here, as in the fourth Act of the *Vikramorvaçī* and in the garden scenes of the *Mālavikāgnimitra*, displays admirably his love for nature and his power of description of all the stock elements of Indian scenery, the mango, the Bimba fruit, the Açoka, the lotus, and his delicate appreciation of the animal world of India. In the last Act of the *Çakuntalā* also we have the graceful picture of the appearance of the earth viewed in perspective from the celestial car of Mātali.

The humour of the Vidūṣaka is never coarse; his fondness for food is admitted; cakes and sugar suggest themselves to him when the hero admires the moon or is sick of love; heroics he despises: the king is summarily compared to a thief in his dislike for discovery; if caught, he should imitate the latter who explains that he was learning the art of wall breaking. Or again, he is in his contempt for the ladies of his harem like one sated of sweet dates and desiring the bitter tamarind. Mālavikā is summarily treated; she is like a cuckoo caught by a cat when Dhāriṇī places her in confinement, but he is no more respectful of himself, for, seized by Mātali, he treats himself as a mouse in mortal fear of a cat. Best of all is his description in Act II of the miseries brought on him by Duḥsanta's hunting; the Brahmins were no admirers of the sport, though they had to acquiesce in it in kings, and the Vidūṣaka's picture is vivid in the extreme.

The range of Kālidāsa's technical knowledge is apparent in his skilled use of the dance and song to set off his dramas; the *Mālavikāgnimitra* contains an interesting exposition by the dancing master of the theory of the art and its importance; not only is Mālavikā a dancer, but Çakuntalā shows her skill in movement in Act I. The songs of the trees and of Hansavatī in the same play enable him to add a fresh interest to the drama, and in the *Vikramorvaçī* spectacular effects seem to have been aimed at, while in the Bengālī recension song is prominently introduced in Act IV of the *Vikramorvaçī*.

Admirable as is Kālidāsa's work, it would be unjust to ignore the fact that in his dramas as in his epics he shows no interest in the great problems of life and destiny. The admiration of Goethe and the style of the Shakespeare of India accorded by Sir William Jones,[1] the first to translate the *Çakuntalā*, are deserved, but must not blind us to the narrow range imposed on Kālidāsa's interests by his unfeigned devotion to the Brahmanical creed of his time. Assured, as he was, that all was governed by a just fate which man makes for himself by his own deeds, he was incapable of viewing the world as a tragic scene, of feeling any sympathy for the hard lot of the majority of men, or appreciating the reign of injustice in the world. It was impossible for him to go beyond his narrow range; we may be grateful that, confined as he was, he accomplished a work of such enduring merit and universal appeal as *Çakuntalā*, which even in the ineffective guise of translations has won general recognition as a masterpiece.

4. *The Style*

Kālidāsa represents the highest pitch of elegance attained in Sanskrit style of the elevated Kāvya character; he is master of the Vaidarbha style, the essentials of which are the absence of

[1] See S. D. and A. B. Gajendragadkar, *Abhijñānaçākuntala*, pp. xxxvi ff.; below, chap. xii.

compounds or the rare use of them, and harmony of sound as well as clearness, elevation, and force allied to beauty, such as is conveyed to language by the use of figures of speech and thought. He is simple, as are Bhāsa and the author of the *Mṛcchakaṭikā*, but with an elegance and refinement which are not found in these two writers; Açvaghoṣa, we may be sure, influenced his style, but the chief cause of its perfection must have been natural taste and constant reworking of what he had written, a fact which may easily explain the discrepancies between the recensions of his work. But his skill in the *Çakuntalā* never leads him into the defect of taste which betrayed his successors into exhibiting their skill in the wrong place; skilled as he is in description, and ready as he is to exhibit his power, in the fifth Act he refrains from inserting any of these ornamental stanzas which add nothing to the action, however much honour they may do to the skill of the poet. His language has also the merit of suggestiveness; what Bhavabhūti, the greatest of his successors, expresses at length, he is content to indicate by a touch. He is admirably clear, and the propriety of his style is no less admirable; the language of the policeman and the fisher is as delicately nuanced as that of the domestic priest who argues at once in the best style of the philosophical Sūtras. The Prākrit which he ascribes to the maidens of his play has the supreme merit that it utterly eschews elaborate constructions and long compounds, such as Bhavabhūti places without thought of the utter incongruity in the mouths of simple girls.

The rhetoricians[1] extol the merits of Kālidāsa in metaphor, and they repeatedly cite his skill in the use of figures of speech, sound and thought, which they divide and subdivide in endless variety. He excels in vivid description (*svabhāvokti*) as when he depicts the flight of the antelope which Duḥṣanta pursues to the hermitage:

grīvābhaṅgābhirāmaṁ muhur anupatati syandane baddhadṛṣṭiḥ
paçcārdhena praviṣṭaḥ çarapatanabhayād bhūyasā pūrvakāyam
darbhair ardhāvalīḍhaiḥ çramavivṛtamukhabhraṅçibhiḥ kīrṇa-vartmā
paçyodagraplutatvād viyati bahutaraṁ stokam urvyāṁ prayāti.

[1] See Hari Chand, *Kālidāsa et l'art poétique de l'Inde* (1917), pp. 68 ff. On his suggestiveness, cf. *Ekāvalī*. p. 52.

'His glance fixed on the chariot, ever and anon he leaps up, gracefully bending his neck; through fear of the arrow's fall he draws ever his hinder part into the front of his body; he strews his path with the grass, half chewed, which drops from his mouth opened in weariness; so much aloft he bounds that he runs rather in the air than on earth.' Inferential knowledge is illustrated by a brilliant stanza:[1]

çāntam idam āçramapadaṁ sphurati ca bāhuḥ kutaḥ phalam ihāsya
atha vā bhavitavyānāṁ dvārāṇi bhavanti sarvatra.

'This is the hermitage where all desires are stilled; yet my arm throbs; how can here be found the fruit of such a presage? Nay, the doors of fate are ever open.' The rôle of conscience in human action is finely portrayed:[2]

asaṁçayaṁ kṣatraparigrahakṣamā: yad āryam asyāabhilāṣi me manaḥ
satāṁ hi saṁdehapadeṣu vāstuṣu: pramāṇam antaḥkaraṇapravṛttayaḥ.

'Assuredly the maiden is meet for marriage to a warrior, since my noble mind is set upon her; for with the good in matters of doubt the final authority is the dictate of conscience.' Of the departing Çakuntalā after her rejection the king says:[3]

itaḥ pratyādeçāt svajanam anugantuṁ vyavasitā
muhus tiṣṭhety uccair vadati guruçiṣye gurusame
punar dṛṣṭiṁ bāṣpaprasarakaluṣām arpitavatī
mayi krūre yat tat saviṣam iva çalyaṁ dahati mām.

'When I rejected her she sought to regain her companions, but the disciple, in his master's stead, loudly bade her stay; then she turned on cruel me a glance dimmed by her falling tears, and that now burns me like a poisoned arrow.' At his son's touch he says:[4]

anena kasyāpi kulāṅkureṇa: spṛṣṭasya gātreṣu sukhaṁ mamaivam
kāṁ nirvṛttiṁ cetasi tasya kuryād: yasyāyam aṅgāt kṛtinaḥ prarūḍhaḥ?

'When such joy is mine in the touch on my limbs of a scion of some other house, what gladness must not be his, from whose

[1] *Çakuntalā*, i. 15.
[2] *Ibid.*, i. 20.
[3] *Ibid.*, vi. 9.
[4] *Ibid.*, vii. 19.

loins, happy man, this child is sprung?' The punishment of the king for his disloyalty is severe:[1]

prajāgarāt khilībhūtas tasyāḥ svapne samāgamaḥ
bāṣpas tu na dadāty enāṁ draṣṭuṁ citragatām api.

'My sleeplessness forbids the sight of her even in a dream; my tears deny me her pictured form.' On reunion the picture is very different:[2]

çāpād asi pratihatā smṛtirodharūkṣe: bhartary apetatamasi prabhutā tavaiva
chāyā na mūrchati malopahataprasāde: çuddhe tu darpaṇatale sulabhāvakāçā.

'Thou wert rejected by thy husband, cruel through the curse that robbed him of memory; now thy dominion is complete over him whose darkness is dispelled; on the tarnished mirror no image forms; let it be cleaned and it easily appears.'

There is pathos in Purūravas's reproach to Urvaçī:[3]

tvayi nibaddharateḥ priyavādinaḥ: praṇayabhañgaparāñmukhacetasaḥ
kam aparādhalavam mama paçyasi: tyajasi mānini dāsajanaṁ yataḥ?

My delight was ever in thee, my words ever of love; what suspicion of fault dost thou see in me that, O angry one, thou dost abandon thy slave?' The metrical effect is here, as usual, extremely well planned. His vain efforts to attain his beloved are depicted forcibly:[4]

samarthaye yat prathamam priyām prati: kṣaṇena tan me parivartate 'nyathā
ato vinidre sahasā vilocane: karomi na sparçavibhāvitapriyāḥ.

'Whatever I deem to be my beloved in a moment assumes another aspect. I will force my eyes to be sleepless, since I have failed to touch her whom I adore.' There are no limits to the strength of his love:[5]

idaṁ tvayā rathakṣobhād añgenāñgaṁ nipīḍitam
ekaṁ kṛti çarīre 'smiñ çeṣam añgam bhuvo bharaḥ.

[1] *Ibid.*, vi. 22.
[2] *Ibid.*, vii. 32.
[3] *Vikramorvaçī*, iv. 55.
[4] *Ibid.*, iv. 68.
[5] *Ibid.*, iii. 11; for the text see Hari Chand, *Kālidāsa*, p. 231.

'In this body no member has value save that which, thanks to the movement of the chariot, she has touched; all else is a mere burden to the earth.' Hyperbole [1] is permissible.

sāmantamaulimaṇirañjitapādapīṭham: ekātapatram avaner
na tathā prabhutvam
asyāḥ sakhe caraṇayor aham adya kāntam: ājñākaratvam
adhigamya yathā kṛtārthaḥ.

'Despite the radiance shed on my footstool by the jewelled diadems of vassal princes, despite the subjection of the whole earth to my sway, not so much joy did I gain from attaining kingship as the satisfaction won from paying homage to the feet of that lady, O my friend.' The recovery of the nymph from her faint caused by the savage onslaught upon her is described in a happy series of similes: [2]

āvirbhūte çaçini tamasā ricyamāneva rātrir
naiçasyārcir hutabhuja iva cchinnabhūyiṣṭhadhūmā
mohenāntar varatanur iyaṁ lakṣyate mucyamānā
gañgā rodhaḥpatanakaluṣā gacchatīva prasādam.

'As the night, freed from the darkness when the moon has appeared, as the light of a fire in the evening when the smoke has nearly all gone, so appears this lady fair, recovering from her faint, and winni g back her calmness, like the Ganges after her stream has been troubled by the falling of her banks.'

The *Mālavikāgnimitra*, it is true, has far fewer beauties of diction than the other two dramas, but it contains many verses which are unmistakably the work of Kālidāsa, though they present much less than the maturity of his later style. The figure of discrepancy (*viṣama*) is illustrated by the description of the god of love whose bow, so innocent in seeming, can yet work such ill: [3]

kva rujā hṛdayapramāthinī: kva ca te viçvasanīyam āyudham
mṛdutīkṣṇataraṁ yad ucyate: tad idam manmatha dṛçyate
tvayi.

'How strange the difference between this pain that wrings the heart, and thy bow to all seeming so harmless. That which is

[1] *Vikramorvaçī*, iii. 19.

[2] *Ibid.*, i. 9. The parallelism, is, of course, complete in Sanskrit, but inexpressible directly in English.

[3] *Mālavikāgnimitra*, iii. 2.

most sweet and most bitter at once is assuredly found in thee, O God of Love.' Agnimitra is ready enough with a pun, when Mālavikā, on being bidden to show fearlessly her love towards him, slyly reminds him that she has seen him as terrified as herself of the queen :[1]

dākṣiṇyaṁ nāma bimboṣṭhi baimbikānāṁ kulavratam
tan me dīrghākṣi ye prāṇās te tvadāçānibandhanāḥ.

Politeness, O Bimba-lipped one, is the family tradition of the descendants of Bimbaka ; nevertheless, what life I have depends entirely on the hope of thy favour.' The excellent Kauçikī consoles and comforts Dhāriṇī with her approval of her acts :[2]

pratipakṣeṇāpi patiṁ sevante bhartṛvatsalāḥ sādhvyaḥ
anyasaritām api jalaṁ samudragāḥ prāpayanty udadhim.

'Even to the extent of admitting a rival, noble ladies, who love their spouses, honour their husbands ; the great rivers bear to the ocean the waters of many a tributary stream.' There is an amusing directness and homeliness in the king's utterance on learning of the true quality of Mālavikā :[3]

preṣyabhāvena nāmeyaṁ devīçabdakṣamā satī
snānīyavastrakriyayā patrorṇaṁ vopayujyate.

'This lady, fit to bear the title of queen, has been treated as a maid-servant, even as one might use a garment of woven silk for a bathing cloth.' But Kālidāsa shows himself equal to the expression of more manly sentiments as well ; the nun thus tells of her brother's fall in the effort to save Mālavikā when the foresters attack them :[4]

imām parīpsur durjāte parābhibhavakātarām
bhartṛpriyaḥ priyair bhartur ānṛṇyam asubhir gataḥ.

'Eager in this misfortune to protect her, terrified by the enemy's onslaught, he paid with his dear life his debt of affection to the lord whom he loved.' The king's reply is manly: *bhagavati tanutyajām īdṛçī lokayātrā : na çocyaṁ tatrabhavān saphalīkṛtabhartṛpiṇḍaḥ.* 'O lady, such is the fate of brave men ; thou must not mourn for him who showed himself thus worthy of his master's salt.'

[1] *Ibid.*, iv. 14.
[2] *Ibid.*, v. 19.
[3] *Ibid.*, v. 12.
[4] *Ibid.*, v. 11.

5. *The Language and the Metres*

In Kālidāsa we find the normal state of the Prākrits in the later drama, Çauraseni for the prose speeches, and Māhārāṣṭrī for the verses.[1] The police officers and the fisher in the *Çakuntalā* use Māgadhī, but the king's brother-in-law, who is in charge of the police and is a faint echo of the Çakāra, speaks, as we have the drama, neither Çākārī nor Māgadhī nor Dākṣiṇātyā but simply Çauraseni. By this time, of course, we may assume that Prākrit for the drama had been stereotyped by the authority of Vararuci's Prākrit grammar, and that it differed considerably from the spoken dialect; there would be clear proof if the Apabhrança verses of the *Vikramorvaçī* could safely be ascribed to Kālidāsa. The Māhārāṣṭrī unquestionably owes its vogue to the outburst of lyric in that dialect, which has left its traces in the anthology of Hāla and later texts, and which about the period of Kālidāsa invaded the epic.[2]

Kālidāsa's Sanskrit is classical; here and there deviations from the norm are found, but in most instances the expressions are capable of defence on some rule or other, while in others we may remember the fact of the epic tradition which is strong in Bhāsa.

The metres of Kālidāsa show in the *Mālavikāgnimitra* a restricted variety; the Āryā (35) and the Çloka (17) are the only metres often occurring. In the *Vikramorvaçī* the Āryā (29) and the Çloka (30) are almost in equal favour, while the Vasantatilakā (12) and the Çārdūlavikrīḍita (11) make a distinct advance in importance. In the *Çakuntalā* the Āryā (38) and Çloka (36) preserve their relative positions, while the Vasantatilaka (30) and Çārdūlavikrīḍita (22) advance in frequency of use, a striking proof of Kālidāsa's growing power of using elaborate metrical forms. The Upajāti types increase to 16. The other metres used in the drama are none of frequent occurrence; common to all the dramas are Aparavaktra,[3] Aupacchandasika,[4] and Vaitālīya, Drutavilambita, Puṣpitāgrā, Pṛthvī, Mandākrāntā, Mālinī, Vançasthā, Çārdūlavikrīḍita, Çikhariṇī, and Hariṇī; the *Mālavikāg-*

[1] Traces of Çauraseni in verses appear in the *Çakuntalā*. Cf. Hillebrandt, *Mudrārākṣasa*, p. iii; GN. 1905, p. 440.

Cf. Pravarasena's *Setubandha*. On Hāla and Kālidāsa, cf. Weber's ed., p. xxiv.

[3] ∪∪∪∪∪∪–∪–∪– ¦ ∪∪∪∪–∪∪–∪–∪– *bis*.

[4] 16 + 18 *bis*: normal type ∪∪–∪∪–∪–∪–– | ∪∪––∪∪–∪–∪––.

nimitra and the *Çakuntalā* share also Praharṣiṇī, Rucirā,[1] Çālinī, and Sragdharā; the latter adds the Rathoddhatā,[2] the *Vikramorvaçī* a Mañjubhāṣiṇī.[3] The earliest play has one irregular Prākrit verse, the second two Āryās, and 29 of varied form of the types measured by feet or morae, and the last seven Āryās and two Vaitālīyas. The predominance of the Āryā is interesting, for it is essentially a Prākrit metre, whence it seems to have secured admission into Sanskrit verse.

Not unnaturally, efforts[4] have been made on the score of metre to ascertain the dates of the plays *inter se*, and in relation to the rest of the acknowledged work of Kālidāsa. The result achieved by Dr. Huth would place the works in the order *Raghuvança*, *Meghadūta*, *Mālavikāgnimitra*, *Çakuntalā*, *Kumārasambhava*, and *Vikramorvaçī*. But the criteria are quite inadequate; the *Meghadūta* has but one metre, the Mandākrāntā, which occurs so seldom in the other poems and plays that any comparison is impossible,[5] and the points relied upon by Dr. Huth are of minimal importance; they assume such doctrines as that the poem which contains the fewest abnormal caesuras is the more metrically perfect and therefore the later, while the poem which has the largest number of abnormal forms of the Çloka metre is artistically the more perfect and so later. A detailed investigation of the different forms of abnormal caesuras reveals the most perplexing counter-indications of relative date, and the essential impression produced by the investigations is that Kālidāsa was a finished metrist, who did not seriously alter his metrical forms at any period of his career as revealed in his poems, and that there is no possibility of deducing any satisfactory conclusions from metrical evidence. The fact that the evidence would place the mature and meditative *Raghuvança*,[6] which bears within it unmistakable proofs of the author's old age, before the *Meghadūta* and long before the *Kumārasambhava*, both redolent of love and youth, is sufficient to establish its total untrustworthiness.

[1] ⏑–⏑–, ⏑⏑⏑⏑–⏑–⏑–.

[2] –⏑–⏑⏑⏑–⏑–⏑–.

[3] ⏑⏑–⏑–, ⏑⏑⏑–⏑––⏑–.

[4] Huth, *op. cit.*, Table.

[5] Hillebrandt (*Kālidāsa*, p. 157) points out the complexity of the position.

[6] H. A. Shah (*Kauṭilya and Kālidāsa* (1920), p. 5), argues that *Raghuvança*, ix. 53 shows a more advanced view of hunting as a useful sport when regulated (*Arthaçāstra*, p. 329) than the *Çakuntalā*. But the dramatic propriety of the passage of the *Çakuntalā* renders the contention uncertain. Whether Kālidāsa knew precisely our *Arthaçāstra* is also uncertain.

VII

CANDRA, HARṢA, AND MAHENDRAVIKRAMAVARMAN

1. *Candra or Candraka*

SOME mystery exists as to the identity and character of Candra as a dramatist.[1] We have in a Tibetan version a *Lokānanda*, a Buddhist drama telling of a certain Maṇicūḍa, who handed over his wife and children to a Brahmin as a sign of supreme generosity, which is ascribed to Candragomin, the grammarian, in whose *Çiṣyalekhā* is found a verse ascribed to Candragopin in the *Subhāṣitāvali*. If this is the dramatist Candaka or Candraka, who is placed by Kalhaṇa under Tuñjina of Kashmir, and who rivalled the author of the *Mahābhārata* in a drama, is wholly uncertain. The grammarian must have lived before A.D. 650, as he is cited in the *Kāçikā Vṛtti* though not by name; a more precise date it is impossible to give, for his reference to a victory of a Jarta over the Hūṇas cannot be made precise until we know what Jāṭ prince is referred to, though Yaçodharman has been suggested. The identification by Lévi of Candra with a person of that name mentioned by I-Tsing as living in his time is seemingly impossible, though I-Tsing ascribes to him the verse found in the *Çiṣyalekhā* mentioned above; the verse is lacking in the Tibetan version and I-Tsing may have made a slip. His contemporary seems to have been a Candradāsa, and to have dramatized the Viçvantara legend.

To Candaka is ascribed in the *Subhāṣitāvali*[2] a fine verse of martial tone:

eṣā hi raṇagatasya dṛḍhā pratijñā: drakṣyanti yan na ripavo
jaghanaṁ hayānāṁ
yuddheṣu bhāgyacapaleṣu na me pratijñā: daivaṁ yad icchati
jayaṁ ca parājayaṁ ca.

[1] Lévi, BEFEO. iii. 38 f.; Liebich, *Das Datum des Candragomin und Kalidasas*; Konow, ID. pp. 72 f.; GIL. iii. 185, 399 f.

[2] v. 2275.

'I go to battle, and I swear that my foes shall never see the backs of my steeds; for the rest, fate directs the destiny of the wavering fight; I promise nothing, but shall take defeat or victory as it pleases destiny.' A verse of love is:[1]

prasāde vartasva prakaṭaya mudaṁ saṁtyaja ruṣam
priye çuṣyanty aṅgāny amṛtam iva te siñcatu vacaḥ
nidhānaṁ saukhyānāṁ kṣaṇam abhimukhaṁ sthāpaya mukham
na mugdhe pratyetum bhavati gataḥ kālahariṇaḥ.

'Be gentle; show a little joy; lay aside thy anger; beloved, my limbs are dried up, let thy speech pour ambrosia upon them. Turn to me for a moment thy face, the abode of happiness; foolish one, time is an antelope which, gone, cannot be recalled.' The other citations we have show skill both in tragic and erotic sentiment.

Candraka was evidently admired by the authorities on poetics; we find in the commentary on the *Daçarūpa*[2] a verse, elsewhere ascribed to him, cited as an example where diverse sentiments blend but where one, that of coming parting of lovers, is predominant:

ekenākṣṇā paritataruṣā vīkṣate vyomasaṁstham
bhānor bimbaṁ sajalalulitenāpareṇātmakāntam
ahnaç chede dayitavirahāçaṅkinī cakravākī
dvau saṁkīrṇau racayati rasau nartakīva pragalbhā.

'With one angry eye she gazes on the orb of the sun as it tarries on the horizon; with the other, dimmed by her tears, she looks on her soul's beloved; thus the mate of the Cakravāka, feeling the approach at nightfall of separation from her dear one, expresses two emotions, even as a clever actress.'

Curiously enough we have no less than four stanzas of benediction ascribed to him, which illustrate a formal feature of the Sanskrit drama, the introduction of each play with one or more stanzas involving divine favour. The verses are interesting, not so much for the intrinsic merits of their poetry, which frankly are not great, but because of the curious manner in which Indian poetry treats its deities; the greatest of gods nevertheless in his sportive moods is yet made the prototype of the human lover:[3]

[1] v. 1629.
[2] p. 163; *Subhāṣitāvali*, 1916; *Çārṅgadhara*, cxvii. 14; text uncertain.
[3] *Subhāṣitāvali*, 66.

cyutāṁ indor lekhāṁ ratikalahabhagnaṁ ca valayaṁ
çanair ekīkṛtya hasitamukhī çailatanayā
avocad yaṁ paçyety avatu sa çivaḥ sā ca girijā
sa ca krīḍācandro daçanakiraṇapūritatanuḥ.

'Smiling, the daughter of the mountain wrought into one a digit fallen from the moon and a bracelet broken in a love quarrel, and said to her lord, "Behold my work". May he, Çiva, protect you, and the lady of the mountain, and that moon of dalliance all covered with bites and rays.'

mātar jīva kiṁ etad añjalipuṭe tātena gopāyyate
vatsa svādu phalaṁ prayacchati na me gatvā gṛhāṇa svayaṁ
mātraivaṁ prahite guhe vighaṭayaty ākṛṣya saṁdhyāñjalim
çambhor bhinnasamādhir uddharabhaso hāsodgāmaḥ pātu vaḥ.

'O mother.—My life.—What is it that my father guards so carefully in the palm of his hand?—Dear one, it is a sweet fruit.—He will not give me it.—Go thyself and take it.—Thus urged by his mother, Guha seizes the closed hands of his sire as he adores the Twilight and drags them apart; Çiva, angry at the interruption of his devotion, stays his wrath at sight of his son and laughs: may that laughter protect you.'[1]

2. *The Authorship of the Dramas ascribed to Harṣa*

Three dramas, as well as some minor poetry, have come down to us under the name of Harṣa, unquestionably the king of Sthāṇvīçvara and Kanyakubja, who reigned from about A.D. 606 to 648,[2] the patron of Bāṇa who celebrates him in the *Harṣacarita* and of the Chinese pilgrim Hiuan-Tsang who is our most valuable source of information on his reign. That the three plays are by one and the same hand is made certain in part by the common ascription in a verse in the prologue mentioning Harṣa as an accomplished poet, partly by the recurrence of two verses in the *Priyadarçikā* and the *Nāgānanda* and of one in the former play and the *Ratnāvalī*, and above all by the absolute similarity of style and tone in the three works, which renders any effort to

[1] *Subhāṣitāvali*, 69.

[2] M. Ettinghausen, *Harṣa Vardhana*, Louvain, 1905; S. P. Paṇḍit, *Gaüdavaho*, pp. cvii ff.; K. M. Panikkar, *Sri Harsha of Kanauj*, Bombay, 1922. It is impossible to connect the dramas with any definite incident of his reign such as the Prayāga festival celebrated by Hiuan-Tsang.

dissociate them wholly impossible. The question of their actual authorship was raised in antiquity; for, while Mammaṭa in his *Kāvyaprakāça*[1] merely refers to the gift of gold to Bāṇa—or Dhāvaka in some manuscripts—by Harṣa, the commentators explain this of the *Ratnāvalī*, which was passed off in Harṣa's name. This is, however, not in any way borne out by early tradition; I-Tsing[2] clearly refers to the dramatization of the subject of the *Nāgānanda* by Harṣa and its performance, and in the *Kuṭṭanīmata*[3] of Dāmodaragupta, who lived under Jayāpīḍa of Kashmir (A.D. 779–813), a performance of the *Ratnāvalī*, ascribed to a king, is mentioned. The ascription to Bāṇa has nothing even plausible in it, so disparate are the styles of the dramas and the *Harṣacarita*, and we have the option of believing that Harṣa wrote them himself with such aid as his Paṇḍits might give, or of accepting them as the work of some unknown dramatist, who allowed the king to claim the credit for them.

3. *The Three Dramas*

The *Ratnāvalī* and the *Priyadarçikā* are closely connected both in subject-matter and form; they are Nāṭikās, each in four Acts; their common hero is Udayana, whom Bhāsa already celebrated, and the common theme one of his numerous amourettes. The *Ratnāvalī*,[4] in special, has found favour in the text-books of the drama, and has served to illustrate the technical rules.

The ubiquitous Yaugandharāyaṇa, insatiable in seeking his master's welfare, has planned marriage for him with the daughter of the king of Ceylon, but to attain this end has been difficult; to avoid vexing the queen Vāsavadattā, he has kept her in the dark, and has spread a rumour which he has had conveyed by Bābhravya, the king's chamberlain, of the death of Vāsavadattā in a fire at Lāvāṇaka. The king of Ceylon then yields the hand of his daughter, and dispatches her in the care of the chamberlain and his minister Vasubhūti to Vatsa, but, wrecked at sea, she is rescued by a merchant of Kauçāmbī, taken there, and handed

[1] i. 2. Cf. Soḍhala (A.D. 993) in *Kāvyamīmāṅsā* (GOS. i), p. xii.

[2] Trs. Takakusu, pp. 163 f.

[3] vv. 856 ff.

[4] Ed. C. Cappeller, Böhtlingk, *Sanskrit-Chrestomathie*, 3rd ed., pp. 326 ff.; trs. Wilson, ii. 255 ff.; L. Fritze, Schloss Chemnitz, 1878. It was performed at a spring festival of Kāma.

over to Vāsavadattā who, seeing her beauty, decides to keep her from contact with her inconstant spouse. But fate is adverse; at the spring festival which she celebrates with Vatsa, Sāgarikā, as the princess is called from her rescue from the sea, appears in the queen's train; hastily sent away, she lingers concealed, watches the ceremony of the worship of the god Kāma, thinking Vatsa is the god in bodily presence, but is undeceived by the eulogy of the herald announcing the advent of evening. In Act II Sāgarikā is presented with her friend Susaṁgatā; she has depicted the prince on a canvas, and Susaṁgatā in raillery adds her beside him; she admits her love, but the confidence is broken by the alarm created by the escape of a monkey from the stables. In its mad rush it breaks the cage in Sāgarikā's keeping, and the parrot escapes. The king and the Vidūṣaka enter the grove where the bird is, hear it repeat the maidens' talk, and find the picture. The maidens returning for the picture overhear the confidences of the king and the Vidūṣaka, until Susaṁgatā sallies out and brings the lovers face to face. Their meeting is cut short by the advent of the queen, who sees the picture, realizes the position, and departs without manifesting the deep anger which she feels and which the king vainly seeks to assuage. In Act III the Vidūṣaka proves to have devised a scheme to secure a meeting of the lovers; Sāgarikā dressed as the queen and Susaṁgatā as her attendant are to meet Vatsa, but the plot is overheard, and it is Vāsavadattā herself who keeps the rendezvous; she listens to Vatsa's declarations of love, and then bitterly reproaches him, rejecting his attempts to excuse himself. Sāgarikā, who had come on the scene too late, hears the king's plight; weary, she ties a noose to her neck, when she is saved by the advent of the Vidūṣaka and the king, who naturally mistakes her for Vāsavadattā whom he fears his cruelty has driven to suicide. He joyously recognizes his error, but the queen, who, ashamed of her anger, has returned to make friends with her husband, finds the lovers united, and in violent anger carries off the maiden and the Vidūṣaka captive. But in Act IV we find the Vidūṣaka released and forgiven, but Sāgarikā in some prison, the king helpless to aid her. Good news, however, arrives; the general Rumaṇvant has won a victory over the Kosalas and slain the king. A magician enters and is allowed to display his art, but the spectacle is interrupted by the advent of Vasubhūti and Bābhravya, who also have escaped the shipwreck. They tell their tale of disaster, when another interruption occurs; the harem is on fire; Vāsavadattā, shocked, reveals that Sāgarikā is there; Vatsa rushes to aid her, and emerges with her in chains, for the fire has been no more than a device of the magician. Bābhravya and Vasubhūti recognize in Sāgarikā the princess, and Yaugandharāyaṇa arrives to confess his management of the whole plot and the magician's device. Vāsavadattā gladly gives the king to Ratnāvalī, since her husband will thus be lord of the earth, and Ratnāvalī is her full cousin.

The *Priyadarçikā*[1] introduces us in a speech by his chamberlain, Vinayavasu, to the king Dṛḍhavarman, whose daughter is destined for wedlock with Vatsa despite the demand for her hand made by the king of Kaliñga, who revenges himself during Vatsa's imprisonment at the court of Pradyota by attacking and driving away Dṛḍhavarman. The maid is carried away by the chamberlain and is received and sheltered by Vindhyaketu, her father's ally, but he offends Vatsa, is attacked and killed by his general Vijayasena, who brings back as part of the booty the unlucky Priyadarçikā; the king allots her to the harem as attendant on Vāsavadattā with the name Āraṇyikā (Āraṇyakā). In Act II we find the king, who has fallen in love with the maiden, seeking to distract himself with his Vidūṣaka. Āraṇyikā enters, to pluck lotuses, with her friend; she tells her love, which the king overhears; a bee attacks her when her friend leaves her, and in her confusion she runs into the arms of the king. Vatsa rescues her, but retires when her confidante returns. Act III tells that the aged confidante of the queen, Sāṁkṛtyāyanī, has composed a play on the marriage of Vatsa and Vāsavadattā which the queen is to see performed; the rôle of queen is to be played by Āraṇyikā, and Manoramā is to act the part of king, but she and the Vidūṣaka have arranged to let the king take the part. The performance causes anxiety to the queen, so ardent is the love-making, though Sāṁkṛtyāyanī reminds her it is but play-making; she leaves the hall, and finds the Vidūṣaka asleep; rudely wakened, he lets out the secret and the queen refuses to listen to Vatsas's lame excuses. Act IV reveals Āraṇyikā in

[1] Ed. R. V. Krishnamachariar, Srirangam, 1906; trs. G. Strehly, Paris, 1888.

prison, the king in despair, and the queen in sorrow, as she has learned from a letter from her mother that Dṛḍhavarman, her aunt's husband, is in bondage, needing Vatsa's aid. But Vijayasena brings news of the defeat of the Kaliñga king and the re-establishment of Dṛḍhavarman, and the chamberlain of the latter brings his thanks, his one sorrow being his daughter's loss. Manoramā enters in terror; Āraṇyikā has poisoned herself, Vāsavadattā, filled with remorse, has her fetched, as Vatsa can cure her; the chamberlain recognizes his princess, Vatsa's magic arts bring her back to consciousness, and Vāsavadattā recognizes in her her cousin, and grants her hand to the king.

The *Nāgānanda*,[1] performed at a festival of Indra, perhaps in the autumn, differs from these dramas in its form, for it is a Nāṭaka in five Acts, and in its inspiration; those are variants by Harṣa on the theme of Vatsa's loves, this is the dramatization of a Buddhist legend, the self-sacrifice of Jīmūtavāhana, which was told in the *Bṛhatkathā*, whence it appears in the later versions of that text[2] and in the *Vetālapañcaviñçati*.[3] Jīmūtavāhana is a prince of the Vidyādharas, who hasinduced his father to resign his kingship, and give himself up to a life of calm; he has made the acquaintance of Mitrāvasu, the prince of the Siddhas, who has a sister. She has had a dream in which Gaurī has revealed to her her future husband, and Jīmūtavāhana hidden behind a thicket overhears her confiding this dream to her friend; the Vidūṣaka forces a meeting on the timid lovers, who shyly confess their affection, when an ascetic from the hermitage arrives to take the maiden away. In Act II Malayavatī is love-sick, resting on a stone seat in the garden; a sound makes her move away, when the king enters, equally oppressed, declares his love and paints his fancy. Mitrāvasu comes to offer him his sister's hand; the king declines it, ignorant of whom he loves; she deems herself disdained and seeks to hang herself, but her friends rescue her and call for aid. Jīmūtavāhana appears, and proves that she is his love by showing the picture. The two exchange vows, and the marriage is concluded. In Act III, after a comic interlude, we find them walking in the park in happiness; Jīmūtavāhana is

[1] Ed. Calcutta, 1886; TSS. 1917; trs. P. Boyd, London, 1872; A. Bergaigne Paris, 1879; E. Tèza, Milan, 1904.

[2] KSS. xxii. 16–257; xc. 3–201; BKM. iv. 50–108; ix. 2. 776–930.

[3] xv.

apprised of the seizure of his kingdom, but accepts the news gladly. But the last two Acts change the topic. While strolling with Mitrāvasu one day, Jīmūtavāhana sees a heap of bones and learns that they are the bones of serpents daily offered to the divine bird Garuḍa; he resolves to save the lives of the serpents at the cost of his own, gets rid of Mitrāvasu, and goes to the place of offering. He hears the sobs of the mother of Çañkhacūḍa, whose son is about to be offered, consoles her by offering himself in ransom, but is refused with admiration for his gallantry. But, when the two have entered the temple to pray before the offering, he gives himself to Garuḍa as substitute and is borne away. The last Act opens with the anxiety of the parents of Jīmūtavāhana, to whom and his wife is borne a jewel fallen from his crown; Çañkhacūḍa, also, emerged from the temple, finds the sacrifice made and reveals to Garuḍa his crime. It is too late; the hero expires as his parents arrive. Garuḍa is ashamed, and Gaurī appears to cut the knot, revive the prince, and re-establish him in his realm, in order to keep faith with Malayavatī; by a shower of ambrosia the snakes slain by Garuḍa revive, and he promises to forego his cruel revenge.

4. *Harṣa's Art and Style*

Comparison with Kālidāsa is doubtless the cause why Harṣa has tended to receive less praise than is due to his dramas. The originality of his Nāṭikās is not perhaps great, but he has effectively devised the plot in both; the action moves smoothly and in either play there is ingenuity. The scene of the magician's activity in the *Ratnāvalī* is depicted with humour and vivacity; the parrot's escape and its chatter are sketched with piquancy, and the exchange of costumes in the *Ratnāvalī* is natural and effective. The double comedy in the *Priyadarçikā* is a happy thought, the intrigue in Act IV is neatly conducted, so as to show us Vāsavadattā in the light of an affectionate niece, and the scene with the bee is attractive. It is true that the plays are full of reminiscences of the *Mālavikāgnimitra*, such as the escape in the *Ratnāvalī* of the monkey, and the monkey that there frightens the little princess while Sāṁkṛtyāyanī is Kauçikī revived. But in this artificial comedy elegance is sought, not originality,[1] and Harṣa is a clever borrower. The similarity of development of both plays is perhaps more to be condemned; they are too obviously variations of one theme.

The dominant emotion in either is love of the type which appertains to a noble and gay (*dhīralalita*) hero, who is always courteous, whose loves, that is to say, mean very little to him, and who does not forget to assure the old love of his devotion while playing with the new. This is a different aspect of Vatsa's character from that displayed by Bhāsa, and admittedly a much inferior one. Vāsavadattā suffers equal deterioration, for she is no longer the wife who sacrifices herself for her husband's good; she is rather a jealous, though noble and kind-hearted woman, whose love for her husband makes her resent too deeply his inconstancy. The heroines are *ingénues* with nothing but good looks and willingness to be loved by the king, whom they know, though he does not, to be destined by their fathers as their husband. In neither case is any adequate reason[2] suggested for the failure to declare themselves in their true character, unless we are to assume that they would not, in the absence of sponsors, have been believed. Susaṁgatā, the friend of the heroine in the *Ratnāvalī*, is a pleasant, merry girl who makes excellent fun of her mistress. The Vidūṣaka[3] in both plays is typical in his greediness, but his figure lacks comic force; he is, however, a pleasant enough character, for his love for his master is genuine; he is prepared to die with him in the *Ratnāvalī*, though he thinks his action in rushing into the fire quixotic. The magician is an amusing and clever sketch of great pretensions allied to some juggling skill.

The *Nāgānanda* reveals Harṣa in a new light in the last two Acts. His liking for the marvellous is exhibited indeed in the last Acts of both the Nāṭikās in accord with the theory, but it has a far wider scope in the *Nāgānanda*, where the supernatural freely appears, and, though the drama be Buddhist in inspiration, Gaurī is introduced to solve the difficulty of restoring

[1] Many traces of the *Svapnavāsavadattā* can be seen in the *Ratnāvalī*, especially in the characterization of the Vidūṣaka.

[2] Āraṇyikā suggests that assertion would be undignified, seeing her actual condition. In the *Mālavikāgnimitra* a prophecy is made to do service as a motif.

[3] Cf. Schuyler, JAOS. xx. 338 ff.

Jīmūtavāhana. Harṣa here rises to the task of depicting the emotions of self-sacrifice, charity, magnanimity, and resolution in the face of death; Jīmūtavāhana, however bizarre his setting, is one of the ideals of Buddhism, a man seized with the conviction that to sacrifice oneself for others is the highest duty. Çañkhacūḍa and his mother too appear as noble in character, far superior to the savage Garuḍa. There is, it must be admitted, a decided lack of harmony between the two distinct parts of the drama, but the total effect is far from unsuccessful. Perhaps as a counterpoise to the seriousness of the last part, Harṣa has introduced effective comedy in Act III. The Vidūṣaka, Ātreya, is hideous and stupid; as he lies sleeping, covered by a mantle to protect him from the bees, the Viṭa, Çekharaka, sees him, mistakes him for his inamorata, embraces him and fondles him. Navamālikā enters, and, indignant, the Viṭa makes the Vidūṣaka, though a Brahmin, bow before her and drink alcohol. A little later Navamālikā makes fun of him before the newly married couple by painting his face with Tamūla juice.

Harṣa is fond of descriptions in the approved manner; the evening, midday, the park, the hermitage, the gardens, the fountain, the marriage festival, the hour for the bath, the mountain Malaya, the forest, the palace, are among the ordinary themes beloved in the Kāvya. In imagination and grace he is certainly inferior to Kālidāsa, but he possesses the great merit of simplicity of expression and thought; his Sanskrit is classical, and precise; his use of figures of speech and thought restrained and in good taste. There is fire in his description of a battle:[1]

astravyastaçirastraçastrakaṣaṇaiḥ kṛttottamāñge muhur
vyūḍhāsṛksariti svanatpraharaṇair gharmodvamadvahnini
āhūyājimukhe sa Kosalādhipatir bhagne pradhāne bale
ekenaiva Rumaṇvatā çaraçatair mattadvipastho hataḥ.

'Heads were cleft by the blows of swords on helmets sore smitten; blood flowed in torrents, fire flashed from the ringing strokes; when his main host had been broken, Rumaṇvant challenged in the forefront of the battle the lord of Kosala, who rode on a maddened elephant, and alone slew him with a hundred arrows.' The matching of the sound to the sense

[1] *Ratnāvalī*, iv. 6.

is admirable, while a delicate perception is evinced in the line describing the king's success in soothing the wounded queen:[1]

savyājaiḥ çapathaiḥ priyeṇa vacasā cittānuvṛttyādhikam
vailakṣyeṇa pareṇa padapatanair vākyaiḥ sakhīnāṁ muhuḥ
pratyāsattim upāgatā na hi tathā devī rudatyā yathā
prakṣālyeva tayaiva bāṣpasalilaiḥ kopo 'panītaḥ svayam.

'It was not so much by my false oaths of devotion, my loving words, my coaxing, my depths of dejection, and falling at her feet, or the advice of her friends, that the queen was appeased as that her anger was wiped away by the cleansing water of her own bitter tears.' Pretty, if not appropriate, is the king's address to the fire:[2]

virama virama vahne muñca dhūmānubandham: prakaṭayasi
kim uccair arciṣāṁ cakravālam?
virahahutabhujāhaṁ yo na dagdhaḥ priyāyāḥ: pralayadahana-
bhāsā tasya kiṁ tvaṁ karoṣi?

'Stay, stay, fire; cease thy constant smoke; why dost thou raise aloft thy circle of flames? What canst thou avail against me, whom the fire of severance from my beloved, fierce as the flame that shall consume the universe, could not consume?' There is excellent taste and propriety in Vatsa's address to the dead Kosala king:[3] *mṛtyur api te çlāghyo yasya çatravo 'py evaṁ puruṣakāraṁ varṇayanti.* 'Even death for thee is glorious when even thy foes must thus depict thy manly prowess.' Such a phrase may reveal to us the true Harṣa himself, the winner of many victories, and the hero of one great disaster.

The *Nāgānanda* strikes varied notes; there is fire and enthusiasm in the assurances which Mitrāvasu gives the prince of the swift overthrow of his enemy, Matañga, at the hands of his faithful Siddhas, will he but give the word:[4]

saṁsarpadbhiḥ samantāt kṛtasakalaviyanmārgayānair vimānaiḥ
kurvāṇāḥ prāvṛṣīva sthagitaravirucaḥ çyāmatāṁ vāsarasya
ete yātāç ca sadyas tava vacanam itaḥ prāpya yuddhāya siddhāḥ
siddhaṁ codvṛttaçatrukṣayabhayavinamadrājakaṁ te svarājyam.

'With their chariots, meeting together and o'erspreading the whole surface of the sky as they speed along, darkening the day

[1] *Ratnāvalī*, iv. 1. [2] *Ibid.*, iv. 16.
[3] *Ibid.*, iv. 6/7. Cf. *Priyadarçikā*, i. on Vindhyaketu's death.
[4] iii. 15.

as when the sun's rays are hidden in the rain, my Siddhas await but the bidding to fare forthwith hence to the battle; but say the word and thy haughty foe shall fall, and thy kingdom be restored to thee, while the princes bow before thee in fear of his fate.'

Jīmūtavāhana, however, has other views of his duty:[1]

svaçarīram api parārthe yaḥ khalu dadyām ayācitaḥ kṛpayā
rājyasya kṛte sa katham prāṇivadhakrauryam anumanye?

'Gladly, unasked, would I give my own life for another in compassion; how then could I consent to the cruel slaughter of men merely to win a realm?' The saying is essential to the drama, for it leads immediately to the determination of the prince to sacrifice himself for the Nāga.

There is dignity and force in the admonition addressed by the dying hero to the repentant Garuḍa who begs him to command him:[2]

nityam prāṇātipātāt prativirama kuru prākkṛte cānutāpam
yatnāt puṇyapravāhaṁ samupacinu diçan sarvasattveṣv abhītim
magnaṁ yenātra nainaḥ phalati parimitaprāṇihiṅsāttam etad
durgāḍhāpāravārer lavaṇapalam iva kṣiptam antar hradasya.

'Cease for ever from taking life; repent of thy past misdeeds; eagerly accumulate a store of merit, freeing all creatures from fear of thee, so that, lost in the infinite stream of thy goodness, the sin of slaying creatures, in number limited, may cease to fructify, even as a morsel of salt cast in the unfathomable depths of a great lake.'

Though Buddhist the drama, the benediction is enough to show how effectively the spirit of the Nāṭikā has been introduced into the legend:[3]

dhyānavyājam upetya cintayasi kāṁ unmīlya cakṣuḥ kṣaṇam?
paçyānaṅgaçarāturaṁ janaṁ imaṁ trātāpi no rakṣasi
mithyākāruṇiko 'si nirghṛṇataras tvattaḥ kuto 'nyaḥ pumān?
serṣyam Māravadhūbhir ity abhihito Buddho[4] *jinaḥ pātu vaḥ.*

'"Feigned is thy trance; of what fair one dost thou think? Open thine eyes for a moment and gaze on us whom love doth

[1] iii. 17. [2] v. 25. [3] i. 1.
[4] Or *bodhau*, 'on his enlightenment.'

drive mad. Protector art thou; save thou us. False is thy compassion; could there be any man more pitiless than thou?" May he, whom Māra's beauties thus addressed, the Buddha, the conqueror, protect you.'

But Harṣa's chief merit is undoubtedly shown in erotic verses as in the description of the shyness of the new-made bride in the *Nāgānanda*:[1]

dṛṣṭā dṛṣṭim adho dadhāti kurute nālāpam ābhāṣitā
çayyāyām parivṛtya tiṣṭhati balād āliṅgitā vepate
niryāntīṣu sakhīṣu vāsabhavanān nirgantum cvehate
jātā vāmatayaiva me 'dya sutarām prītyai navoḍhā priyā.

'Looked at, she casts down her face; addressed, she gives no reply; with head averted she lies on the couch; forcibly embraced, she trembles; when her maidens leave her chamber, she seeks also to depart; perverse though she be, my new-wed love delights me more and more.' The accuracy of the aim of love as an archer is described in the *Ratnāvalī*:[2]

manaḥ prakṛtyaiva calaṁ durlakṣyaṁ ca tathāpi me
anaṅgena kathaṁ viddhaṁ samaṁ sarvaçilīmukhāiḥ.

'Mind is naturally mobile and hard to find; nevertheless mine has been pierced by love at once with all his darts.' In entire harmony with Indian taste Harṣa dwells on the points of physical perfection in the adored one in the *Nāgānanda*:[3]

khedāya stanabhāra eṣa kim u te madhyasya hāro 'paras
tāmyaty ūruyugaṁ nitambabharataḥ kāñcyānayā kim punaḥ
çaktiḥ padayugasya noruyugalaṁ voḍhuṁ kuto nūpurau
svāṅgair eva vibhūṣitāsi vahasi kleçāya kiṁ maṇḍanam?

'The burden of thy bosom serves to weary thy waist; why then add the weight of thy necklace? Thy thighs are wearied by the bearing of thy hips; why then thy girdle of bells? Thy feet can barely carry the load of thy thighs; why add thine anklets? When in every limb thou dost possess such grace, why dost thou wear ornaments to thy weariness?' Harṣa is also capable of expressing a deeper side of love, as when the king in the *Ratnāvalī*[4] fancies that Vāsavadattā has been driven to suicide by his faithlessness:

[1] iii. 4. [2] iii. 2.
[3] iv. 7. [4] iii. 15.

samārūḍhaprītiḥ praṇayabahumānād anudinam
vyalīkaṁ vīkṣyedaṁ kṛtam akṛtapūrvaṁ khalu mayā
priyā muñcaty adya sphuṭam asahanā jīvitam asau
prakṛṣṭasya premṇaḥ skhalitam aviṣahyaṁ hi bhavati.

'My beloved, whose love for me waxed daily because of my affection and respect, has seen my falsity which she has never known before, and now assuredly she seeks to lay life aside in despair; for unendurable is a wrong against a noble love.'

5. *The Language and the Metres of Harṣa's Dramas*

Harṣa's Sanskrit is of the usual classical type, eschewing any deviation from the beaten paths, and his Prākrits, mainly Çauraseni with Māhārāṣṭrī in the verses, offer nothing of special interest, beyond evidence of his careful study of Prākrit grammar.[1]

His use of metrical forms, on the other hand, marks the tendency to reject the simplicity of the earlier dramatists, and to insist on the use of the more elaborate metres, which in themselves are wholly undramatic, but give a much wider range of opportunity for the exhibition of merits of description. Harṣa's favourite is the Çārdūlavikrīḍita, which occurs 23 times in the *Ratnāvalī*, 20 times in the *Priyadarçikā*, and 30 times in the *Nāgānanda*; the Sragdharā takes second place with 11, 8, and 17 occurrences. The Çloka occurs in the *Ratnāvalī* (9), and the *Nāgānanda* (24), the frequency in the latter being due to the more epic character of the piece; its absence from the *Priyadarçikā* is marked. The Āryā occurs 9 times each in the Nāṭikās, and 16 times in the *Nāgānanda*. The *Priyadarçikā* suggests by its content immaturity, and its poverty in metres supports this view; it has but seven in all, including Indravajrā, Vasantatilaka (6), Mālinī, and Çikhariṇī. The *Nāgānanda* has also Çālinī and Hariṇī, in common with the *Ratnāvalī*, and Drutavilambita, while the *Ratnāvalī* adds Puṣpitāgrā, Pṛthvī, and Praharṣiṇī. That play has 5 Prākrit Āryās and 1 Gīti, the other two 3 Āryās apiece, while the *Ratnāvalī* contains a pretty pair of rhymed verses, each with Pādas of 12 morae.

[1] Māgadhī is found in the *Nāgānanda* spoken by the servant. On the variation of forms in the northern and southern editions see Barnett, JRAS. 1921, p. 589.

6. *Mahendravikramavarman*

Almost a contemporary to a day of Harṣa was Mahendravikramavarman, son of the Pallava king Siṅhaviṣṇuvarman, and himself a king with the styles of Avanibhājana, Guṇabhara, and Mattavilāsa, all alluded to in his play,[1] who ruled in Kāñcī, the scene of his drama, in the first quarter of the seventh century A.D.[2] Chance rather than any special merit has preserved for us his Prahasana,[3] which is so far the only early farce published, and which has special interest as it comes from the south, and, as we have seen, shows signs of the same technique as that of Bhāsa. Thus the play is opened by the director at the close of the Nāndī, which is not preserved, and the prologue is styled Sthāpanā, and not, as usual, Prastāvanā. We have also a reference to Karpaṭa as the writer of a text-book for thieves, as in the *Cārudatta* of Bhāsa, but there is an essential difference in the fact that great care is taken in the prologue to set out at length the merits of the author as well as the name of the drama.

The director introduces the play by a dialogue in which he by skilled flattery induces his first wife to aid him in the work, despite her annoyance at his taking to himself of a younger bride, and the transition to the actual drama is accomplished as in Bhāsa by his being interrupted in the midst of a verse by a cry from behind the scene, which leads him to complete his stanza by mentioning the appearance of the chief actor and his companion. They are a Çaiva mendicant of the skull-bearing order, a Kapālin, and his damsel, Devasomā by name. Both are intoxicated, and the maiden asks for her companion's aid to prevent her from falling; he would hold her if he could, but his own condition hinders aid; in remorse he proposes to forswear strong drink, but the lady entreats him not for her sake thus to break

[1] The *Mattavilāsa*, ed. TSS. lv. 1917.

[2] EI. iv. 152; *South Ind. Inscr.* i. 29 f.; G. Jouveau-Dubreuil, *The Pallavas*, pp. 37 ff.

[3] A *Sarvacarita* is attributed to a Bāṇa in Rājarāma Çāstrin's *Sūcīpatra*, but it may really be Vāmana Bhaṭṭa Bāṇa's as is the *Pārvatīpariṇaya* (against Ettinghausen, *Harṣa Vardhana*, pp. 122 f.). The *Mukuṭatāḍitaka* of Bāṇa is cited in Caṇḍapāla's comm. on the *Nalacampū*, p. 227.

his penance, and he joyfully abandons the rash project, praising instead his rule of life:[1]

peyā surā priyatamāmukham īkṣitavyam: grāhyaḥ svabhāvalalito 'vikṛtaç ca veṣaḥ
yenedam īdṛçam adṛçyata mokṣavartma: dīrghayur astu bhagavān sa pinākapāṇiḥ.

'Long live the god who bears the trident and who has revealed to men this as the way of salvation, to drink brandy, to gaze on the face of one's beloved, to wear beautiful and becoming raiment.' He is reminded by his companions that the Arhants have a very different definition of the path of salvation, but he has little trouble in disposing of them:

karyasya niḥsaṁçayam ātmahetoḥ: sarūpatāṁ hetubhir abhyupetya
duḥkhasya kāryaṁ sukham āmanantaḥ: svenaiva vākyena hatā varākāḥ.

'They establish that an effect, as self-caused, is of the same nature as its causes; when, therefore, they declare that pleasure is the effect of pain, the poor fools contradict their own dogmas.' There follows a complimentary description of Kāñcī, and a careful parallel between the tavern where the pair are seeking more charity and a scene of sacrifice; the Kapālin also discovers that Surā has a celestial origin; it is none other than the form taken by the god of love when burnt by the flame from Çiva's eye, a conclusion heartily accepted by his friend. The two are successful in attaining alms, but the tragic discovery is made that the skull, which serves as begging bowl, and which seems indeed at first to be the *raison d'être* of the Kapālin, is lost, though he consoles himself by reflecting that it was only a sign and that his occupation is still intact. A search through Kāñcī follows, and suspicion falls on a Buddhist monk, Çākyabhikṣu, who is lamenting the fact that despite the excellent fare he has received the law forbids the enjoyment of strong drink and women; he concludes that the true gospel of the Buddha contained no such ridiculous restrictions, and expresses his desire to benefit the whole community by discovering the authentic text.

[1] This verse is attributed to Bhāsa by Somadeva in his *Yaçastilaka*; Peterson, *Reports*, ii. 46.

Naturally, when challenged, he denies that his begging bowl is that of the Kapālin, and blesses the master for his good sense in insisting on shaving the head, since it prevents the damsel from succeeding in her well-meant effort to aid her companion by pulling his hair. His arguments as to the identity of his bowl are unconvincing to the Kapālin:

> *dṛṣṭāni vastūni mahīsamudra—: mahīdharādīni mahānti mohāt*
> *apahnuvānasya sutaḥ kathaṁ tvam: alpaṁ na nihnotum alaṁ kapālam?*

'Thou art the son of one who denies in his folly things that we see, the earth, the ocean, mountains and so forth; how then art thou not ready to deny so small a thing as a bowl?' Moreover, when the Buddhist, politely and with commendable charity, picks up Devasomā when her fruitless assault on his locks lands her on the ground, he accuses him of taking her in marriage and invokes punishment on this violator of the rights of Brahmins. A Pāçupata, a more respectable type of Çaiva sectarian, comes on the scene and is appealed to as an arbitrator, but finds the task too difficult; both claimants proudly assert their adherence to a creed which forbids lying, and the Buddhist recites in addition the whole list of moral rules which makes up the Çikṣāpada. The obvious arguments from colour and shape in favour of the Buddhist are made out by his rival to be no more than signs of his skill in changing objects at pleasure. Finally the Pāçupata suggests that they must take the matter before a court. *En route*, however, a diversion is made by an Unmattaka, or madman, who has rescued the skull from a dog, the real thief; he first appears willing to give it as a present to the Pāçupata, who haughtily rejects the horrible object, but suggests the Kapālin as the recipient; then he changes his mind, but, annoyed by the cry of 'mad', asks the Kapālin to hold the skull and to show him the madman; the Kapālin, nothing loth, accepts the skull, and misdirects the madman. All are now happy; the Kapālin makes a handsome apology to the Buddhist monk, and the usual Bharatavākya with a reference to the ruling king, the author, concludes the work.

The author undoubtedly shows a considerable knowledge of the tenets of the Buddhists, and the play is not unamusing, though the subject is much too trivial for the pains taken to deal with it. The style is certainly appropriate to the subject-matter; it is like that of Harṣa, simple and elegant, while many of the verses are not without force and beauty. In the prose speeches of the Kapālin, however, we have occasional premonitions [1] of the unwieldy compounds of Bhavabhūti. There is, as in all the later Prahasanas, a certain incongruity between the triviality of the subject-matter and the elaboration of the form but the king has the merit of avoiding the gross vulgarity which marks normally the later works of this type.

Short as is the play, it shows a variety of Prākrits, for of the *dramatis personae* only the Kapālin and the Pāçupata speak Sanskrit, while the madman, the Buddhist, and Devasomā talk in Prākrit. That of the Buddhist and of Devasomā is practically Çauraseni, but the madman uses Māgadhī.[2] The Prākrits show some of the signs of antiquity which have been seen in Bhāsa's dramas; thus forms of the plural in *āṇi* and *ññ* in lieu of *ṇṇ* are found, doubtless as a result of the influence of Bhāsa. The frequency of such forms as *aho nu khalu* and *kiṁ nu khalu* is precisely in the manner of Bhāsa, and mention may be made of the employment of *mā* with the infinitive in Prākrit in a prohibition.

The variety of metres is large in view of the brief extent of the play. There are nine different stanzas employed; five each of the Çloka and Çārdūlavikrīḍita, three each of Indravajrā type and Āryā, two each of Vaṅçasthā type and Vasantatilaka, the solitary Prākrit verse being of the former kind, and one each of Rucirā, Mālinī, and Sragdharā.[3]

[1] pp. 7, 8, 9.

[2] So the Unmattaka in the *Pratijñāyaugandharāyaṇa* of Bhāsa.

[3] Antiquity is claimed by the editors of *Caturbhāṇī* (1922) for the Bhāṇas, *Ubhayābhisārikā* of Vararuci, *Padmaprābhṛtaka* of Çūdraka, *Dhūrtaviṭasaṁvāda* of Īçvaradatta, *Pādatāḍitaka* of Ārya Çyāmilaka, but no reliance can be placed on the first two ascriptions, and none of the plays need be older than 1000 A. D. Their technique is similar to that of the *Mattavilāsa*.

VIII

BHAVABHŪTI

1. *The Date of Bhavabhūti*

Bhavabhūti tells us in his prologues that he belonged to a family of Brahmins styled Udumbaras, of Padmapura, apparently in Vidarbha, who were of the Kāçyapa Gotra and followed the Taittirīya school of the Black Yajurveda. His full name was Çrīkaṇṭha Nīlakaṇṭha, son of Nīlakaṇṭha and Jātūkarṇī, grandson of Bhaṭṭa Gopāla, fifth in descent from Mahākavi, a Vājapeya sacrificer, famed for his scholarship. He was skilled in grammar, rhetoric, and logic, or perhaps in grammar, logic, and Mīmāṅsā,[1] if we may believe the legend that he was a pupil of Kumārila preserved in one manuscript of the *Mālatīmādhava*, which complicates the matter by styling the author also Umvekācārya, a commentator on Kumārila's works. As he expressly mentions his knowledge of the Vedas, the Upaniṣads, Sāṁkhya and Yoga, and gives Jñānanidhi as his teacher, we may probably discard this suggestion. The whole three of his plays were performed for the feast of the Lord Kālapriya, who is normally identified with Mahākāla of Ujjayinī, though the scene of the *Mālatīmādhava* is laid in Padmāvatī. We may conjecture, therefore, that he left his home and proceeded to Ujjayinī or Padmāvatī in search of fortune. From the silence in his dramas on any good luck, it is strange to find that Kalhaṇa in the *Rājataraṅgiṇī*[2] expressly asserted that he was a member of the entourage of Yaçovarman of Kanyakubja, who was defeated by Muktāpīḍa Lalitāditya of Kashmir, not earlier, probably, than A.D. 736. A further indication of date is afforded by the

[1] *Pādavākyapramāṇajña*; see Belvalkar, HOS. XXI. xxxvi. ff. where the attempt to identify Padmapura with Padmāvatī as Pavāyā near Narvār and the shrine of Kālapriya with Kālp on the Jumna is disproved. On his Vedic studies, see Keith, JRAS. 1914, pp. 729 f. He knew the *Kāmasūtra*; JBRAS. xviii. 109 f.

[2] iv. 144. On the dates, see Stein's Intr., § 85, and notes on iv. 126 and 134.

reference in Vākpati's *Gaüḍavaha*[1] to Bhavabhūti's ocean of poetry; the poem is a prelude to a description in Prākrit of Yaçovarman's defeat of a Gauḍa king, and, as it seems never to have been finished, it presumably was interrupted by the king's own defeat. We must, therefore, place Bhavabhūti somewhere about A.D. 700. The silence of Bāṇa regarding him suggests that he was not known to him, while it is certain that he knew Kālidāsa; the first writer on poetics to cite him is Vāmana.[2] Verses not in our extant dramas are ascribed to him, so he may have written other works than the three dramas, two Nāṭakas on the Rāma legend and a Prakaraṇa, which we have. His friendship with actors is a trait to which he himself refers, and efforts have been made to trace in his works evidence of revision for stage purposes.

2. *The Three Plays*

Perhaps the earliest of the works is the *Mahāvīracarita*, but the evidence for this is uncertain, and there is no reason to assign it definitely to an earlier date than the *Mālatīmādhava*; both antedate, perhaps considerably, the *Uttararāmacarita*. The *Mālatīmādhava*,[3] as a Prakaraṇa, should have a plot invented by the author, and this is true to the extent that the combination of elements which make up the intrigue is clearly the poet's, though the main motif of the story and the chief episodes can all be paralleled in the Kathā literature even as we have it.

Bhūrivasu, minister of the king of Padmāvatī, has asked an old friend, now turned nun, Kāmandakī, to arrange a marriage between his daughter, Mālatī, and Mādhava, son of an old friend Devarāta, minister of the king of Vidarbha, who has sent his son to Padmāvatī, mainly in the hope that Bhūrivasu would remember a compact of their student days to marry their children to each other. The obstacle in the way is the desire of

[1] v. 799.

[2] i. 2. 12 (anonymous). That Bhavabhūti knew Bhāsa may be assumed; his use of the rare Daṇḍaka metre may be borrowed, and similarities between *Uttararāmacarita*, Act II and *Svapnavāsavadattā*, Act I, &c., exist.

[3] Ed. R. G. Bhandarkar, Bombay, 1876 (2nd ed., 1905); trs. Wilson, ii. 1 ff.; G. Strehly, Paris, 1885; L. Fritze, Leipzig, 1884. Cf. Gawroński, *Les sources de quelques drames indiens*, pp. 43 ff.; Cimmini, *Osservacioni sul rasa nel Mālatīmādhava*, Naples, 1915.

Nandana, the king's boon companion (*narmasuhṛd*), to wed Mālatī with the king's approval. Kāmandakī, therefore, decides to arrange the meeting of the young people and their marriage, so as to be able to present the king with a *fait accompli.* Both hero and heroine have friends, Makaranda and Madayantikā, sister of Nandana, and, after Acts I and II have made the main lovers sufficiently enamoured, in Act III, when the lovers are meeting in a temple of Çiva, Madayantikā is in danger of death from an escaped tiger, and is rescued by Makaranda, not without injury. These two then are deeply in love. But Act IV shows us the king resolved on the mating of Mālatī and Nandana; Mādhava, despairing of success through Kāmandakī's aid alone, decides to win the favour of the ghouls of the cemetery by an offering of fresh flesh; this leads him in Act V to a great adventure, for on his ghastly errand he hears cries from a temple near by, and rushes in just in time to save Mālatī whom the priest Aghoraghaṇṭa and his acolyte Kapālakuṇḍalā were about to offer in sacrifice to the goddess Cāmuṇḍā. He slays Aghoraghaṇṭa. In Act VI Kapālakuṇḍalā swears revenge, but for the moment all goes well; Mālatī is to wed Nandana, but by a clever stratagem Makaranda takes her place at the temple where she goes to worship before her marriage, and, while Mādhava and Mālatī flee, Makaranda is led home as a bride. In Act VII we hear how poor Nandana has been repulsed by his bride; Madayantikā comes to rebuke her sister-in-law, finds her lover, and elopes. But they are pursued, as they make their way to rejoin their friends, and in Act VIII we learn that the fugitives were succoured by Mādhava and so splendidly routed their foes that the king, learning of it, gladly forgives the runaways. But in the tumult Mālatī has been stolen away by Kapālakuṇḍalā, and Act IX is devoted to Mādhava's wild search with his friend to find her, which would have been fruitless, had not Saudāminī, a pupil of Kāmandakī, by good fortune come on Kapālakuṇḍalā and rescued her victim. A scene of lament at the beginning of Act X is interrupted by the return of the lovers, and the king approves the marriage.

The source of the *Mahāvīracarita*[1] is very different; it is an

[1] Ed. F. H. Trithen, London, 1848; NS. 1901; trs. J. Pickford, London, 1892.

effort to describe the main story of the *Rāmāyaṇa* by the use of dialogue narrating the main events, but a deliberate bid for dramatic effect is made through treating the whole story as the feud of Rāvaṇa, and his plots to ruin Rāma. The motif is introduced in Act I; at Viçvāmitra's hermitage Rāma and Lakṣmaṇa see and love Sītā and Ūrmilā, daughters of Janaka of Videha. Rāvaṇa, however, sends a messenger to demand Sītā's hand in marriage, but Rāma defeats the demon Tāḍakā, and Viçvāmitra gives him celestial weapons, and summons Çiva's bow, which, if he bends, he may have Sītā. The bow is broken and Rāvaṇa's envoy departs in rage. In Act II Rāvaṇa's minister Mālyavant plots with his sister Çūrpaṇakhā how to make good the defeat sustained; a letter from Paraçurāma suggests a means; they incite him to avenge the breaking of Çiva's bow. Paraçurāma acts on the hint in his usual haughty pride; he arrives at Mithilā, insults Rāma and demands a conflict. In the next Act the exchange of insults continues; Vasiṣṭha, Viçvāmitra, Çatānanda, Janaka, and Daçaratha in vain seek to avoid a struggle between the youth and the savage Brahmin, slayer of his own mother and exterminator of Kṣatriyas, but they fail. Act IV reveals that Paraçurāma has been defeated, and has saluted with respect the victor; Mālyavant bethinks him of a new device, Çūrpaṇakhā will assume the dress of Mantharā, servant of Kaikeyī, Daçaratha's favourite wife, and destroy the concord of the royal family. That family is in excellent spirits; Rāma is at Mithilā with his father-in-law when the supposed Mantharā appears, bearing an alleged letter from Kaikeyī asking him to secure Daçaratha's fulfilment of two boons he had once granted her; these are the selection of her son Bharata as crown prince and Rāma's banishment for fourteen years. Meanwhile Bharata and his uncle Yudhājit have asked Daçaratha to crown Rāma forthwith; he is only too willing, but Rāma arrives, reports the demands of Kaikeyī and insists on leaving for the forest, accompanied by Sītā and Lakṣmaṇa, while Bharata is bidden remain, though he treats himself but as vicegerent. In Act V a dialogue between the aged vultures Jaṭāyu and Sampāti informs us of Rāma's doings in the forest and destruction of demons; Sampāti is uneasy and bids Jaṭāyu guard Rāma well. Jaṭāyu fares on his duty, sees Sītā stolen by Rāvaṇa, and is slain in her defence.

We see Rāma and Lakṣmaṇa in mourning; they wander in the forest, save, and receive tidings from, an ascetic; Vibhīṣaṇa, brother of Rāvaṇa, exiled from Lañkā, wishes to meet them at Ṛṣyamukha where also are the jewels dropped by Sītā in her despair. Vālin, however, on the instigation of Mālyavant, seeks to forbid their entry; Rāma persists and slays his foe, who bids his brother Sugrīva lend his aid to Rāma's search. In Act VI Mālyavant appears desolated by the failure of his plans; he hears of Hanumant's setting Lañkā on fire. Rāvaṇa appears, doting on Sītā; in vain Mandodarī warns him of the advance of the enemy, but his disbelief is rudely dispelled; Añgada bears terms of surrender of Sītā and humiliation before Lakṣmaṇa; he refuses, and seeks to punish the envoy, who escapes. He then goes out to battle, described at length by Indra and Citraratha, who, as divine, can watch it from the sky; Rāvaṇa performs feats of valour, but Hanumant revives with ambrosia Rāma and his comrades, and Rāvaṇa finally falls dead beside his gallant son, Meghanāda. In Act VII the cities Lañkā and Alakā, represented by their deities, exchange condolences; it is reported that Sītā has by the fire ordeal proved her chastity. The whole of Rāma's party are now triumphant; an aerial journey carries them to the north, where they are welcomed by Rāma's brothers and Daçaratha's widows, and Viçvāmitra crowns Rāma.

The *Uttararāmacarita* [1] is based on the last and late book of the *Rāmāyaṇa*. Janaka has departed; Sītā *enceinte* is sad and Rāma is consoling her. News is brought from Vasiṣṭha; he bids the king meet every wish of his wife, but rank first of all his duty to his people. Lakṣmaṇa reports that the painter, who has been depicting the scenes of their wanderings, has finished; they enter the gallery, and live over again their experiences, Rāma consoling Sītā for her cruel separation from her husband and friends; incidentally he prays the holy Gañgā to protect her and that the magic arms he has may pass spontaneously to his sons. Sītā, wearied, falls asleep. The Brahmin Durmukha, who has been sent to report on the feeling of the people, reveals that they doubt Sītā's purity. Rāma has already promised Sītā to let her visit again the forest, scene of her wanderings; he now decides

[1] Ed. and trs. S. K. Belvalkar, HOS. xxi–xxiii; trs. C. H. Tawney, Calcutta, 1874; P. d'Alheim, Bois-le-Roi, 1906.

that, when she has gone, she must not return, and the command is obeyed. Act II shows an ascetic Ātreyī in converse with the spirit of the woods, Vāsantī; we learn that Rāma is celebrating the horse sacrifice, and that Vālmīki is bringing up two fine boys entrusted to him by a goddess. Rāma enters, sword in hand, to lay an impious Çūdra Çambūka; slain, the latter, purified by this death, appears in spirit form and leads his benefactor to Agastya's hermitage. In Act III two rivers Tamasā and Muralā converse; they tell us that Sītā abandoned would have killed herself but Gañga preserved her, and entrusted her two sons, born in her sorrow, to Vālmīki to train. Then Sītā in a spirit form appears, unseen by mortals; she is permitted by Gañgā to revisit under Tamasā's care the scenes of her youth. Rāma also appears. At the sight of the scene of their early love, both faint, but Sītā, recovering, touches unseen Rāma who recovers only to relapse and be revived again. Finally Sītā departs, leaving Rāma fainting.

The scene changes in Act IV to the hermitage of Janaka, retired from kingly duties; Kauçalyā, Rāma's mother, meets him and both forget self in consoling each other. They are interrupted by the merry noises of the children of the hermitage; one especially is pre-eminent; questioned, he is Lava, who has a brother Kuça and who knows Rāma only from Vālmīki's work. The horse from Rāma's sacrifice approaches, guarded by soldiers. Lava joins his companions, but, unlike them, he is undaunted by the royal claim of sovereignty and decides to oppose it. Act V passes in an exchange of martial taunts between him and Candraketu, who guards the horse for Rāma, though each admires the other. In Act VI a Vidyādhara and his wife, flying in the air, describe the battle of the youthful heroes and the magic weapons they use. The arrival of Rāma interrupts the conflict. He admires Lava's bravery, which Candraketu extols; he questions him, but finds that the magic weapons came to him spontaneously. Kuça enters from Bharata's hermitage, whither he has carried Vālmīki's poem to be dramatized. The father admires the two splendid youths, who are, though he knows it not, his own sons.

In Act VII all take part in a supernatural spectacle devised by Bharata and played by the Apsarases. Sītā's fortunes after her abandonment are depicted; she weeps and casts herself in the Bhāgīrathī; she reappears, supported by Pṛthivī, the earth goddess, and Gaṅgā, each carrying a new-born infant. Pṛthivī declaims against the harshness of Rāma, Gaṅgā excuses his acts; both ask Sītā to care for the children until they are old enough to hand over to Vālmīki, when she can act as she pleases. Rāma is carried away, he believes the scene real, now he intervenes in the dialogue, now he faints. Arundhatī suddenly appears with Sītā, who goes to her husband and brings him back to consciousness. The people acclaim the queen, and Vālmīki presents to them Rāma's sons, Kuça and Lava.

Indian tradition asserts that of the *Mahāvīracarita* Bhavabhūti wrote only up to stanza 46 of Act V, the rest being completed by Subrahmaṇya Kavi; if this were to be taken as certain, it would be a sign that that drama was never completed, and so was the last work of the author, but the maturity ot the *Uttararāmacarita* makes it clear that, whatever there may be of truth in the story, the incompleteness cannot have been due to lack of time.

3. *Bhavabhūti's Dramatic Art and Style*

It is difficult to doubt that Bhavabhūti must have been induced to write his Prakaraṇa in an effort to vie with the author of the *Mṛcchakaṭikā*. It is true that no such humour as lightens that drama is found in the *Mālatimādhava*, but that was doubtless due to Bhavabhūti's own temperament; conscious that he had no gift[1] in that direction, he omitted boldly the part of the Vidūṣaka which he could clearly not have handled effectively. But in doing so he lessened greatly his resources, and has to select for his theme in lieu of comic relief incidents of the terrible and horrible type blended with the supernatural. The main love-story, with the episode of the two young lovers, whose desires are thwarted by interposition of a powerful suitor, and whose affairs are mixed up with those of two other lovers, both affections ending in elopements, occurs in the *Kathāsarit-*

[1] The deplorable effort in Act IV of the *Uttararāmacarita* at deliberate humour shows his weakness in this regard. A certain measure of irony of situation is all that he ever attains, e.g. in connexion with Rāma's ignorance of the identity of his sons, cf. *Uttararāmacarita*, iv. 22/3; vi. 19/20.

sāgara,[1] and in that collection as elsewhere[2] we find the motifs of the sacrifice of a maiden by a magician and the offering of flesh to the demons to obtain their aid. But the credit is due to Bhavabhūti of combining them in an effective enough whole, and of producing in Act V a spectacle at once horrible and exciting. He has also improved his authorities in detail; the escaped tiger replaces the more conventional elephant; and the intrigue is more effectually welded together by making Madayantikā the sister of Nandana, the king's favourite. Further, he has introduced the machinery of Kāmandakī and her assistants Avalokitā and Saudāminī. This again is taken from the romance; Daṇḍin, as Brahmanical an author as Bhavabhūti himself, adopts Buddhist nuns as go-betweens, and Kāmandakī's offices are perfectly honourable; she merely undertakes, at the request of the parents, to subtract Mālatī from marriage with one unworthy of her and not her father's choice. The influence of Kālidāsa explains Act IX, which is a manifest effort to rival Act IV of the *Vikramorvaçī*, which it excels in tragic pathos, if it is inferior to it in grace and charm. The same Act has a flagrant imitation of the *Meghadūta* in Mādhava's idea of sending a cloud message to his lost love, and is full of verbal reminiscences of that text.

The plot, however interesting, is extremely badly knit together; the action is dependent to an absurd degree on accident; Mālatī twice on the verge of death is twice saved by mere chance. Moreover, the characters live apart from all contact with real life; they are in a city like the characters of the *Mṛcchakaṭikā*, but seem to exist in a world of their own in which the escape of tigers and the abduction of maidens with murderous intent cause no surprise. There is little individuality in hero or heroine, though the shy modesty of the latter contrasts with the boldness of Madayantikā, who flings herself at Makaranda's head. A friend of Mādhava, Kalahaṅsa, is asserted later[3] to be a Viṭa, but has nothing characteristic, and probably the assertion is without ground.

The *Mahāvīracarita* lacks the novelty of the *Mālatīmādhava*,

[1] xiii.

[2] KSS. xviii.; xxv. (Açokadatta and the Rākṣasas): cxxi. (Kāpālika and Madanamañjarī); DKC. vii. (Mantragupta and Kanakalekhā).

[3] Kumārasvāmin, *Pratāparudrīya*, i. 38.

but Bhavabhūti's effort to give some unity to the plot is commendable, though it is unsuccessful. The fatal error, of course, is the narration of events in long speeches in lieu of action. The conversations of Mālyavant and Çūrpaṇakhā, of Jaṭāyu and Sampāti, of Indra and Citraratha, and of Alakā and Lañkā are wholly undramatic; the word-painting of the places of their adventures, as seen from the aerial car on the return home, has not the slightest conceivable right to a place in drama. The elaborate exchange of passionate and grandiose defiances between Rāma and Paraçurāma which drags through two Acts does credit to the rhetorical powers of the dramatist, but is wearisome and a mere hindrance to the action. On the other hand, the scene where Bharata determines to act as vicegerent and that between Vālin and Sugrīva are effective, while with excellent taste Vālin is made an enemy, who opposes Rāma under bad advice, and the treachery and fraternal strife of the *Rāmāyaṇa* disappear for good. The characterization is feeble; Rāma and Sītā are tediously of one pattern without shadow on their virtue, and neither Mālyavant nor Rāvaṇa surpasses mediocrity.

The *Uttararāmacarita* reaches no higher level as a drama; he has a period of twelve years to cover, as he had fourteen in the *Mahāvīracarita,* and to produce effective unity would be hard for any author; Bhavabhūti has made no serious effort to this end; he has contented himself with imagining a series of striking pictures. The first Act is admirably managed; the tragic irony of Sītā's gazing on the pictures of a sorrow over for good just on the verge of an even crueller fate, and of asking for a visit to see the old scenes of her unhappiness as well as her joy, which affords the king the means of immediately abandoning her, is perfectly brought out. Yet excuses are made for the king; it is the voice of duty that he hears; his counsellors who might have stayed his rash act are away. The scene in Act III, when Sītā sees and forgives her spouse, is admirable in its delicacy of the portrayal of her gradual but generous surrender to the proof that, though harsh, he deeply loved her. Lava again is a fine study in his pride, followed by submission to the great king when approached with courtesy, but the Vidyādhara's tale of the use of the magic weapons, doubtless an effort to vie with Bhāravi's *Kirātārjunīya*, is ineffective. The last Act, however, reveals

Bhavabhūti at his best; the plain tale of the *Rāmāyaṇa* makes Kuça and Lava recite the story of the *Rāmāyaṇa* at a sacrifice and be recognized by their father; here a supernatural drama with goddesses as actors leads insensibly to a happy ending, for Bhavabhūti again defies tradition to attain the end, without which the drama would be defective even in our eyes. Sītā and Rāma are splendidly characterized; the one in his greatness of power and nobility of spirit, the other ethereal and spiritual, removed from the gross things of earth. Janaka and Kauçalyā are effectively drawn; their condolences have the accent of sincerity, but the other characters—there are twenty-four in all—present nothing of note. It was not within Bhavabhūti's narrow range to create figures on a generous scale; in his other dramas they are reduced to the minimum necessary for the action.

As a poem the merits of the *Uttararāmacarita* are patent and undeniable. The temper of Bhavabhūti was akin to the grand and the inspiring in nature and life; the play blends the martial fervour of Rāma and his gallant son with the haunting pathos of the fate of the deserted queen, and the forests, the mountains, the rivers in the first three Acts afford abundant opportunity for his great ability in depicting the rugged as well as the tender elements of nature; what is awe-inspiring and magnificent in its grandeur has an attraction for Bhavabhūti, which is not shown in the more limited love of nature in Kālidāsa. He excels Kālidāsa also in the last Act, for the reunion of Sītā and Rāma has a depth of sentiment, not evoked by the tamer picture of the meeting of Duḥṣanta and Çakuntalā; both Rāma and Sītā are creatures of more vital life and deeper experience than the king and his woodland love.

We find, in fact, in Bhavabhūti, in a degree unknown to Kālidāsa, child of fortune, to whom life appeared as an ordered joyous whole, the sense of the mystery of things; 'what brings things together', he says, 'is some mysterious inward tie; it is certainly not upon outward circumstances that affection rests'.[1] Self-sacrifice is a reality to Bhavabhūti; Rāma is prepared to abandon without a pang affection, compassion, and felicity, nay Sītā herself, for the sake of his people,[2] and he acts up to his resolve. Friendship is to him sacred; to guard a friend's interests

[1] *Uttararāmacarita*, vi. 12. [2] *Ibid.*, i. 12.

at the cost of one's own, to avoid in dealings with him all malice and guile, and to strive for his weal as if for one's own is the essential mark of true friendship.[1] Admirable also is his conception of love, far nobler than that normal in Indian literature; it is the same in happiness and sorrow, adapted to every circumstance of life, in which the heart finds solace, unspoiled by age, mellowing and becoming more valuable as in course of time reserve dies away, a supreme blessing attained only by those that are fortunate and after long toil.[2] The child completes the union; it ties in a common knot of union the strands of its parents' hearts.[3] Bhavabhūti was clearly a solitary soul; this is attested by the prologue of the *Mālatīmādhava*:

ye nāma kecid iha naḥ prathayanty avajñām: jānanti te
kim api tān prati naiṣa yatnaḥ
utpatsyate 'sti mama ko 'pi samānadharmā: kālo hy ayam
anavadhir vipulā ca pṛthvī.

'Those that disparage me know little; for them my effort is not made; there will or does exist some one with like nature to mine, for time is boundless and the earth is wide.' Yet we may sympathize with those who felt[4] that his art was unfit for the stage, for Bhavabhūti's style has many demerits in addition to the defects of his technique.

Bhavabhūti in fact proclaims here as his own merit richness and elevation of expression (*prauḍhatvam udāratā ca vacasām*) and depth of meaning, and we must admit that he has no small grounds for his claims. The depth of thought and grandeur which can be admitted in the case of Bhavabhūti must be measured by Indian standards, and be understood subject to the grave limitations which are imposed on any Brahmanical speculation as to existence by the orthodoxy which is as apparent in Bhavabhūti as it is in the lighter-hearted Kālidāsa. When, therefore, we are told[5] that 'with reference to Kālidāsa he holds a position such as Aeschylus holds with reference to Euripides', we must not take too seriously the comparison. No poet, in fact, suggests less readily comparison with Euripides than does Kālidāsa. He has nothing whatever of the questioning mind of the

[1] *Mahāvīracarita*, v. 59. Cf. *Uttararāmacarita*, iv. 13, 14.
[2] *Ibid.*, i. 39.
[3] *Uttararāmacarita*, iii. 18.
[4] Cf. *ibid.*, i. 5.
[5] Ryder, *The Little Clay Cart*, p. xvi.

Greek dramatist, contemporary of the Sophists, and eager inquirer into the validity of all established conventions. In style again he aims at a level of perfection of achievement, which was neither sought nor attained by Euripides. Unquestionably, if any parallel were worth making, Kālidāsa would fall to be ranked as the Sophokles of the Indian drama, for as far as any Indian poet could, 'he saw life steadily and saw it whole', and was free from the vain questionings which vexed the soul of Euripides. Bhavabhūti again cannot seriously be compared with Aischylos, for he accepted without question the Brahmanical conceptions of world order, unlike the great Athenian who sought to interpret for himself the fundamental facts of existence, and who found for them no solution in popular belief or traditional religion. There can, moreover, be no greater contrast in style than that between the simple strength of Aischylos, despite his power of brilliant imagery,[1] and the over-elaboration and exaggeration of Bhavabhūti. The distinction between Kālidāsa and his successor is of a different kind. Both accepted the traditional order, but Kālidāsa, enjoying, we may feel assured, a full measure of prosperity in the golden age of India under the Gupta empire, viewed with a determined optimism all that passed before him in life, in strange contrast to the bitterness of the denunciations of existence which Buddhism, then losing ground, has set forth as its contribution to the problems of life. Bhavabhūti, on his part, recognized with a truer insight, sharpened perhaps by the obvious inferiority of his fortunes and failure to enjoy substantial royal favour, the difficulties and sorrows of life; his theme is not the joys of a pleasure-loving great king or the vicissitudes of a Purūravas, too distant from humanity to touch our own life, but the bitter woes of Rāma and Sītā, who have for us the reality of manhood and womanhood, as many a touch reminds us:[2]

kim api kim api mandam mandam āsattiyogād: avicalitakapolaṁ jalpatoç ca krameṇa
açithilaparirambhavyāpṛtaikaikadoṣṇor: aviditagatayāmā rātrir evaṁ vyaraṅsīt.

'As slowly and gently, cheek pressed against cheek, we whispered soft nothings, each clasping the other with warm embrace, the night, whose watches had sped unnoticed, came to an end.'

[1] G. Norwood, *Greek Tragedy*, pp. 121 ff. [2] i. 27.

As regards the formal side of Bhavabhūti's style we must unquestionably admit his power of expression, which is displayed equally in all three dramas. To modern taste Bhavabhūti is most attractive when he is simple and natural, as he can be when it pleases him. Thus in Act VI of the *Mālatīmādhava* we have a pretty expression of Mādhava's joy at the words of love of him uttered by Mālatī when she has no idea of his presence near her:

mlānasya jīvakusumasya vikāsanāni : saṁtarpaṇāni sakalendriyamohanāni
ānandanāni hṛdayaikarasāyanāni : diṣṭyā mayāpy adhigatāni vacomṛtāni.

'Fortune has favoured me, for I have heard the nectar of her words that make to bloom again the faded flower of my life, delightful, disturbing every sense, causing gladness, sole elixir for my heart.' The deliberate rhyming effect is as appropriate as it is uncommon in such elaboration, and it is characteristic that the same effect is shortly afterwards repeated. Effective simplicity and directness also characterize the speech, in Sanskrit contrary to the usual rule, of Buddharakṣitā in Act VII, when she clinches the argument in favour of the elopement of Madayantikā and Makaranda:

preyān manorathasahasravṛtaḥ sa eṣaḥ : suptapramattajanam etad amātyaveçma
prauḍhaṁ tamaḥ kuru kṛtajñatayaiva bhadram : utkṣiptamūkamaṇinūpuram ehi yāmaḥ.

'Here is thy beloved, on whom a thousand times thy hopes have rested; in the minister's palace the men are asleep or drunken; impenetrable is the darkness; be grateful and show thy favour; come, let us silence our jewelled anklets by laying them aside, and depart hence.' Equally effective is the expression of the admirable advice tendered to Mādhava and Mālatī at the moment when Kāmandakī has succeeded in securing their union:

preyo mitram bandhutā vā samagrā : sarve kāmāḥ çevadhir jīvitaṁ vā
strīṇām bhartā dharmadārāç ca puṁsām : ity anyonyaṁ vatsayor jñātam astu.

'Know, my dear children, that to a wife her husband and to a husband his lawful wife are, each to each, the dearest of friends, the sum total of relationships, the completeness of desire, the perfection of treasures, even life itself.' Pretty again are the terms in which Kāmandakī laments Mālatī in Act X when she learns of her disappearance:

ā janmanaḥ pratimuhūrtaviçeṣaramyāṇy: āceṣṭitāni tava samprati tāni tāni
cāṭūni cārumadhurāṇi ca saṁsmṛtāni: dehaṁ dahanti hṛdayaṁ ca vidārayanti.

'My body is aflame and my heart torn in sunder by the memory of thy childish movements which grew more delightful every hour from thy birth, and of the beauty and sweetness of thy loving words.'

It is, therefore, the more to be regretted that Bhavabhūti was not content with simplicity, but is often too fond of elaborate and overloaded descriptions, which are fatally lacking in simplicity and intelligibility and can be fully comprehended only after careful study and examination. We must, however,. it is clear, admit that Bhavabhūti definitely improved in taste as the years went on. The latest of his dramas, the *Uttararāmacarita*, is far less obnoxious to criticism for defects of judgement than the *Mālatīmādhava*, which may be set down as an adventure in a genre unsuited to the poet's talent. There is an admirable touch in the scene in Act I of the play where Sītā, wearied, falls to rest on the pillow of Rāma's arm, that arm which no other woman can claim and which has ever lulled her to sleep, and he gazes on her in fond admiration:[1]

iyaṁ gehe lakṣmīr iyam amṛtavartir nayanayor
asāv asyāḥ sparço vapuṣi bahulaç candanarasaḥ
ayaṁ kaṇṭhe bāhuḥ çiçiramasṛṇo mauktikasaraḥ
kim asyā na preyo yadi param asahyas tu virahaḥ.

'She is Fortune herself in my home; she is a pencil of ambrosia for the eyes; her touch here on my body is as fragrant as sandal juice; her arm round my neck is cool and soft as a necklace of pearls; what in her is there that is not dear, save only the misery of separation from her?' Scarcely are the words said than the attendant enters with the word, 'It has come', which on her lips is to announce the advent of the spy whose report is to lead to Sītā's banishment, while the audience, following the words, applies it at once to the separation which Rāma was deploring,

[1] i. 38.

and which to him was the parting in the past when Rāvaṇa stole his bride.

The spontaneous regard which springs up for each other in the hearts of the two princes Lava and Candraketu when they meet is admirably depicted:[1]

yadṛcchāsampātaḥ kim u guṇagaṇānām atiçayaḥ
purāṇo vā janmāntaranibiḍabandhaḥ paricayaḥ
nijo vā sambandhaḥ kim u vidhivaçāt ko 'py avidito
mamaitasmin dṛṣṭe hṛdayam avadhānaṁ racayati?

'Is it this chance encounter, or his wealth of splendid qualities, or an ancient love, firm bound in a former birth, or a common tie of blood unknown through the might of fate, which draws close my heart to him even at first sight?'

The rebuke which Vāsantī addresses to Rāma for his treatment of Sītā, despite the loyalty of the queen, is effectively broken off by a faint:[2]

tvaṁ jīvitaṁ tvam asi me hṛdayaṁ dvitīyam
tvaṁ kaumudī nayanayor amṛtaṁ tvam aṅge
ity ādibhiḥ priyaçatair anurudhya mugdhām
tām eva çāntam athavā kim ataḥ pareṇa.

'"Thou art my life, my second heart, thou the moonlight of my eyes, the ambrosia for my body thou": with these and a hundred other endearments didst thou win her simple soul, and now alas—but what need to say more?'

Elsewhere we have less simplicity, but in these cases we must distinguish carefully between those instances in which the difficulty and complexity of expression serve to illustrate the thought, and those in which the words are made to stand in lieu of ideas. In many cases Bhavabhūti may justly claim to have achieved substantial success, even when he is not precisely simple. The effect of love on Mādhava is effectively expressed:[3]

paricchedātītaḥ sakalavacanānām aviṣayaḥ
punarjanmany asminn anubhavapathaṁ yo na gatavān
vivekapradhvaṅsād upacitamahāmohagahano
vikāraḥ ko 'py antar jaḍayati ca tāpaṁ ca kurute.

'An emotion, evading determination, inexpressible by words, never before experienced in this birth of mine, wholly confusing

[1] v. 16. [2] iii. 27. [3] i. 29.

because of the impossibility of examination, is at once numbing me within and filling me with a torment of fire.'

The poet's command of the philosophical conceptions of his day is shown in the verse following:

paricchedavyaktir bhavati na puraḥsthe 'pi viṣaye
bhavaty abhyaste 'pi smaraṇam atathābhāvavirasam
na saṁtāpacchedo himasarasi vā candramasi vā
mano niṣṭhāçūnyam bhramati ca kim apy ālikhati ca.

'Though an object be before one's gaze, determination is not easy; brought back, memory intervenes to introduce an element of falsity; neither in the cool lake nor in the moonbeams can passion be quenched; my mind, powerless to attain a fixed result, wanders, and yet records something.'

We have a further effective picture of the physical effect of love on Mādhava when he seeks to assuage his sorrows by depicting his beloved from memory:[1]

vāraṁ vāraṁ tirayati dṛçor udgamam bāṣpapūras
tatsaṁkalpopahitajaḍima stambham abhyeti gātram
sadyaḥ svidyann ayam aviratotkampalolāṅgulīkaḥ
pāṇir lekhāvidhiṣu nitarāṁ vartate kiṁ karomi.

'Time after time the tears that stream from my eyes blind my sight; my body is paralysed by the numbness born of the thought of her; when I seek to draw, my hand grows moist and trembles incessantly; ah, what is there that I can do?'

It is, however, easy to pass into exaggeration, as in:[2]

līneva pratibimbiteva likhitevotkīrṇarūpeva ca
pratyupteva ca vajralepaghaṭitevāntarnikhāteva ca
sā naç cetasi kīliteva viçikhaiç cetobhuvaḥ pañcabhiç
cintāsaṁtatitantujālanibiḍasyūteva ca lagnā priyā.

'So have I grasped my dear one that she is as it were merged in me, reflected in me, depicted in me, her form mingled in me, cast into me, cemented with adamant to me, planted within me, pinned to my soul by the five arrows of love, firmly sewn into the fabric of my thought *continuum*.'

A stanza like this, whatever credit it may do to the ingenuity of its author, hardly gives any high opinion of his literary taste, but we are undoubtedly forced to assume that he believed deliberately in the merits of the style he adopted, which as

[1] i. 34. [2] v. 10.

contrasted with that of Kālidāsa belongs to the Gauḍī type,[1] which loves compounds in prose, and aims at the grandiose rather than sweetness and grace. The adoption of such a style, possibly under the influence of the reputation of Bāṇa, is wholly unjustified in drama; the prose, which normally in the plays moves freely and easily, is hampered by compounds of ridiculous length which must have been nearly as unintelligible to his audiences as they are now without careful study. The defect, it is true, gradually diminishes; the *Uttararāmacarita* is far freer from sins of this type. In the verse the theory does not make such demands for compounds, so that the poetry is often better than the prose; especially in his latest drama it gains clearness and intelligibility. Sanskrit, however, was clearly in large measure an artificial language to Bhavabhūti; he employs far too freely rare terms culled from the lexicons, honourable to his scholarship but not to his taste, and the same lack of taste is displayed in the excess of his exaggerations. Of the sweetness and charm of Kālidāsa he has as little as of the power of suggestion displayed by his predecessor; but he excels in drawing with a few strokes the typical features of a situation or emotion. He seeks propriety in his characters' utterances; Janaka shows his philosophical training, as do the two ascetics in Act IV; Lava manifests his religious pupilship under Vālmīki; Tamasā as a river goddess uses similes from the waters. Effective is the speech of the old chamberlain who addresses the newly-crowned Rāma as 'Rāma dear' to remember the change and fall back on 'Your Majesty'. It may be admitted also that in many passages Bhavabhūti does produce effective concatenations of sounds, but only at the expense of natural expression and clearness of diction. The appreciation which he has excited in India is often due not to his real merits, but to admiration of these linguistic *tours de force*, such as the following:

dordaṇḍāñcitacandraçekharadhanurdaṇḍāvabhañgodyataṣ
ṭañkāradhvanir āryabālacaritaprastāvanāḍiṇḍimaḥ
drākparyastakapālasampuṭamiladbrahmāṇḍabhāṇḍodara—
bhrāmyatpiṇḍitacaṇḍimā katham aho nādyāpi viçrāmyati.

'The twang, emanating from the broken staff of Çiva's bow, bent by his staff-like arms, is the trumpet sound proclaiming to the

[1] Vāmana, i. 2.12; SD. 627; *Kāvyādarça*, i. 40 ff.

world the youthful prowess of my noble brother; it ceases not yet, its reverberations enhanced by its rumbling through the interstices of the fragments of the universe rent asunder by the dread explosion.' It may readily be admitted that the sound effect of such a verse is admirable, but it is attained only at the sacrifice of clearness and propriety of diction.

4. *The Language and the Metres*

Bhavabhūti, with his limited scope, confines himself to Çaurasenī, and models his style on Sanskrit, so that the speakers of Prākrit are committed to the absurdity of elaborate style in what is supposed to be a vernacular. For him doubtless as for later poets the production of Prākrit was a mechanical task of transforming Sanskrit according to the rules of Vararuci or other grammarians.

In metre the *Mahāvīracarita* shows a free use of the Çloka, as is inevitable in an epic play; it is found 129 times; the Çārdūlavikrīḍita (75), Vasantatilaka (39), Çikhariṇī (31), and Sragdharā (28) are the other chief metres; the Upajāti, Mandākrāntā, and Mālinī are not rare, but the Āryā (3) and Gīti (1) are almost gone, and there are only sporadic Aupacchandasika, Puṣpitāgrā, Pṛthvī, Praharṣiṇī, Rathoddhatā, Vaṅçasthā, Çālinī, and Hariṇī. The *Uttararāmacarita* has the same metres, save the Sragdharā, a curious omission; it adds the Drutavilambita and Mañjubhāṣiṇī; the occurrences of the Çloka are 89, the Çikhariṇī is second (30), Vasantatilaka third (26), and Çārdūlavikrīḍita fourth (25). The *Mālatīmādhava* has the same metres as the *Uttararāmacarita* plus the Narkuṭaka[1] and a Daṇḍaka of six short syllables and sixteen amphimacers; here the Vasantatilaka takes first place (49), Çārdūlavikrīḍita (32), Çikhariṇī (21), and Hariṇī (12). The Mālinī (21) and Mandākrāntā (15) take on greater importance, while the Çloka is negligible (14). The fact that there are only 8 Āryās reflects the changed character of Bhavabhūti's versification from that of Kālidāsa.

[1] ⏑⏑⏑⏑–⏑– ⏑⏑⏑–⏑⏑–⏑⏑–.

IX

VIÇĀKHADATTA AND BHAṬṬA NĀRĀYAṆA

1. *The Date of Viçākhadatta*

A CURIOUS vagueness besets our knowledge of Viçākhadatta or Viçākhadeva, son of the Mahārāja Bhāskaradatta or the minister Pṛthu, grandson of the feudatory Vaṭeçvaradatta. None of these persons are elsewhere known, and for his date we are reduced to conjectures. The play ends with a stanza mentioning Candragupta as would be natural in a play of which he is hero, but there are variants in the manuscripts, including Dantivarman, Rantivarman, and (A)vantivarman. The last has been utilized to fix the date, but in two different ways; Avantivarman might be the Maukhari king whose son married Harṣa's daughter, or the king of Kashmir (A.D. 855–83); Jacobi[1] identifies the eclipse referred to in the play as that of December 2, 860, when, he holds, Çūra, the king's minister, had the play performed. There is no conclusive argument for or against this clever combination. Konow[2] sees in Candragupta the ruler of the Gupta line, and would make the poet a younger contemporary of Kālidāsa, but this is fantasy. We have some evidence of imitation of Ratnākara by Viçākhadatta, but it is possibly not conclusive as to date. Still less weight attaches to the fact that in one manuscript the Nāndī is supposed to be over before the play begins, for that is merely a habit of South Indian manuscripts, true to the Bhāsa tradition. There is nothing that prevents a date in the ninth century, though the work may be earlier.[3]

[1] VOJ. ii. 212 ff.; *contra* Dhruva, VOJ. v. 25; Charpentier, JRAS. 1923, pp. 585 f.

[2] ID. pp. 70 f. Cf. Antani, IA. li. 49 f.; Winternitz, GIL. iii. 210.

[3] Keith, JRAS. 1909, pp. 145 f.; Hertel, ZDMG. lxx. 133 ff. It is later than the *Mṛcchakaṭikā*, the *Raghuvaṅça* (vii. 43 as compared with v. 23), and the *Çiçupālavadha* (i. 47 as compared with the last verse).

2. *The Mudrārākṣasa*

Whatever its date, the *Mudrārākṣasa*[1] is one of the great Sanskrit dramas, although in India itself its merits have long been underrated, because it does not conform to the normal model. It is a drama of political intrigue, centred in the person of Rākṣasa, formerly minister of the Nandas, who is now sworn to revenge their destruction on Cāṇakya, the Brahmin who vowed to ruin them, and who, in pursuance of this end, secured an alliance between Candragupta, their rival, and Parvateça[2] and attacked Pāṭaliputra. Rākṣasa seeing resistance vain surrendered the city; the last of the royal house, Sarvārthasiddhi, retired to an ascetic life, and Rākṣasa left to weave plots elsewhere. His effort by a poison maiden to slay Candragupta miscarried; instead, Parvateça fell a victim through Cāṇakya's cunning. This so far aided Rākṣasa that his son Malayaketu left Candragupta and is now his ally, preparing with the aid of a host of motley origin, including princes of Kulūta, Malaya, Kashmir, Scind, and Persia to attack the capital. Act I shows Cāṇakya's schemes; in a monologue he expresses his detestation of the Nandas and his determination to secure Rākṣasa as minister for his lord, for he is convinced of Rākṣasa's worth and has no desire himself to rule. Nipuṇaka, his spy, enters; he has found a Jain Jīvasiddhi hostile to the king—he is in reality Cāṇakya's agent; the scribe Çakaṭadāsa is a real enemy, as is the jeweller Candanadāsa, in whose house are Rākṣasa's wife and child; by good fortune he has secured the signet ring of Rākṣasa, dropped by the former in pulling indoors the child. Cāṇakya sees his chance; he writes a letter, has it copied in good faith by Çakaṭadāsa and sealed with Rākṣasa's seal; Çakaṭadāsa is then arrested, but on the point of impalement is rescued by Siddhārthaka, another spy of the minister's, who flees to Rākṣasa; Jīvasiddhi is banished in ignominy to the same destination, and Candanadāsa is flung into prison, to await death for having harboured Rākṣasa's family, which has escaped. Finally, it is reported that Bhāgurāyaṇa and others of the court are also fled,

[1] Ed. A. Hillebrandt, Breslau, 1912; trs. Wilson, ii. 125 ff.; L. Fritze, Leipzig, 1886; V. Henry, Paris, 1888.

[2] Or Parvataka. For an effort to extract history, see CHI. i. 470 ff. It must be regarded as very dubious.

news received by Cāṇakya with admirable composure, for they are also his emissaries.

Act II shows Rākṣasa's counter-plots. Virādhaka, in a serpent-charmer's disguise, bears him news of ill import: the scheme to murder Candragupta, as he passed under a coronation arch, has failed, Vairodhaka, uncle of Malayaketu, who stayed when his nephew fled and had been crowned also as lord of half the realm, being slain in lieu of Candragupta; Abhayadatta, who offered him poison, has been forced to drink the draught; Pramodaka, the chamberlain, has flaunted the wealth sent to him to use in bribes, and is dead in misery; the bold spirits, who were to issue from a subterranean passage into the king's bedchamber, have been detected by the king through the sight of ants bearing a recent meal, and burnt in agony in their hiding place; Jīvasiddhi is banished, Çakaṭadāsa condemned to the stake, Candanadāsa to the same fate. The tale of woe is interrupted by the advent of Çakaṭadāsa with Siddhārthaka, who restores his seal to Rākṣasa, saying he had picked it up at Candanadāsa's house, and begs permission to remain in his train. Virādhaka now gives the one piece of good news: Candragupta is tired of Cāṇakya. At this moment Rākṣasa is asked if he will buy some precious jewels, and hastily bids Çakaṭadāsa see to the price, little knowing that they are sent by Cāṇakya to entrap him. Act III displays Cāṇakya at his ablest; a fine scene takes place between him and Candragupta, on the score that he has forbidden all feasting without telling the king; the monarch finally upbraids him, the minister taunts him with ingratitude and insolence, resigns office, and leaves in high dudgeon; none but the chief actors know the whole is but a ruse, and Rākṣasa's fortunes seem again fair. In Act IV the bright prospect begins to darken; Bhāgurāyaṇa, for the officials who have deserted to Malayaketu, explains to that monarch that they desire to deal direct with him, not Rākṣasa; the latter, they suggest, is no real foe of Candragupta; if Cāṇakya were out of the way, there would be nothing to hinder his allying himself with Candragupta. The king is perplexed, and his doubt increases when he overhears a conversation between Rākṣasa and a courier who bears the glad tidings of the split between the king and Cāṇakya; Rākṣasa eagerly exclaims that Candragupta is now in the palms of his hands (*hastatalagata*), a phrase which unhappily lends itself to the suspicious interpretation that he meditates alliance with that king. Malayaketu's conversation with Rākṣasa, which ensues, leaves him half-hearted for an advance, for he cannot rid himself of his suspicions of the minister. The Act ends with Jīvasiddhi's admission to see Rākṣasa, who asks him in vain for intelligible advice as to the time for an advance, receiving in lieu much astrological lore and what is really a presage of disaster. This is achieved in Act V. First Jīvasiddhi approaches Bhāgurāyaṇa, who is entrusted with the grant of permits to leave the camp, and admits—with feigned reluctance—in order to get a permit, that he fears Rākṣasa, who used him formerly when he was arranging for the poisoning of Parvateça, but now seeks to slay him. The king, who overhears this, is wild with rage; he had deemed his father slain by Cāṇakya, and Bhāgurāyaṇa has great difficulty in persuading him that Rākṣasa's action might be deemed justifiable, and that at any rate vengeance must wait. Siddhārthaka, however, now appears a prisoner, caught trying to escape without a passport; beaten, he finally gives evidence against Rākṣasa in the shape of the letter written in Act I by Çakaṭadāsa, which he asserts he was to bear from Rākṣasa to Candragupta, a jewel sealed, like the letter, with Rākṣasa's seal —one given by Malayaketu to Rākṣasa and by him to Siddhārthaka for rescuing Çakaṭadāsa, and a verbal message, stating the terms demanded by the allied kings for their treachery, and Rākṣasa's own demand, the removal of Cāṇakya. The king confronts Rākṣasa with the proofs, and the minister has made his case worse from the start, for, asked the order of march proposed, he assigns to the allied kings the proud duty of guarding the king's person, which Malayaketu interprets as a device to facilitate their treachery. Rākṣasa is bewildered; he can deny the message, but the seal and the writing are genuine; can Çakaṭadāsa have turned traitor through fear? The argument against him is clinched by the king's seeing that he wears a fine jewel, one of those purchased at the close of Act II; it was the king's father's, and must, he insists, be the price of the minister's treachery. Incensed, the foolish king gives orders to bury alive those allied kings who craved territory as their reward, and to trample under elephants those who sought them as their share.

All is confusion, and Rākṣasa, insolently spared, slips away to fulfil his duty of rescuing his friend Candanadāsa.

Act VI reveals Rākṣasa in the capital deeply soliloquizing on the failure of all his ends, and the fate of his friend. A spy of Candragupta's approaches him, and passes himself off as one seeking death, in despair for Candanadāsa's fate, on which Candragupta's mind is relentlessly set. He warns Rākṣasa that he may not attempt a rescue, for, when they fear one, the executioners slay the victim out of hand, and Rākṣasa sees that nothing save self-sacrifice is left for him. The net is now firmly cast; Act VII sees Candanadāsa led out to death, his wife and child beside him, a scene manifestly imitated from the *Mṛcchakaṭikā*; the wife is determined to die also, but Rākṣasa intervenes; Cāṇakya and Candragupta come on the scene, and Rākṣasa decides to accept the office of minister pressed on him by both, when thus alone he can save, not his own life, but that of Candanadāsa and his friends. They, indeed, are in sore case, for Malayaketu's massacre of the kings has broken the host into fragments, and the apparent rebels have taken the moment to capture him and his court. As minister, Rākṣasa is permitted to free Malayaketu and restore his lands, Candanadāsa is rewarded, and a general amnesty approved.

The interest in the action never flags; the characters of Cāṇakya and Rākṣasa are excellent foils. Each in his own way is admirable; Cāṇakya in his undying and just hatred of the Nandas, and Rākṣasa in his unsparing devotion to their cause, his noble desire to save Candanadāsa, and his fine submission, for the sake of others, to a yoke he had purposed never to bear. The maxims of politics in which both delight may amuse us; they are essentially the Indian views of polity and give the play a contact with reality which Professor Lévi[1] wrongly denies; the plots and counterplots of both ministers are the type in which Indian polity has ever delighted. The minor figures are all interesting; Siddhārthaka and Samiddhārthaka, gentlemen who even disguise themselves as Caṇḍālas in the last Act, so that they may serve Cāṇakya's aims; Nipuṇaka, whose cleverness in finding the seal justifies the name he bears; the disguised Virādhaka, the honest Çakaṭadāsa, the noble Candanadāsa and

[1] TI. i. 226 f.

his wife, the one female figure in the play. The kings Candragupta and Malayaketu represent the contrast of ripe intelligence with youthful ardour, and the weak petulance of one who does not know men's worth, and who rashly and cruelly slays his allies on the faith of treachery. Bhāgurāyaṇa, who is the false friend deluding Malayaketu in Candragupta's interest, is a carefully drawn figure; he dislikes the work, but dismisses his repulsion as essentially the result of dependence which forbids a man to judge between right and wrong.

Viçākhadatta's diction is admirably forcible and direct; the martial character of his dramas reflects itself in the clearness and rapidity of his style, which eschews the deplorable compounds which disfigure Bhavabhūti's works. An artist in essentials, he uses images, metaphors, and similes with tasteful moderation; alone of the later dramatists, he realizes that he is writing a drama, not composing sets[1] of elegant extracts. Hence is explained the paucity of citations from him in the anthologies, which naturally find little to their purpose in an author of a more manly strain than is usual in the drama. It is significant that the *Subhāṣitāvali* cites but two stanzas, under his name, as Viçākhadeva, both pretty but undistinguished; the second[2] is graceful:

sendracāpaiḥ çṛtā meghair nipatannirjharā nagāḥ
varṇakambalasaṁvītā babhur mattadvipā iva.

'The mountains, with their leaping waterfalls, girt with rainbow clouds, shone like rutting elephants clad in raiment of bright hue.'

More characteristic is the terse and effective phraseology in which he describes the dilemma of Malayaketu when his mind has been poisoned against Rākṣasa:[3]

bhaktyā Nandakulānurāgadṛḍhayā Nandānvayālambinā
kiṁ Cāṇakyanirākṛtena kṛtinā Mauryeṇa saṁdhāsyate
sthairyam bhaktiguṇasya vā vigaṇayan satyasandho bhavet
ity ārūḍhakulālacakram iva me cetaç ciraṁ bhrāmyati.

'His loyalty was founded on his love for the family of Nanda, it rested on a scion of that house; now that the cunning Maurya is severed from Cāṇakya, will he make terms with him? Or,

[1] His ability in this regard can be seen in the jingle of Malayaketu's lament in v. 16.
[2] v. 1728.
[3] *Mudrārākṣasa*, v. 5.

faithful ever in loyalty, will he keep his pact with me? Perplexed with these thoughts my mind revolves as on a potter's wheel.'

There is effective gravity in the manner in which the aged chamberlain handles the regular topic of his failing powers in old age:[1]

rūpādīn viṣayān nirūpya karaṇair yair ātmalābhas tvayā
labdhas teṣv api cakṣurādiṣu hatāḥ svārthāvabodhakriyāḥ
aṅgāni prasabhaṁ tyajanti paṭutām ājñāvidheyāni me
nyastam mūrdhni padaṁ tavaiva jarayā tṛṣṇe mudhā tāmyasi.

'Sight, alas, and the other organs, wherewith aforetime I was wont to grasp for myself the sights and objects of desire which I beheld, have lost their power of action. My limbs obey me not and suddenly have lost their cunning; thy foot is placed on my head, old age; vainly, O desire, dost thou weary thyself.'

Rākṣasa's name inevitably demands the usual play on its sense of demoniac, but Malayaketu's feeling redeems the use from triviality:[2]

mitram mamāyam iti nirvṛtacittavṛttim
viçrambhatas tvayi niveçitasarvakāryam
tātaṁ nipātya saha bandhujanākṣitoyair
anvarthasaṁjña nanu Rākṣasa rākṣaso 'si?

'My father's mind rested secure in thy friendship; in his confidence he entrusted to thee the whole burden of his affairs; when, then, thou didst bring him low midst the tears of all his kin, didst thou not act, O Rākṣasa, like the demon whose name thou dost bear?'

The martial spirit of Rākṣasa is admirably brought out in Act II:[3]

prakārān paritaḥ çarāsanadharaiḥ kṣipram parikṣipyatām
dvāreṣu dvipadaiḥ pratidvipaghaṭābhedakṣamaiḥ sthīyatām
muktvā mṛtyubhayam prahartumanasaḥ çatror bale durbale
te niryāntu mayā sahaikamanaso yeṣām abhīṣṭaṁ yaçaḥ.

'Around the ramparts be the archers set at once; station at the portals the elephants, strong to overthrow the host of the foeman's herd; lay fear aside, in eagerness to smite the host of the foe that cannot withstand us, and issue forth with me with one

[1] iii. 1. [2] v. 7. [3] ii. 14.

accord, all to whom glory is dear.' The burden of duty is expressed admirably:[1]

kiṁ Çeṣasya bharavyathā na vapuṣi kṣāṁ na kṣipaty eṣa yat
kiṁ vā nāsti pariçramo dinapater āste na yan niçcalaḥ
kiṁ tv aṅgīkṛtam utsṛjan kiraṇavac chlāghyo jano lajjate
nirvyūḍhiḥ pratipannavastuṣu satām ekaṁ hi gotravratam.

'Is it because Çeṣa feels not the pain of the burden of the earth that he flings it not aside? Is it that the sun feels no weariness that he does not stand still in his course? Nay, a noble man feels shame to lay aside the duty he has taken on him, like a meaner creature; for the good this is the one common law, to be faithful to what one has undertaken.' The minister's resolve to save his friend is forcibly put:[2]

audāsīnyaṁ na yuktaṁ priyasuhṛdi gate matkṛtām eva ghorām
vyāpattiṁ jñātam asya svatanum aham imāṁ niṣkrayaṁ kalpayāmi.

'Indifference is impossible since my dear friend has fallen into this disaster for my sake; I have it: my own life do I set as ransom for his.' There is grim humour in the command of the infuriated Malayaketu:[3] 'Those who desired my land, take and cast into a pit and cover with dust; those two who sought my army of elephants slay by an elephant,' and in the Caṇḍāla's remark[4] when he bids his friend impale Candanadāsa: 'His family will go off quickly enough of their own accord.' The revelation of Jīvasiddhi's treachery wrings from Rākṣasa the cry:[5] 'My very heart has been made their own by my foes (*hṛdayam api me ripubhiḥ svīkṛtam*).' Proverbs are aptly used, as in the same context the Sanskrit equivalent for an accumulation of evils (*ayam aparo gaṇḍasyopari sphoṭaḥ*).

3. *The Language and the Metres of the Mudrārākṣasa*

The Sanskrit of the *Mudrārāksasa* is classical, and the Prākrits number three, for, in addition to the normal Çaurasenī and Māhārāṣṭrī, Māgadhī is used by the Jain monk, by Siddhārthaka and Samiddhārthaka as Caṇḍālas, by a servant and an envoy. We may take it that Viçākhadatta wrote from the grammars, and this is confirmed by the fact that we find in some

[1] ii. 19. [2] vi. 21. [3] p. 154. [4] p. 189. [5] p. 153.

of the manuscripts traces of the carrying through of characteristic Māgadhī features, *ññ* for *ṇṇ* for Sanskrit *ny*; *ẖk* for *kṣ*; *çc* for *cch*, *st* for *sth*, *sṭ* for *ṣṭ* and for *ṣṭh*, and the usual *ç*, *l*, and *e*. It is possible, of course, that these are no more than restorations by scribes, but they may easily be more venerable. It is also interesting to note that there appear traces of Çaurasenī verses, which is perfectly possible, as the theory does not necessitate all persons who use Çaurasenī in prose singing in Māhārāṣṭrī; that is given as requisite for women only, and in this play they are men who use these Çaurasenī verses.

The metres most used are Çārdūlavikrīḍita (39), Sragdharā (24), Vasantatilaka (19), and Çikhariṇī (18); the Çloka occurs also 22 times. Other metres are sporadic, save Prākrit Āryās; they include Upajāti, Aupacchandasika, Puṣpitāgrā, Praharṣiṇī, Mālinī, Mandākrāntā, Rucirā, Vaṅçasthā, Suvadanā (iv. 16), and Hariṇī.

4. *The Date of Bhaṭṭa Nārāyaṇa*

The age of Bhaṭṭa Nārāyaṇa, Mṛgarājalakṣman is unknown. But he is cited by Vāmana (iv. 3. 28) and Ānandavardhana [1] and so is before A.D. 800. Tradition, preserved in the Tagore family, makes him out to be a Brahmin summoned from Kanyakubja to Bengal by Ādisūra, the founder of a dynasty of eleven kings, who are supposed to have reigned before the Pāla dynasty came to the throne in the middle of the eighth century A.D. It has been suggested[2] that it was identical with the Guptas of Magadha since Ādityasena, son of Mādhavagupta of Magadha, made himself independent of Kanyakubja; this would make Ādisūra Ādityasena, who was alive in A.D. 671. The date, however, is clearly conjectural for the present.

5. *The Veṇīsaṁhāra*

Bhaṭṭa Nārāyaṇa has chosen as his topic [3] one episode from the great epic and has endeavoured to make it capable of dramatic representation. One of the worst of the insults heaped on Draupadī in the gambling scene of the epic is the dragging of her by the hair before the assembly by Duḥçāsana, one of the

[1] Ed. KM. pp. 80, 150. [2] Konow, ID. p. 77.

[3] Ed. J. Grill, Leipzig, 1871; Bombay, 1905; trs. S. M. Tagore, Calcutta, 1880. Traces of different recensions exist.

Kauravas. Draupadī vows never to braid her hair again until the insult is avenged, as it ultimately is.

Act I shows Bhīma in conversation with Sahadeva as they await the result of Kṛṣṇa's visit as an envoy to seek to settle the fued between Pāṇdavas and Kauravas; Bhīma shows his insolent confidence in his power and his bitter anger, by declaring that he will break with Yudhiṣṭhira if he makes peace before the insult to Draupadī has been avenged. Sahadeva in vain seeks to appease him, and Draupadī adds to his bitterness by relating a fresh insult in a careless allusion by Duryodhana's queen. Kṛṣṇa returns, nothing effected; indeed he has had to use his magic arms to escape detention in the enemies' camp. War is inevitable, but Draupadī, more human now, bids her husbands take care of their lives against the enemy. Act II opens with an ominous dream of Bhānumatī, Duryodhana's queen; an ichneumon (*nakula*) has slain a hundred serpents; it is a presage that the Pāṇḍavas—of whom Nakula is one—will slay the hundred Kauravas. The king, overhearing but not understanding, thinks he is betrayed; learning the truth, at first he inclines to fear, but shakes off the temporary depression. The queen offers oblation to the sun to remove the evil omen; the king appears to comfort her: a storm arises, and they seek security in a pavilion, where they indulge in passages of love. Then appears the mother of Jayadratha of Sindhu, slayer of Abhimanyu, son of Arjuna, who fears the revenge of the Pāṇḍavas; Duryodhana makes light of her fears; he despises the resentment of the Pāṇḍavas, gloating over the remembrance of the insults heaped on Draupadī. Finally he mounts his chariot for the battle. Act III presents an episode of horror but also of power; a Rākṣasī and her husband feed on the blood and flesh of the dead on the battlefield; they have been summoned thither, for Ghaṭotkaca, son of Hiḍimbā by Bhīma, is dead, and his demon mother has bidden them attend Bhīma in his revenge on the Kuru host. They see the first-fruits in Droṇa's death at the hands of Dhṛṣṭadyumna, when he lets fall his arms, deceived by the lie of his son's death. They retire before Açvatthāman who advances, but is filled with grief when he learns of the treacherous device which cost his father's life. His uncle Kṛpa consoles him, and bids him ask Duryodhana for the command in the battle. But in the meantime Karṇa has poisoned Duryodhana's mind; Droṇa had fought, only to win the imperial authority for his son, and has sacrificed his life in disappointment at the failure of his plans. Kṛpa and Açvatthāman come up; Duryodhana condoles, Karṇa sneers, Açvatthāman asks for the command, but is refused it, as Karṇa has been promised it. Açvatthāman quarrels with Karṇa, and a duel is barely prevented; Açvatthāman accuses Duryodhana of partiality, and will fight no more. Their disputes are interrupted by Bhīma's boast that he will now slay Duḥçāsana; Karṇa at Açvatthāman's instigation makes ready to rescue him, Duryodhana follows suit, Açvatthāman would go also, but is stayed by a voice from heaven and can only bid Kṛpa lend his aid.

In Act IV Duryodhana is brought in wounded; recovering, he learns of Duḥçāsana's death and a Kuru disaster; a messenger from Karṇa tells in a long Prākrit speech of the death of Karṇa's son, and gives an appeal for aid written in Karṇa's blood. Duryodhana makes ready for battle, but is interrupted by the arrival of his parents, Dhṛtarāṣṭra and Gāndhārī with Sañjaya, whose advent begins Act V. The aged couple and Sañjaya urge in vain Duryodhana to peace; he refuses, and again, hearing of Karṇa's death, unaided, is ready to part for the field, when Arjuna and Bhīma appear; Bhīma insists on their saluting with insults their uncle; Duryodhana reproves them, but Arjuna insists that it is just retribution for the acquiescence of the aged king in Draupadī's ill-treatment. Duryodhana defies Bhīma, who would fight, but Arjuna forbids, and Yudhiṣṭhira's summons takes them away. Açvatthāman arrives, and seeks reconciliation with Duryodhana, who receives him coldly; he withdraws, followed by Sañjaya, bidden by Dhṛtarāṣṭra to appease him.

Act VI tells us from an announcement to Yudhiṣṭhira and Draupadī of Duryodhana's death at Bhīma's hands. But a Cārvāka comes in, who tells a very different story; Bhīma and Arjuna are dead. Yudhisṭhira and Draupadī resolve on death, and the Cārvāka, who is really a Rākṣasa, departs in glee. When, however, they are about to die, a noise is heard; Yudhiṣṭhira, deeming it Duryodhana, rushes to arms, while Draupadī runs away, and is caught by her hair by Bhīma, whom Yudhiṣṭhira seizes. The ludicrous error is discovered, and Draupadī binds up at last her locks. Arjuna and Vāsudeva arrive, the Cārvāka has been slain by Nakula, and all is well.

The play is on the whole undramatic, for the action is choked by narrative, and the vast abundance of detail served up in this form confuses and destroys interest. Yet the characterization is good; Duryodhana, as in the later Indian tradition, is unlovable; he is proud and arrogant, self-confident, vain, and selfish; he laughs at Bhānumatī's fears and has no sympathy for the maternal anxiety of Jayadratha's mother. He is suspicious of Droṇa and Açvatthāman, and thus deprives himself of their effective aid; Karṇa, whose jealous advice he accepts, he leaves to perish. Bhīma again is a bloodthirsty and boastful bully; Arjuna is equally valiant, but he is less an undisciplined savage, while Kṛṣṇa intervenes with wise moderation. Yudhiṣṭhira is, as ever, grave and more concerned with the interest of his subjects than his personal feelings. Horror and pathos are not lacking, but the love interest is certainly not effective, and it may be that it was forced on the author by tradition rather than any thought of producing a real interest of itself. Bhaṭṭa Nārāyaṇa's slavish fidelity to rule brought him censure even from Indian critics.

The style of the play is clear and not lacking either in force or dignity: dismayed by the dream of Bhānumatī Duryodhana comforts himself.[1] Añgiras says:

> *grahāṇāṁ caritaṁ svapno nimittāny upayācitam*
> *phalanti kākatālīyaṁ tebhyaḥ prajñā na bibhyati.*

'The movements of the planets, dreams, omens, oblations, bear fruit by accident; therefore wise men fear them not.' Graceful is his address to Bhānumatī if out of place:[2]

> *kuru ghanoru padāni çanaiḥ çanair: api vimuñca gatiṁ parivepinīm*
> *patasi bāhulatopanibandhanam: mama nipīḍaya gāḍham uraḥsthalam.*

'O firm-limbed one, make slow thy steps; stay thy trembling gait; thou dost fall into the shelter of my arms; clasp me closely in thine embrace.' But any display of tenderness is abnormal in Duryodhana; he rebukes his aged mother when she urges him to save his life by coming to terms with the enemy:[3]

> *mātaḥ kim apy asadṛçaṁ vikṛtaṁ vacas te: sukṣatriyā kva bhavatī kva ca dīnataiṣā*
> *nirvatsale sutaçatasya vipattim etām: tvaṁ nānucintayasi rakṣasi mām ayogyam.*

[1] ii. 41. [2] ii. 47. [3] v. 120.

'O mother, strange and unseemly is thy bidding. Ill accord thy noble birth and this faintness of spirit. Shame on thee, without natural affection, in that thou dost forget the cruel fate of thy hundred sons in seeking to save my life.' In vain is Dhṛtarāṣṭra's manly appeal to him:[1]

dāyādā na yayor balena gaṇitās tau Droṇabhīṣmau hatau
Karṇasyātmajam agrataḥ çamayato bhītaṁ jagat Phālgunāt
vatsānāṁ nidhanena me tvayi ripuḥ çeṣapratijño 'dhunā
krodhaṁ vairiṣu muñca vatsa pitarāv andhāv imau pālaya.

'Slain are Droṇa and Bhīṣma whose peers none were deemed in might; all shrank in terror before Arjuna as he slew Karṇa's son before his eyes; my dear ones slain, the foe's whole aim is against thee now; lay aside thine anger with thy foes, and guard these thy blind parents.' Admirably expressed is Bhīma's wild fury when he disdains Yudhiṣṭhira's effort to secure peace:[2]

mathnāmi Kauravaçataṁ samare na kopād: Duḥçāsanasya
rudhiraṁ na pibāmy urastaḥ
saṁcūrṇayāmi gadayā na Suyodhanoru: sandhiṁ karotu
bhavatāṁ nṛpatiḥ paṇena.

'Shall I not in anger crush the hundred Kauravas in battle; shall I not drink the blood from Duḥçāsana's breast; shall I not break with my club the thighs of Duryodhana, although your master buy peace at a price?' Admirable also is his description of the sacrifice of battle:[3]

catvāro vayam ṛtvijaḥ sa bhagavān karmopadeṣṭā hariḥ
saṁgrāmādhvaradīkṣito narapatiḥ patnī gṛhītavratā
Kauravyāḥ paçavaḥ priyāparibhavakleçopaçāntiḥ phalam
rājanyopanimantraṇāya rasati sphītaṁ yaçodundubhiḥ.

'We are the four priests, and the blessed Hari himself directs the rite; the king has consecrated himself for the sacrament of battle, the queen has taken on herself the vow; the Kauravyas are the victims, the end to be achieved the extinction of our loved one's bitterness of shame at the insult done her; loudly the drum of fame summons the warrior to the fray.' Equally effective is his summing up of his feat:[4]

bhūmau kṣiptaṁ çarīraṁ nihitam idam asṛk candanam
Bhīmagātre

[1] v. 122. [2] i. 15. [3] i. 25. [4] vi. 197.

lakṣmīr ārye niṣaṇṇā caturudadhipayaḥsīmayā sārdham urvyā
bhṛtyā mitrāṇi yodhāḥ Kurukulam akhilaṁ dagdham etadraṇāgnau
nāmaikaṁ yad bravīṣi kṣitipa tad adhunā Dhārtarāṣṭrasya çeṣam.

'His body is cast upon the ground; his blood is smeared as sandal paste on Bhīma's limbs; the goddess of fortune, with the earth bounded by the waters of the four oceans, rests on my noble brother's lap; servants, friends, warriors, the whole house of the Kurus has been burned in this fire of battle; the name alone, O king, is left of Dhṛtarāṣṭra's race.' Effective is the appeal which Dhṛtarāṣṭra bids the faithful Sañjaya address to the righteously indignant Açvatthāman:[1]

smarati na bhavān pītaṁ stanyaṁ cirāya sahāmunā
mama ca malinaṁ kṣaumam bālye tvadaṅgavivartanaiḥ
anujanidhanasphītāc chokād atipraṇayāc ca tad—
vikṛtavacane māsmin krodhaç ciraṁ kriyatāṁ tvayā.

'Forget not the milk which thou didst so long drink from the same breast with him; forget not my robe that thy childish feet so often soiled in play; his grief is bitter for the death of the younger brother whom he loved so dearly; be not, therefore, wroth for the unjust words he hath spoken to thee.'

On the other hand, we find in Bhaṭṭa Nārāyaṇa many of the defects of Bhavabhūti, in special the fondness for long compounds both in Prākrit and in Sanskrit prose[2] and the same straining after effect which gives such a description of the battle as that vouchsafed to Draupadī by Bhīma, when she warns him nor to be overrash in battle:[3]

anyonyāsphālabhinnadviparudhiravasāmāṅsamastiṣkapaṅke
magnānāṁ syandanānām upari kṛtapadanyāsavikrāntapattau
sphītāsṛkpānagoṣṭhīrasadaçivaçivātūryanṛtyatkabandhe
saṁgrāmaikārṇavāntaḥpayasi vicaritum paṇḍitāḥ Pāṇḍuputrāḥ.

'The sons of Pāṇḍu are well skilled to disport in the waters of the ocean of the battle, wherein dance headless corpses to the music of the unholy jackals, that yell in joy as they drink the thick blood of the dead, and the footmen in their valour leap over the chariots that are sunk in the mud of the blood, fat,

[1] v. 157. [2] E.g. vi, p. 87 (Sanskrit); v, p. 59 (Prākrit). [3] i. 27.

flesh, and brains of the elephants shattered in mutual onslaught.' The adaptation of sound to sense here is doubtless admirable, and the picture drawn is vivid in a painful degree, but the style is too laboured to be attractive to modern taste.

None the less Nārāyaṇa has the merit, shared by Viçākhadatta, of fire and energy; much of the fierce dialogue is brutal and violent, but it lives with a reality and warmth which is lacking in the tedious contests in boasting, which burden all the descriptions in the Rāma dramas of the meeting of Rāma and Paraçurāma. Duryodhana is not behind Bhīma himself in insolence, though perhaps more subtle than that of the violent son of the Wind-god: [1]

kṛṣṭā keçeṣu bhāryā tava tava ca paços tasya rājñas tayor vā
pratyakṣam bhūpatīnām mama bhuvanapater ājñayā dyūtadāsī
tasmin vairānubandhe vada kim apakṛtaṁ tair hatā ye narendrā
bāhvor vīryātibhāradraviṇagurumadam mām ajitvaiva darpaḥ.

'Thy wife—whether thine, O beast, or that king's or the twins'—was seized by the hair, in the presence of all the princes, by my command as lord of the earth, she won as my slave at the dice. With this abiding cause of hatred between us, say what wrong was wrought by the kings whom thou hast slain? When thou hast not conquered me, why vainly dost thou boast of the cumbrous strength of thy huge arms?'

Violent as is the language, there is some excuse for it in the extraordinarily heartless character of Bhīma's address to the ill-fated Dhṛtarāṣṭra, which almost justifies the recalling of the disgraceful slight put on Draupadī: [2]

nihatāçeṣakauravyaḥ kṣībo Duḥçāsanāsṛjā
bhañktā Duryodhanasyorvor Bhīmo 'yaṁ çirasā nataḥ.

'Bhīma bows low his head before thy feet, Bhīma who has slain all the scions of Kuru, who is drunk with the blood of Duḥçāsana, and who shall shatter the thighs of Duryodhana.' Effectively contrasted is the stern, but courteous rebuke addressed by Yudhiṣṭhira to Kṛṣṇa's elder brother: [3]

jñātiprītir manasi na kṛtā kṣatriyāṇāṁ na dharmo
rūḍhaṁ sakhyaṁ tad api gaṇitaṁ nānujasyārjunena
tulyaḥ kāmam bhavatu bhavataḥ çiṣyayoḥ snehabandhaḥ
ko 'yam panthā yad asi vimukho mandabhāgye mayi tvam?

[1] v. 146. [2] v. 144. [3] vi. 178.

'Thou hast forgotten the love due to kindred blood, thou hast violated the law of the warrior, thou hast ignored the deep friendship between thy younger brother and Arjuna. Granted that thy love for both thy pupils may be equal, nevertheless what is the cause that thou dost show hostility to me in my misfortune?'

These and many other passages are cited by the writers on poetics who find in the *Veṇīsaṁhāra* an inexhaustible mine of illustration of the theory which doubtless deeply affected the author in his composition. They do not, however, eulogize him blindly; the love scene with Bhānumatī is definitely treated as out of place.[1]

6. *The Language and the Metres of the Veṇīsaṁhāra.*

The Sanskrit and the Prākrits offer no special features of interest. The latter is mainly in Çaurasenī, but the speeches of the Rākṣasa and his wife at the beginning of Act III are clearly in Māgadhī; they show the characteristic signs of *e* for the nominative singular, both masculine and neuter, of *a*-stems; *l* for *r*, and *ā* in the vocative of *a*-stems. The suggestion of Grill[2] that the dialect is more precisely Ardha-Māgadhī is not necessary, for the points enumerated—the presence of *s* beside *ç*, the variation of *o* and *aṁ* in the nominative for *e*, and the use of *jj* for *ry*, and not *yy*—can be explained readily by the error of the scribes or the mistakes of the author. The freedom with which those worthies acted is seen clearly enough in the fact that one representative of the Bengālī as opposed to the Devanāgarī recension of the text has systematically rewritten the Prākrit into Çaurasenī.

The metrical treatment is noteworthy for the almost equal use of Vasantatilaka (39), Çārdūlavikrīḍita (32), Çikhariṇī (35), and Sragdharā (20). There are 53 Çlokas, and a few stanzas of Mālinī, Puṣpitāgrā, Praharṣiṇī, and one each of Aupacchandasika, Vaitālīya, Indravajrā, and Drutavilambita, with 6 Āryās, and 2 Prākrit Vaitālīyas. The versification is thus decidedly of the later type.

[1] SD. 408. Lévi, however, is in error (TI. i. 35, 224) in suggesting that SD. 406 censures as inappropriate Duryodhana and Karṇa's dialogue in Act III.

[2] pp. 139, 140.

X

MURĀRI, RĀJAÇEKHARA, THEIR PREDECESSORS AND SUCCESSORS

1. *The Predecessors of Murāri*

WE know definitely of very few dramatists of the eighth and ninth centuries. Kalhaṇa[1] mentions expressly Yaçovarman of Kanyakubja as a patron of literature, who, as we have seen, patronized Bhavabhūti and Vākpati, and we learn of his drama *Rāmābhyudaya*, which is mentioned by Ānandavardhana in the *Dhvanyāloka*, by Dhanika and Viçvanātha, but has not yet been found. To Kalhaṇa[2] also we are indebted for knowledge of the period of Çivasvāmin, who lived under Avantivarman of Kashmir (A.D. 855–83) and was a contemporary of the poet Ratnākara. He wrote many Nāṭakas and Nāṭikās, and also Prakaraṇas, but save an occasional verse in the anthologies his fame is lost.

Anañgaharṣa Mātrarāja,[3] on the other hand, is known to Ānandavardhana and Abhinavagupta, and his play *Tāpasavatsarājacarita* is a variation on the theme of the ruse of Yaugandharāyaṇa to secure the marriage of Vatsa and Padmāvatī, in face of the deep love of the king for Vāsavadattā. Vatsa in this drama, which is of little poetic or dramatic value, becomes an ascetic on learning of his queen's supposed fate, whence the title of the play. Padmāvatī, who had become enamoured of the king from a portrait sent by the minister, follows suit. Eventually Vāsavadattā and Vatsa are united in Prayāga when each is about to commit suicide in sorrow at separation, and the usual victory is reported by Rumaṇvant to give a happy ending.

[1] See Aufrecht, ZDMG. xxxvi. 521.

[2] v. 36; Lévi, TI. ii. 87. The citations are mainly from his *Kapphiṇābhyudaya*; Thomas, *Kavīndravacanasamuccaya*, p. 111.

[3] Pischel, ZDMG. xxxix. 315; Hultzsch, GN. 1886, pp. 224 ff.

There seems little doubt that the author used the *Ratnāvalī*, which gives the upper limit of his date. His father's name is given at Narendravardhana.

Māyurājā[1] has been less fortunate in that his *Udāttarāghava* is known only by reference. Rājaçekhara represents him as a Karaculi or Kulicuri, which suggests the possibility that he was a king of the Kalacuri dynasty, of which unhappily we know little during the period in which he is probably to be set. He seems to have known Bhavabhūti. Like him he eliminated treachery from the slaying of Vālin by Rāma, and he represents Lakṣmaṇa as first to follow the magic gazelle, and Rāma as going later in pursuit. He is cited more than once in Dhanika's commentary on the *Daçarūpa*.

No other dramatist of this period is known with any certainty; the *Pārvatīpariṇaya* once ascribed to Bāṇa is now allotted to Vāmana Bhaṭṭa Bāṇa (*c.* A.D. 1400), and the *Mallikāmāruta*, wrongly thought to be Daṇḍin's, is the work of one Uddaṇḍin of the seventeenth century.

Of these dramatists Yaçovarman has had the honour of being considered worthy of quotation by the writers on theory who have preserved for us some interesting verses:[2]

ākrandāḥ stanitair vilocanajalāny açrāntadhārāmbhubhis
tvadvicchedabhuvaç ca çokaçikhinas tulyās taḍidvibhramaiḥ
antar me dayitāmukhaṁ tava çaçī vṛttiḥ samāpy āvayoḥ
tat kim mām aniçaṁ sakhe jaladhara dagdhum evodyataḥ.

'My moans are like thy thunder, the floods of my tears thy ever-streaming showers, the flame of my sorrow at severance from my beloved thy flickering lightning, in my mind is her face reflected, in thee the moon; like is our condition; why then, O friend, O cloud, dost thou ever seek to consume me with the burning pangs of love?'

This is decidedly pretty, and there is elegance and beauty in another verse:[3]

yat tvannetrasamānakānti salile magnaṁ tad indīvaram
meghair antaritaḥ priye tava mukhacchāyānukāraḥ çaçī
ye 'pi tvadgamanānukāragatayas te rājahaṅsā gatās
tvatsādṛçyavinodamātram api me daivena na kṣamyate.

[1] Bhattanatha Svamin, IA. xli. 139 f.; Bhandarkar, *Report* (1897), pp. xi, xviii; Peterson, *Report*, ii. 59. The name is variously given as Māyūrāja.

[2] *Subhāṣitāvali*, 1766.

[3] *Ibid.*, 1366.

'The blue lotus which rivalled thine eyes in beauty is now sunk in the lake; the moon which imitated the fairness of thy face, beloved, is hidden by the clouds; the royal swans which aped thy lovely gait are departed; cruel fate will not grant me even the consolation of thy similitude.'

This verse is appropriated by the *Mahānāṭaka*, and so is the following,[1] which deals elegantly enough with the commonplace contrast between the sad lover and the Açoka tree, whose name is interpreted as 'sorrowless', and which flowers, as the poets never weary in telling us, when touched by the foot of a fair lady especially one young:

raktas tvaṁ navapallavair aham api çlāghyaiḥ priyāyā guṇais
tvām āyānti çilīmukhāḥ smaradhanurmuktāḥ sakhe mām api
kāntapādatalāhatis tava mude tad api mamāvayoḥ
sarvaṁ tulyam açoka kevalam ahaṁ dhātrā saçokaḥ kṛtaḥ.

'Thou are proud in thy new shoots, I in the glorious excellences of my beloved; the bees resort to thee, to me the arrows shot from love's bow; like me thou dost delight in the touch of thy dear one's foot; all is alike for us both save only that, O tree Sorrowless, the creator hath made me a man of sorrows.'

kāmavyādhaçarāhatir na gaṇitā saṁjīvanī tvaṁ smṛtā
no dagdho virahānalena jhaṭiti tvatsaṁgamāçāmṛtaiḥ
nīto 'yaṁ divaso vicitralikhitaiḥ saṁkalparūpair mayā
kiṁ vānyad dhṛdaye sthitāsi nanu me tatra svayaṁ sākṣiṇī.[2]

'I have not recked of the wound given by love, the hunter, for the memory of thee hath been my elixir; the fire of separation hath not consumed me straightway because of the nectar of the hope of union with thee; all this day hath been spent by me in limning thy fancied form; nought else have I done, as thou thyself art witness, for dost thou not live in my heart?' We may regret the loss of a work which contained verses as pretty as these, even on the outworn topic of Rāma and Sītā.

It might be interesting to know whether Yaçovarman was successful in introducing any new element into the established plot. The play is cited in the commentary on the *Daçarūpa*[3] to illustrate the device called deception or humiliation (*chalana*) and the parallel cited is that of the treatment of Vāsavadattā in the

[1] *Ibid.*, 1364. [2] *Ibid.*, 1634.
[3] i. 42; SD. 390; N. xix. 94; Lévi, TI. ii. 9.

Ratnāvalī. The definitions of the theory leave this idea far from clear; Viçvanātha seems to treat it as the bearing of insult for the sake of the end to be reached, and the allusion in the case of Sītā may be to her abandonment by Rāma as an act of duty.

A much less favourable impression is left by the few fragments of the *Udāttarāghava* which are preserved. The poet seems to have affected the horrible, as two of his few stanzas deal with it; the better is: [1]

jīyante jayino 'pi sāndratimiravrātair viyadvyāpibhir
bhāsvantaḥ sakalā raver api rucaḥ kasmād akasmād amī
etāç cograkabandharandhrarudhirair ādhmāyamānodarā
muñcanty ānanakandarānalamucas tīvrā ravāḥ pheravāḥ.

'The victors are vanquished; thick darkness invades the sky and triumphs over the brilliant rays of the sun; why this inexplicable event? Why do these jackals, whose bellies are swollen with the blood sucked from the wounds of bleeding corpses, and whose gaping jaws belch flame, utter these piercing cries?

A somewhat flat passage illustrates the conflict of thought in Rāma's mind when appealed to by Citramāya on the score that Lakṣmaṇa is in danger from a Rākṣasa: [2]

vatsasyābhayavāridheḥ pratibhayam manye kathaṁ rākṣasāt
trastaç caiṣa munir virauti manasaç cāsty eva me sambhramaḥ
mā hāsīr Janakātmajām iti muhuḥ snehād gurur yācate
na sthātuṁ na ca gantum ākulamater mūḍhasya me niçcayaḥ.

'The boy is an ocean of valour; how can I fear danger for him from a Rākṣasa? Yet the sage here is terrified and calls for aid, and my own mind is confused; my master too in his affection ever begs me not to leave Janaka's daughter alone; my heart is troubled, and in my confusion I cannot resolve either to go or to stay.'

Another Rāma drama, the *Chalitarāma*, is also referred to by Dhanika in his comment on the *Daçarūpa*; it may belong to this period, or fall somewhat later: we have from it a picture of the leading captive of Lava: [3]

yenāvṛtya mukhāni sāma paṭhatām atyantam āyāsitam
bālye yena hṛtākṣasūtravalayapratyarpaṇaiḥ krīḍitam
yuṣmākaṁ hṛdayaṁ sa eṣa viçikhair āpūritāṅsasthalo
mūrchāghoratamaspraveçavivaço baddhvā Lavo nīyate.

[1] DR. ii. 54 comm. [2] DR. iv. 26 comm. [3] DR. i. 41 comm.

'He who caused such trouble to the Sāman reciters turning to look at him in his childish play, who amused himself by stealing and giving back strings of beads and bracelets, he, your heart's joy, his shoulder pierced by arrows, powerless through entry into the dread darkness of fainting, is being led away bound, even Lava.'

Another stanza refers to Bharata; Rāma returning to Ayodhyā in the celestial chariot declines thus to enter the town, since it is not his, but under the rule of Bharata; scarcely has he descended when he sees before him his brother:[1]

ko 'pi siṅhāsanasyādhaḥ sthitaḥ pādukayoḥ puraḥ
jaṭāvān akṣamālī ca cāmarī ca virājate.

'There stands some one, below the lion throne, before a pair of sandals, wearing his hair long, bearing a rosary, resplendent beneath the chowrie.'

The same play[2] contains an amusing slip by Sītā where she bids her boys go to Ayodhyā and tender their respects to the king. Lava naturally replies by asking why they should become members of the king's entourage, and Sītā answers because the king is their father, a slip which she explains away as well as she can by saying that the king is father of the whole earth.

Yet another drama of which we know nothing else is revealed to us by Dhanika, the *Pāṇḍavānanda*, from which is cited a stanza interesting in its series of questions and answers, a literary form of which the dramatists are fond:[3]

kā çlāghyā guṇināṁ kṣamā paribhavaḥ ko yaḥ svakulyaiḥ kṛtaḥ
kiṁ duḥkhaṁ parasaṁçrayo jagati kaḥ çlāghyo ya āçrīyate
ko mṛtyur vyasanaṁ çucaṁ jahati ke yair nirjitāḥ çatravaḥ
kair vijñātam idaṁ Virāṭanagare channasthitaiḥ Pāṇḍavaiḥ.

'For the good what is there praiseworthy? Patience. What is disgrace? That which is wrought by those of one's own blood. What is misery? Recourse to another's protection. Who in the wor' ' is enviable? He to whom one resorts for aid. What is death, Misfortune. Who escape sorrow? Those who conquer their foes. Who learned this lesson? The Pāṇḍavas when they dwelt in concealment in the city of Virāṭa.'

We learn also from Dhanika of two further dramas, of un-

[1] DR. iii. 13 comm. [2] DR. iii. 17 comm. [3] DR. iii. 12 comm.

known authorship and date; they are mentioned [1] as illustrating the two kinds of Prakaraṇa as a dramatic form, the basis of distinction being whether the heroine is the wife of the hero and therefore a lady of good family or whether she is a courtesan. Of the latter class we have an example in the *Tarañgadatta*, and of the former in the *Puṣpadūṣitaka*; the latter name occurs in the slightly altered form of Puṣpabhūṣita in the *Sāhityadarpaṇa*. As an example of the Samavakāra the *Daçarūpa* [2] mentions the *Samudramanthana*, a title doubtless as well as the description of the drama in question.

2. *Murāri*

Murāri tells us that he was the son of Çrīvardhamānaka of the Maudgalya Gotra and of Tantumatī; he claims to be a Mahākavi, and arrogates the style of Bāla-Vālmīki. His date is uncertain; he is certainly later than Bhavabhūti since he cites from the *Uttararāmacarita*,[3] while we have evidence from the anthologies that he was reckoned by some as superior to Bhavabhūti, apparently his predecessor. A further suggestion as to date may be derived from the Kashmirian poet Ratnākara,[4] who in his *Haravijaya* makes a clear reference to Murāri as a dramatist, for the effort of Bhattanatha Svamin to disprove the reference must be deemed completely unsuccessful. As Ratnākara belongs to the middle of the ninth century A.D., this gives us that period as the latest date for Murāri. Curiously enough, Professor Konow,[5] who accepts the disproof of the reference to Murāri in Ratnākara, admits that the reference to Murāri in Mañkha's *Çrīkaṇṭhacarita* [6] (*c.* A.D. 1135) suggests that he was regarded by that author as earlier than Rājaçekhara, a fact which accords excellently with his priority to Ratnākara, and is far more important than the fact that he is not cited by the authors on theory of the eleventh century A.D. A further effort to place him late is that of Dr. Hultzsch,[7] who infers from verse 3 of the *Kaumudīmitrāṇanda* of Rāmacandra, pupil of Hemacandra, that that

[1] DR. iii. 38 comm.; SD. 512.

[2] DR. iii. 56 f. comm.; SD. 516.

[3] vi. 30/31 is cited in i. 6/7.

[4] xxxviii. 68. For his date cf. Bühler, *Kashmir Report*, p. 42. See Bhattanatha Svamin, IA. xli. 141; Lévi, TI. i. 277.

[5] ID. p. 83. Dhanika (DR. ii. 1) cites, anonymously as usual, iii. 21.

[6] xxv. 74.

[7] ZDMG. lxxv. 63.

dramatist was a contemporary of Murāri. But the evidence is clearly inadequate; the words used are perfectly compatible with the fact that Murāri was dead, and there are grave chronological difficulties in the way of the theory. It is practically impossible that a contemporary of Rāmacandra could have been cited by Mañkha at the date of the *Çrīkaṇṭhacarita*. Moreover Murāri seems to have been imitated by Jayadeva in the *Prasannarāghava*.[1]

Of his place of activity we know nothing definite. He mentions, however, Māhiṣmatī as the seat of the Kalacuris, and it has been suggested that this indicates that he lived under the patronage of a prince of that dynasty at Māhiṣmatī, now Māndhātā on the Narmadā.

3. *The Anargharāghava*

Murāri declares in the prologue to the solitary drama, the *Anargharāghava*,[2] which has come down to us, though quotations show that he wrote other works, that his aim is to please a public tired of terror, horror, violence, and marvels, by a composition elevated, heroic, and marvellous throughout, not merely at the close. He defends his choice of the banal subject of Rāma; his character adds elevation and charm to the poet's work, and it would be folly to lay aside so splendid a theme. The *Anargharāghava*, however, does little to justify the poet's confidence in his choice of topic. The theme, treated already at length by Bhavabhūti, offered no chance of success save for a great poet, and Murāri was not such a poet save in the estimate of occasional later writers who extol his depth (*gambhīratā*) without any shadow of justification.

Act I shows us Daçaratha in conversation with Vāmadeva. The arrival of the sage Viçvāmitra is announced; he exchanges with the king hyperbolic compliments of the most tedious type, but proceeds to business by demanding the aid of Rāma against the Rākṣasas which are troubling his hermitage. The king hesitates to send one so young and dear into danger. The sage insists on his obeying the call of duty, and he hands over Rāma and Lakṣmaṇa to the care of the ascetic. The herald announces

[1] ii. 34, as compared with vii. 83.

[2] Ed. KM. 1894; cf. Baumgartner, *Das Rāmāyaṇa*, pp. 125 ff.

midday, and the king mourns the loss of his son. In Act II we have first a long-drawn-out conversation between Çunaḥçepha and Paçumeḍhra, two pupils of Viçvāmitra, which serves to enlighten us on the history of Vālin, Rāvaṇa, the Rākṣasas, Jāmbavant, Hanumant, and Tāḍakā. The entr'acte is followed by the appearance of Rāma and Lakṣmaṇa who describe the hermitage and the doings of its occupants, and then the heat of midday. Time, however, does not trouble the dramatist ; though there is no further action and no interruption in the dialogue, we find ourselves transported to the evening ; Viçvāmitra enters and describes in converse with the boys the sunset. A cry behind the scene announces the approach of the demoness Tāḍakā ; Rāma hesitates to slay a female, but finally departs for the necessary duty ; on his return he has to describe the rising of the moon. Viçvāmitra then suggests a visit to Janaka of Mithilā, affording an opportunity for a description of the city and its ruler.

In Act II only do we reach the motif which Bhavabhūti with far greater skill made the leading idea of the drama, thus giving it effective unity, so far as the story permits. The chamberlain of Janaka in conversation with Kalahaṅsikā, one of Sītā's suite, lets us know that the princess is now ripe for marriage, and Rāvaṇa seeks her hand. In the scene that follows the king accompanied by Çatānanda receives Rāma, but hesitates to put him to the severe test involved in bending Çiva's bow. Çauṣkala, Rāvaṇa's envoy, arrives to demand the maiden's hand, but indignantly declines the request that his master should bend the bow. He eulogizes Rāvaṇa whom Rāma depreciates. Rāma is at last allowed to make the trial ; those who remain on the stage describe his wonderful deed in breaking the bow. He is promised Sītā's hand, while the other sons of Daçaratha are also awarded consorts. Çauṣkala departs, menacing revenge. Act IV shows us Rāvaṇa's minister Mālyavant lamenting the failure of his scheme to win Sītā. Çūrpaṇakhā arrives from Videha and tells of the union of Rāma and Sītā. Mālyavant recognizes that Rāvaṇa will insist on seeking to separate the pair, and he counsels Çūrpaṇakhā to assume the disguise of Mantharā, the maid of Kaikeyī, with the view of securing the banishment of Rāma to the forest, where he will be more vulnerable to attack.

He is also cheered by the news given by Çūrpaṇakhā of the approach of Paraçurāma to Mithilā, whence some gain may accrue to his cause. The following scene shows us Rāma and Paraçurāma in verbal contest; Rāma is even more polite than in the *Mahāvīracarita* which is obviously imitated, while the friends of Rāma carry on a vituperative dialogue behind the scene without actually appearing. Finally they resolve to fight, for Rāma has annoyed his rival by reminding him that the flag of his fame won by his destruction of the Kṣatriyas is worn out and challenging him to mount a new one. The fight itself takes place off the stage; Sītā, we learn from a voice behind the scenes, is apprehensive lest Rāma be drawing again his bow to win another maiden. The rivals then appear on excellent terms; Paraçurāma exchanges farewells with his former interlocutors and disappears. Then enter Janaka and Daçaratha. The latter is determined to resign his kingdom to Rāma, but Lakṣmaṇa enters introducing Mantharā who bears a fatal missive from Kaikeyī, bidding the king grant the two boons of the banishment of Rāma and the coronation of Bharata. The kings faint; Rāma sends Lakṣmaṇa to tell Sītā, and commends his father to Janaka.

In Act V a conversation between Jāmbavant and an ascetic lady, Çravaṇā, tells of the doings of Rāma until his advent in the forest. Çravaṇā goes to Sugrīva to bespeak a kindly welcome for the wayfarers, while Jāmbavant overhears a dialogue between Rāvaṇa, disguised as a juggler, and Lakṣmaṇa. The vulture Jaṭāyu then appears with the grave news that he has seen Rāvaṇa and Mārīca in the forest; Jāmbavant goes to warn Sugrīva of the danger, while Jaṭāyu sees the rape of Sītā and pursues the ravisher. After this entr'acte Rāma and Lakṣmaṇa enter, wandering in grief in vain search. They are interrupted by a cry and see the friendly forest chief, Guha, assailed by the headless Kabandha. Lakṣmaṇa rescues him, but, in doing so, knocks off the tree, on which it was suspended, the skeleton of Dundubhi, to the annoyance of Vālin, who appears, and after a lengthy conversation challenges Rāma to battle. The fight is described from the stage by Lakṣmaṇa and Guha; the enemy is slain. Voices from behind the scenes report the coronation of Sugrīva and his determination to aid Rāma in the recovery of

Sītā, and Lakṣmaṇa and his friend leave the stage to rejoin their party. In Act VI Sāraṇa and Çuka, two spies of Rāvaṇa's describe to Mālyavant the building of the bridge over the ocean and the advent of Rāma's army. Voices from behind announce the departure of Kumbhakarṇa and Meghanāda for battle; in the same way we learn of their fall and the last exit of Rāvaṇa, whom Mālyavant decides to follow to the field. The final struggle is described with tedious and tasteless prolixity by two Vidyādharas, Ratnacūḍa and Hemāñgada, and with this the Act closes.

In Act VII we have a determined effort to vie with the close of the *Mahāvīracarita*. Rāma, Sītā, Lakṣmaṇa, Vibhīṣaṇa, and Sugrīva proceed in Kubera's celestial car to Ayodhyā. But the route is diversified from the simplicity of the model, for the travellers are taken to the celestial regions to view in all its aspects the mythical mountain Sumeru and the world of the moon; only then do they commence their journey in its terrestrial aspect by a description of Siṅhala, distinguished as usual from Lañkā; the route then passes over the Malaya mountains, the forest, the mountain Prasravaṇa, the Godāvarī, mount Mālyavant, Kuṇḍinīpura in the Mahārāṣṭra country, Kāñcī, Ujjayinī, Māhiṣmatī, the Yamunā, the Ganges, Vārāṇasī, Mithilā and Campā; the car goes then west to Prayāga, and later turns east to Ayodhyā, where the priest Vasiṣṭha waits with Rāma's brothers to crown him king.

The demerits of the poem are obvious; there is no attempt to improve on the traditional narrative, though Vālin is honourably killed; the characters are as stereotyped as ever. The author, however, delights to overload and elaborate the theme; hyperbole marks every idea; his mythological knowledge is adequate to enable him to abound in conceits and plays on words, when he does not sink, as largely in Act III, to mere commonplace. The taste which invents the visit to the world of the moon and Sumeru is as deplorable as that which substitutes the dull dialogue between Jāmbavant and Jaṭāyu for the vigorous conversation of Jaṭāyu and Sampāti in the *Mahāvīracarita*. For dialogue in general Murāri has no taste at all, and what merit his work has lies entirely in the ability which he shows to handle the Sanskrit language and to frame sentences of harmonious sound in effective metrical forms. His knowledge of the lexica is obvious, while his love of the recondite in grammar has won him the fame of being used to illustrate rare forms by the author of the *Siddhāntakaumudī*. These linguistic merits have secured him the preference shown for him by modern taste. Nor indeed can his power of expression be justly denied:[1]

dṛçyante madhumattakokilavadhūnirdhūtacūtāñkura—
prāgbhāraprasaratparāgasikatādurgās taṭībhūmayaḥ
yāḥ kṛcchrād atilañghya lubdhakabhayāt tair eva reṇūtkarair
dhārāvāhibhir asti luptapadavīniḥçañkam eṇīkulam.

There are seen the towering slopes as of sand where the pollen tilts off from the mango shoots, shaken by the female cuckoos, maddened by the intoxication of spring; scarce can the antelopes in their fear of the hunter leap over them, but the dust which they raise in showers accords them security by concealing the path of their flight.' The idea is certainly trivial enough, but the expression, which defies reproduction in English, is in its own way a masterpiece of effect.

A pretty erotic verse is found in Act VII:[2]

anena rambhoru bhavanmukhena: tuṣārabhānos tulayā dhṛtasya
ūnasya nūnam pratipūraṇāya: tārā sphuranti pratimāna-khaṇḍāḥ.

'When the moon is placed in the scales, fair-limbed one, against thy face, assuredly it is found wanting, and to make good the deficit the stars must shine as make-weights.'

Not a bad example of more elaborate, yet graceful, eulogy is found in the following stanza:[3]

gotre sākṣād ajani bhagavān eṣa yat padmayoniḥ
çayyotthāyaṁ yad akhilam ahaḥ prīṇayanti dvirephān
ekāgrāṁ yad dadhati bhagavaty uṣṇabhānau ca bhaktim
tat prāpus te sutanu vadanaupamyam ambhoruhāṇi.

'Since manifestly in their family has been born the blessed one, sprung from the lotus; since all day long they delight the bees as they rise from their bed; since their whole faith they devote to the blessed lord of the sharp rays, thus, O lovely one, the flowers that spring from the water attain the likeness of thy face.'

[1] v. 6. [2] vii. 87. [3] vii. 82.

Happy also is another erotic stanza :[1]

abhimukhapatayālubhir lalāṭa— : çramasalilair avadhūta-
pattralekhaḥ
kathayati puruṣāyitaṁ vadhūnām : mṛditahimadyutidur-
manāḥ kapolaḥ.

'Its painted mark obliterated by the moisture which streams from the wearied brow over the face, the cheek reveals the longing of women, melancholy as the wan moon.'

udeṣyatpīyūṣadyutirucikaṇārdrāḥ çaçimaṇi—
sthalīnām panthāno ghanacaraṇalākṣālipibhṛtaḥ
cakorair uḍḍīnair jhaṭiti kṛtaçañkāḥ pratipadaṁ
parācaḥ saṁcārān avinayavatīnāṁ vivṛṇate.

'Footprints on pavements of moonstone, marked with the lac that dyes deep the feet, wet with drops that have the radiance of rising cream, made with anxiety at every step as the Cakoras fly up disturbed, mark the departure of ladies who violate decorum.'[2]

A further stanza in some manuscripts of the poem occurs in the drama, while elsewhere it seems to be treated as a verse about Murāri :[3]

devīṁ vācam upāsate hi bahavaḥ sāraṁ tu sārasvataṁ
jānīte nitarām asau gurukulakliṣṭo Murāriḥ kaviḥ
abdhir lañghita eva vānarabhaṭaiḥ kiṁ tv asyā gambhīratām
āpātālanimagnapīvaratanur jānāti manthācalaḥ.

'Many serve the goddess speech, but the essence of eloquence Murāri alone knows to the full, that poet who long toiled in the house of his teacher; even so the monkey host leapt over the ocean, but its depth the Mount of Churning alone knows, for its mighty mass penetrated down even to the realms below.'

4. *The Date of Rājaçekhara*

Rājaçekhara, with the usual prolixity of bad poets, is voluble on his personality; he was of a Mahārāṣṭra Kṣatriya family of the Yāyāvaras, who claimed descent from Rāma; son of the minister Durduka or Duhika, and of Çīlavatī; grandson of Akālajalada, and descendant of Surānanda, Tarala, and Kavirāja, all

[1] vii. 107. [2] vii. 90. [3] Ed. p. 1, note.

poets of name. He married Avantisundarī of the Cāhamāna family, and was a moderate Çaiva.[1]

In the *Karpūramañjarī*, probably his first play since it was produced at the request of his wife, and not a king, he refers to himself as the teacher of Nirbhaya or Nirbhara, who was clearly the Pratihāra king, Mahendrapāla of Mahodaya or Kanyakubja, of whom we have records in A.D. 893 and 907. The *Bālarāmāyaṇa* was produced at his request. But he seems then to have visited another court, for the *Viddhaçālabhañjikā* was produced for the Kalacuri king, Yuvarāja Keyūravarṣa of Tripurī. But, as the unfinished *Bālabhārata* was written for Mahīpāla, successor of Mahendrapala, whose records begin in A.D. 914, we may assume that he returned to the court of the Pratihāras and died there. In the *Bālarāmāyaṇa* he speaks of six of his works, not apparently including the *Viddhaçālabhañjikā* and the *Bālabhārata*, and in fact we have many stanzas from him regarding famous authors, though of course the proof of derivation from this Rājaçekara is not always complete.

The *Bālarāmāyaṇa* shows to perfection Rājaçekhara's own estimate of himself. He traces his poetic descent from Vālmīki, through Bhartṛmeṇṭha and Bhavabhūti, but it is not clear that Bhartṛmeṇṭha must be assumed to have dramatized the work, and the little we know of this obscure person merely shows that he wrote an epic, the *Hayagrīvavadha*, while his date is involved in the problems of Vikramāditya and Mātṛgupta.[2]

5. *The Dramas of Rājaçekhara*

The *Bālarāmāyaṇa*[3] is a Mahānāṭaka, that is one in ten acts, and the author, to add to the horror of the length, has expanded the prologue to almost the dimensions of an act, celebrating his non-existent merits, and has expanded each act to almost the dimensions of a Nāṭikā. The whole has 741 stanzas, and of these no less than 203 are in the 19-syllable Çārdūlavikrīdita and 89 in the Sragdharā, which has two more syllables in each pada or 84 in a stanza. The play has a certain novelty, because

[1] Konow, *Karpūramañjarī*, pp. 177 ff.; Hultzsch, IA. xxxiv. 177 ff.; V. S. Apte, *Rājaçekhara*, Poona, 1886. Of special virtue is his *Kāvyamīmānsā* on rhetoric, which is better than his dramas.

[2] Winternitz, GIL. iii. 47; Lévi, TI. i. 183 f.

[3] Ed. Calcutta, 1884.

the author has made the love of Rāvaṇa the dominating feature. He appears in person in the first act, but declines to test himself by drawing Çiva's bow, and departs, menacing evil to any husband of Sītā. In Act II he seeks the aid of Paraçurāma, but is insulted instead, and a battle barely prevented by intervention of friends. In Act III the marriage of Sītā is enacted before him to distract his amorous sorrow, but the attempt is as little a success as it deserved to be; he interrupts, and finally the scene has to be broken off. In Act IV the duel of Rāma and Paraçurāma is disposed of, but in Act V we find another ludicrous effort to amuse Rāvaṇa; dolls with parrots in their mouths are presented to him as Sītā and his foster sister; he is deceived until he finds that his grasp is on wood; distracted, he demands his beloved from nature, the seasons, the streams, and the birds, as does Purūravas in the *Vikramorvaçī*. The arrival of Çūrpaṇakhā, his sister, who has suffered severely from her attack on Rāma, brings him to a condition of more manly rage. A tedious Act then carries matters down to the death of the sorrowing Daçaratha. In Act VII the problem of inducing the ocean to accept the burden of the bridge is solved; Dadhittha and Kapittha, two monkeys, describe at length its construction to Rāma. A momentary terror is caused by a stratagem of Mālyavant; the severed head of Sītā seems to be flung on the shore, but it speaks and reveals the fraud; it is the head of the speaking doll. In Act VIII we have Rāvaṇa's impressions as disaster after disaster is announced; he sends out Kumbhakarṇa, but sees even him helpless, despite his magic weapons, before Rāma. In Act IX Indra himself describes the last desperate duel of Rāma and Rāvaṇa. In Act X the party of Rāma makes the usual aerial tour of India, including the world of the moon, and ending with the inevitable consecration.

The *Bālabhārata*[1] is mercifully unfinished; it covers the marriage of Draupadī, and the gambling scene with the ill usage of Draupadī. The other two plays are really Nāṭikās, but the first, the *Karpūramañjarī*[2] is classed by the theory as a Saṭṭaka, simply because it is in Prākrit, none of the characters

[1] Ed. C. Cappeller, Strassburg, 1885; Weber, IS. xviii. 481 ff.

[2] Ed. S. Konow, trs. C. R. Lanman, HOS. iv. 1901; J. Charpentier, *Monde oriental*, ii. 226 ff.

speaking Sanskrit. It is the old story; here the king is Caṇḍapāla, possibly a compliment to Mahendrapāla, and his beloved the Kuntala princess, Karpūramañjarī, who is really a cousin of the queen. In Act I a magician, Bhairavānanda, displays the damsel to the king and queen; the apparition tells her tale, and the queen decides to add her to the number of her attendants. The king and the maiden fall at once in love. In Act II a letter from the maiden avows her passion, and the Vidūṣaka and her friend Vicakṣaṇā arrange to let the king see her swinging and also producing by her touch the blossoming of the Açoka. Between the Acts we must assume that the queen has found out the love, and has confined the maiden, while the king has secured the making of a subterranean passage giving access to her prison. In Act III by this means the princess and the king enjoy a flirtation in the garden, when the queen discovers them. In Act IV we find that the end of the passage giving on the garden has been blocked, but another passage has been made to the sanctuary of Cāmuṇḍā, the entrance concealed behind the statue. Thus the prisoner can play a game of hide-and-seek with the queen, and this enables her to carry out a clever ruse invented by the magician to secure the queen's blessing for the wedding. The queen is induced to demand that the king shall marry a princess of Lāṭa who will secure him imperial rank. She is still at her home, but the magician will fetch her to the place. The wedding goes on merrily, but the princess is no other than Karpūramañjarī, and the queen has unwittingly accomplished the lovers' desires.

The same motif is repeated in the *Viddhaçālabhañjikā*,[1] which is a regular Nāṭikā. Act I tells us that Candravarman of Lāṭa, vassal of Vidyādharamalla, has sent to the court of his overlord his daughter Mṛgāñkāvalī in the guise of his son and heir. The king, Vidyādharamalla, recounts a dream in the truthful hours of the morning, in which a beautiful maid had cast a collar of pearls round his neck; he is haunted by her, and next finds her in sculptured form (*çālabhañjikā*) in the picture gallery. He has a further glimpse of her in the flesh but no more, before the heralds announce midday. In Act II we learn that the queen proposes to marry Kuvalayamālā of Kuntala to the pretended

[1] Ed. Poona, 1886; trs. L. H. Gray, JAOS. xxvii. 1 ff.

boy, while the Vidūṣaka has been promised by her foster-sister, Mekhalā, marriage with a lady of the seductive name of Ambaramālā, Air Garland. Imagine his disgust when she turns out to be a mere slave; the king has to calm him, and together they watch in hiding Mṛgāñkāvalī playing in the garden, and hear her reading a letter of love. The heralds proclaim the evening hour. In Act III we are told that the dream of the king was reality, devised by Bhāgurāyaṇa, his minister, who knew that the husband of the heroine would attain imperial rule. The Vidūṣaka punishes Mekhalā's ruse by another; he bids a woman hide herself and call out a warning to Mekhalā of evil to befall her unless she crawl between a Brahmin's limbs. The queen begs the Vidūṣaka to permit this ceremony, and, it over, he avows the plot to the great indignation of the queen. The Vidūṣaka and the king then have an interview with the heroine. In Act IV we learn of a plot of the queen to punish the king. She induces him to agree to marry the sister of the pretended boy, meaning that he should find that he has married a boy. The king agrees; the marriage is completed; news comes from Candravarman that a son is born, begging the queen to dispose in marriage of his daughter, who may resume her sex. The queen, tricked and deceived, makes the best of her situation; with dignity and hauteur she bestows on her husband both Mṛgāñkāvalī and Kuvalayamālā, while news is brought that the last rebels are subdued and the king's suzerainty is recognized everywhere.

There can be no doubt of the demerits of Rājaçekhara's works; he is devoid of the power to create a character: Vidyādharamalla is stiff and uninteresting beside his model, the gay and gallant Vatsa; the queen is without the love or the majesty of Vāsavadattā; Bhāgurāyaṇa is a feeble Yaugandharāyaṇa, whose magician is borrowed in the *Karpūramañjarī* and spoiled in the borrowing. The heroines are without merit; the Vidūṣaka in the *Karpūramañjarī* is tedious, but Cārāyaṇa in the *Viddhaçālabhañjikā* has merits; he has plenty of sound common sense, though he is simple and capable of being taken in by others. The intrigue in both Nāṭikās is poorly managed; the confusion of exits and entrances in the *Karpūramañjarī* is difficult to follow and probably more difficult to act, while in the *Viddhaçālabhañjikā* the queen is induced to arrange a marriage out of a puerile incident affecting the Vidūṣaka only. The taste of giving two brides to the king at once is deplorable, as is the failure to explain why the king accepts the suggested marriage when ignorant of its true import.

In all his dramas, however, Rājaçekhara is merely concerned with exercises in style. The themes he frankly tells us in the prologue to the *Karpūramañjarī* are the same; the question is the expression, and the language is indifferent; therefore Prākrit being smooth, while Sanskrit is harsh, the language of women as opposed to men, can be used as a medium of style by one who boasts himself an expert in every kind of language. We have, therefore, elaborate descriptions in equally elaborate verses, of the dawn, midday, sunset, the pleasures of the harem, the game of ball, the swing, a favourite enjoyment of the Indian maidens, and in the Nāṭakas pictures *ad nauseam* of battles with magic weapons, and appalling mythical geography and topography. His allusions to local practices and customs may be interesting to the antiquarian, but are not poetical. More praiseworthy is his real accomplishment in metres, especially the Çārdūlavikrīḍita, his facility in which Kṣemendra justly praises, the Vasantatilaka, Çloka, and Sragdharā. His ability to handle elaborate Prākrit metres is undeniable; in 144 stanzas in the *Karpūramañjarī* he has 17 varieties. If poetry consisted merely of harmonious sound, he must be ranked high as a poet. He is fond of proverbs: *varaṁ takkālovaṇadā tittirī ṇa uṇa diahantaridā morī*, which gives our 'A bird in hand is worth two in the bush'; he introduces freely words from vernaculars, including Marāṭhī. But, despite his parade of learning, he cannot distinguish accurately Çaurasenī and Māhārāṣṭrī in his drama; in the former we find such forms as *laṭṭhi* for *yaṣṭi*, *ammi* in the locative and *hiṁto* in the ablative singular of *a*-stems, and *esa* for the pronoun. Important as he is lexicographically for both Sanskrit and Prākrit, it is undeniable that both were utterly dead languages for him, which he had laboriously learned. Forms like *ḍhilla* equivalent to *çithila* in the *Karpūramañjarī* show how far the vernaculars had advanced beyond the Prākrits of the drama.

It would, however, be quite unjust to deny to Rājaçekhara the power of effective expression; like all the later dramatists he is capable of producing elegant and attractive verses, which are largely spoiled in their context by their being embedded in masses of tasteless matter. Thus the benediction of the *Viddhaçālabhañjikā* is decidedly graceful:

kulagurur abalānāṁ kelidīkṣāpradāne
paramasuhṛd anaṅgo rohiṇīvallabhasya
api kusumapṛṣatkair devadevasya jetā
jayati suratalīlānāṭikāsūtradhāraḥ.

'Family preceptor of young maidens for the bestowal of the sacrament of love, the bodyless one, dearest friend of Rohiṇī's lover, he that with his flower arrows overthrew the god of gods, he is victorious ever, the director of the comedy of the play of love's mysteries.'

The description of summer is also pretty if banal:

rajaniviramayāmeṣv ādiçantī ratecchām
kim api kaṭhinayantī nārikelīphalāmbhaḥ
api pariṇamayitrī rājarambhāphalānām
dinapariṇatiramyā vartate grīṣmalakṣmīḥ.

'This is the glorious season of summer, delightful in the length of the days, when the royal plantain fruits are ripened, and the milk in the coco-nut is hardened, and the season bids us enjoy the delight of love in the closing watches of the night.'

The signs of a maiden distracted by unfulfilled affection are quaintly described:

candraṁ candanakardamena likhitaṁ sā mārṣṭi daṣṭādharā
bandhyaṁ nindati yac ca manmatham asau bhaṅktvāgrahastāṅgurīḥ
kāmaḥ puṣpaçaraḥ kileti sumanovargaṁ lunīte ca yat
tat kāmyā subhaga tvayā varatanur vātūlatāṁ lambhitā.

'Biting her lip, she wipes out the figure of the moon sketched in sandal paste; snapping her finger-tips she mocks at love as barren; to flout his darts, the flowers she gathers she tears in shreds; assuredly the fair one whom thou shouldst love hath been brought by thee to madness.'

antastāraṁ taralitatalāḥ stokam utpīḍabhājaḥ
pakṣmāgreṣu grathitapṛṣataḥ kīrṇadhārāḥ krameṇa
cittātaṅkaṁ nijagarimataḥ samyag āsūtrayanto
niryānty asyāḥ kuvalayadṛço bāṣpavārām pravāhāḥ.

'Rippled on the surface of the pupil, slightly foaming, forming drops on the tips of the lashes, then slowly issuing in streams, betokening by their weight her heart's sorrow, there pour forth from the lotus-eyed one the floods of her tears.'

Of all the plays the *Karpūramañjarī* is undoubtedly that which contains the most substantial evidence that Rājaçekhara had some real poetic talent, despite the banality and stupidity of his conception of love in Act III. The swing scene contains really effective lines of word-painting, in harmonious metre: [1]

vicchaanto ṇaararamaṇīmaṇḍalassāṇaṇāiṁ
viccholanto gaaṇakuharaṁ kantijoṇhājaleṇa
pecchantīṇaṁ hiaaṇihiaṁ ṇiddalanto a dappaṁ
dolālīlāsaralataralo dīsae se muhendū.

'Paling the face of every beauty here, making the sky's vault to ripple with the liquid moonlight of her loveliness, and breaking the haughty pride in the hearts of maids that regard her, appeareth the moon-like orb of her face as she moveth straight to and fro in her sport on the swing.' The effective alliteration and paronomasia of this stanza are surpassed by the metrical perfection of the next but one, where the Pṛthvī metre, with 'its jingling tribrachs and bell-like, chiming cretics', is employed in a stanza which admirably conveys by its sound the sense at which it aims:

raṇantamaṇiṇeuraṁ jhaṇajhaṇantahāracchaḍaṁ
kaṇakkaṇiakiṅkiṇīmuhalamehalāḍambaraṁ
vilolavalaāvalījaṇiamañjusiñjāravaṁ
ṇa kassa maṇomohaṇaṁ sasimuhīa hindolaṇaṁ.

'With the tinkling jewelled anklets,
With the flashing jewelled necklace,
With the show of girdles garrulous
From their ringing, ringing bells
With the sound of lovely jingles
From the rows of rolling bangles,
Pray whose heart is not bewildered
While the moon-faced maiden swings?'

Excellent also is the king's address [2] to the Açoka when made to blossom by the touch of the foot of his young beloved, but more characteristic in his comment,[3] inspired by the Vidūṣaka's

[1] ii. 30. The translation of this and the next verse is taken from Lanman's version.
[2] ii. 47. [3] ii. 49.

ungallant comparison of the fresh beauty of the maiden with the *passée* comeliness of his queen:

bālāu honti kuūhaleṇa emeya cavalacittāo
daralasiathaṇīsu puṇo ṇivasai maaraddhaarahassaṁ.

'Though maidens in their young zest for life are fickle of faith, yet it is with them—their breasts just budding—that the mystery of the dolphin-bannered doth abide.'

For technique Rājaçekhara is of interest, because he uses in the *Karpūramañjarī* the old form of prologue quite openly, with the Nāndī recited doubtless by the Sūtradhāra, followed by the advent of the Sthāpaka who recites two verses. It is noteworthy that the manuscripts often alter the Sthāpaka to the Sūtradhāra despite the clear sense of the text. The late *Pārvatīpariṇaya* likewise has a Nāndī before the Sūtradhāra speaks a verse. It is probable that the older technique long persisted in the south.

Rājaçekhara's indebtedness to his predecessors is wholesale; the influence of Kālidāsa, Harṣa, and Bhavabhūti is obvious, and it is probably an indication of his contemporaneity with, or slight posteriority to, Murāri that he does not seem to have known his writings. Influence of the vernacular or of Prākrit is to be seen in his occasional use of rhyme, such as is found in the later *Gītagovinda* or the *Mohamudgara*.

6. *Bhīmaṭa and Kṣemīçvara*

A verse attributed to Rājaçekhara mentions the five dramas of Bhīmaṭa, of which the *Svapnadaçānana* won him chief fame. He is described as a Kaliñjarapati, whence the suggestion has been made that he was a connection of the Candella king Harṣa of Jejākabhukti, who, we know, was a contemporary of Mahīpāla of Kanyakubja, patron of Rājaçekhara, but we have no ground for positive assertion.[1]

The case is different with Kṣemīçvara, who in his *Caṇḍakauçika* wrote for Mahīpāla, doubtless the king of Kanyakubja, patron of Rājaçekhara. Kṣemīçvara asserts his patron's victory over the Karṇāṭas, which was doubtless the view taken in royal circles of the contest against the Rāṣṭrakūṭa Indra III, who for his part claims victory over Mahodaya, or Kanyakubja.[1] A

[1] Konow, ID. p. 87; Peterson, *Reports*, ii. 63; Bhandarkar, *Report* (1897), p. xi.

variant of the name is Kṣemendra, but he is not to be identified with the Kashmirian poet of that name. His great-grandfather was called Vijayakoṣṭha or Vijayaprakoṣṭha, who is designated as both Ārya and Ācārya, and was, therefore, a learned man of some sort.

Kṣemīçvara has left two dramas. The *Naiṣadhānanda*[1] in seven acts deals with the legend of Nala, famous in the epic and later. The *Caṇḍakauçika*[2] reveals the stupid story of Hariçcandra, who, seeing as he thought the sacrifice of a damsel on the fire rebukes the Kauçika Viçvāmitra, and in return for his gallant action is cursed by the irascible sage, who was merely bringing the sciences under his control. He secures pardon by the surrender of the earth and a thousand gold pieces ; to secure the latter he sells wife and child to a Brahmin, and himself to a Caṇḍāla as a cemetery keeper. One day his wife brings the dead body of their child, but it turns out merely to be a trial of his character ; his son is alive and is crowned king. The plot is as poor as the execution of the piece. He shows in metre a special fondness for the Çikhariṇī, which occurs 20 times, nearly as often as the Çārdūlavikrīḍita (23), while the Vasantatilaka appears 27 times and the Çloka 36. His Prākrits, Çaurasenī and a few Māhārāṣṭri stanzas, are artificial.

The compilers of anthologies make little of Kṣemīçvara, with sufficient reason, for his verses do not rise above mediocrity. The second stanza of the three-verse benediction in the *Naiṣadhānanda* is on a common theme, but not unhappily expressed ; it follows a verse in honour of Puruṣottama and Çrī, with the usual impartiality of this period :

asthi hy asthi phaṇī phaṇī kim aparaṁ bhasma bhasmaiva tac
carmaiva carma kiṁ tava jītaṁ yenaivam uttāmyasi
naitāṁ dhūrta paṇīkaroṣi satatam mūrdhni sthitāṁ Jāhnavīm
ity evaṁ Çivayā sanarmagadito dyūte Haraḥ pātu vaḥ.

'A skull is but a skull, a serpent a serpent ; what more ? The ashes and the skin also which thou dost wear are but ashes and skin. What of thine hast thou lost that thus thou art outworn ? Ah, rogue, it is that thou wilt not stake Jahnu's daughter that

[1] Peterson, *Reports*, iii. 340 f.

[2] Ed. Calcutta, 1884; trs. L. Fritze, Leipzig, 1883. On the same theme is Rāmacandra's *Satyahariçcandra* (twelfth cent.); see Keith, JRAS. 1914, pp. 1104 f.

rests ever on thy crest. May Hara guard you, Hara to whom Çivā once spake playfully when they diced.'

This amusing play on the unwillingness of Çiva to prolong the dicing after he has unsuccessfully staked his necklace of skulls and serpents, and his clothing of ashes and hide, is followed by a wearisome eulogy of the glances of the god in the Tāṇḍava dance, alluding to the great moments in his history. Similar bad taste is shown in the curious and unusual form of the last verse of the drama:

yenādiçya prayogaṁ ghanapulakabhṛtā nāṭakasyāsya harṣād
vastrālaṁkārahemnām pratidinam akṛçā rāçayaḥ sampradattāḥ
tasya kṣattraprasūter bhramatu jagad idaṁ Kārttikeyasya kīrtiḥ
pāre kṣīrāmbhusindho ravikaviyaçasā sārdham agresareṇa.

'Through all the universe beyond the ocean of milk, heralded by the fame of his bard, the sun, may the fame wander of that scion of heroism, that god of war, who bade this drama be performed and who in keen delight at the pleasure he found in it gave daily to the poet abundant store of raiment, jewels and gold.' Such a mode of immortalizing himself, and his patron can hardly be regarded as precisely dignified, and it certainly is not in harmony with the traditions of the drama.

XI

THE DECLINE OF THE SANSKRIT DRAMA

1. *The Decadence of the Drama*

WE have seen already in Murāri and Rājaçekhara the process which was depriving the drama of real dramatic quality. The older poets were, indeed, under the influence of the epic; they lived in the atmosphere of the poetry of the court and their dramatic instincts had always to fight against the tendency to introduce epic and lyric verses into their works, heedless of the ruin thus wrought on the drama. Had the stage been a more popular one, this defect might have been counteracted, but the audience for whose approval a poet looked was essentially one of men of learning, who were intent on discerning poetic beauties or defects, and who, as the theory proves, had singularly little idea of what a drama really means.

Other factors doubtless helped the decline of the drama. The invasion of the Mahomedans into northern India, which began in earnest with the opening of the eleventh century, was a slow process, and it could not immediately affect the progress of the dramatic art. But gradually, by substituting Mahomedan rulers—men who disliked and feared the influence of the national religion, which was closely bound up with the drama—for Hindu princes, the generous and accomplished patrons of the dramatists, it must have exercised a depressing effect on the cultivation of this literary form. The drama doubtless took refuge in those parts of India where Moslem power was slowest to extend, but even there Mahomedan potentates gained authority, and drama can have been seldom worth performing or composing, until the Hindu revival asserted the Indian national spirit, and gave an encouragement to the renewal of an ancient national glory.

Yet a further and most important consideration must have lain in the ever-widening breach between the languages of the drama and those of real life. In Bhāsa's days and even those of Kālidāsa we may imagine that there was not too great difficulty in following the main features of the drama both in Sanskrit and in Prākrit, but the gulf between the popular languages and those of learning went on widening every year, and Rājaçekhara, as we have seen, was, despite his boasted studies, of which we have no reason to doubt, unable to discriminate correctly his Prākrits. It in no wise disproves this view that the *Lalitavigraharājanāṭaka* of Somadeva shows a close connexion with the language as laid down in Hemacandra's grammar, for, as that work preceded the play in date and was produced at the court of Aṇhilvāḍ, which was in close connexion with that of Sambhār, where Somadeva lived, we need not doubt that copies of Hemacandra's work were available for the production of artificial Prākrit.

It was clearly a very different thing to compose in Sanskrit and Prākrit in A.D. 1000, when the vernaculars were beginning to assume literary form, than in A.D. 400, and the difficulty of composition in any effective manner must have rapidly increased with the years, and the growth of the realization that it was idle to seek fame under modern circumstances by the composition of dramas, for which there was no popular audience and only a limited market. What is amazing is that for centuries the Sanskrit drama continued to be produced in very substantial numbers, as the existence of manuscripts proves, and that so strong was the force of tradition that the first attempt to introduce the vernacular into the drama by Bidyāpati Ṭhākur in Behar took the form of producing works in which the characters use Sanskrit and Prākrit and the songs only are in Maithilī. So powerful has been the strength of the Sanskrit drama that it is only in the nineteenth century that vernacular drama has exhibited itself in Hindi, and in general it is only very recently that the drama has seemed proper for vernacular expression. But the writing in artificial languages has revenged itself on the writers ; their works are reminiscent of modern copies of Greek or Latin verses, which only too painfully reveal through all the artifices suggested by careful study the impossibility of the production of real poetry, not to mention drama, in dead languages. It is significant in this regard that perhaps the most interesting of later dramas is the *Prabodhacandrodaya* of Kṛṣṇamiçra, a drama of allegory on philosophical topics, which claim as their right Sanskrit as a mode of expression. The Sanskrit of the author thus represents the medium of his habitual use in discussions and is appropriate to the matters dealt with.

This is essentially the period when the dramatic rules, strong in their hold earlier over the minds of dramatists, attain even greater sway. It is to this that we owe the few specimens we have of the rarer types of drama which are not represented among the scanty remains of the classical drama. There is no reason to suppose that these types were popular among the earlier dramatists; they had, it seems, their vogue in the time before the *Nāṭya-çāstra* assumed its present form, but were rejected as unsuitable by the classical drama. We have also specimens of types which may have been regularly produced in classical times, but none of which are represented in the extant literature. Finally, we have specimens of new forms, the result of efforts to introduce into Sanskrit dramatic forms which had sprung up in more popular circles.

2. *The Nāṭaka*

The Nāṭaka remains throughout the post-classical period of the drama the natural exponent of the higher form of the dramatic art. No change of importance appears in its character; it merely steadily develops those features which we have seen in full process of production in Murāri and Rājaçekhara, the subordination of action to description, and the degeneration of the description into a mere exercise in style and in the use of sounds.

The character of the decline is obvious enough in the *Prasannarāghava*,[1] a Nāṭaka in seven Acts, in which the logician Jayadeva (*c.* A. D. 1200), son of Mahādeva and Sumitrā, of Kuṇḍina in Berar, endeavours to tell again the story of the *Rāmāyaṇa*.[2] In Act I a disciple of Yājñavalkya appears and repeats from the speech of two bees heard behind the scene the news they are discussing; the Asura Bāṇa is to rival Rāvaṇa for the hand of

[1] Ed. Bombay, 1894; Poona, 1894; cf. Baumgartner, *Das Râmâyaṇa*, pp. 129 ff.

[2] Cf. Peterson, *Subhāṣitāvali*, pp. 38 f.; Keith, *Indian Logic*, pp. 33 f. The verses common to the play and the *Mahānāṭaka* are clearly not evidence of prior date, despite Lévi, TI. ii. 48; Konow, ID. p. 88. He is later than Murāri; Hall's (DR. p. 36 n.) suggested reference to Jayadeva in comm. on DR. ii. 10 is incorrect. He is known to R. (*c.* A. D. 1330); iii. 171 f., and the *Çārṅgadharapaddhati*.

Sītā. Two heralds then appear to describe the suitors for the maiden's hand; they are interrupted and insulted by a gross and rough arrival who casts a contemptuous eye on the bow which the suitor must bend, and would forcibly seize the prize. The heralds soothe him, but he assumes the monstrous form of Rāvaṇa with his ten heads. Bāṇa then appears, tries in vain the bow, insults Rāvaṇa and retires. In Act II we have a ludicrous scene in which Rāma watches Sītā and her friend; both he and she describe the beauties of the union of the Vāsantī creeper and the mango-tree, an allusion to their own state to be, and confronted shyly whisper love. In Act III we have an intolerable series of compliments exchanged by all the parties, Viçvāmitra, Çatānanda, Janaka, Daçaratha, Rāma, and Lakṣmaṇa; Viçvāmitra bids Rāma bend the bow of Çiva, though a message from Paraçurāma deprecates such an insult. The bow is broken, there is great joy, and the marriage is celebrated. In Act IV Paraçurāma himself arrives; his great feats are set out in a dialogue of Rāma and Lakṣmaṇa; he encounters them, exchanges harangues, is dissuaded by Janaka, Çatānanda, and Viçvāmitra from battle, but an insult of his to Viçvāmitra breaks down Rāma's patience; they fight, Rāma is victor, but falls at his rival's feet and asks his blessing. In Act V we have a new and picturesque conception and one wholly aloof from drama. The river goddess Yamunā tells Gañgā of her grief at Vālin's act in exiling his brother, Sugrīva. Sarayū joins them and reports the fate of Rāma until his departure for exile; her flamingo arrives to carry on the tale until Rāma's fatal departure in pursuit of a golden deer. Anxious, the rivers hasten to the ocean, Sāgara, to learn the news; they find Godāvarī in converse with Sāgara; she tells of the rape of Sītā, the death of Jaṭāyu, the fall of Sītā's jewels and their transport to Ṛṣyamukha. The Tuñgabhadrā arrives with her tale; Rāma has slain Vālin and made alliance with Sugrīva and Hanumant. Suddenly a great mass flies over the ocean. Is it the Himālaya? the Vindhya? Sāgara goes out to see and the rivers follow. In Act VI we find that sorrow has all but driven Rāma mad; he asks the birds, the moon, for his beloved. Fortunately two Vidyādharas by magic art are able to show him the events in Lañkā; Sītā appears, saddened lest Rāma suspect, or be faithless to her; Rāvaṇa seeks her love; she despises him; angry, he reaches out his hand for his sword to slay her, but receives in it the head of his son, Akṣa, slain by Hanumant, who it is who has leaped the ocean and attacked Lañkā. Sītā is desperate; she seeks to burn herself on a funeral pyre, but the coal changes to pearl, and Hanumant consoles her by news of Rāma's fidelity. In Act VII Rāvaṇa is given by Prahasta a picture sent by Mālyavant showing the details of the enemy's attack and the bridge; he refuses to regard it as more than a painter's fancy; Mandodarī, his wife, enters; she has received an oracular response which terrifies her and also Prahasta, but Rāvaṇa scorns it. At last, however, he realizes that the city is attacked, sends Kumbhakarṇa and Meghanāda to their death, and at last himself issues forth to die; his fate is described by a Vidyādhara and his mate. Then enter Rāma, Sītā, Lakṣmaṇa, Vibhīṣaṇa, and Sugrīva, who all describe in turn the setting of the sun and the rise of the moon; they mount the aerial car, describe a few points of interest in the country over which they pass in their journey north, and then in turn solemnly describe the rising of the sun.

The play is typical of the later drama; its one merit is Act V where the spectacle of the river goddesses grouped round the ocean affords admirable scope for an effective tableau, but it is wholly out of harmony with dramatic action. As usual, the author is fond of the long metres, though the Vasantatilaka is his favourite; then comes the Çārdūlavikrīḍita, Çloka, Çikhariṇī, and Sragdharā, while he shows decided fondness for the Svāgatā, which occurs a few times in Rājaçekhara and the *Mahānāṭaka*, but is not employed in the earlier drama. The drama is superior in merit to the other very popular Rāma drama, the *Jānakīpariṇaya*[1] by Rāmabhadra Dīkṣita, who flourished and wrote many bad works at the end of the seventeenth century. The number of Rāma dramas already known is enormous; any one of merit appears still to be unearthed. The commentary on the *Daçarūpa* knows a *Chalitarāma* which would probably date before A.D. 1000, but its preservation is problematical. The *Adbhutadarpaṇa*[2] of Mahādeva, son of Kṛṣṇa Sūri, a contemporary of Rāmabhadra Dīksita, shows Jayadeva's influence in that it presents the events

[1] Ed. Madras, 1892; trs. by L. V. Ramachandra Aiyar, Madras, 1906.
[2] Ed. KM. 1896.

at Laṅkā as happening by means of a magic mirror. Its ten acts cover only the period from Aṅgada's mission to Rāvaṇa to the coronation of Rāma, and it introduces, contrary to the rule in Rāma dramas, the figure of the Vidūṣaka.

The Kṛṣṇa legend naturally attracted not less note; the Kerala prince Ravivarman, born in A.D. 1266, is the author of a *Pradyumnābhyudaya*.[1] The minister of Husain Shāh Rūpa Gosvāmin wrote about A.D. 1532 the *Vidagdhamādhava*[2] and the *Lalitamādhava*[3] in seven and ten Acts respectively on the theme of the loves of Kṛṣṇa and Rādhā, in pursuance of his eager support of the movement of Caitanya. For the son of Ṭodar Mall, Akbar's minister, Çeṣa Kṛṣṇa wrote the *Kaṅsavadha*[4] which in seven Acts covers the ground of Bhāsa's *Bālacarita*, as well as other plays on the Rāma legend. The winning of Rukmiṇī by Kṛṣṇa is the theme of the *Rukmiṇīpariṇaya*[5] by Rāmavarman of Travancore (1735–87), and Kṛṣṇa's generosity to a poor friend, though in a surprising shape, is recounted by Sāmarāja Dīkṣita in the *Çrīdāmacarita*[6] written in A.D. 1681.

The number of dramas based on the *Mahābhārata* is decidedly smaller. We have not the *Citrabhārata* of the indefatigable Kṣemendra of Kashmir, who wrote in the middle of the eleventh century. But from that century probably are the *Subhadrādhanaṅjaya* and *Tapatīsaṁvaraṇa*[7] of the Kerala king Kulaçekharavarman, and from about A.D. 1200 the *Pārthaparākrama*,[8] a Vyāyoga, to be discussed hereafter, of Prahlādanadeva, a Yuvarāja, brother of Dhārāvarṣa, lord of Candrāvatī.

Of other mythological subjects we have the *Harakelināṭaka*[9] of the Cāhamāna king Vīsaladeva Vigraharāja, of whom we have an inscription of A.D. 1163, and whose work is partially preserved on stone. The *Pārvatīpariṇaya*[10] of Vāmana Bhaṭṭa Bāṇa, who wrote about A.D. 1400 under the Reḍḍi prince Vema of Koṇḍavīḍu, owes its fame to its being mistaken for a work of Bāṇa. The *Haragaurīvivāha*[11] of Jagajjyotirmalla of Nepal (1617–33) is interesting, because it is rather an opera than a play and the

[1] Ed. TSS. 1910. [2] Ed. KM. 1903.
[3] Ed. Murçidābād, 1880 f. [4] Ed. KM. 1888. [5] Ed. KM. 1894.
[6] Wilson, ii. 404. [7] Ed. TSS. 1912 and 1911. [8] Ed. GOS. 1917.
[9] Kielhorn, *Bruchstücke indischer Schauspiele*, Berlin, 1901.
[10] Ed. R. Schmidt, Leipzig, 1917; trs. K. Glaser, Trieste, 1886. Cf. GIL. iii. 248, n. 4.
[11] Lévi, *Le Népal*, ii. 242.

vernacular verses are its only fixed element, but this is not likely to be a primitive feature.

Of dramas with lesser personages of the saga as heroes we have the *Bhairavānanda*[1] of the Nepalese poet Maṇika from the end of the fourteenth century, and at least a century later the *Bhartṛharinirveda*[2] of Harihara, which is interesting, as it shows the popularity of Bhartṛhari; he is represented as desolated by his wife's death, through despair on a false rumour of his own death, but, consoled by a Yogin, he attains indifference, so that, when his wife is recalled to life, neither she nor their child has any attraction for him.

Of historical drama we have little, and that of small value. The *Lalitavigraharājanāṭaka*,[3] preserved in part in an inscription, is a work of the latter part of the twelfth century by Somadeva in honour of Vīsaladeva Vigraharāja, the Cāhamāna. The *Pratāparudrakalyāṇa*[4] by Vidyānatha, inserted in his treatise on rhetoric as an illustration of the drama, celebrates his patron, a king of Warangal about A.D. 1300.

More interesting is the *Hammīramadamardana*,[5] written between A.D. 1219 and 1229 by Jayasiṅha Sūri, the priest of the temple of Munisuvrata at Broach. It appears that Tejaḥpāla, brother of Vastupāla, minister of Vīradhavala of Gujarāt, visited the temple, and, with the assent of his brother, complied with the request of Jayasiṅha for the erection of twenty-five golden flagstaffs for Devakulikās. As a reward Jayasiṅha not merely celebrated the brothers in a panegyric, of which a copy has been preserved along with his drama, but wrote, to please Jayantasiṅha, son of Vastupāla, the play for performance at the festival of the procession of the god Bhīmeçvara at Cambay. He claims that it includes all nine sentiments, in contrast to Prakaraṇas, exploiting the sentiment of fear, with which the audience has been surfeited.

In Act I, after the introductory dialogue between the Sūtradhāra and an actor, Vīradhavala is brought in, conversing with Tejaḥpāla, the theme being the extraordinary merits of Vastu-

[1] Haraprasād, *Nepal Catal.*, p. xxxvii.

[2] Ed. KM. 1900; trs. L. H. Gray, JAOS. xxv. 197 ff.

[3] Ed. Kielhorn, *op. cit.*

[4] Ed. Bombay, 1891.

[5] Ed. *Gaekwad's Oriental Series*, no. x, 1920. On the merits of Vastupāla see also Arisiṅha's *Sukṛtasaṁkīrtana* and Someçvara's *Kīrtikaumudī*.

pāla as a statesman. But times are still troublous; the realm is menaced by the Turuṣka Hammīra, by the Yādava Siṅhana,[1] who may hope for aid from Saṁgrāmasiṅha, nephew of Siṅha, lord of Lāṭa. Vastupāla enters, and extols the skill of Tejaḥpāla's son Lāvaṇyasiṅha, whose spies bring in valuable information. He then with Tejaḥpāla compliments the king, who tells them of his proposed attack on Hammīra. Vastupāla warns him against excessive valour in pursuit, and counsels him to secure the aid of the Mārvār princes. In Act II we find that the advice has been followed with success, as related by Lāvaṇyasiṅha, who has an opportunity of repaying the compliments showered on him by his uncle. The spy Nipuṇaka then enters with a tale of success; he has entered Siṅhana's camp, passed himself off as a spy on Vīradhavala's movements, reported that that king was making ready an attack on Hammīra, and persuaded Siṅhana to wait in the forest of the Tapti a favourable opportunity to attack Vīradhavala, after his forces have been weakened by battle with Hammīra. In the meantime Nipuṇaka's brother Suvega, who has been serving Devapāla of Mālava, steals the best steed of his master and presents it to Saṁgrāmasiṅha, who is leading Siṅhana's army. He then presents himself in the guise of a Tāpasa to Siṅhana, but runs away when the king goes to pay him due honour. Suspicion is thus aroused, and Suvega is seized; from his matted locks is extracted a letter addressed to Saṁgrāmasiṅha. It refers to the horse which it treats as a present from Devapāla to Saṁgrāmasiṅha, and advises him to attack Siṅhana when he has entered Gujarāt, the Mālava king engaging to assail him at that moment. Siṅhana asks Nipuṇaka to ascertain the truth about the horse, and he has no difficulty through Suvega in terrifying Saṁgrāmasiṅha into flight. We then find Vastupāla on the stage; his spy Kuçalaka reports that Saṁgrāmasiṅha menaces Cambay; Vastupāla takes precautions for its defence, and summons Bhuvanapāla, Saṁgrāmasiṅha's minister, with whom he arrives at an understanding, assuring Vīradhavala of that prince's aid. In Act III Vīradhavala and Tejaḥpāla hear from a spy Kamalaka the fate of Mewār's king Jayatala; attacked by the Mlecchas, the people in despair flung

[1] Usually Siṅghaṇa or Siṅhaṇa. Cf. Bhandarkar, *Report* (1907), pp. 15 ff., who equates Mīlacchīkāra with Shamsu-d-din (1210–35).

themselves into wells, burned themselves in their houses or hanged themselves, until he had heartened them and discouraged the foe by announcing the approach of Vīradhavala, at whose name the Turuṣkas fled in terror. Vīradhavala extols the cleverness of Vastupāla, who has enabled him to dispose of all his enemies save the Mlecchas, and Tejaḥpāla assures him of succes even against these foes. What Vastupāla is doing is shown by a conversation between two spies, Kuvalayaka and Çīghraka, which forms the entr'acte to Act IV; he has induced the Kaliph of Baghdad by a false report to instruct Kharpara Khāna to send Mīlacchrīkāra to him in chains, and he has won over various Gūrjara princes by promising them the lands of the Turuṣkas when they are defeated. We then find Mīlacchrīkāra discussing his situation with his minister Gorī Īsapa; Kharpara Khāna, on the one hand, and Vīradhavala press him hard; the king declines, however, even to think of retreat, but both king and minister flee hastily before the sound of the approach of Vīradhavala's army and the voice of the king, who is disappointed not to capture his foes, but obeys loyally Vastupāla's counsel against rash pursuit. Act V shows us the triumphant return of the king, his reunion with his wife Jayataladevī, and exchange of felicitations with Vastupāla and Tejaḥpāla. We learn that Vastupāla has accomplished a further feat; he has intercepted at sea Radī and Kadī, Mīlacchrīkāra's preceptors, returning from Baghdad, and the king has been forced, in order to secure their safety, to enter into friendly relations. Finally the king enters Çiva's temple, where the god presents himself before him, and grants him a boon; the king, however, has little that is not formal to ask, so fortunate is he in his ministers.

Neither as history nor as poetry does the work claim any high merit. Its chief aim is to provide unlimited eulogy for Vastupāla and Tejaḥpāla, and secondarily for the king who is lucky enough to have in his retinue these remarkable models of intelligence and skill. It must be admitted, however, that the author does not exactly convey the impression of the real success of his objects of admiration; the impression is rather one of minor successes and a good deal of rather obvious diplomacy. Style, Prākrit, and metres are decidedly stereotyped.

A certain number of dramas of similar type has been preserved.[1] Gaṅgādhara's *Gaṅgadāsapratāpavilāsa*[2] celebrates the struggle of a Campānīr prince against Muhammed II, Shāh of Gujarāt (A. D. 1443–52). The stream, though scanty, flows continuously to the *Ḍillīsāmrājya*[3] of Lakṣmaṇa Sūri of 1912.

The adaptation of English drama is seen in R. Kṛṣṇamachari's adaptation in 1892 of the *Midsummer Night's Dream* in his *Vāsantikasvapna*.[4]

3. *The Allegorical Nāṭaka*

We cannot say whether Kṛṣṇamiçra's *Prabodhacandrodaya*[5] was a revival of a form of drama, which had been practised regularly if on a small scale since Açvaghoṣa or whether it was a new creation, as may easily have been the case. At any rate, his work can be dated with precision; it was produced for one Gopāla in the presence of the Candella king Kīrtivarman of Jejākabhukti, of whom we have an inscription of A.D. 1098. Gopāla had restored, we learn, Kīrtivarman after his defeat by Karṇa of Cedi, who was living in A.D. 1042, but we can only guess that he was a general. The play in its six Acts is devoted to the defence of the Advaita form of the Viṣṇu doctrine, a combination of Vedānta with Viṣṇuism.

The supreme reality which is truly one, but is united with illusion, has a son, Spirit, who again has two children, Discrimination (*viveka*) and Confusion (*moha*); the posterity of the latter has largely gained in strength, and the position of the former and his offspring is menaced. This is told us at the outset of the drama by Love in converse with Desire; the former is sure he has done much to attain the result. The one danger is the old prophecy that there will arise Knowledge (*prabodha*) and Judgement or Science (*vidyā*) from the union of Discrimination and Theology, Upaniṣad, but these two are long since parted, and their reunion seems unlikely. The two, however, flee before the approach of the king Discrimination who is talking with Reason

[1] We hear of a *Rājarājanāṭaka* performed annually in a temple of Çiva by order of the Cola Rājarāja I of Tanjore in the eleventh century, but of its content we know nothing; H. Krishna Sastri in Ridgeway's *Dramas*, &c., p. 204.

[2] *India Office Catal.*, no. 4194.

[3] Ed. Madras, 1912.

[4] Kumbhakonam, 1892.

[5] Ed. Bombay, 1898; trs. J. Taylor, Bombay, 1893. Cf. J. W. Boissevain, *Prabodhacandrodaya*, Leiden, 1905.

(*mati*), one of his wives; to his joy he finds that she is all in favour of his reunion with Theology which she is fain to bring about. In Act II we find Confusion in fear of overthrow; he hastens by the use of Falsity (*dambha*) to secure Benares as the key of the world; Egoism, grandfather of Falsity, visits the city and discovers to his joy his relative. Confusion enters in triumphant pomp his new capital; the Materialist Cārvāka supports him. But there is bad news; Duty is rising in revolt; Theology meditates reunion with Discrimination; Confusion bids his minions cast Piety, daughter of Faith (*çraddhā*) in prison and orders Heresy (*mithyādṛṣṭi*) to separate Theology and Faith. In Act III Piety appears supported by her friend Pity; she has lost her mother Faith and is in sad plight, even dreaming of suicide, from which Pity dissuades her. In Digambara Jainism, Buddhism, and Somism she searches in vain for Faith; each appears with a wife claiming to be Faith, but she cannot recognize her mother in these distorted forms. Buddhism and Jainism quarrel; Somism enters, makes them drunk with alcohol and pleasure, and takes them off in search of Piety, the daughter of Faith. In Act IV Faith in great distress tells of a danger; she and Duty have escaped from a demoness who would have devoured them but for Trust in Viṣṇu, who has saved them. She brings a message to Discrimination to start the battle. He musters his leaders, Contemplation, Patience, Contentment, and himself goes to Benares, which he describes. In Act V the battle is over; Confusion and his offspring are dead. But Spirit is disconsolate, mourning the loss of Confusion and Activity. The doctrine of Vyāsa, the Vedānta, appears, disabuses his mind of error, and he resolves to settle down as a hermit with the one wife worthy of him, Inactivity. Act VI shows us the ancestor of all Being; he is still under the influence of Confusion, who, before dying, dispatched to him spirits to confuse him, and his companion, Illusion, favours their efforts. But his friend Reasoning shows him his error, and he drives them away. Peace of heart reunites Theology and Discrimination; she tells of her mishaps with Cult and Exegesis, Nyāya and Sāṁkhya, and reveals to Being that he is the Supreme Lord. This, however, is too much for his intellect, but the difficulty is cleared away by Judgement, which is the immediate supernatural child of the reunion of the spouses. The appearance of Trust (*bhakti*) in Viṣṇu to applaud the result terminates the drama.

No one can doubt the cleverness with which the strife of races of one stock in the *Mahābhārata* and the plot and love interest of the usual Nāṭikā are combined, nor the ingenuity of fitting in the Vedānta doctrine of the Absolute and the devotion of the Vaiṣṇava creed. There is certainly some comedy in the exchange of views of Egoism and Falsity, who are perfect examples of hypocrisy, and the scenes between Buddhism, Jainism, and Somism are distinctly funny. None the less it would be idle to pretend that the play has any dramatic force. Its chief merits are its effective and stately stanzas of moral and philosophical content. Kṛṣṇamiçra is an able master of the Çārdūlavikrīḍita, his favourite metre; he has also effective Vasantatilakas, and rhymed Prākrit stanzas.

Kṛṣṇamiçra's example has caused the production of numerous dramas of the same type, but of much less value. The *Saṁkalpasūryodaya*[1] of Veṅkaṭanātha of the fourteenth century is excessively dreary, but it is better than the famous *Caitanyacandrodaya*[2] of Kavikarṇapūra, which is an account of Caitanya's success, but which wholly fails to convey any suggestion of his spiritual power. He turns out as a long-winded discourser of a muddled theology, surrounded by obedient and unintelligent pupils. Two Çaiva dramas are the *Vidyāpariṇayana*[3] and *Jīvānandana*[4] written at the end of the seventeenth and beginning of the eighteenth century. They have no merits.

An example of a Jain allegory of comparatively early date is afforded by the *Moharājaparājaya*,[5] the conquest of King Confusion, describing the conversion of the Caulukya king of Gujarāt, Kumārapāla, to Jainism, his prohibition of the killing of animals, and his cessation from the practice of confiscating the property of persons dying without heirs in the realm, as a result of the

[1] Ed. Kāñcī, 1914; trs. K. Narayanacharya and D. Raghunathaswamy Iyengar, vol. i. Srirangam, 1917.

[2] Ed. KM. 1906; analysed by Lévi, TI. i. 237 ff. Date, *c.* A.D. 1550.

[3] Ed. KM. 1893. Another imitation is the *Amṛtodaya* of Gokulanātha, Haraprasād, *Report* (1901), p. 17.

[4] Ed. KM. 1891. For the author of the *Vidyāpariṇayana* (Vedakavi, nominally Ānandarāya) see KM. xliv. Pref. p. 9.

[5] Ed. *Gaekwad's Oriental Series*, no. ix. 1918.

efforts of the famous sage, Hemacandra. The author, Yaçaḥpāla, was the son of a minister Dhanadeva and Rukmiṇī, of the Moḍha Bania caste, and he served the Cakravartin Abhayadeva or Abhayapāla, who reigned after Kumārapāla from A.D. 1229–32. The play is in five Acts, and all the personages save the king, Hemacandra, and the Vidūṣaka, are personifications of qualities, good and evil. The play was performed on the occasion of the festival of the idol of Mahāvīra at the Kumāravihāra, or temple erected by Kumārapāla, at Thārāpadra, where the author seems to have been governor or resident.

The play begins with an invocation in three stanzas of the Tīrthakaras, Ṛṣabha, Pārçva, and Mahāvīra, followed by the usual dialogue of the Sūtradhāra and the actress, his wife. Then are introduced Kumārapāla with the Vidūṣaka, to whom enter Jñānadarpaṇa, the Mirror of Knowledge, the spy who has been sent to report on the affairs of King Confusion. He reports the successful siege by Confusion of the city of Man's Mind, whose king, Vivekacandra, the Moon of Discrimination, has been forced to flee accompanied by his bride Calm, and his daughter Kṛpāsundarī, in whom Compassion is incorporated, and of whose escape Kumārapāla learns with joy. The spy further reports a meeting with Kīrtimañjarī, the Garland of Fame, daughter of Good Conduct by his wife Polity, and herself wife of Kumārapāla. She complains that the king has turned from her and her brother, Pratāpa, Valour, owing to the efforts of a Jain monk. She has, therefore, sought the aid of Confusion and he is preparing to attack Kumārapāla. The spy, however, disappoints her by answering her inquiry as to the victory in the struggle by insisting that it will be Confusion that must fall. The king expresses his determination to overthrow Confusion, and the announcement of the hour of worship by bards terminates the Act.

An entr'acte then tells us through Puṇyaketu, the Banner of Merit, minister of the king, that Discrimination has arrived at the penance grove of Hemacandra, and has met the king, who has looked favourably at his daughter. The Act itself shows us in the accustomed mode the king with the jester spying on Kṛpāsundarī and Somatā, Gentleness,[1] her companion, and ultimately

[1] This is probably the nuance intended, as in *saumyatā*.

speaking to them; as usual the queen, Rājyaçrī, the Royal Fortune, with her companion, Raudratā, Harshness, intervenes, and the king vainly craves pardon. In Act III Puṇyaketu overcomes the obstacle to the match by a clever device; he stations one of his servants behind the image of the goddess to which the queen goes to seek the boon of the disfigurement of her rival, and thus, through apparent divine intervention, the queen is taught that by marriage with Kṛpāsundarī alone can the king overcome Confusion, and is induced to beg Discrimination for the hand of his daughter. Discrimination consents, but insists that to please his daughter the seven vices must be banished, and the practice of confiscating the property of those dying without heirs shall be abolished, terms to which the queen consents. The king also agrees, and the Act ends in his action in forgoing the property of a millionaire believed dead, who, however, opportunely turns up with a new bride in an aerial car.

In Act IV we have the fulfilment of the pledge to banish the seven vices. It first tells of the meeting of the Fortune of the City with that of the Country; the former persuades the latter to accept the tenets of Jainism. Then appears Kṛpāsundarī who is annoyed by the noises of hunting and fishing, but consoled by the appearance of the police officer, who proceeds to the business of banishing vices. Gambling, Flesh-eating, Drinking, Slaughter, Theft, and Adultery must depart, despite the plea that the king's predecessors permitted them, and that they bring revenues to the State; Concubinage may remain if she will. In Act V the king, armed by Hemacandra with his *Yogaçāstra*, which is his armour, and the *Vītarāgastuti*, which serves to make him invisible, inspects the strong places of Confusion, and finally rendering himself visible does battle with the adversary and wins a great victory. He restores Discrimination to his capital, and pronounces a benediction in which praise of the Jina and of Hemacandra blend with the desire of close union with Kṛpā and Discrimination, and the hope that 'my fame, allied with the moon, may prevail to dispel the darkness of Confusion'.

The play is certainly not without merits; in the main it is written in simple Sanskrit, free from the artifices which disfigure more pretentious plays, and it has also the merit of bringing vividly before us the activities of Jainism in its regulation of

Kumārapāla's kingdom, casting an interesting light on what is known from inscriptions and other sources of the history of Gujarāt. The marriage of the king with Kṛpāsundarī is recorded by Jinamaṇḍana in his *Kumārapālaprabandha* as taking place in A.D. 1159. Interesting details are given of the forms of gambling, including chess, and of the sects which approve slaughter. The Prākrits are, of course, deeply influenced by Hemacandra's grammar, and include Māgadhī and Jain Māhārāṣṭrī.

4. *The Nāṭikā and the Saṭṭaka*

The Nāṭikā differs in no real essential from a Nāṭaka save in the number of Acts, but its type continues to be rigidly restricted to that set by Harṣa. The *Karṇasundarī*[1] of Bilhaṇa belongs to the period about A.D. 1080–90. It seems to have been written out of compliment to Karṇadeva Trailokyamalla of Aṇhilvāḍ (1064–94), and to celebrate his wedding in advanced age with Miyāṇalladevī, daughter of the Karṇāṭa king, Jayakeçin. The story runs that the Cālukya king is to marry Karṇasundarī, daughter of the Vidyādhara king. The minister introduces her into the harem, and the king first sees her in a dream, then in a picture. He falls in love, and the queen is jealous; she breaks in on their meeting, and once assumes Karṇasundarī's guise to present herself to the king. Next she tries to marry the king to a boy in Karṇasundarī's clothes, but the minister adroitly substitutes the real for the feigned damsel, and the usual tidings of triumph abroad ends the play, which is a patent jumble of reminiscences of Kālidāsa, Harṣa, and Rājaçekhara.

Madana Bālasarasvatī, preceptor of the Paramāra Arjunavarman of Dhārā, wrote the *Vijayaçrī* or *Pārijātamañjarī*,[2] a Nāṭikā in four Acts, of which two are preserved on stone at Dhārā. A garland falls on the breast of Arjunavarman after his victory over the Cālukya king, Bhīmadeva II, and becomes a maiden, who is handed over to the charge of the Chamberlain. She is the daughter of the Cālukya, and the usual sequence of events leads to her wedlock with the king. There is doubtless a historical reference; the date of the play is early in the thirteenth century.

[1] Ed. KM. 1888. Cf. Keith, *Sansk. Lit.*, pp. 64 ff.

[2] Ed. E. Hultzsch, Leipzig, 1906; cf. GGA. 1908, pp. 98 ff.

Rather less commonplace is Mathurādāsa's effort in the *Vṛṣabhānujā*[1] to make a Nāṭikā of the love of Kṛṣṇa and Rādhā. He was a Kāyastha of Suvarṇaçekhara on the Ganges and Yamunā, and he uses the motive of the jealousy of Rādhā for a portrait of a lady which Kṛṣṇa has, but which turns out to be one of herself. A philosophic play is Narasiṅha's *Çivanārāyanabhañjamahodaya*, in honour of a prince of Keonjhor.

The Saṭṭaka with its demand for Prākrit was too exacting for the average poet; we have only the *Ānandasundarī*[2] of the tedious Ghanaçyāma, minister of the Marāṭha Tukkojī and the *Çṛṅgāramañjarī*[3] of the Almora poet Viçveçvara of the eighteenth century.

5. *The Prakaraṇa*

The example of the *Mṛcchakaṭikā* induced few imitations, doubtless because would-be imitators had the sense to realize the appalling difficulties of producing anything worthy of setting beside that masterpiece. There is, however, a servile redaction of the same idea as that of the *Mālatimādhava* of Bhavabhūti in the *Mallikāmāruta*[4] of Uddaṇḍin or Uddaṇḍanātha, who has had the quite undeserved honour of being taken for Daṇḍin, but who was really no more than the court poet of the Zemindar of Kukkuṭakroḍa or Calicut in the middle of the seventeenth century. The plot follows that of Bhavabhūti's play almost slavishly. The magician Mandākinī is eager to arrange a marriage between Mallikā, daughter of the minister of the Vidyādhara king and Māruta, son of the minister of the king of Kuntala. She arranges an interview between the two, who fall in love, but the match is disturbed by the desire of the king of Ceylon for Mallikā's hand. Māruta's friend Kalakaṇṭha is also in love with Ramayantikā. In Act III there is the usual temple scene, and a couple of elephants are let loose to frighten the two maidens and cause two rescues. Then Māruta is told by an emissary of the king of Ceylon that Kalakaṇṭha is dead, and is only saved from suicide by his friend's appearance. In

[1] Ed. KM. 1895. The late *Mṛgāṅkalekhā* of Viçvanātha son of Trimaladeva, is summarized in Wilson, ii. 390 f.

[2] Hultzsch, *Reports*, no. 2142. He wrote a Nāṭaka, a Bhāṇa, a Prahasana, and the *Ḍamaruka* in ten Alaṁkāras; *Madras Catal.* xxi. 8403 ff.

[3] KM., Part 8, p. 51.

[4] Ed. Calcutta, 1878.

Act V Māruta tries conjuring up spirits; he finds Mallikā stolen by a Rākṣasa, rescues her, but is himself stolen, and finally overcomes the demon. But the marriage is to proceed, so that we have the elopement of Māruta and Mallikā, and the usual deception of the bridegroom, while the other couple follow the example set and elope also. The inevitable second abduction of Mallikā takes place, with the necessary search for her, which at last is rewarded; all are united under Mandākinī's protection, and the king and the parents accord their sanction.

The work is metrically interesting, because the author shows a remarkable preference for the Vasantatilaka (118), and, while he is fond of the Çārdūlavikrīḍita and employs a great variety of metres, he, unlike most later authors, uses freely the Āryā in its different forms (74).

We know also of Prakaraṇas written by Jain writers.[1] Rāmacandra, pupil of the great Hemacandra, who perished under the reign of Ajayapāla, nephew and successor of Hemacandra's patron, Kumārapāla, between A.D. 1173 and 1176, wrote, besides other plays, the *Kaumudīmitrāṇanda*[2] in ten Acts. The work is wholly undramatic and is really the working up in the form of a play of a number of Kathā incidents, presenting a result not unlike the plot of a modern pantomime. We first learn of a merchant's son, Mitrāṇanda, who on the island of Varuṇa attains as wife the daughter, Kaumudī, of the head of a monastery, after he and his friend have freed from durance the Siddha king, cruelly nailed to a tree by Varuṇa. She reveals to him the fact that the ascetics are frauds, and that the fate of her husbands is normally to be flung into a pit under the nuptial chamber; in this case, however, attracted to her husband by the love charm he had received from Varuṇa, she agrees to flee with him and the treasure collected from former spouses to Ceylon. There the pair would have been in evil plight, since Mitrāṇanda is taken for a thief by the police, had he not cured from death by snakebite the crown prince Lakṣmīpati with the aid of the magic spell given to him to revive the dead by the goddess Jāṅgulī on the occasion of his marriage. The king in gratitude entrusts the pair to the minister, who, however, is enamoured of Kaumudī and anxious to get rid of her husband. The opportunity is given

[1] Hultzsch, ZDMG. lxxv. 61 ff.

[2] Ed. Bhāvnagar, 1917.

by a human sacrifice which a vassal of the king wishes to offer; Mitrāṇanda is sent by the minister with a letter intended to secure his being the victim, but luckily is recognized by Maitreya, his companion, who had won the vassal's favour by curing him by a magic herb. Kaumudī in the meantime is expelled from the minister's house by his jealous wife, and wanders until she meets Sumitrā, daughter of a merchant, and her family; all are captured by a prince of the aborigines Vajravarman, to whom also is brought one Makaranda, who turns out to be a friend of Mitrāṇanda. A letter from Lakṣmīpati arrives to ask for the welfare of Mitrāṇanda and Kaumudī, and the latter takes advantage of it to induce Vajravarman to celebrate the marriage of Makaranda and Sumitrā. The three then have an adventure at Ekacakrā with a Kāpālika, who induces the women to go into a subterranean cave, while he asks Mitrāṇanda's aid against a Vidyādhara, described as eager after women. He breathes life into a corpse which takes a sword in its hand, but Mitrāṇanda by a magic formula induces it to strike the Kāpālika, who disappears. In Act IX Makaranda has to establish before Lakṣmīpati his claim to his own caravan, which a certain Naradatta claims; the dispute is settled by the appearance of Vajravarman and Mitrāṇanda, while Act X disposes of the piece by uniting husband and wife in the abode of the Siddha king. The work is, of course, wholly without interest other than that presented by so many marvels appealing to the sentiment of wonder in the audience. The author refers to Murāri in such a way as to suggest to Dr. Hultzsch[1] his contemporaneity with him, but this in no wise rendered necessary by the wording of the passage cited, and, secondly, would very badly agree with the fact that Mañkha knew and cites Murāri about A.D. 1135, for it takes some time for an author to reach the stage of being treated as an authority.

Another Jaina composition is the *Prabuddharauhiṇeya*[2] of one Rāmabhadra Muni, pupil of Jayaprabha Sūri, of the school of Deva Sūri, the famous writer on Nyāya, who died in A.D. 1169. It was written for performance in a temple of Yugādideva, that is the Tīrthakara Ṛṣabha, on the occasion of a procession

[1] ZDMG. lxxv. 63. See above, chap. x. § 2.

[2] Ed. Bhāvnagar, 1917.

festival. It is in six Acts. In Act I Rauhiṇeya, who is a bold bandit, steals away Madanavatī, a married woman, while his helper, a Çabara, who speaks Māgadhī, keeps her lover at bay. In the next Act he dresses up as the mother of a youth Manoratha, and abducts him for the sake of his ornaments, terrifying the bystanders with a snake made out of rags. The next three Acts tell of the complaints of these robberies made to Çreṇika of Magadha, and the efforts of his minister Abhayakumāra to find the guilty man, ending ultimately in the arrest of the robber, who, however, stoutly maintains his innocence, though he fails in succeeding in winning his discharge. In Act VI women and musicians under the control of Bharata, a teacher of dancing, endeavour to deceive him into the belief that he is in heaven, and thus to win a confession of his misdeeds from him. But he sees through the play, for he remembers a verse which he had heard spoken by Vardhamāna Svāmin before his captivity, in which the characteristics[1] of the gods, freedom from perspiration, unfaded garlands, and feet that do not touch the ground, were set out. The miscreant thus is pronounced innocent, but, liberated, manifests his penitence by taking the king and the minister to the mount Vaibhāra, in which are the treasures he has stolen and the missing boy and woman. The topic is one handled by Hemacandra in the matter illustrating his *Yogaçāstra*.

Quite different is the character of the *Mudritakumudacandra*[2] of Yaçaçcandra, son of Padmacandra, grandson of Dhanadeva of the Dharkaṭa family, who was, it seems, the minister of a prince of Çākambharī in Sapādalakṣa. The play describes the controversy which took place in A.D. 1124 between the Çvetāmbara Jaina teacher Deva Sūri, mentioned above, and the Digambara Kumudacandra, in which the latter was silenced, whence the title of the piece.

6. *The Prahasana and the Bhāṇa*

Popular as the Prahasana or farce must have been, we have in this period no example preserved certainly older than the *Laṭakamelaka*,[3] written in the earlier part of the twelfth century under Govindacandra of Kanyakubja by Çaṅkhadhara Kavirāja. The

[1] Famous from the *Nala* onwards. [2] Ed. Benares, Vīrasaṁvat, 2432.

[3] Ed. KM. 1889. R. iii. 271, &c., cites an *Ānandakoça*.

nature of the play is characteristic; the action passes at the house of the go-between Danturā, to which come all sorts of people anxious to buy the affection of the fascinating Madanamañjarī. Comic relief is further provided by the arrival of doctor Jantuketu to extract a fish-bone from the damsel's throat. He is perfectly incompetent and his methods absurd, but they affect their purpose indirectly, since, through laughing at his antics, the bone is happily dislodged. The bargaining of the lovers is satirized, and the marriage which is actually arranged is one between the go-between herself and a Digambara, a type doubtless sure to raise a laugh.

Of much later date is the well-known *Dhūrtasamāgama*[1] of Jyotirīçvara Kaviçekhara, son of Dhaneçvara, grandson of Rāmeçvara, of the family of Dhīreçvara who wrote under the Vijayanagara king Narasiṅha (A.D. 1487–1507), though a Nepalese manuscript makes his father Dhīrasiṅha and his patron Harasiṅha, who has been identified, implausibly, with Harisiṅha of Simraon (A.D. 1324). The first part of the play relates the contest of the religious mendicant Viçvanagara and his pupil Durācāra, whose names are significant, over the beautiful Anañgasenā; the pupil has every reason to complain, since it was he who saw the fair one and confided his love to his master, who meanly seeks to secure the damsel's favour in lieu. She insists on the matter being referred to arbitration, and in the second part the Brahmin Asajjāti, Impure Race, an expert at dealing with delicate matters of casuistry, undertakes the duty, and wisely decides to impound the damsel for himself, though, while he is deliberating, his Vidūṣaka seeks to secure the prize for himself. The case over, the barber Mūlanāçaka, Root Destroyer, turns up to demand payment of a debt from Anañgasenā. She refers him to Asajjāti, who pays him with his pupil's purse; he then demands the barber's care; the latter ties him up and leaves him to be rescued by the Vidūṣaka.

Very popular is Jagadīçvara's *Hāsyārṇava*.[2] The king, Anayasindhu, Ocean of Misrule, is devastated because all goes ill in his realm: Caṇḍālas make shoes, not Brahmins, wives are chaste, husbands constant, and the good respected. He asks his minister where best he can study the character of his people, and is

[1] Ed. in Lassen's *Anth. Sanscr.*, Bonn, 1838. Cf. Haraprasād, *Nepa Catal.*, p. xxxvii.
[2] Ed. Calcutta, 1896. Cf. Wilson, ii. 408 f.

advised to go to the house of the go-between, Bandhurā, who presents to him her daughter, Mṛgāñkalekhā. The court chaplin enters with his pupil, and are attracted to the damsel. A comic doctor is called in for Bandhurā, who feels ill; his remedies are worse than the disease, and he has to run away. A series of other figures are introduced. Then a barber, who has cut a patient; the latter demands damages, but is nonsuited; then comes the chief of police, Sādhuhiṅsika, Terror to the Good, the comic general Raṇajambuka, the astrologer Mahāyātrika, who indicates as the time for a journey the conjunction of stars presaging death. The king disappears at the end of the first Act; the second deals with the efforts of the chaplain and his pupil to obtain the damsel; but rivals come in the form of another man of religion and his pupil; finally the two older reprobates secure the damsel, while the boys content themselves with Bandhurā, who is delighted with the turn of events. But the celebration of these double marriages is left to another holy man, Mahānindaka, who also desires to share the hetaera. The date of the piece is unknown, as is that of the *Kautukasarvasva*[1] of Gopīnātha Cakravartin, written for the autumn festival of the Durgāpūjā in Bengal. It is more amusing and less vulgar than most of these pieces; the king, Kalivatsala, who is licentious, addicted to every kind of vice, and a lover of hemp juice, ill-treats the virtuous Brahmin Satyācāra, who finds that everything is wrong in the state, even the people being valiant in oppression, skilled in falsehood, and persevering only in contempt for the pious. The general is valiant: he can cleave a roll of butter with his blade, and trembles at the approach of a mosquito. Play is made with the immoralities recounted in the Purāṇas; the objections of the Ṛṣis to vice are put down to the fact that they censured in others what they themselves were too old to enjoy. The king proclaims free love, but becomes himself involved in a dispute over a hetaera. He is summoned back to the queen, which so annoys the hetaera that every one hastens to console her, and the king, obligingly to please her, banishes all Brahmins from the realm.

The *Dhūrtanartaka*[2] of Sāmarāja Dīkṣita is of the seventeenth century. It deals with one Mureçvara, who, though a Çaiva ascetic, is a devotee of a dancing girl whom he entrusts to his

[1] Ed. Calcutta, 1828; Wilson, ii. 410 f. [2] Wilson, ii. 407.

pupils on having to go away. They seek to secure the favours of the damsel and, failing in this, denounce him to the king, but Pāpācāra, Bad Conduct, is merely amused and allows the saint to keep the damsel. Rather earlier is the *Kautukaratnākara*[1] by the chaplain of Lakṣmaṇa Māṇikyadeva of Bhūluyā, which centres in the carrying off of the queen, though the chief of police sleeps beside her to guard her, and the adventures of the hetaera who is to take her place at the spring festival.

The Bhāṇa, despite its antiquity, attested by the theory, is not represented early in the history of the drama. To Vāmana Bhaṭṭa Bāṇa, about A.D. 1500, we owe the *Çṛñgārabhūṣaṇa*,[2] which is typical of the class. The chief Viṭa, Vilāsaçekhara, comes out to pay a visit to the hetaera Anañgamañjarī on the evening of the spring festival. He goes into the street of the hetaerae, and takes part in a series of imaginary conversations, giving the answers himself to his own questions, or pretending to listen to some one out of sight and then repeating the answers. He describes the hetaerae, ram-fights, cock-fights, boxing, a quarrel between two rivals, the different stages of the day, and the pleasures of the festival. Much on the same lines is the *Çṛñgāratilaka*[3] or *Ayyābhāṇa* of Rāmabhadra Dīkṣita, which was written to rival the *Vasantatilaka*[4] or *Ammābhāṇa* of Varadācārya or Ammāl Ācārya, the Vaiṣṇava. The play was written for performance at the festival of the marriage of Mīnākṣī, the deity of Madurā. Bhujañgaçekhara, the hero, is vexed at the departure of his beloved Hemāñgī, but is assured of meeting her again, despite her return to her husband. He makes the usual promenade in the hetaerae's street, has the usual imaginary conversations and describes the ordinary sights, including snake charmers and magic shows of gods and their mountains and so forth. Finally he succeeds in rejoining Hemāñgī. We have similar lengthy descriptions in the *Çāradātilaka*[5] of Çañkara, who places the scene in the feigned city of uproar, Kolāhalapura, and whose satire extends to the Jañgamas or Çaivas and the Vaiṣṇavas. Nallā Kavi (*c.* A.D. 1700) is responsible for the *Çṛñgārasarvasva*,[6]

[1] Cappeller, *Gurupūjākaumudī*, pp. 62 f.

[2] Ed. KM. 1896. R. iii. 248 gives an unknown *Çṛñgāramañjarī* as a specimen. See p. 185, n. 3.

[3] Ed. KM. 1894.

[4] Ed. Madras, 1874.

[5] Wilson, ii. 384.

[6] Ed. KM. 1902.

which deals with Anañgaçekhara, who has to part from his beloved Kanakalatā, but he is helped to meet her by the advent of an elephant which terrifies all the others in the street, but is worshipped by the lover as Gaṇeça and Çiva's answer to his prayer for help. A slight variant is presented by the *Rasasadana*[1] by a Yuvarāja from Koṭiliñga in Kerala; the hero here is a chief Viṭa who has promised his friend Mandāraka to look after his loved one for him. He goes about with her to a temple, and then to his house; wanders out into the street, talks and describes at large, and finally, after accepting the invitation of a lady from a neighbouring town to pay her a visit, goes back home to find the lovers united again.

The Prahasanas and Bhāṇas are hopelessly coarse from any modern Europe standpoint, but they are certainly often in a sense artistic productions. The writers have not the slightest desire to be simple; in the Prahasana their tendency to run riot is checked, as verse is confined to erotic stanzas and descriptions, and some action exists. In the Bhāṇa, on the other hand, the right to describe is paramount, and the poets give themselves full rein. They exhibit in this comic monologue precisely the same defects as are seen in the contemporary Nāṭaka; all is reduced to a study of stylistic effects, especially as regards sound. They rejoice in exhibiting their large command of the Sanskrit vocabulary, as obtained from the lexica, and the last thing desired is simplicity or perspicuity. Nothing more clearly indicates the close connexion of the two styles than the fact that we find a type of mixed Bhāṇa in the *Mukundānanda*[2] of Kāçipati Kavirāja, who is certainly not earlier than the thirteenth century. The adventures recounted by Bhujañgaçekhara, the hero, allude also to the sports of Kṛṣṇa and the cowherdesses, a double allusion which explains the difficulty of the style asserted by the author.

7. *Minor Dramatic Types*

The Vyāyoga seems not to have been often written, despite the example of Bhāsa. The *Pārthaparākrama*[3] of Prahlādanadeva falls in the period between A.D. 1163 and half a century

[1] Ed. KM. 1893; JRAS. 1907, p. 729. [2] *Ibid.*, 1889.

[3] Ed. in *Gaekwad's Oriental Series*, no. iv. 1917.

later, for its author was the brother of Dhārāvarṣa, son of Yaçodhavala, and lord of Candrāvatī, whose reign ranks honourably in the records of the Paramāras of Mount Ābu. It was acted on the occasion of the festival of the investment of Acaleçvara, the tutelary deity of Mount Ābu with the sacred thread, and claims to exhibit the sentiment of excitement (*dīptarasa*). The story, taken from the Virāṭa Parvan of the *Mahābhārata*, is the well-known one of the recovery by Arjuna of the cows of Virāṭa, raided by the Kauravas, and the defeat of the raiders. It accords, therefore, well with the definition in the text-books, for the struggle which it describes is not caused by a woman, the feminine interest is restricted to the colourless figures of Draupadī and Uttarā, and the hero is neither a divine being nor a king. The poet, whose fame as a warrior and whose princely generosity are extolled by Someçvara, claims for his poetry the merits of smooth composition and clearness, and these may be admitted, though the play does not rise above mediocrity. Technically the play is of some interest, in so far as after the Nāndī the Sthāpaka enters, recites a couple of stanzas, and then an actor comes on the stage who addresses him, but is answered by the Sūtradhāra; apparently the two terms were here synonymous to the author of the play or the later tradition. Moreover the final benediction is allotted, not to Arjuna, the hero of the play, but to Vāsava, who appears at the close of the play in a celestial chariot in company with the Apsarases to bestow applause and blessing. Prahlādana wrote other works, of which some verses are preserved in the anthologies, and must have been a man of considerable ability and merit.

The *Kirātārjunīya*[1] is a Vyāyoga based on Bhāravi's epic by Vatsarāja, who calls himself the minister of Paramardideva of Kālañjara, who reigned from A.D. 1163 to 1203. Vatsarāja is interesting as a good specimen of the poet of decadence; we have from him six plays illustrating each a different type of drama. The *Karpūracaritra* is a Bhāṇa of orthodox type; the gambler Karpūraka describes in monologue his revelry, gambling, and love. The *Hāsyacūḍāmaṇi* is a farce in one act which has as its hero an Ācārya of the Bhāgavata school, styled Jñānarāçi, who professes the possession of supernatural know-

[1] Ed., with the other five plays, *Gaekwad's Oriental Series*, no. viii. 1918.

ledge, enabling him to trace lost articles and buried treasure, and who carries out his professions by various tricks and fooleries. He has an irresistible pupil, who is sadly lacking in respect for his teacher, and delights in interpreting literally his remarks. The *Kirātārjunīya* has no special merit, but is technically interesting; after a Nāndī celebrating Çiva's consort, the Sūtradhāra enters, immediately followed by the Sthāpaka, who insists on his reciting a further Nāndī of the trident of Çiva, on the score that the play is heroic in sentiment and should be appropriately introduced. This play was produced later than the other five, for it came out under Trailokyavarmadeva, successor of Paramardi. The other three plays, an Īhāmṛga, Ḍima, and Samavakāra will be noticed below.

We have also a Vyāyoga by Viçvanātha, the *Saugandhikāharaṇa*,[1] of about A.D. 1316, which deals with Bhīma's visit to Kubera's lake to fetch water-lilies for Draupadī, his struggle first with Hanumant and then with the Yakṣas, and his final victory; the Pāṇḍavas meet at Kubera's home and Draupadī obtains her desired flowers. Of unknown date is the *Dhanaṁjayavijaya*[2] of Kāñcana Paṇḍita, son of Nārāyaṇa, which deals with the prowess of Arjuna in the defeat of Duryodhana and the Kauravas when they raid the cattle of Virāṭa, evidently a special favourite of the dramatic authors. The description of the contest in which Arjuna uses magic weapons is given by Indra and a couple of his celestial entourage; the play ends with the giving to Arjuna's son Uttarā, daughter of the king Virāṭa, in marriage. A manuscript of A.D. 1328 is extant of the *Bhīmavikramavyāyoga*[3] of Mokṣāditya, while the *Nirbhayabhīma*[4] of Rāmacandra belongs to the second half of the twelfth century A.D.

Of the type Īhāmṛga we have a specimen by Vatsarāja in the *Rukmiṇīharaṇa*, which in four Acts deals with the success of Kṛṣṇa in depriving Çiçupāla of Cedi of Rukmiṇī, his promised bride. The play opens with a dialogue between the Sūtradhāra who enters, after a Nāndī in a couple of stanzas has been pronounced, and the Sthāpaka, which tells us that the play was performed at moonrise during the festival of Cakrasvāmin. The action of the play is languid, and the author has had trouble to

[1] Ed. KM. 1902. Cf. SD. 514.
[2] Ed. KM. 1885; Wilson, ii. 374.
[3] Bendall, *Brit. Mus. Catal.*, p. 273.
[4] Hultzsch, ZDMG. lxxv. 62 f.

spread it out over four Acts; the characters are conventional; Rukmiṇī the heroine is a nonentity, and neither Çiçupāla nor Rukmin, the objects of Kṛṣṇa's enmity, has any distinct characterization. Kṛṣṇa goes into a state of trance on the stage in Act IV to produce the presence of Tārkṣya to enable him to complete his victory. The female character, Subuddhi, uses Sanskrit in lieu of Prākrit.

Other dramas of this type[1] are the late *Vīravijaya* of Kṛṣṇamiçra, and the *Sarvavinodanāṭaka* of Kṛṣṇa Avadhūta Ghaṭikāçata Mahākavi.

To Vatsarāja also we owe a specimen of the Ḍima, the *Tripuradāha* in four Acts, which describes the destruction of the capital of Tripurāsura by Çiva. The idea of writing such a piece was doubtless given by the mention of a work of this name in the *Nāṭyaçāstra*, and the play is extremely insipid; the numerous figures who crowd the stage are lifeless, and the celestial weapons which overcome the Asuras lack reality; the convenances are duly observed; Kumāra in the full flight of his triumph is stayed by his father's commands, and Çukra delightedly records this act of courtesy on the part of the god, despite his anger with the Dānavas. The play closes with the homage paid by the gods and the seers alike to Maheça, who is bashful, and the benediction is pronounced by Indra, not by the hero of the drama.

Other Ḍimas are late; thus we have one by the ubiquitous Ghanaçyāma, the *Kṛṣṇavijaya* of Veṅkaṭavarada, and the *Manmathonmathana*[2] of Rāma, a drama of 1820.

Vatsarāja is also responsible for a Samavakāra, the *Samudramathana*, in three Acts, which again owes its existence doubtless to the naming of a work with a kindred title in the *Nāṭyaçāstra* as the model of a Samavakāra. Here again we find after a Nāndī of two stanzas the Sūtradhāra and the Sthāpaka engaged in conversation. The former and his eleven brothers seek simultaneously to attain wealth; how is this possible? The Sthāpaka suggests either homage to Paramardi or to the ocean, a statement duly caught up by a voice behind the stage, which asserts that from the ocean comes the fulfilment of wishes, followed by the entry of Padmaka. The play is based on the legend of the

[1] Konow, ID. p. 114.

[2] Schmidt, ZDMG. lxiii. 409 f, 623 f.

churning of the ocean by the gods and demons with its sequel, the winning by Viṣṇu of Lakṣmī and the gaining of other desired objects by the participators in the enterprise. The treatment fails to rise above the commonplace; Lakṣmī appears in Act I with Lajjā and Dhṛti, her companions, in the normal occupation of gazing on a picture of her beloved, who later appears also on the scene. The artificiality of the type is proved by the absence of other dramas of this kind.

The Añka, or one-Act play, is represented by very few specimens. The term is often applied to denote a play within a play, in the *Bālarāmāyaṇa* the name Prekṣaṇaka is applied generally to such plays. The same name is also given to the *Unmattarāghava*[1] of Bhāskara Kavi, of unknown date, though the Vidyāraṇya mentioned in it may be Sāyaṇa or his contemporary. The play is a stupid imitation of Act IV of the *Vikramorvaçī*; while Rāma and Lakṣmaṇa pursue the golden gazelle, Sitā, by the curse of Durvāsas, is changed into a gazelle herself; Rāma returns and wanders miserably in search of her, but finally wins her by the help of Agastya.

The term Prekṣaṇaka is also applied to the *Kṛṣṇābhyudaya* of Lokanātha Bhaṭṭa, written for the raintime procession of the Lord of Hastigiri, Viṣṇu, in Kāñcī. A number of modern plays, which may be styled Añkas, are also known, while the *Çarmiṣṭhāyayāti* in the *Sāhityadarpaṇa* may be identical with the work of that name by Kṛṣṇa Kavi.[2]

Of the types of Uparūpaka, other than the Nāṭikā and Saṭṭaka, there are very few represented, and these only obviously written in accord with the text-book definitions. Thus Rūpa Gosvāmin has left a Bhāṇikā, the *Dānakelikaumudī*,[3] among his varied efforts to adapt the drama to the tenets of his faith, and the *Subhadrāharaṇa*[4] of Mādhava, son of the Maṇḍaleçvara Bhaṭṭa and Indumatī, and brother of Harihara, styles itself a Çrīgadita. As it describes itself in terms similar to those used in the *Sāhityadarpaṇa*, it is quite possibly posterior to that work, and, on the other hand, there exists a manuscript of A.D. 1610. The story of the play is the old legend of the elopement of Kṛṣṇa's friend Arjuna with Subhadrā, whom he meets

[1] Ed. KM. 1889.
[2] Konow, ID. p. 118.
[3] Ed. Murçidābād, 1881 f.
[4] Ed. KM. 1888.

by going to her father's house as a beggar. The presence of a narrative verse has suggested comparison with a shadow-drama, but for this there is inadequate evidence.

8. *The Shadow Play*

It is extremely doubtful at what date the shadow-drama appeared in India; the first play which we can be certain was represented in this way is the *Dharmābhyudaya*[1] of Meghaprabhācārya, which in the stage direction mentions once clearly a puppet (*putraka*) and calls itself a Chāyānāṭyaprabandha. Unluckily the age of this work does not seem to be ascertainable with any certainty.

It is natural to suggest, as did Pischel, that the *Dūtāñgada* of Subhaṭa, which is styled a Chāyānāṭaka, really was a shadow play. On the other hand, Rājendralālamitra[2] suggested that the drama was perhaps simply intended as an entr'acte, and this may be justified on the interpretation of the term of drama in the form of a shadow: i.e. reduced to the minimum for representation in such a form. The play itself unluckily contains nothing to help us to a decision as to its real character. It was represented in A.D. 1243 in honour of the dead king Kumārapala at the court of Tribhuvanapāla, a Caulukya of Aṇahilapāṭaka, and it has come down to us in various forms. A longer and shorter recension may be distinguished, though not very definitely; in the longer form occur epic verses, and an introduction is prefixed in thirty-nine stanzas, partly placed in the mouths of Rāma and Hanumant, describing the finding of Sītā's hiding-place. The story is the simple one of Añgada's mission as an ambassador to Rāvaṇa to demand back Sītā; Rāvaṇa endeavours to persuade Añgada that Sītā is in love with him. Añgada is not deceived, and leaves Rāvaṇa with threats, and we learn shortly afterwards that Rāvaṇa has met his doom. The merits of the work are negligible.

We have no other play of which we can say with even the slightest plausibility that it was a real shadow-drama. There are three works by Vyāsa Çrīrāmadeva from the fifteenth

[1] See above, ch. ii. § 4.

[2] *Bikaner Catal.*, p. 251. It is trs., Gray, JAOS. xxxii. 59 ff. The play borrows from the *Bālarāmāyaṇa* (ix. 58 f. = verses 52 f.), and the *Mahānāṭaka*.

century, his patrons being Kalacuri princes of Raypur. The first, the *Subhadrāpariṇayana*, produced under Brahmadeva or Haribrahmadeva, deals with the threadworn topic of the winning of Arjuna'a bride; the second, the *Rāmābhyudaya* appeared under the Mahārāṇa Meru, and deals with the conquest of Lañkā, the fire ordeal of Sītā, and the return to Ayodhyā; the third, the *Pāṇḍavābhyudaya*, written under Raṇamalladeva, describes in two Acts Draupadī's birth and marriage. But that these were really shadow-dramas is not indicated by anything save the title, for they resemble ordinary dramas in all other respects. The *Sāvitrīcarita* of Çañkaralāla, son of Maheçvara, calls itself a Chāyānāṭaka, but the work, written in 1882, is an ordinary drama, and Lüders[1] is doubtless right in recognizing that these are not shadow dramas at all. On the other hand, he adds to the list the *Haridūta*, which tells the story given in the *Dūtavākya* of Bhāsa of the mission of Kṛṣṇa to the Pāṇḍavas' enemies to seek to attain peace. This drama, however, does not describe itself as a Chāyānāṭaka, and the argument is, accordingly, without value. But what is most significant, there is no allusion to this sort of drama in the theory which suggests that its introduction was decidedly late.

9. *Dramas of Irregular Type*

Professor Lüders[2] adds to the almost non-existing list of shadow dramas, the *Mahānāṭaka.* He does this on the strength of the fact that it is written mainly in verse, with little of prose; that the verse is decidedly at times of the narrative as opposed to the dramatic type; there is no Prākrit; the number of persons appearing is large, and there is no Vidūṣaka, and these characteristics are found in the *Dūtāñgada,* which is a Chāyānāṭaka in name. The argument is clearly inadequate in the absence of any real evidence, and the *Mahānāṭaka* can be explained in other ways.

The history of this play is curious. It is preserved in two recensions, one in nine or ten Acts redacted by Madhusūdana and one in fourteen by Dāmodaramiçra. The stories given by the commentator Mohanadāsa and the *Bhojaprabandha,* agree in effect that the play was put together by order of Bhoja from

[1] SBAW. 1916, pp. 698 ff. [2] *Loc. cit.*

fragments found on rocks, which were fished out of the sea; the tradition was that Hanumant himself wrote the work, which, therefore, is called *Hanumannāṭaka*, but that to please Vālmīki, who recognized that it would eclipse his great epic, the generous ape permitted his rival to cast into the sea the drama which he had inscribed on the rocks. This certainly suggests that some old matter was embodied in the play, and this view has been strengthened by the fact that Ānandavardhana cites three verses out of the play, but without giving any source, as also do Rājaçekhara in the *Kāvyamīmāṅsā* and Dhanika in his *Daçarūpāvaloka*, so that the evidence is not of much worth, for the work, as we have it, plagiarizes shamelessly from the dramas of Bhavabhūti, Murāri, and Rājaçekhara, and even from Jayadeva's *Prasannarāghava*, unless we are to suppose that in the latter case the borrowing is the other way. The question which is the earlier of the two recensions is unsolved; the one with fewer Acts has 730 as opposed to 581 verses, and of these about 300 are in common.[1]

There is a brief benediction, but no prologue, and narrative follows down to the arrival of Rāma at Mithilā for the winning of Sītā by breaking the bow of Çiva; this part of the action is given in a dialogue between Sītā, Janaka, Rāma, and others. More narrative leads up to a scene with Paraçurāma, then narrative follow to Sītā's marriage. Act II is undramatic, being a highly flavoured description of Sītā's love passages with Rāma. Act III again is mainly descriptive, carrying the story down to the departure of Rāma and Lakṣmaṇa in chase of Mārīca in deer shape. Act IV carries the story down to Rāma's return to the deserted hut; in Act V Rāma seeks Sītā and sends Hanumant to Laṅkā; in the next Act Hanumant consoles Sītā and returns; in Act VII the host of apes crosses the ocean; in Act VIII, which is much more dramatic than usual, we have Aṅgada's mission to Rāvaṇa; and the rest of the Acts drag out the wearisome details of the conflict, often in so imperfect a manner as to be unintelligible without knowledge of the *Rāmāyaṇa* and the earlier dramas. The two versions generally correspond, but not with any precision in detail.

[1] For the slightly different legend of Madhusūdana—current in Bengal—see SBAW. 1916, pp. 704 ff. The number of verses varies greatly in the manuscripts. The apparent citation by name in DR. comm. ii. 1 is only in some manuscripts.

The exact purpose of such a play is not obvious, but it looks rather like a literary *tour de force*, possibly in preparation for some form of performance [1] at which the dialogue was plentifully eked out by narrative by the director and the other actors. It is incredible, however, that, as we have it, it can ever have served any practical end, and its chief value, such as it is, is to reflect possibly the form of drama of a period when the drama had not yet completely emerged from the epic condition. We should thus have the old work of the Granthikas reinforced by putting part of the dialogue in the mouths of real actors. But it would be dangerous in so late a production to lay any stress on the possibility of deriving hence evidence for the growth of the early drama. It is, however, legitimate to note that there are similarities between the type and that of the performance of a Tamil version of the *Çakuntalā*.[2] The curious number of Acts has been suggested as indicating that the original was otherwise divided than a normal drama, but on this it would be dangerous to lay much stress.

The metre of the play exhibits the extraordinary fact of 253 Çārdūlavikrīḍita stanzas to 109 Çloka, 83 Vasantatilaka, 77 Sragdharā, 59 Mālinī, and 55 Indravajrā type. This fact, in the version of Madhusūdana, is sufficient to show how far we are removed from anything primitive.

The type of the *Mahānāṭaka* may be compared with the *Gītagovinda*,[3] which, written by Jayadeva under Lakṣmaṇasena in the twelfth century A.D., exhibits songs sung by Kṛṣṇa, Rādhā, and her companion, intermingled with lyric stanzas of the poet, describing their position, or the emotions excited, and addressing prayer to Kṛṣṇa. The work is a poem, and can be enjoyed simply as such, but it is also capable of a quasi-dramatic presentment. It reveals a highly-developed outcome of the simple Yātrās of the Kṛṣṇa religion.

In the *Gopālakelicandrikā*[4] of Rāmakṛṣṇa of Gujarāt, of unknown date, but certainly later than the *Mahānāṭaka* and the *Bhāgavata Purāṇa*, we have an irregular drama whose form has

[1] Lüders's attempt to read, in Madhusūdana's recension only, *saubhyāḥ*, shadow players, is clearly absurd; ZDMG. lxxiv. 142, n. 3.

[2] Lévi, TI. i. 244; G. Devèze, *Çakuntalā*, Paris, 1888.

[3] Lévi, TI. i. 235 ff.; Keith, *Sansk. Lit.*, pp. 121 ff.

[4] Ed. W. Caland, Amsterdam, 1917. Cf. ZDMG. lxxiv. 138 ff.; IA. xlix. 232 f.

excited a large number of conjectures, including the inevitable but absurd solution of a shadow play. The nearest parallel of those suggested in this case and in that of the *Mahānāṭaka*[1] is the Swāng of North-West India, in that the actors recite the narrative parts as well as take part in the dialogue. There seems no special reason to doubt that the same thing might have taken place in this case, though it is conceivable that it was an imitation of the type of entertainment in which a Brahmin says the spoken parts, while his small pupils go through the action of the drama, possibly a far-off parallel to the Çaubhikas as far as the action is concerned. But it is quite possibly no more than a literary exercise, and the same judgement may apply to the *Mahānāṭaka*. The fact that both talk as if there were action is no sign of real representation. The modern written drama is full of stage directions, though it may never succeed in obtaining a performance on the stage, and we have not the slightest reason to deny the existence of the literary drama in India.[2] The piece is highly stylized, and could only be understood, if at all, by a cultivated audience.

The connexion of the play with the *Hanumannāṭaka* is expressly admitted in the prologue; the actress, who enters with the usual inquiry in Prākrit as to the business to be undertaken, is informed by the Sūtradhāra that this is not a case for Prākrit, but for Sanskrit, alone worthy of an audience of Viṣṇu devotees. The actress, not unnaturally, asks how a drama is possible without Prākrit, to be comforted by the parallel of the *Hanumannāṭaka*. This seems a clear enough indication that the work is a literary exercise rather than a genuine stage play representing a living form of dramatic representation. From an ordinary play it is distinguished by the fact that we have stanzas and prose of merely narrative character, and we learn from one passage that these parts are directed by the Sūcaka to the spectator. The Sūcaka may be equated, on the authority of Hemacandra, with the Sūtradhāra, and if we assume that the play was actually

[1] The Swāng, unlike the play, is metrical throughout; R. C. Temple, *Legends of the Panjab*, I. viii, 121.

[2] In Greece, despite the great advantages of a public representation, plays to be read only arose early; Aristotle, *Rhetoric*, iii. 12. 2. Most of the dramas of the last few years seem literary.

performed,[1] all we need do is to assume that the director thus intervened from time to time to help on the action of the play. We are, in any case, very far from the primitive drama, as the long compounds of the prose show, reminding us of the worst eccentricities of Bhavabhūti.

The work begins with an act of religious devotion, the performance of the ceremony of the waving of a lamp in honour of Kṛṣṇa, who appears in the vesture of a herdsman, and thus receives in person the worship of his votaries. The play is essentially religious and mystic, despite the fact that the sports of Kṛṣṇa and his comrades, and of Rādhā and her friends, are duly introduced. In Act III we have from the mouth of Vṛndā, that is Lakṣmī, a series of verses setting out the mystic doctrine of the identity of Kṛṣṇa and Rādhā; Kṛṣṇa is the highest being, descended to earth in the guise of a herdsman, and Rādhā represents his Çakti. In Act IV we have the usual scene of the theft by Kṛṣṇa of the clothes of the maidens when they bathe in the Yamunā, but the restoration is made a test of their faith; Kṛṣṇa demands their devotion as the price of their garments, and asserts that faith in him is superior to the Vedas, to asceticism, and to sacrifice as a means of securing knowledge of him. In the last Act we find the spirits of the night of full moon and of autumn lamenting that the maidens are not dancing the Rāsa with Kṛṣṇa, who appears, and whom they remind of this duty of his. He summons his magic power (*yogamāyā*) and bids her proceed to the station of the herders to summon the maidens to the dance. Then it is narrated how he himself goes there, and with his flute draws out the maidens to join him, while the gods come in multitudes to pay him honour. Many verses from the *Bhāgavata Purāṇa* are here borrowed. Finally the god accepts the homage of the maidens and leads them in the dance, as is described again in narrative, until the director breaks off the piece with the assertion that it is impossible to represent adequately the greatness of the god. We can see at once, even if we were not told, that the author was under the influence of Rāmānuja, and the fact that his father bears the name of Devajī[2] suggests a decidedly modern date.

[1] Cf. perhaps the nineteenth-century *Citrayajña*, described by Wilson, ii. 412 ff.

[2] Devajīti as read by the editor and Winternitz is a quaint misreading.

A glimpse into a form of entertainment not represented by any Sanskrit drama so far published is given by the changes made in the fourth Act of the *Vikramorvaçī* at an unknown date. The Apabhrança stanzas introduced into that Act cannot be assigned to the period of Kālidāsa, unless we are to rewrite the history of the language; Apabhrança represents not a vernacular but a definitely literary language in which the vocabulary is based on Prākrit, and the inflexions on a vernacular with free use of Prākrit forms as well. Guhasena of Valabhī, of whom we have inscriptions of A.D. 559–69, was celebrated as a composer in Apabhrança as well as in Sanskrit and Prākrit, and the new literary form may have arisen in the sixth century A.D. as an effort to produce something nearer the vernacular than Prākrit, but yet literary, much as the modern dialects have evolved literatures largely by reliance on Sanskrit. It can hardly be doubted that the Apabhrança stanzas represent the libretto of a pantomime (*nṛtya*). Such pantomimes are well known as a form of the nautch at Rājput courts; the dancers perform a well-known scene, and sing verses to a musical accompaniment; the chief element, however, is the gestures and postures. In the case of the pantomime based on the *Vikramorvaçī*, the verses placed in the mouth of the king may have been sung by an actor, while those regarding the forsaken elephant and the Haṅsas may have been sung by singers, male or female, acting under him. There is an introduction in Prākrit for the libretto, which very possibly as inserted in the drama has not come down to us in full, though in any case the libretto in such instances is of only secondary importance and never adequate. It is a plausible suggestion that the introduction of the libretto into the *Vikramorvaçī* was the outcome of the difficulty felt by the ordinary audience in picking up the sense of the fourth Act of the play, which contains in overwhelming measure Sanskrit stanzas, and, therefore, must have been extremely difficult for the audience to follow. The date of the change is uncertain; on linguistic grounds it has been placed after Hemacandra and before the date of the *Prākṛta Piṅgala*.[1]

[1] See Jacobi, *Bhavisattakaha*, p. 58 n. Influence by the Yātrās is probable; Windisch, *Sansk. Phil.* p. 407.

XII

THE CHARACTERISTICS AND ACHIEVEMENT OF THE SANSKRIT DRAMA

THE Sanskrit drama may legitimately be regarded as the highest product of Indian poetry, and as summing up in itself the final conception of literary art achieved by the very self-conscious creators of Indian literature. This art was essentially aristocratic; the drama was never popular in the sense in which the Greek drama possessed that quality. From an early period in Indian history we find the distinction of class reflected in a distinction of language; culture was reserved largely for the two higher castes, the Brahmin and the Kṣatriya or ruling class. It was in this rarified atmosphere that the Sanskrit drama came into being, and it was probably to litterati of high cultivation that its creation from the hints present in religion and in the epic was due. The Brahmin, in fact, much abused as he has been in this as in other matters, was the source of the intellectual distinction of India. As he produced Indian philosophy, so by another effort of his intellect he evolved the subtle and effective form of the drama. Brahmins, it must be remembered, had long been the inheritors of the epic tradition, and this tradition they turned to happy use in the evolution of the drama.

The drama bears, therefore, essential traces of its connexion with the Brahmins. They were idealist in outlook, capable of large generalizations, but regardless of accuracy in detail, and to create a realistic drama was wholly incompatible with their temperament. The accurate delineation of facts or character was to them nothing; they aimed at the creation in the mind of the audience of sentiment, and what was necessary for this end was all that was attempted. All poetry was, in the later analysis, which is implicit in the practice of the earlier poets, essentially a means of suggesting feeling, and this function devolved most of all on the drama. Nothing, therefore, is of value save what tends to this end, and it is the function of the true dramatist to lay aside everything which is irrelevant for this purpose.

It follows from this principle that the plot is a secondary element[1] in the drama in its highest form, the heroic play or Nāṭaka. To complicate it would divert the mind from emotion to intellectual interest, and affect injuriously the production of sentiment. The dramatist, therefore, will normally choose a well-known theme which in itself is apt to place the spectator in the appropriate frame of mind to be affected by the appropriate emotion. It is then his duty by the skill with which he handles his theme to bring out in the fullest degree the sentiment appropriate to the piece. This is in essentials the task set before themselves by the great dramatists; Kālidāsa makes subtle changes in the story of Çakuntalā, not for the sake of improving the plot as such, but because the alterations are necessary to exhibit in perfection the sentiment of love, which must be evoked in the hearts of the audience. The crudities of the epic tale left Çakuntalā a business-like young woman and Duḥṣanta a selfish and calculating lover; both blemishes had to be removed in order that the spectator might realize within himself, in ideal form, the tenderness of a girl's first affection, and the honourable devotion of the king, clouded only by a curse against which he had no power.

The emotions which thus it was desired to evoke were, however, strictly limited by the Brahminical theory of life. The actions and status of man in any existence depend on no accident; they are essentially the working out of deeds done in a previous birth, and these again are explained by yet earlier actions from time without beginning. Indian drama is thus deprived of a motif which is invaluable to Greek tragedy, and everywhere provides a deep and profound tragic element, the intervention of forces beyond control or calculation in the affairs of man, confronting his mind with obstacles upon which the greatest intellect and the most determined will are shattered. A conception of this kind would deprive the working of the law of the act of all validity, and, however much in popular ideas the inexorable character of the act might be obscured by notions of

[1] Contrast Aristotle's doctrine of plot as the soul of tragedy (*Poetics*, 1450 *a* 38).

an age before the evolution of the belief of the inevitable operation of the act, in the deliberate form of expression in drama this principle could not be forgotten. We lose, therefore, the spectacle of the good man striving in vain against an inexorable doom ; we lose even the wicked man whose power of intellect and will make us admire him, even though we welcome his defeat. The wicked man who perishes is merely, in the view of the Sanskrit drama, a criminal undergoing punishment, for whose sufferings we should feel no sympathy whatever ; such a person is not a suitable hero for any drama, and it is a mere reading of modern sentiment into ancient literature to treat Duryodhana in the *Ūrubhañga* as the hero of the drama.[1] He justly pays the full penalty for insolence and contempt of Viṣṇu.

It follows, therefore, that the sentiments which are to be evoked by a Sanskrit Nāṭaka are essentially the heroic or the erotic, with that of wonder as a valued subordinate element, appropriate in the *dénouement*. The wonderful well consorts with the ideal characters of legend, which accepts without incredulity or discomfort the intervention of the divine in human affairs, and therefore follows with ready acceptance the solution of the knot in the *Çakuntalā* or the *Vikramorvaçī*. Heroism and love, of course, cannot be evoked without the aid of episodes which menace the hero and heroine with the failure to attain their aims ; there must be danger and interference with the course of true love, but the final result must see concord achieved. Hence it is impossible to expect that any drama shall be a true tragedy ; in the long run the hero and the heroine must be rewarded by perfect happiness and union. The *Nāgānanda* of Harṣa illustrates the rule to perfection ; the sublimity of self-sacrifice suggests real tragedy, but this would be wholly out of harmony with the spirit of India, and the intervention of Gaurī is invoked to secure that the self-sacrifice is crowned by a complete and immediate reward in this life. The figure of an Antigone might have been paralleled in Indian life ; it would not be acceptable to the spirit of Indian drama.

Idealist as it is, the spirit of the drama declines to permit of a division of sentiment ; it will not allow the enemy of the hero to rival him in any degree ; nothing is more striking than the

[1] See above, pp. 38, 96, 106.

failure to realize the possibility of a great dramatic creation presented by the character of Rāvaṇa as the rival of Rāma for Sītā's love. Rāvaṇa varies in the hands of the dramatists, but all tend to reduce him to the status of a boastful and rather stupid villain, who is inferior at every point to his rival. Equally effectively the drama banishes from the possibilities the conception of a struggle of conscience in the mind of the hero or the heroine;[1] if this were represented, it would create a similar struggle in the mind of the audience, and destroy the unity and purity of the sentiment, which it is the part of the drama to generate.

The style similarly is explained and justified by the end of suggesting sentiment. The lyric stanzas, at first sight strangely undramatic,[2] find their full explanation when it is remembered how effective each is in exciting the appropriate emotion in the mind of the audience, which, deeply versed in Sanskrit poetry, is keen to appreciate the effect of each stanza. The simplicity or even negligence of the prose of the drama is thus also explained and excused. It is not necessary to excite sentiment; it serves merely as the mode of communicating facts, and of enabling the audience to follow the action, until an opportunity is afforded to excite feeling by the melody of a verse, all the more effective from its sudden emergence from the flatness of its environment. The same consideration explains the importance of those elements of which we can form so faint an impression, the dance, music, song, and the mimetic art. The elaborate code of gestures laid down in the theory, and unquestionably bulking large in practice, was all intended to produce in cultivated spirits the sentiments appropriate to the play.

The ideal character of the heroic drama extends itself even to the Nāṭikā, where a closer approach to real life might be expected. The dramatists, however, make no attempt at realism; they choose their subjects from the legend, and they cast over the trivial *amourettes* of their heroes the glamour derived from the assurance that the winning in marriage of a maiden will

[1] Contrast Aristotle's doctrine of ἁμαρτία (*Poetics*, 1453 *a* 10 ff.), as in Euripides's *Hippolytos*; G. Norwood, *Greek Tragedy*, pp. 209 f., 213 f.

[2] Greek tragedy progressively reduced the lyric element in the drama, in harmony with the rhetorical trend of the Greek intellect, and approximated in language to ordinary speech; Aristotle, *Poetics*, 1450 *b* 9; *Rhetoric*, iii. 1 and 2; Haigh, *The Tragic Drama of the Greeks*, ch. vi, § 3.

assure them universal rule. The action of the play is thus not suffered to degenerate into a portrayal of the domestic difficulties of the harem system under polygamic conditions; the dramatists do not seek realism, but are content to reproduce a stereotyped scheme of love, jealousy, parting, and reunion, a sequence well calculated to evoke the sentiment of love in the mind of the audience. Even in the Prakaraṇa, in which realism might be expected, seeing that it condescends to heroes of less than royal or divine status, there is no actual exception: though the author of the *Mṛcchakaṭikā* has had the power to infuse a semblance of life and actuality into his characters, Bhavabhūti shows us in the *Mālatīmādhava* nothing but types suggesting the erotic sentiment. Equally ideal is the Vyāyoga with its suggestion of heroism and its deliberate selection of its subject from the epic tradition.

Tragedy proper is denied us by these conditions of Indian thought, and comedy in any of its higher forms is also difficult; it might legitimately be expected to prevail in the Nāṭikā or the Prakaraṇa, but it is unduly subordinated to the erotic sentiment and, though not absent, is comparatively undeveloped. The Prahasana and the Bhāṇa indeed appeal to the comic sentiment, but only in an inferior and degraded form, a fact expressed in the failure of the classical drama to preserve a single specimen of either form of composition.

Limited by the nature of the intellectual movement which produced it, the Sanskrit drama could never achieve the perfection of Greek tragedy or comedy. Kālidāsa, greatest of Indian dramatists, experiences no uneasiness at the structure of life or the working of the world. He accepts without question or discontent the fabric of Indian society. When Goethe writes of him:

> Willst du die Blüthe des frühen, die Früchte des späteren Jahres,
> Willst du, was reizt und entzückt, willst du, was sättigt und nährt,
> Willst du den Himmel, die Erde, mit einem Namen begreifen,
> Nenn' ich Çakuntalā dich, und so ist alles gesagt,

the praise is doubtless just in a measure, but it may easily be pressed further than is justifiable. For the deeper questions of human life Kālidāsa has no message for us; they raised, so far as we can see, no question in his own mind; the whole Brahmanical system, as restored to glory under the Guptas, seems to have satisfied him, and to have left him at peace with the universe. Fascinating and exquisite as is the *Çakuntalā*, it moves in a narrow world, removed far from the cruelty of real life, and it neither seeks to answer, nor does it solve, the riddles of life. Bhavabhūti, it is true, shows some sense of the complexity and difficulty of existence, of the conflict between one duty and another, and the sorrow thus resulting, but with him also there prevailed the rule that all must end in harmony. Sītā, who in the older story is actually finally taken away from the husband who allowed himself to treat her as if her purity were sullied by her captivity in Rāvaṇa's hands, is restored to Rāma by divine favour, an ending infinitely less dramatic than final severance after vindication. How serious a limitation in dramatic outlook is produced by the Brahmanical theory of life, the whole history of the Sanskrit drama shows.[1] Moreover, acceptance of the Brahmanic tradition permits the production of such a play as the *Caṇḍakauçika*, where reason and humanity are revolted beyond measure by the insane vengeance taken by the sage Viçvāmitra on the unfortunate king for an act of charity.

The drama suffered also from its close dependence on the epic, and the failure of the poets to recognize that the epic subjects were often as a whole undramatic. Hence frequently, as in the vast majority of the Rāma dramas and those based on the *Mahābhārata*, we have nothing but the recasting of the epic narrative into a semi-dramatic form, without real dramatic structure. There was nothing in the theory to hint at the error of such a course; on the contrary, to the poets the subject was one admirably suitable, since in itself it suggested the appropriate sentiments, and therefore left them merely the duty of heightening the effects. This led on the high road to the outward signs of the degradation of the drama, the abandoning of any interest in anything save the production of lyric or narrative stanzas of perfection of form, judged in accordance with a taste which progressively declined into a rejection of simplicity and

[1] Contrast Greek tragedy; Butcher, *Greek Genius*, pp. 105 ff.; G. Norwood, *Greek Tragedy*, pp. 97 f., 114 f., 128 f., 177, 318, 324; W. Nestle, *Euripides* (1901).

the search for what was recondite. To the later poets the drama is an exercise in style, and that, as contrasted with the highest products of Indian literature, a fantastic and degraded one.

To the Brahmin ideal individuality has no appeal; the law of life has no room for deviation from type; the caste system is rigid, and for each rank in life there is a definite round of duties, whence departure is undesirable and dangerous. The drama likewise has no desire for individual figures, but only for typical characters. The defect from the Aristotelian as from the modern point of view of the Rāma dramas is simply that Rāma is conceived as an ideal, a man without faults, and therefore for us lacking in the essential traits of humanity. Similarly, in the style of the drama we are denied any differentiation of individuals as contrasted with classes. The divergence in the use of Sanskrit or Prākrit, and in the different kinds of Prākrit, marks the essential distinction of men and women, and of those of high and those of humble rank, but beyond this characterization does not go. We are treated to an artificial court speech, which assorts with stereotyped emotions, refined, elegant, sentimental, rich in the compliments of court gallantry, often pathetic, marked with a distinct strain of philosophical commonplace, and fond of suggested meanings and *double entendres*, hinting at the events yet to come. But the dramatists made no serious attempt to create individual characters, and to assign to them a speech of their own; they vary greatly in merit as regards characterization, but even the best dramas paint types, not individuals.

Indifference to individuality necessarily meant indifference to action, and therefore to plot, and this lies at the basis of the steady progress by which the dialogue was neglected in favour of the stanzas. The latter express the general; they draw highly condensed, but also often extremely poetical, pictures of the beauty of nature in one of its many aspects, or of the charms of the beloved; or they enunciate the Brahmanical solutions of the problems of life and conduct. In them the individual has no place; the beloved may be described, but she is merely typical. These stanzas appealed to the audience; we have no echo in India of the criticisms which were levelled in Greece against Euripides, for the introduction of sentiments unfitted to his characters and the scenes involved, and we have no hint that

Indian theory ever recognized that the drama by the tenth century A.D. was in a state of decadence.

The peculiar and limited view of the drama was intimately connected with its Brahmanical character. The drama of Greece was popular; it appealed to all free Athenian citizens,[1] an infinitely wider class than that for which the dramas of India in Sanskrit and Prākrit were composed, and it was written in a language easily comprehended by all those who viewed the spectacle. From the period of the earliest dramas known to us the full comprehension of the words can have been confined to a limited section of the audience, which, however, had sufficient pleasure in the spectacle, in the song, the pantomimic dances, and the music, and sufficient general comprehension of the drama to follow it adequately enough. Such an audience, however, acted as a stimulus to refinement and elaboration; the dramatist could neglect the prime necessity of being understood which weighed on the Greek dramatist, and indulge in the production of something recondite, calculated to manifest his skill in metrical form and management of words. The fact that Sanskrit was not a normal living language presented him with the temptation, to which none of the later dramatists rises superior, of the free use of the vast store of alleged synonyms presented by the lexica,[2] freed from any inconvenient necessity, such as exists in every living language, of using words only in that precise nuance which every synonym possesses in a living dialect.

The same tendency to artificiality was undoubtedly stimulated by the fact that plays for their reputation must have depended largely on being read, not witnessed, however important it may have been for the poet to secure the honour of public performance. The popularity and number of the Kāvyas which have come down to us attests the existence of an effective public which, if it did not read the works, at least enjoyed having them read aloud, and the dramatist was thus encouraged, while adhering to the dramatic form, to vie in this genre of literature with the effects produced in the Kāvya. The Kāvya, however,

[1] For its extension and popularity outside Athens, see Haigh, *The Tragic Drama of the Greeks*, chap. vi, § 4.

[2] Gawroński, *Les sources de quelques drames indiens*, pp. 1 ff.

was undergoing throughout its history a tendency to seek mere stylistic effects, and this influence must largely have contributed to the elaboration of style of the drama. It is significant that the Kāvyas and dramas of Kālidāsa show a relative simplicity which contrasts effectively with the complexities of Bhavabhūti in drama, and Bhāravi and Māgha in the Kāvya.

To understand the Indian drama we have aid from a work of curious character and importance, the *Kāmaçāstra* or *Kāmasūtra* of Vātsyāyana,[1] which was doubtless familiar to the dramatists from Kālidāsa onwards. The world which produced the classical drama was one in which the pessimism of Buddhism, with its condemnation of the value of pleasure, had given way to the worship of the great sectarian divinities Çiva and Viṣṇu, in whose service the enjoyment of pleasure was legitimate and proper. The Buddhists themselves admittedly felt the force of the demand for a life of ease; we have preserved verses satirizing their love of women, wine, soft living, and luxury, and there is abundant evidence of the decline of austerity in the order. The eclecticism of Harṣa is sufficiently significant; the policy which at the great festival at Prayāga reported by Hiuan Tsang resulted in the dedication of a statue to the Buddha on the first day, to the sun, the favourite deity of his father, on the second, and to Çiva on the third, excludes any possibility of belief in the depth of Harṣa's Buddhist beliefs. If there were any doubt as to the strange transformation of feeling among Buddhists, it would be removed by the benediction which opens the *Nāgānanda*, where the Buddha is invoked as rallied on his hardheartedness by the ladies of Māra's train. The process of accommodation had evidently gone very far. The philosophy of the age shows equally the lack of serious interest in the old tenets of Buddhism; we have the great development of logical studies in lieu of insistence on the truths of misery and the path to its removal, while the *chef-d'œuvre* of the period outside Buddhist circles is the complicated and fantastic system of the Sāṁkhya philosophy, which adequately reflects the artistic spirit of the time in its comparison of nature with a dancer who makes her début, and gracefully retires from the stage when she has satisfied her audience. The spirit of Açoka has entirely disap-

[1] See also Schmidt's *Beiträge zur indischen Erotik*.

peared from the royal families of India, and the courts demanded amusement with refinement, just as they sought for elegance in art. The interests of this world are centred in the pleasures of life, the festivals which amused the court and the people by the pomp of their celebration from time to time, and in the intervals the amusements of the palace and the harem, sports in the water, the game of the swing, the plucking of flowers, song, dance, pantomime, and such other diversions as were necessary to while away the endless leisure of princes, who left the business of their realms to ministers and soldiers, while they spared themselves any fatigue more serious than that of love encounters. The manners of their princes were aped by their rich subjects, and there was no dearth of courtiers and parasites to aid them in their diversions. The man about town (*nāgaraka*) as sketched by the *Kāmasūtra*[1] is rich and cultivated; devoted to the niceties of attire and personal adornment, perfumed, pomaded, and garlanded; he is a musician, and a lover of books; cage-birds afford him pleasure of the eyes, and diversion in teaching them speech; a lovely garden with an arbour presents facilities for amusement and repose. In the daytime the care of the toilet, cock fights, ram fights, excursions in the neighbouring country, fill his time; while at night, after a concert or ballet, there are the joys of love, in which the *Kāmasūtra* gives him more elaborate instruction than the *Ars Amoris* ever contemplated. The luxury of polygamy did not suffice such a man; he is allowed to enjoy the society of courtesans, and in them, as in Athens, he finds the intellectual interests which are denied to his legitimate wives. With them and the more refined and cultured of the band of hangers-on, high and low, with whom he is surrounded, he can indulge in the pleasures of the discussion of literature, and appreciate the fine efforts of the poets and dramatists. From such a nature, of course, anything heroic cannot be expected, and the poets recognize this state of affairs; but it demands refinement, beauty, luxury, and the demand is fully met. Love is naturally a capital theme, but the dramatists suffer from one grave difficulty from the condition of the society which they depict. The ideal of a romantic love between two persons free and independent, masters of their own destinies, is in great measure denied

[1] pp. 57 ff.; Keith, *Sansk. Lit.* pp. 29 ff.

to them, and they are reduced to the banality of the intrigue between the king and the damsel who is destined to be his wife, but who by some accident has been introduced into his harem in a humble position.

For the dramatists the favour of a king was the chief object to be aimed at, and kings were evidently very willing to lend their names to dramatic and other compositions, whatever part they actually took in their production. The persistence of the rumour which regards Harṣa as winning his fame in part at the expense of Bāṇa, may be unjust to the king, but at any rate it expresses what was popular belief in the possibility of such a happening in poetical circles, and it is indeed incredible that a king should have been so scrupulous as to refuse any aid in his literary toils from his court poets. Competitions in exhibitions of poetry were in favour with monarchs, but they were not the only patrons; their actions excited imitation,[1] and even in Buddhist and Jain circles the desire to adopt the expedient of drama in connexion with religion was evinced. But even when applied by Brahmins, Buddhists, or Jains to philosophy or religion, the drama bore throughout the unmistakable stamp of its original predominance in circles whose chief interest was gallantry: the *Nāgānanda* bears eloquent evidence of this for Buddhist ideas the *Prabodhacandrodaya* for Brahmin philosophy, and the *Moharājaparājaya* for Jainism.

A society of this kind was certain to encourage refinement and elegance in poetry; it was equally certain to lead to artificiality and unreality. But we may be certain that true poetic taste existed; it is attested not merely by the existence and fame of such dramas as those of Kālidāsa, but in the kindred sphere of music it has an interesting exposition in the third Act of the *Mṛcchakaṭikā*, in which, following with slight changes the precedent of Bhāsa, Cārudatta is made to express to the unresponsive ears of Maitreya, his one faithful friend, the effect produced on his ears by the sweet singing of Rebhila, which has come to console him in the midst of his sorrow:[2]

> The notes of love, peace, sweetness, could I trace,
> The note that thrills, the note of passion too,

[1] Mañkha, *Çrīkaṇṭhacarita*, xxv; *Bhojaprabandha*; *Vikramā¯kadevacarita*; *Kāvyamīmāṅsā*, pp. 49 ff.

[2] The translation by Ryder.

The note of woman's loveliness and grace,
Ah, my poor words add nothing, nothing new.
But as the notes in sweetest cadence rang,
I thought it was my hidden love who sang.
The melody of song, the stricken strings,
In undertone that half unconscious clings,
More clearly sounding as the passions rise,
But ever sweeter as the music dies.
Words that strong passion fain would say again,
Yet checks their second utterance—in vain;
For music sweet as this lives on until
I walk as hearing sweetest music still.

To Rājaçekhara[1] we owe a full account of the studies which went to make up the finished poet, who had the choice of Sanskrit, Prākrit, Apabhrança, and Paiçācī, or the speech of the goblins (*bhūtabhāṣā*), as his modes of composition. Knowledge of grammar, of the dictionary, poetics, and metrics are demanded, as well as skill in the sixty-four acts; purity of mind, speech, and body are requisite, as well as most attractive surroundings. The poet's male attendants are to speak Apabhrança, the female Māgadhī, while those within the harem itself are to use Prākrit and Sanskrit, and his friends to exercise themselves in all forms of speech. With pardonable lack of historical truth, we are told anecdotes of kings who forbade the use in their harems of certain letters, and combinations of sounds, on grounds of euphony, and the poet may imitate their usage. We also learn that Sanskrit was affected among the people of Bengal, in Lāṭa Prākrit, in Mārwār, and by the Ṭakkas and Bhādānakas, Apabhrança, while in Avantī, Pariyātra, and Daçapura Bhūtabhāṣā prevailed. The people of Surāṣṭra and the Travaṇas are credited elsewhere[2] with intermingling Sanskrit and Apabhrança, while unkind comments are made on the mode of pronouncing Sanskrit among the excellent poets of Kashmir, and on the nasal accent of the north as opposed to the music of that in Pañcāla. We learn also[3] that poets were wont to make journeys, and to utilize the knowledge of other places thus gained in their works.

Rājaçekhara[4] is also emphatic regarding the capacity of women:

[1] *Kāvyamīmāṅsā*, pp. 49 ff.
[2] *Ibid.*, p. 33.
[3] *Ibid.*, p. 78.
[4] *Ibid.*, p. 53.

daughters of kings or ministers, courtesans, and wives of jesters, were skilled as poets, the capacity which brings about the ability to compose being a matter affecting the soul, and not, therefore, bound up with sex. To Rājaçekhara the ability to write poems is largely due to experiences in previous births, and he logically denies that sex can affect this. But though verses are cited from the poetesses in the anthologies, and not a few names are known, and Avantisundarī, Rājaçekhara's own wife, appears to have been an authority on poetics, it is certain that no drama of importance has come down to us which is written by a woman. The explanation for this would seem rather to lie in social conventions, as in Greece, for there is no reason to suppose that the clever women mentioned by Rājaçekhara, and doubtless not rare in the courts, could not have composed plays of merit.

III

DRAMATIC THEORY

XIII

THE THEORY OF THE DRAMATIC ART

1. *The Treatises on Dramatic Art*

PĀṆINI, whose date falls doubtless before 300 B.C., alludes in his grammar to the *Naṭasūtras*, books of rules for Naṭas, compiled by Çilālin and Kṛçāçva, and Professor Hillebrandt[1] has suggested that we should recognize in these works the earliest text-books of the Indian drama. But we have no other suggestion that Pāṇini knew of dramatic performances, and the only legitimate conclusion is that these rules were laid down for the guidance of dancers or, perhaps, pantomimes, and with this accords admirably the fact that the dramatic tradition knows nothing of these names, and instead makes the sage Bharata the eponymous hero of the drama. True it was Brahmā, highest of gods, himself who, at the instance of the gods, produced as a counterpart to the four Vedas, which contain the science of religion and magic, the more mundane Nāṭya-Veda, consecrated to the drama, but this Veda is not current among men. Bharata, on the other hand, whose task it was to direct the production by the Apsarases in heaven of plays for the delight of the gods and who thus had practical experience of the art, has set forth for men the principles of the drama in the *Nāṭyaçāstra* which, if not inspired, has at least a measure of sanctity, and thus supplies an authoritative basis for practice.

The legend is interesting because it precisely interprets the spirit of India towards authority; Bharata occupies in the theory of the drama a place analogous to that of Pāṇini in grammar, but unfortunately the *Nāṭyaçāstra* has fared badly in comparison with the *Aṣṭādhyāyī*, which has, through the care of its commentators, come down to us in a form but little changed from that it assumed in the hands of its author. The

[1] AID., pp. 3 ff.; above, p. 31.

work, which we have under the title *Bhāratīya Nāṭyaçāstra*,[1] is extremely badly preserved in the manuscript tradition, a fact due in part to the comparatively late date of any commentary upon it. We have only a few references to an exposition of the *Nāṭyaçāstra* by Mātṛgupta, a somewhat mysterious figure with a more or less legendary connexion with Kālidāsa, with whom he has even been identified;[2] if we are to place any faith in his contemporaneity with Kālidāsa, he may date from the close of the fourth century A.D. It is significant that tradition makes him for a time king of Kashmir, for it is to that country we owe the commentaries of Çañkuka, who wrote the epic *Bhuvanābhyudaya* under Ajitāpīḍa (A.D. 813–50), and of Bhaṭṭa Nāyaka, who belongs to the period of Çañkaravarman (A.D. 883–902). In the same line of tradition is the great work of Abhinavagupta, the *Abhinavabhāratī*, which has been lucky enough to come to light after long oblivion, and which represents the erudition of the close of the tenth century.

The treatise, as we have it, is elaborate, covering the whole ground connected with the drama. It deals with the architecture of the theatre, the scenery, and the dress and equipment of the actors; the religious ceremonial to be observed at every representation; the music, the dance, the movements and gestures of the actors, and their mode of delivery; the division of rôles; the general characteristics of poetry; the different classes of drama, and the emotions and sentiments which form a vital element in the drama. There is confusion, complexity, and repetition in the work, but that much of it is old cannot be doubted. It appears clearly to be based on the examination of a dramatic literature which has been lost, eclipsed by the more perfect dramas of Kālidāsa and his successors. In the description of classes of drama we seem to have hasty generalizations on insufficient material; the Samavakāra, for instance, is described in terms

[1] Ed. KM. 1894, i–xiv; by J. Grosset, Paris, 1898; xviii–xx, xxxiv in F. Hall's *Daçarūpa*; xv–xvii (xiv–xvi), in Regnaud, *Annales du Musée Guimet*, i and ii; xxviii in Grosset's *Contribution à l'étude de la musique hindoue*, Paris, 1888; vi and vii in Regnaud, *Rhétorique sanskrite*.

[2] Bhau Daji, JBRAS. vi. 218 ff. Lévi (TI. ii. 4) suggests that the *Çāstra* is largely made out of a versified comment on original Sūtras. For various guesses as to Mātṛgupta, cf. JRAS. 1903, p. 570; see Peterson, *Subhāṣitāvali*, p. 89. It is probable that the *Çāstra* is related to an original Sūtra in the same way as the *Kāmandakīya Nītiçāstra* to the *Arthaçāstra*. Cf. S. K. De, SP. i. 27 ff.

which, with the precise definition of the time to be occupied by the acts, can be interpreted only as based on a single drama, and the Ḍima seems to have a similar origin. The elaborate description of the preliminary scene or Pūrvarañga, which is practically non-existent in the classical drama, suggests a period of a less cultivated taste. A more definite result may be derived from comparison of the *Nāṭyaçāstra* with the works of Açvaghoṣa and of Bhāsa. The Prākrits recognized by the *Nāṭyaçāstra* are clearly later than those of Açvaghoṣa and more akin to those found in Bhāsa; again the *Nāṭyaçāstra* recognizes the use of Ardha-Māgadhī, found in these two dramatists, but not later, while, like them, he ignores the Māhārāṣṭrī of the later dramas. Moreover Bhāsa expressly alludes to a *Nāṭyaçāstra*,[1] and it is most probable that both he and Kālidāsa had knowledge of the prototype of the present text. That Bhāsa by no means slavishly adheres to the rules of the *Nāṭyaçāstra*, either as regards the formal mode of terminating his dramas or the exclusion of scenes of death from the stage,[2] merely shows that when he wrote the Çāstra had not attained any binding force. There is nothing to contradict the date thus vaguely indicated,[3] for the treatment of poetics in general is simple and early, and it is impossible to draw any conclusion as to date from the remarks on music, apart altogether from the constant possibility that incidental additions and alterations have been made in the work.

It was inevitable that the complicated and confused work of Bharata should be superseded for many purposes by something more accessible and easy to follow, and this need was supplied by the *Dāçarūpa* of Dhanaṁjaya, son of Viṣṇu, and *protégé* of the ill-fated king Muñja of Dhārā (974–95). The work takes its name from the ten primary forms of drama recognized in the *Nāṭyaçāstra*, which is followed closely by Dhanaṁjaya, his deviations being unimportant and trivial, such as a new division of types of heroine or of the erotic sentiment. On the other hand, Dhanaṁjaya omits by far the greater part of the topics of

[1] *Avimāraka*, ii. A treatise on drama is also attributed to him: *Arthadyotanikā*, 2.

[2] That in the *Çāstra* itself there is contradiction in this regard between x. 83 f. and xviii. 19 f. is shown by Lindenau, BS., p. 34.

[3] Cf. Jacobi, *Bhavisattakaha*, pp. 83 ff., who suggests the third century; the Prākrit seems anterior to Māhārāṣṭrī in development; Jacobi suggests Ujjayinī as a possible location in view of the affinity to Māhārāṣṭrī and Çaurasenī. Cf. GIL. iii. 8.

his model; his four books of wooden verses treat first of the subject-matter and plot; then of the hero, the heroine, and other characters, and the language of the drama; thirdly of the prologue and the different kinds of drama; and lastly of the emotions and sentiments, thus concentrating attention on the essential dramatic features. The text is naturally often unintelligible save in the light of the *Nāṭyaçāstra* itself and of the commentary, *Avaloka*, which is ascribed to Dhanika, son of Viṣṇu, and minister of Utpaladeva, a term which is an alias of Muñja. The identity of the two writers is suggested by the fact that later writers ascribe passages of the *Daçarūpa* itself to Dhanika, and that without the commentary the work is in a sense incomplete. But, on the other hand, in a few passages the commentator more or less distinctly differs from the text, and it seems sufficient to assume that they may have been brothers. The *Avaloka* must have been completed after Muñja's death, since it cites Padmagupta's *Navasāhasāñkacarita*, which was written under Sindhurāja, and this throws some doubt on the identification of Dhanika with the Dhanika Paṇḍita to whose son, Vasantācārya, a land grant was made by Muñja in A.D. 974. Dhanika quotes stanzas of his own in Sanskrit and Prākrit and also a treatise, *Kāvyanirṇaya*, elsewhere unknown.[1]

Of the fourteenth century in all probability are three works of unequal importance and merit. The *Pratāparudrīya*[2] of Vidyānātha is a mediocre compilation from the *Daçarūpa* and the *Kāvyaprakāça* of Mammaṭa, covering the whole field of poetics; it illustrates the formal rules of the drama by the composition of a wretched drama in honour of Pratāparudra of Warangal, whose inscriptions show dates from A.D. 1298 to 1314. Of much greater interest is Vidyādhara's *Ekāvalī*;[3] like Vidyānātha, the author celebrates in his illustrations of his text his patron, in this case Narasiṅha II of Orissa, perhaps A.D. 1280–1314; as a poet his merits are negligible, but he shows a lively interest in his subject and intelligence in his views. Of greater popularity than either

[1] Ed. F. Hall, Calcutta, 1865; trs. G. C. O. Haas, New York, 1912. Jacobi (GGA. 1913, p. 301) presses for the identity of the writers, but the difference of the name is fatal.

[2] Ed. K. P. Trivedī, Bombay, 1909.

[3] Ed. K. P. Trivedī, Bombay, 1903 cf. R. G. Bhandarkar, *Report* (1897) pp. lxviii f.

is Viçvanātha Kavirāja, the author of the *Sāhityadarpaṇa*,[1] a general treatise on poetics. His handling of the drama is based largely on the *Daçarūpa* and its commentary, but he introduces a good deal of matter from the *Nāṭyaçāstra* in his sixth chapter, including details of the characteristics and ornaments of the drama, which the *Daçarūpa* omits. In this Viçvanātha indicates his servile character, which, however, renders his work the more valuable as an exposition of the orthodox doctrine. Of his ancestry and his own works he makes free mention, but the most definite evidence of his date is the existence in the library at Jammu of a manuscript of his work whose date appears to be A.D. 1383. The lack of order and the errors in his work are made the basis of criticism by Rūpa Gosvāmin in the early part of the sixteenth century, but his own *Nāṭakacandrikā* shows little improvement on the work of his predecessor, whence it draws much of its material; its real purpose is to eulogize the saint Caitanya, whose disciple Rūpa was and in whose honour he composed dramas of no merit. Equally dependent on Viçvanātha and the *Daçarūpa* is Sundaramiçra, whose *Nāṭyapradīpa* was composed in A.D. 1613. Many other treatises on drama are known by name or exist in manuscript, but none apparently of any great importance or repute. Of the fourteenth century also is the *Rasārṇavasudhākara*[2] of Çiṅga Bhūpala, lord of Rājācala and the land between the Vindhya and Çrīçaila about A.D. 1330, who cites Vidyādhara.

The development of a theory of drama progressed in the closest relation to the general theory of poetics, for the Indian theory of poetry does not admit any distinction in essence between the aesthetic pleasure produced by the drama and any other form of poetry. Thus we find in Abhinavagupta in full application to the drama the theory of suggestion, Dhvani, as the essence of poetry, which appeared in strength about A.D. 800 and was rendered popular by Ānandavardhana (A.D. 850) and by Abhinavagupta himself in his comment on the *Dhvanyāloka* of the former. Attacked by Mahiman Bhaṭṭa, author of the *Vyaktiviveka* (A.D. 1050), the doctrine was again developed with special

[1] Ed. BI. with trs., 1851–75; in part by P. V. Kane, Bombay, 1910.

[2] Ed. TSS. no. L, 1916. It freely uses the *Daçarūpa*. Cf. Seshagiri, *Report for 1896–97*, pp. 7 ff. Many verses by the author are cited.

care by the Kashmirian Mammaṭa[1] at the close of the eleventh century. In slightly varied forms it appears in Vidyānātha, Vidyādhara, and Viçvanātha.

Apart from this important development, which, however, has no special application to the drama, there is little progress in the course of the literature. The later authorities are bound by the authority of the *Nāṭyaçāstra*; they repeat unintelligently its descriptions of literary forms such as the Dima, the Samavakāra, the Īhāmṛga, the Vīthī, and the Añka, which had ceased to be in popular use, if indeed the definitions of the *Nāṭyaçāstra* were not merely hasty generalizations from a single play or so in every one of these cases. The most that they do is to omit or to vary details, but not in independence; normally the changes can be traced to variants in the text of the Çāstra or to maxims current under Bharata's name, though not included in the Çāstra as we have it. Often the authors differ in the definition of terms in the Çāstra which, as often in Sanskrit technical phrases, present ambiguity and admit of various renderings. These divergences are especially frequent in the long lists of characteristics and ornaments or the different means of effecting dramatic results; the Indian love of meaningless subdivision here can indulge itself to its fullest and least profitable extent. A rich variety of such ambiguities is apparent in the verses in which the *Agni Purāṇa*[2] describes the drama, including dancing and the mimetic art, true to its aim to constitute itself a treasure-house of all learning, popular as well as divine. The chief value of the work is the occasional light which it throws on the variants in the text of the Çāstra, and its comparative antiquity, for it is cited in the *Sāhityadarpaṇa* and is probably some centuries older.

2. *The Nature and the Types of the Drama*

A drama is the imitation or representation of the conditions or situations (*avasthānukṛti*)[3] in which the personages who form the subject of treatment are placed from time to time, by means of gesture, speech, costume, and expression, and, one version of

[1] For the authorship of the *Kāvyaprakāça* see Hari Chand, *Kālidāsa*, pp. 103 ff.

[2] cc. 337–41. On Dhvani see Keith, *Sansk. Lit.* ch. x.

[3] Bharata cited in Rucipati's comm. on *Anargharāghava*, 9. Cf. DR. i. 7; SD. 274.

the definition adds, the situations must be such as to produce pleasure or pain, that is, they must be tinged with emotion. It is the presence of these ancillaries which distinguishes the drama from an ordinary poem ; a poem appeals to the ear only, a drama is also a spectacle to delight the eyes ; hence the term Rūpa or Rūpaka as applied generically to the drama, for Rūpa primarily denotes the object of vision, though the Indian tradition gives the artificial explanation that Rūpaka denotes a drama because the actors are credited with different parts.

Further light is shown on the nature of drama (*nāṭya*) by the discrimination of it from dance (*nṛtta*) and mimetic art (*nṛtya*), which united with song and speech serve to make up the drama.[1] The dance is based on time and rhythm ; the mimetic art is concerned with representing the feelings or emotions (*bhāva*), while the essence of the drama is the sentiment (*rasa*) which it evokes in the spectator, a fact which places it on a higher level than either of its handmaidens. But there may be dramas in which these auxiliaries take first place, and on this fact is based a distinction between the primary forms, Rūpakas, in which the poetry is the dominant element and the secondary forms, Uparūpakas. Of Rūpakas ten are distinguished, Nāṭaka, Prakaraṇa, Bhāṇa, Prahasana, Ḍima, Vyāyoga, Samavakāra, Vīthī, Aṅka, and Īhāmṛga, which vary in regard to subject-matter (*vastu*), hero or heroine, and sentiment.

3. *The Subject-Matter and the Plot*

The scene of the plot must be laid in India, and the period must be one of the three ages succeeding the Golden Age, for pleasure and pain, essential elements as we have seen in the drama, cannot be experienced elsewhere than in Bhāratavarṣa, and even there they do not exist in the age of happiness unalloyed.[2] Otherwise the choice is free; the poet may take an incident familiar from tradition (*prakhyāta*), or may invent his plot (*utpādya*) or may combine both forms (*miçra*). But, if he follows a current legend, it is necessary that he shall not ruin the effect of it by incongruous invention ; he must confine his ingenuity to episodes, for otherwise the audience will be painfully disturbed

[1] Cf. Hall, DR. pp. 6 f.

[2] N. xviii. 89; xix. 1 ; AP. cccxxxvii. 18, 27.

by departure from tradition. On the other hand, it is not merely legitimate but also necessary that the dramatist should ennoble his hero, if tradition assigns to him deeds incompatible with the character which he normally exhibits.[1] The epic is not encumbered with such considerations; it can represent Duḥṣanta as merely forgetful of his vows to Çakuntalā, but Kālidāsa must clear the character of the king from this seeming baseness by attributing his loss of memory to a curse provoked by a negligence of the heroine herself. The *Rāmāyaṇa* admits, and seeks to explain, if not convincingly, the death of Vālin, king of the monkeys, at the hands of the virtuous Rāma; Māyurāja in the *Udāttarāghava* passes over the episode in silence, while Bhavabhūti, with greater boldness, in the *Mahāvīracarita* perverts tradition to represent Vālin as an ally of Rāvaṇa, and as slain by Rāma in legitimate self-defence, and exonerates Kaikeyī.

The subject-matter takes two forms, the principal (*ādhikārika*) and the incidental (*prāsañgika*) actions. The first owes its name to the fact that it is connected with the attainment (*adhikāra*) of the purpose of the hero, whether that be love, or some material interest, or duty, or two or all of these. In the incidental action the end achieved is not that aimed at by the hero, but it serves as a means towards the fruition of his aims.[2] The incidental action may take the dimension of an episode (*patākā*), as is the case with the exploits of Sugrīva as an ally of Rāma, or it may be a mere incident (*prakarī*), as in Act VI of the *Çakuntalā* the scene in which the two attendants converse.[3]

An action, when developed in full, as normally it is in the Nāṭaka, the most perfect of forms of drama, involves of necessity five stages of development (*avasthā*);[4] there must be as the beginning (*ārambha*) the desire to attain some end, which leads on to the determined effort (*prayatna*) to secure the object of desire; this leads to the stage in which success is felt to be possible (*prāptyāçā, prāptisambhava*) having regard to the means available and the obstacles in the way of achievement; then arrives the certainty of success (*niyatāpti*), if only some specific

[1] DR. i. 15; iii. 20–22.
[2] N. xix. 2–6, 25 f.; DR. i. 11, 12, 16; SD. 296 f., 323.
[3] N. xix. 23; DR. i. 13; SD. 320–3; R. iii. 13 f.
[4] N. xix. 7–13; DR. i. 18–20; SD. 324–9; R. iii. 22–5.

difficulty can be surmounted; and finally the object is attained (*phalāgama*). Thus in the *Çakuntalā* we have the king's first anticipation of seeing the heroine, then his eagerness to find a device to meet her again; in Act IV we learn that the anger of the sage, Durvāsas, has in some measure been appeased, and the possibility of the reunion of the king and Çakuntalā now exists; in Act VI the discovery of the ring brings back to the king remembrance, and the way for a reunion is paved, to be attained in the following act. The *Ratnāvalī*, no less perfect an example of the minor type, the Nāṭikā, reveals to us the aims of the minister to secure the union of the heroine and the king; a definite step to this end is taken when the heroine decides to depict the face of Vatsa on the canvas; in Act II the lovers are united for the moment, but subject to the risk of discovery by the queen; then the king recognizes that his success in love depends on winning the queen's favour, which is successfully accomplished in the last act.

There are also five elements of the plot (*arthaprakṛti*),[1] which the theory not very accurately parallels with the five stages of the action. The first is the germ (*bīja*), whence springs the action, as in the *Ratnāvalī* from Yaugandharāyaṇa's scheme to secure the princess for the king. The second, with change of metaphor, is the drop (*bindu*), which spreads out as oil on water; the course of the drama, which has seemed to be interrupted, is again set in activity; thus in the *Ratnāvalī*, when the festival of the god of love is over, the princess gives a decisive impulse to the motion of the drama by recognizing in him, whom she deemed the god himself, the king for whom she was destined as a bride. The other three elements are the episode, the incident, and the *dénouement* (*kārya*).

Based on these parallel sets is a third division of the junctures[2] (*sandhi*), which carry each of the stages of the action to its natural close. They are the opening (*mukha*), progression (*pratimukha*),

[1] N. xix. 19–21; DR. i. 16 f.; SD. 317–19. The parallelism is faulty: neither episode nor incident is necessary nor corresponds to Prāptyāçā and Niyatāpti nor Garbha and Vimarça; Dhanika, DR. i. 33, admits this in effect; there is no episode in *Ratnāvalī*, III. Cf. R. iii. 22.

[2] N. xix. 16, 35 ff.; DR. i. 22 ff.; SD. 330 ff. Hall (DR., p. 11 n.) suggests *nibarhaṇa* as correct (N. xix. 36), wrongly. Cf. R. iii. 26–74. The precise parallelism of the Sandhis and Avasthās in the *Bālarāmāyaṇa* is given in R. iii. 23–5.

development (*garbha*), pause (*vimarça*), and conclusion (*nirvahaṇa*), corresponding clearly and closely with the stages,[1] set out above. Thus in the *Çakuntalā* the opening extends from Act I to the point in Act II where the general departs; the progression begins with the king's confession to the Vidūṣaka of his deep love, and extends to the close of Act III. The development occupies Acts IV and V, up to the point where Gautamī uncovers the face of Çakuntalā; at this moment the curse darkens the mind of the king, who, instead of rejoicing in reunion with his wife, pauses in reflection, and this pause in the action extends to the close of Act VI, while the conclusion is achieved in the last Act. In the *Ratnāvalī* the opening extends to that point in Act II, where Ratnāvalī decides to depict the king as the only means of gazing on him whom she loves, but from whom she is jealously kept by the queen; the progression extends then to the close of the Act; the development occupies Act III, while the pause, due to the intervention of the queen, is brought to an end by the mock fire of the palace in Act IV, and the remaining portion of that Act gives the conclusion.

So far there is obviously force and reason in the analysis, which, if in needless elaboration, recognizes the essential need of a dramatic conflict, of obstacles to be overcome by the hero and heroine in their efforts to secure abiding union. The classification of elements of the plot is perhaps superfluous beside the junctures; its parallelism to the other two divisions is faulty, for it is admitted that the episode is not confined to the development, as it should be, but may extend into the pause and even into the conclusion.[2] The episode again is credited with subjunctures, to be fewer in number than the junctures, and even the incident is permitted on one view to have incomplete junctures.[3] But far more complex is the insistence on the subdivision of the five junctures into 64 members (12, 13, 12, 13, and 14 respectively). The distribution, however, has no real value, for, though Rudraṭa[4] asserts that the members should only be used

[1] Abhinavagupta (*Dhvanyāloka*, p. 140) frankly treats the Avasthās as the Sandhis as parts of the story, and distinguishes the Arthaprakṛtis. DR. is responsible for the doctrine that each Sandhi rests on an Avasthā and an Arthaprakṛti, accepted in *Pratāparudrīya*, iii. 3; GGA. 1913, pp. 306–8; R. iii. 26 f.

[2] SD. 321.

[3] N. xix. 28; DR. i. 33.

[4] N. xix. 103; SD. 406.

in the juncture to which they are assigned, other authorities decline to admit this view, on the score of the usage of the dramatists, which is the supreme norm. Not all of these members need be used; it is a fault in the *Veṇīsaṁhāra* that the poet drags in the separation of Duryodhana from Bhānumatī in Act II for no better reason than to comply with the rules.[1] When used, they should be essentially subservient to the sentiment which the piece seeks to create;[2] they should either treat the subject chosen, expand the plot, increase interest, produce surprise, represent the parties in action, or conceal what should be concealed; the hero or his rival should appear in them, or at any rate they should flow from the germ and lead up to the *dénouement*. Some must be included in any drama, since one without any would be like a man without limbs, and, adroitly used, they may give merit to a mediocre subject-matter. But the definitions and the classifications are without substantial interest or value.

A distinction must be made between such things as can properly be shown on the stage, and such as must only be alluded to.[3] What is seen should essentially serve to produce the sentiment aimed at, and it must avoid offending the feelings of the audience. Hence it is improper to portray on the stage such events as a national calamity, the downfall of a king, the siege of a town, a battle, killing, or death, all of them painful. It is equally forbidden to depict a marriage or other[4] religious rite, or such domestic details as eating, sleeping, bathing, or anointing the body, amorous dalliance, scratching with nails or teeth, or such ill-omened things as curses. But these rules are not without exception early or late; if Bhāsa does not hesitate as in the *Ūrubhaṅga* to depict death on the stage, Rājaçekhara in his *Viddhaçālabhañjikā* describes the marriage ceremonial in Act III, and in the following Act shows us the wife of Cārāyaṇa asleep, while the author of the *Pārvatīpariṇaya* does not hesitate to choose as his theme the nuptials of Çiva and Pārvatī. Nor do dramatists decline to represent death if the dead person is restored to life, as in the *Nāgānanda*.[5] A long journey, or calling

[1] N. xix. 50 f.; SD. 407.
[2] SD. 342, 407.
[3] N. xviii. 16 ff.; DR. i. 51; iii. 31 f.; SD. 278.
[4] The rule is dubious; see Dhanika on DR. iii. 32, where he allows the performance of essential religious rites.
[5] Jackson, AJP. xix. 247 ff.

from a distance,[1] is excluded from representation for obvious reasons of practicability.

Such matters as are appropriate for presentation must be presented in Acts, and each Act must contain only such events as can naturally, or by skilful management, be made to occupy the duration of a single day,[2] a requisite which is obeyed by Bhavabhūti in his *Mahāvīracarita* and by Rājaçekhara in his *Bālarāmāyaṇa* despite the difficulties presented by the effort thus to condense the epic. But it is essential that the events described shall not be disconnected; they must flow from the same cause, or issue naturally from one another. There should be an effective development of the plot within the Act; at the time when it comes to an end by the departure of the actors—three or four at most, one of whom should be the hero—at the moment when they seemed to have attained their immediate aims, a new motive should come into play, and a fresh impetus be given to the movement of the drama. But it is neither necessary nor usual that Act should follow Act without interval; on the contrary, anything up to a year may intervene between the action of one Act and that of the next; if the events as recorded in history covered more than that time, as in the case of Rāma's fourteen years of banishment in the forest, the poet must reduce the period to a year or less. To reveal to the audience the events during such intervals the theory permits a choice of five forms of scenes of introduction (*arthopakṣepaka*), which serve also to narrate things, whose performance on the stage is forbidden by the etiquette of the drama.[3]

Two of these are the Viṣkambha or Viṣkambhaka and the Praveçaka, which are both explanatory scenes, but between which the theory draws fine distinctions. The Viṣkambhaka is performed by not more than two persons,[4] never of chief rank; it serves to explain the past or the future, and it may be used at the beginning of a drama where it is not desired to arouse sentiment at the outset. It is pure (*çuddha*) if the performers are of

[1] SD. 278, no doubt by misreading.

[2] N. xviii. 14 f., 22-4; DR. iii. 27, 32-4; SD. 278; R. iii. 205; JAOS. xx. 341 ff.

[3] N. xviii. 28, 34 f.; xix. 109-16; DR. i. 52-6; SD. 305-13; R. iii. 178 ff.

[4] Bhāsa has three in several cases; Lindenau, BS. p. 40 says Prākrit is never used alone, as stated by Lévi, TI. i. 59, and Konow, ID. p. 13, but see Vatsarāja's *Tripuradāha*, II.

middle rank and speak Sanskrit; mixed (*saṁkīrṇa*) when the characters are of middle and inferior class and use also Prākrit. The Praveçaka cannot be used at the beginning of a drama, and is confined to inferior characters, who use Prākrit. Thus in the *Çakuntalā* Act III is introduced by a Viṣkambhaka, in which a young disciple of the sage Kaṇva tells us in Sanskrit of the king's stay at the hermitage, while in Act VI a Praveçaka gives the episode of the fisherman and the police. An abbreviated mode of producing the same result is the Cūlikā,[1] in which a voice from behind the curtain narrates some essential event, as when in Act IV of the *Mahāvīracarita* we learn thus of the defeat of Paraçurāma by Rāma. In the Aṅkamukha, or anticipatory scene, at the close of one Act a character alludes to the subject of the following Act; thus at the end of Act II in the *Mahāvīracarita* Sumantra announces the arrival of Vasiṣṭha, Viçvāmitra, and Paraçurāma, and these three open Act III. A different view is taken by Viçvanātha, who makes it out to be a part of an Act in which allusion is made to the subject-matter of the following Acts and the whole plot, as is done in the dialogue of Avalokitā and Kāmandakī in Act I of the *Mālatīmādhava*. This is evidently an attempt to justify the treatment of this form of scene as revealing matters which cannot conveniently be depicted on the stage, as well as to distinguish it from the Aṅkāvatāra or continuation scene, in which the action is continued by the characters in the next Act without any break, other than the technical one of the departure of the actors and their return, as at the close of Act I of the *Mālavikāgnimitra*. Such a scene obviously in no way answers the purpose of explanation, and its assignment to such an end is clearly erroneous.

Various devices are recognized to help the movement of the intrigue, five of which are classed as internal junctures (*antara-sandhi*).[2] The first of these is the dream, as in the *Veṇīsaṁhāra* where Bhānumatī is terrified by a vision in which she sees an ichneumon (*nakula*) slay a hundred snakes, dread presage of the fall of the hundred Kauravas before the attack of Nakula and his

[1] R. iii. 185 f. calls Khaṇḍacūlikā an exchange of words between one on and one off the stage at the beginning only of an act; e. g. *Bālarāmāyaṇa*, VII.

[2] Mātṛgupta in *Arthadyotanikā*, 20.

brothers. The letter serves in the *Çakuntalā*, Act III, to allow the heroine to express her feelings towards the king; she reads it aloud and he overhears it and breaks in upon her; more often it serves the important end of conveying news, leading to dramatic action. A message serves the same end, as when in the *Çakuntalā,* Act VI, Mātali brings to the king Indra's message imploring aid against the demons. A voice from behind the scene (*nepathyokti*) in Act I of that play warns Duḥṣanta not to kill the gazelle of the hermitage, and a voice in the air (*ākāçabhāṣita*) in Act IV makes known to Kaṇva on his return the important news of Çakuntalā's marriage and approaching motherhood. The *Nāṭyaçāstra*[1] ignores the term internal junctures, but has the term special junctures or divisions of junctures (*sandhyantara*) which includes the dream, the letter, and the message, among many other miscellaneous elements; two of these are akin to those already mentioned. The picture is used in the *Ratnāvalī* as the mode by which the heroine satisfies her longing for her beloved, while Vāsavadattā discovers Vatsa's infidelity through seeing the portrait of Sāgarikā, painted beside that of the king by the mischievous Susaṁgatā. Intoxication (*mada*) may result as in the *Mālavikāgnimitra*, Act III, in the letting fall of imprudent words by an important character. Other devices might have been included in the list, such as that of assuming a disguise on the stage, a device used by Harṣa in the *Ratnāvalī* and the *Priyadarçikā* in order to secure the inconstant king uninterrupted interviews with the objects of his temporary affections. The latter play contains in Act III a good example of the embryo Act (*garbhāñka*),[2] which is recognized by the theory but not classed as a species of juncture; in it Vāsavadattā causes her maids of honour to perform before her a play representing her early adventures with Vatsa. So in the *Uttararāmacarita* Vālmīki has performed by the Apsarases before Rāma and Lakṣmaṇa the adventures of Sītā since her banishment, and the events of her marriage are described in this form in the *Bālarāmāyaṇa*, Act III.

Similarly the theory recognizes as a separate element the pro-episode (*patākāsthānaka*),[3] an equivocal speech or situation which

[1] xix. 53–7, 105–9; R. iii. 95; 79–92.

[2] SD. 279.

[3] N. xix. 30–4; DR. i. 14; SD. 299–303; R. iii. 15–17. where N. is cited with variant readings.

foreshadows an event whether near at hand or distant. The *Nāṭyaçāstra* distinguishes four kinds of equivoke. An ambiguous situation may result in bringing about the aim of the hero; thus in Act III of the *Ratnāvalī*, when Vatsa hastens to save Vāsavadattā, as he thinks, from hanging herself, he finds to his equal joy and surprise that he has rescued none other than Sāgarikā herself.[1] Or the equivocation may lie in words, whose sense the spectator alone grasps in its deeper application; thus in Act II of the *Çakuntalā* a voice behind the scene bids the female Cakravāka say farewell to her spouse, a command whose application to the case of the king and the heroine is immediately appreciated by the audience alone. Or the equivocation may be deliberately conveyed in the response of the actor, whose words apply not merely to the immediate matter in hand, but allude to the future; in the *Veṇīsaṁhāra*, Act II, Duryodhana is told of the mishap of the breaking of his standard by the fierce (*bhīma*) wind in words which presage his own fall, his thigh broken by Bhīma's blow. Finally we may have a *double entendre* which later is destined to find a third application; in the *Ratnāvalī* Vatsa playfully suggests that his earnest gaze on the creeper, which has borne blossoms out of season, may cause jealousy in the queen; his words apply equally to a maiden, and in the sequel the queen is made furiously angry by his ardent gaze at Sāgarikā. The *Daçarūpa* contents itself with two species, equivocation of situation and deliberate equivocation of phrase, but there is general agreement that pro-episodes may be used in any part of the play and not merely in the first four junctures.

Importance attaches to the conventions which enable the author to surmount difficulties inseparable from the dramatic form.[2] Normally, of course, the actors speak aloud (*prakāçam*), to be heard by all those on the stage as well as by the audience, but asides (*svagatam*, *ātmagatam*) are frequent, meant to be heard by the audience alone. If the need arises for making a remark to be heard by one actor only, it is made in the form of a confidence (*apavāritam*, *apavārya*), while a private conversation (*janāntikam*) is arranged by the actors holding up three

[1] This is differently taken by R. iii. 16 as an allusion to Vāsavadattā's anger to come.

[2] DR. i. 57–61; SD. 425; R. iii. 200 ff.

fingers, the thumb and ring finger being curved inwards. Or, it is possible to avoid bringing on a person by speaking in the air (*ākāçabhāṣita*), pretending to hear the reply, and repeating it before answering it, while a similar purpose can be served by a voice from behind the scene.

The number of Acts which a play should contain varies according to the nature of the drama ; in the Nāṭaka the number must be at least five, and may be ten ; in other cases one Act suffices. Normally the Acts are simply numbered ; in some cases, as in that of the *Mṛcchakaṭikā*, names are given, doubtless not by the poet.

4. *The Characters*

The hero owes his name, Nāyaka, to the fact that it is he who leads (*nī*) the events to the conclusion which he has set before him, in so far as such a result is permitted by human frailty and the force of circumstances. His good qualities are innumerable[1]; he must be modest as is Rāma in depreciating his own prowess in comparison with that of Paraçurāma whom he has vanquished ; handsome, generous like Jīmūtavāhana, prompt and skilled in action, affable, beloved of his people, of high family, ready of speech, and steadfast. He must be young, and endowed with intelligence, energy, a good memory, skill in the arts, and just pride ; a hero, firm, glorious, skilled in the sciences, and an observer of law. More useful is the distinction drawn between types of hero[2]; all are noble or self-controlled (*dhīra*), a characteristic not universally found in heroines, but they are distinguished as light-hearted or gay (*lalita*), calm (*çānta*) exalted (*udātta*), and haughty or vehement (*uddhata*).

The light-hearted hero is one free from care, a lover of the arts, and above all a devotee of love ; he is normally a king whose public burdens are confided to others, and whose one business it is to secure union with a new favourite by overcoming the obstacles interposed by the not unnatural jealousy of his queen or queens ; such beyond all is Vatsa in Bhāsa and Harṣa's dramas. The calm hero differs primarily from the light-hearted hero by reason of his birth, for he is a Brahmin or merchant, such

[1] DR. ii. 1 ; SD. 64 ; R. i. 61 ff.

[2] N. xxiv. (Hall, xxxiv.) 4-6 ; DR. ii. 3-5 ; SD. 67-9 ; R. i. 72-8.

as Mādhava in the *Mālatīmādhava* and Cārudatta in the *Daridracārudatta* and the *Mṛcchakaṭikā*; the hero of the Prakaraṇa, or comedy of manners, normally is of this class. The exalted hero is a character of great strength and nobility, firm of purpose, but free from vanity, forbearing, and without egotism. Of such a type are generals, ministers and high officials, and Jīmūtavāhana in the *Nāgānanda*. An instructive controversy rages round this description of Jīmūtavāhana; to be exalted, it is argued, implies the desire of superiority, but Jīmūtavāhana renounces every dream of empire and is a model of calm, of boundless pity, and freedom from passion save, indeed, as regards his love for Malayavatī, which is inconsistent with the general nature of his character. He should really be ranked among the calm heroes, with the Buddha himself, disregarding the meaningless convention which excludes kings from that category. Dhanika[1] effectively defends the classification of Jīmūtavāhana by insisting that he is not without desire, namely that of saving others at the cost of his own life; the desires he lays aside are wishes for personal advantage which Kālidāsa rightly censures in a king; his love for Malayavatī is wholly inconsistent with calmness, which, on the contrary, is in fact as in drama a characteristic of Brahmins, and it distinguishes him absolutely from the Buddha, who is exempt from passion. The haughty hero is a victim of pride and jealousy, an adept in magic arts and ruses, self-assertive, fickle, irascible, and boastful; Paraçurāma illustrates this character.

The chief hero in any drama must be essentially true to one or other of those types; any change would spoil the unity of the development of the drama, and, if necessary, changes must be made in the plot, as in the case of Rāma's dealings with Vālin, to preserve the unity of character. In the case of the secondary hero there is no need for such consistency; he may change in different situations, and his lack of consistency tends merely to heighten the impression caused by the constancy of the hero. Thus Paraçurāma appears in the *Mahāvīracarita*[2] as exalted in his attitude to the evil Rāvaṇa, as haughty towards the untried Rāma, and as calm when he has experienced the superior prowess of that hero. It is obvious that there is difficulty in conceiving as a chief hero

[1] DR. ii. 4

[2] ii. 10, 16; iv. 22.

one of the haughty type, and the theory does not provide us with one, for Paraçurāma is only a secondary hero.

As the Sanskrit drama deals usually with love, the theory has another division of types of hero based on their attitude to women.[1] The courteous (*dakṣiṇa*) hero is one who can find room in his heart for more loves than one; he seeks another to the deep grief of the old, but he does not cease to feel affection for his earlier love; such are the heroes of the Nāṭikā, or short heroic comedy, like Vatsa. He may not be regarded as either deceitful (*çaṭha*), or shameless (*dhṛṣṭa*), for these two types represent heroes who have ceased to love their former flame, and differ only in so far as they seek to deceive her, or are indifferent to her anger and bear open traces of the new attachment. Men like Vatsa never allow passion to dominate them; if a woman spurns them they are ready to leave her. The fourth type is the loyal (*anukūla*) lover who is faithful to one woman only, as is Rāma. As these four types are applicable to each class of hero, there are sixteen possible kinds of hero, and the theory adds the further complication that each of these may be a high class, middle class, or inferior person, giving forty-eight types.

As if the enumeration of the general characteristics of the hero were insufficient, a set of eight special excellencies[2] is enumerated separately as springing from his character (*sāttvika*). These are brilliance (*çobhā*), including compassion for inferiors, emulation with superiors, heroism, and cleverness; vivacity (*vilāsa*), including a firm step and glance and a laughing voice; grace (*mādhurya*) manifested in the display of but slight change of demeanour in trying circumstances; impassivity (*gāmbhīrya*) or superiority to emotion; steadfastness (*sthairya*) in accomplishing his object despite obstacles; the sense of honour (*tejas*) which will punish insult even at the cost of life itself; lightheartedness as grace of deportment; and nobility (*audārya*) exhibited in sacrifice for the sake of the good.

The enemy of the hero (*pratināyaka*)[3] is self-controlled and vehement (*dhīroddhata*); but he is also avaricious, stubborn, criminal, and vicious; such are Rāvaṇa and Duryodhana as con-

[1] DR. ii. 6; SD. 71-5; R. i. 80-2. R. i. 79, 83-8 has a division into husbands, adulterers (*upapati*), and the connoisseur of hetaerae (*vaiçika*). For the courteous lover, see p. 205.

[2] DR. ii. 9-13; SD. 89-95; R. i. 215-19; 64, 69.

[3] DR. ii. 8; SD. 159.

trasted with Rāma and Yudhiṣṭhira. On the other hand, the hero of the episode, the companion (*pīṭhamarda*)[1] of the hero, is to possess, but in a less degree, the qualities of the hero; he is to be intelligent, ever in attendance on the hero, and devoted to his interests, as are Makaranda in the *Mālatīmādhava* and Sugrīva in the dramas based on the Rāma legend. The term, however, is unknown to these plays, while in the *Mālavikāgnimitra* the nun Kauçikī is styled a Pīṭhamardikā, and serves as a trusted go-between. The theory here seems to have stereotyped a relationship commoner in an older type of drama.

The heroine, Nāyikā,[2] plays a part in the economy of the drama similar to that of the hero, and not of less importance. The types of heroine depend primarily on her relation to the hero; she may be his wife (*svā, svīyā*), or belong to another (*anyā, anyastrī*) or be a hetaera. The hero's wife must be upright and of good character, but she may be inexperienced (*mugdhā*), partly experienced (*madhyā*), or fully experienced and bold (*pragalbhā*). The inexperienced wife is shy in her love and gentle in her anger with her spouse's infidelities. The partly experienced is full of the love of youth, and even faints in her passion; when angry, if self-controlled, she chides her husband with *double entendres*; if but partly controlled, she allows her tears to aid her reproaches; if uncontrolled, she adds harsh words. The bold wife is frantically in love, fainting at the first embrace; when angry, if self-controlled, she adopts an attitude of haughty reserve and indifference to the pleasures of life; if lacking in self-control, she uses threats and blows; if partly self-controlled, she employs the weapons of raillery and equivoque. A further division is possible, for each of these three kinds of heroine may be subdivided according as the lady is the earlier or later of the loves of the husband.

A woman, who is in the power of another, may be the wife of another man or a maiden. An amour with a married woman may not form the subject of the dominant sentiment in the play, but that for a maiden may occur as an element in the principal or the secondary action. Even when a parent or guardian is willing to permit a maiden's marriage, there may be other obstacles, as in the case of the love of Mālatī and Mādhava and

[1] DR. ii. 7; SD. 76. Cf. *Kāmasūtra*, p. 60; R. i. 89, 90.

[2] DR. ii. 14 f.; SD. 96–100; R. i. 94–120, who takes the unusual view that Irāvatī in the *Mālavikāgnimitra* is a hetaera.

in Vatsa's numerous amours. The woman who is common to all (*sādhāraṇī*) is a courtesan, skilled in the arts, bold, and cunning; she accepts as lovers the rich, the foolish, the self-willed, the selfish, and the impotent so long as their money lasts, then she has them turned out of doors by her mother, who acts as go-between. If she is a heroine, she must be represented as in love, like Vasantasenā in the *Mṛcchakaṭikā*, except in a Prahasana or farce, where she can be depicted as fleecing her lovers for comic effect; she must not figure as a heroine if the hero is divine or royal.

The heroine may occupy eight different relations to her lover.[1] She may be his absolute mistress (*svādhīnapatikā*), and he her obedient slave; she may be awaiting him in full dress (*vāsaka-sajjā*); she may be distressed by his involuntary absence (*virahotkaṇṭhitā*), enraged (*khaṇḍitā*) at discovering him disfigured by the marks of her rival's teeth and nails, or be severed from her beloved by a quarrel (*kalahāntaritā*) and suffer remorse, or be deceived (*vipralabdhā*) by a lover who fails to meet her at the rendezvous which she has named. Her lover may be absent abroad (*proṣitapriyā*), or she may have to seek him out or press him to come to her (*abhisārikā*), giving as meeting-place a ruined temple, a garden, the house of a go-between, a cemetery, the bank of a stream, or in general any dark place. The first two classes of heroine are bright and gay, the others are wearied, tearful, changing colour, sighing, and wear no ornaments as token of their dejection. A woman, who is subject to another, cannot stand in all these relations to a lover; she may be distressed at his absence, deceived, or driven to seek him out, but she cannot be enraged, for she is not the mistress of her lover, and thus the king's courtesy to Mālavikā in Kālidāsa's play is not to be treated as an effort to appease an enraged heroine.

The heroine is accorded even a more generous allowance of excellencies than the hero.[2] The first three are physical, the first display of emotion in a nature previously exempt (*bhāva*), the movement of eyes and brows betokening the awakening of love (*hāva*), and the still more open manifestation of affection. The next seven are inherent characteristics of the heroine; the brilliance of youth and passion; the added touch of loveliness

[1] N. xxii. 197–206; DR. ii. 22–5; SD. 113–21; R. i. 121–51.

[2] N. xxii. 4–29; DR. ii. 28–39; SD. 126–55; R. i. 190–214, with Bhoja's views.

given by love, sweetness, radiance, courage, dignity, and self-control. Then come ten graces; the sportive imitation of the movements or words of the beloved one, the swift change of aspect at his arrival, tasteful arrangement of one's ornaments to increase radiance of appearance, studied confusion of ornaments, hysteria (*kilakiñcita*), in which anger, fear, joy, and tears mingle, manifestations of affection (*moṭṭāyita*) on hearing the beloved mentioned or seeing his portrait, pretended anger (*kuṭṭamita*) on the lover touching hair or lip, affected indifference (*bibboka*), born of excess of pride, a graceful pose (*lalita*), and the bashfulness which forbids speech even when an opportunity presents itself. To these twenty Viçvanātha adds eight more graces; the pride which is vain of youth and beauty, the ennui which besets the maiden in her lover's absence, the *naïveté* which displays itself in pretended ignorance and innocence, the distraction evinced by ornaments in disorder, wandering glances, and truant words, curiosity, the meaningless laugh of youth and high spirits, the tremors of fear causeless but common in the presence of the lover, and the sportive play of young affection. The same source gives us in great detail the modes in which the different types of heroine display their affection, in maidenly modesty or in shameless boldness, an analysis showing keen and deep insight into all the outward manifestations of love at an Indian court. Less praiseworthy is the perverse ingenuity which enumerates the different types of heroine, and educes first 128 from the combination of the eight forms of relationship to the lover with the sixteen kinds based on the division of wife, another's, and hetaera. These are then multiplied by three on the basis of the division of all characters as high class, middle class, and low class.

The same division of classes is applied to all the other characters (*pātra*) which can appear in a play, but a much more fundamental classification is that by sex, masculine, feminine, and neuter. Most of the rôles are such as are incidental to the life of a palace, for the normal drama deals with the amours of a king, and his entourage and that of the queen account for practically all the normal characters of the drama.

The king's confidant and devoted friend is the Vidūṣaka,[1] a Brahmin, ludicrous alike in dress, speech, and behaviour. He is a

[1] N. xii. 121 f.; xxi. 126; xxiv. 106; DR. ii. 8; SD. 79; R. i. 92.

misshapen dwarf, baldheaded, with projecting teeth and red eyes, who makes himself ridiculous by his silly chatter in Prākrit, and his greed for food and presents of every kind. It is a regular part of the play for the other characters to make fun of him, but he is always by the king's side, and the latter makes him his confidant in all his affairs of the heart, while the Vidūṣaka repays him by willing, if frequently incompetent or unlucky, attempts at service. The theorists offer no explanation of the anomaly of a Brahmin in such a curious position, but Açvaghoṣa already has the figure, as has Bhāsa, though not in his epic dramas, and later he is established as almost an essential feature in all dramas not derived from the epic; the chief exception is the *Mālatīmādhava*, where, however, his place is taken by the hero's friend in sport (*narmasuhṛd*).

A much less common, but an interesting character is that of the Viṭa,[1] who resembles, though distantly, the parasite of the Greek drama; he is a poet skilled in the arts, especially music, acquainted *au fond* with the ways of hetaerae, in short a perfect man of the world with literary and artistic culture to boot. He is an essential figure in the Bhāṇa, or monologue, in which he relates his own shady adventures, but in other forms of drama he plays but a small part; Kālidāsa and Bhavabhūti ignore him, and, while Harṣa depicts him in the *Nāgānanda*, his position there is episodic; in the *Mṛcchakaṭikā* alone does he attain full development in his relation to the boastful Çakāra. Both these figures appear also in the *Cārudatta*, Çūdraka's model. The Çakāra,[2] brother of a royal concubine, is of low caste, easily angered and appeased, fond of fine raiment, and proud of his office, in which, however, he shows himself corrupt and incompetent. He is found also in an episode of the *Çakuntalā*, but then fades from the drama leaving, however, a clear suggestion of its early history.

The king requires in his amours the aid of a messenger (*dūta*)[3] as well as for more serious affairs. The holder of this rôle must be possessed of loyalty, energy, courage, a good memory, and adroitness; he may be given full powers to act as seems best in each emergency, or have limited authority, or be a mere bearer

[1] N. xii. 97; xxiv. 104; DR. ii. 8; SD. 78; *Kāmasūtra*, p. 58; Schmidt, *Beiträge zur indischen Erotik*, pp. 200 ff.

[2] N. xii. 130; xxiv. 105; DR. ii. 42; SD. 81.

[3] SD. 86 f., 158.

of a message. Others intimately associated with the royal household are the servants (*ceṭa*),[1] the mercenaries, Kirātas or Mlecchas, the chaplain, priest, and other theologians. There are also those employed in the government of the realm, which the king is only too pleased to neglect.[2] The minister (*mantrin, amātya*) is of good family, of high intelligence, skilled in affairs human and divine, and devoted to the interests of the country. The general (*senāpati*) is also of high birth, incapable of weakness, skilled in both the theory and the practice of war, and kind of speech; ready to note the weakness of the enemy and to direct at the suitable moment a campaign against him. The judge (*prāḍvivāka*) must be master of the laws and of judicial procedure, absolutely impartial, devoted to his duty, free from anger or pride, master of himself. The other officers are required to possess high qualities of intelligence, activity, and devotion to duty, while for less important work the king commands the services of foresters, military officers, and soldiers. The prince royal (*kumāra*) and the friend are also mentioned in the *Nāṭyaçāstra*, but without detail.

Of women's rôles[3] the most important in dignity is that of the chief queen (*mahādevī*), the equal in age and rank of her husband, whose lapses in affection wound her, without robbing her of her sense of self-respect or dignity. In good fortune or evil she is devoted to him and seeks ever his welfare. The queen (*devī*) is also a daughter of a king, but she is more proud than dignified, and, intoxicated by her youth and beauty, her mind is set on the pleasures of love. The favourite (*svāminī*) is the daughter of a general or a minister, seductive by her beauty and intelligence, honoured by the king and others. There are other types of concubine (*sthāyinī* and *bhoginī*) with characteristics but little distinctive. The harem includes also the chief attendants (*āyukta*), who are charged with the supreme oversight of some department of the court, the king's personal attendant who is always with him (*anucārikā*), the maid who performs his toilet and holds over him the umbrella of state, the women—called sometimes Yavanīs, once Greek maidens—who act as his bodyguard, and those aged women who are skilled in political tradi-

[1] N. xxiv. 107; DR. ii. 41; SD. 82.
[2] N. xxiv. 60 ff.
[3] N. xxiv. 15 ff. The *Kāmasūtra*, of course, covers much the same ground.

tions and are respected on that score. There are also the princess, *ingénue* and modest, and the duenna (*mahattarā*), who among other things sees to the punctual performance of auspicious rites, and the more humble adepts in the dance, in song, in handicrafts, in acting, and in the favourite amusement of swinging the ladies of the harem. The hetaera is painted in attractive colours; she is thoroughly well educated, exempt from the normal defects of women, kind of heart, adroit, active, a born coquette, and seductive in every way. Special importance among these feminine rôles attaches to that of the heroine's messenger, the counterpart of the hero's agent. She may be a friend, a slave, a foster-sister, a neighbour, a workwoman, or an artiste, or strangely enough, a nun, usually of Buddhist connexions, a curious and interesting sidelight on Indian views of the devotees of that faith. The doorkeeper (*pratīhārī*) has the function of announcing to the king such political events as the declaration of war and the conclusion of peace.

The neuter rôles[1] are filled by men who have either taken vows of chastity, or have been deprived of virility in order to permit of their employment in the harem. The Snātaka is a Brahmin, who has completed his course of religious study, is familiar with religious and social affairs; he resides within the palace. The chamberlain (*kañcukin*) is an old Brahmin, worn out in the service of the king, but still mentally alert and skilled in his business of conveying the royal orders in the palace. The eunuchs (*varṣadhara*, *nirmuṇḍa*, *upasthāyika*) are effeminate and cowardly but not lacking in *savoir faire*; they find employment in the king's amours.

The nomenclature[2] of the characters is in some measure regulated by rule; the name of a hetaera should end in *dattā*, *senā*, or *siddhā*, as does that of Vasantasenā in the *Cārudatta*; that of a merchant in *datta* as in Cārudatta; that of the Vidūṣaka from spring or a flower, but in the *Avimāraka* he is styled Saṁtuṣṭa; that of a servant, male or female, should be derived from some object, which occurs in descriptions of the seasons, &c., as in the names Kalahaṅsa and Mandārikā in the *Mālatīmādhava*; those of Kāpālikas, a species of ascetics, should end in *ghaṇṭa* as in Aghoraghaṇṭa in the same play.

[1] N. xxiv. 50 ff. [2] SD. 426. R. iii. 323-38 gives very elaborate details.

There is also an elaborate etiquette[1] as to the mode of addressing the diverse personages. A king is styled thus by ascetics, but Deva or Svāmin by his courtiers; his charioteer and Brahmins generally hail him as Āyuṣmant 'long-lived', while inferiors style him Bhaṭṭa, 'master'. The crown prince is styled Svāmin, like his father; the other princes of the blood (*bhartṛdāraka*), but also common people, Bhadramukha or Saumya, preceded by *he* in the latter case, terms designed to conciliate by attributing to those addressed the qualities they are desired to show.[2] The style Bhagavant, 'blessed', is appropriate to the gods, to great sages and saints; Ārya, 'noble', is appropriate to Brahmins, ministers, and elder brothers, while a wife should address her husband as Āryaputra. Sages address an ascetic as Sādhu; ministers are styled Amātya or Saciva; the king calls his Vidūṣaka, and is called by him, Vayasya, 'friend'. Sugṛhītābhidha, 'well named one', is the address[3] of a pupil to his master, a son to a father, or a younger to an elder brother, while the latter in return uses Tāta or Vatsa, both affectionate and condescending terms, suitable also for use to a son, or any person who owes one respect. Heretics should be given the styles they affect, thus a Buddhist should be hailed as Bhadanta; Çakas should be styled by such terms as Bhadradatta. The interjection Hañho may be used between men of middle rank, Haṇḍe between common people. The Vidūṣaka addresses the queen and her ladies as Bhavatī; otherwise the queen is styled Bhaṭṭinī or Svāminī, a wife as Āryā, a princess Bhartṛdārikā, a hetaera Ajjukā, a go-between or aged dame Ambā; Halā is used between friends of equal rank, Hañjā is addressed to a servant.

5. *The Sentiments*

The most original and interesting part of dramatic theory is the gradual definition of the nature of the sentiment which it is the aim of the performance to evoke in the mind of the audience.[4]

[1] N. xvii. 73 ff.; DR. ii. 62 6; SD. 431 ff.; Lévi, TI. i. 129, corrected JA. sér. 9, xix. 97 f.; R. iii. 306–22.

[2] A child may thus be addressed by persons of low rank, SD. 431; cf. *Mṛcchakaṭikā*, x. p. 160.

[3] For another style, cf. *Hāsyacūḍāmaṇi*, p. 124; *Upādhyāya*, R. iii. 309.

[4] P. Regnaud, *Rhétorique Sanskrite*, pp. 266 ff.; Jacobi, DMG. lvi. 394 f.; M. Lindenau, *Beiträge zur altindischen Rasalehre*, Leipzig, 1913. See N. vi. and vii.; DR. iv.; SD. iii.; R. . 298–ii. 265.

The statement of the *Nāṭyaçāstra* is simple. Sentiment is produced from the union of the determinants (*vibhāva*), the consequents (*anubhāva*), and the transitory feelings (*vyabhicārin*). The determinants fall in the later classification into two divisions, the fundamental determinants (*ālambana*) and the excitant determinants (*uddīpana*); fundamental determinants comprise such things as the heroine or the hero, for without them there can be no creation of sentiment in the audience; excitant determinants are such conditions of place and time and circumstance as serve to foster sentiment when it has arisen, for instance the moon, the cry of the cuckoo, the soft breeze from Malaya, all things which foster the erotic sentiment. The consequents are the external manifestations of feeling, by which the actors exhibit to the audience the minds and hearts of the persons of the drama, such as sidelong glances, a smile, a movement of the arm, and—though this is but slightly indicated in later texts—his words.[1] A special class is later made of those consequents, which are the involuntary product of sympathetic realization of the feeling of the person portrayed, and hence are called Sāttvika, as arising from a heart which is ready to appreciate the sorrows or joys of another (*sattva*); these are paralysis, fainting, horripilation, perspiration, change of colour, trembling, weeping, and change of voice. The transitory or evanescent feelings are given as thirty-three; they are discouragement, weakness, apprehension, weariness, contentment, stupor, joy, depression, cruelty, anxiety, fright, envy, indignation, arrogance, recollection, death, intoxication, dreaming, sleeping, awakening, shame, epilepsy, distraction, assurance, indolence, agitation, deliberation, dissimulation, sickness, insanity, despair, impatience, and inconstancy. But these factors are not sufficient to account for sentiment, nor does the *Nāṭyaçāstra* intend this. It recognizes that an essential element in the production of sentiment is the dominant emotion (*sthāyibhāva*) which persists throughout the drama amid the variations of the transitory feelings; it stands to the other factors in the position of the king to his subjects or a master to his pupils, as the Çāstra says; it is, says the *Daçarūpa*, the source of delight, and brings into harmony with itself the transitory states of feeling.

[1] Mātṛgupta (Hall, DR., p. 33) subdivides sentiment as *vācika*, produced by words; *nepathya*, generated by appropriate garlands, ornaments, clothes, &c.; *svābhāvika*, produced by such natural excellencies as beauty, youth, grace, firmness, courage, &c.

It is the dominant emotions which in some fashion determine or become sentiments even in the view of the *Nāṭyaçastra*, though in it there is clearly difficulty in conceiving the precise signification of the process, a fact revealed in a tendency to confuse the terms emotion and sentiment, Bhāva and Rasa. In Bhaṭṭa Lollaṭa[1] we have a determined effort to make clear the implication of the doctrine. The dominant emotion of love, for instance, generated by a fundamental determinant such as a maiden, inflamed by an excitant determinant such as a pleasant garden, made cognizable by consequents such as sidelong glances and embraces, and strengthened by transitory feelings such as desire, becomes the erotic sentiment first of all in the hero of the drama, e.g. Rāma. The sentiment is subsequently attributed to the actor who imitates the hero in form, dress, and action, and so it becomes the source of charm to the audience. The fatal objection to this theory is clear; it fails to recognize that the sentiment must be that of the spectator himself; he cannot have enjoyment of a sentiment which exists merely in the actor as a secondary outcome of its existence in Rāma. Moreover, the actor whose chief aim is to please the audience and earn money need not feel at all the emotions of Rāma, while, if he does so, he is then in the same position as a spectator.

The view of Lollaṭa, which is classed as one of the production (*utpatti*) of sentiment and regarded as that of the Mīmāṅsā school, is opposed by the doctrine of Çrīçañkuka, regarded as the Naiyāyika view, which interprets the manifestation of sentiment as a process of inference. The emotions, love, &c., are inferred to exist in the actor, though not really present in him, by means of the determinants, &c., cleverly exhibited in his acting; the emotion thus inferred, being sensed by the audience, through its exquisite beauty, adds to itself a peculiar charm and thus finally develops into the state of a sentiment in the spectator. This view, however, is open to the fatal objection that it is commonly admitted that it is not inference, or any other derivative mode of knowledge, which produces charm, but perception alone, and no adequate ground exists for disregarding this general truth in this case.

[1] *Ekāvalī*, iii, pp. 86 ff.; *Kāvyaprakāça* (ed. 1889), pp. 86 ff. Cf. R., pp. 173-5.

In Bhaṭṭa Nāyaka[1] we find yet a different point of view, which denies either the production (*utpatti*) of sentiment, its perception or apprehension (*pratīti*) or its revelation (*abhivyakti*). If sentiment is perceived as appertaining to another, then it cannot personally affect oneself. But it cannot be perceived as present in oneself as a result of study of a work about Rāma; there are no factors present in the self to produce any such result; it is impossible to hold that an emotion dormant in oneself is called to life by seeing or reading the story of Rāma; experience shows that one's own beloved does not come up to one's mind to raise love, nor could a tale of a goddess evoke the picture of a mortal amour; again, such marvellous deeds as Rāma's have nothing common to mortal efforts so as to be able to awake conceptions of acts of our own. Thus sentiment cannot be apprehended. Nor is it a case of production; if so, no one would go twice to a play of a pathetic type, since one would experience actual misery as the result, in lieu of a pleasant melancholy; again the sight of lovers united does not in real life produce sentiment. Nor is a case of the revelation of something existing potentially (*çakti-rūpa*). If this were so, then, when the potential emotions were let loose, they would occupy their field of action in diverse degrees—thus contradicting the nature of sentiment as one; moreover there would be the same difficulties as in the case of apprehension as to whether revelation applied to the hero or oneself. The true solution, therefore, is to ascribe to a poem a peculiar threefold potency of its own, the power of denotation (*abhidhā*), which deals with what is expressed, the power of realization (*bhāvakatva*), which relates to the sentiment, and the power of enjoyment (*bhojakatva*), which has regard to the audience. If denotation were all, there would be no difference between poetic figures and manuals, there would be absence of the distinctions produced by divergence of literal and metaphorical sense, and the avoidance of harsh sounds would be needless. As it is, we have the second function of realization of sentiment, which causes the expressed sense to serve as the basis of the sentiment, and confers on the determinants, &c., the essential feature of being appropriated by the audience as universal. From this comes the appreciation by the audience

[1] See also Abhinavagupta, *Dhvanisaṁketa*, pp. 67 f.; *Alaṁkārasarvasva*, p. 9.

of the sentiment, an appreciation consisting in a mental condition made up entirely of the element of goodness or truth (*sattva*), uninfluenced by the other elements of passion (*rajas*) and dullness (*tamas*), that is, entirely free from desire, comparable with meditation on the absolute. This condition is the vital element; the enjoyment ranks above the aesthetic equipment[1] which renders it possible. To this theory which is sometimes ascribed to the Sāṁkhya,[3] and called the Bhuktivāda, doctrine of the enjoyment of sentiment, the objection is made that the two powers ascribed to poetry, realization, and enjoyment, have no legitimate foundation.

The view finally adopted by the theorists is that defended, but not first enunciated, by Abhinavagupta, based on the general doctrine of suggestion (*vyañjanā*) as lying at the basis of all poetic pleasure. The spectator's state of mind must be considered; it is in him that from experience of life there come into being emotional complexes, which lie dormant, ready to be called into activity by the reading of poems or by seeing plays performed. Those whose life has left them barren of impressions of emotions are, accordingly, incapable of relishing dramas, a fate which awaits men whose minds are intent merely on grammar or on the complexities of the Mīmāṅsā. The sentiment thus excited is peculiar, in that it is essentially universal in character; it is common to all other trained spectators, and it has essentially no personal significance. A sentiment is thus something very different from an ordinary emotion; it is generic and disinterested, while an emotion is individual and immediately personal. An emotion again may be pleasant or painful, but a sentiment is marked by that impersonal joy, characteristic of the contemplation of the supreme being by the adept, a bliss which is absolutely without personal feeling. There is in fact a close parallel between the man of taste (*sahṛdaya*)[3] and the adept (*yogin*); both have in them the possibility of attaining this bliss, and, to make it real, the one must investigate the determinants, &c., while the other must apply himself to concentration on the absolute. It is

[1] The term is *vyutpatti*; it is explained by Abhinavagupta, *op. cit.*, p. 70; GGA. 1913, p. 305, n. 1.

[2] The reference to Brahman shows that we have here the same fusion of doctrine as in Sadānanda's *Vedāntasāra*.

[3] In the same sense we have *rasika* and *bhāvaka* (e.g. R., p. 170).

this peculiar nature of sentiment which forbids it being created as the result of denotation or indication by speech, of perception, inference, or recollection. It cannot exist without determinants, &c., but these are not in the normal sense causes; an effect can exist when its causes have disappeared, but sentiment exists only while the determinants, &c., last; the terms used in this regard are one and all distinct from the normal terminology of causation. Sentiment is something supernatural (*alaukika*); its relations to the factors may be compared with that of a beverage to the black pepper, candied sugar, camphor, &c., which compose it, but of which as such no trace remains in the liquor as produced. This characteristic enables us to understand how it is that the list of sentiments includes that of horror or odium (*bībhatsa*) and that of fear (*bhayānaka*), as well as the pathetic sentiment. These are awakened into life by things which cause disgust, fear, and grief in ordinary life, and these emotions in real life are far from pleasant in any sense of that term. But, conveyed as ideal and generic, they produce this supernatural pleasure or happiness, which is not to be compared with normal pleasure, just as the joy of the contemplation of the absolute is not to be described as pleasure in the ordinary sense. Bhānudatta, in his *Rasataraṅgiṇī*, a work composed before A. D. 1437, distinguishes Rāsa as natural (*laukika*) and supernatural or transcendental; the former is the emotion experienced in ordinary life—which may more conveniently be distinguished as Bhāva,—the latter includes the emotion experienced in dream experiences, in the building of castles in the air, and in the appreciation of poetry, and he is careful to emphasize the totally different nature of the natural and the transcendental emotion.

The doctrine set out in Abhinavagupta is also that of the *Daçarūpa*, although it is rendered more obscure there by the brevity of its exposition. The process of transformation of an emotion to a sentiment is formally described; 'a dominant feeling or emotion becomes a sentiment when it is transformed into an object of enjoyment through the co-operation of the determinants, the consequents, including the involuntary manifestations of feeling, and the transitory feelings'.[2] The sense is made

[1] vi. 7 ff.; Huizinga, *De Vidūṣaka in het indisch tooneel*, pp. 67 ff.

[2] *vibhāvair anubhāvaiç ca sāttvikair vyabhicāribhiḥ*
ānīyamānaḥ svādyatvaṁ sthāyī bhāvo rasaḥ smṛtaḥ. (iv. 1.) Cf. R. ii. 169.

further precise by the assertion[1] that the dominant emotion becomes a sentiment, because it is enjoyed by the spectator of taste, and he is actually at present in existence; the sentiment is not located in the hero whose actions are represented, for he belongs to the past, nor does it appertain to the poem, for that is not the object of the poem—its function being to set out the determinants, &c., through which the dominant emotion is brought out and generates the sentiment,—nor is sentiment the apprehension by the spectator of the emotions enacted by the actor, since in that case spectators would feel not sentiment, but an emotion varying in the different individuals, just as in real life from seeing a pair in union those who see them feel according to their nature shame, envy, desire, or aversion. The position of the spectator is compared to that of the child which, when it plays with its clay elephants—the ancient equivalent of our tin soldiers—experiences the sensation of its own energy as pleasant; the deeds of Arjuna arouse a like feeling in the spectator's mind. This experiencing sentiment is a manifestation of that joy which is innate as the true nature of the self, and this manifestation comes into being as the result of the pervasion of the mind of the spectator with the dominant emotion and the determinants, &c., in combination.

An effort is made to describe the precise nature of the mental activity involved in the enjoyment of sentiment, and to base upon it a division of the sentiments. The four sentiments of love, heroism, horror, and fury are taken as primary, and brought into connexion with mental conditions described as the unfolding (*vikāsa*), expansion (*vistara*), agitation (*kṣobha*), and movement to and fro (*vikṣepa*) of the mind.[2] These are evidently mental conditions, believed to be reached by introspection, and they have the merit of giving a quasi-psychological rationale for the doctrine of four primary and four secondary sentiments found in the *Nāṭyaçāstra*.[3] But there was no early agreement on this piece of psychology; Abhinavagupta,[4] with Bhaṭṭa Nāyaka, accepts only three aspects of mental condition as involved, the melting (*druti*), expansion, and unfolding, a division which is applied also in the theory of poetics to justify the doctrine of the

[1] iv. 36 ff.

[2] iv. 41; R., p. 175, l. 1.

[3] vi. 39–41.

[4] *Dhvanisaṁketa*, pp. 68, 70.

existence of three qualities only of words.[1] On Dhanaṁjaya's view the sentiment of calm which he denies for drama,[2] if it exists at all, must be regarded as combining all the four mental aspects above distinguished.

It is now possible to understand clearly the essential relation of the spectator to the actors; we see on the stage, for instance, Rāma and Sītā, who excites his affection, aided by suitable circumstances of time and place; this affection is intimated by speech and gesture alike, which indicate both the dominant emotion of love and its transient shapes in the various stages of love requited. The spectacle evokes in the mind of the spectator the impressions of the emotion of love which experience has planted there, and this ideal and generic excitation of the emotion produces in him that sense of joy which is known as sentiment. The fullness of the enjoyment depends essentially on the nature and experience of the spectator, to whom it falls to identify himself with the hero or other character, and thus to experience in ideal form his emotions and feelings. He may even succeed in his effort to the extent that he weeps real tears, feels terror and sorrow, but the sentiment is still one of exquisite joy. We may compare the thrill of pleasure which the most terrifying narration excites in us, and we are all conscious of the sweetness of sad tales.

Viçvanātha insists very strongly on the necessity of the identification of the spectator with the personages depicted, a process which enables him to accept without any difficulty such episodes of extraordinary character as Hanumant's leap over the ocean.[3] He must not treat the emotion of love as his own, for in that case it would never become a sentiment; it would remain a feeling, and in the case of fear, for instance, it would cause pain, not joy. Nor must he regard it as belonging solely to the hero, for then it would remain his feeling, and in no wise affect the spectator or become a sentiment. Similarly, the determinants, &c., are not to be treated as pertaining to the hero alone; they must be felt as generic. This generic action (*sādhāraṇī kṛti*) is the essential feature, replacing the generic power which Bhaṭṭa Nāyaka attributes to poetry. We can now

[1] See § 6 below. [2] iv. 33. Cf. R., p. 171.
[3] SD. 41. This possibility is denied by Bhaṭṭa Nāyaka.

see clearly the position of the actor; the *Nāṭyaçāstra*[1] bids him as far as possible to assume the emotions of the person whom he represents, and to depict them by costume, speech, movements, and gestures as his own, but Viçvanātha[2] is more anxious to insist that the sentiment is not necessarily to be found in the actor, who often merely performs mechanically his part according to rote and rule; if he actually does experience the feelings he portrays, then he becomes in so far a spectator.[3] Further, he points out the simultaneous presence of all the factors is by no means essential, for the existence of one will revive the others by force of the association of ideas. He insists also on the necessity of experience and cultivation of the power of imagination in one who seeks to enjoy sentiment; as we are by virtue of the doctrine of transmigration—or if we prefer to modernize, by heredity—endowed with the germs of the capacity of appreciation, we can normally by study of poetical works develop the capacity, but, if we devote ourselves to the study of grammar or philosophy, we shall certainly deaden our susceptibilities. The difficult problem, why much study of poetry leaves some still unable to relish the sentiment, is explained by the convenient hypothesis that demerit in a previous birth intervenes to frustrate present effort. He refutes at length the effort of Mahiman Bhaṭṭa[4] to destroy the whole doctrine of suggestion in poetry by the doctrine of inference; doubtless by inference we could arrive at a belief in the existence of an emotion in the hero's mind but that inference would not produce any effect in us or arouse sentiment; a logician might make the inference and draw the correct conclusion, but would remain cold and unmoved. Suggestiveness, he shows, is absolutely essential as a function of words and as the characteristic of poetry, giving it power to create sentiment. What is expressed may be understood by every one; the man of taste alone appreciates the suggestion and enjoys the flavour resulting.

Now sentiment is one, it is a single, ineffable, transcendental joy, but it can be subdivided, not according to its own nature,

[1] xxvi. 18 f. Cf. Aristotle, *Poetics*, xvii. 1455 *a* 30.

[2] SD. 50 ff. So such a great actress as Sarah Bernhardt might feel emotion in acquiring her part, but not in the daily performance.

[3] *Ekāvalī*, p. 88; DR. iv. 40.

[4] *Vyaktiviveka* (*Trivandrum Sanskrit Series*, no. v).

but according to the emotions which evoke it. Thus the *Nāṭya-çāstra* recognizes the existence of eight emotions or dominant feelings; love (*rati*), mirth (*hāsa*), anger (*krodha*), sorrow (*çoka*), energy (*utsāha*), terror (*bhaya*), disgust (*jugupsā*), and astonishment (*vismaya*), and corresponding to these eight emotions we have eight forms of sentiment. The erotic sentiment (*çṛṅgāra-rasa*) is of two kinds, the union (*sambhoga*) or sundering (*vipra-lambha*) of two lovers, according to the Çāstra and the great mass of theorists, but the *Daçarūpa*[1] distinguishes three cases, privation (*ayoga*), sundering (*viprayoga*), and union. Privation denotes the inability of two young hearts to secure union, because of obstacles to their marriage; such love passes through ten stages,[2] longing, anxiety, recollection, enumeration of the loved one's merits, distress, raving, insanity, fever, stupor, and death. Sundering may be due to absence or resentment, and this in its turn may be caused by a quarrel between two determined lovers, or indignation at finding out, by sight, hearing or inference, that one's lover is devoted to another. The hero may counteract anger by conciliation, by winning over her friends, by gifts, by humility, by indifference, and by distracting her attention. Absence again may be due to business, to accident, or a curse; if the reason is death the love sentiment cannot, in Dhanaṁjaya's view, be present, though others allow of a pathetic variety of this sentiment.[3] In union the lover should avoid vulgarity or annoyance.

The heroic (*vīra*) sentiment corresponds to the emotion of energy; it may take the three forms of courage in battle as in Rāma; compassion as in Jīmūtavāhana; and liberality as in Paraçurāma. Assurance, contentment, arrogance, and joy are the transitory states connected with it. The sentiment of fury (*raudra*) is based on anger; its transitory states are indignation, intoxication, recollection, inconstancy, envy, cruelty, agitation, and the like. The comic (*hāsya*) sentiment depends on mirth, which is caused by one's own or another's strange appearance, speech, or attire.[4] The transitory states in connexion with it are

[1] iv. 47 ff. Cf. R. ii. 170 ff.

[2] Cf. Haas, DR., pp. 133, 150; R. ii. 178–201, where a list of twelve, with desire and eagerness prefixed, is rejected.

[3] Cf. R., pp. 189 f.

[4] Cf. Aristotle, *Poetics*, v. 1449 *a* 36.

sleeping, indolence, weariness, weakness, and stupor. The sentiment of wonder (*adbhuta*) is based on astonishment; the transitory states are usually joy, agitation, and contentment. The sentiment of terror (*bhayānaka*) is based on terror; the states associated with it are depression, agitation, distraction, fright, and the like. The pathetic (*karuṇa*) sentiment is based on sorrow; its associated states are sleeping, epilepsy, depression, sickness, death, indolence, agitation, despair, stupor, insanity, anxiety, and so forth. The sentiment of horror or odium (*bībhatsa*) is based on disgust; its associated states are agitation, sickness, apprehension, and the like. In each case the theorists give in full the determinants and the consequents of each emotion, which becomes a sentiment, and a special colour is ascribed to each; it is not surprising to find that red is associated with fury, black with fear; whiteness may, in association with the comic sentiment, be explained by the flashing teeth of a laughing maiden, and the dark (*çyāma*) colour of the erotic sentiment is a reflex of the favoured hue of the beloved; grey accords with pathos, but the connexion of yellow with wonder, dark blue with horror, and orange with heroism is not obvious. It is also artificial to find four primary and four secondary sentiments laid down; the erotic, the furious, the heroic, and that of horror, whence in order are supposed to develop the comic, the pathetic, that of wonder and that of terror. The *Nāṭyaçāstra* recognizes these eight only,[1] but later authorities add the sentiment of calm (*çānta*) based on indifference to worldly things (*nirveda*), although this is in the Çāstra merely a transitory feeling. Those who follow the Çāstra contend tnat there is no such sentiment, for it is impossible to destroy utterly love, hatred, and other feelings, which have been operative from time without beginning; others admit the existence of the sentiment, as does Mammaṭa, but not in drama, on the ground that indifference to all worldly things is incapable of being represented. But this also is erroneous; the actor's power of representing indifference is not in point, as it is the spectator who is to feel the sentiment, and the fact that the Çāstra places it first in the list of transitory states, though that would normally be an inauspicious beginning, indicates that it was meant to serve both as an emotion and a transitory feeling,

[1] Save for a late reading in vi. 15.

and it is fully recognized by Vidyādhara, Viçvanātha, and Jagannātha, though Dhanaṁjaya barely admits it.[1] The interrelations of the sentiments, their possible combinations, their harmonies and conflicts, are detailed at length.

The sentiments may all be employed in drama, but there are rules affecting their use. In each play there should be a dominant sentiment; in the Nāṭaka it should be the erotic or the heroic; other sentiments are merely auxiliary, but that of wonder is especially appropriate in the *dénouement*; indeed something in the way of supernatural intervention is often convenient to extricate the plot. An excess of sentiments is as bad as a defect; if there are too many they destroy the unity of the whole and detach it into a series of ill-connected fragments, while the excessive use of action and of rhetorical display is equally destructive to the merit of a piece.

The *Çakuntalā* illustrates excellently the sentiment of love as the ruling motive of the play; the heroic sentiment appears in the verses in Act II in which the hermits extol the king; the horrible in Act VI in the scene in which Mātali menaces the Vidūṣaka; terror is evoked by the description of the dusk at the close of Act III; the whole play from the arrival of Kaṇva in Act IV to the departure of Çakuntalā produces the sentiment of pathos, while that of fury is called into being by the close of Act VI from the despairing cries of the Vidūṣaka to the entry of Mātali; finally wonder is aroused by the strange incident at the close when the king picks up the bracelet fallen from the arm of the child which, unknown to him, is his own son by the wife whom he has in ignorance repudiated. The Nāṭikās afford excellent examples of the erotic sentiment; Harṣa, in complete accord with the rules of the drama, helps out his plot in both the *Ratnāvalī* and the *Priyadarçikā* by the use of incidents evoking the sentiment of wonder; the imprisonment of Sāgarikā in the former play evokes the sentiment of pathos, while terror is excited by the description in Act II of the wild confusion caused by the monkey's escape from the royal mews. The sentiment of fury is frequently evoked in the *Mahāvīracarita* and the

[1] See Dhanika, DR. iv. 33; SD. 240; *Ekāvalī*, pp. 96 ff. Other sentiments are sometimes recognized, such as friendship, faith, and devotion; cf. *Rasagaṅgādhara*, p. 45. Bhoja admits love only. An example of calm is the *Prabodhacandrodaya*. Cf. Jacobi, ZDMG. lvi. 395; R., p. 171.

Veṇīsaṁhāra ; the *Mālatīmādhava* affords excellent illustrations evoking horror, while the *Mahāvīracarita* is permeated by the sentiment of heroism. The *Nāgānanda* reveals heroism in another aspect, that of the perfection of compassion and nobility, for, as we have seen, Jimūtavāhana is not to be regarded as a hero in whom calm prevails.

There is doubtless pedantry in the theory of sentiment; the choice of eight emotions, the subordination to them of transitory states, the enumeration of determinants and consequents, are largely dominated by empiricism, and not explained or justified. But in its essentials the theory may be admitted to be a bold and by no means negligible attempt to indicate the essential character of the emotional effect of drama.

6. *The Dramatic Styles and Languages*

Plot, characters, and sentiment are not the only constituent elements of drama ; the poet must be an adept in adopting the appropriate manner[1] or style (*vṛtti*), for each action of the hero; the style adds to the play the indefinable element of perfection which is present in the highest beauty of feature or dress. The manners allowed by the *Nāṭyaçāstra* are four, the graceful (*kaiçikī*), the grand (*sāttvatī*), the violent (*ārabhaṭī*), and the verbal (*bhāratī*), which owes its name to the fact that, unlike the others, it depends for its effect on words, not action.

The graceful manner is appropriate to the erotic sentiment; it employs song, dance, and lovely raiment, admits both male and female rôles, and depicts love, gallantry, coquetry, and jesting. It admits of four varieties. The first is pleasantry (*narman*), which is based on what is comic in speech, dress, or movement in the actors ; the pleasantry may be purely comic, or be mingled with love, or even with fear, as when Susaṁgatā makes fun of Sāgarikā and adds that she will tell the queen of the episode of the picture.[2] When love is mingled, it may serve to evince affection, or to ask for a response, or to impute a fault on the lover's part. A comedy of costume is seen in the *Nāgānanda* where the Viṭa, misled by his

[1] N. xx. 25–62; DR. ii. 44–57; iii. 5; SD. 285. 410–21; R. i. 244–94, which expressly denies a fifth manner composed of the four.

[2] *Ratnāvalī*, ii. R. i. 275 gives *pā pā pāhi hi hiti* as an instance of comic fear exhibited in speech.

garments, mistakes the Vidūṣaka for a woman; a comedy of action in the *Mālavikāgnimitra* where Nipunikā punished the Vidūṣaka by dropping on him a stick which he takes, naturally enough, for a snake. The second form is the outburst of affection (*narmasphūrja*)[1] at the first meeting of lovers, which ends in a note of fear, as in the meeting of the king and Mālavikā in Act IV of the *Mālavikāgnimitra.* Thirdly, there is the manifestation of a recent love by physical signs (*narmasphoṭa*),[2] and, fourth, the development of affection (*narmagarbha*), illustrated by the adoption of a disguise by the hero to attain his end, as when Vatsa in the *Priyadarçikā* comes on the scene in the garb of Manoramā.[3]

The grand manner is appropriate to the sentiments of heroism, wonder, and fury, and in a less degree to the pathetic and erotic. Virtue, courage, self-sacrifice, compassion, and righteousness are its subjects, not sorrow. Its divisions are the challenge (*utthāpaka*), as in the *Mahāvīracarita*, Act V, Vālin defies Rāma; breach of alliance (*saṁghātya*) among one's foes, which may be brought about by deliberate stratagem, as in the *Mudrārākṣasa*, or by fate, as in the Rāma dramas Vibhīṣaṇa severs himself from Rāvaṇa; change of action (*parivartaka*) as when in the *Mahāvīracarita* Paraçurāma offers to embrace Rāma, whom he came to overthrow; and the dialogue (*saṁlāpa*) of warriors such as that of Rāma and Paraçurāma in the same play.

The violent manner accords with the sentiments of fury, horror, and terror. It employs magic, conjuration, conflicts, rage, fury, and underhand devices. Its elements include, first, the almost immediate construction (*saṁkṣipti*) of some object by artificial means, such as the elephant of mats made to contain Udayana's men in the lost *Udayanacarita*; but others interpret this member as a sudden change of hero, whether real, as in the substitution of Vālin for Sugrīva, or merely a change of heart on the hero's part, as in Paraçurāma's submission to Rāma; in either case only a secondary hero can change or be changed, else the unity of the drama would disappear. The other elements are the creation of an object by magic means (*vastūtthāpana*); the angry meeting of

[1] Or *narmasphañja.*

[2] An alternative is love enjoyment interrupted, as in the *Ratnāvalī*, ii. 17; R. i. 278.

[3] A variant ascribed to Bharata is given in R. i. 279, where a hero dies and another fills his place, e. g. Rāvaṇa replaced by Vibhīṣaṇa.

two persons who end by fighting (*sampheṭa*), as do Mādhava and Aghoraghaṇṭa in the *Mālatīmādhava*; and a scene of tumultuous disturbance (*avapāta*), such as that when the monkey escapes in the *Ratnāvalī* or of the attack on Vindhyaketu in the *Priyadarçikā*, Act I.

The verbal manner is based on sound, as the other three are on sense. The voice only is its means of expression; women may not use it, and the men must speak Sanskrit; these actors bear the name Bharata, which is appropriated to this manner. It is adapted to all the sentiments, or, according to the *Nāṭyaçāstra*, only to those of heroism, wonder, and fury. Its elements are, in true scholastic fashion, likewise reckoned as four; two of them, the propitiation (*prarocanā*), and the introduction (*āmukha*, *prastāvanā*), essentially belong to the prologue of the drama, and will be considered in that connexion; the other two are given as the garland (*vīthī*) and the farce, which are species of drama. But the theorists agree that the elements (*aṅga*) of the garland[1] are applicable in any part of the drama, especially the first juncture, and they are evidently an essential part of the verbal manner.

The first element is the abrupt dialogue (*udghātya*), which takes either the form of a series of questions and answers in explanation of something not at once understood, or a monologue of question and reply. The second is continuance (*avalagita*) of one section by another in substitution, as where, when Sītā has decided to go to the forest for pleasure, Rāma is persuaded to let her go indeed, but into exile, or, according to Dhanaṁjaya alone, where there is a sudden turn in an event in progress.[2] The third is the Prapañca, which passes for a comic dialogue, in which two actors frankly set out each other's demerits,[3] or, according to Viçvanātha, such a clever ruse as that of Nipuṇikā in the *Vikramorvaçī*, Act II, where she worms out from the Vidūṣaka the king's infatuation. The triple explanation (*trigata*), a term which is used in a different sense in the rule regarding the prologue, seems to denote guesses made at the cause of a sound, which in its character is ambiguous and may be, e.g. the hum of the bees, the cry of the cuckoo, or the music

[1] N. xviii. 106–16; DR. iii. 11–18; SD. 289, 293, 521–32; R. i. 164–74.

[2] The first kind is illustrated by *Uttararāmacarita*, i; the second by a citation from the *Chalitarāma*.

[3] As in the *Vīrabhadravijṛmbhaṇa*, R. i. 168.

made by celestial maidens.[1] Cheating (*chala*) denotes the use of words of seeming courtesy but boding ill, as in the inquiry for Duryodhana, their foe, by Bhīma and Arjuna in the *Veṇīsaṁhāra*, Act V. The repartee (*vākkelī*) produces comic effect in a series of questions and answers ; but the same term is applied to the interruption of a sentence by Dhanaṁjaya, and by Viçvanātha to a single reply to many questions. Outvying (*adhibala* or *atibala*) applies to a dialogue in which those conversing vie with one another in violence, as in the discussion of Arjuna, Bhīma, and Duryodhana in the *Veṇīsaṁhāra*, Act V. The abrupt remark (*gaṇḍa*) is one which intervenes vitally in the tale; thus in the *Uttararāmacarita* Rāma has just declared that separation from Sītā would be unbearable, when the porteress announces Durmukha, the spy of the king, who comes to destroy the king's happiness. Reinterpretation (*avasyandita*) is the taking up of an expression which has escaped one in a different sense; thus in the *Chalitarāma*, Sītā carelessly tells her sons to go to Ayodhyā and greet their father, and seeks to remedy this slip by insisting that the king is father of his people. The enigma (*nālikā*) conceals the sense under joking words. Incoherent talk (*asatpralāpa*) is the speech of one just awake, drunk, asleep, or childish; such are the hero's words in *Vikramorvaçī*, Act IV. In another sense, admitted by Viçvanātha, it denotes good advice thrown away, as in the *Veṇīsaṁhāra*, Act I, Gāndhārī's admonition of Duryodhana. Humorous speech (*vyāhāra*) is a remark made for the sake of some one else, which provokes a laugh, as when the Vidūṣaka in the *Mālavikāgnimitra*, Act II, by his chatter makes the damsel laugh, and permits the king longer to gaze on her charms. Mildness (*mṛdava*) denotes the turning of evil into good, or *vice versa*, as when in the *Çakuntalā*, Act II, the virtues of hunting, a vice in the eyes of the sacred law, are extolled.

It is an essential defect of Indian theory in all its aspects that it tends to divisions which are needless and confusing. Besides the elements of the garland we find thirty-three dramatic ornaments (*nāṭyālaṁkāra*)[2] and thirty-six characteristics or beauties (*lakṣaṇa*),[3] which cannot be distinguished as two classes on any

[1] As in the *Abhirāmarāghava*. [2] SD. 471–503.
[3] N. xvii. 6–39; SD. 435–70; 36 *bhūṣaṇāni*, R. iii. 97–127.

conceivable theory,[1] for both consist largely of modes of exposition and figures of thought and diction, while they also contain, as recognized by Dhanaṁjaya, a number of feelings which fall within the sphere of sentiment and its discussion. Thus we find as ornaments the benediction, the lamentation, raillery, the use of argument to support a view (*upapatti*), the prayer, the expression of resolution, the reproach, the provocation, the adduction of a common opinion in order to administer covertly a rebuke, the request, the narrative, reasoning, and the telling of a story. The beauties again include the combination of merits of style with poetic figures; the grouping of letters to make up a name; the use of analogy and example; the citation of admitted facts to refute incorrect views; the fitting of expression to the sense; the explanation by reasoning of a fact which is not capable of sense perception; the description of an object from the point of view of place, time, or shape; the indication of a characteristic which serves to distinguish two objects otherwise alike; the allusion to the truth of the literal meaning of a name; the use of the names of famous persons in a eulogy of some living being; the expression unconsciously, under the influence of passion, of the contrary of what one means; the statement in succession (*mālā*) of several means to attain a desired object; the expression of two different views, one of which in reality strengthens the other; the reproach; the question; the use of commonplaces; eulogy; the employment of a comparison to convey a sense which it is not desired directly to express; the indirect expression of desire; the veiled compliment; and the address of gratitude. Unfortunately no scientific attempt at orderly arrangement or examination of the principles on which these matters are based is attempted.

The *Nāṭyaçāstra*[2] adds an account of four ornaments of the drama (*nāṭakālaṁkāra*), which the *Daçarūpa* ignores, doubtless for the adequate reason that these matters appertain to poetics in general, and they are treated of in vast detail by the text-books of that science. The first is simile, defined as a comparison based on the similarity of characteristics in two objects; there

[1] The *Saṁgītadāmodara* merges them in one (Lévi, TI. i. 104). Cf. DR. iv. 78.

[2] xvii. 40 ff. The Alaṁkāra doctrine later develops enormously; cf. Jacobi, GN. 1908, pp. 1 ff.

are five kinds, the simile which extols, that which condemns, that with an imagined thing, as when the elephant is likened to a winged mountain, that based on similarity, and that on partial similarity, as in 'Her face is like the full moon, her eyes like the blue lotus'. The metaphor is an abridged comparison which unites the two objects so as to efface their distinction, as 'The fisher Love casts on the ocean of this world his lure, woman'. The illuminator (*dīpaka*) is the figure of speech, which uses but one verb to express the connexion between a subject series and a string of qualifications. Of forms of alliteration (*yamaka*), the repetition of vowels and consonants forming different words and meanings, there are enumerated ten kinds, a striking proof of the importance attached to these verbal jingles in early poetics.

The Çāstra[1] adds some vague and valueless suggestions as to the use of these ornaments and metrical effects in connexion with the expression of the sentiments. The erotic sentiment demands metaphors and Dīpakas, and prefers the Āryā metre. The heroic affects short syllables, similes, and metaphors; in passages of lively dialogue the metres[2] Jagatī, Atijagatī, and Saṁkṛti; in scenes of battle and violence, the Utkṛti. The sentiment of fury adopts the same metres, and also favours short syllables, similes, and metaphors. The Çakvarī and Atidhṛti metres are appropriate to the pathetic sentiment; it prefers long syllables, a liking shared by the sentiment of horror.

An effort is made by later writers on poetics to apply to the doctrine of the sentiments the theory of excellencies (*guṇa*), which is laid down generally in Daṇḍin, Vāmana, Bhoja, and other writers. In Daṇḍin[3] we find assigned to the Vaidarbha style a miscellaneous number of qualities, ten in all, which are defined in terms sometimes vague and unsatisfactory; these qualities include both those of sense and sound (*artha* and *çabda*). They include strength or majesty (*ojas*), elevation (*udāratva*), clearness (*prasāda*), precision of exposition (*arthavyakti*), beauty or attractiveness (*kānti*), sweetness or elegance (*mādhurya*), metaphorical language (*samādhi*), and in the use and combination of sounds homogeneity (*samatā*), softness (*sukumāratā*), and a natural flow (*çleṣa*). The chief opponent of the Vaidarbha style is given as the Gauḍa; it is vaguely credited with the possession

[1] xvii. 99 ff. [2] See Weber, IS. viii. 377 ff. [3] i. 41 ff.

of features the opposite of those of its rival; more specifically, we find it credited with the fondness for the use of long compounds both in prose and verse, while the Vaidarbha objects to such compounds in verse at least, and with affecting alliterations. Vāmana [1] develops the doctrine by distinguishing ten qualities of sense and ten of sound, and he ascribes all the qualities to the Vaidarbha style; to the Gauḍa he allots reliance on force and beauty, to the exclusion of sweetness and softness, while he recognizes as a third style the Pāñcāla, which is marked with sweetness and softness, and therefore is rather feeble. In Mammaṭa [2] and later we find a new view of the qualities; those of sense are explained away as being rather the absence of defects (*doṣa*), so that the qualities are reduced to the sphere of sound alone. In this regard they are further reduced from ten to three, sweetness, strength, and clearness, and these are now brought into effective connexion with the sentiments.

Sweetness, the source of pleasure, causing as it were the melting of the heart, is appropriate in the sentiments of love in enjoyment, pathos, love in separation, and calm; it is normal in love in union, and rises in degree successively in the other three forms of sentiment; unmixed in the others, in that of calm it is combined with a small degree of strength, because of the relation of the sentiment of calm to the emotion of disgust. Strength causes the expansion of the heart; it rises in vehemence in the sentiments of heroism, horror, and fury, and it is found also in that of terror. The quality of clearness is appropriate to all the sentiments, and is that which causes the sense to become intelligible, pervading the mind as fire does wood or water a cloth, as the outcome of merely hearing the words. The precise mode in which sweetness is produced is by the use of mutes other than cerebrals, with their appropriate nasals, *r* and *ṇ* with short vowels, and no compounds or short compounds; strength results from the use of compound letters, doubled letters, conjunct consonants of which *r* forms part, cerebrals other than *ṇ*, palatal and cerebral sibilants, and long compounds. The older names, Vaidarbha, Gauḍa, and Pāñcāla are now given up in favour of refined (*upanā-*

[1] iii. 1 and 2; cf. Regnaud, *Rhétorique Sanskrite*, ch. v.

[2] *Kāvyaprakāça*, pp. 542 ff.; *Ekāvali*, pp. 147–9; *Alaṁkarasarvasva*, pp. 20 f. R. i. 229–43 has the ten Guṇas and *komalā*, *kaṭhinā*, and *miçrā* as the three names.

garikā), harsh (*paruṣā*), and soft (*komalā*). But Mammaṭa reminds us that in drama very long compounds are undesirable, a rule ignored largely by the later dramatists.

More important than these technical details, which are illustrated often enough in the verses composed by the later dramatists, and no doubt possess considerable antiquity, is the changed view [1] which brings the qualities in the new sense into relation with the sentiment. Sentiment is the very soul of poetry, and the relation of the qualities to it may be most effectually compared with that of such virtues as heroism to the soul of man. They serve to heighten the effect of the sentiment, and therefore they cannot be considered save in close relation to that sentiment. However soft and sweet the verbal form of a work, none the less it cannot be said to possess the quality of sweetness, unless it has a sentiment to which sweetness is appropriate. To give it the name of sweet, if the sentiment is incompatible with sweetness, is compared with regarding a tall man as brave on the strength of his appearance only. The sounds, therefore, produce the qualities only as instruments, for the real cause is the sentiment, even as the soul is the true cause of the heroism and other qualities of a man.

The case of figures, whether of sound or sense, is somewhat similarly handled; the figures are compared with the ornaments which, placed on a man's body, and through this union with him, gratify the soul; the figures adorn words and meanings which are parts of poetry by their union with them, and thus serve to heighten the sentiment, provided one exists. If there is no sentiment, through the defective ability of the poet, then the figures serve merely to lend variety to the composition, and even when sentiment exists the figures may fail to be appropriate to it. Both figures and qualities thus are in a very intimate relation with the sentiment, but that does not mean that the two are identical.

From this doctrine, which makes sentiment essentially the main element in poetry, the view of Vāmana,[2] who laid down that style was the soul of poetry and that the qualities give the essential beauty or distinction (*çobhā*) to a poem, while the figures

[1] Mammaṭa, *Kāvyaprakāça*, viii. 1 ff; *Ekāvali*, v.; *Sāhityadarpaṇa*, viii; *Alaṁkārasarvasva*, p. 7.

[2] iii. 1. 1–3.

increase such distinction, is necessarily regarded as inadequate. If the doctrine is interpreted to mean that it is the possession of all the qualities which makes a poem, then all compositions in the Gauḍa and Pāñcāla styles would be denied the rank of poetry; if the presence of a single quality gave the right to the style of poem, then a perfectly prosaic verse passage containing the quality of strength would have to be dubbed a poem, while a stanza containing elegant figures, but no qualities, would be denied that style, which in point of fact is regularly accorded by usage and must be recognized as valid.

As regards language we have, as often in the theory, no explanation of a principle which is laid down as accepted, the divergent use of Sanskrit and Prākrit in the same play. Yet it cannot be held that, when the theory was developed in such works as the *Daçarūpa*, and very possibly in the *Nāṭyaçāstra* itself, the usage of the plays could be put down simply to the copying of the actual practice in real life. That such was its origin we may believe in the general way; the Vidūṣaka in the *Mṛcchakaṭikā* derides a woman using Sanskrit as resembling a young cow with a rope through her nose; but there is evidence that already in the time of the *Kāmaçāstra*[1] the use of Prākrit was artificial. We are there told that the cultured man about town (*nāgaraka*) in social meetings (*goṣṭhī*), should neither confine himself to Sanskrit nor to the vernacular (*deçabhāṣā*) if he is to win repute for good manners. We have here a sign that matters were already, at the time of the *Kāmaçāstra*, much in the same condition as in modern India, where the use of Sanskrit terms with the vernacular is a regular sign of education. Now Vātsyāyana tells us clearly that those who frequent such gatherings are hetaerae, Viṭas, Vidūṣakas, and Pīṭhamardas, in short the wits of the court, and to them in the theory is assigned Çaurasenī and kindred Prākrit dialects. We are justified, therefore, in assuming that at Vātsyāyana's epoch in actual life, as opposed to the conventional existence of the stage, Prākrits were definitely out of employment. The same text includes in the requisites of the knowledge of a hetaera the knowledge of the local speech, and, as there is no doubt of the knowledge of the Andhras as kings by Vātsyāyana, it is interesting to note that in the famous passage

[1] pp. 57, 60. Cf. Jacobi, *Bhavisattakaha*, pp. 68

in which Somadeva tells of the reason why the *Bṛhatkathā*[1] was written in Paiçācī he treats as the three forms of human speech contemporaneous with Sātavāhana, whose name shows his connexion with the Andhras, Sanskrit, Prākrit, and the vernacular.

The date of Vātsyāyana thus becomes of interest, but unluckily it is still undefined with any precision.[2] It certainly seems, however, that Kālidāsa was familiar with a text very similar to and perhaps identical with the *Kāmaçāstra*, and this reasonably may be regarded as giving A.D. 400 as the lower limit of date. That the *Kauṭilīya Arthaçāstra* has been used by Vātsyāyana gives no precise result, in view of the difficulty of dating exactly that text. But the mention by Vātsyāyana of the Ābhīras[3] and Andhras certainly suggests, taken into conjunction with his silence as to the Guptas, that he wrote before the power of the latter had established itself in western India, and we may assign his work to approximately A.D. 300. If so we must believe that already in Kālidāsa's age the Prākrits of his characters were more or less artificial, and with this well accords his introduction of Māhārāṣṭrī for the verses of those to whom Çaurasenī is assigned in prose, an obviously literary device.

Elaborate rules for the use of language[4] by the characters are given in the *Nāṭyaçāstra* and, in much less detail, by the *Daçarūpa*. The use of Sanskrit is proper in the case of kings, Brahmins, generals, ministers, and learned persons generally; the chief queen is assigned it, and so also ministers' daughters, but this rule is not in practice observed. On the other hand, it is used by Buddhist nuns, hetaerae, artistes, and others on occasion. It is a rule that in the description of battles, peace negotiations, and omens Sanskrit shall be resorted to, and this is done by Bṛhannalā in Bhāsa's *Pañcarātra*. The use of Sanskrit by allegorical female types is also found both early and late.

The general rule for women and persons of inferior rank[5] is

[1] vi. 147. Cf. *Kāvyamīmānsā*, pp. 48 ff.

[2] Jacobi, GN. 1911, pp. 962 f.; 1912, pp 841 f.

[3] Jacobi, *Bhavisattakaha*, pp. 74, 76. Cf. Haranchandra Chaklardai, *Vātsyāyana* (1921).

[4] N. xvii. 31 ff.; DR. ii. 58–61; SD. 432; R. iii. 299–305.

[5] Including, of course, persons assuming such rôles, e.g. in the *Pratijñāyaugandharāyaṇa* and *Mudrārākṣasa*. For the use of Sanskrit by women, usually in verse, as by Vasantasenā in the *Mṛcchakaṭikā*, and by inferior characters, see Pischel, *Prākrit Grammatik*, pp. 31 f.

the use of Prākrit, but it may be resorted to as a means of self-aid by persons of higher position. The types of Prākrit to be used are described with much confusion in the *Nāṭyaçāstra*, and the amount of variation contemplated is large. Thus the use of Çaurasenī is permitted in the Çāstra in lieu of the dialect of the Barbara, Andhra, Kirāta, and Draviḍa, though these may be used. The Çāstra gives seven different Prākrits as in use. Çaurasenī is the speech of the land between the Yamunā and the Gaṅgā or Doab; it is to be used by the ladies of the play, their friends and servants, generally by ladies of good family and many men of the middle class. Prācyā is assigned to the Vidūṣaka, but in fact he speaks practically Çaurasenī, and therefore the term can only denote an eastern Çaurasenī dialect. Āvantī is ascribed to gamblers or rogues (*dhūrta*), but is only an aspect of Çaurasenī, as spoken at Ujjayinī, and the Prākrit grammarian Mārkaṇḍeya calls it a transition between Çaurasenī and Māhārāṣṭrī. Māhārāṣṭrī is unknown to the Çāstra; it is assigned to the verses of persons who use Çaurasenī by the *Daçarūpa*, while the *Sāhityadarpaṇa* limits it to the verses of women; normally, but not absolutely, it is used in all verses,[1] though Çaurasenī verses occasionally occur, and possibly were more frequent originally. The earlier drama of Açvaghoṣa and Bhāsa has no clear evidence of Māhārāṣṭrī at all. Ardha-Māgadhī is prescribed for slaves (*ceṭa*), Rājaputras and guildsmen (*çreṣṭhin*) by the Çāstra, but, save in Açvaghoṣa and possibly the *Karṇabhāra* of Bhāsa, it is unknown to our dramas. Māgadhī, on the other hand, is important in theory, and of some consequence in practice; it is ascribed to all those men who live in the women's apartments, diggers of underground passages, keepers of drink shops, watchers, and is used in time of danger by the hero, and also by the Çakāra, according to the Çāstra. The *Daçarūpa* assigns it and Paiçācī to the lowest classes, which accords with facts as regards Māgadhī, but Paiçācī is not found clearly in the dramas.

The *Nāṭyaçāstra* provides for the use of Dākṣiṇātyā in the case of soldiers (*yodha*), police officers (*nāgaraka*), and gamblers (*dīvyant*), and there are slight traces in the *Mṛcchakaṭikā* of the existence of this dialect. Bālhīkā is assigned by the same

[1] R. iii. 300 assigns it as Prākṛta to low persons and Jains. He assigns Apabhraṅça to Caṇḍālas, Yavanas, &c., but admits that others give Māgadhī, &c.

authority to the Khasas and the northerners, but has not yet been traced in any drama.

We learn also from the Çāstra and from Mārkaṇḍeya in special of a number of Vibhāṣās,[1] which seem to be modified forms of the more normal Prākrits, as stereotyped for use by certain characters in the drama. Thus the Çāstra attributes Çākārī to the Çakas, Çabaras, and others, while the *Sāhityadarpaṇa* accords Çābarī to these persons. The Çāstra ascribes Çābarī to charcoal-burners, hunters, wood-workers, and partly also to forest dwellers in general, and Ābhīrī is ascribed with the option of Çābarī to herdsmen, Cāṇḍālī to Caṇḍālas, and Drāviḍī to Draviḍas, while Oḍri, mentioned by the Çāstra, is left unascribed; presumably it was assigned to men of Orissa. Something of this is seen in the *Mṛcchakaṭikā*, where Çākārī, Cāṇḍālī, and a further speech Ḍhakkī or Ṭākkī appear. They all have nothing very marked as to their characteristics; the first two may be allied to Māgadhī, the last is more dubious.

The addition of Chāyās or translations in Sanskrit to explain the Prākrit is normal in the manuscripts of the dramas, and it is certain that it is old, for it is alluded to by Rājaçekhara in his *Bālarāmāyaṇa*. Evidently, even so early as A.D. 900, there was no public which cared for Prākrit without a Sanskrit explanation.

On the subject of the use of stanzas, as opposed to prose, the text-books are curiously and unexpectedly silent.[2] This indicates how entirely empirical they are in these matters. The use of Prākrits in the dramas obviously varied, and something had to be said regarding this point, but the alternation of prose and verse is accepted as something established, on which comment is unnecessary. The fact is recognized, but its implications and purpose remain unexplored. In the stanzas themselves, it is clear, we must distinguish between those which were sung and those which were simply recited; recitation must clearly have been the normal form of use, and as sung we have normally at any rate only some of the stanzas in Māhārāṣṭrī which are placed in the mouths of women. Çaurasenī stanzas, on the other hand,

[1] Grierson, JRAS. 1918, pp. 489 ff. Cf. R. i. 297 which has seven; Çabara, Dramiḷa, Andhraja, Çakāra, Abhīra, Caṇḍāla, foresters.

[2] Contrast the Aristotelian doctrine as to the use of the lyric choruses; *Poetics*, 1456*a* 25 ff.; G. Norwood, *Greek Tragedy*, pp. 75–80; Haigh, *The Tragic Drama of the Greeks*, ch. v, § 6.

we may assume to have been recited, but the distinction has practically vanished from the texts preserved.

7. *The Dance, Song, and Music*

Of the part played by the song, dance, and music in the drama the theorists curiously enough tell us comparatively little of interest, though it is certain that both were most important elements in the production of sentiment. The types of dance recognized in the *Nāṭyaçāstra* are two, the violent dance of men, invented by Çiva himself, the Tāṇḍava, and the tender and voluptuous dance of Pārvatī, the Lāsya. The latter alone, by reason of its special importance, is carefully analysed into ten parts by the Çāstra,[1] which shows the essential union of song and dance. The first is the song proper, which is sung by one seated, to the accompaniment of a lute, without dancing; the recitation standing (*sthitapāṭhya*) is a declamation in Prākrit by a woman pacing rapidly under the influence of love, or it may also mean, according to Abhinavagupta, a declamation by a woman in anger. The recitation sitting (*āsīna*) is performed by a woman lying down, under the stress of sorrow, without musical accompaniment. In the Puṣpagaṇḍikā various metres are used; Sanskrit may be employed; men act as women and *vice versa*, and there is a musical accompaniment. In the Pracchedaka a woman sings to the lute her grief at her lover's infidelity. The Trigūḍha is the acting of a man in woman's dress, as of Makaranda in the *Mālatīmādhava*, Act VI. The Saindhava is a song to a clear accompaniment of a lady whose love has failed to keep his tryst. The Dvigūḍhaka is a harmonious song, full of sentiment, in dialogue form. The Uttamottaka is a song filled with the bitterness of a troubled love. The Uktapratyukta is a duet, in which one lover addresses to the other feigned reproaches. These divisions, of course, appear to ignore their nature as parts of a dance, but it must be remembered that the motions of the performers are essential in the performance.

[1] xviii. 117–29; DR. iii. 47 f.; SD. 504–9. On gesture see the *Abhinayadarpaṇa* of Nandikeçvara, trs. Cambridge, Mass., 1917. R. iii. 236–48 gives other details of the Lāsya from the *Çṛṅgāramañjarī*; dialect is allowed in the Saindhāva. He follows N. in having Trimūḍhaka as expressing male emotions in smooth words, and has Dvimūḍhaka.

The music of the drama is not described at length in the later theorists; what is clear is that each sentiment has its special appropriate music, and each action its special accompaniment. Thus the Dvipadikās accompanied the performance of the rôles of persons distressed, unwell, and unhappy; the Dhruvās were chosen so as to intimate at once to the audience the quality of the new arrival on the stage.[1]

8. *The Preliminaries and the Prologue*

The *Naṭyaçāstra*[2] prescribes an elaborate series of preliminaries (*pūrvaranga*) which must be performed before the actual drama begins; they are intended to secure divine favour for the performance, each act having a definite share in the result, and doubtless they present us with a reminiscence of the early theatre in the mingling of music, dance, and song. First there is the beat of drum (*pratyāhāra*) announcing the beginning of the performance, and the carpet is spread out for the orchestra; the singers and the musicians then enter and take their places (*avataraṇa*): then the chorus try their voices (*ārambha*); the musicians try their instruments (*āçrāvaṇā*); they tune up their wind and string instruments, and manipulate their hands to make them ready for the work; then an instrumental concert follows, succeeded by the appearance and practice steps of the dancers.[3] A song follows, to please the gods; then the Tāṇḍava is performed, increasing in violence as it proceeds; then a song accompanies the raising by the Sūtradhāra of the banner (*jarjara*) of Indra; he scatters flowers and purifies himself with water from a pitcher borne by an attendant, while another carries the banner; there follows a perambulation of the stage, the praise of the world guardians, and homage to the banner. Then comes the Nāndī or benediction; it is followed by the recitation by the Sūtradhāra of a verse in honour of the god whose festival it is,

[1] Lévi, TI. ii. 18 f. For N. xxviii see J. Grosset, *Contribution a l'étude de la musique hindoue*, Paris, 1888. The hints as to musical accompaniment in *Vikramorvaçi* iv. and the *Gītagovinda* are unfortunately largely unintelligible. Cf. also Çivarāma on *Nāgānanda*, i. 15.

[2] v. 1 ff.; Konow, ID., pp. 23 ff.

[3] These nine acts gratify the Apsarases, Gandharvas, Daityas, Dānavas, Rakṣases, Guhyakas, and Yakṣas. They are performed behind the curtain according to Konow, but cf. Lévi, TI. i. 376.

or the king or a Brahmin ; then comes the Raṅgadvāra, which is said to mark the beginning of the dramatic action (*abhinaya*), the Sūtradhāra reciting another verse, and bowing before the banner of Indra. There follow steps and movements of erotic character (*cārī*) in honour of Umā, and more violent movements of the same kind in honour of the Bhūtas. A discussion (*trigata*) between the Sūtradhāra, the Vidūṣaka, who talks nonsense, and an attendant follows. Finally the Prarocanā announces the content of the drama, and the Sūtradhāra and his two attendants leave the stage, and the preliminaries are ended.

Immediately after, according to the *Nāṭyaçāstra*, another person, similar in appearance and qualities to the Sūtradhāra, is to enter and introduce the play, a function which gives him the style of introducer, Sthāpaka.[1] His costume should indicate the nature of the drama, as dealing with divine or human affairs. An appropriate song greets his entrance, he dances a Cārī, praises the gods and Brahmins, propitiates the audience by verses alluding to the subject of the play, mentions the name of the author and the play, and describes some season in the verbal manner, thereby opening the prologue (*prastāvanā*, *āmukha*, *sthāpanā*)[2] of the play. The essential feature of the prologue is an address by the director with an attendant (*pāripārçvika*) or an actress or the Vidūṣaka on some personal business which indirectly hints at the drama. The mode of connexion is given by Dhanaṁjaya as threefold, as in the *Nāṭyaçāstra* ; the words of the director may be caught up (*kathodghāta*) by a character in the drama, entering from behind the curtain, as in the *Ratnāvalī* Yaugandharāyaṇa catches up the consolation offered to the actress which is applicable to his own scheme, and in the *Veṇīsaṁhāra* Bhīma brusquely denounces the benediction of his adversaries. Or a person may enter (*pravṛttaka*), who has just been mentioned by the director in a comparison with the season of the year, as in the *Priyadarçikā*. Excess of representation (*prayogātiçaya*) is taken in the *Daçarūpa* as applying to a case where the director actually mentions the entry of a character of the drama, as at the beginning of the *Çakuntalā*, where he assures the actress that her song has enchanted him, as the

[1] N. v. 149 ff. ; DR. iii. 2 ff. ; SD. 283 ff. Cf. R. iii. 150 ff.

[2] An effort to discriminate Prastāvanā and Sthāpanā is made, R. iii. 158.

gazelle enchants Duḥṣanta, who just then enters. Viçvanātha, on the other hand, treats this form as an instance of continuance (*avalagita*), and interprets the phrase as denoting the supersession of the director's action; thus, in the lost *Kundamālā*, about to call on the actress to dance, he hears the word, 'Lady, descend', and realizes that it is a reference to Sītā, who is being led into exile. He admits also the abrupt dialogue (*udghātya*) as a means of connexion; thus in the *Mudrārākṣasa* the director alludes to the demon of eclipse as eager to triumph over Candra, the moon, and Cāṇakya behind the scenes calls out, 'Who then while I live claims to triumph over Candragupta?' and enters a moment later. The theorist Nakhakuṭṭa is also credited with the view that a voice behind the scenes or from the air may be used to introduce the chief personage.

This account of the preliminaries and the prelude presents obvious difficulties both in itself and in connexion with the actual specimens of the Sanskrit drama. The *Daçarūpa* and Viçvanātha alike give no details of the preliminaries, and the *Nāṭyaçāstra* indicates that, in addition to the complete form of Pūrvaranga, there might be an abbreviated form and also an extended form with additional ceremonials. There is an obvious overlapping between the Pūrvaranga and the rest of the performance, for the last element of the former, the giving the content of the drama in the Prarocanā, is essentially an element in the latter. We are quite definitely told by Viçvanātha that in his time there was not a complete performance of the preliminaries; when, therefore, we find in Bhāsa's dramas that there is no mention of the name of the author or the drama in the prologue, we may safely assume that it was after his time that the practice grew up of transferring from the preliminaries, which were not a matter for the poet, the substance of the Prarocanā, and embodying it in the poet's own work. In Viçvanātha's time also we are told that the Sūtradhāra or director performed the whole of the work assigned in the theory to him and the Sthāpaka. But it is extremely difficult to say how far back this goes; the extant dramas with occasional exceptions,[1] such as Rājaçekhara's *Kar-*

[1] These are more common than formerly thought; the Sthāpaka is found in various connexions in the *Pārthaparākrama* of Prahlādana, and Vatsarāja's *Kirātārjunīya*, *Rukmiṇīharaṇa*, *Samudramathana*. But the *Rasārṇavasudhākara* ignores him.

pūramañjarī and Mādhava's *Subhadrāharaṇa* mention only the Sūtradhāra, and Pischel[1] suggested that it was Bhāsa who banished the Sthāpaka, in view of the reference in Bāṇa to his dramas as begun by the Sūtradhāra. It is uncertain, however, what precisely the sense of this reference is. The *Daçarūpa* expressly provides for the activity of the Sthāpaka, but then proceeds to style him Sūtradhāra, and there is agreement that he is to have the attributes of the Sūtradhāra, so that the use of the name may merely be explained by this reason. This is certainly supported by the express reference in the *Sāhityadarpaṇa* to the transfer of his functions to the Sūtradhāra and the silence of the *Daçarūpa* on this head. The point would be of importance only if it meant that Bhāsa dropped the Pūrvaraṅga as part of the drama; nothing, however, even hints at this; as we have seen, his omission to name himself or his play in the prologue tells strongly in favour of the view that the old Prarocanā was still in use.

More complex still is the question of the Nāndī or benediction. Most Sanskrit dramas open with a verse or verses of this type, followed by the remark, 'At the close of the Nāndī the Sūtradhāra enters,' but in Bhāsa's dramas, in old manuscripts of the *Vikramorvaçī*, and now and then in South Indian manuscripts of such plays as the *Nāgānanda*, the *Mudrārākṣasa*, and other more modern dramas,[2] we find the play begun with these words, and a verse or verses following. We have also the direct testimony of Viçvanātha, who tells us that some authorities held that the introductory verse in the *Vikramorvaçī* which normally passes for the Nāndī was not that at all, but was the Raṅgadvāra, with which, according to the *Nāṭyaçāstra*, the play properly begins, as in it we first find acting in the shape of a combination of speech and action; that verse, they argued, could not be reconciled with the definition of the extent of the Nāndī given in the *Nāṭyaçāstra*; others, however, on the authority of Abhinavagupta repelled this objection. Viçvanātha adopts as the definition of Nāndī what is recited in praise of a deity, Brahmin, king

Çivarāma's comm. on *Nāgānanda*, i. 1 shows that great doubt then existed both as to the preliminaries (p. 2), and the Sūtradhāra, Sūcaka, or Sthāpaka (pp. 6, 7). Cf. p. 273.

[1] GGA. 1883, p. 1234; 1891, p. 361. Bhāsa's use of Sthāpanā for the prologue suggests accord with the *Daçarūpa*.

[2] E. g. *Tapatīsaṁvaraṇa* and *Subhadrādhanaṁjaya*, where Sthāpanā is used.

or the like, and is accompanied by a benediction, consisting of twelve inflected words (with nominal or verbal endings) or eight lines (quarter-verses); this would exclude the beginning of the *Vikramorvaçī*, but Abhinavagupta permits of a greater variety of forms. In Viçvanātha's view the Nāndī is part of the preliminaries, which must be preserved, however much these are shortened. It is clear, therefore, that gradually the benediction, like the Prarocanā with its appeal to the benevolence of the audience,[1] came to be worked into the play by the author himself, though the period when the custom became normal cannot be stated with any precision, and in the south of India, at any rate, the older practice of leaving the benediction to the Sūtradhāra seems to have been sometimes followed. There can, indeed, be little doubt that the extent to which the preliminaries were retained differed from time to time; Viçvanātha evidently contemplates their almost total disappearance, but the *Amṛtodaya* of Gokulanātha in the sixteenth century assumes their presence; the authority of the *Nāṭyaçāstra* told heavily in their favour, and the stock phrase, 'Enough of this ceremony,' which occurs frequently at the opening of the plays, doubtless refers to the dance, song, and music with which the drama was prefaced.[2]

These facts explain the confusion[3] of the notices of the theorists as to the actor by whom the benediction is to be recited. We find ascribed to Bharata the view that a special actor, the Nāndī, should recite it, or that duty should be performed by the Sūtradhāra; another authority permits the Sūtradhāra or any other actor to recite it. The situation is complicated by the rule that at the end of the preliminaries the Sūtradhāra is supposed to leave the stage and the Sthāpaka to come on, while our dramas, as a rule, have the benediction followed by the entry of the Sūtradhāra, or rarely, as in the *Pārthaparākrama*, the Sthāpaka. The theory, therefore, suggests that the benediction is recited by the Sūtradhāra or

[1] A classification of poets on the basis of their confidence in themselves as expressed in this place is given in R. i. 246 f.; Kālidāsa is elevated (*udātta*) in the *Mālavikāgnimitra*; Bhavabhūti haughty (*uddhata*) in the *Mālatīmādhava*; self assertion (*prauḍha*) is seen in the *Karuṇākandala*; modesty (*vinīta*) in the *Rāmānanda*.

[2] Konow, ID. p. 25.

[3] Lévi, TI. i. 135, 379; ii. 26 f., 64, 66. Cf. *Harivaṅça*, ii. 93; *Kuṭṭanīmata*, 856 ff.

Sthāpaka (called Sūtradhāra by reason of similarity of function and character) behind the curtain, and then he enters on the stage. The matter is not cleared up by the practice followed in the embryo dramas introduced into others: in that included in the *Bālarāmāyaṇa* the Sūtradhāra recites a benediction of twelve inflected words, and then proceeds with the prologue without a break; in the *Jānakīpariṇaya* it is one of the actors who does so, as in Ravivarman's *Pradyumnābhyudaya*, the director then beginning the play; in the *Caitanyacandrodaya* the benediction is recited behind the curtain, but that is stated to be because the piece to be acted is a Bhāṇa or Vyāyoga, implying that in other cases it normally was recited on the stage, presumably by an actor other than the director.

The extent of the benediction was, as we have seen, disputed.[1] Bharata's rule of eight or twelve Padas does not stand alone, for he is credited with mentioning four or sixteen as possible numbers, and Pada may mean inflected word, line, or proposition. Abhinavagupta allows three, six, or twelve Padas in a benediction of three times; four, eight, or sixteen in one of four times; and definitely takes Pada as proposition; illustrations of eight- and twelve-Pada benedictions of this type are given by Abhinavagupta and Bharata. The dramas differ; the *Çakuntalā* has one of eight propositions or four lines; the *Ratnāvalī* four stanzas; the *Mālatīmādhava* and the *Mudrārākṣasa* eight lines each; the *Uttararāmacarita* twelve words.

Harmony between the benediction and the character of the drama is naturally demanded by the theory, and is observed largely in practice; thus the *Prabodhacandrodaya*, a philosophic drama, begins with an adoration of the sole reality, the *Mudrārākṣasa*, a drama of political intrigue, with a verse as tortuous as the diplomacy of Cāṇakya. It is a characteristic of the determination to carry matters to extremes which distinguishes Indian theory that attempts are made to extract from the benediction not merely a general harmony with the theme, but also a reference both to the main characters and to the chief events.[2]

[1] Lévi, TI. i. 132 f.; ii. 24 f.; Hall, DR., pp. 25 f. The *Veṇīsaṁhāra* has six stanzas. R. iii. 137 f. takes Pada as word, giving the *Mahāvīracarita*, *Abhirāmarāghava*, and *Anargharaghāva* as examples of 8, 10, and 12 Padas.

[2] For a general reference see *Pañcarātra*, i. 1. In a Jain drama like the *Moharājaparājaya*, the benediction is addressed to the three Tīrthakaras; in the *Nāgānanda* to the Buddha.

9. *The Types of Drama*

The types of drama are distinguished by the theorists according to the use which they make of the various dramatic elements enumerated. The highest of the ten main forms, Rūpakas, is the Nāṭaka or heroic comedy. The term is generic; it may denote any representation whether by pictures or dumb show, but it has also the more important specific sense of the drama proper.

The subject of a Nāṭaka [1] should be drawn from tradition, not invented; the hero should be a king, royal sage, or god, who may appear in human form; the dominant sentiment must be the heroic or the erotic, but all may be illustrated, and that of wonder is well suited for the *dénouement*, which should be led up to through the whole series of stages of the action and junctures. The end must be happy; tragedy is forbidden, though the prohibition is unexplained. The prose should be simple without elaborate compounds; the verses clear and sweet; the Prākrits should be varied; the whole style noble and harmonious, with full use of all the beauties and the adventitious attractions of the song and the dance as well as music. The number of acts should be from five to ten; if a play contains every kind of episode, it is styled a Mahānāṭaka, if it has ten acts. The rule is generally obeyed, but late dramas styling themselves Nāṭakas are known of one (Ravidāsa's *Mithyājñānaviḍambana*), two (Vedāntavāgīça's *Bhojacarita*), three, or four acts,[2] and one comparatively early work exists in one version of fourteen acts, without any passage in Prākrit, the *Mahānāṭaka*; the *Adbhutārṇava* of a Kavibhūṣaṇa has twelve acts. The name of a Nāṭaka should be derived from the hero or the subject-matter, and this is regularly the case. Four or five is the number of chief personages permitted.

The bourgeois comedy, Prakaraṇa,[3] is a comedy of manners of a rank below royalty, which in the main follows the laws of construction of the Nāṭaka. The subject-matter is to be framed at his good pleasure by the poet. The hero should be

[1] N. xviii. 10 ff.; DR. iii. 1–34; SD. 278, 433, 510; R. iii. 130 ff.

[2] Ghanaçyāma's *Navagrahacarita* has three acts; Madhusūdana's *Jānakīpariṇaya* (A. D. 1705) has four.

[3] N. xviii. 41 ff.; DR. iii. 35–8; SD. 511 f.; R. iii. 214–18, who gives *Kāmadatta* as the name of a hetaera drama.

a Brahmin, minister, or merchant, who has fallen on evil days and is seeking through difficulties to attain property, love, and the performance of duty, in which he at last succeeds. The heroine may be of three types, a lady of good family, as in the lost *Puṣpadūṣita* (°*bhūṣita*); a hetaera as in the lost *Taraṅgadatta*; or a lady of good family may share the honours with a hetaera, with whom, however, she may not come in contact, as in the *Cārudatta* and the *Mṛcchakaṭikā*. The drama offers an appropriate place for slaves, Viṭas, merchant chiefs, and rogues of various kinds. The erotic sentiment should dominate, though Dhanaṁjaya allows also the heroic, and the structure should include all five junctures. The number of acts should be as in the Nāṭaka, and the name be derived from the hero or heroine or both, as in the *Mālatīmādhava* and the *Çāriputraprakaraṇa* of Açvaghoṣa. It must, however, be noted that the *Pratijñāyaugandharāyaṇa* has but four acts, and the *Mṛcchakaṭikā*, unlike the *Cārudatta*, does not follow the rule as to name.

The supernatural drama, Samavakāra,[1] is described in our sources obviously on the basis of a single play, the *Amṛtamanthana*, the churning of the ocean to obtain the ambrosia, at which all participants attained their desires. The precise duration of each of its three acts is given, at twelve, four, and two Nāḍikās (of forty-eight minutes). The subject must be taken from a tale of the gods and demons. The juncture, pause, is omitted, and the expansion (*bindu*) as an element of the plot. The number of heroes may reach twelve, each pursuing an object which he attains. The heroic sentiment dominates. Each act exhibits one type of cheating, tumultuous action, and love. The graceful manner is excluded, or but faintly developed; the Uṣṇih, Kuṭila, and Anuṣṭubh metres are appropriate. The description fits but loosely Bhāsa's *Pañcarātra*, the only old drama to which that name may plausibly be applied.

The Īhāmṛga,[2] of which no old example is known, owes its name, according to the *Daçarūpāvaloka* to the fact that in it a maiden as hard to attain as a gazelle (*mṛga*) is sought after (*īhā*). The subject is one partly derived from legend and partly

[1] N. xviii. 57–70; xix. 43 f.; DR. iii. 56–61; SD. 515 f.; R. iii. 249–64.

[2] N. xviii. 72–6; xix. 44 f.; DR. iii. 66–8; SD. 518; R. iii. 284–8 (type *Māyākuraṅgikā*).

the poet's imagination; in special, if the legend relates the death of a great man, this result must be avoided. The essence of the drama is that some one seeks to deprive the hero, who on one view may be divine or human, on another divine only, of a heavenly maiden; the result is a conflict of wills, but actual fighting is to be avoided by artifice. The hero and his rival must both be of the noble and haughty type; the latter must do wrong in error. Only the first two and the last junctures are allowed, and the graceful style is excluded. There are four acts, but Viçvanātha mentions a view which allows one act only and makes the hero a god, or six rivals for a divine maiden's hand.

The Ḍima[1] is also little known, though the *Nāṭyaçāstra* cites a *Tripuradāha* as a specimen. Its subject is to be legendary; there is to be no pause juncture. The heroes are sixteen gods, demi-gods, and demons, all of the haughty type; magic, sorcery, combats, eclipses of the sun and moon are in place. The erotic and comic sentiments are excluded, that of fury is predominant. There are four acts without introductory scenes of any kind, but the late *Manmathonmathana* of Rāma has them. The graceful manner is forbidden. It is clear that the type is described on the basis of inadequate material; it may represent a popular form of entertainment which did not attain full recognition. The origin of the name is unknown, for no root *ḍim*, to wound, is found in the language, though Dhanika asserts its existence.

The Vyāyoga[2] is, as its name suggests, a military spectacle. Its subject must be legendary, its hero a god or royal sage, but Dhanaṁjaya allows a man. It is in one act, the action not extending over a day, and it is filled with strife and battle, the intervention of women as the cause of battle being excluded. The first two and last junctures alone are permitted, the erotic and comic sentiments are barred, and the graceful manner. The type is old, for it is found in Bhāsa and revives later.

The Act or Isolated Act (Aṅka, Utsṛṣṭikāṅka)[3] is a single-act piece, whose longer style serves to discriminate it from an act of

[1] N. xviii. 78–82; xix. 43 f.; DR. iii. 51–3; SD. 517; R. iii. 280–4 (type *Vīrabhadravijṛmbhaṇa*).

[2] N. xviii. 83–5; xix. 44 f.; DR. iii. 54 f.; SD. 514; R. iii. 229–32 (type *Dhanaṁjayajaya*).

[3] N. xviii. 86–9; xix. 45 f.; DR. iii. 64 f.; SD. 519 R. iii. 224–8 (type *Karuṇākandala*) who differs.

a normal drama. Its subject is taken from legend, but may be developed by the poet; the first and last junctures alone are permitted. The hero should be human, of the common folk, according to the later theory. The sentiment should be the pathetic, and the style the verbal. The laments of women should accompany the description of battles and fights, but these should not take place on the stage. Viçvanātha gives the *Çarmiṣṭhāyayāti* as an example, but the type is not represented by any early play.

The farce, Prahasana,[1] on the other hand, has every sign of popular origin and vogue. The subject is the poet's invention; it deals essentially with the tricks and quarrels of low characters of every kind. There is but one act, and only the first and last junctures; the comic sentiment predominates. The *Daçarūpa* recognizes three kinds; the pure is that in which heretics, Brahmins, men- and maid-servants and parasites are represented in appropriate costume and language; the modified represents eunuchs, chamberlains, and ascetics in the garb, and with the speech, of lovers; and the mixed is styled so because it contains the elements of the Vīthī, and is filled with rogues. Only the first and last are recognized by the *Nāṭyaçāstra*, the second being included in the third, while Viçvanātha recognizes the possibility of there being only one hero or several, and allows the use of two acts in such a case, as in the *Laṭakamelaka*. The graceful and violent manners are excluded.

The monologue, Bhāṇa,[2] has also an obviously popular character and origin. The subject-matter is invented by the poet; a parasite sets forth his own or another's adventures, appealing to both the heroic and the erotic sentiments by descriptions of heroism and beauty in the verbal manner. There are only the first and last junctures, and but one act. The actor speaks in the air, repeating answers supposed to be received. The elements of the Lāsya are specially in place, a fact which shows that we have here a formal version of a primitive mimetic performance. Viçvanātha gives as example the *Līlāmadhukara*; the *Çāradātilaka* is one of the best known.

[1] N. xviii. 93–8; xix. 45 f.; DR. iii. 49 f.; SD. 534–8; R. iii. 268–79 (type *Ānandakoça*).

[2] N. xviii. 99–101; xix. 45 f.; DR. iii. 44–6; SD. 513; R. iii. 232–5

The garland, Vīthī,[1] has a certain similarity to the Bhāṇa in that it includes frequent speeches in the air, and is in one act. But it is played by one or two actors, or, according to Viçvanātha on one view found in the *Nāṭyaçāstra*, by three, one of each station in rank. The leading sentiment is the erotic, but others are hinted at. The graceful manner is forbidden by the *Nāṭyaçāstra*, but enjoined by the other authorities, and the elements of the garland are available. Only the first and last junctures are employed, but all the elements of the plot are present. The theorists are sadly at a loss to explain the name garland; it is suggested that the several sentiments are gathered into it as into a garland, or the meaning 'way' or 'road' is accepted in lieu. The only example given by Viçvanātha is the *Mālavikā*, which is not the *Mālavikāgnimitra*; the first act of the *Mālatīmādhava* is styled Bakulavīthī, but is in no sense even taken by itself an example of this type.

The later theory as seen in Viçvanātha[2] adds descriptions of eighteen minor forms of drama, Uparūpakas, which represent refinements on the original scheme. Needless to say, though omitted in the *Nāṭyaçāstra*, quotations are found ascribing to Bharata the doctrine, though he mentions in them but fifteen with several variations of name;[3] the *Agni Purāṇa*[4] mentions eighteen with some variants of name, while a verse cited by Dhanika[5] names seven forms of mimetic dramas, which it classes in conjunction with the Bhāṇa. The age of these divisions is, therefore, uncertain; the *Daçarūpa* condescends to mention only the Nāṭikā, but obviously knows of the existence of others, confining its scope to the main forms, as its title indicates.

The *Nāṭyaçāstra*[6] mentions, in a passage suspected of interpolation, but without special cause, a type of dramas Nāṭī, which later is styled Nāṭikā, or lesser heroic comedy. The subject-matter in this view may be either legendary or invented; the later opinion requires it to be invented as in the Prakaraṇa, which is the model for the Nāṭikā in this regard. The hero is to be

[1] N. xviii. 102 f.; xix. 45 f.; DR. iii. 62 f.; SD. 520. Konow (ID. p. 32) is in error as to N. R. iii. 265–70 has *Mādhavī-Vīthikā*.

[2] SD. 276.

[3] Hall, DR., p. 6.

[4] cccxxxvii. 2–4. R. iii. 218–23 denies the separate character of the Nāṭikā or Prakaraṇikā.

[5] DR. i. 8.

[6] xviii. 54–6; DR. iii. 39–43; SD. 539.

that of the Nāṭaka, a gay king, and the intrigue consists of his efforts to attain marriage with the heroine, who is an *ingénue* of royal family, whom he is destined to marry, but who by some accident or design has been introduced into the harem in an inferior capacity. The lovers have to strive against the jealousy of the queen, a lady of mature character and devotion to the king, who at last is induced to sanction the nuptials. The life of the court gives opportunity for introducing music, song, and the dance as elements in the entertainment. The graceful manner is appropriate, and the erotic sentiment is prescribed; by an excess of zeal, when the drama as usual has four acts, they are in theory to contain each one of the four members of the graceful style. A lesser number of acts is allowed by Dhanaṁjaya. There is certainly not much difference between such a Nāṭaka as the *Mālavikāgnimitra* and the normal Nāṭikā, save the length, as expressed in the number of the acts, but it would be unwise to assert that the distinction is based on this alone. It is a fact that both in the *Priyadarçikā* and the *Ratnāvalī* the poet has freely enough invented his episodes, and this is a fact justifying the discrimination.

The little bourgeois comedy, the Prakaraṇikā,[1] is precisely of the same character as the Nāṭikā, save that its hero and heroine are of the merchant class. It is clear that it is due merely to a false desire for symmetry, as it is merely a Prakaraṇa when judged by the three determinants of plot, character, and sentiment, and Dhanika rightly rejects it as a species, though Viçvanātha admits it.

A variant of the Nāṭikā is the Saṭṭaka,[2] which differs from it merely by being all in Prākrit, in having no introductory scenes of any kind, and in having the acts called Javanikāntara. As the name denotes a form of dance, it is quite possible that it owes its origin as a species to the use of such dances in these plays. We have an example in Rājaçekhara's *Karpūramañjarī*.

The Troṭaka[3] or Toṭaka is merely a variant of the Nāṭaka; the Bengālī recension of the *Vikramorvaçī* which contains Apabhrança verses and an appropriate dance of the distracted

[1] SD. 554.

[2] SD. 542. Cf. the Bharhut bas-relief of a dance, *Sāḍika*; Hultzsch, ZDMG. xl 66, no. 50.

[3] SD. 540

king alone gives the name. The term denotes both a dance and confused speech, and the origin of the species need be sought only in this peculiarity. The other manuscripts call it a Nāṭaka.

The other species enumerated have no representatives in the old literature, nor is this wonderful, for they show the character rather of pantomime with song, dance, and music than of serious drama; the Goṣṭhī [1] has nine or ten men and five or six women as actors; the Hallīça [2] is clearly a glorified dance; the Nāṭyarāsaka [3] a ballet and pantomime; the Prasthāna,[4] in which hero and heroine are slaves, is based on a mimetic dance; so also apparently are the Bhāṇikā,[5] or little Bhāṇa, and the Kāvya, both one-act pieces; the Rāsaka, of the same general type, includes dialect in its language. The Ullāpya may have one or three acts, and its hero is of high rank, while battles form part of its subject, as they do also in the Saṁlāpaka, which may have one, three, or four acts. The Durmallikā has four acts, a hero of low rank, and a precise time-table of duration of acts. The Vilāsikā has one act, but is interesting in that the hero has, to support him, not only the Vidūṣaka, but also the parasite and a friend (*pīṭhamarda*); the sentiment is erotic. The Çilpaka is mysterious, for it has four acts, allows all the manners, has a Brahmin as hero with a man of lower rank as secondary hero, excludes the calm and comic sentiments, and has twenty-seven most miscellaneous constituents; if a pantomime, it was clearly not amusing. The Preñkhaṇa, or Prekṣaṇa, is a piece in one act, with a hero of low birth, full of combats and hard words; it has no introductory scenes, and both the benediction and the Prarocanā are performed behind the scenes, but none of the late works which bear approximately this title conforms to type. The Çrīgadita is in a single act, the story legendary, the hero and heroine of high rank, the manner verbal; the word Çrī is often mentioned, or the goddess is presented seated and singing some verse. The only play known of that name is the *Subhadrāharaṇa* of Mādhava before A.D. 1600, which is much like an ordinary play, but contains a narrative verse, suggesting connexion with the shadow-drama. It is characteristic that the theory ignores wholly this type.

[1] SD. 541. Cf. Hall, DR., p. 6.
[2] SD. 555. [3] SD. 543. [4] SD. 544.
[5] SD. 556; for the others see 546 ff. Names of plays are given, but they are lost, and were probably late.

10. *The Influence of Theory on Practice*

Though we cannot say precisely at what date the *Nāṭyaçāstra* obtained definite form, we can be assured that by the time of Kālidāsa it was not merely known, but its authority was already accepted as binding on poets. The mere fact that Kālidāsa's dramas exhibit a marvellous fidelity to the rules of the Çāstra might be explained by the theory that it drew its principles from them rather than *vice versa*. But in his epics Kālidāsa, in due accord with the duty of a poet to display every form of his erudition, has emphatically shown a far-reaching competence in the terminology of the Çāstra. In the *Kumārasambhava*[1] Çiva and Pārvatī watched the performance in honour of their nuptials of a Nāṭaka in which the different dramatic manners were combined with the junctures, the modes of the music corresponded with the sentiments, and the Apsarases displayed their grace of form. There are similar references in the *Raghuvañça*.[2] The knowledge of the Çāstra by later writers goes without saying. The author of the *Mudrārākṣasa*[3] depicts Rākṣasa as comparing political combinations with the work of a dramatist and giving a brief plan of the structure of the drama, and Bhavabhūti[4] and Murāri[5] alike show familiarity with the terminology of the Çāstra as well as with its rules. The most complete proof, however, of the domination of the theory is the absence of any original creations in dramatic form. There must, it is certain, have been a time when the genius of Indian poetry was active in trying and developing the new instrument of drama, but with the appearance of the *Nāṭyaçāstra* this creative epoch came to all intents and purposes to a close, and the writers of the classical drama accept without question the forms imposed upon them by authority, although that authority rests on no logical or psychological basis, but represents merely generalizations, often hasty, from a limited number of plays.

The Nāṭaka, accordingly, remains the form of drama *par excellence*, a pre-eminence due to its comparative freedom from narrow

[1] vii. 90 f.; xi. 36.
[2] ii. 18.
[3] iv. 3.
[4] *Mālatīmādhava*, p. 79.
[5] vi. 48, and see pp. 108 f.; Lévi, TI. ii. 38.

restrictions as well as to the submissive spirit of the dramatists. The form serves very different purposes; it accommodates itself not only to the grace and charm of Kālidāsa, but to the unmeasured and irregular genius of Bhavabhūti; it permits of the political drama of Viçākhadatta, as well as the philosophical disquisitions of Kṛṣṇamiçra and the devotional fervour of Kavikarṇapūra's *Caitanyacandrodaya*.

The Prakaraṇa is essentially similar to the Nāṭaka save in the social status of the hero and heroine; the distinction between the *Mālatīmādhava* and a Nāṭaka is far less important than the similarity. The *Mṛcchakaṭikā*, indeed, departs from type, but that is not surprising now that it is known that it is based on Bhāsa's *Cārudatta*, which is not merely the work of a man of unusual talent, but came into being before the rules of the drama had attained the binding force they later achieved. The Nāṭikā, however, which is likewise closely allied to the Nāṭaka, became stereotyped at an early stage, leaving no room for serious innovation; the charms of the song and dance appear to have prevailed, and to have dissuaded efforts at originality of plot. The Vyāyoga is hardly more than an aspect of the Nāṭaka; the spirit of such works as those of Bhāsa in this genre is reflected in many passages of the *Mahāvīracarita* and the *Veṇīsaṁhāra*.

The farce and the monologue, of which we have many specimens in the later drama, are confined to representations of the lower and coarser side of life; but curiously enough they fail entirely to achieve what might have seemed the legitimate aim of a vivid portrayal of the lives and manners of contemporary society; tradition has proved too strong for the dramatists whose works deal with types, not individuals. On the other hand, we find practically no living tradition of the construction of dramas of the other five classes of the theory, Ḍima, Samavakāra, Īhāmṛga, Vīthī, and Utsṛṣṭikāṅka. We may legitimately assume that these were types erected on little foundation of fact, and that, while the theory could restrict enterprise, it could not induce life in forms which had no real vitality of their own. The mere fact that later poets occasionally patronize these forms is sufficient evidence of the strength of the authority of the Çāstra. It is amazing, however, that we find no serious effort to produce pure comedy; the farce and the monologue may hover on the borders of that form; they certainly never attain it.

To the force of the tradition is presumably to be ascribed the absence of any effort at tragedy, though its absence undoubtedly coincides with the mental outlook of the Indian people and their philosophy of life. Bhāsa has indeed been claimed as a tragedian, but with complete disregard for the facts; there is in fact in his dramas disregard of the rule which objects to death on the stage, but the slain are always evil men, whose death is just punishment; the *Ūrubhaṅga* may to us be tragic, but that is because we are not adorers of Viṣṇu who regard with relish the fate of the enemy of that god, the evil Duryodhana. The tragic sentiment is nowhere recognized, for the term (*raudra*), which is unhappily often so rendered, is the sentiment which is based on anger, and has nothing truly tragic in it. The idea is, indeed, entirely wanting in the theory as it is in the practice.

To the developed thought of India, as it existed during the vogue of the drama, there was little possibility of a realization of the elements of which Greek tragedy is composed. The conception of human activity striving with circumstance, endeavouring to assert itself in the teeth of forces superhuman in power and uncontrollable, and meeting with utter ruin, but yet maintaining its honour, which affords the spring of tragedy in Greece, is alien to Indian thought. Fate is nothing outside man; he is subject to no alien influences; he is what he has made himself by acts in past lives; if he suffers evil he has deserved it as just retribution, and to sympathize with him, to feel the pathos of his plight, is really unthinkable. Death, therefore, by violence is merely a just punishment of crime, and it is a more refined taste than that of Bhāsa which bids us banish from the stage the spectacle of what is no more than an execution, a scene as ill-suited to the decorum and good taste of the serious drama[1] as to the rude merriment of the farce or monologue.

[1] Cf. the later view in Rome, which forbids death on the stage, Horace, *Ars Poetica*, 183 ff., with Aristotle, *Poetics*, 1452 *b* 10 ff., which approves the presentation of death and other acts on the stage.

11. *Aristotle and the Indian Theory of Poetics*

It is natural that contemporaneously with the effort to prove the Greek origin of the Indian drama efforts [1] should have been made to establish the indebtedness of the *Nāṭyaçāstra* to Aristotle's theory of drama.[2] There is no doubt of the many parallels between the two theories. The unity of action is fully recognized in the Çāstra, and the rule which insists that the events described in an Act shall not exceed in duration a day has a certain similarity to the unity of time in Aristotle,[3] and is much more significant than such agreement as there is as to unity of place. The doctrine that the drama is an imitation (*anukṛti*) does not differ from the doctrine of Mimesis, but there is an essential distinction in what is imitated or represented; in the Çāstra it is a state or condition, in Aristotle it is action, a distinction absolutely in accord with the different geniuses of the two peoples. The importance of acting is common in both schemes, but Aristotle makes little of the dance. Both stress the plot, which the Çāstra recognizes as the body of the drama. The Indian division of characters as high, middle, and low has a certain parallelism to the Aristotelian distinctions of modes of depicting character as ideal, real, and inferior. The Çāstra, like Aristotle, shows appreciation of the distinction between male and female characters. To some degree we find in the Çāstra the recognition of the necessity of conflict in drama, and of the emotions of pity and fear in the sentiment of pathos and in the element of the development known as Vidrava. The Çāstra also touches on the relation of the feelings aroused in the actor and in the audience as in the *Poetics*. Both recognize the use of significant names, and deal with the linguistic aspects of style.

Other suggestions of Greek influence may also be adduced; thus we have the mention of what seems a derivative of the Greek caryatides in the description of the theatre; the monologue may be based on the Greek Mime, and we have the actual

[1] M. Lindenau, *Festschrift Windisch*, pp. 38 ff.

[2] *Poetics*, 1449 *b sq.* with Butcher's trs. and Bywater's notes.

[3] *Poetics*, 1449 *b* 13. For time analysis in Kālidāsa, see Jackson, JAOS. xx. 341–59; in Harṣa, xxi. 88–108.

mention in a passage of the Çāstra of Yavanas, while the description of the Viṭa suggests derivation from the Greek parasite. But it is impossible to take these pieces of evidence as conclusive proof of borrowing; we are, in fact, faced with the usual difficulty that, if there were borrowing, the Indian genius has known how to recast so cleverly and to adapt what it borrowed so effectively that the traces which would definitely establish indebtedness cannot be found. In all the instances enumerated there is no doubt similarity, but there is also essential difference such as renders independent development of the Indian doctrine at least as probable as borrowing.

IV

DRAMATIC PRACTICE

XIV

THE INDIAN THEATRE

1. *The Theatre*

THE Sanskrit drama of the theorists is, despite its complexity, essentially intended for performance, nor is there the slightest doubt that the early dramatists were anything but composers of plays meant only to be read. They were connoisseurs, we may be certain, in the merits which would accrue to their works from the accessories of the dance, music, song, and the attractions of acting; the *Vikramorvaçī* must, for instance, have had much of the attraction of an opera, and as a mere literary work loses seriously in attraction.

On the other hand, the existence of regular theatres for the exhibition of drama is not assumed in the theorists. A drama was, it is clear, normally performed on an occasion of special rejoicing and solemnity, such as a festival of a god, or a royal marriage, or the celebration of a victory, and the place of performance thus naturally came to be the temple of the god or the palace of the king. We learn often in the drama and tales of the existence of dancing halls and music rooms in the royal palace where the ladies of the harem were taught these pleasing arts, and one of these could easily be adapted for a dramatic performance. But we have from the second century B.C. the remains of a cave which seems to have been used, if not for the performance of plays, at any rate for purposes of recitation of poems or some similar end; it is found in the Rāmgarh hill[1] in Chota Nagpur, and, although it is quite impossible to prove that it had anything to do with plays, it is interesting to note that the *Nāṭyaçāstra* states that the play-house should have the form of a mountain cave and two stories.

[1] Bloch, *Arch. Survey of India Report*, 1903–4, pp. 123 ff.

According to the Çāstra,[1] the play-house as made ready for performance may be of three types, the first for the gods, 108 hands (18 inches) long; the second rectangular, 64 hands long and 32 broad; the third triangular, 32 hands long, the second being praised on acoustic grounds. The house falls into two parts, the places for the audience and the stage. The auditorium is marked off by pillars, in front a white pillar for the seats for the Brahmins, then a red pillar for the Kṣatriyas, in the north-west a yellow pillar marks the seats for the Vaiçyas, while the Çūdras have a blue-black pillar in the north-east. The seats are of wood and bricks, and arranged in rows. In front beside the stage is a veranda with four pillars, apparently also for the use of spectators. In front of the spectators is the stage (*rañga*), adorned with pictures and reliefs; it is eight hands square in the second form of play-house; its end is the head of the stage (*rañgaçīrṣa*), decorated by figures, and there offerings are made.[2]

Behind[3] the stage is the painted curtain (*paṭī, apaṭī, tiraskaraṇī, pratisīrā*), to which the name Yavanikā (Prākrit, Javanikā) is given, denoting merely that the material is foreign, and forbidding any conclusion as to the Greek origin of the curtain itself or the theatre. When one enters hastily, the curtain is violently thrown aside (*apaṭīkṣepa*). Behind the curtain are the actors' quarters (*nepathyagṛha*) or tiring rooms. Here are performed the sounds necessary to represent uproar and confusion which cannot be represented on the stage; here also are uttered the voices of gods and other persons whose presence on the stage is impossible or undesirable.

The colour of the curtain is given in some authorities as necessarily in harmony with the dominant sentiment of the play, in accordance with the classification of sentiments already given, but others permit the use of red in every instance. Normally the entry of any character is effected by the drawing aside of the curtain by two maidens, whose beauty marks them out for this

[1] ii; cf. JPASB. v. 353 ff.; *Çilparatna* (ed. TSS.), pp. 201 ff. Cf. *Kāvyamīmāṅsā*, p. 54.

[2] For the Greek theatre, which presents certain points of similarity but many of difference, see Dorpfeld, *Das griechische Theater*; Haigh, *Attic Theatre* (3rd ed.); a brief summary is given in Norwood, *Greek Tragedy*, pp. 49 ff.

[3] The theory of a transverse curtain (Wilson, I. lxviii) is not supported by evidence of any clear kind. Cf. p. 113, n. 1.

employment (*dhṛtir yavanikāyāḥ*). The term Nepathya has suggested an erroneous deduction as to the relative elevation of the stage and the foyer, for it is conceivable that it denotes a descending (*ni-patha*) way, and it has been concluded[1] that it was, therefore, below the level of the stage. But the regular phrase of the entry of an actor on the stage (*rañgāvataraṇa*) would suggest exactly the opposite, a descent from the foyer to the stage. In the case of stages hastily put together, often for merely very temporary aims, it would clearly be absurd to expect any fixed practice, nor can we say what was the normal height of the stage platform. In the case of a play within a play, in the *Bālarāmāyaṇa* of Rājaçekhara, we find that both a stage and a tiring room are erected on the original stage, though we may assume that these were of a very simple structure.

The number of doors leading to the tiring room from the stage is regularly given as two,[2] and apparently the place of the orchestra was between them.

2. *The Actors*

The normal term for actor is Naṭa, a term which has the wider sense of dancer or acrobat; terms like Bharata, or Bhārata, Cāraṇa,[3] Kuçīlava, Çailūṣa, or Çaubhika have interest practically only for the history of the drama. The chief actor, whose name Sūtradhāra doubtless denotes him as primarily the architect of the theatre, the man who secures the erection of the temporary stage, is occasionally styled 'troop-head of actors (*naṭagāmaṇi*)',[4] and he is essentially the instructor of the other actors in their art (*nāṭyācārya*), so that his title Sūtradhāra can be used topically as equivalent to Professor. For this high position his qualifications were to be numerous; he was supposed to be learned in all the arts and sciences, to be acquainted with the habits and customs of all lands, to combine the completeness of technical knowledge with practical skill, and to be possessed of all the

[1] Weber, IS. xiv. 225. Cf. Lévi, TI. i. 374; ii. 62.

[2] The Greek number was three, later five. The Chinese stage, which resembles the Indian in its primitive character, but has no curtain, has two doors, one for entry, one for exit; Ridgeway, *Dramas*, &c., pp. 274 f.

[3] W. Crooke, *The Tribes and Castes of the N. W. Provinces and Oudh*, ii. 20 ff.

[4] Hillebrandt, AID., p. 12; cf. *naṭagrāma*, *Epigr. Ind.* i. 381.

moral qualities which an Indian genius can enumerate. To him falls not merely the very important function of introducing the play, but also of taking one of the chief parts; thus he plays Vatsa in the *Ratnāvalī*, and in the *Mālatīmādhava* Kāmandakī, the nun, who powerfully affects the current of the drama. He is normally the husband of one of the actresses (*naṭī*), who aids him in the opening scene, and who is compelled, poor woman, to combine the arduous life of an actress with the domestic duty of looking after her husband's material wants. She is represented as devoted to him, fasting to secure reunion in another life, preparing his meal and seeking to remove by her good works the dangers which threaten him, and compelled to play her parts, although anxious, as in the *Ratnāvalī*, over the difficulty of securing the marriage of her daughter to a fiancé who has gone overseas, or, as in the *Jānakīpariṇaya*, over the wickedness of another actor in seeking to take her daughter from her.

The Sthāpaka, according to the theory, is to resemble in his attributes the Sūtradhāra; as we have seen, to what extent he really in the dramas known to us was employed as distinct from the Sūtradhāra, it is impossible to say; the name suggests that he aided him in the structure of the stage, and then in his actor's duties. But there is no ground to assume that he really had disappeared as a living figure before the classical drama; the occasional mention of him in actual dramas as well as in the theory need not be artificial. We have, however, a much more common attendant of the Sūtradhāra in the Pāripārçvika, who appears in the prologue of many plays, and in addition acted the parts of persons of middle rank. He receives the orders of his master and passes them on to the other actors, and directs the operations of the chorus, as in the *Veṇīsaṁhāra*. He is addressed by his master as Mārṣa, and he greets him as Bhāva.

The other actors, of whom there must often have been many in pieces with crowds introduced, are to have the qualities of the Sūtradhāra in as generous a measure as may be; they are divided, however, according to their qualifications into superior, medium, and third-rate actors.[1] The principal parts in any drama are, however, few; the king, the Vidūṣaka, the parasite, the heroine, and a companion are stock types. The division of

[1] xxiv. 85 f.

rôles is seldom shown in the prologues, whence are derived most of the details of our knowledge of actual performances. The Sūtradhāra in the *Ratnāvalī* and the *Priyadarçikā* plays the part of Vatsa, his younger brother that of Yaugandharāyaṇa in the former play and that of Dṛḍhavarman in the latter; the Sūtradhāra and the Pāripārçvika take in the *Mālatīmādhava* the rôles of Kāmandakī and her pupil Avalokitā respectively. This taking of women's parts by men is not by any means the normal practice; the Naṭī normally plays an important female part;[1] in the embryo drama in the *Priyadarçikā* we find that the heroine's part is played by Āraṇyikā, and the hero's part was to have been performed by another girl Manoramā, but Vatsa, without the queen's knowledge, insinuated himself into the scene *in propria persona*. In the legend of Bharata's exhibition of the *Lakṣmīsvayaṁvara* the nymph Urvaçī is represented as playing the chief rôle, and in Dāmodaragupta's *Kuṭṭanīmata*, where an actual representation of the *Ratnāvalī* is described, we find a woman in the rôle of the princess. The *Nāṭyaçāstra*[2] expressly admits of three modes of representation; the rôles may be filled by persons of appropriate sex and age; the rôles of the old may be taken by the young and *vice versa*; and the rôles of men may be played by women and *vice versa*. The taking of women's parts by men has, curiously enough, a very early piece of evidence, for the *Mahābhāṣya* mentions the word Bhrūkuṅsa, which was used to denote a man who made up as a female.[3]

We are, it is clear, to conceive of the troupe of actors under the Sūtradhāra as ready to wander hither and thither in search of a favourable opportunity of exhibiting their powers as interpreters. The performance of a drama became, it is clear, in later times at any rate, a worthy adornment of a festive occasion such as a religious festival, the consecration of a king, a marriage, the taking possession of a town or a new estate, the return of a traveller, and the birth of a son. The best patrons of the actors might be kings, but there was evidently no lack of appreciation of their services among men of lesser rank but of large means. The later prologues give us details of the rivalry between different troupes. In the *Anargharāghava* the actor declares that

[1] Cf. *Karpūramañjarī*, i. 12, 13.
[2] xxvi.; cf. xii. 166 f.
[3] Weber, IS. xiii. 493.

he has come to exhibit a superior sort of drama to that played by a rival, and asserts that the dearest desire of a player is to satisfy the public and to win back the favour he has lost. Rājaçekhara twice introduces the motive of a competition between actors to win the hand of an actress who has been offered by her father in marriage to the most adept of her suitors. Jayadeva invents a pleasing tale of an actor who won great success and reputation, inducing a comedian of the south to claim his name and steal his renown. The actor in revenge went south, and, striking up a partnership with a singer, won both repute and profit in the courts of the Deccan.

The reputation of actors and actresses was low and unsavoury; they are reputed to live on the price of their wives' honour (*jāyājīva*, *rūpājīva*), and Manu imposes only a minor penalty on illicit relations with the wife of an actor on the score of their willingness to hand over their wives to others and profit by their dishonour.[1] The *Mahābhāṣya* gives equally clear testimony of the lack of chastity among the actresses or their predecessors.[2] The law book of Viṣṇu[3] treats them as Āyogavas, a mixed caste representing the fruit of alliances, improper and undesirable, between Çūdras and the daughters of the Vaiçya; to be an actor or a teacher of the art is ranked as a lesser sin in Baudhāyana.[4] The Kuçīlava is described as a Çūdra, who ought to be banished;[5] his evidence, and indeed that of any actor, is not to be accepted in law,[6] and Brahmins may not accept food offered by an actor,[7] a fact attested by the Sūtradhāra in the prologue to the *Mṛcchakaṭikā* who can find no one in Ujjayinī to accept his hospitality. Actors again are classed in Manu with wrestlers and boxers. An actress was often, if not necessarily, one of the great army of courtesans; Vasantasenā, the hetaera of the *Cārudatta* and *Mṛcchakaṭikā*, is herself skilled in acting, and has in her household maidens learning to act, and Daṇḍin includes lessons in this art in his account of the education of the perfect courtesan in the *Daçakumāracarita*.

On the other hand, we have traces of a higher side of the

[1] viii. 362; cf. *Rāmāyaṇa*, ii. 30. 8; *Kuṭṭanīmata*, 855.
[2] vi. 1. 13.
[3] xvi. 8.
[4] ii. 1. 2. 13.
[5] *Kauṭilīya*, p. 7.
[6] Manu, viii. 65; Yājñ. ii. 70.
[7] Manu, iv. 215; Yājñ. i. 161.

profession, which doubtless can quite fairly be connected with the gradual elevation of the drama from humble origins to the rank of an elaborate and refined poetry. Bharata, the alleged founder of the *Nāṭyaçāstra*, ranks as a Muni, or holy sage, and Urvaçī, a divine nymph, is treated as an actress. What is more important is that Bāṇa definitely enumerates in the *Harṣacarita* among his friends an actor and an actress; Bhartṛhari[1] refers to their friendship with kings, which is also attested in the legend of Vasumitra, son of Kālidāsa's hero Agnimitra, who was slain amidst his actors by his enemy. Kālidāsa himself represents Agnivarṇa, king of Raghu's line, as pleased to compete with actors in their own speciality. Vatsa, in the *Priyadarçikā*, is prepared to play a part without question, and Bhavabhūti in two of his prefaces asserts his friendship with his actors. In truth, men who could effectively declaim the stanzas of Bhavabhūti must have possessed both education and culture in a high degree, and have been very different from the acrobats and jugglers, dancers, and others whose humble occupations account for the censures of the law books and the *Arthaçāstra*.

3. *The Mise-en-scène and Representation of the Drama*

We have no trace in the drama of any attempt to introduce scenery into the representation. The curtain remained as a background throughout the entertainment, and it was in the main left to the imagination of the spectator, aided by the descriptions of the poet, to conceive the beauties of the situation supposed to be presented to his eyes. We have for this conclusive proof, if any were needed beyond the silence of the text-books, in the abundant stage directions which accompany the text of our dramas, and are found even in the fragments of Açvaghoṣa. When actions such as watering a plant were ascribed to an actress, no serious effort was made to bring in plants and perform the ceremonial of watering; on the contrary, she went through a mimicry of the process, which was enough to satisfy the audience. The king may mount a chariot, but no effort is made to bring one for this purpose; he merely goes in

[1] iii. 57.

elaborate pantomime through the action of getting up off the ground, and the audience, trained and intelligent, realizes what has happened. At the beginning of the *Çakuntalā* the gazelle which Duḥṣanta follows is not a real animal, but the Sūtradhāra tells us that the king is pursuing a gazelle, and the actor, who represents the monarch, by his eager gaze and his gestures reveals himself as in the act of seeking to shoot the deer. To pluck flowers is merely to imitate the movements of one who really does so, and an actress with any skill has no difficulty in persuading an audience by her marks of agitation that she is escaping from the attacks of a bee.

There is thus no tedious attempt at realism, though the dramatists vary in the care with which they avoid the absurd in their use of conventions; the works of Bhāsa show doubtless an excessive tendency to allow of strain being placed on the credulity of the audience. The exits and entrances of the characters are often abrupt and unnatural, but the drama was not primarily intended as a realistic copy of events, and doubtless was not felt unsatisfactory by the audience. Nor, it may be remembered, has perfection in detail in any form of ceremonial ever made a strong appeal to Indian minds; in the most gorgeous celebrations there will occur, without exciting surprise or comment, strange deviations from western canons of good taste and elegance.

To a limited extent, however, use was made of minor properties, which are classed under the generic style of model work (*pusta*).[1] The *Nāṭyaçāstra* distinguishes three forms of such objects; they may be made up (*sandhima*) from bamboos covered with skins or cloths; or mechanical means might be employed (*vyājima*); or merely clothes (*veṣṭita*) used. We hear of the making of an elephant in the *Udayanacarita*; the *Mṛcchakaṭikā* owes its name to the toy cart which appears in it; the *Bālarāmāyaṇa* has mechanical dolls, and doubtless there were represented houses, caves, chariots, rocks, horses, and so on; monsters with animal heads and many arms could be made of clay and bamboos, and covered with cloths; we are expressly told that weapons must not be made of hard material, but that

[1] N. xxi. 5 ff. Masks may have been used for animals, but not normally as in Greece; cf. ZDMG. lxxiv. 137, n. 2.

stocks of grass, bamboos, and lac may be made to serve, and naturally gestures served in lieu of hard blows.

The dress[1] of the actors is carefully regulated, especially as regards colour, which evidently was regarded as an important item in matters of sentiment. Ascetics wear garments of rags or bark; those in charge in the harem red jackets, kings gay garments or, if there are portents described, garments without colour. Ābhīra maidens wear dark blue clothes; in other cases dirty or uncoloured garments are prescribed. Dirty clothes indicate madness, distraction, misery, or a journey; uncoloured garb, one engaged in worship or some solemn religious service, an interesting survival of antique custom, while gods, Dānavas, Gandharvas, Uragas, Yakṣas, and Rakṣases, as well as lovers and kings, normally wear gay clothing.

Colour,[2] however, is by no means confined to garments; the actors are expected to adorn themselves with paint of hues appropriate to the rôles they play. There are, on one theory, four fundamental colours, white, blue-black, red, and yellow, from which others are developed, for instance pigeon colour by mixing the first two; a reddish yellow (*gaura*) from mixing the last two is also recorded. It or dark (*çyāma*) is given as suited for kings, while happiness is indicated by it. Kirātas, Barbaras, Andhras, Draviḍas, the people of Kāçi and Kosala, Pulindas, and the people of the Deccan are to be black (*asita*); the Çıkas, Yavanas, Pahlavas, and Bālhikas[3] are to be reddish yellow; Pāñcālas, Çūrasenas, Māhiṣas, Uḍras, Māgadhas, Aṅgas, Vaṅgas, and Kaliṅgas are to be dark (*çyāma*), as also Vaiçyas and Çūdras in general, while Brahmins and Kṣatriyas are to be reddish-yellow.

Naturally the hair[4] attracts attention; Piçācas, madmen, and Bhūtas wear it loose; the Vidūṣaka is bald; boys have three tufts of hair, and so also servants if it is not cut short; the maidens of Avantī, and usually those of Bengal, wear ringlets, in the case of women of the north it is worn high on the head, and otherwise plaits are usual. The beard may be bright in hue, dark, or bushy. There is also the same tendency to stereotype

[1] N. xxi.

[2] N. xxi. 62 ff.; Lévi, TI. i. 388; ii. 69. Cf. the *Mahābhāṣya*, iii. 1. 26; Yājñavalkya, iii. 162.

[3] Also read Pāhravas and Bāhlikas. Cf. *Kāvyamīmāṅsā*, pp. 96 f.

[4] N. xxi.

the ornaments, made out of copper, mica, or wax, and the garlands carried by the various personages; Vidyādharīs, Yakṣīs, Apsarases and Nāgīs carry pearls and jewels, while the latter are at once recognizable by the snake's hood rising over their heads, as are Yakṣas by a large tuft of hair.

The dress and appearance of the actor thus serve in some measure to carry out his duty of representation (*abhinaya*), of presenting before our eyes the states or conkitions of the personage for whom he stands. This is the Āhāryābhinaya, the first of the four agencies enumerated by the *Nāṭyaçāstra*. He has also to perform the duty of representation by speech (*vācika*), using his voice to convey the dramatist's words, and by exhibiting *in propria persona* the appropriate physical counterparts of the feelings and emotions of the characters (*sāttvikābhinaya*). Finally, he has specially to concentrate on the expression by gesture (*āṅgikābhinaya*) of the feelings which he is supposed to experience. In this regard most detailed rules are given, doubtless from the technique of a period when more importance attached to gestures than later seems natural. Each member of the body is singled out for description; deep significance lies in the mode in which the head is shaken, the eyes glance, the brows move; cheek, nose, lip, chin, and neck can all be used to convey subtle senses. The hands are invaluable for this purpose; the different manœuvres with the fingers can convey almost any possible combination of meanings to the person sufficiently acquainted with the *Nāṭyaçāstra* to understand them. But other parts of the body down to the feet are valuable; great care is bestowed on their postures, and the gait is invaluable in distinguishing classes of persons and their deeds. Darkness need not artificially be induced; movements of hands and feet to indicate groping are enough; one set of movements shows the mounting of a chariot, another the climbing up to the top of a palace; if the garments are pulled up, the crossing of a river is plainly shown; if the motions of swimming are mimicked, clearly the river is too deep to wade; a dexterous movement of the hands shows that one is driving, and similarly one can mount an elephant or a horse.[1]

[1] Cf. the *Abhinayadarpaṇa* of Nandikeçvara, trs. by A. Coomaraswamy and G. K. Duggirala, Cambridge, Mass., 1917.

It is characteristic of the nature of the Indian theory that, while it descends into enormous detail, it leaves alone to all intents and purposes the obvious duty of defining precisely the relation of the varieties of representation described as Sāttvika and Āñgika. The true relation is that under the head of Sāttvika are described the physical states, which are deemed appropriate to feelings and emotions, while the Āñgika prescribes the precise physical movements which express most effectively both psychic states and physical movements, which cannot be conveniently presented on the stage. The division accordingly is unscientific, and, acute as is the investigation of the *Nāṭyaçāstra* in detail, it is far from satisfying as a whole.

The importance of such accessories to the representation as garlands, ornaments, and appropriate garments, is emphasized by Mātṛgupta, who admits a specific form of sentiment styled Nepathyarasa, a fact which illustrates the effect produced in the mind of the spectator by the details of the *mise-en-scène*. The same impression may be derived from the elaboration of the stage directions in the dramas, comparable only to such as are given, for instance, in Mr. Bernard Shaw's productions. It is clear that they were intended not only for the direction of the actors in actually performing one of the pieces, but as instruments to aid the reader of the drama in realizing mentally the form of the representation and in appreciating, therefore, the dramatic quality of what he studied. Moreover, we have independent evidence which aids us in seeing how complete these directions are. A fortunate chance has preserved in Dāmodaragupta's *Kuṭṭanīmata*,[1] written in the reign of Jayāpīḍa of Kashmir in the eighth century A.D., an account of the performance of the *Ratnāvalī* of Harṣa. The description is incomplete, but it is perfectly clear that it was played exactly in accordance with the stage directions which have come down to us, embedded in the text of the drama as we have it.

The actual performance of the play was preceded, as we have seen in describing the theory of the drama, by preliminaries, the essential aim of which was the securing of the favour of the gods for the play to be represented. Of the varied elements of the preliminaries special importance seems to have attached to the

[1] 856 ff. Cf. the accounts in the *Harivaṅça*, ii. 88–93.

praise of the world guardians (*dikpālastuti*), and the reverence paid to Indra's banner. A reed with five knots is selected which is called Jarjara; the five sections are painted white, blue-black, yellow, red, and a mixture of hues; banners of every colour are tied to it, and the supplication is made to Gaṇeça, the god who removes obstacles and favours literature, and to the guardians of the quarters of the world.

A religious aspect is given also to the mingling of the pigments, the materials employed being yellow arsenic, lamp black, and red among others. The arsenic is formally addressed as being created by Svayambhū for the purpose of serving as a pigment; then it is placed on a board with fragments of brick, the whole reduced to fine powder, and mingled, and then used as pigment.[1]

The time of the performance is not in many cases stated, but in a number of plays, including the *Mālatīmādhava*, *Karṇasundarī*, and the embryo drama in the *Priyadarçikā*, we find it assumed to be the moment when the sun is just appearing.[2] The beat of drum announces the beginning of the drama, the preliminaries, often reduced to little more than a vocal and instrumental concert of brief duration, are completed, and the benediction pronounced, to be followed by the prologue proper and the drama.

4. *The Audience*

A drama like the Sanskrit demanded the full attention of a cultivated audience, and it is assumed or expressly asserted, as in the dramas of Kālidāsa, Harṣa, and Bhavabhūti, that the spectators are critical and experienced. The *Nāṭyaçāstra*[3] requires from the ideal spectator (*prekṣaka*) keen susceptibility and excellent judgement, with ability to make his own the feelings and emotions of the characters depicted by the actors. But it is admitted that there are the usual degrees among the spectators, good, medium, and indifferent; the question of the success of a drama depends on the judgement of the critic

[1] *Saṁgītadāmodara*, 39.

[2] Cf. Nīlakaṇṭha's reason for the alleged abbreviation of the *Mṛcchakaṭikā* (Lévi, TI. i. 210).

[3] xxvii. 51 ff.; Lévi, TI. ii. 62 ff.

(*prāçnika*), who is to possess every possible good quality to fit him for the delicate task. The audience, as it is to share the feelings of the characters, is expected to show them by the usual outward signs; laughter, tears, cries, hair standing on end, jumping up from their seats, clapping with the hands and other manifestations of pleasure, horror, fear, and other sentiments are both proper and natural.

The rules for placing the patron at whose bidding the drama is performed, Sabhāpati, and his guests, are elaborate.[1] He sits himself on the Lion Throne, the equivalent of the royal box, with the ladies of his harem on the left, and on the right the personages of highest importance, such as the vassal princes of a great king like Harṣa. Behind the latter are the treasurer and other officers, and near them the learned men of the court, civil and religious, including the poets, and in their midst the astrologers and physicians. On the left again are the ministers and other courtiers; all around are maidens of the court. In front again of the king are Brahmins, behind the bearers of fans, radiant in youthful beauty. On the left in front are the reciters and panegyrists, eloquent and wise. Guards are present to protect the sacred person of the sovereign.

How far the dramas were viewed by the public in general we cannot say; the rules regarding the play-house contemplate the presence of Çūdras, but that is a vague term, and may apply to a very restricted class of royal hangers on. We have the general rule[2] that barbarians, ignorant people, heretics, and those of low class should not be admitted, but such prescriptions mean very little. There must, it is clear, have been the utmost variation in the character of the audience according to the place and circumstances of representation. At great festivals, when plays were given in the temples, there must have been admission for as many as could be crowded in; in private exhibitions the audience may well have been more select. The fact that the dramas must have been largely unintelligible to all save a select few of the audience would not matter much; a drama was essentially a spectacle; in many cases its subject was perfectly familiar to the

[1] *Saṁgītaratnākara*, 1327 ff.; Lévi, TI. i. 375 ff. Cf. *Kāvyamīmāṅsā*, pp. 54 f.

[2] Tagore, *Eight Principal Rasas*, p. 61. That women as such were excluded (Wilson, ii. 212) cannot have held good for the early stage.

audience, and the elaborate use of conventional signs must have been enough to aid many of the audience in following roughly the nature of the proceedings.

When such dramatic exhibitions became rare we do not know; it is certain that in the eleventh century in Kashmir they were not uncommon; Kṣemendra advised aspirants to poetic fame to improve their taste by the study of such representations.[1] Doubtless the Mahomedan conquest seriously affected the vogue of the classical drama, which was obnoxious to Mahomedan fanaticism as being closely identified both with the national religion and the national spirit of India. The kings, who had been the main support of the actors and poets alike, disappeared from their thrones or suffered grave reverses in fortune. The tradition of dramatic performances gradually vanished. Other causes contributed to this end; the divorce between the language of the stage and that of the people steadily increasing with the passage of time made the Sanskrit drama more and more remote to the public, and the Mahomedans made it lose its position as the expression of the official and court life of the highest circles.[2]

[1] *Kavikaṇṭhābharaṇa*, p. 15.

[2] A certain revival of displays occurred in the nineteenth century; e.g. the *Citrayajña* of Vaidyanātha Vācaspati Bhaṭṭācārya, written for the festival of Govinda by request of the Rājā of Nadiyā about A.D. 1820. The Cakkyars of Malabar still act Çaktibhadra's *Āçcaryamañjarī* and Kulaçekharavarman's plays, as well as Act III of the *Pratijñāyaugandharāyaṇa*, under the style of *Mantrāṅkanāṭaka*, and the *Nāgānanda*; JRAS. 1910, p. 637; *Pratimānāṭaka* (ed. TSS.), p. xl; A. K. and V. R. Pisharoti, *Bulletin of School of Oriental Studies*, III. i. 107 ff., who maintain the impossible view that Bhāsa's plays are compilations or adaptations of the eighth century, or later, holding that the *Cārudatta* is an adaptation of the *Mṛcchakaṭikā* (contrast p. 131), the *Pratimānāṭaka* is later than Kālidāsa, and the *Avimāraka* than Daṇḍin. The genealogy of Rāma in the *Pratimā* (iv. 9 f.) is that of Kālidāsa, but is also Purāṇic, and Daṇḍin, of course, is not the inventor of the Kathā. Barnett (*Bulletin*, III. i. 35) accepts Pisharoti's views, holding the *Nyāyaçāstra* of Medhātithi (*Pratimā*, v. 8/9) to be the *Manubhāṣya* (tenth century), but this is wholly against the context, and Barnett's view is surely incompatible with the priority of the *Cārudatta* to the *Mṛcchakaṭikā* which he admits, and the absence of Māhārāṣṭrī. Cf. also p. 341.

ENGLISH INDEX

Abhayadatta, in the *Mudrārākṣasa*, 206.
Abhayadeva, king (A. D. 1229–32), 254.
Abhayakumāra, minister of Çreṇika, 260.
Abhayapāla, king, 254.
Abhimanyu, son of Arjuna, 96, 97, 117, 213.
Abhinavagupta, writer on poetics, 103, 220, 291, 294, 318, 319, 320, 338, 342, 343, 344.
Abhirāma, commentator on the *Çakuntalā*, 154.
Ābhīras, a people, 129, 335, 337, n. 1.
Abrupt dialogue (*udghātya*), 328, 341.
Abrupt remark (*gaṇḍa*), 329.
Abuse, in ritual, as one source of drama, 24, 25.
Achievements of the Sanskrit drama, 276-88.
Active, for middle, and *vice versa*, in Bhāsa, 120.
Actors and Actresses, 360-4; number of, 66, 110, 345, 346, 347; opening dialogue of, 340; feelings aroused in, 316, 320, 321, 324, 355; see also *Granthikas*, *Çaubhikas*, *Çailūṣa*.
Acts, 60, 61, 301, 305, 345-51.
Address, conventional modes of, 314; as evidence of date of dramatic origin, 69–71.
Ādisūra, of Bengal, 212.
Ādityasena, of Magadha (A. D. 671), 212.
Adultery, as an allegorical character, 255.
Advaita form of Viṣṇu doctrine, 251, 252.
Aerial car, journeys in an, 190, 229, 233, 246, 255.
Agastya, a seer, dialogues of, in the *Ṛgveda*, 14.
Aghoraghaṇṭa, a priest, 188, 313, 328.
Agni, god of fire, dialogue of, with the gods, 21; saves Avimāraka, 101; saves Sītā, 105.
Agnimitra, a prince, hero of the *Mālavikāgnimitra*, 147–9, 165, 364.
Agnivarṇa, a prince, 364.
Agon, dramatic contest, essential to drama, 45.
Aihole inscription (A. D. 634), mentions Kālidāsa, 146.
Aischylos, 75, n. 2, 196, 197.
Ajayapāla, king (A. D. 1173–6), 258.
Ajitāpīḍa (A. D. 813–50), king of Kashmir, 291.
Ājīvika, in drama, 85.
Akālajalada, grandfather of Rājaçekhara, 231.
Akṣa, son of Rāvaṇa, 246.
Alakā, a city, 190, 194.
Alexander of Macedonia, his love of drama, 59.
Alexandria, as source of Greek influence on India, 60.
Alkestis, dramatic silence of, compared with that of Sītā, 110.
Allegorical drama, Buddhist, 83, 84; later, 251–6.
Allegorical personages, in Bhāsa, 112.
Alliteration, 238, 331; a characteristic of the Gauḍa style, 332.
Ammāl Ācārya, author of the *Vasantatilaka*, 263.
Aṇahilapāṭaka, 269, *and see* Aṇhilvāḍ.
Ānandarāya, author of the *Jīvānandana*, 253.
Ānandavardhana, writer on poetics, 212, 220, 294.
Anaṅgaharṣa Mātrarāja, author of *Tāpasavatsarājacarita*, 220.
Anaṅgamañjarī, a hetaera, 263.
Anaṅgaçekhara, a *Viṭa*, 264.
Anaṅgasenā, a hetaera, 361.
Anasūyā, friend of Çakuntalā, 153, 158.
Anayasindhu, an evil king, 261, 262.
Andhrabhṛtyas, dynasty, 129.
Andhraja, speech, 337, n. 1.
Andhras, a people, 335, 336; colour of, 366.
Aṅgada, envoy to Rāvaṇa, 119, 190, 247, 269.
Aṅgas, a people, colour of, 366.
Anger (*krodha*), as basis of sentiment, 323.
Aṇhilvāḍ, literary activity at court of, 243; *and see* Aṇahilapāṭaka.
Anticipatory scene (*aṅkamukha*), 302.
Antigone, of Sophokles, possibly known in India, 59, n. 2.
Antigone, a character impossible in Sanskrit drama, 278.
Apabhrança, 89, 122, 151, 175, 187, 336, n. 1, 350.
Apatouria, 38.

Apsarases, divine nymphs, 17, 40, 48, 96, 100, 112, 114, 265, 303, 339, n. 3, 352, 367.
Āraṇyakā or Āraṇyikā, heroine of the *Priyadarçikā*, 173, 174, 176, 362.
Arhants, views of, on the path of salvation, 183.
Ariṣṭa, a demon killed by Kṛṣṇa, 99, 106.
Arisiṁha, author of the *Sukṛtasaṁkīrtana*, 248, n. 7.
Aristotle, 39, 64, 279, n. 1, 287, 337, n. 2, 354, n. 1, 355.
Arjuna, a demon, 99.
Arjuna, a Pāṇḍava, 48, 96, 97, 213, 214, 215, 218, 265, 266, 268, 320, 329.
Arjunavarman, Paramāra of Dhārā (A.D. 1211), 256.
Arrian, notes Indian love for song and dance, 44, n. 2.
Ars Amoris, of Ovid, 285.
Arsenic, used for pigments, 369.
Art of Bhāsa, 105–10; *Mṛcchakaṭikā*, 134; Kālidāsa, 155–60; Harṣa, 175–7; Mahendravikramavarman, 182, 183; Bhavabhūti, 192–6; Viçākhadatta, 208, 209; Bhaṭṭa Nārāyan, 214, 215; Yaçovarman, 222, 223; Murāri, 229, 230; Rājaçekhara, 235, 236; Jayadeva, 246; Kṛṣṇamiçra, 253.
Arundhatī, in the *Uttararāmacarita*, 192.
Āryabhaṭa, astronomer (A.D. 499), 146.
Āryaka, in the *Mṛcchakaṭikā*, 64, 129, 130, 132, 133, 135.
Aryan, conquers Çūdra, in the Mahāvrata ritual, 24.
Açokadatta, and the Rākṣasas, 193, n. 2.
Açokan dialect, compared with that of Açvaghoṣa, 86, 87.
Açvaghoṣa, dramatist, 43, 58, 70, 72, 74, 77, 80–90, 93, 94, 95, 158, 161, 251, 292, 311, 336.
Açvajit and Çāriputra, 81.
Asajjāti, a comic Brahmin, 261.
Ascetics, how addressed, 314; appropriate to a Prahasana, 348.
Asides, 304.
Aspirates, reduced in Bhāsa, but not in Açvaghoṣa, to *h*, 121.
Astonishment (*vismaya*), as the basis of the sentiment of wonder, 323.
Astrologers, where placed in the auditorium, 370.
Asura Maya, magic craftsman, 52.
Asuras, demons, 41, 267.
Atharvan, dialogue of, 15.
Ātreya, the *Vidūṣaka* of Jīmūtavāhana, 177.
Ātreyī, an ascetic, 191.
Audience, 369–71, *and see* Spectators.
Auditorium, 359, 370.
Aulularia, form of name, 64.
Auçinarī, wife of Purūravas, 156.
Authenticity of Bhāsa's dramas (very ineffectively attacked in BSOS. III. i. 107 ff.), 91–3.
Avadhūta, *see* Kṛṣṇa.
Avalokitā, pupil of Kāmandakī, 193, 303, 362.
Avanibhājana, epithet of Mahendravikramavarman, 182.
Avantī, use of *Bhūtabhāṣā* in, 287.
Avantisundarī, wife of Rājaçekhara, 232, 288.
Avantivarman (A.D. 855–83) of Kashmir, patron of poets, 204, 220.
Āyogavas, actors ranked as, 363.
Āyus, son of Urvaçī, 62, 151, 156, 157.

Bābhravya, chamberlain of Vatsa, 171, 173.
Bāhlika, or Bālhika, a people, colour of, 366.
Bakchai, of Euripides, 59.
Baktria, Greek rule in, 57.
Baladeva, 48.
Bāla-Vālmiki, sobriquet of Murāri, 225.
Bali, binding of, performed in a dramatic manner, 32, 36, n. 1.
Ballet, 48, 275, 351.
Bāṇa, the Asura, 242, 243.
Bāṇa, writer (A.D. 625), 29, 76, 91, 171, 182, n. 3, 366.
Bāṇa, *see* Vāmana Bhaṭṭa Bāṇa.
Bandhurā, a go-between, 262.
Barbaras, speech of, 336; excluded from theatres, 370.
Barygaza, Bharukacchā, as port through which Greek influence came, 60.
Battles, in the drama, 347, 351.
Baudhāyana, censures actors, 363.
Bearer of fans, where placed in the auditorium, 370.
Benediction, see *Nāndī* and *Bharatavākya*.
Bengal, Sanskrit used in, 287.
Bengālī recension, of the *Vikramorvaçī*, 151; the *Çakuntalā*, 154, 155; the *Veṇīsaṁhāra*, 219.
Bernhardt, Sarah, 322, n. 2.
Bhādānakas, use of Apabhrança by, 287.
Bhadravatī, elephant, 108.
Bhāgurāyaṇa, in the *Mudrārākṣasa*, 205, 235.
Bhariavānanda, a magician, 234.
Bhāmaha, writer on poetics, 102.
Bhānudatta, views on sentiment, 319.
Bhānumatī, queen of Duryodhana, 213, 215, 219, 300.
Bharata, alleged author of the *Nāṭyaçāstra*, 12, 41, 150, 191, 343, 344, 349, 362, 364.
Bharata, brother of Rāma, 189, 224.

Bharata, son of Duḥṣanta, 154, 157.
Bhārata tribe, 30.
Bhāravi, poet, 265, 284.
Bharhut sculptures, dance represented on, 350, n. 2.
Bhartṛhari, poet, 366; celebrated in the *Bhartṛharinirveda*, 248.
Bhartṛmeṇṭha, 232.
Bhāsa, dramatist, 42, 51, 66, 70, 73, 74, 87, 91–126, 147, 161, 185, 187, n. 2, 243, 270, 286, 292; 300, 301, n. 4, 305, 311, 335, 336, 341, 342, 346, 347, 353, 354, 371, n. 2.
Bhāskaradatta, a Mahārāja, 204.
Bhāskara Kavi, author of the *Unmattarāghava*, 268.
Bhāṭ, reciters, 30.
Bhaṭṭa Gopāla, grandfather of Bhavabhūti, 186.
Bhaṭṭa Lollaṭa, doctrine of sentiment, 316.
Bhaṭṭa Nārāyaṇa, author of the *Veṇīsaṁhāra*, 83, 212–19.
Bhattanatha Svamin, on date of Murāri, 225.
Bhaṭṭa Nāyaka, writer on poetics, 291, 317, 318, 320, 321.
Bhavabhūti, dramatist, 42, 139, 161, 186–203, 209, 217, 225, 226, 227, 232, 239, 247, 257, 271, 281, 284, 297, 301, 311, 343, n. 1, 352, 353, 364.
Bhīma, a Pāṇḍava, 95, 96, 97, 109, 213, 214, 215, 216, 218, 266, 304, 329, 340.
Bhīmadeva II, the Cālukya, 256.
Bhīmaṭa, author of *Svapnadaçānana*, 239.
Bhīmeçvara, procession of the god, 248.
Bhīṣma, preceptor of the Kauravas, 97.
Bhoja (11th cent.), writer on poetics (JRAS. 1923, p. 545 ff.), 143, 325, n. 1, 331.
Bhujaṅgaçekhara, a *Viṭa*, 263, 264.
Bhūrivasu, a minister, 187.
Bhtūas, honoured in the preliminaries of the drama, 340.
Bhuvanapāla, minister of Saṁgrāmasiṅha, 249.
Bidyāpati Ṭhākur, Maithilī dramatist, 243.
Bilhaṇa, author of the *Karṇasundarī*, 256.
Bimbisāra, king of Magadha, 43.
Bloch, Th., on the Greek origin of the Indian theatre, 67.
Bourgeois Comedy, see *Prakaraṇa* and *Prakaraṇikā*.
Boy, suggested marriage to, as a motif, 234, 235, 256.
Bṛhannalā, a eunuch, 335.
Brahmā, as creator of the *Nāṭyaçāstra*, 12, 13, 41.
Brahmadeva, of Raypur, 270.
Brahmin and hetaera, dialogue of, 39, 73.
Brahminical supremacy, in Bhāsa, 110; in Kālidāsa, 160; in Bhavabhūti, 197; theory of life, 281.
Brahmin, 81, 276, 277, 281, 282, 283, 306; as the *Vidūṣaka*, 310, 311; address of, 314; as hero of the *Prakaraṇa*, 346; the *Çilpaka*, 351; seats for, 359; colour of, 366; where placed in the auditorium, 370.
Brajbhāshā, 41.
Breach of alliance (*saṁghātya*), 327.
Buddha, the, 81, 82, 87, 179; statues of the, 58; as a dramatic character, 306.
Buddharakṣitā, in the *Mālatīmādhava*, 198.
Buddhism, disapproved, 252, 253.
Buddhist monk, 135; nun, 193, 335.
Buddhists, and the drama, 42, 44, 174, 175, 284; addressed as Bhadanta, 314.

Cāhamāna, Vīsaladeva Vigraharāja, 248.
Caitanya, the saint, 247, 294.
Cakkyars, or Cākyārs, performance of plays by, 371, n. 1.
Cakora, Candraketu, prince of, 129.
Cakrasvāmin, festival of, 266.
Calm, as a character, 254; hero, 305, 306.
Calm (*çānta*), sentiment, 324, 332, 351.
Cambay, 248, 249.
Cāmuṇḍā, the goddess, 188, 234.
Cāṇakya, in the *Mudrārākṣasa*, 62, 205 ff., 341, 344.
Caṇḍabhārgava, curse of, 125.
Caṇḍālas, 99, 133, 336, n. 1, 337.
Caṇḍālī, 99.
Candanadāsa, in the *Mudrārākṣasa*, 205 ff.
Candanaka, Prākrit used by, 141.
Caṇḍapāla, a king, 234.
Candra, Candraka, or Candaka, dramatist, 168–70.
Candradāsa, an author, 168.
Candragupta, in the *Mudrārākṣasa*, 205 ff., 341.
Candragupta II, probable patron of Kālidāsa, 146.
Candraketu, prince of Cakora, 129.
Candraketu, rival of Lava, 191, 200.
Candraçekhara, commentator on the *Çakuntalā*, 154.
Candravarman, of Lāṭa, 234, 235.
Candrāvatī, 247, 265.
Cāṇūra, slain by Kṛṣṇa, 48, 100, 110.
Captivi, of Plautus, 64.
Cārāyaṇa, a Vidūṣaka, 235, 300.
Cārudatta, hero of the *Cārudatta*, 104, 116, 131, 132, 133, 134, 135, 136, 137–40, 306.
Cārvāka, atheist, philosopher, 214, 252.
Caryatides, possibly imitated in the Indian theatre, 355.
Caṣṭana, a Kṣatrapa, 69.

Caste system, denounced by Açvaghoṣa, 80.
Causative, and simple verbal forms, confused in Bhāsa, 120, 121.
Cave, mountain, similarity of theatre to, 358.
Cedi era, 129.
Cerebral sibilants, produce strength of style, 332.
Cerebralization of *n*, in Açvaghoṣa's Prākrits, 86, 87, 88, 121.
Cerebrals, other than *ṇ*, produce strength of style, 332.
Ceylon, king of, father of Ratnāvalī, 171.
Challenge (*utthāpaka*), 327.
Chamberlain (*kañcukin*), 313; appropriate to the *Prahasana*, 348.
Change of action (*parivartaka*), 327.
Character drawing, 282; in Bhāsa, 110; *Mṛcchakaṭikā*, 134, 135, 137; Kālidāsa, 155–9; Harṣa, 176, 177: Bhavabhūti, 193, 194; Viçākhadatta, 208, 209; Bhaṭṭa Nārāyaṇa, 215; Rājaçekhara, 235.
Characters in the drama, 305–14, 355.
Characteristics of the Sanskrit drama, 276–88.
Charcoal burners, speech of, 337.
Cheating (*chala*), 329; in the *Samavakāra*, 346.
Chess, 256.
Child, mode of address of, 314, n. 2.
Chinese stage, 360, note 2.
Cistellaria, form of name, 64.
Citramāya (Citramāyu), friend of Rāma, 223.
Citraratha, associated with Indra, 190, 194.
Clay elephants, children play with, 320.
Clearness, of style, 331, 332.
Coarseness of the *Prahasanas* and *Bhāṇas*, 264.
Cock-fights, 263, 285.
Colour of curtain, 359; dress of actors, 366; participators in dramatic performances, 35, 36, 37, 366; sentiments, 324; Indra's banner, 369; pillars of the auditorium, 359.
Combats, in the *Ḍima*, 347; the *Preñkhaṇa*, 351.
Comedy, Greek, origin of, 39, n. 2; influence of, on Sanskrit drama, 58–66.
Comedy, Sanskrit drama deficient in higher forms of, 280, 354, and see *Nāṭaka*, *Nāṭikā*, and *Prakaraṇa*.
Comic dialogue (*prapañca*), 328.
Comic (*hāsya*) sentiment, 323, 324, 347, 348, 351.
Compassion, as a character, 254.
Compensatory lengthening of a vowel, with reduction of consonant groups, in Bhāsa, 121.
Competitions for poets, 286.
Compound letters, produce strength of style, 332.
Compounds, 217, 274, 332, 333; irregular forms in Bhāsa, 121.
Conclusion (*nirvahaṇa*) as fifth juncture of the drama, 299.
Concubinage, as an allegorical character, 255.
Confiscation of property of persons dying without heirs, 253.
Conflict in character, un-known to Indian drama, 278, 279.
Confusion, as an allegorical character, 251, 252, 254, 255.
Conjunct consonants, produce strength of style, 332.
Conscience, struggle of, unknown in Sanskrit drama, 279.
Consequents (*anubhāva*), in dramatic theory, 315 ff.
Construction, immediate, of an object by artificial means (*saṁkṣipti*), 327.
Contemplation, as an allegorical character, 252.
Contentment, as an allegorical character, 252.
Contest, as essential element of the drama, 45, 278.
Continuance (*avalagita*), 328.
Continuation scene (*añkāvatāra*), 302.
Contractions, irregular, in Bhāsa's Sanskrit, 120.
Cora Indians, dramatic ritual of, 18, 19.
Corpse, revival of, as dramatic motif, 259.
Cosmopolitan character, ascribed to the *Mṛcchakaṭikā*, 139, 140.
Courteous, hero, 307.
Courtesans, *see* Hetaerae.
Courtiers, where placed in the auditorium, 370.
Courts, as patrons of the drama, 285, 362.
Crassus, Iason and the head of, 59.
Creation of object by magic (*vastūtthāpana*), 327.
Creeper, Urvaçī transformed into a, 150, 151, 156.
Critique of life, lacking in Sanskrit drama, 160, 195, 196, 197, 280, 281, 354.
Cult, as an allegorical character, 252.
Curse, as a dramatic motif, 125, 153, 157, 158.
Curtain of theatre, 61, 67, 68, 113, n. 1; colour of, 359 (cf. Elizabethan curtain, with colours varying as in India according to subject, GIL. iii. 177, n. 1).

Dadhittha, a monkey, 233.
Daityas, propitiated in the preliminaries of the drama, 339, n. 3.
Dakṣiṇāvartanātha, commentator on the *Meghadūta*, 145.
Dāmodara, 99, *and see* Kṛṣṇa.
Dāmodaragupta, author of the *Kuṭṭanīmata*, 171, 362, 368.
Dāmodaramiçra, redactor of the *Mahānāṭaka*, 270.
Dānavas, demons, 267, 339, *n.* 3, 366.
Dance, 12, 15, 16, 25, 26, 42, 44, 45, 50, 57, 58, 112, 160, 291, 296, 338, 350, 351.
Daṇḍin, author, 104, 129, 193, 221, 330, 363.
Dantivarman, dubious name of a king, 204.
Danturā, a go-between, 261.
Daçapura, use of *Bhūtabhāṣā* in, 287.
Daçaratha, a king, 100, 101, 189, 226, 228, 232, 245.
Daçārha festival, 42.
Date of Bhāsa's dramas, 93-5.
Dead, worship of, and drama, 46, 47.
Death on the stage, 105, 110, 140, 292, 354.
Deccan, colour of people of the, 366; dramatic performances in the, 363.
Deceitful hero, 307.
Decline of the drama, causes of, 242-4.
Demi-gods, as heroes of the *Ḍima*, 347
Demons, as heroes of the *Ḍima*, 347, *and see* Daityas, Dānavas, Rākṣasas.
Dénouement (*kārya*), as an element of the plot, 298; wonder appropriate in the, 325.
Desire, as a character, 251.
Determinants (*vibhāva*), in dramatic theory, 315 ff.
Deus ex machina, Gaurī as, 175, 176.
Devajī, father of Rāmakṛṣṇa, 274.
Devakī, mother of Kṛṣṇa, 40, 98.
Devanāgarī recension, of the *Çakuntalā*, 154, 155; the *Vikramorvaçī*, 151; the *Veṇīsaṁhāra*, 219.
Devapāla of Mālava, 249.
Devarāta, a minister, 187.
Devasomā, a damsel attached to a Çaiva mendicant, 182, 185.
Deva Sūri, Jain sage, 259, 260.
Development (*garbha*), third juncture of the drama, 299.
Development of affection (*narmagarbha*), 327.
Devil, in mediaeval mystery plays, 24, 39.
Devotion, as a sentiment, 325, n. 1.
Dhanadeva, father of Yaçaḥpāla, 254, 260.
Dhanaṁjaya, writer on poetics, 292, 321, 325, 328, 329, 340, 347.
Dhānaṁjaya, in a Buddhist drama, 84.
Dhaneçvara, father of Jyotiriçvara, 261.
Dhanika, writer on poetics, 220, 223, 271, 293, 350, 366.
Dhanika Paṇḍita, 293.
Dhārāvarṣa, prince of Candrāvatī, 247, 265.
Dhāriṇī, a queen, 148, 149, 155, 159, 163, 165.
Dhāvaka, misreading for Bhāsa, 171.
Dhīrasiṅha, father of Jyotiriçvara, 261.
Dhīreçvara, family, 261.
Dialogue (*saṁlāpa*), 327.
Dialogues of the Veda, alleged dramatic character of the, 13-23.
Digambara Jainism, 252.
Diggers of underground passages, speech of (cf. JRAS. 1923, p. 591), 88, 336.
Dignāga, alleged enemy of Kālidāsa, 145.
Dionysos, Greek god, 66.
Dionysos, Indian, i.e. Çiva, 42, n. 1.
Dionysos Melanaigis, 38.
Discrimination, as a character, 251, 252, 254, 255.
Disguise, of girl as boy, as motif, 234, 235.
Disguise, assumed on the stage, 303.
Disgust (*jugupsā*), as the basis of the sentiment of horror, 323.
Dithyramb, and drama, 39.
Division into acts, 60, 61.
Division of sentiment, not allowed in the drama, 278, 279.
Doors of the stage, number of, 360.
Double consonant, with short vowel, in place of single consonant and long vowel, 121.
Double entendre, 304.
Dṛḍhavarman, uncle of Vāsavadattā, 173, 174, 360.
Dhṛṣṭadyumna, slays Droṇa, 213.
Dhṛtarāṣṭra, a king, 96, 106, 117, 214, 216, 218.
Double letters, produce strength of style, 332.
Dramatic elements in Vedic ritual, 23-7.
Dramilas, speech of the, 337, n. 1, *and see* Draviḍas.
Draupadī, wife of the Pāṇḍavas, 63, 97, 212, 213, 214, 218, 233, 265, 266, 270.
Draviḍas, speech of, 336, 337; colour of, 366.
Dream, as motif, 303; truthful in early hours of morning, 234.
Dress of actors, 366.
Drinking, as an allegorical character, 255.
Droṇa, preceptor of the Kauravas, 97, 213.
Drop, or expansion (*bindu*), as an element of the plot, 298.

Duhika, variant of Durduka, 231.
Duḥçāsana, 212, 214, 216.
Duḥṣanta (Duṣyanta), a king, hero of the *Çakuntalā*, 152–5, 297, 341, 365.
Dumb actors, 53, 273.
Dundubhi, 228.
Durācāra, a pupil, 261.
Duration of acts of certain dramas, 346, 351.
Durduka, father of Rājaçekhara, 231.
Durgāpūjā, festival in Bengal, 262.
Durmukha, in the *Uttararāmacarita*, 190, 329.
Durvāsas, an ascetic, 153, 158, 268, 298.
Duryodhana, chief of the Kauravas, 38, n. 2, 96, 97, 106, 110, 111, 114, 212, 214, 215, 216, 218, 266, 278, 300, 304, 309, 329, 354.
Duty, as superior to private interest, in Kālidāsa, 153, 154.

Eclecticism of classical age of Sanskrit literature, 284.
Egoism, as a character, 252.
Ekbatana, Greek artistes at, 59.
Elements of the plot (*arthaprakṛti*), 298, 299.
Elephant, artificial, to contain men, 327; terrifies people in the street, 264.
Elephants, escape of, as dramatic motif, 193, 257.
Elision of consonants, not in Açvaghoṣa, 86; in Bhāsa, 121; with compensatory lengthening, 121.
Emotion (*bhāva*), 277, 278, 296, 316–26.
Energy (*utsāha*), as basis of heroic sentiment, 323.
Enigma (*nālikā*), 329.
Epics, and the drama, 27, 28–31, 42, 45, 47, 49, 58, 63, 75, 76, 281, 282, 297, original form of, 21–3.
Epidicus, of Plautus, 64.
Episode (*patākā*), 297, 298, 299.
Equivoke, as dramatic motif, 304.
Erotic (*çṛñgāra*), sentiment, 278, 323, 324, 346, 347, 349, 350, 351; metre and style appropriate to, 331, 332.
Eunuchs, 313; in the *Prahasana*, 348.
Euripides, 59, 196, 197, 279, n. 1, 282.
Exalted, hero, 305, 306.
Excitement, sentiment of, 265.
Exegesis, as an allegorical character, 252.
Expansion (*bindu*), as element of the plot, 298, 346.

Fainting, as a dramatic motif, 192, 224, 228.
Faith, as a character, 252; as a sentiment, 325, n. 1.
Faith in Viṣṇu, as a character, 253.
Falsity, as a character, 252.
Farce (*prahasana*), 182–5, 260–3, 280, 296, 309, 348.
Fate, 140, 277, 278.
Fear, sentiment of, 319, 324, 325.
Festivals, occasions of performance of dramas, 362.
Fifth manner, existence of, denied, 328, n. 1.
Fifth Veda, nature of the, 12, 13
Fighting (*sampheṭa*, 328.
Figures of speech, 116, 117, 211, 330, 331, 333, 334.
Fire, imaginary, as a dramatic motif, 103, 173.
Fleet, Dr. J. F., theory of origin of Cedi era, 129.
Flesh-eating, as an allegorical character, 255.
Flesh-offering, to the ghouls of the cemetery, 188.
Forest dwellers, speech of, 347.
Fortune of the City, as an allegorical character, 255.
French borrowings from the classics, 68.
Friendship, in Bhavabhūti, 195, 196; sentiment of, 325, n. 1.
Frog hymn (RV. vii. 103), 19.
Funeral games, and the origin of drama, 47.
Fury, sentiment of, 320, 323, 324, 347; metre and style appropriate to, 331, 332.

Gamblers (*dīvyant*), language of, 141, 336.
Gambler's hymn (RV. x. 24), 19.
Gambling, as an allegorical character, 255.
Gaṇadāsa, a dancing-master, 148.
Gandhāra, art of, relation to Greek art, 58.
Gāndhārī, wife of Dhṛtarāṣṭra, 214.
Gandharvas, 17, 23, 40, 100, 112, 339, n. 3; dress of, 366.
Gaṇeça, propitiated in the preliminaries of the drama, 369.
Gañgā, river-goddess, 190, 191, 192, 245.
Gañgādhara, author of the *Gañgadāsapratāpavilāsa*, 251.
Garland, *see Vīthī*.
Garland of Fame, an allegorical character, 254.
Garuḍa, 79, 100, 175, 179.
Gātrasevaka, in the *Pratijñāyaugandharāyaṇa*, 108.
Gauḍa, or Gauḍī, style, 202, 331, 335.
Gaurī, the goddess, 174, 175, 176, 278.
Gautama, the *Vidūṣaka* of Agnimitra, 148, 155.
Gay, hero, 305.

Gazelle, magic, in the Rāma legend, 221.
Gedrosians, knew Greek drama, 59.
Geldner, Prof. K., theory of dialogue hymns in Veda, 22, 23.
General (*senāpati*), exalted hero, 306, 312.
Gentleness, as an allegorical character, 254.
Germ (*bīja*), as an element of the plot, 298.
Gesture, 279, 338, n. 1, 364, 365, 367.
Ghanaçyāma, author of the *Ānandamañjarī*, 257.
Ghaṭikāçata, *see* Kṛṣṇa.
Ghaṭotkaca, son of Bhīma and Hiḍimbā, 95, 106, 109, 111, 213.
Gobaṁ°, a character, 85; Prākrit used by, 86, 87.
Godāvarī, river goddess, as a character, 245.
Gods, as heroes of the *Ḍima*, 347; in the *Samavakāra*, 346; dress of, 366; characteristics of, 260.
Goethe, views of, on Kālidāsa, 160, 280.
Goha, in the *Mṛcchakaṭikā*, 136.
Gokulanātha, author of the *Amṛtodaya*, 253, n. 3, 343.
Good Conduct, as an allegorical character, 254.
Gopāla, father of Āryaka, 129.
Gopāla, patron of Kṛṣṇamiçra, 251.
Gopīnātha Cakravartin, author of the *Kautukasarvasva*, 262.
Gopīs, cowherdesses, loved by Kṛṣṇa, 40, 274.
Gori Īsapa, a Mahomedan, 250.
Graceful (*kaiçikī*) manner, 326, 327, 346, 347, 349, 350.
Graces, of the heroine, 310.
Grammarians, evidence of, as to drama, 31–6.
Grammatical, peculiarities, in Sanskrit, 85, 86; in Prākrit, 86–9, 121, 122.
Grandeur, 195, 196.
Great Dionysia, plays produced at, 66.
Greece, absence in the main of female dramatists, 288.
Greek astrology, known to Kālidāsa, 146.
Greek drama, compared with Indian, 276, 277, 279, n. 2, 280, 281, 311; origin of, 37–39; stage for, 360.
Greek influence on the Sanskrit drama, 57–68, 355, 356.
Guards, present in the auditorium, 370.
Guha, a forest chief, 228.
Guha, son of Çiva, 170.
Guhasena, of Valabhī, 275.
Guhyakas, propitiated in the preliminaries, 339, n. 3.
Guildsmen, or rich merchants (*çreṣṭhin*), language of, 87, 141, 336.
Guṇabhara, epithet of Mahendravikramavarman, 182.
Guṇāḍhya, author of the *Bṛhatkathā*, 52, 102.
Guptas, dynasty, 60, 144, 281, 334; of Magadha, 212.

Hair, how worn on the stage, 366, 367.
Hāla, or Sātavāhana, 74, 76; refers to drama, 45, n. 1.
Hamartia, Aristotelian doctrine of, 279, n. 1.
Hammīra, a Mahomedan invader, 248, 249, 250.
Haṅsavatī, a queen of Duḥṣanta, 158, 160.
Hanumant, 63, 111, 113, 190, 227, 245, 246, 266, 269.
Happy ending, necessary in drama, 38, n. 2, 140, 278, 354.
Hara, the god, 240, 241.
Haradatta, on *Mahābhāṣya*, 34.
Harem life, effect on drama, 65, 280.
Haribrahmadeva, of Raypur, 270.
Hāricandra, a poet, 91.
Harihara, author of the *Bhartṛharinirveda*, 248.
Harihara, brother of Mādhava, 268.
Hariçcandra, tale of, 240.
Harisiṅha, of Simraon, 261.
Harlequin, origin of the character of the, 39.
Harṣa, dramatist, of Kanyakubja (A.D. 606–48), 42, 85, 103, 155, 170–81, 204, 239, 256, 278, 284, 303, 305, 311, 325, 355, n. 3, 368.
Harṣa, Candella, king of Jejākabhukti, 239.
Harshness, as an allegorical character, 255.
Hastigiri, lord of, 268.
Haughty, hero, 305, 306, 307, 347; enemy of the hero, 307, 308.
Hemacandra, Jain author, 225, 243, 254, 255, 258, 260, 273, 275.
Hemakūṭa, place of abode of Mārīca, 154.
Hemāṅgada, a Vidyādhara, 229.
Hemāṅgī, a heroine, 263.
Herakleidai, of Euripides, known in India, 59.
Heresy, as a character, 252.
Heretics, parodied in the *Prahasana*, 348; excluded from spectacles, 370.
Hero, in Sanskrit drama, 305–7, 323; should be on stage during each Act, 140, 301; appropriate to several types of drama, 345–51.
Heroic comedy, see *Nāṭaka* and *Nāṭikā*.
Heroic (*vīra*) sentiment, 320, 323, 346;

metre and style appropriate to, 331, 332.
Heroine, in New Comedy, 62; in Sanskrit drama, 308–10; in different types of play, 346–8, 350, 351.
Heroism, 165, 168, 177, 195, 211, 278.
Hertel, Prof. J., theory of the origin of the drama, 16–18.
Hetaera drama, Buddhist, 84, 85.
Hetaerae, 62, 133, 313, 334, 335, 346; form of names of, 313.
Hiḍimbā, wife of Bhīma, 95, 96, 106, 109, 213.
Hillebrandt, Prof. A., view of origin of drama, 25, 35, 36, n. 1, 39, 49, 50, 51, 52, 53.
Hindi, vernacular drama in, 243.
Hindu revival under the Guptas, 60.
Hippolytos, of Euripides, 279, n. 1.
Historical drama, 248–51.
Hiuen Tsang, 170, 284.
Hoernle, Dr. A. F. R., theory as to identity of Vikramāditya, 144.
Holi festival, 41.
Horrible, descriptions of the, 192, 223.
Horror, sentiment of, 319, 320, 324, 325; metre and style appropriate to, 331, 332.
Horse sacrifice, ritual abuse in, 25; of Agnimitra and Samudragupta, 149.
Hultzsch, Prof. E., on date of Murāri, 225, 259.
Human sacrifice, as motif, 259.
Humorous speech (*vyāhāra*), 329.
Humour, 136, 159, 160, 177, 192, 211.
Hūṇas, 144, 145, 168.
Hunters, speech of, 347.
Hunting, miseries of, 152, 160.
Huth, G., views on date of Kālidāsa, 145, n. 1; on order of his poems, 167.

Iason, actor, 59.
Idealism of Sanskrit drama, 276.
Illuminator (*dīpaka*), a figure of speech, 331.
Imitation, of Açvaghoṣa (*Buddhacarita*, xiii. 60), by Bhāsa, 118.
of Bhāsa, by Kālidāsa, 124–6; by Bhavabhūti, 187, n. 2; in the *Mṛcchakaṭikā*, 131, 140.
of Kālidāsa, by Harṣa, 175, 176; by Bhavabhūti, 193.
of the *Mṛcchakaṭikā* (wrongly questioned in JRAS., 1923, p. 592), by Viçākhadatta, 208.
Incident (*prakarī*), 297, 298, 299.
Incoherent talk (*asatpralāpa*), 329.
Indian philosophy, the product of the Brahmins, 276.
Individuality, of characterization, not aimed at in Sanskrit drama, 282, 353.
Indra, dialogues introducing, 14, 15, 19; monologue of drunken, 18, 19; referred to, 267, 303.
Indra's banner, origin of drama in festival of, 41, 369.
Indra III, Rāṣṭrakūṭa, 239.
Infinitive, form of, in Açvaghoṣa, 87.
Internal junctures, see *Antarasandhi*.
Interval of time, between Acts, 301.
Intoxication (*mada*), as a dramatic motif, 303.
Introduction (*āmukha*), 328.
Invention of the poet, when allowed, 277, 296, 297, 346, 348, 349.
Ionian, equivalent to Greek, and also used more widely, 61.
Irāvatī, a queen, in the *Mālavikāgnimitra*, 148, 149, 155, 157.
Irony, in Bhāsa, 119; in Bhavabhūti, 192, n. 1, 194.
Irregularities of Sanskrit, in Açvaghoṣa, 85, 86; in Bhāsa, 120, 121.
Īçvarasena, an Ābhīra prince, 129.
I-Tsing, 168, 171.

Jagadīçvara, author of the *Hāsyārṇava*, 261, 262.
Jagajjyotirmalla, *Haragaurīvivāha* by, 76, n. 2, 247, 248.
Jagannātha, writer on poetics, 325.
Jain Māhārāṣṭrī, 256.
Jaina allegorical drama, 253–6.
Jainism, 252, 253–6.
Jains, and drama, 45, 46, 253–6, 286.
Jāmbavant, a bear, 227, 228, 229.
Janaka, of Videha, 189, 190, 202, 223, 227, 228, 245, 271.
Jaṅgamas, criticism of the, 263.
Jantuketu, a doctor, 261.
Jarta, victory of, over Hūṇas, 168.
Jaṭāyu, a vulture, 100, 189, 194, 228, 229, 245.
Jātūkarṇī, mother of Bhavabhūti, 186.
Javan drama, 57.
Jayadeva, author of the *Gītagovinda*, 40, 272.
Jayadeva, author of the *Prasannarāghava*, 226, 242, 244–6, 271, 363.
Jayadratha, of Sindhu, 96, 213, 215.
Jayakeçin, the Karṇāta, 256.
Jayantasiṅha, son of Vastupāla, 248.
Jayaprabha Sūri, teacher of Rāmabhadra Muni, 259.
Jayasiṅha Sūri, author of the *Hammīramadamardana*, 248–50.
Jayatala, king of Mewār, 249.
Jayataladevī, wife of Vīradhavala, 250.
Jayāpīḍa (A.D. 779–813), of Kashmir, 171, 368.
Jester, see *Vidūṣaka*.
Jhāṁkīs, of Bombay and Mathurā, 33.

Jīmūtavāhana, hero of the *Nāgānanda*, 174, 175, 177, 179, 305, 306, 323, 326.
Jinamaṇḍana, author of the *Kumārapālaprabandha*, 256.
J vasiddhi, in the *Mudrārākṣasa*, 205, 207.
Jñānanidhi, teacher of Bhavabhūti, 186.
Jñānarāçi, a Bhāgavata, 263.
Jogīmārā cave, 54, 86, 89.
Jones, Sir William, 160.
Judgement, as a character, 251, 252.
Juncture (*sandhi*), 298-300, 346-51.
Jyotirīçvara Kaviçekhara, author of the *Dhūrtasamāgama*, 261.

Kabandha, headless demon, 228.
Kādī, or Kadī, Mīlacchrikāra's preceptor, 250.
Kaikeyī, wife of Daçaratha, 100, 101, 189, 227, 228.
Kaiyaṭa, on the *Mahābhāṣya* 33.
Kalacuris, a royal house, 226, 232.
Kalahaṅsa, in the *Mālatīmādhava*, 193, 313.
Kalakaṇṭha, friend of Māruta, 257.
Kālapriya, probably Mahākāla, the deity of Ujjayinī, 186.
Kalhaṇa, historian, 129, 168, 220.
Kālidāsa, dramatist, 42, 58, 65, 76, 91, 93, 115, 120, 124-6, 127, 129, 139, 143-67, 196, 197, 239, 243, 256, 275, 280, 281, 284, 291, 292, 297, 309, 311, 334, 343, n. 1, 352, 353, 355, n. 3, 364.
Kaliṅga, king, enemy of Vatsa, 173, 174.
Kaliṅgas, colour of, 366.
Kaliñjarapati, Bhīmaṭa described as, 239.
Kaliph of Baghdad, 250.
Kalivatsala, a licentious king, 262.
Kāliya, a demon foe of Kṛṣṇa, 99, 106.
Kāma, worship of, 172.
Kāmandakī, in the *Mālatīmādhava*, 187, 188, 193, 302, 361, 362.
Kanakalatā, a heroine, 264.
Kanakalekhā, a princess saved by Mantragupta, 193, n. 2.
Kanarese words, found in a Greek comedy, 60, n. 2.
Kāñcana Paṇḍita, author of the *Dhanaṁjayavijaya*, 266.
Kāñcī, described in the *Mattavilāsa*, 183.
Kaniṣka, king, 58, 70, 72.
Kaṅsa, uncle of Kṛṣṇa, 32, 33, 34, 35, 36, 37, 38, 40, 45, 48, 73, 98, 99, 116.
Kaṇva, foster-father of Çakuntalā, 152, 153, 302, 303, 325.
Kapālakuṇḍalā, a sorceress, 188.
Kāpālika, in the *Mitrānanda*, 259; endeavours to sacrifice *Madanamañjarī*, 193, n. 2.
Kāpālikas, 313.
Kapālin, in the *Mattavilāsa*, 182, 184.
Kapittha, a monkey, 233.
Karṇa, ally of the Kauravas, 96, 106, 115, 213, 214, 215.
Karṇa, king of Cedi, 251.
Karṇadeva Trailokyamalla, of Aṇhilvāḍ, 256.
Karṇapūraka, slave of Vasantasenā, 141.
Karṇasundarī, a princess, 256.
Karṇīsuta, text-book by, on gambling, 134.
Karpaṭa, an authority on thieves' practice, 182.
Karpūramañjarī, a princess, 234, 235.
Kārtyāyanī, a deity, 99.
Kāçi, colour of people of, 366.
Kāçīpati Kavirāja, author of the *Mukundānanda*, 264.
Kāçmīrī, recension of the *Çakuntalā*, 154.
Kashmir, dramatic exhibitions in, 371; pronunciation of Sanskrit in, 287; Hūṇas in, 144.
Kāṭayavema, commentator on Kālidāsa, 151, 154.
Kātyāyana, the grammarian, 31.
Kaumudī, heroine of the *Kaumudīmitrānanda*, 258, 259.
Kauṇḍinya, in the *Çāriputraprakaraṇa*, 82.
Kauravas, 265, 302.
Kauçalyā, mother of Rāma, 191, 195.
Kauçāmbī, scene of the *Ratnāvalī*, 171.
Kauçikī, in the *Mālavikāgnimitra*, 148, 155, 156, 162, 165, 308.
Kavikarṇapūra, author of the *Caitanyacandrodaya*, 84, 85, 353.
Kaviputra, or Kaviputrau, dramatists, 91, 127, 128, 147.
Kavirāja, an ancestor of Rājaçekhara, 231.
Kāvya, Sanskrit, 71, 75, 76; style, 115, 283, 284.
Keepers of drink shops, speech of, 88, 336.
Keçava, 48.
Keçin, a demon foe of Kṛṣṇa, 99.
Keyūravarṣa, Yuvarāja, of Tripurī, 232.
Khāravela of Kaliṅga, 89.
Kharpara Khāna, a Mahomedan, 250.
Khasas, a people, speech of, 337.
Kīcaka, death of, 63, 97.
Killing of animals forbidden by Kumārapāla, 253.
Kings, as patrons of literature, 286; of actors, 362; as heroes of the drama, 345, 347, 350, 366.
Kirātas, 312; colour of, 366; speech of, 336.
Kīrtivarman, king of Jejākabhukti, 251.
Kolāhalapura, city of uproar, 263.
Komudagandha, a *Vidūṣaka*, 84.

Konow, Professor Sten, theory of origin of drama, 25, 49, 54; various views of, 66, 81, 92, 94, 95, 129, 130, 141, 204, 225.
Kordax, 42, n. 1.
Korybantes, 20.
Kosala, king, enemy of Vatsa, 172, 177, 178.
Kosalas, a people, colour of, 366.
Koṭiliñga, Yuvarāja of, 264.
Kouretes, 20.
Kṛpa, ally of the Kauravas, 213, 214.
Kṛpāsundarī, a princess, 254, 255.
Kṛçāçvins, followers of Kṛçāçva, 31.
Kṛṣṇa, 17, 26, 32, 35, 36, 37, 38, 40, 41, 42, 45, 48, 49, 50, 73, 83, 97, 98–100, 106, 107, 110, 130, 213, 215, 247, 257, 264, 266, 267, 270, 272, 274, *and see* Vāsudeva *and* Viṣṇu.
Kṛṣṇa Avadhūta Ghaṭikāçata Mahākavi, author of the *Sarvavinodanāṭaka*, 267.
Kṛṣṇa Kavi, author of the *Çarmiṣṭhāyayāti*, 268.
Kṛṣṇamachari, R., author of the *Vāsantikasvapna*, 251.
Kṛṣṇamiçra, author of the *Prabodhacandrodaya*, 84, 85, 112, 251–3, 353.
Kṛṣṇamiçra, author of the *Vīravijaya*, 267.
Kṛṣṇa Sūri, father of Mahādeva, 246.
Krakucchanda, a Buddha, 43.
Kṣatriya, 66, 81, 276; colour of, 366; seats for, 359.
Kṣemendra, of Kashmir, 236, 240, 247, 371.
Kṣemīçvara, or Kṣemendra, dramatist, 239–41.
Kulaçekharavarman, author of the *Tapatīsaṁvaraṇa* and *Subhadrādhanaṁjaya*, 247, 371, n. 2.
Kumāra, the god, 267; grove of, 150.
Kumāradāsa of Ceylon, alleged connexion with Kālidāsa, 143.
Kumāragiri, king of Koṇḍavīḍu, 151.
Kumārapāla, Caulukya, king of Gujarāt, 253, 254, 258.
Kumāravihāra, at Thārāpadra, 254.
Kumārila, alleged to be a teacher of Bhavabhūti, 186.
Kumbhakarṇa, son of Rāvaṇa, 228, 233, 246.
Kumbhīlaka, servant of Vasantasenā, 141.
Kumudacandra, a Digambara teacher, 260.
Kumudikā, a hetaera, 133.
Kuntibhoja, a king, 101, 109.
Kurañgī, a princess, 101, 109.
Kurus, 96, 97, 106.
Kuça, son of Rāma, 30, 31, 191, 192.
Kuçalaka, a spy, 249.
Kuṣana, Kuṣāṇa, dynasty, 59.
Kuvalayā, an actress, 43.
Kuvalayamālā, princess of Kuntala, 234, 235.

Ladies, of the harem, where placed in the auditorium, 370; *see also* Heroines *and* Hetaerae.
Lagidai, rule of, in Alexandria, 60.
Lakṣmaṇa, brother of Rāma, 42, 100, 105, 115, 119, 189, 190, 223, 226, 227, 228, 229, 245, 246, 269, 271, 303.
Lakṣmaṇa Māṇikyadeva, patron of, author of the *Kautukaratnākara*, 263.
Lakṣmaṇa Sūri, author of the *Dillīsāmrājya*, 251.
Lakṣmī, the goddess, 268, 274.
Lakṣmīpati, a prince, 258, 259.
Laments, of women, permitted in the *Añka*, 348.
Language, of Açvaghoṣa, 85–9; Bhāsa, 120–2; *Mṛcchakaṭikā*, 140–2; Kālidāsa, 166; Harṣa, 181; Mahendravikramavarman, 185; Bhavabhūti, 203; Viçākhadatta, 211, 212; Bhaṭṭa Nārāyaṇa, 219; Rājaçekhara, 236.
Lañkā, mythical home of Rāvaṇa, not Ceylon, 190, 194.
Lāṭa, use of Prākrit in, 287.
Lava, son of Rāma, 31, 191, 192, 194, 195, 223, 224.
Lāvaṇyasiṅha, son of Tejaḥpāla, 249.
Legendary origin of the dramatic art, 12, 13; of the theory of drama, 290.
Legends, altered in the drama, 297, 346, 348.
Letter, as a dramatic motif, 63, 303.
Lévi, Prof. S., *Théâtre indien* of, 5; theory of origin of the drama, 15; views on the origin of the *Vidūṣaka*, 66; the Çakas and the drama, 69–72; other references to, 128, 208.
Life, lack of criticism on, 160, 195, 196, 197, 280, 281, 354.
Light-hearted, hero, 305.
Lion throne, royal box, 370.
Literary antecedents of, and influences on, the Sanskrit drama, 75–7.
Literary drama, 56, 273.
Lokanātha Bhaṭṭa, author of the *Kṛṣṇābhyudaya*, 268.
Lopāmudrā, legend of, 14, 19.
Loss of memory, as a dramatic motif, 153, 297.
Love, as a character, 151.
Love, as a dramatic motif, 278, 285, 286, 310; as basis of sentiment, 323, 324; in Bhāsa, 107; *Mṛcchakaṭikā*, 130, 138; Kālidāsa, 159; Candaka, 169; Harṣa, 180; Bhavabhūti, 196, 198, 199; Bhaṭṭa Nārāyaṇa, 219; Rājaçekhara, 238.

Lovers, kinds of men, and women, 307–9.
Low moral character of actors, 55, 363.
Loyal, hero, 307.
Lüders, Prof. Heinrich, theory of origin of the drama, 33, 34, 35, 53, 272, n. 1.
Lyric choruses, Aristotle's view as to, 337, n. 2.
Lyric stanzas, in the drama, 279, 281, 282, *and see* Verse.

Madana Bālasarasvatī, author of the *Pārijātamañjarī*, 256.
Madanamālā, a hetaera, 134.
Madanamañjarī, and a Kāpālika, 193, n. 2; a hetaera, 261.
Madanavatī, a female character, 260.
Madanikā, in the *Mṛcchakaṭikā*, 135.
Madayantikā, in the *Mālatīmādhava*, 188, 193.
Mādhava, author of the *Subhadrāharaṇa*, 268, 342, 357.
Mādhava, hero of the *Mālatīmādhava*, 62, 139, 187 ff., 306, 308.
Mādhavasena, a prince, 147.
Madhuka, a seer, 99.
Madhusūdana, redactor of the *Mahānāṭaka*, 270, 271, n. 1, 272.
Madhyama, in the *Madhyamavyāyoga*, 96.
Madness, of Purūravas, as a dramatic motif, 150.
Magadhavatī, a hetaera, 84.
Māgha, poet (date, Jacobi, SBAW., 1923, p. 214), 284.
Magic, 111, 234.
Magic arts, in the *Ratnāvalī*, 172, 173; in the *Priyadarçikā*, 174; in the *Nāgānanda*, 175.
Magic gazelle, in the Rāma legend, 221.
Magic ring, conferring invisibility, 101, 112.
Magicians, tricks of, 112, 172, 173, 176, 234.
Mahādeva, author of the *Adbhutadarpaṇa*, 246, 247.
Mahādeva, father of Jayadeva, 244.
Mahākāla, deity of Ujjayinī, 186.
Mahākavi, ancestor of Bhavabhūti, 186.
Mahānindaka, a holy man, 262.
Mahārāja Bhāskaradatta, father of Viçākhadatta, 204.
Mahārāṇa Meru, of Raypur, 270.
Māhārāṣṭrī lyric, 146.
Mahāsena, Pradyota, 102, 130.
Mahāvīra, speech of, 87; idol of, 254.
Mahāvrata rite, relation of, to drama, 21, 24, 26, 37, 39, 45, 51, 73, 112.
Mahāyāna school, 80; Greek influence on the, 58.
Mahāyātrika, a comic astrologer, 262.
Mahendrapāla, of Mahodaya, 232.
Mahendravikramavarman, an author, 93, 182–5.
Maheçvara, father of Çaṅkaralāla, 270.
Mahiman Bhaṭṭa, writer on poetics, 294, 322.
Mahīpāla, of Mahodaya, 232.
Māhiṣas, colour of, 366.
Māhiṣmatī, capital of the Kalacuris, 226.
Mahomedan influence on decadence of Hindu drama, 242, 371.
Maitreya, a character in the *Kaumudīmitrāṇanda*, 259.
Maitreya, Cārudatta's *Vidūṣaka*, 139.
Makaranda, in the *Mālatīmādhava*, 188, 193, 308, 338.
Makaranda, friend of Mitrāṇanda, 259.
Mālatī, in the *Mālatīmādhava*, 187 ff., 308.
Mālava era, 144.
Mālavikā, heroine of the *Mālavikāgnimitra*, 62, 63, 148, 149, 158, n. 1, 159, 165, 309.
Malayaketu, in the *Mudrārākṣasa*, 205 f.
Malayavatī, heroine of the *Nāgānanda*, 174, 306.
Mallikā, heroine of the *Mallikāmāruta*, 257, 258.
Mallinātha, commentator on Kālidāsa, 145.
Mālyavant, minister of Rāvaṇa, 189, 190, 194, 227, 228, 229, 233, 246.
Mammaṭa, writer on poetics, 171, 295, 323, 324.
Man about town, 285.
Man of taste, 318, 368, 370.
Mandākinī, a magician, 257, 258.
Maṇḍaleçvara Bhaṭṭa, father of Mādhava, 268.
Mandara, Mount, 98.
Mandārikā, a friend of a *Viṭa*, 264.
Mandārikā, a servant, 313.
Mandasor Praçasti (A.D. 473), imitates Kālidāsa, 146.
Mandodarī, wife of Rāvaṇa, 190, 246.
Maṇicūḍa, legend of, 168.
Manifestation of affection (*narmasphoṭa*), 327.
Maṇika, author of the *Bhairavānanda*, 248.
Maṅkha, poet, 75, n. 3, 225, 259.
Manners or styles (*vṛttis*), 12, 331, 332; in relation to types of dramas, 346–51.
Manoramā, an attendant in the *Priyadarçikā*, 174, 362.
Manovatī, acts part of Rambhā, 49.
Mantharā, a slave woman, 189, 227, 228.
Mantragupta, and Kanakalekhā, 193, n. 2.
Manu, censures actors, 363.
Māra, enemy of the Buddha, 180, 284.
Mārīca, in the *Çakuntalā*, 126, 154, 158; in the Rāma legend, 271.

Mārkaṇḍeya, Prākrit grammarian, 336.
Marriage, celebrated by painting scene of it, 102, 203.
Māruta, hero of the *Mallikāmāruta*, 257, 258.
Maruts and Indra, dialogue of, 14, 19, 20.
Mārwār, use of Apabhrança in, 287.
Masks, possible use of, 365, n. 1.
Mātali, charioteer of Indra, 154, 157, 160, 303, 325.
Matañga, enemy of Jīmūtavāhana, 178.
Māthura, in the *Mṛcchakaṭikā*, 135.
Mathurā, as home of drama, 41, 70, 74.
Mathurādāsa, author of the *Vṛṣabhānujā*, 257.
Mātṛgupta, a poet, 291, n. 2, 232, 315, n. 1, 360.
Mātrarāja, *see* Anañgaharṣa.
Matrona, of Greco-Roman drama, 65.
Mattavilāsa, epithet of Mahendravikramavarman, 182.
Matters unfit for stage representation, 300, 301.
Maudgalyāyana, a disciple of the Buddha, 81, 84.
Maukhari king, Avantivarman, 204.
Max Müller, theory of origin of the drama, 15.
May-day merriment, in England, 41.
Māyurāja, author of *Udāttarāghava*, 221, 223, 297.
Māyūrāja, variant of Māyurāja, 221, n. 1.
Megasthenes, refers to the Kordax, 42, n. 1.
Meghanāda, son of Rāvaṇa, 190, 229, 246.
Meghaprabhācārya, dramatist, 55, 269.
Mekhalā, a maidservant. 235.
Melanthos, legend of, 37, 38.
Men, play women's parts, 36, 362.
Menakā, mother of Çakuntalā, 152.
Menander, comedy of, 60.
Menander, king, conquests of, 59, 60.
Mercenary soldiers, reflected in figure of *Çakāra*, 66.
Merchants, or guildsmen, speech of, 87, 141, 336; form of names, 313; as heroes of the *Prakaraṇa*, 346; the *Prakaraṇikā*, 348.
Meru, Mahārāṇa of Raypur, 270.
Message, as dramatic device, 303.
Messenger, of hero, 311, 312; of heroine, 313.
Metre, influence of lyrics on, 77; of Açvaghoṣa, 89, 90; Bhāsa, 123, 124; *Mṛcchakaṭikā*, 142; Kālidāsa, 167, 168; Harṣa, 181; Mahendravikramavarman, 185; Bhavabhūti, 203; Viçākhadatta, 212; Bhaṭṭa Nārāyaṇ, 219; Rājaçekhara, 234, 236, 238; Kṣemīçvara, 240; Jayadeva, 246; Kṛṣṇamiçra, 253; Uddaṇḍin, 258; use of, in accord with sentiments, 331; in the *Samavakāra*, 346.
Mewār, defeat of Jayatala of, by the Mahomedans, 249, 250.
Middle, for active, in Bhāsa, 120.
Midsummer Night's Dream, Sanskrit version of, 251.
Mīlacchrīkāra, a Mahomedan, 250.
Mildness (*mṛdava*), 329.
Miles gloriosus, of Greco-Roman drama, 65; Rāvaṇa as a, 105.
Military spectacle, see *Vyāyoga*.
Mīmāṅsā view of sentiment, 316.
Mime, Greek, alleged influence of, on Indian drama, 67, 68.
Mimes, in India, 49, 57.
Mimesis, Aristotelian doctrine of, 355.
Mimetic art, 12, 296.
Mind, movements of, as related to the sentiments, 320.
Minister, appropriate hero for a *Prakaraṇa*, 306, 346; how addressed, 314; where placed in the auditorium, 370.
Mirror of knowledge, an allegorical character, 254.
Mirth (*hāsa*), as the basis of the comic sentiment, 323.
Mise-en-scène, 364–9.
Mitrāṇanda, hero of the *Kaumudīmitrāṇanda*, 258, 259.
Mitrāvasu, prince of the Siddhas, 174, 175, 178.
Miyāṇalladevī, a princess, 256.
Mlecchas, 249, 312.
Mohanadāsa, commentator on the *Mahānāṭaka*, 270.
Mōkos, compared with *Vidūṣaka*, 67.
Mokṣāditya, author of the *Bhīmavikramavyāyoga*, 266.
Monkey, escape of, as a dramatic motif, 175.
Monmohan Chakravarti, on date of Kālidāsa, 144.
Monologue, see *Bhāṇa*.
Moon of Discrimination, an allegorical character, 254.
Mṛgāñkalekhā, a hetaera, 262.
Mṛgāñkāvalī, a princess, 234, 235.
Mṛgarājalakṣman, 212.
Mudgala hymn (RV. x. 102), 18.
Muhammad II, of Gujarāt, 251.
Muktāpīḍa Lalitāditya, of Kashmir, defeats Yaçovarman of Kanyakubja, 186.
Mūlanāçaka, a barber, 261.
Munisuvrata, temple of, 248.
Muñja (A.D. 974–95), a king, of Dhārā, 292, 293.
Muralā, a river, 191.
Murāri, author of the *Anargharāghava*, 225–31, 242, 244, 259, 271, 352.

Mureçvara, a Çaiva ascetic, 262, 263.
Muṣṭika, slain by Kṛṣṇa, 100, 110.
Music, 16, 25, 44, 49, 50, 291, 292, 339, 350, 351, 352.
Mystery of things, in Bhavabhūti, 195.

Nāgas, pair of kings, 43; destroyed by Garuḍa, 174, 175, 179.
Nāgīs, how shown on the stage, 367.
Nahapāna, a Western Kṣatrapa, 69.
Naiyāyika view of sentiment, 316.
Nakhakuṭṭa, a theorist, 341.
Nakula, a Pāṇḍava, 214.
Nala and Damayantī, 63, 240.
Nalakūbara, 49.
Nallā Kavi, author of the *Çṛñgārasarvasva*, 263, 264.
Names of the Acts of a drama, 305; the drama, 345, 346; the characters, 85, 313, 355.
Nanda, the cowherd, 98.
Nandana, in the *Mālatīmādhava*, 188, 193.
Nandas, a dynasty, 205.
Nandikeçvara, *Abhinayadarpaṇa* by, 338, 367, n. 1.
Nārada, a sage, 48, 98, 100, 101, 110, 126, 151.
Narasiṅha, of Vijayanagara, 261.
Narasiṅha II, of Orissa, 293.
Narasiṅha, author of the *Çivanārāyaṇabhañjamahodaya*, 257.
Nārāyaṇa, father of Kāñcana Paṇḍita, 266.
Nārāyaṇa, 97, 98, *and see* Kṛṣṇa *and* Viṣṇu.
Narendravardhana, father of Anañgaharṣa Mātrarāja, 220.
Narration, in lieu of action dialogue, 194.
Narrative verses, 270, 271, 273, 351.
Nature, described in the drama, *Mṛcchakaṭikā*, 138, 139; Kālidāsa, 159; Bhavabhūti, 195.
Navamālikā, in the *Nāgānanda*, 177.
Nema Bhārgava, a seer, 14.
Neuter plural of *a*-nouns, in Açvaghoṣa's and Bhāsa's Prākrit, 87, 122.
Neuter rôles, 313.
New Comedy, alleged influence on Indian drama, 60–7.
Nicula, alleged friend of Kālidāsa, 145.
Nīlakaṇṭha, alters the last scene of the *Mṛcchakaṭikā*, 135, 369, n. 2.
Nīlakaṇṭha, on the shadow play, 55, 56.
Nipuṇaka, in the *Mudrārākṣasa*, 205, 208; in the *Hammīramadamardana*, 249.
Nipuṇikā, 328.
Nirbhaya, or Nirbhara, pupil of Rājaçekhara, 232.
Noble, hero as always, 305.
Nominative singular, of *a*-stems, in *e* and *o*, in Açvaghoṣa, 86, 87, 88; in Bhaṭṭa Nārāyaṇa, 219.
Northern Thrace, dramatic performance in, 38.
Number, of Acts in a drama, 305, 345–51; actors, 66, 87, 110, 345, 346, 347, 351.

Officers, of the Court, 312; where placed in the auditorium, 370.
Officials, high, as exalted heroes, 306.
Oldenberg, Prof. H, theory of *Ākhyāna*, 21–3.
Omission of consonants in Prākrit, 86, 87, 88, 121.
Opening (*mukha*), as a juncture, 298, 299.
Opera, *Haragaurīvivāha*, 76, n. 2.
Ornaments, worn by the actors, 367.
Orodes of Parthia, Greek drama at Court of, 59.
Outburst of affection (*narmasphañja*), 327.
Outvying (*ati-*, or *adhi-bala*), 329.
Oxus, Hūṇas on the, 144.

Padmacandra, father of Yaçaçcandra, 260.
Padmagupta, cited by Dhanika, 293.
Padmāvatī, a heroine, 103, 107, 113, 125, 220.
Padmāvatī, place, 186.
Pahlavas, colour of, 366.
Painting, of actors' faces, 37, 366.
Pālaka, king of Ujjayinī, 129, 133.
Palatal sibilants, produce strength of style, 332.
Pāli, 87, 89.
Pañcāla, music of speech of, 287.
Pāñcāla style, 332, 335.
Pāñcālas, colour of, 366
Pāṇḍavas, 95, 96, 97, 266, 270.
Panegyrists, where placed in the auditorium, 370.
Pāṇini, the drama in, 31; his position in grammatical literature, 290.
Paṇis and Saramā, dialogue of, 14, 19, 21.
Pantomime, 58, 258, 275, 351, and see *Naṭa*.
Pāpācāra, a bad king, 263.
Paramardideva, of Kālañjara, 265.
Paraçurāma, 96, 189, 194, 228, 233, 245, 271, 302, 319, 323, 327.
Parasite, in Greco-Roman drama, 65; in Indian drama, see *Viṭa*.
Pariyātra, use of *Bhūtabhāṣā* in, 287.
Paronomasia, 238.
Pārçva, a Tīrthakara, 254.
Parthians, invaders of India, 60, *and see* Pahlava.
Partnership, of actor and singer, 363.
Parvateça, a king, 205 f.

Pārvatī, the goddess, 300, 338, 352; and the *Lāsya* dance, 12.
Paçumeḍhra, a student, 227.
Pāçupata, a monk in the *Mattavilāsa*, 184.
Pāçupatas, a Çaiva sect, 42.
Patañjali (B.C. 150), the grammarian, 32–5, 52, 71, 72, 77, 98.
Pathak, Prof. K. B., on date of Kālidāsa, 144.
Pathos, in *Mṛcchakaṭika*, 136; in Kālidāsa, 159, 161; in Bhavabhūti, 193, 195; as a sentiment, 319, 323, 324, 325, 348; metre and style appropriate to, 331. 332.
Patience, as an allegorical character, 252.
Pause (*vimarça*), the fourth juncture of the drama, 299.
Persians, alleged to have knowledge of Greek tragedy, 59.
Phallic dances, as sources of drama, 16.
Phallic deities, 16, 21.
Phallic orgies, 41.
Philostratos, life of Apollonios of Tyana, 59.
Physicians, where placed in the auditorium, 370.
Picture, as dramatic motive, *see* Portrait.
Piety, as an allegorical figure, 252.
Pigments, mingling of, 369.
Pillars, as marking off places in the auditorium, 359.
Piçācas, demons, hair of, 366.
Pischel, Prof. Richard, theory of *Itihāsa*, 21; suggestion as to origin of the drama in the puppet play, 52–6; on the authorship of the *Mṛcchakaṭikā*, 128; on Bhāsa and the *Sthāpaka*, 342.
Pity, as a character, 252.
Plautus, 64.
Play within a play, 303; in the *Priyadarçikā*, 173; the *Uttararāmacarita*, 191, 192; the *Bālarāmāyaṇa*, 233.
Pleasantry (*narman*), as part of the graceful manner, 326.
Pleasure, as connected with the primitive drama, 50; as a characteristic of the classical period of the Sanskrit drama, 284; supernatural character of aesthetic, 318, 319, 320, 321.
Plot, 277, 296–305, 355.
Plutarch, on drama in Parthia, 59.
Poetics, 169 and Part III.
Poets, when placed in the auditorium, 370.
Police officials (*nāgaraka*), speech of, 141, 336.
Polity, as an allegorical character, 254.
Portraits, as dramatic device, 154, 174, 257, 303, 326.
Poverty, evils of, 137.
Pṛthu, father of Viçākhadatta, 204.
Pṛthvīdhara, on Prākrits of the *Mṛcchakaṭikā*, 141.
Practice of drama, influenced by theory, 352–4.
Pradyota Mahāsena, 102, 130.
Pradyumna, 48, 49.
Prahasta, ally of Rāvaṇa, 246.
Prahlādanadeva, author of the *Pārthaparākrama*, 83, n. 1, 247, 264, 265, 341, n. 1.
Prākrits, 40, 46, 50, 58, 243, 273, 275, 287, 301, 302, 311, 333, 336–8; evidence of, as to origin of drama, 72–5; of Açvaghoṣa, 86–9; Bhāsa, 121, 122, *Mṛcchakaṭikā*, 140–2; Kālidāsa, 161, 166; Harṣa, 181; Mahendravikramavarman, 185; Bhavabhūti, 203; Viçākhadatta, 211, 212; Bhaṭṭa Nārāyaṇa, 219; Rājaçekhara, 236; Kṣemīçvara, 240; Yaçaḥpāla, 256.
Prākrit drama, 65, 66, 69–72, 236, 257; translation of Prākrit passages into Sanskrit, 337.
Prākrit Kāvya, later than Sanskrit Kāvya, 71, 77.
Prākrit stanzas, 253.
Pralamba, a demon, 48, 99.
Pramodaka, in the *Mudrārākṣasa*, 206.
Pratāparudra, of Warangal, 293.
Pratiṣṭhāna, 129.
Preliminaries, of the drama, 51, 66, 111, 339–44, 368, 369.
Previous birth, influence on ability to write poems, 288.
Privation, as an aspect of love, 323.
Priyadarçikā, a heroine, 173, 174.
Priyaṁvadā, friend of Çakuntalā, 153, 159.
Problems of life, ignored in Sanskrit drama, 160, 195, 196, 197, 280, 281, 354.
Progression (*pratimukha*), as the second juncture, 298, 299.
Prologue, 66, 111, 114, 239, 339–44, 369.
Pronominal forms, in Açvaghoṣa's and Bhāsa's Prākrits, 87, 122.
Propitiation (*prarocanā*), 328.
Prose, 23, 50, 51, 58, 73, 76, 202, 337; narrative style, 273; simple in the *Nāṭaka*, 345.
Protagonist, compared to *Sūtradhāra*, 66.
Proverbial phrases, affected by Bhāsa, 120.
Proverbs, 211, 236.
Public, dramas and, the, 370, 371.
Pulindas, a people, colour of, 366.
Puṇyaketu, a character, 254, 255.
Puppet play, relation to drama, 52, 53.
Purūravas, a hero, 14, 22, 62, 149, 151, 156, 157, 233.

Puruṣamedha, 25.
Puruṣottama, name confused with that of Purūravas, 150; celebrated, 240.
Puṣpaka, car, 101.
Puṣyagupta, described as a Rāṣṭriya, 69.
Puṣyamtia, a king, 149.
Pūtanā, demoness killed by Kṛṣṇa, 99.

Qualities, of words, theory of, 321, 332, 333, 334.
Queen, character of the, 312.

Ṛṣabha, a Tīrthakara, 254, 259.
Ṛṣis, hypocritical objections of, to vice, 262.
Ṛṣyaçṛṅga, tale of, 48.

Radanikā, servant of Cārudatta, 141.
Rādhā, beloved of Kṛṣṇa, 40, 100, 247, 257, 272, 274.
Radī, Mīlacchrīkāra's preceptor, 250.
Rāghavabhaṭṭa, commentator on the *Çakuntalā*, 154.
Raghu, *Digvijaya* of, 144.
Rājācala, 294.
Rājarāja I, of Tanjore, 251, n. 1.
Rājaçekhara, dramatist and critic, 52, 91, 103, 155, 225, 231–9, 242, 243, 244, 246, 256, 271, 287, 288, 300, 301, 337, 341, 350, 360, 363.
Rājaçekhara, the younger, 129.
Rājasiṅha, 93.
Rājendralālamitra, referred to, 269.
Rājputs, Rājaputras, language of, 87, 141, 336.
Rākṣasa, hero of the *Mudrārākṣasa*, 62, 205 ff., 352.
Rākṣasas, or Rakṣases, demons, 48, 223. 258; dress of, 366.
Rāma, 30, 42, 47, 63, 100, 101, 105, 111. 116, 119, 189, 190, 191, 192, 194, 195, 197, 199, 223, 224, 227, 228, 229, 233, 245, 246, 247, 269, 271, 279, 281, 282, 297, 303, 305, 307, 308, 316, 317, 323, 327, 328, 329.
Rāma, author of the *Manmathonmathana*, 267, 347.
Rāmabhadra Dīkṣita, author of the *Jānakīpariṇaya*, 246; the *Çṛṅgāratilaka*, 263.
Rāmabhadra Muni, author of the *Prabuddharauhiṇeya*, 259, 260.
Rāmacandra, dramatist, 225, 258, 259.
Rāmakṛṣṇa, author of the *Gopālakelicandrikā*, 272–4.
Rāmānuja, philosopher, 274.
Rāmavarman, author of the *Rukmiṇīpariṇaya*. 247.
Rambhā, a nymph, 49.
Rāmeçvara, grandfather of Jyotirīçvara, 261.
Rāmila, dramatist, 127, 129.
Ram-fights, 263, 285.
Rām-Līlā festival, 42.
Raṇajambuka, a comic general, 262.
Raṇamalladeva, of Raypur, 270.
Raṅganātha, commentator on the *Vikramorvaçī*, 151.
Rantivarman, *v. l.*, for Avantivarman, 204.
Ratnacūḍa, a Vidyādhara, 229.
Ratnākara, a poet, 220, 225; perhaps imitated by Viçākhadatta, 204.
Ratnāvalī, princess of Ceylon, 63, 298, 299, *and see* Sāgarikā.
Rauhiṇeya, hero of the *Prabuddharauhiṇeya*, 260.
Rāvaṇa, 49, 52, 100, 101, 105, 111, 116, 189, 190, 194, 227, 233, 242, 245, 246, 247, 269, 271, 279, 297, 306, 307, 317.
Ravidāsa (before A.D. 1812), *Mithyājñānaviḍambana*, 345.
Ravivarman (born A.D. 1266), *Pradyumnābhyudaya*, 344.
Reason, a character, 251, 252.
Recensions of the *Mālavikāgnimitra*, 147, n. 2; of the *Çakuntalā*, 154, 155; of the *Vikramorvaçī*, 151; of the *Veṇīsaṁhāra*, 212, n. 3.
Recitation, as opposed to singing, 12, 20, 27, 337, 338.
Reciters, where placed in the auditorium, 370.
Recognition, in Greek and Indian drama, 62, 63.
Reed, banner of Indra, 369.
Reich, Prof. E., theory of mime, 67, 68.
Reinterpretation (*avasyandita*), 329.
Religion and the drama, 36–49, 339, 340, 369.
Repartee (*vākkelī*), 329.
Representation, of the drama, 364–9.
Revata, 48.
Rhyme, 239.
Ridgeway, Prof. Sir William, theory of origin of drama, 46, 47.
Ring, motif of lost, in the *Çakuntalā*, 62, 153; magic, 101, 112.
Ritual cathartic cursing, and Greek comedy, 39, n. 2.
Rogue, peculiarly appropriate to the *Prakaraṇa*, 346; the *Prahasana*, 348.
Rohasena, son of Cārudatta, 132, 137, 141.
Rohiṇī, beloved of the Moon, 237.
Roman borrowing from Greece, 68; drama, 60, 64.
Royal Fortune, as an allegorical character, 99, 112, 255.
Rudens, of Plautus, 63.

Rudra, the god, 17, *and see* Çiva.
Rudradāman (A.D. 151), use of Sanskrit in inscriptions of, 69.
Rudrasena, use of word Bhadramukha by, 69, 71.
Rudrasiṅha, a Kṣatrapa, 94, 95.
Rudraṭa, writer on poetics, 299.
Rukmin, enemy of Kṛṣṇa, 267.
Rukmiṇī, bride of Kṛṣṇa, 247, 266, 267.
Rukmiṇī, mother of Yaçaḥpāla, 254.
Rumaṇvant, a general, 108, 172, 177, 220.
Rūpa Gosrāmin, author of the *Dānakelikaumudī*, 268; of the *Vidagdhamādhava*, and the *Lalitamādhava*, 247, 294.

Çabaras, speech of, 337.
Çailālins, followers of Çilālin, 31.
Çaiva dramas, 253.
Çaivas, criticism of, 263.
Çākambharī, in Sapādalakṣa, 260.
Çakas, and Sanskrit drama, 60, 69–72; defeated by a Vikramāditya, 143; mode of address in the drama, 314; speech of, 337; colour of, 366.
Çakaṭa, a demon, 99.
Çakaṭadāsa, in the *Mudrārākṣasa*, 205 f.
Çakti, female energy of Çiva, 42.
Çakuntalā, an Apsaras, 152–5, 193, 297, 298, 299, 303.
Çākyabhikṣu, in the *Mattavilāsa*, 183.
Çālivāhana, 129, *and see* Sātavāhana.
Çalya, king of the Madras, ally of the Kauravas, 96, 115.
Çambhūka, a Çūdra, 191.
Çañkara, author of the *Çāradātilaka*, 263.
Çañkara, commentator on the *Çakuntalā*, 154.
Çañkaralāla, author of the *Sāvitrīcarita*, 270.
Çañkaravarman (A.D. 883–902), of Kashmir, 291.
Çañkhacūḍa, a snake, 175, 177.
Çañkhadhara Kavirāja, author of the *Laṭakamelaka*, 260, 261.
Çañkuka, a writer on poetics, 291, 316.
Çañkukarṇa, in the *Abhiṣekanāṭaka*, 111.
Çāntā, and Ṛṣyaçṛñga, 48.
Çāradvata, a hermit, 159.
Çāriputra, 81, 82, 84.
Çārñgarava, a hermit, 159.
Çarvilaka, a thief in the *Mṛcchakaṭikā*, 64, 114, 131, 132, 135.
Çātakarṇis, use of Prākrit by the, 69.
Çatānanda, friend of Janaka, 189, 227, 245.
Çaunaka, views as to character of certain Vedic hymns, 15.
Çauṣkala, envoy of Rāvaṇa, 227.
Çekharaka, the *Viṭa* of Jīmūtavāhana, 177.
Çesakṛṣṇa, author of the *Kaṅsavadha*, 247.
Çīghraka, a spy, 250.
Çīlavatī, mother of Rājaçekhara, 231.
Çiñga Bhūpāla, author of the *Rasasudhārṇava*, 294.
Çiçupāla, of Cedi, 266, 267.
Çiva, 12, 17, 26, 41, 42, 47, 66, 183, 189, 227, 233, 241, 250, 267, 271, 284, 300, 338, 352.
Çivā, wife of Çiva, 241.
Çivadatta, an Ābhīra prince, 129.
Çivasvāmin, dramatist and poet, 220.
Çobhāvatī, capital of Çūdraka, 43, 129.
Çramaṇa, in the *Çāriputraprakaraṇa*, 82.
Çramaṇaka, guise adopted by Rumaṇvant, 108.
Çravaṇā, an ascetic, 228.
Çreṇika, of Magadha, 260.
Çrī, celebrated, 240.
Çrīkaṇṭha Nīlakaṇṭha, or Bhavabhūti, 186.
Çrīrāmadeva, Vyāsa, dramatist, 269, 270.
Çrīvardhamānaka, father of Murāri, 225.
Çūdra, a seller of Soma, 24; struggle with Aryan in the Mahāvrata, 24.
Çūdraka, alleged author of the *Mṛcchakaṭikā*, 42, 51, 129–42.
Çūdras, Nāṭyaçāstra shared by, 12; colour of, 366; seats for, 359, 370; referred to, 37, 73, 98, 99, 363.
Çuka, a spy, 229.
Çukra, in the *Tripuradāha*, 267.
Çunaḥçepa, tale of, 22; a student, 227.
Çuñga dynasty, 149.
Çūra, minister of Avantivarman, 204.
Çūrasenas, colour of, 366.
Çūrpaṇakhā, enemy of Rāma, 189, 194, 227, 233.

Sadānanda, *Vedāntasāra*, syncretism in, 318, n. 2.
Sādhuhiṅsika, a chief of police, 262.
Saffron, in Kashmir, 144.
Sāgara, and the rivers, 245, 246.
Sāgarikā, *alias* of Ratnāvalī, 172, 173, 303, 304, 325, 326.
Sahadeva, a Pāṇḍava, 213.
Sajjalaka, a thief, 104.
Salu, 20.
Sāmarāja Dīkṣita, author of the *Dhūrtanartaka*, 262, 263; of the *Çrīdāmacarita*, 247.
Sāmba, 48, 49.
Saṁgrāmasiṅha, a prince, 249.
Samiddhārthaka, in the *Mudrārākṣasa*, 208.
Sāṁkṛtyāyanī, confidante of Vāsavadattā, 173, 175.

Sampāti, 189, 194.
Saṁsthāna, in the *Cārudatta*, 104.
Saṁsthānaka, in the *Mṛcchakaṭikā*, 131, 132, 133, 134, 136, 140.
Saṁtuṣṭa, a *Vidūṣaka*, 313.
Samudragupta, Gupta Emperor, horse sacrifice of, 149.
Sānchi, *Kathakas* on relief at, 30.
Sañjaya, in the *Veṇīsaṁhāra*, 214, 217.
Sanskrit, Çakas and, 69–72; of Açvaghoṣa, 85, 86; Kālidāsa, 166; Harṣa, 181; Kṛṣṇamiçra, 243, 244; Yaçaḥpāla, 255; and Prākrit, 243, 244, 255, 273, 282, 283, 287, 333, 335, 336.
Saramā and the Paṇis, legend of, 14, 19, 21.
Sāraṇa, a spy, 229.
Sārasvata school of grammarians, 145, n. 2.
Sarayū, river, 245.
Sātavāhana, 129, 333, *and see* Hāla.
Satyabhāmā, in the Kṛṣṇa legend, 48.
Satyācāra, a Brahmin, 262.
Saudāminī, pupil of Kāmandakī, 62, 188, 193.
Saumilla, Somila, a dramatist, 91, 127, 129, 147.
Sauvīra, king, 101, 102.
Sāyaṇa, commentator on the *Ṛgveda*, 15, 268.
Scenes of introduction (*arthopakṣepaka*), 301, 302.
Schroeder, Prof. L. von, theory of origins of drama, 16–21.
Secular origin of the drama, 49–57.
Self-sacrifice in Harṣa, 177, 278; in Bhavabhūti, 195.
Senex, of Greco-Roman comedy, 65.
Sense, figures of (*arthālaṁkāra*), 331.
Sentiment, produced by drama, 12, 296, 314–26, 334, 335, 366, 368; in relation to types of drama, 346–51; in connexion with the qualities of style, 332; blending of, 169.
Servants (*ceṭa*), speech of, 87, 141, 336; kind of names of, 313.
Servus currens, of Greco-Roman drama, 65.
Seven vices, banished, 255.
Shadow plays, and dramatic origins, 53–7; 269, 270, 351.
Shakespeare of India, Kālidāsa as, 160.
Shameless, hero, 307.
Shamsu-d-din, probable original of Hammīra, 249, n. 1.
Shaw, Bernard, stage directions in plays of, 366.
Sibilants, treatment of, in Açvaghoṣa, 86, 87, 88; in Bhāsa, 122; in Bhaṭṭa Nārāyaṇa, 219.
Siddhārthaka, in the *Mudrārākṣasa*, 205, 208.
Siddhas, 178, 179.
Similes, 330, 331.
Simple, and causative verbal forms, confused, in Bhāsa, 120, 121.
Simplicity of Indian theatrical apparatus, 50, 358–60.
Siṅha, lord of Lāṭa, 249.
Siṅhana (Siṅghaṇa, Siṅhaṇa), the Yādava, 249.
Siṅhaviṣṇuvarman, a Pallava king, 182.
Siparium, in Roman mime, 67.
Sītā, wife of Rāma, 30, 42, 52, 63, 100, 101, 105, 110, 115, 119, 189, 190, 191, 192, 194, 195, 197, 199, 218, 219, 224, 227, 228, 229, 233, 243, 244, 270, 271, 279, 281, 303, 328, 329.
Sītābeṅgā cave, 54, 67, 89.
Skandagupta, Emperor, 144.
Slaughter, as an allegorical character, 255.
Slaves (*ceṭa*), speech of, 87, 141, 336; in the *Prakaraṇa*, 346; as hero and heroine in the *Prasthāna*, 351.
Softening of hard letters, in Prākrit, 86, 87, 88, 89, 121.
Soma rite, 30, 51.
Somadatta, a *Nāyaka*, 84.
Somadeva, author of the *Lalitavigraharājanāṭaka*, 243, 248.
Somaçarman, in Cambodia, 29.
Someçvara, *Kīrtikaumudī*, 248, n. 7.
Somila, *see* Saumilla.
Somism, 252, 253.
Song, in relation to the drama, 12, 16, 20, 25, 44, 49, 50, 160, 338, 350, 351.
Sophokles, 59, 197.
Sorrow (*çoka*), as the basis of the pathetic sentiment, 323.
Sound, figures of (*çabdālaṁkāras*), 331.
Sound effects, in Bhavabhūti, 202, 203; Bhaṭṭa Nārāyaṇa, 218; Murāri, 230; Rājaçekhara, 236.
South Indian recension, of the *Vikramorvaçī*, 151; the *Çakuntalā*, 154, 155.
Spectators, 35–7, 369–71; relation to actors, 316, 317, 318, 320, 321, 322.
Spirit, as an allegorical character, 251.
Stage, 359; matters excluded from representation on, 300, 301.
Stage directions, 86, 113, 364, 366.
Stage properties, 365, 366.
Stages of the development of the action (*avasthā*), 297–9.
Stanzas, *see* Lyric Stanzas.
Sthāvaraka, servant of Saṁsthānaka, 141.
Strength (*ojas*), of style, 331.
Struggle of conscience, unknown in the Sanskrit drama, 279.
Style, of Bhāsa, 114–20; *Mṛcchakaṭikā*,

136–9; Kālidāsa, 160–5; Harṣa, 177–81; Mahendravikramavarman, 185; Bhavabhūti, 196–203; Viçākhadatta, 209–11; Bhaṭṭa Narāyaṇa, 215–19; Yaçovarman, 221–3; Murāri, 230, 231; Rājaçekhara, 236–9; Kṣemīçvara, 240; theoretical views of qualities of, 331–3, 334; *see also* Gauḍa style, Vaidarbha style.
Styles, dramatic (*vṛtti*), doctrine of the, 326–9.
Subandhu, author, 76, 91.
Subhadrā, taken away by Arjuna, 268.
Subhaṭa, dramatist, 55, 269.
Subjunctures, in the episode, 299.
Subrahmaṇya Kavi, author of part of the *Mahāvīracarita*, 192.
Subterranean passages, referred to, 206, 234.
Sudarçanā, wife of the king of Kāçi, 101, 110.
Sudeṣṇā, wife of Virāṭa, 63.
Suggestion, in poetry, 276, 277, 318, 322; in Kālidāsa as opposed to Bhavabhūti, 161.
Sugrīva, brother of Vālin, 100, 105, 190, 194, 228, 229, 245, 246, 297, 308, 327.
Suicide, motif, 107.
Sumeru, description of, 229.
Sumitrā, mother of Jayadeva, 242.
Sundaramiçra, author of the *Nāṭyapradīpa*, 294.
Sundering of lovers, 323.
Supernatural, 159, 192, *and see* Wonder.
Surānanda, an ancestor of Rājaçekhara, 231.
Surāṣṭra, speeches used in, 287.
Susa, people of, know Greek dramas, 59.
Susaṁgatā, confidante of Ratnāvalī, 172, 176, 303, 325, 326.
Sūtas, slain by Bhīma, 97, n. 1.
Suvarṇākṣī, mother of Açvaghoṣa, 80.
Suvarṇaçekhara, on the Ganges, 257.
Suvega, a spy, 249.
Svayaṁbhū, creator of the pigments, 369.
Swāng of North-West India, 273.
Sweetness of style, 331, 332.
Swinging, 313; description of, 234, 238.
Synonyms, free use of, 283.

Tāḍakā, a demoness, 227.
Ṭakkas, use of Apabhrança by, 287.
Tales, close connexion of, with the drama, 76, 258, and see *Kathāsaritsāgara*.
Tamasā, river, goddess, as a dramatic character, 191, 202.
Tantras, 42.
Tantumatī, mother of Murāri, 225.
Tārā, wife of Vālin, 105.
Tarala, an ancestor of Rājaçekhara, 231.
Tārkṣya, 267.
Tears, of the auditor, 321, 368.
Technique, of Açvaghoṣa, 82–5; Bhāsa, 110–14; Kālidāsa, 126, 160; Yaçovarman, 222, 223; Rājaçekhara, 239; Prahlādanadeva, 265; certain irregular dramas, 270–5; according to the writers on theory, 296–305.
Tejaḥpāla, brother of Vastupāla, 248, 249, 250.
Ten qualities of style, 331, 332.
Ten stages of love, 323.
Ten types of drama, 345–9.
Terror (*bhaya*), as the basis of the sentiment of terror, 323.
Terror, sentiment of, 192, 278, 324, 325, 332.
Thārāpadra, 254.
Theatre, buildings, 67, 358–60.
Theft, as an allegorical character, 255.
Theories of the Secular Origin of the Drama, 49–57.
Theory of the drama, 290–351; influence of, on dramatic practice, 352–4; possible influence of Aristotle on, 355, 356.
Tibet, drama in, 44.
Tiger, escape of, as dramatic motif, 188, 193.
Time, of performance of plays, 369; unity of, 64, 65, 301, 355.
Tīrthakaras, invocation of the, 254.
Ṭodar Mall, Akbar's minister, 247.
Tradition, as the fifth Veda, 12, 13.
Traditional account of the origin of Sanskrit drama, 12, 13; of dramatic theory, 290.
Tragedy, 38, n. 2, 278, 280, 345, 354.
Trailokyavarmadeva, of Kālañjara, 266.
Transitory (*vyabhicārin*), feelings, 315.
Transmigration, as explaining sensibility to poetry, 322.
Transverse, curtain, 113, n. 1, 359.
Travaṇas, speech of people of, 287.
Triads, Bhāsa's fondness for, 111.
Tribhuvanapāla, of Aṇahilapāṭaka, 269.
Triple explanation (*trigata*), 328.
Tukkojī, 257.
Tumultuous action or disturbance (*avapāta*), 328, 346.
Tuṅgabhadrā, river, as a dramatic character, 245.
Tuñjina, of Kashmir, patron of Candraka, 168.
Turfan, fragments of Buddhist dramas, 80.
Twelve stages of love, 323, n. 2.
Types of drama, 345–51.

Typical, not individual, characters, found in Sanskrit drama, 282, 353.

Udayana, 94, 102, 103, 107, 108, 125, 327, *and see* Vatsa.
Uddaṇḍanātha or Uddaṇḍin, author of the *Mallikāmāruta*, 221, 257, 258.
Uḍras, a people, colour of, 366.
Udumbaras, family of Bhavabhūti, 186.
Ugrasena, king, 100.
Ujjayinī, importance of, in Indian history, 60; for Sanskrit drama, 70, 71, 74, 94; speech used in, 70, 336.
Umā, dance in honour of, 340.
Umvekācārya, alleged identity of, with Bhavabhūti, 186.
Union of lovers, 323.
Unities, dramatic, of subject, 297–300; of time, 64, 65, 301, 355; of place, 355.
Uragas, snakes, clothing of, 366.
Ūrmilā, daughter of Janaka, 189.
Urvaçī, a nymph, 14, 114, 149–51, 156, 362, 364.
Uṣavadāta (A.D. 124), 69.
Utpaladeva, *alias* Muñja, 293.
Uttarā, a princess, 265, 266.

Vaibhāra, mount, 260.
Vaidarbha style, 161, 331, 332.
Vairantya, capital of Kuntibhoja, 109.
Vairodhaka, in the *Mudrārākṣasa*, 206.
Vaiçya, 37, 38, 73, 363; colour of, 366; seats of, 359; in the Mahāvrata rite, 24.
Vaiṣṇavas, 263.
Vajranābha, in the Kṛṣṇa legend, 48, 49.
Vajravarman, an aboriginal prince, 259.
Vākpati, author of the *Gauḍavaha*, 91, 92, 187.
Vālin, a monkey king, 100, 105, 110, 114, 119, 189, 190, 194, 228, 229, 245, 297, 306, 327.
Vallabhadeva, commentator on the *Meghadūta*, 145.
Vālmīki, author of the *Rāmāyaṇa*, 114, 191, 192, 232, 303.
Valour, as an allegorical character, 254
Vāmadeva, a seer, 14, 226.
Vāmana, a writer on poetics, 92, 102, 103, 104, 145, 330, 332.
Vāmana Bhaṭṭa Bāṇa, author of the *Pārvatīpariṇaya*, 221, 247, 263, 264.
Vaṅgas, a people, colour of, 366.
Varadācārya, author of the *Vasantatilaka*, 263.
Varāhamihira, date of, 144.
Vardhamāna, capital of Çūdraka, 129.
Vardhamānaka, servant of Cārudatta, 141.
Vardhamāna Svāmin, 260.
Varuṇa and Indra, dialogue of, 15, 21.
Vasantācārya, son of Dhanika Paṇḍita, 293.
Vasantasenā, heroine of the *Mṛcchakaṭikā*, 104, 131, 132, 133, 134, 135, 136, 139, 140, 309, 313, 335, n. 3, 363.
Vāsantī, in the *Uttararāmacarita*, 191, 200.
Vāsava, 83, n. 1, 265, *and see* Indra.
Vāsavadattā, queen of Udayana, 102, 107, 108, 109, 113, 119, 125, 171–4, 176, 220, 235, 303, 304.
Vasiṣṭha, a sage, 189, 229, 302; dialogue of, in the *Ṛgveda*, 14, 17.
Vassal princes, where placed in the auditorium, 370.
Vasubandhu, the Buddhist philosopher, 145, 146.
Vasubhūti, a minister, 171, 173.
Vasudeva, 40, 98, 99, 214, 264.
Vāsudeva, 32, 34, *and see* Kṛṣṇa.
Vasukra, dialogue with Indra, 14.
Vasulakṣmī, a princess, in the *Mālavikāgnimitra*, 148.
Vasumatī, a queen of Duḥṣanta, 158.
Vasumitra, of the Çuñga dynasty, defeats the Yavanas, 149; favours actors, 364.
Vastupāla, minister of Vīradhavala of Gujarāt, 248, 249, 250.
Vaṭeçvaradatta, the feudatory (*sāmanta*), grandfather of Viçākhadatta, 204.
Vatsa, or Udayana, 102, 108, 171–4, 176, 220, 235, 298, 303, 304, 305, 307, 309, 327, 361, 362, 364.
Vatsabhaṭṭi, imitates Kālidāsa, 146.
Vatsarāja, dramatist, 265, 266, 301.
Vātsyāyana, author of the *Kāmaçāstra*, 332, 335.
Veda, the fifth, 12, 13.
Vedakavi, author of the *Vidyāpariṇayana*, 253, n. 4.
Vedānta, in the *Prabodhacandrodaya*, 251–3.
Vedāntavāgīça, *Bhojacarita*, 345.
Vedic ritual, dramatic elements in the, 23–7.
Vegetation ritual, and drama, 45.
Vema, prince of Koṇḍavīḍu, 247.
Veṅkaṭanātha, author of the *Saṁkalpasūryodaya*, 253.
Veṅkaṭavarada, author of the *Kṛṣṇavijaya*, 267.
Verbal (*bhāratī*) manner, 326, 328, 329, 344; in the *Bhāṇa*, 348.
Vernaculars, use of, 243, 334.
Vernacular drama, 243.
Verse, in drama, 23, 56, 58, 73, 76, 90, 279, 281, 282, 337.
Vibhīṣaṇa, brother of Rāvaṇa, 190, 229, 246, 327.

Vidiçā, 147.
Vidyādhara, writer on poetics, 293, 294, 295, 325.
Vidyādharamalla, hero of the *Viddhaçālabhañjikā*, 234, 235.
Vidyādharas, 111, n. 3, 174, 191, 245, 256.
Vidyādharīs, wear jewels on the stage, 367.
Vidyānātha, author of the *Pratāparudrīya*, 248, 293, 295.
Vidyāraṇya, perhaps Sāyaṇa, 268.
Vigraharāja, *see* Vīsaladeva.
Vijayakoṣṭha, or Vijayaprakoṣṭha, ancestor of Kṣemīçvara, 240.
Vijayasena, general of Vatsa, 173.
Vijñānavāda school, 80.
Vikramāditya, 130, 143.
Vikramasiṅha, a prince, 133.
Vilāsaçekhara, a *Viṭa*, 263.
Vinayavasu, a chamberlain of Dṛḍhavarman, 173.
Vindhyaketu, a prince, 173.
Violent (*ārabhaṭī*) manner, 326, 327, 328.
Virādhaka, in the *Mudrārākṣasa*, 206, 208.
Vīradhavala, king of Gujarāt, 248, 249, 256.
Vīraka, a policeman, 141.
Virāṭa, a king, 97, 265, 266.
Viçākhadatta, dramatist (date as a younger contemporary of Kālidāsa supported, but inconclusively, by J. Charpentier, JRAS., 1923, pp. 585 ff.), 204–12, 218, 253.
Viçvāmitra, a sage, 189, 190, 226, 227, 240, 245, 281, 302; father of Çakuntalā, 152; dialogue of, with the rivers in the *Ṛgveda*, 14, 17, 20.
Viçvanagara, a mendicant, 261.
Viçvanātha, author of the *Mṛgāṅkalekhā*, 257, n. 1.
Viçvanātha, author of the *Sāhityadarpaṇa*, 220, 223, 294, 295, 302, 310, 321, 322, 325, 328, 329, 341, 342, 343, 347, 348, 349, 350.
Viçvanātha, author of the *Saugandhikāharaṇa* (not, as Winternitz, GIL. iii. 248, suggests, the writer on poetics, who does not cite the work as his), 266.
Viçvantara, legend of, 168.
Viçveçvara, author of the *Çṛṅgāramañjarī*, 257.
Viṣṇu, 12, 17, 26, 98, 105, 106, 112, 268, 284, 354.
Viṣṇu, censure of actors, 363.
Viṣṇu, father of Dhanaṁjaya and Dhanika, 292, 293.
Vīsaladeva Vigraharāja, 248; author of the *Harakelināṭaka*, 247.
Visions of the dying, 114.
Vocative of *a* stems in *ā*, in Bhaṭṭa Nārāyaṇa, 219; *ṛ* stems in *ā*, in Açvaghoṣa, 88.
Voice in the air, 303; in the *Bhāṇa*, 348.
Vṛndā, or Lakṣmī, 274.
Vṛndā, wood, 99.
Vṛṣākapi, comparison of, with the *Vidūṣaka*, 51, n. 1.
Vṛṣākapi, hymn, 14, 18.
Vṛṣṇis, Kṛṣṇa born in the family of the, 98.
Vyāsa, Çrīrāmadeva, dramatist, 269, 270.

Warriors (*yodha*), speech of, 141, 336.
Watchers, speech of, 88, 336.
Weber, Prof. Albrecht, as to origin of drama, 32, 33, 57.
Western Kṣatrapas, alleged influence of, on drama, 69–72.
Wife, characteristics of a, 308, 309.
Windisch, Prof. E., theory of epic, 21; on Greek origin of the drama, 57–64; on the plot of the *Mṛcchakaṭikā*, 130.
Winternitz, Prof. M., 33, n. 1.
Woman, disguised as a boy, 234, 235, 256; using Sanskrit as comic, 334; may use it in various cases, 335.
Women, as poets, 287, 288; as spectators, of the drama, 370.
Women's apartments, speech of those living in, 88, 336.
Women's roles, played sometimes by men, 362.
Wonder, sentiment of, 278, 324.
Wood-workers, speech of, 337.
Words, qualities of, 321, 332, 333, 334.
Worship of the dead, alleged origin of drama in the, 46, 47.

Xanthos, legend of, 37, 38.

Yādavas, drama among the, 48, 49.
Yajñasena, a prince, 147.
Yakṣas, 266, 339, n. 3; dress of, 366; hair of, 367.
Yakṣīs, carry jewels, 367.
Yama and Yamī, dialogue of, 13, 14, 19, 20.
Yamala and Arjuna, demons, 99.
Yamunā, 245.
Yaçaḥpāla, author of the *Moharājaparājaya*, 254–6.
Yaçaçcandra, author of the *Mudritakumudacandra*, 260.
Yaçodā, wife of Nanda, 98.
Yaçodharman, conqueror of the Hūṇas, 144.
Yaçovarman, of Kanyakubja, as a dramatist, 186, 187, 220, 221, 222.

Yāska, 15.
Yātrās, 16, 17, 40, 51, 272.
Yaugandharāyaṇa, 102, 103, 107, 108, 113, 171, 173, 220, 235, 240, 262.
Yavanas, 356, 366; defeated by Vasumitra, 149; Apabhrançа assigned to, 336, n. 1; see also *Yavanānī*.
Yavanīs, in king's harem, 61, 62.
Yāyāvara family, 231.
Yudhājit, uncle of Bharata, 189.
Yudhiṣṭhira, oldest of the Pāṇḍavas, 83, 214, 215, 308.
Yugādideva, the Tīrthakara Ṛṣabha, 259.

Zēlotypos, compared with *Çakāra*, 67.

SANSKRIT INDEX

Agni Purāṇa, 295, 349.
Aṅka, act, 301.
Aṅka, one act play, 268, 295, 296, 347, 348.
Aṅkamukha, anticipatory scene, 302.
Aṅkāvatāra, continuation scene, 302.
Ajjukā, style of a hetaera, 314.
Atijagatī, metre, appropriate to lively dialogue, 331.
Atidhṛti, metre, appropriate to the pathetic sentiment, 331.
Atibala, outvying, 329.
Attāṇaṁ, in Bhāsa for *attāṇaaṁ*, 122.
Atharvaveda, 12, 15.
Adaṇḍārako, in Açvaghoṣa, 88.
Adbhuta, wonder, as a sentiment, 324.
Adbhutadarpaṇa, by Mahādeva, 246, 247.
Adbhutārṇava, by Kavibhūṣaṇa, 345.
Adhikāra, attainment of hero's purpose, 297.
Adhibala, outvying, 329.
Anargharāghava by Murāri, 226–31, 344, n. 1, 362.
Anukūla, loyal (hero), 307.
Anukṛti, mimesis, 355, and see *Avasthānukṛti*.
Anucārikā, king's attendant, 312.
Anubhāvas, consequents of sentiments, 315.
Anuçāsana Parvan, allusion to drama in, 28.
Anuṣṭubh, metre, 346.
Antarasandhi, nature of, 302, 303.
Anyā, *anyastrī*, heroine as wife of another, 308.
Apaṭī, curtain, 61, 359.
Aparavaktra, metre, 166.
Apavāritam, confidentially, 304.
Abhijñāna, recognition, as motif, 62.
Abhijñānaçakuntala, (drama) of Çakuntalā (recognized) by a token of recognition, see *Çakuntalā*.
Abhidhā, power of denotation, 317.
Abhinayadarpaṇa, by Nandikeçvara, 338, n. 1, 367, n. 1.
Abhinavabhāratī, by Abhinavagupta, 291.
Abhirāmarāghava, 329, n. 1, 344, n. 1.
Abhivyakti, revelation of sentiment, 317.
Abhiṣekanāṭaka, by Bhāsa, 94, 101, 105, 110, 111, 113, 114, 115.
Abhisārikā, type of heroine, 309.
Amātya, minister, 312.
Amṛtodaya, by Gokulanātha, 253, n. 3, 343.
Ambā, style of a go-between, 314.
Ammābhāṇa, by Varadācārya, 263.
Amhāaṁ, genitive plural in Bhāsa, 122.
Amhe, in Kālidāsa, 122.
Ayoga, privation, as form of the erotic sentiment, 323.
Ayyābhāṇa, by Rāmabhadra Dīkṣita, 263.
Arthaprakṛti, elements of the plot, 298, 299.
Arthavyakti, precision of exposition, 331.
Arthaçāstra, *Kauṭilīya*, 102, 291, n. 2, 334, 364; whether known by Kālidāsa, 167, n. 6.
Arthāntaranyāsa, a figure, 125.
Arthopakṣepaka, scenes of introduction, 301, 302.
Ardha-Māgadhī, a Prākrit, 74, 87, 122, 141, 219, 336.
Arh, epenthetic vowel in Prākrit of Açvaghoṣa, 88.
Alaṁkāras, poetic figures, 330, 331; see also *Nāṭakālaṁkāra* and *Nāṭyālaṁkāra*.
Alaukika, sentiment as supernatural, 319.
Avataraṇa, entry of performers, 339, and see *Raṅgāvataraṇa*.
Avadānaçataka, 43.
Avantikā, a Prākrit, 141.
Avapāta, disturbance, 328, 346.
Avalagita, continuance, 328.
Avaloka, Dhanika's commentary on the *Daçarūpa*, 293.
Avasthā, stage of development of the action of the drama, 297–9.
Avasthānukṛti, as nature of drama, 295.
Avasyandita, re-interpretation, 329.
Avimāraka, by Bhāsa, 94, 101, 102, 107, 108, 109, 112, 113, 125, 313.
Açoka, tree, 159, 222, 234, 238.
Açvattha, tree, 96, 213, 214, 215, 217.
Aṣṭādhyāyī, careful preservation of the, 290.
Asatpralāpa, incoherent talk, 329.
Ahakaṁ, *ahake*, in Açvaghoṣa, 86; *ahake* in Bhāsa, 122.
Ākāçabhāṣita, a voice in the air, 303, 348.
Ākhyāna, theory of certain Vedic hymns, 21–3.

Ākhyāyikā, romance, 76.
Āngikābhinaya, expression by gesture, 367, 368.
Āṇi, *āni*, and *ā* in neuter plural of *a*-stems, 87, 122.
Ātmagatam, aside, 304.
Ādhikārika, principal (action), 297.
Ānandakoça, a farce, 260, n. 3, 348, n. 1.
Ānandamañjarī, by Ghanaçyāma, 257.
Ābhīrī, speech, 337.
Āma, in assertions in Bhāsa, 120.
Āmukha, introduction, 328, 340.
Āyāraṁga Sutta, 44, n. 2.
Āyukta, attendants, 312.
Āyuṣmant, as style of the king, 314.
Ārabhaṭī, violent (manner), 326, 327, 328.
Ārambha, voice testing by chorus, 339.
Ārambha, first stage of development in drama, 297.
Ārttha, in Açvaghoṣa for *artha*, 85.
Āryaputra (*ajjaütta*), style of a husband, 314.
Āryā (*ajjā*), style of a wife, 314.
Āryā, metre, 124, 142, 167, 181, 185, 203, 212, 258; appropriate to the erotic sentiment, 331.
Ālambana, fundamental determinants of sentiment, 315.
Āvantī, a Prākrit, 141, 333.
Āçcaryamañjarī, by Çaktibhadra (BSOS. III. i. 116 f.), 371, n. 2.
Āçrāvaṇā, trying of instruments, 339.
Āsīna, a kind of recitation, 338.
Āhi, as instrumental in Açvaghoṣa's Prākrit, 87.

Itihāsa, 12; Prof. Pischel's theory of the, 21.
Indravajrā, metre, 142, 181, 185, 272.
Iyaṁ, in Açvaghoṣa, 88.
Īhāmṛga, 266, 267, 295, 296, 346, 347, 353.

Uktapratyukta, a duet, 338.
Ucca, used by Kālidāsa, 146.
Utkṛti, metre, appropriate to scenes of violence, 331.
Uttamottaka, a kind of song, 338.
Uttararāmacarita, by Bhavabhūti, 66, 139, 190–2, 194, 196, 199, 202, 203, 225, 303, 329, 344.
Utthāpaka, challenge, 327.
Utpatti, production of sentiment, 317.
Utpādya, invented (plot), 296.
Utsāha, energy, as basis of sentiment, 323.
Utsṛṣṭikāñka, a kind of drama, 347, 348, 363.
Udayanacarita, 327, 365.
Udātta, exalted (hero), 305, 306.
Udāttarāghava, by Māyurāja, 221, 223, 297.
Udāratā vacasām, claimed by Bhavabhūti, 196.
Udāratva, elevation of style, 331.
Udghātya, abrupt dialogue, 328; in the prologue, 341.
Uddīpana, excitant determinants, 315.
Uddhata, haughty (hero), 305, 306, and see *Dhīroddhatta*.
Unmattaka, disguise of, adopted by Yaugandharāyaṇa, 108, 184, 185.
Unmattarāghava, by Bhāskara Kavi, 268.
Upagīti, metre, 123.
Upajāti, metre, 123, 142, 166, 203, 212.
Upanāgarikā, style, 332, 333.
Upaniṣad, Theology, 251, 252.
Upapati, adulterer, 307, n. 1.
Upapatti, use of argument, 330.
Uparūpaka, minor dramatic forms, 268, 269, 349–51.
Upasthāyika, eunuch, 313.
Ummadantijātaka, alleged dramatic character of, 43, n. 1.
Ullāpya, a form of drama, 351.
Uṣṇih, metre, 346.
Ūrubhañga, by Bhāsa, 38, 94, 96, 106, 114, 278, 300, 354.

Ṛgveda, 12, 13, 15, 17, 18, 20, 21, 22, 23, 26.
Ṛtusaṁhāra, by Kālidāsa, 147, n. 3.

E, as masculine nominative of *a*-stems, in Açvaghoṣa, 86, 87.
Ekāvalī, by Vidyādhara, 293.
Ekka, in Bhāsa's Prākrit, 122.
Edisa, in Açvaghoṣa's Prākrit, 89.
Evva, *evvaṁ*, in Bhāsa's Prākrit, 121.

Ai, interjection, in Açvaghoṣa's Prākrit, 88.
Aitareya Brāhmaṇa, 77; tale of Çunaḥçepa, 22.
Aindrajālika, juggler, 55.

Ojas, strength, 331.
Oḍrī, speech, 337.

Audārya, nobility, as a quality of the hero, 307.
Aupacchandasika, metre, 142, 166, 203, 212, 219.

Ka, suffix, lengthening of vowel before, 87.
Kaṅsavadha, 37, 38.
Kaṅsavadha, by Çeṣakṛṣṇa, 247.
Kacci, in Bhāsa's Prākrit, 122.
Kañcukin, chamberlain, 313.
Kaṭhinā, style, 332, n. 2.

Kathakas, reciters, 29, 30.
Kathā, tale, 76, 258.
Kathāsaritsāgara, by Somadeva, 52, 129, 134, 192, 193.
Kathodghāta, form of prologue, 340.
Kadua, not in Bhāsa, 122.
Kapphiṇābhyudaya, poem by Çivasvāmin, 220, n. 2.
Kariya, gerund of *kṛ* in Açvaghoṣa, 88.
Karuṇa, pathos, as a sentiment, 323, 325.
Karuṇākandala, 343, n. 1.
Karotha, anomalous strong form in Açvaghoṣa, 88.
Karṇabhāra, by Bhāsa, 87, 96, 106, 122, 336.
Karṇasundarī, by Bilhaṇa, 256, 369.
Karpūracaritra, by Vatsarāja, 265.
Karpūramañjarī, by Rājaçekhara, 232, 233, 234, 235, 239, 342, 350.
Kalahāntaritā, type of heroine, 309.
Kaleti, in Açvaghoṣa, 87.
Kādambarī, by Bāṇa, 129.
Kānti, beauty of style, 331.
Kāmandakīya Nītiçāstra, 291, n. 2.
Kāmaçāstra, by Vātsyāyana, 284, 285, 334, 335.
Kārya, dénouement, 298.
Kāla, equivalent to *Horā*, 146.
Kālanā, in Açvaghoṣa, 86.
Kāvya, as influencing drama, 283, 284.
Kāvya, a type of drama, 351.
Kāvyanirṇaya, by Dhanika, 293
Kāvyaprakāça, by Mammaṭa, 171, 295, n. 1.
Kāvyamīmāṅsā, by Rājaçekhara, 232, 271, 287, 288.
Kāvyādarça, by Daṇḍin, 104.
Kāçikā Vṛtti, cites Candra's grammar, 168.
Kāçirājñe, irregular compounds in Bhāsa, 121.
Kirātārjunīya, by Bhāravi, 194.
Kirātārjunīya, by Vatsarāja, 265.
Kilakiñcita, hysteria, 310
Kiçça, in Açvaghoṣa, 86.
Kissa, in Bhāsa, 122.
Kīrti, fame, 84.
Kīrtikaumudī, by Someçvara, 248, n. 7.
Kīrtimañjarī, an allegorical character, 254.
Kuṭila, metre, 346.
Kuṭṭanīmata, by Dāmodaragupta, 171.
Kuṭṭamita, pretended anger, 310.
Kundamālā, 341.
Kumāra, prince royal, 312.
Kumārasambhava, by Kālidāsa, 75, 146, 147, 167, 284, 285, 312, 352.
Kuçīlava, actor, 31, 360, 363.
Kṛṣṇavijaya, by Veṅkaṭavarada, 267.
Kṛṣṇābhyudaya, by Lokanātha Bhaṭṭa, 268.
Kaiçikī ('of the Kaiçikas', Lévi, TI, i. 333), graceful (manner), 326, 327.
Komalā, style, 333.
Komudagandha, 86.
Kauṭilīya Arthaçāstra, 102, 291, n. 2, 334, 364.
Kautukaratnākara, written under Lakṣmaṇa Māṇikyadeva, 263.
Kautukasarvasva, by Gopīnātha Cakravartin, 262.
Kaumudīmitrāṇanda, by Rāmacandra, 225, 258, 259.
Krimi, Buddhist irregularity for *kṛmi*, 86.
Krodha, anger, as basis of sentiment, 323.
Kṣ, treatment of, in various Prākrits, 86, 88, 122, 212.
Kṣobha, agitation of mind, 320.
Khaṇḍacūlikā, nature of, 302, n. 1.
Khaṇḍitā, enraged (heroine), 309.
Khu, after vowels in place of *kkhu*, in Açvaghoṣa, 89.

Gauḍavaha, by Vākpati, 187.
Gaṅgadāsapratāpavilāsa, by Gaṅgādhara, 251.
Gacchia, and *gadua* in Bhāsa, 122.
Gaḍu, obscure term, 35.
Gaṇḍa, abrupt remark, 329.
Gaṇhadi, in Bhāsa for *geṇhadi* in Açvaghoṣa, 122.
Gambhīratā, depth, 226.
Garbha, third juncture, 299.
Garbhāṅka, embryo act, 303.
Gahītaṁ, in Açvaghoṣa, 89.
Gāmbhīrya, impassivity, as quality of the hero, 307.
Gītagovinda, by Jayadeva, 17, 40, 239, 272, 339, n. 1.
Gīti, metre, 142, 203.
Guṇa, excellencies, theory of, 331, 332, 333, 334.
Gṛhya, irregular form in Bhāsa, 121.
Gai, sing, used of *Sāmaveda*, 20.
Gopālakelicandrikā, by Rāmakṛṣṇa, 272-4.
Goṣṭhī, a type of drama, 351.
Granthikas, reciters, 32-5, 38, 39, 45, 272.
Granthin, owner of a book, 35, n. 2.

Cakravāka, grief at separation from his mate, 169.
Caṇḍakauçika, by Kṣemīçvara, 239, 240, 281.
Candakinnarajātaka, alleged dramatic character of, 43, n. 1.
Cāṇḍālī, a Prākrit, 141, 142, 337.
Cāraṇa, actor, 360.
Cārī, a dance, 340.

Cārudatta, by Bhāsa, 64, 65, 67, 85, 92, 93, 103, 104, 107, 116, 122, 128, 130, 182, 311, 313, 346, 363.
Citrabhārata, by Kṣemendra, 247.
Citrayajña, by Vaidyanātha Vācaspati Bhaṭṭācārya, 274, n. 1, 371, n. 2.
Cūlikā, nature of, 302.
Ceṭa, servants, 312; speech of, 336.
Caitanyacandrodaya, by Kavikarṇapūra, 133, n. 6, 253, 344, 353.
Cch, in Māgadhī as *çc*, 122, 212.
Chaḍḍ, in Açvaghoṣa, 88.
Chaddantajātaka, alleged dramatic character of, 43, n. 1.
Chala, cheating, 329.
Chalana, deception, 222.
Chalitarāma, 223, 224, 246, 329.
Chāyā, Sanskrit version of Prākrit, 337.
Chāyānāṭaka, shadow drama, 55–7, 269, 276.
Chāyānātya, shadow drama, 55, 269.

Jagatī, metre, appropriate to lively dialogue, 331.
Janāntikam, in private conversation, 304.
Jarjara, banner (of Indra), 41, 369.
Javanikā, see *Yavanikā*.
Javanikāntara, name of acts in the *Saṭṭaka*, 350.
Jātakas, 22, 23, n. 1.
Jānakīpariṇaya, by Rāmabhadra Dīkṣita, 246, 344, 361.
Jāmitra, diameter, used by Kālidāsa, 146.
Jāyājīva, one who lives on (the beauty) of his wife, 55.
Jīvānandana, by Ānandarāya, 253.
Jugupsā, disgust, as basis of sentiment, 323.
Jovvana, in Bhāsa's Prākrit, 121.
Jñ, treatment of, in Prākrit, 88, 121.
Jñānadarpaṇa, mirror of knowledge, as a character, 254.

Ṭakki or *Ṭākkī*, a Prākrit, 141, 337.

Ḍamaruka, by Ghanaçyāma, 257, n. 2.
Ḍim, alleged root, 347.
Ḍima, 266, 267, 292, 295, 296, 347, 353.
Ḍillīsāmrājya, by Lakṣmaṇa Sūri, 251.
Ḍhakkī, a Prākrit, 141, 337.

Ṇ, and *n* in the Prākrits, 86, 87, 88, 121; as affecting the quality of style, 332.
Ṇevaccha, see *Nevaccha*.
Ṇy, altered to *ññ* or *ṇṇ* in Bhāsa, 121.

T normally retained in Açvaghoṣa's Prākrits, 89.
Tapatīsaṁvaraṇa, by Kulaçekharavarman, 247, 342, n. 2.
Tamas, element of dullness, 318.
Taraṅgadatta, a *Prakaraṇa*, 225, 346.
Tava, in Açvaghoṣa, 88.
Tāṇḍava, dance, 12, 42, 241, 338, 339.
Tāta, as style of address, 314.
Tāpasavatsarājacarita, by Anaṅgaharṣa Mātrarāja, 2 0.
Tiraskaraṇī or *Tiraskariṇī*, curtain, 359.
Tumhākaṁ, in Açvaghoṣa, 89.
Tulyadharma, irregular compound in Bhāsa, 121.
Tuvaṁ, in Açvaghoṣa, 88.
Tejas, honour as a quality of the hero, 307.
Toṭaka, see *Troṭaka*.
Trigata, various senses of, 111, n. 2, 328, 340.
Trigūḍha, a kind of song, 338.
Tripuradāha, by Vatsarāja, 267, 347.
Trimūḍhaka, a kind of song, 338.
Troṭaka, a type of drama, 151, 350, 351.
Theragāthā (866 ff.), alleged dramatic character of, 43, n. 1.
Therīgāthā, 43, n. 1, 54.

Dakṣiṇa, courteous (hero), 307.
Daṇḍaka, metre, 123, 187, n. 2, 203.
Dambha, falsity, as a character, 252.
Daridracārudatta, 104, 306, and see *Cārudatta*.
Darç, in Bhāsa's Prākrit, 122.
Daçakumāracarita, by Daṇḍin, 55, 129, 133, 363.
Daçarūpa, by Daṇḍin, 71, 169, 221, 223, 292, 293, 294, 304, 315, 319, 320, 330, 334, 335, 336, 341, 342, 348, 349.
Daçarūpāvaloka, by Dhanaṁjaya, 346.
Dākṣiṇātyā, a Prākrit, 141, 166, 336.
Dānakelikaumudī, by Rūpa Gosvāmin, 268.
Dāni, *dāṇi*, Prākrit forms, 88, 89.
Dikpālastuti, praise of the world guardians, 369.
Digvijaya, conquest of the earth, of Raghu, 144.
Dissadi, in Açvaghoṣa, 89; *dīsadi*, in Bhāsa, 121.
Dīpaka, a figure of speech, 331.
Dīptarasa, sentiment of excitement, 265.
Dīvyant, gamblers, speech of, 141, 336.
Duguṇa, irregular form in Açvaghoṣa, 88.
Durmallikā, a form of drama, 351.
Duṣṭa, a character in Buddhist drama, 74, 84; Prākrit of, 86.
Duhitṛkā, puppet, 53.
Dūta, messenger, 311, 312.
Dūtaghaṭotkaca, by Bhāsa, 94, 97, 98, 106, 107.
Dūtavākya, by Bhāsa, 73, 94, 106, 111, 270.

Dūtāṅgada, by Dhanaṁjaya, 55, 56, 269, 270.
Deva, as style of the king, 314.
Devī queen, 312.
Devva, in Bhāsa's Prākrit, 122.
Deçabhāṣā, vernacular, when used, 334.
Doṣa, defects of style, 332.
Dy, represented in Açvaghoṣa by *yy*, 88.
Drāviḍī, speech, 337.
Drutavilambita, metre, 123, 160, 181, 203, 219.
Druti, melting, as a mental condition, 320.
Dvigūḍhaka, harmonious song, 338.
Dvipadās. music, 339.
Dvimūḍhaka, a kind of song, 338.
Dhanaṁjayajaya, 347, n. 2.
Dhanaṁjayavijaya, by Kāñcana Paṇḍita, 266.
Dharmaçarmābhyudaya, by Haricandra, 75, n. 3.
Dharmābhyudaya, by Meghaprabhācārya, 55, 269.
Dhārakas, expounders of epic, 29.
Dhīra, noble, as characteristic of heroes, 305. 306.
Dhīralalita, type of hero, 305, 306.
Dhīraçānta, type of hero, 305, 306.
Dhīrodātta, type of hero, 305, 306.
Dhīroddhata, type of hero, 305, 306, 307, 347; of enemy of hero, 307, 308.
Dhūrtanartaka, by Sāmarāja Dikṣita, 262, 263.
Dhūrtas, gamblers or rogues, speech of, 141, 336.
Dhūrtasamāgama, by Jyotirīçvara Kaviçekhara, 261.
Dhṛti, firmness, as an allegorical character, 84, 268.
Dhṛtir yavanikāyāḥ, the holding apart of the curtain, 360.
Dhṛṣṭa, shameless (hero), 307.
Dhruvās, in music, 339.
Dhvajamaha, banner festival (of Indra), 41.
Dhvanyāloka, by Ānandavardhana, 294.

N and *ṇ* in the Prākrits, 86, 87, 88, 121.
Nacca, 43.
Naṭa, actor, 25, 28, 31, 36, 45, 49, 50, 52, 67.
Naṭasūtras, in Pāṇini, 31, 290.
Naṭī, actress, 51, 66, 361.
Narkuṭaka, metre, 203.
Nartaka, dances, 28, 29, 50.
Narmagarbha, development of affection, 327.
Narman, pleasantry 326.
Narmasuhṛd, boon companion, 188, 311.
Narmasphañja, outburst of affection, 327
Narmasphoṭa, manifestation of affection, 327.
Navagrahacarita, by Ghanaçyāma, 345, n. 2.
Navasāhasāṅkacarita, by Padmagupta, 293.
Nāgaraka, character of, 285; speech of, 334.
Nāgānanda, by Harṣa, 62, 85, 170, 174, 175, 180, 278, 284, 286, 300, 305, 311, 326, 339, n. 1, 342, 344, n. 2, 371, n. 2.
Nāṭaka, a type of drama, 28, 29, 95, 244–56, 278, 279, 296, 297, 345, 352, 353.
Nāṭakacandrikā, by Rūpa Gosvāmin, 294.
Nāṭakālaṁkāra, dramatic ornaments, 330, 331.
Nāṭikā, a type of drama, 62, 63, 71, 233, 234, 256, 257, 279, 280, 298, 305, 325, 349, 350, 353.
Nāṭī, a type of drama, 349.
Nāṭya, drama, 296.
Nāṭyapradīpa, by Sundaramiçra, 294.
Nāṭyarāsaka, a ballet, 351.
Nāṭyaçāstra, 12, 36, 42, 51, 65, 69, 75, n. 1, 81, 84, 95, 110, 141, 244, 267, 289–92, 293, 294, 295, 304, 312, 315, 320, 323, 324, 326, 328, 330, 331, 334, 335, 336, 340, 341, 343, 347, 348, 349, 352, 355, 358, 362, 364, 367, 369.
Nāṭyācārya, professor, 360.
Nāṭyālaṁkāra, dramatic ornaments, 329, 330.
Nāndī, benediction at beginning of play, 85, 111, 126, 182, 204, 239, 265, 266, 267, 339, 342, 343, 369; pronounced behind the scenes in the *Bhāṇa*, the *Vyāyoga*, 344; the *Preṅkhaṇa* or *Prekṣaṇa*, 351.
Nāyaka, hero, 84, 85, 305–7.
Nāyikā, heroine, 308–10.
Nālikā, enigma, 329.
Nikkhanta, in Açvaghoṣa, 89.
Nidarçanā, a figure, 125.
Niyatāpti, fourth stage of development in drama, 297.
Nirussāsaṁ, in Açvaghoṣa, 88.
Nirbhayabhīma, by Rāmacandra, 266.
Nirmuṇḍa, eunuch, 313.
Nirvahaṇa, conclusion, as last juncture, 299.
Nirveda, indifference, as basis of sentiment, 324.
Nṛt, dance, origin of *Naṭa*, 57.
Nṛtu, dancer, 25, n. 7.
Nṛtta, dance, 25, n. 7, 296.
Nṛtya, pantomime, 275, 296.
Nepathya, as form of sentiment, 315, n. 1, 368.
Nepathyagṛha, tiring room, 54, 359, 360.

Nepathyokti, a voice from behind the scene, 303.
Nevaccha (*Ṇevaccha*), Prākrit equivalent of *Nepathya*, 54.
Naipāṭhya, alleged origin of *Nepathya*, 54.
Naiṣadhānanda, by Kṣemīçvara, 240, 241.
Ny, altered to *ññ* in Açvaghoṣa's Prākrit, to *ññ* or *ṇṇ* in Bhāsa; to *ṇṇ* in Kālidāsa, 88, 121; to *ññ* in the *Mudrārākṣasa*, 212.

Pañcarātra (ed., with trans. by W. G. Urdhwareshe, Indore, 1920), by Bhāsa, 94, 110, 112, 119, 122, 123, 335, 344, n. 2, 346.
Paṭī, curtain, 61, 389.
Patākā, episode, 297; subjunctures of, 290.
Patākāsthānaka, pro-episode, 303, 304.
Padas, number of, in prologue, 344.
Padhānasutta, alleged dramatic character of, 43, n. 1.
Pabbajjāsutta, alleged dramatic character of, 43, n. 1.
Parivartaka, change of action, 327.
Paruṣā, style, 333.
Palinata, in Açvaghoṣa for *pariṇata*, 87.
Pāñcālī, (puppet) from Pañcāla, 53.
Pāṭhakas, repeaters of epic passages, 29.
Pāṇḍavānanda, 224.
Pāṇḍavābhyudaya, by Vyāsa Çrīrāmadeva, 270.
Pātra, character, 310.
Pādavākyapramāṇajña, sense of, 186.
Pāripārçvika, attendant, 85, 340.
Pārthaparākrama, by Prahlādana, 83, n. 1, 247, 264, 265, 341, n. 1.
Pārvatīpariṇaya, by Vāmana Bhaṭṭa Bāṇa, 221, 239, 247, 300.
Pīṭhamarda, companion of the hero, 308, 334, 351.
Pīṭhamardikā, confidante of the heroine, 308.
Puttalī, *Puttalikā*, puppet, 53.
Putraka, puppet, 269.
Putrikā, puppet, 53.
Pupphā, in Açvaghoṣa, 87.
Puruva, in Bhāsa for *pūrva*, 122.
Purusa, in Bhāsa, 122.
Puṣpagaṇḍikā, a kind of song, 338.
Puṣpadūṣitaka, a *Prakaraṇa*, 225, 346.
Puṣpabhūṣita, a *Prakaraṇa*, 225, 346.
Puṣpitāgrā, 123, 142, 166, 203, 212, 219.
Pusta, stage properties, 365.
Pūrvaraṅga, preliminaries of drama, 292, 341, 342.
Pṛthivī, in the *Uttararāmacarita*, 192.
Pṛthvī, metre, 123, 167, 181, 203, 238.
Pekkhā, spectacle, 43.
Paiçācī, a Prākrit, 102, 287, 335, 336.
Prakaraṇa, a type of drama, 82, 102, 187, 225, 248, 257-61, 264, 280, 296, 306, 345, 346, 353.
Prakaraṇikā, a type of drama, 349, n. 4, 350.
Prakarī, incident, 297.
Prakhyāta, traditional (plot), 296.
Pragalbhā, bold (heroine), 308.
Pracaṇḍapāṇḍava, see *Bālabhārata*.
Pracchedaka, a kind of song, 338.
Pratāpa, valour, as a character, 254.
Pratāparudrakalyāṇa, by Vidyānātha, 248.
Pratāparudrīya, by Vidyānātha, 293.
Pratijñāyaugandharāyaṇa, by Bhāsa, 92, 94, 95, 108, 110, 113, 114, 118, 119, 122, 130, 185, n. 2, 335, n. 3, 371, n. 2.
Pratināyaka, the enemy of the hero, 307, 308.
Pratimānāṭaka, by Bhāsa, 94, 100, 101, 105, 117, 124, 125.
Pratimukha, second juncture, 298, 299.
Pratisīrā, curtain, 359.
Pratigṛhita, irregular form in Açvaghoṣa, 86.
Pratīti, apprehension of sentiment, 317.
Pratīhārī, door-keeper, 313.
Pratyāyati, irregular form in Bhāsa, 121.
Prathamakalpa, misunderstood term, 112, n. 2.
Pratyāhāra, beat of drum to begin performance, 339.
Pradyumnābhyudaya, by Ravivarman, 247, 344.
Pradvesam, Buddhist irregularity for *pradoṣam*, 86.
Prapañca, comic dialogue, 328.
Prabuddharauhiṇeya, by Rāmabhadra Muni, 259, 260.
Prabodha, knowledge, as a character, 251.
Prabodhacandrodaya, by Kṛṣṇamiçra, 55, 84, 112, 243, 251-3, 286, 325, n. 1, 344.
Prayatna, second stage of development of drama, 297.
Prayogātiçaya, form of prologue, 340.
Prarocanā, part of preliminaries, 328, 340, 341, 343; pronounced behind the scenes, 351.
Pravṛttaka, form of prologue, 340.
Praveçaka, introductory scene, 110, 301, 302.
Prasannarāghava, by Jayadeva, 109, 151, 226, 244-6, 271.
Prasāda, clearness, 331.
Prastāvanā, prologue, 111, 328, 340.
Prasthāna, a form of drama, 351.
Praharṣiṇī, metre, 167, 181, 203, 212, 219.

Prahasana, farce, 182–5, 260–3, 280, 296, 309, 348.
Prācyā, a Prākrit, 88, 141, 336.
Prāḍvivāka, judge, 312.
Prāptyāçā, third stage of development of drama, 297.
Prāçnika, critic, 370.
Prāsañgika, incidental (action), 297.
Priyadarçikā, by Harṣa, 170, 171, 173, 174, 175, 303, 325, 328, 340, 350, 362, 364, 369.
Prekṣaka, spectator, 369, 370.
Prekṣaṇa, a form of drama, 351.
Prekṣaṇaka, a form of drama, 268.
Preñkhaṇa, a form of drama, 351.
Proṣitapriyā, type of heroine, 309.
Prauḍhatva, of style, claimed by Bhavabhūti, 196.
Phalāgama, attainment of end in drama, 298.

Bakulavīthi, 349.
Bambhaṇa, in Açvaghoṣa, 86.
Bāḍham, indicating assent, in Bhāsa, 120.
Bālacarita (ed. and trs. by H. Weller, Leipzig, 1922), by Bhāsa, 38, 94, 98–100, 104, 106, 112, 122, 247.
Bālabhārata, or *Pracaṇḍapāṇḍava*, by Rājaçekhara, 232, 233.
Bālarāmāyaṇa, by Rājaçekhara, 52, 151, 232, 268, 269, n 2, 303, 337, 360, 365.
Bālhikā (*Bāhlīkā*), speech of Khasas, 336, 337.
Bindu, second element of the plot, 298.
Bibboka, affected indifference, 310.
Bīja, first element of the plot, 298.
Bībhatsa, horror, as a sentiment, 319, 324.
Buddhacarita, by Açvaghoṣa, 80, 81, 82.
Buddhi, wisdom, 84.
Bṛhatkathā, by Guṇāḍhya, 52, 102, 133, 174; why written in *Paiçācī*, 335.
Bhakti, trust (in Viṣṇu), as a character, 252, 253.
Bhagavant, as style of address, 314.
Bhagavāṁ, Buddhist irregularity for *bhagavān*, 86.
Bhaṭṭa, as style of the king, 314.
Bhaṭṭā, vocative of *bhartṛ* in Açvaghoṣa, 88.
Bhaṭṭidālaka, style of princes of the blood, 84, and see *Bhartṛdāraka*.
Bhaṭṭinī, style of the queen, 314.
Bhaṇ, conjugated in the 9th class, 88.
Bhadradatta, as style of Çakas, 314.
Bhadramukha, title in dramas, 69, 71, 314.
Bhaya, terror, as basis of sentiment, 323.
Bhayānaka, fear, as a sentiment, 319, 324.
Bharatavākya, at close of the drama, 82, 83, 111, 265.
Bhartṛdāraka, style of princes of the blood, 314, and see *Bhaṭṭidālaka*.
Bhartṛdārikā, style of a princess, 314.
Bhartṛharinirveda, by Harihara, 248.
Bhavatī (Prākrit, *bhodi*), as style of the queen and her ladies, 314.
Bhavāṁ, as nominative in Açvaghoṣa, 88.
Bhāgavata Purāṇa, 100, 272, 274.
Bhāṇa, monologue, 263, 264, 280, 296, 311, 344, 348.
Bhāṇikā, 268, 351.
Bhārata, a rhapsode or comedian, 29, 30.
Bhāratī, verbal (manner), 326, 328, 329, 344; in the *Bhāṇa*, 348.
Bhāratīya Nāṭyaçāstra, see *Nāṭyaçāstra*.
Bhāva, emotion, 296, 309, 316, 319.
Bhāva, mode of address, 361.
Bhāvaka, man of taste, 318, n. 3.
Bhāvakatva, power of realization, 317.
Bhāsanāṭakacakra, 92, n. 2.
Bhikkhunīsaṁyutta, alleged dramatic character of, 43, n. 1.
Bhīmavikramavyāyoga, by Mokṣāditya, 266.
Bhuktivāda, doctrine of the enjoyment of sentiment, 318.
Bhujañgaprayāta, metre, 123.
Bhuṁjitaye, in Açvaghoṣa, 87.
Bhuvanābhyudaya, by Çañkuka, 291.
Bhūtabhāṣā, use of, 287.
Bhairavānanda, by Maṇika, 248.
Bhoginī, concubine, 312.
Bhojakatva, power of enjoyment, 317.
Bhojacarita, by Vedāntavāgīça, 345.
Bhrūkuṅsa, man playing female part, 36, 362.

Makkaṭaho, dubious form in Açvaghoṣa, 89.
Mati, reason, as a character, 251, 252.
Matta, in Bhāsa, later *metta*, 122.
Mattavilāsa, by Mahendravikramavarman, 93, 182–5.
Matsya Purāṇa, 156.
Mada, intoxication, as an internal juncture, 303.
Madd, in Açvaghoṣa, 88, 89.
Madhyamavyāyoga, by Bhāsa, 94, 106, 111, 123.
Madhyā, partly experienced (heroine), 308.
Mantrāñkanāṭaka, Act III of the *Pratijñāyaugandharāyaṇa*, 371, n. 2.
Mantrin, minister, 312.
Mandākrāntā, metre, 166, 203, 212.
Manmathonmathana, by Rāma, 267, 347.
Mallikāmāruta, by Uddaṇḍin or Uddaṇḍanātha, 221, 257, 258.
Mahattarā, duenna, 313.
Mahājanakajātaka, alleged dramatic character of, 43, n. 1.

Mahādevī, chief queen, 312.
Mahānāṭaka, type of drama, 232, 345.
Mahānāṭaka or *Hanumannāṭaka*, 56, 151, 244, n. 2, 246, 270-2, 273, 345.
Mahābhārata, 52, 54, 95, n. 2, 97, 105, 157, 247, 253, 265, 281.
Mahābhāṣya, 28, 36, 45, 48, 49, 53, 56, 57, 58, 71, 362, 363; evidence of, as to existence of the drama, 31-3.
Mahāyānaçraddhotpāda, by Açvaghoṣa, 80.
Mahāvaṅsa, 44.
Mahāvīracarita, by Bhavabhūti, 187, 188, 192, 193, 194, 203, 228, 229, 297, 302, 306, 325, 326, 327, 344, n. 1, 353.
Mā, with the gerund, in Bhāsa, 122.
Māgadhī, a Prākrit, 70, 74, 86, 87, 88, 122, 141, 142, 166, 185, 211, 212, 219, 256, 287, 336.
Mādhurya, grace as a quality of the hero, 307.
Mādhurya, sweetness of style, 331.
Māyākuraṅgikā, a specimen of the *Īhāmṛga*, 346, n. 2.
Mārasaṁyutta, alleged dramatic character of, 43, n. 1.
Mārṣa, as mode of address, 361.
Mālatīmādhava, by Bhavabhūti, 62, 66, 82, 131, 151, 186, 187, 188, 192, 193, 199, 203, 257, 280, 302, 306, 308, 311, 313, 326, 338, 343, n. 1, 344, 349, 353, 361, 369.
Mālavikā, a specimen of the *Vīthī*, 349.
Mālavikāgnimitra, by Kālidāsa, 42, 124, 127, 147-9, 155, 156, 159, 160, 164, 167, 175, 302, 303, 327, 329, 343, n. 1, 349, 350.
Mālā, statement in succession, 330.
Mālinī, metre, 123, 142, 166, 181, 185, 203, 212, 219, 272.
Māhārāṣṭrī, a Prākrit, 70, 73, 89, 130, 141, 146, 166, 181, 211, 212, 236, 240, 256, 335, 336, 337.
Mithyājñānaviḍambana, by Ravidāsa, 345.
Mithyādṛṣṭi, heresy, as a character, 252.
Milindapañha, 54.
Miçra, combined (plot), 296.
Miçrā, style, 332, n. 2.
Mukuṭatāḍitaka, by Bāṇa, 182, n. 3.
Mukundānanda, by Kāçīpati Kavirāja, 264.
Mukha, first juncture of the plot, 298.
Mugdhā, inexperienced (heroine), 308.
Mudrārākṣasa, (the drama of) Rākṣasa and his seal-ring, by Viçākhadatta, 62, 66, 205-12, 327, 335, n. 3, 341, 342, 344, 352.
Mudritakumudacandra, (the drama of) Kumudacandra put to silence, by Yaçaçcandra, 260.
Mṛgāṅkalekhā, by Viçvanātha, son of Trimaladeva, 257, n. 1.
Mṛcchakaṭikā (for an implausible conjecture as to date (7th or 8th cent.) and author, see J. Carpentier, JRAS., 1923, pp. 597 ff.), 62, 63, 64, 65, 66, 67, 69, 70, 74, 77, 82, 84, 92, 93, 104, 107, 123, n. 3, 128-42, 153, 161, 192, 193, 280, 286, 305, 309, 311, 314, n. 2, 335, n. 3, 336, 337, 346, 363, 365, 369, n. 2.
Mṛdava, turning of evil into good, 329.
Meghadūta, by Kālidāsa, 76, 145, 167; imitated by Bhavabhūti, 193.
Moṭṭāyita, manifestations of affection, 310.
Moha, confusion, as a character, 251, 252.
Mohamudgara, 239.
Moharājaparājaya, by Yaçaḥpāla, 84, n. 1, 253-6, 344, n. 2.

Y retained in Açvaghoṣa's Prākrits, 88; altered to *j* in Bhāsa, 121.
Yajurveda, 12, 25, 26.
Yamaka, alliteration, 331.
Yavanikā (Prākrit, *Javanikā*), refers to material of curtain, 61, 68, 359, 360.
Yudh, as a masculine noun, in Bhāsa, 121.
Yuvarāja, style of, in drama, 71.
Yeva, in Açvaghoṣa's Prākrit, after long vowels, 87.
Yogamāyā, as a character, 274.
Yogaçāstra, by Hemacandra, 255.
Yogin, adept, 316.
Yodha, soldier, speech of, 141, 336.

R and *l* in the Prākrits, 86, 87, 88, 122, 212, 219; as affecting the quality of style, 332.
Raghuvaṅça, by Kālidāsa, 75, 144, 162, 352.
Raṅgadvāra, part of preliminaries, 340, 342.
Raṅgāvataraṇa, appearing on the stage, 55.
Rajas, element of passion, 318.
Rati, love, as basis of sentiment, 323.
Ratnāvalī, by Harṣa, 55, 62, 103, 170, 171, 173, 175, 180, 221, 298, 299, 304, 325, 328, 340, 350, 361, 362, 368.
Rathoddhatā, metre, 167, 203.
Rasa, sentiment, 296, 314-26.
Rasataraṅgiṇī, by Bhānudatta, 319.
Rasārṇavasudhākara, by Çiṅga Bhūpāla, 294.
Rasika, men of taste, 318, n. 3.
Rājaputras, speech of, 87, 141, 336.
Rājapraçniya, 44, n. 2.
Rājarājanāṭaka, 251, n. 1.
Rājaçrī, the kingly fortune, personified 99, 112.

Rājyaçrī, the royal fortune, 255.
Rāmānanda, 343, n. 1.
Rāmābhyudaya, by Vyāsa Çrīrāmadeva, 270.
Rāmāyaṇa, by Vālmīki, 28, 29, 30, 42, 48, 50, 63, 76, 101, 105, 114, 150, n. 1.
Rāṣṭriya, as title in dramas, 69, 71.
Rāsa, a dance, 274.
Rāsamaṇḍala, 40.
Rukmiṇīpariṇaya, by Rāmavarman, 247.
Rukmiṇīharaṇa, by Vatsarāja, 266, 267.
Rasasadana, a *Bhāṇa*, 264.
Rucirā, metre, 166, 185, 212.
Rudantī, irregular form in Bhāsa, 121.
Rūpa, in Açoka's edict, 54; object of vision, source of *Rūpaka*, 296.
Rūpaka, generic name of the drama as a spectacle, 296, 345.
Rūpadakkha, meaning of, 54.
Rūpājīva, epithet of actors, 363.
Rūpopajīvana, sense of, 54.
Rūpopajīvin, one who lives on the beauty (of his wife), 55.
Raudra, fury as a sentiment, 323, 354.
Raudratā, harshness, as a character, 255.
Ry becomes *yy* in Açvaghoṣa and Bhāsa, *jj* in Kālidāsa, 122; but *jj* in Açvaghoṣa's *Māgadhī*, 86; in Bhaṭṭa Nārāyaṇa, 219.

L and *r* in the Prākrits, 86, 87, 88, 122, 212, 219.
Lakṣaṇa, beauties of the drama, 329, 330.
Lajjā, allegorical character, 268.
Laṭakamelaka, by Çaṅkhadhara, 5; Kavirāja, 260, 261, 348.
Lalita, light-hearted (hero), 305.
Lalitamādhava, by Rūpa Gosvāmin, 247.
Lalitavigraharājanāṭaka, by Somadeva, 243, 248.
Lalitavistara, allusion to the drama in, 43.
Lāsya, dance, 12, 42, 338, 348.
Līlāmadhukara, a *Bhāṇa*, 348.
Lūpadakkha, meaning of, 54.
Laukika, sentiment as natural, 319.

Vaaṁ, *vayaṁ*, 'we', in Açvaghoṣa's and Bhāsa's Prākrits, 89, 122.
Vaṅçasthā, metre, 123, 142, 166, 185, 203, 212.
Vaṅkṣū, Oxus, 144, n. 5.
Vajrasūcī, by Açvaghoṣa, 80.
Vat, nominative of stems in, 87.
Vatsa, as style of address, 314.
Vannikāhi, in Açvaghoṣa, 87.
Vayasya, as style of address, 314.
Vara, frequent use of, in Bhāsa, 120.
Varṇānyatva, change of colour or difference of colour, 35.
Varṣadhara, eunuch, 313.
Vasantatilaka, metre, 123, 142, 166, 181, 185, 203, 212, 219, 236, 240, 246, 253, 258, 272.
Vasantatilaka, by Varadācārya, 263.
Vastu, plot, 296–305.
Vastūtthāpana, creation of an object, 327.
Vācika (sentiment), produced by words, 315, n. 1.
Vācikābhinaya, expression by words, 367.
Vāsakasajjā (heroine), in full dress, 309.
Vāsantikasvapna, by R. Kṛṣnamachari, 251.
Vāsavadattā, by Subandhu, 76.
Vikāsa, expansion of the mind, 320.
Vikramorvaçī, by Kālidāsa, 62, 66, 124, 126, 146, 147, 149–52, 156, 157, 159, 160, 167, 193, 233, 268, 275, 278, 328, 329, 339, n. 1, 342, 343, 350.
Vikrāntaçūdraka, a drama, 129, n. 4.
Vikṣepa, movement to and fro of the mind as connected with sentiment, 320.
Vijayaçrī, by Madana Bālasarasvatī, 256.
Viṭa, parasite, 65, 132, 135, 136, 177, 193, 263, 311, 326, 334, 346, 356.
Vidagdhamādhava, by Rūpa-Gosvāmin, 247.
Vidūṣaka, jester, 28, 39, 40, 50, 51, 52, 53, 56, 62, 65, 66, 67, 73, 81, 82, 84, 107, 108, 133, 141, 156, 158, 159, 160, 176, 177, 234, 235, 237, 254, 263, 264, 270, 299, 310, 311, 313, 314, 326, 328, 334, 340, 351, 361.
Vidyā, as a character, 251, 252.
Vidyāpariṇayana, by Vedakavi, 253.
Vidyunmālā, metre, 142.
Viddhaçālabhañjikā, by Rājaçekhara, 232, 234, 235, 300.
Viprayoga, sundering, as form of the erotic sentiment, 323.
Vipralabdhā, deceived (heroine), 309.
Vipralambha, sundering, as form of erotic sentiment, 323.
Vibhāva, determinants of sentiment, 315.
Vibhāṣās, conventional dialects used in drama, 337.
Vimadda, in Açvaghoṣa for *vimarda*, 89.
Vimarça, fourth juncture of the plot, 299.
Vimoktukāma, irregular form in Bhāsa, 121.
Viya, in Açvaghoṣa, 88.
Virahotkaṇṭhitā, type of heroine, 309.
Vilāsa, vivacity as quality of the hero, 307.
Vilāsikā, a form of drama, 351.
Viveka, discrimination, 251, 252.
Vivekacandra, as allegorical character, 254.
Viṣkambha or *Viṣkambhaka*, introductory scene, 110, 301, 302.

Viṣṇu Purāṇa, 100.
Visūkadassana, spectacle, 43.
Vistara, expansion of the mind, 320.
Vismaya, astonishment, as basis of sentiment, 323.
Vījanti, irregular form in Bhāsa, 120.
Vītarāgastuti, by Hemacandra, 255.
Vīthī, 'garland', 295, 296, 328, 329, 348, 349, 353.
Vīra, heroism as a sentiment, 323.
Vīrabhadravijṛmbhaṇa, 328, n. 3.
Vīravijaya, by Kṛṣṇamiçra, 267.
Vṛttis, dramatic styles, 326–9.
Vṛddhi, sense of, 36, n. 1.
Vṛṣabhānujā, by Mathurādāsa, 257.
Veṇīsaṁhāra, by Bhaṭṭa Nārāyaṇa, 83, 212–9, 300, 304, 326, 328, 340, 344, n. 1, 353, 361.
Vetālapañcaviṅçati, 129, 174.
Vedāntasāra, by Sadānanda, 318, n. 2.
Veṣṭita, stage costumes, 365.
Vaitālīya, metre, 123, 167.
Vaiçika, connoisseur of hetaerae, 307, n. 1.
Vaiçvadevī, metre, 123, 142.
Vyaktiviveka, by Mahiman Bhaṭṭa, 294.
Vyañjanā, the doctrine of suggestion, 318.
Vyabhicārin, transitory (feelings), 315.
Vyājima, kind of stage properties, 365.
Vyāmiçraka, possible reference to plays, 29.
Vyāyoga, a type of drama, 95, 96, 247, 264–6, 296, 344, 347, 353.
Vyutpatti, aesthetic equipment, 318.
Vyūḍhoras, irregular compound in Bhāsa, 121.

Ç, for *s* in *Māgadhī*, 86, 122, 212.
Çaṅs, recite, used of *Ṛgveda*, 20.
Çakāra, *miles gloriosus*, 65, 69, 134, 166, 311, 336.
Çakuntalā, by Kālidāsa, 62, 66, 70, 124, 139, 147, 152–5, 157–9, 160, 161, 167, 272, 278, 281, 297, 298, 299, 302, 303, 304, 311, 325, 329, 340, 344, 365.
Çakvarī, metre, appropriate to the pathetic sentiment, 331.
Çaṭha, deceitful (hero), 307.
Çatapatha Brāhmaṇa, tale of Purūravas in, 22.
Çarmiṣṭhāyayāti, by Kṛṣṇa Kavi, 268.
Çākārī, a Prākrit, 141, 142, 166, 337.
Çānta, calm (hero), 305, 306; sentiment, 324.
Çānti Parvan, allusion to drama in, 28.
Çābarī, a Prākrit, 337.
Çāradātilaka, by Çaṅkara, 263, 348.
Çāradvatīputraprakaraṇa or *Çāriputraprakaraṇa*, by Açvaghoṣa, 80, 83, 85, 346.
Çārdūlavikrīḍita, metre, 123, 142, 166, 181, 185, 203, 212, 219, 232, 236, 240, 253, 258, 272.
Çālabhañjikā, statue, 234.
Çālinī, metre, 123, 168, 181, 203.
Çikṣāpada, moral rules of the Buddhists, 184.
Çikhariṇī, metre, 123, 142, 166, 181, 203, 212, 219, 240, 246.
Çilpaka, a form of drama, 351.
Çivanārāyaṇabhañjamahodaya, by Narasiṅha, 257.
Çiṣyalekhā, by Candra, 168.
Çuddha, type of *Viṣkambhaka*, 301.
Çūdrakavadha, a *Parikathā*, 129, n. 4.
Çṛṅgāra, love as a sentiment, 323.
Çṛṅgāratilaka, by Rāmabhadra Dīkṣita, 263.
Çṛṅgārabhūṣaṇa, by Vāmana Bhaṭṭa Bāṇa, 263.
Çṛṅgāramañjarī a *Bhāṇa*, 263, n. 2.
Çṛṅgāramañjarī, a *Saṭṭaka*, by Viçveçvara, 257.
Çṛṅgāramañjarī, cited in the *Kasārṇavasudhākara*, 338, n. 1.
Çṛṅgārasarvasva, by Nallā Kavi, 263, 264.
Çṛṇvam, in Açvaghoṣa for *çṛṇvan* (*çṛṇvaṁ*), 86.
Çailāli Brāhmaṇa, 31.
Çailūṣa, actor, 25, 360.
Çoka, sorrow, as basis of sentiment, 323.
Çobhanikas, actors, 32–5.
Çobhā, brilliance as quality of the hero, 307.
Çobhā, distinction of poem, 334.
Çaubhikas, kind of actors, 32–5, 45, 53, 55, 273, 360.
Çaurasenī, a Prākrit, 41, 70, 73, 74, 88, 89, 141, 166, 181, 185, 203, 211, 212, 219, 236, 240, 335, 336, 367.
Çyāma, dark colour of the erotic sentiment, 324.
Çraddhā, faith, as a character, 252.
Çrīkaṇṭhacarita, by Maṅkha, 75, n. 3, 225.
Çrīgadita, a type of drama, 268, 351.
Çrīdāmacarita, by Sāmarāja Dīkṣita, 247.
Çreṣṭhin, guildsmen, or rich merchants, speech of, 87, 141, 336.
Çleṣa, flow of style, 331.
Çloka, metre, 123, 142, 166, 181, 185, 203, 212, 219, 236, 240, 246, 272.

Sṭ and *ṣṭh*, treatment of, in Prākrit, 86, 122, 212.

S, alone preserved in certain Prākrits, 87, 88, 122.
Saṁlāpa, dialogue, 327.
Saṁlāpaka, a form of drama, 351.
Saṁkalpasūryodaya, by Veṅkaṭanātha, 253.

Saṁkīrṇa, mixed form of *Viṣkambhaka*, 302.
Saṁkṛti, metre, appropriate to lively dialogue, 331.
Saṁkṣipti, construction of object, 327.
Saṁgamamaṇi, stone of reunion, 62.
Saṁgītadāmodara, unites ornaments and beauties, 330, n. 1.
Saṁghātya, breach of alliance, 327.
Saciva, as style of a minister, 314.
Saṭṭaka, a type of drama, 233, 350.
Sattva, element of goodness or truth, 318.
Saddharmapuṇḍarīka, dramatic form of the, 43.
Sandhi, junctures of the plot, 298–300.
Sandhima, kind of stage properties, 365.
Sandhyantara, divisions of junctures, 303.
Sabhāpati, patron of the drama, 370.
Samajja or *Samāja*, form of entertainment, 43, 85.
Samatā, homogeneity of style, 331.
Samavakāra, a type of drama, 97, 225, 266, 267, 268, 291, 346, 353.
Samāja, 85, and see *Samajja*.
Samādhi, metaphorical language, 331.
Samāçvāsitum, irregular form in Bhāsa, 121.
Samudramathana, by Vatsarāja, 267, 268.
Samudramanthana, a *Samavakāra*, 225.
Sampheṭa, fighting, 328.
Sambhoga, union, as part of erotic sentiment, 323.
Sarvacarita, by Bāṇa, 182, n. 3.
Sarvarājñaḥ, irregular compound in Bhāsa, 121.
Sarvavinodanāṭaka, by Kṛṣṇa Avadhūta Ghaṭikāçata Mahākavi, 267.
Sassirīkaṁ, for *saçrīkaṁ*, in Açvaghoṣa, 88.
Sahṛdaya, man of taste, 318.
Sāttvatī, correctly *Sātvatī*, grand (manner), 326, 327.
Sāttvika, of excellencies of hero, 307.
Sāttvika, class of consequents, 315.
Sāttvikābhinaya, nature of, 367, 368.
Sāḍika, dance, 350, n. 2.
Sātvatī ('of the Satvants', cf. Lévi, TI. i, 332), grand (manner), 326, 327.
Sādhāraṇī, courtesan, 309.
Sādhāraṇī kṛti, generic power of poetry, 321.
Sādhu, style of address, 314.
Sāmaveda, 12, 15, 20, 26.
Sāvitrīcarita, by Çaṅkaralāla, 270.
Sāhityadarpaṇa, by Viçvanātha, 71, 225, 268, 294, 295, 336, 342.
Siddhāntakaumudī, cites Rājaçekhara for grammar, 230.
Sukumāratā, softness of style, 331.
Sukṛtasaṁkīrtana, by Arisiṅha, 248, n. 7.
Sugṛhītanāman, as title in dramas, 69, 71.
Sugṛhītābhidha, as style of address, 71, 314.
Sudhanāvadāna, 150, n. 1, 156, n. 1.
Suparṇādhyāya, character of the, 17, 21.
Subuddhi, a female character, 267.
Subhadrādhanaṁjaya, by Kulaçekharavarman, 247, 342, n. 2.
Subhadrāpariṇayana, by Vyāsa Çrīrāmadeva, 270.
Subhadrāharaṇa, by Mādhava, 268, 342, 351.
Subhāṣitāvali, 168, 209.
Surada, for *surata*, an isolated form, in Açvaghoṣa, 89.
Surā, origin of, 183.
Suvadanā, metre, 123, 212.
Sūcaka, part undertaken by the, 273, 274.
Sūtradhāra, 51, 52, 56, 65, 66, 91, 92, 126, 232, 248, 254, 265, 266, 267, 273, 339, 340, 341, 342, 343, 344, 360, 361, 362, 363, 365.
Sūtrālaṁkāra, by Açvaghoṣa, 80, 81.
Senāpati, general, 306, 312.
Saindhava, a kind of song, 338.
Sobhiya, Prākrit for *Çaubhika*, 55.
Somatā, gentleness, as a character, 254.
Saugandhikāharaṇa, by Viçvanātha, 266.
Saundarananda, by Açvaghoṣa, 80, 81.
Saubhya, misreading for *Saumya*, 272, n. 1.
Saumya, as style of address, 314.
Skanda Purāṇa, 129.
Sthāpaka, 36, n. 1, 52, 56, 126, 239, 265, 266, 267, 340, 341, 342, 343, 344, 361.
Sthāpanā, prologue, 111, 112, 182, 340, 342, n. 1.
Sthāyinī, concubine, 312.
Sthāyibhāva, dominant emotion, 315, 320.
Sthitapāṭhya, standing recitation, 338.
Sthairya, steadfastness as a quality of the hero, 307.
Snātaka, as a character, 313.
Sragdharā, metre, 123, 142, 167, 181, 185, 203, 212, 219, 232, 236, 246, 272.
Sravati, irregular form in Bhāsa, 120.
Svagatam, aside, 304.
Svapnadaçānana, by Bhīmaṭa, 239.
Svapnavāsavadattā, by Bhāsa, 91, 92, 94, 95, 103, 107, 113, 117, 118, 119, 123, 125, 187, n. 2.
Svabhāvokti, vivid description, 161.
Svā, *svīyā*, heroine as wife, 308.
Svādhīnapatikā, absolute mistress, 309.
Svābhāvika, natural (sentiment), 315, n. 1.
Svāmin, as style of the Crown Prince, 69, 71, 314.
Svāminī, style of the queen, 314.
Svāminī, favourite, 312.

Hañho, as term of address, 314.
Hake, hago, in Açvaghoṣa, 86.
Hañgho, in Açvaghoṣa, 86.
Hañjā (voc., *Hañje*), as term of address, 314.
Haṇḍe, as term of address, 314.
Hanumannāṭaka, see *Mahānāṭaka*, 271.
Hammīramadamardana, by Jayasiṅha Sūri, 248–50.
Hayagrīvavadha, epic by Bhartṛmeṇṭha, 232.
Harakelināṭaka, by Vīsaladeva Vigraharāja, 247.
Haragaurīvivāha, by Jagajjyotirmalla, 76, n. 2, 247, 248.
Hariṇī, metre, 123, 142, 166, 181, 203, 212.
Haridūta, 56, 270.
Harivaṅça, 28, 47, 48, 100.
Harṣacarita, by Bāṇa, 76, 129, 170, 364.
Halā, as term of address, 314.
Hallīça, a type of drama, 351.
Hallīçaka, dance, 99.
Hāva, awakening of love, 309.
Hāsa, mirth, as basis of sentiment, 323.
Hāsya, the comic sentiment, 323.
Hāsyacūḍāmaṇi, by Vatsarāja, 265.
Hāsyārṇava, by Jagadīçvara, 261, 262, 314, n. 3.
Horā, or *Kāla*, 146.